BYRON
A Self-Portrait

LETTERS AND DIARIES
1798 TO 1824

EDITED BY
PETER QUENNELL

OXFORD UNIVERSITY PRESS
1990

Oxford University Press, Walton Street, Oxford OX2 6DP

*Oxford New York Toronto
Delhi Bombay Calcutta Madras Karachi
Petaling Jaya Singapore Hong Kong Tokyo
Nairobi Dar es Salaam Cape Town
Melbourne Auckland*

*and associated companies in
Berlin Ibadan*

Oxford is a trade mark of Oxford University Press

© *John Murray 1950*

*First published 1950 (in two volumes) by John Murray
First issued as an Oxford University Press paperback 1990*

British Library Cataloguing in Publication Data

Byron, George Gordon Byron, (Baron 1788–1824
*Byron: a self portrait: letters and diaries 1798–1824.
(Oxford letters and memoirs)*
1. *Poetry in English. Byron, George Gordon Byron, Baron
1788–1824, Shelley, Percy Bysshe, 1792–1822*
I. *Title* II. *Quennell, Peter, 1905–*
821.709

ISBN 0–19–282754–5

Library of Congress Cataloging in Publication Data

*Byron, George Gordon Byron, Baron, 1788–1824.
Byron, a self-portrait: letters and diaries, 1798 to 1824/edited by Peter Quennell.
p.   cm.*
1. *Byron, George Gordon Byron, Baron, 1788–1824— Correspondence.*
2. *Byron, George Gordon Byron, Baron, 1788–1824— Diaries.* 3. *Poets,
English— 19th century— Correspondence.* 4. *Poets, English— 19th
century— Diaries.* I. *Quennell, Peter, 1905–   .   II. Title.*
821'.7— dc20   PR4381.A4 1990   90–6773 [B]

ISBN 0–19–282754–5

*Printed in Great Britain by
Richard Clay Ltd.
Bungay, Suffolk*

CONTENTS

NOTE: *Letters unpublished at time of first hardback edition of this book are marked in the text
by a star; letters to which passages have been restored, by a dagger.*

FOREWORD

Ay me! what perils do environ
The man that meddles with Lord Byron!

murmured a volatile acquaintance caught in the web of the
strange Byronic destiny. It is a complaint that every
biographer of Byron must now and then have echoed;
for, although Byron is the most alluring of themes, and
although there is no other great man who appears at first
sight to reveal himself more readily, his character, if we study
him closely enough and follow him hard enough, often seems,
as our knowledge increases, to be among the most elusive. We
possess a vast quantity of information about his habits, tastes
and antecedents; and yet, it may presently strike us, some
essential clues are lacking. We know much, possibly too
much, about his various troubled love-affairs; but we can
only guess at the nature of that decisive early experience
which caused him to feel that he had anticipated adult life,
and that he had begun to squander his capital before he had
reached an age when he could gather in the interest. Other
problems are equally insoluble. Byron, who had an odd, at
times a slightly distorted, sense of humour, was never averse
from mystifying his intimates; and that he might mystify
readers yet unborn was an idea that, in freakish and provocative
moods, evidently appealed to him. Their correspondence, he
wrote to his friend Lady Melbourne, on November 6th, 1812,
might be expected to " puzzle posterity " when, after a hundred
years' interval, it eventually burst forth !

That particular section of his private papers (edited and
published by John Murray under the title of *Lord Byron's
Correspondence*) as he had prophesied finally burst upon the
world in 1922. It added not a little to our understanding of
his temperament, and heightened the impression made by his
Letters and Journals, edited in six volumes by R. E. Prothero
(later Lord Ernle) at the end of the last century. But a mass
of documents, some of them unusually illuminating, still
remained unpublished. A large number are preserved at

50 Albemarle Street, in a house that Byron often visited, among the Murray archives: others repose in the British Museum, or have been acquired by collections, both private and public, in England and America. Because the pleasures of becoming acquainted with Byron far outweigh the perils, we have been tempted to make a new selection of the poet's scattered prose-writings, the letters he dashed off to his friends and the wonderful diaries and journals in which, for his own amusement, he composed a partial and fragmentary, but extremely vivid, self-portrait. Together with material already published, we have included fifty-six letters hitherto unprinted; while to the published text of some thirty-six we have restored passages, ranging in length from a few lines to several solid paragraphs, suppressed or omitted by Byron's previous editors. It has been a stimulating, at times a perplexing, task. So strong was Byron's personality that everything he produced, down to the smallest and least studied notes, seems impregnated with his character; and his was a character that, however attentively we observe it, at length defies analysis. Thus he was the most self-conscious of men; yet the chief characteristic of his private outpourings is their reckless spontaneity. He did not labour to create an effect; yet he can seldom have been unaware of the effect he was creating. He was usually prepared to live for the moment, but always inclined to see the moment against a background of eternity: for his religious sense, though undeveloped, was strong and ineradicable. Opportunist and amorous adventurer, he had in him the makings (as Walter Scott once remarked) of an ascetic and a devotee.

All these aspects of his temperament appear in rapid succession, sometimes brightly, sometimes flickeringly, throughout the pages of his correspondence. We watch the evolution of a human being—from the little boy who informs his aunt, Mrs. Parker, that the " potatoes are now ready ", and the angry schoolboy bursting with a complication of adolescent grievances, to the disillusioned and exhausted man, struggling to perform an impossible task amid the gloom of Missolonghi, while rain thrashes down into the muddy street and the Suliot mercenaries in the courtyard chant their dismal warsongs. He grows up; he changes perpetually; yet neither triumph nor disgrace, neither satisfaction nor disillusionment, can alter or obliterate the underlying outline. He was a fatalist. "Like Sylla", he wrote in *Detached Thoughts*, the journal of miscellaneous reflections he compiled in 1821, "I have always believed that all things depended upon Fortune, and nothing upon ourselves. I am not aware of any one thought or action worthy of being called good to myself or others, which is not to be attributed to the Good Goddess, Fortune!" But his pagan fatalism had a Christian colouring. Brought up by a Calvinist nurse, he never quite shook off the dogma of predestination in which he had been educated; and to these ideas a strain of private superstition gave added picturesqueness. All the Byrons, he was convinced, were doomed—the "Wicked Lord", "Foulweather Jack" (the admiral whose mere presence seemed to have attracted hurricanes) and himself, offspring of a handsome, dissolute father and a foolish, ill-educated, violent-tempered mother. They shared a mysterious ancestral curse. To those whom he loved, Byron sometimes asserted, his love was always fatal.

With these hereditary factors Byron, at least as a young man, combined a strain of vehement personal ambition and romantic self-assertiveness. Take, for example, this passage from a letter (hitherto unpublished) written to his mother from Harrow, presumably during the year 1804: "I . . . am equal", he rages, "if not superior to most of my school-fellows, and if my fortune is narrow it is my misfortune, not my fault. But, however, the way *to riches*, *to greatness* lies before me. I can, I will cut myself a path through the world or perish in the attempt. . . . I will carve myself a passage to Grandeur, but never with Dishonour. These, Madam, are my intentions."

Yet Byron the arch-Romantic is but a single aspect of the complex and fascinating being whom his private letters show us. Equally conspicuous is Byron the man of the world— rake and diner-out and jocular companion, than whom (as he was wont to observe, somewhat plaintively, when the dark Byronic legend became too oppressive or too embarrassing) nobody could laugh more! Byron's correspondence, on the other hand, does not deserve attention merely because it builds up into the portrait of an extraordinarily gifted and unusually complex personality; it is also memorable because this intimate record of his moods and thoughts and doings is conveyed in a prose-style at once sensitive and vigorous, a style which is frequently slipshod but at times rises to the height of imaginative literature. The letters of Pope, Gray and Walpole are deliberate works of art, copied out and carefully revised and often begged back from the recipient for further literary polishing. Byron, however, agreed with Dorothy Osborne that the real charm of a letter was its freedom from any deliberate literary artifice; " all letters [she had remarked] . . . should be free and easy as one's discourse, not studied as an oration, nor made up of hard words like a charm ". Byron's epistles have always this quality: at their best, they are admirable *talk*—delivered by a talker of genius, who had explored life energetically and mused upon it passionately, even though (as his detractors may suggest) he had not seen it steadily. English prose is much the richer for the constant need Byron felt, whether at home or abroad, to communicate his feelings; and it is an odd fact that the most eloquent appreciation of his merits as a letter-writer should have been composed neither by a contemporary nor ·by a twentieth-century admirer, but by a great Victorian prophet. Ruskin's criticism is both just and generous. In the eighth chapter of *Praeterita*, after describing the benefit that during his youth he had received from Byron's poetry, he proceeds to expatiate at considerable length on the virtues of his prose-work :

" Read . . .", Ruskin advises, " the sentence on Sheridan, in his letter to Thomas Moore, from Venice, June 1st (or dawn of June 2nd !), 1818. ' The Whigs abuse him; however, he never left them, and such blunderers deserve neither credit nor compassion. As for his creditors,—remember, Sheridan *never had* a shilling, and was thrown, with great powers and passions, into the thick of the world, and placed upon the pinnacle of success, with no other external means to support him in his elevation. Did Fox * * * *pay his* debts? or did Sheridan take a subscription ? Was the * *'s drunkenness more excusable than his ? Were his intrigues more notorious than those of all his contemporaries ? and is his memory to be blasted and theirs respected ? Don't let yourself be led away by clamour, but compare him with the coalitioner Fox, and the pensioner

Burke, as a man of principle; and with ten hundred thousand in personal views; and with none in talent, for he beat them all *out* and out. Without means, without connexion, without character (which might be false at first, and make him mad afterwards from desperation), he beat them all, in all he ever attempted. But, alas poor human nature! Good-night or rather, morning. It is four, and the dawn gleams over the Grand Canal, and unshadows the Rialto '.

" Now, observe, that passage is noble primarily because it contains the utmost number that will come together into the space, of absolutely just, wise, and kind thoughts. But it is more than noble, it is *perfect*, because the quantity it holds is not artificially or intricately concentrated, but with the serene swiftness of a smith's hammer-strokes on hot iron ; and with choice of terms which, each in its place, will convey far more than they mean in the dictionary. Thus, ' however ' is used instead of ' yet ', because it stands for ' howsoever ', or, in full, for ' yet whatever they did '. ' Thick ' of society, because it means, not merely the crowd, but the *fog* of it; ' ten hundred thousand ' instead of ' a million ', or ' a thousand thousand ', to take the sublimity out of the number, and make us feel that it is a number of nobodies. . . . Finally, the dawn ' unshadows '—lessens the shadow on—the Rialto, but does not *gleam* on that, as on the broad water. . . .

" . . . Here at last ", Ruskin concludes, now discussing Byron's prose and verse as facets of the same genius, " I had found a man who spoke only of what he had seen, and known ; and spoke without exaggeration, without mystery, without enmity. ' That *is* so ;—make what you will of it ! ' "

Ruskin's tastes were commendably catholic. All his inherited puritanism did not debar him from conceding Byron's splendid qualities, though they were the qualities of a mind to which his own intelligence bore very little likeness. But each writer had a superb descriptive gift ; and for sheer evocative and descriptive skill Byron's letters composed in Italy—especially the letters written from Venice—would be difficult to improve on. In a few sentences he produced an impression which the average novelist might fail to achieve in many laboured paragraphs:

" That she had a sufficient regard for me in her wild way, I had many reasons to believe. I will mention one. In the autumn, one day, going to the Lido with my Gondoliers, we were overtaken by a heavy Squall, and the Gondola put in peril—hats blown away, boat filling, oar lost, tumbling sea, thunder, rain in torrents, night coming, and wind encreasing. On our return, after a tight struggle, I found her on the open steps of the Mocenigo palace, on the Grand Canal, with her great black eyes flashing through her tears, and the long dark hair, which was streaming drenched with rain over her brows and breast. She was perfectly exposed to the storm ; and the wind blowing her hair and dress about her tall thin figure, and the lightning flashing round her, with the waves rolling at her feet, made her look like Medea alighted from her chariot, or the Sibyl of the tempest that was rolling around her, the only living thing within hail at that moment except ourselves. . . . Her joy at seeing me again was moderately mixed with ferocity, and gave me the idea of a tigress over her recovered Cubs."

But no less beguiling than his broadly dramatic strokes is the verbal wit that Byron compresses into two or three words, or into a single telling epithet. Certain phrases constantly recur to the memory, so felicitous is their summing-up of some familiar human situation. The charm of these jokes is very often their apparent slightness ; and we are reminded that George Bryan Brummell, whose wit struck always a glancing blow, had been one of Byron's early masters. Thus, on September 21st, 1813, describing for Lady Melbourne's benefit the not excessively comfortable household of his friends the Websters, he remarks that " the place is very well, and quiet, and *the children only scream in a low voice*. . . ." And, elsewhere, portraying a Venetian mistress : ". . . She is pretty as an Antelope, is but two-and-twenty years old, has the large, black, Oriental eyes, with the Italian countenance, and dark glossy hair, of the curl and colour of Lady Jersey's. . . . But her great merit is finding out mine—*there is nothing so amiable as discernment*."

Elsewhere a robust satirical humour, expressed in some comic or ludicrous image, suddenly reveals itself. Byron was accounted excellent company by friends who met him in a

laughing mood, and with whom he felt sufficiently at his ease
to discard the haughty and supercilious attitude he sometimes
adopted in mixed or hostile gatherings.   Then there was no
hint of the Byronic melancholy, no indication that this
muscular, talkative and curly-headed young man had any
relationship with the misanthropic wanderer depicted in
Childe Harold.   But, if it is true that he was seldom serious for
long, and that his habitual flippancy shocked solemn admirers
of the stamp of Lady Blessington, who found that he loved to
gossip and rarely troubled to philosophise, it is also true that
the strain of melancholy which ran through his nature was
deep-rooted and pervasive.   It was at least as genuine as his
flippant and ribald humour.   Byron himself accepted both
sides of his temperament, but did not try to reconcile them.
Both coloured his epistolary prose-style, and contribute to the
feeling of fascination with which we turn his pages.   But
where is the *real* Byron? we are occasionally tempted to ask.
Are we to look for this elusive personage among the rich
diversity of letters he sent to Hobhouse, Moore and Kinnaird,
in which he emerges as a generous and warm-hearted friend,
though, when crossed or disappointed, markedly petulant and
short-tempered : among the rancorous letters received by his
wife : the tender letters to Augusta Leigh : or in his protestations
to the other women with whom his fortune linked him ?
Nowhere is Byron revealed in so many contradictory aspects
as in his attitude towards the opposite sex.   Women had
dominated his life : he laughed at and pitied and adored and
often affected to despise them.   " There is something to me ",
he recorded, " very softening in the presence of a woman—
some strange influence, even if one is not in love with them
—which I cannot at all account for. . . ."   Yet if we except
the letters to Augusta Leigh and Lady Melbourne, we find
little evidence of strong affection and numerous traces, as
disillusionment grew upon him, of boredom and satiety.   To
Teresa Guiccioli he was undoubtedly devoted ; but there is a
disconcerting contrast between the carefully penned declara-
tions—copy-book productions in the author's best Italian—with
which at frequent intervals her romantic lover favoured her,
and his irreverent account to Hoppner and Kinnaird of the
progress of their intimacy.   No lover could be less loyal, no

writer less consistent. Yet his inconsistency and emotional instability were as much a part of Byron's character as his melancholy, his fatalism or his wild romantic yearnings; and in his collected correspondence all are fully set forth—and set forth with a freedom and freshness, even with a kind of shamelessness, rarely equalled and never surpassed in European literature. He may not reveal the whole of himself, but he gives us more than any English letter-writer had previously attempted. Indeed, he had more to give. His nature, with its disorderly abundance, its bewildering assemblage of mean and noble attributes, was, as his contemporaries guessed, in the most genuine sense inimitable; and, when he died, young and old understood that a light had been extinguished. " Byron is dead. . . . Byron is dead ", scratched the boyish Tennyson, half stupefied by the news, upon the sandstone slabs of a deserted quarry. " Gentlemen, Lord Byron is dead ! " announced the Duke of Rutland to a gathering of local fox-hunters : and the country gentlemen abandoned their banquet and silently, unquestioningly trooped home.

BIBLIOGRAPHICAL NOTE

This selection of Byron's letters and journals includes forty-nine letters hitherto unpublished, and thirty-eight not hitherto published in full. Unpublished letters are marked by a star; letters to which passages have been restored, by a dagger. A list of sources will be found at the end of the second volume. Many of the manuscripts used by Moore have subsequently disappeared, and his omissions therefore remain. In the interests of propriety, certain brief passages, not in themselves important, have been deleted from letters, of which the manuscript still exists, at the request of their present owners; otherwise every letter appears in its entirety. Nothing, however, has been omitted which throws real light on Byron's career or character. These omissions, like Moore's, are denoted by asterisks. Byron's spelling has been preserved, except where it seemed likely to confuse the general reader.

The printed sources which have been drawn upon are *Correspondence of Lord Byron*, by R. C. Dallas; *Letters and Journals of Lord Byron*, by Thomas Moore; *Byron's Letters and Journals*, edited by R. E. Prothero; *Astarte*, by the Earl of Lovelace; *Lord Byron's Correspondence*, edited by John Murray; *Recollections of a Long Life*, by Lord Broughton; *The Life and Letters of Anne Isabella, Lady Noel Byron*, by Ethel Colburn Mayne; *The Last Attachment*, by the Marchesa Iris Origo. For permission to print unpublished material, we are indebted to the legal personal representative of Lord Byron's Estate, who controls Byron copyrights, apart from some controlled by Sir John Murray, and to owners of Byroniana who have allowed us to make use of their manuscripts; the Trustees of the British Museum; Mr. Russell Ellice; the Count Carlo Gamba; Henry E. Huntingdon Library; Rare Books Collections, the University of Texas and Professor Cline; the Lord Kinnaird; the Marquess of Lansdowne; Sir John Murray; the Historical Society of Pennsylvania; the Pierpont Morgan Library; Yale University Library. The editor wishes to express his gratitude for the generous assistance that he has throughout received; to Mr. Harold Nicolson, and especially to Miss Lilian Mattingly, the author of the index. Finally, he would like to put on record his deep indebtedness to his friend, Mr. John Grey Murray, with whom, in surroundings that the poet knew well, he has passed so many agreeable evening hours. Thanks to Mr. Murray's help, encouragement and sympathetic insight into editorial frailties, sessions at 50 Albemarle Street, beneath the eye of Byron's portrait, have frequently assumed an almost festive colouring.

NOTE TO SECOND PRINTING

Since the appearance of the first edition, Dr. Ehrsam of New York University has been kind enough to draw our attention to evidence proving conclusively that a letter purporting to have been addressed to Sir Godfrey Webster from Pisa on April 12th, 1822, is one of the forgeries of G. G. Byron. Another letter has been inserted in its place. To Professor L. A. Marchand of Rutgers University, New Jersey, we are particularly indebted for several important corrections and suggestions.

1

Childhood and Youth

January 1798 to July 1811

George Gordon Lord Byron was born on January 22nd, 1788, at 16 Holles Street, London, the son of Captain John Byron and of his second wife, the former Miss Catherine Gordon of Gight, once a substantial Scottish heiress. By his previous marriage—to the divorced Lady Carmarthen—Captain Byron had a single surviving child, Augusta, subsequently married to her cousin, Colonel George Leigh. His first marriage was brief; his second was ill-fated. A gambler and spendthrift, by 1786 he had run through his wife's fortune and was obliged to go abroad, where he eventually died in squalor and poverty at Valenciennes. Mrs. Byron had meanwhile returned to London, and thence fell back upon Aberdeen. In that place, amid gloomy and poverty-stricken surroundings, exposed to the tempestuous whims of his ungovernable mother, the little lame boy received his early education. Then, in 1798, his grand-uncle, the " Wicked Lord ", died at Newstead Abbey, and mother and son travelled south to Nottinghamshire to claim the new lord's half-ruined and much-encumbered heritage, the Newstead estates and the disputed Rochdale property. They could not hope to inhabit Newstead itself: the house was dilapidated; their resources were meagre; and for many years they were obliged to make do with a small and unpretentious house in the adjacent town of Southwell. During 1801 Byron was sent to Harrow. At school he made a number of close friends, Clare, Dorset, Delawarr, Wingfield and Long, for whom the feelings he experienced were passionately possessive, ran into several storms, played cricket and swam, but scamped his academic tasks. At home he became desperately enamoured of Mary Chaworth, the " Morning Star of Annesley ", who made light of his protestations and married a dissolute local squire. He would also seem to have had some revealing and disconcerting adventures among the mercenary young ladies whom he met in Southwell drawing-rooms.

Having left Harrow, he went up to Cambridge in the autumn of 1805. At the University, besides his protégé *John Edleston, his friends were Charles Skinner Matthews, Scrope Davies and John Cam Hobhouse. All were high-spirited young men; and it was with their encouragement that, during this period of his life, Byron took his first enthusiastic steps in London dissipation. He was already deep in debt when he came down from Cambridge in July 1808.* English Bards and Scotch Reviewers (*to which he had been provoked by the unkind reception of his juvenile poems,* Hours of Idleness) *appeared in May 1809; and that same spring he gathered his Cambridge friends at Newstead, there to hold profane revels in a romantic mediaeval setting. The Newstead party was to be his farewell to England. In July he sailed from Falmouth, accompanied by John Cam Hobhouse, and visited Portugal, Spain, Sardinia, Malta, Constantinople, Athens and the countries of the Near East. Hobhouse presently returned to England; but Byron remained abroad, eagerly absorbing new impressions and tasting new enjoyments, for exactly two years.*

TO MRS. PARKER[1]   *Newstead Abbey, Nov. 8th, 1798*

DEAR MADAM,—My Mamma being unable to write herself desires I will let you know that the potatoes are now ready and you are welcome to them whenever you please.

She begs you will ask Mrs. Parkyns if she would wish the poney to go round by Nottingham or to go home the nearest way as it is now quite well but too small to carry me.

[1] The recipient of this letter, written by Byron at the age of ten years and ten months, was his aunt, Mrs. Parker, born Charlotte Augusta Byron, the mother of Margaret, one of his earliest loves.

I have sent a young Rabbit which I beg Miss Frances will accept off and which I promised to send before. My Mamma desires her best compliments to you all in which I join.

> I am, Dear Aunt, yours sincerely, BYRON

I hope you will excuse all blunders as it is the first letter I ever wrote.

TO HIS MOTHER *Harrow-on-the-Hill, Sunday, May 1st, 1803*

MY DEAR MOTHER,—I received your Letter the other day. And am happy to hear you are well. I hope you will find Newstead in as favorable a state as you can wish. I wish you would write to Sheldrake to tell him to make haste with my shoes. I am sorry to say that Mr. Henry Drury has behaved himself to me in a manner I neither *can* nor *will bear*. He has seized now an opportunity of showing his resentment towards me. To day in church I was talking to a Boy who was sitting next me ; *that* perhaps was not right, but hear what followed. After Church he spoke not a word to me, but he took this Boy to his pupil room, where he abused me in a most violent manner, called me *blackguard*, said he *would* and *could* have me expelled from the School, and bade me thank his *Charity* that *prevented* him ; this was the Message he sent me, to which I shall return no answer, but submit my case to *you* and those you may think *fit* to *consult*. Is this fit usage for any body ! had I *stole* or behaved in the most *abominable* way to him, his language could not have been more outrageous. What must the boys think of me to hear such a Message ordered to be delivered to me by a *Master* ? Better let him take away my life than ruin my *Character*. My Conscience acquits me of ever *meriting* expulsion at this School ; I have been *idle* and I certainly ought not to talk in church, but I have never done a mean action at this School to him or *any one*. If I had done anything so *heinous*, why should he allow me to stay at the School ? Why should he himself be so *criminal* as to overlook faults which merit the *appellation* of a *blackguard* ? If he had

4

had it in his power to have me expelled, he would long ago have *done* it ; as it is, he has done *worse*. If I am treated in this Manner, I will not stay at this *School*. I write you that I will not as yet appeal to Dr. Drury ;[1] his son's influence is more than mine and *justice* would be *refused* me. Remember I told you, when I *left* you at *Bath*, that he would seize every means and opportunity of revenge, not for leaving him so much as the mortification he suffered, because I begged you to let me leave him. If I had been the Blackguard he talks of, why did he not of his own accord refuse to keep me as his *pupil* ? You know Dr. Drury's first letter, in it were these Words : " My son and Lord Byron have had some disagreements ; but I hope that his future behaviour will render a change of Tutors unnecessary ". Last time I was here but a short time, and though he endeavoured, he could find nothing to abuse me in. Among other things I forgot to tell you he said he had a great mind to expel the boy for speaking to me, and that if he ever again spoke to me he would expel him. Let him explain his meaning ; he abused me, but he neither did nor can mention anything bad of me, further than what every boy else in the School has done. I fear him not ; but let him explain his meaning ; 'tis all I ask. I beg you will write to Dr. Drury to let him know what I have said. He has behaved to me, as also Mr. Evans, very kindly. If you do not take notice of this, I will leave the School myself ; but I am sure *you* will not see me *ill treated* ; better that I should suffer anything than this. I believe you will be tired by this time of reading my letter, but, if you love me, you will now show it. Pray write me immediately. I shall ever remain,

Your affectionate Son, BYRON

P.S.—Hargreaves Hanson [2] desires his love to you and hopes you are very well. I am not in want of any money so will not ask you for any. God bless, bless you.

---

[1] The Reverend Joseph Drury, D.D., was Head-master of Harrow from 1784 to 1805. He was assisted by his son Henry, who afterwards became the poet's close friend.

[2] Son of John Hanson, London solicitor and the Byrons' man of business. He had three sons, Charles, Hargreaves (Byron's contemporary at Harrow) and Newton, and a daughter, Mary Anne, whom the poet gave away when, in 1814, she married the weak-witted Earl of Portsmouth.

TO THE HON. AUGUSTA BYRON

Burgage Manor
March 22d, 1804

Although, My ever Dear Augusta, I have hitherto appeared remiss in replying to your kind and affectionate letters; yet I hope you will not attribute my neglect to a want of affection, but rather to a shyness naturally inherent in my Disposition. I will now endeavour as amply as lies in my power to repay your kindness, and for the Future I hope you will consider me not only as *a Brother* but as your warmest and most affectionate *Friend*, and if ever Circumstances should require it your *protector*. Recollect, My Dearest Sister, that you are *the nearest relation* I have in *the world both by the ties of Blood* and *affection*. If there is anything in which I can serve you, you have only to mention it; Trust to your Brother, and be assured he will never betray your confidence. When You see my Cousin and future Brother George Leigh,[1] tell him that I already consider him as my Friend, for whoever is beloved by you, my amiable Sister, will always be equally Dear to me.

I arrived here today at 2 o'clock after a fatiguing Journey, I found my Mother perfectly well. She desires to be kindly remembered to you; as she is just now Gone out to an assembly, I have taken the first opportunity to write to you, I hope she will not return immediately; for if she was to take it into her head to peruse my epistle, there is one part of it which would produce from her a panegyric on *a friend of yours*, not at all agreeable to me, and I fancy, *not particularly delightful to you*. If you see Lord Sidney Osborne I beg you will remember me to him; I fancy he has almost forgot me by this time, for it is rather more than a year Since I had the pleasure of Seeing him.—Also remember me to poor old Murray;[2] tell him we will see that something is to be done for him, for *while I live he shall never be abandoned In his old Age*. Write to me Soon, my Dear Augusta, And do not forget to love me, In the meantime, I remain, more than words can express, your ever sincere, affectionate   Brother and Friend, BYRON

P.S.—Do not forget to knit the purse you promised me, Adieu my beloved Sister.

[1] Byron's half-sister married her first cousin, Colonel George Leigh of the Tenth Dragoons, in 1807.

[2] Joe Murray, an old servant of the Byron family, to whom Byron afterwards made a small allowance.

6

TO THE HON. AUGUSTA BYRON

Southwell, March 26th, 1804

I received your affectionate letter, my ever Dear Sister, yesterday and I now hasten to comply with your injunction by answering it as soon as possible. Not, my Dear Girl, that it can be in the least irksome to me to write to you, on the Contrary it will always prove my Greatest pleasure, but I am sorry that I am afraid my correspondence will not prove the most entertaining, for I have nothing that I can relate to you, except my affection for you, which I can never sufficiently express, therefore I should tire you, before I had half satisfied myself. Ah, How unhappy I have hitherto been in being so long separated from so amiable a Sister ? but fortune has now sufficiently atoned by discovering to me a relation whom I love, a Friend in whom I can confide. In both these lights, my Dear Augusta, I shall ever look upon you, and I hope you will never find your Brother unworthy of your affection and Friendship.

I am as you may imagine a little dull here ; not being on terms of intimacy with Lord Grey [1] I avoid Newstead, and my resources of amusement are Books, and writing to my Augusta, which, wherever I am, will always constitute my Greatest pleasure. I am not reconciled to Lord Grey, *and I never will.* He was once my *Greatest Friend,* my reasons for ceasing that Friendship are such as I cannot explain, not even to you, my Dear Sister, (although were they to be made known to any body, you would be the first,) but they will ever remain hidden in my own breast.

They are Good ones, however, for although I am *violent* I am not *capricious* in my *attachments*. My mother disapproves of my quarrelling with him, but if she knew the cause (which she never will know,) She would reproach me no more. He Has forfeited all *title to my esteem*, but I hold him in too much *contempt* ever *to hate him*. My mother desires to be kindly

---

[1] Newstead Abbey was let to Lord Grey de Ruthyn from 1803 to 1808. Some light on this quarrel is shed by Hobhouse's pencil note scribbled in the margin of Moore's *Life*. While Mrs. Byron was established at Southwell, Byron often visited Newstead and was on friendly terms with his tenant. " . . . A circumstance occurred during this intimacy [Hobhouse records] which certainly had much effect on his future morals."

remembered to you. I shall soon be in town to resume my studies at Harrow ; I will certainly call upon you in my way up. Present my respects to Mrs. Harcourt ; I am Glad to hear that I am in her Good Graces for I shall always esteem her on account of her behaviour to you, my Dear Girl. Pray tell me If you see Lord S. Osborne, and how he is ; what little I know of him I like very much and If we were better acquainted I doubt not I should like him still better. Do not forget to tell me how Murray is. As to your Future prospects, my Dear Girl, *may they be happy !* I am sure you deserve Happiness and if *you* do not meet with it I shall begin to think it is " a bad world we live in ". Write to me soon. I am impatient to hear from you. God bless you, My amiable Augusta, I remain,

Your ever affectionate Brother and Friend, BYRON

TO THE HON. AUGUSTA BYRON   *Burgage Manor,*
                                                   August 18th, 1804

MY DEAREST AUGUSTA,—I seize this interval of my *amiable* mother's absence this afternoon, again to inform you, or rather to desire to be informed by you, of what is going on. For my own part I can send nothing to amuse you, excepting a repetition of my complaints against my tormentor, whose *diabolical* disposition (pardon me for staining my paper with so harsh a word) seems to increase with age, and to acquire new force with Time. The more I see of her the more my dislike augments ; nor can I so entirely conquer the appearance of it, as to prevent her from perceiving my opinion ; this, so far from calming the Gale, blows it into a *hurricane*, which threatens to destroy everything, till exhausted by its own violence, it is lulled into a sullen torpor, which, after a short period, is again roused into fresh and renewed phrenzy, to me most terrible, and to every other Spectator astonishing. She then declares that she plainly sees I hate her, that I am leagued with her bitter enemies, viz. Yourself, L^d C[arlisle] [1] and Mr. H[anson],

---

[1] Lord Carlisle, former gambler, dandy and friend of George Selwyn, had become Byron's guardian in 1799. He was connected with the Byron family on his mother's side.

and, as I never Dissemble or contradict her, we are all *honoured* with a multiplicity of epithets, too *numerous*, and some of them too *gross*, to be repeated. In this society, and in this amusing and instructive manner, have I dragged out a weary fortnight, and am condemned to pass another or three weeks as happily as the former. No captive Negro, or Prisoner of war, ever looked forward to their emancipation, and return to Liberty with more Joy, and with more lingering expectation, than I do to my escape from this maternal bondage, and this accursed place, which is the region of dullness itself, and more stupid than the banks of Lethe, though it possesses contrary qualities to the river of oblivion, as the detested scenes I now witness, make me regret the happier ones already passed, and wish their restoration.

Such Augusta is the happy life I now lead, such my *amusements*. I wander about hating everything I behold, and if I remained here a few months longer, I should become, what with *envy, spleen and all uncharitableness*, a complete *misanthrope*, but notwithstanding this,

Believe me, Dearest Augusta, ever yours, etc., etc., BYRON

TO HIS MOTHER *   [*Harrow-on-the-Hill, 1804 ?*]

MY DEAR MOTHER,—I received your letter and was very glad to hear that you are well. I am very comfortable here as far as relates to my Comrades, but I have got into two or three scrapes with Drury and the other Masters, which are not very convenient. The other day as he was reprimanding me (perhaps very properly) for my misdeeds he uttered the following words, " it is not probable that from your age and situation in the School your Friends will permit you to remain longer than Summer. But because you are about to leave Harrow, it is no reason you are to make the house a scene of riot and confusion." This and much more said the Doctor ; and I am informed from creditable authority that Dr. Drury, Mr. Evans and Martin Drury said I was a *Blackguard*. That Martin Drury said so I *know*, but I am inclined to doubt the authenticity of the report as to the rest. Perhaps it is true, perhaps not. But thank God they may call me a Blackguard, but they can never make me one. If Dr. Drury can bring one boy or any one else to say that I have committed a dishonourable action, and to prove it, I am content. But otherwise I am stigmatized without a cause, and I disdain and despise the malicious efforts of him and his Brother. His Brother Martin not Henry Drury (whom I will do the justice to say has never since last year interfered with me) is continually reproaching me with the narrowness of my fortune, to what end I know not ; his intentions may be good, but his manner is disagreeable. I see no reason why I am to be reproached with it. I have as much money, as many clothes, and in every respect of appearance am equal if not superior to most of my schoolfellows, and if my fortune is narrow it is my misfortune, not my fault. But, however, the way *to riches*, *to greatness* lies before me. I can, I will cut myself a path through the world or perish in the attempt. Others have begun life with nothing and ended greatly. And shall I, who have a competent if not a large fortune, remain idle ? No, I will carve myself the passage to Grandeur, but never with Dishonour. These, Madam, are my intentions. But why this upstart Son of a Button maker is to reproach me about an estate which, however, is far superior to his own, I know not. But that he should call me a Blackguard is far worse. On account of the former, I can blame only Mr. Hanson (and that officious friend Lord Grey de Ruthyn, whom I shall ever consider as my most inveterate enemy). It is a mere trifle, but the latter I cannot bear. I have not deserved it, and I will not be insulted with impunity. Mr. Martin Drury rides out with his son, sees me at a distance on a poney which I hired to go to the bathing place which is too far for me to walk. He calls out, tells his son I am a Blackguard. This son, who is no friend of mine, comes home, relates the story to his companions, possibly with a few exaggerations. But however the greatest part was true, and I am to be considered as such a person by my comrades. It shall not be. I will say no more. I only hope you will take this into your consideration and remove me at Summer from a place where I am goaded with insults by those from whom I have little deserved it.

I remain your affectionate Son, BYRON

TO THE HON. AUGUSTA BYRON   *Harrow-on-the-Hill,*
                                         October 25th, 1804

MY DEAR AUGUSTA,—In compliance with your wishes, as well as gratitude for your affectionate letter, I proceed as soon as possible to answer it ; I am glad to hear that *any body* gives a good account of me ; but from the quarter you mention, I should imagine it was exaggerated. That you are unhappy, my dear Sister, makes me so also ; were it in my power to relieve your sorrows you would soon recover your spirits ; as it is, I sympathize better than you yourself expect. But really, after all (pardon me my dear Sister), I feel a little inclined to laugh at you, for love, in my humble opinion, is utter nonsense, a mere jargon of compliments, romance, and deceit ; now, for my part, had I fifty mistresses, I should in the course of a fortnight, forget them all, and, if by any chance I ever recollected one, should laugh at it as a dream, and bless my stars, for delivering me from the hands of the little mischievous Blind God. Can't you drive this Cousin of ours out of your pretty little head (for as to *hearts* I think they are out of the question), or if you are so far gone, why don't you give old L'Harpagon (I mean the General) the slip, and take a trip to Scotland, you are now pretty near the Borders. Be sure to Remember me to my formal Guardy Lord Carlisle, whose magisterial presence I have not been into for some years, nor have I any ambition to attain so great an honour. As to your favourite Lady Gertrude, I don't remember her ; pray, is she handsome? I dare say she is, for although they are a *disagreeable, formal, stiff* Generation, yet they have by no means plain *persons*, I remember Lady Cawdor was a sweet, pretty woman ; pray, does your sentimental Gertrude resemble her? I have heard that the duchess of Rutland was handsome also, but we will say nothing about her temper, as I hate Scandal.

Adieu, my pretty Sister, forgive my levity, write soon, and God bless you.

I remain, your very affectionate Brother, BYRON

P.S.—I left my mother at Southwell, some time since, in a monstrous pet with you for not writing. I am sorry to say the old lady and myself don't agree like lambs in a meadow, but I believe it is all my own fault, I am rather too fidgety, which my precise mama objects to, we differ, then argue, and to my shame be it spoken fall out a *little*, however after a storm comes a calm ; what's become of our aunt the amiable antiquated Sophia ? is she yet in the land of the living, or does she sing psalms with the *Blessed* in the other world. Adieu. I am happy enough and Comfortable here. My friends are not numerous, but select ; among them I rank as the principal Lord Delawarr,[1] who is very amiable and my particular friend ; do you know the family at all ? Lady Delawarr is frequently in town, perhaps you may have seen her ; if she resembles her son she is the most amiable woman in Europe. I have plenty of acquaintances, but I reckon them as mere Blanks. Adieu, my dear Augusta.

TO THE HON. AUGUSTA BYRON   *Harrow-on-the-Hill,*
Novr., Saturday, 17th, 1804

I am glad to hear, My dear Sister, that you like Castle Howard so well, I have no doubt what you say is true and that Lord C[arlisle] is much more amiable than he has been represented to me. Never having been much with him and always hearing him reviled, it was hardly possible I should have conceived a very *great friendship* for his L^dship. My mother, you inform me, commends my *amiable disposition* and *good understanding* ; if she does this to you, it is a great deal more than I ever hear myself, for the one or the other is always found fault with, and I am told to copy the *excellent pattern* which I see before me in *herself.* You have got an invitation too, you may accept it if you please, but if you value your own comfort, and like a pleasant situation, I advise you to avoid Southwell.—I thank you, My dear Augusta, for your readiness to assist me, and will in some manner avail myself of it ; I do not however wish to be separated from *her* entirely,

---

[1] Lord Delawarr, like Lord Clare, was one of the bevy of good-looking younger companions whom Byron collected around himself at Harrow.

but not to be so much with her as I hitherto have been, for I do believe she likes me ; she manifests that in many instances, particularly with regard to money, which I never want, and have as much as I desire. But her conduct is so strange, her caprices so impossible to be complied with, her passions so outrageous, that the evil quite overbalances her *agreeable qualities*. Amongst other things I forgot to mention a most *ungovernable appetite* for Scandal, which she never can govern, and employs most of her time abroad, in displaying the faults, and censuring the foibles, of her acquaintance ; therefore I do not wonder, that my precious Aunt, comes in for her share of encomiums ; This however is nothing to what happens when my conduct admits of animadversion ; " then comes the tug of war ". My whole family from the conquest are upbraided ! myself abused, and I am told that what little accomplishments I possess either in mind or body are derived from her and *her alone*.

When I leave Harrow I know not ; that depends on her nod ; I like it very well. The master Dr. Drury, is the most amiable *clergyman* I ever knew ; he unites the Gentleman with the Scholar, without affectation or pedantry, what little I have learnt I owe to him alone, nor is it his fault that it was not more. I shall always remember his instructions with Gratitude, and cherish a hope that it may one day be in my power to repay the numerous obligations, I am under ; to him or some of his family.

Our holidays come on in about a fortnight. I however have not mentioned that to my mother, nor do I intend it ; but if I can, I shall contrive to evade going to Southwell. Depend upon it I will not approach her for some time to come if it is in my power to avoid it, but she must not know, that it is my wish to be absent. I hope you will excuse my sending so short a letter, but the Bell has just rung to summon us together. Write Soon, and believe me,

Ever your affectionate Brother, BYRON

I am afraid you will have some difficulty in decyphering my epistles, but *that* I know you will excuse. Adieu. Remember me to Ld Carlisle.

TO THE HON. AUGUSTA BYRON *Burgage Manor,*
April 23d, 1805

MY DEAREST AUGUSTA,—I presume by this time, that
you are safely arrived at the Earl's, at least I *hope* so ; nor
shall I feel myself perfectly easy, till I have the pleasure of
hearing from yourself of your safety. I myself shall set out
for town this day (Tuesday) week, and intend waiting upon
you on Thursday at farthest ; in the mean time I must console
myself as well as I can ; and I am sure, no unhappy mortal
ever required much more consolation than I do at present.
You as well as myself know the *sweet* and *amiable* temper of a
certain personage to whom I am nearly related ; of *course*,
the pleasure I have enjoyed during my vacation, (although
it has been greater than I expected) yet has not been so *super-
abundant* as to make me wish to stay a day longer than I can
avoid. However, notwithstanding the dullness of the place,
and certain *unpleasant things* that occur In a family not a hundred
miles distant from Southwell, I contrived to pass my time in
peace, till to day, when unhappily, In a most inadvertent
manner, I said that Southwell was not *peculiarly* to my taste ;
but however, I merely expressed this in common conversation,
without speaking disrespectfully of the *sweet* town ; (which,
between you and I, I wish was swallowed up by an earthquake,
provided my *Eloquent mother* was not in it). No sooner had the
unlucky sentence, which I believe was prompted by my evil
Genius, escaped my lips, than I was treated with an Oration
in the *ancient style*, which I have often so *pathetically* described
to you, unequalled by any thing of *modern* or *antique* date ;
nay the *Philippics* against Ld Melville [1] were nothing to it ;
one would really Imagine, to have heard the *Good Lady*, that
I was a most *treasonable culprit*, but thank St. Peter, after undergoing this *Purgatory* for the last hour, it is at length blown over,
and I have sat down under these *pleasing impressions* to address
you, so that I am afraid my epistle will not be the most entertaining. I assure you upon my *honour*, jesting apart, I have
never been so *scurrilously*, and *violently* abused by any person,

---

[1] Henry Dundas, created Viscount Melville in 1802, was accused in 1805 of
misdemeanours connected with the accounts of the naval department. He stood
trial in Westminster Hall during the following year and was acquitted on all
charges.

as by that woman, whom I think I am to call mother, by that being who gave me birth, to whom I ought to look up with veneration and respect, but whom I am sorry I cannot love or admire. Within one little hour, I have not only heard myself, but have heard my *whole family*, by the father's side, *stigmatized* in terms that the *blackest malevolence* would perhaps shrink from, and that too in words you would be shocked to hear. Such, Augusta, such is my mother ; *my mother !* I disclaim her from this time, and although I cannot help treating her with respect, I cannot reverence, as I ought to do, that parent who by her outrageous conduct forfeits all title to filial affection. To you, Augusta, I must look up, as my nearest relation, to you I must confide what I cannot mention to others, and I am sure you will pity me ; but I entreat you to keep this a secret, nor expose that unhappy failing of this woman, which I must bear with patience. I would be very sorry to have it discovered, as I have only one week more, for the present. In the mean time you may write to me with the greatest safety, as she would not open any of my letters, even from you. I entreat then that you will favour me with an answer to this. I hope however to have the pleasure of seeing you on the day appointed, but If you could contrive any way that I may avoid being asked to dinner by Ld C. I would be obliged to you, as I hate strangers. Adieu, my Beloved Sister,

　　　　　　　　　　　　　I remain ever yours, BYRON

TO THE HON. AUGUSTA BYRON　　　　[Address cut out], *Tuesday, July 2d, 1805*

MY DEAREST AUGUSTA,—I am just returned from Cambridge, where I have been to enter myself at Trinity College. —Thursday is our Speechday at Harrow, and as I forgot to remind you of its approach, previous to our first declamation, I have given you *timely* notice this time. If you intend doing me the *honour* of attending, I would recommend you not to come without a Gentleman, as I shall be too much engaged all the morning to take care of you, and I should not imagine you would admire *stalking* about by yourself. You had better be there by 12 o'clock as we begin at 1, and I should like to procure you a good place ; Harrow is 11 miles from town, it will just make a *comfortable* mornings drive for you. I don't know how you are to come, but for *Godsake* bring as few women with you as possible. I would wish you to Write me an answer immediately, that I may know on Thursday morning, whether you will drive over or not, and I will arrange my other engagements accordingly. I *beg*, *Madam*, you may make your appearance in one of his Lordships most *dashing* carriages, as our Harrow *etiquette*, admits of nothing but the most *superb* vehicles, on our Grand *Festivals*. In the mean time, believe me, dearest Augusta,

Your affectionate Brother, BYRON

TO JOHN HANSON   *Harrow, 8 July, 1805*

MY DEAR SIR,—I have just received a Letter from my Mother, in which she talks of coming to Town about the *commencement* of our Holidays. If she does, it will be impossible for me to call on *my Sister*, previous to my leaving it, and at the same time I cannot conceive* what the Deuce she can want at this season in London. I have written to tell her that my Holidays commence on the 6th of August, but however, July the 31st is the proper day.—I beg that if you cannot find some means to keep her in the Country that you at least will connive at this deception which I can palliate, and then I shall be down in the country before she knows where I am. My reasons for this are, that I do *not wish* to be detained in Town so uncomfortably as I know I shall be if I remain with her ; that *I do wish* to see my Sister ; and in the next place she can just as well come to Town after my return to Notts, as I don't desire to be dragged about according to her caprice, and there are some other causes I think unnecessary to be now mentioned. If you will only contrive by settling this business (if it is in your power), or if that is impossible, not mention anything about the day our Holidays commence, of which you can be easily supposed not to be informed : if, I repeat, you can by any means prevent this Mother from executing her purposes, believe me, you will greatly oblige

Yours truly, BYRON

TO CHARLES O. GORDON [1]   *Burgage Manor, Southwell, Notts, August 4, 1805*

Although I am greatly afraid, my Dearest Gordon, that you will not receive this epistle till you return from Abergeldie, (as your letter stated that you would be at Ledbury on Thursday next) yet, that is not my fault, for I have not deferred answering yours a moment, and, as I have just now concluded my Journey, my first, and, I trust you will believe me when I say, most pleasing occupation will be to write to you.

We have played the Eton and were most confoundedly beat; however it was some comfort to me that I got 11 notches the 1st Innings and 7 the 2d, which was more than any of our side except Brockman and Ipswich could contrive to hit. After the match we dined together, and were extremely friendly, not a single discordant word was uttered by either party. To be sure, we were most of us rather drunk and went together to the Haymarket Theatre, where we kicked up a row, As you may suppose, when so many Harrovians and Etonians met at one place; I was one of seven in a single hackney, 4 Eton and 3 Harrow, and then we all got into the same box, and the consequence was that such a devil of a noise arose that none of our neighbours could hear a word of the drama, at which, not being *highly delighted*, they began to quarrel with us, and we nearly came to a *battle royal*. How I got home after the play God knows. I hardly recollect, as my brain was so much confused by the heat, the row, and the wine I drank, that I could not remember in the morning how I found my way to bed.

The rain was so incessant in the evening that we could hardly get our Jarveys, which was the cause of so many being stowed into one. I saw young Twilt, your brother, with

---

[1] Charles Gordon was one of Byron's " juniors and favourites " at Harrow, whom he " spoilt by indulgence ".

Malet, and saw also an old schoolfellow of mine whom I had not beheld for six years, but he was not the one whom you were so good as to enquire after for me, and for which I return you my sincere thanks. I set off last night at eight o'clock to my mother's, and am just arrived this afternoon, and have not delayed a second in thanking you for so soon fulfilling my request that you would correspond with me. My address at Cambridge will be Trinity College, but I shall not go there till the 20th of October. You may continue to direct your letters here, when I go to Hampshire which will not be till you have returned to Harrow. I will send my address previous to my departure from my mother's. I agree with you in the hope that we shall continue our correspondence for a long time. I trust, my dearest friend, that it will only be interrupted by our being some time or other in the same place or under the same roof, as, when I have finished my *Classical Labour*, and my minority is expired, I shall expect you to be a frequent visitor to Newstead Abbey, my seat in this country which is about 12 miles from my mother's house where I now am. There I can show you plenty of hunting, shooting and fishing, and be assured no one ever will be more welcome guest than yourself—nor is there any one whose correspondence can give me more pleasure, or whose friendship yield me greater delight than yours, sweet, dearest Charles, believe me, will always be the sentiments of

Yours most affectionately, BYRON

TO CHARLES O. GORDON *Burgage Manor, August 14, 1805*

Believe me, my dearest Charles, no letter from you can ever be unentertaining or dull, at least to me; on the contrary they will always be productive of the highest pleasure as often as you think proper to gratify me by your correspondence. My answer to your first was addressed to Ledbury; and I fear you will not receive it till you return from your tour, which I hope may answer your expectation in every respect; I recollect some years ago passing near Abergeldie in an excursion through the Highlands, it was at that time a most beautiful place.

I suppose you will soon have a view of the eternal snows that summit the top of Lachin y Gair, which towers so majestically above the rest of our *Northern Alps*. I still remember with pleasure the admiration which filled my mind, when I first beheld it, and further on the dark frowning mountains which rise near Invercauld, together with the romantic rocks that overshadow Mar Lodge, a seat of Lord Fife's, and the cataract of the Dee, which dashes down the declivity with impetuous violence in the grounds adjoining to the House. All these I presume you will soon see, so that it is unnecessary for me to expatiate further on the subject. I sincerely wish that every happiness may attend you in your progress. I have given you an account of our match in my epistle to Herefordshire. We unfortunately lost it. I got 11 notches the first innings and 7 the 2d, making 18 in all, which was more runs than any of our side (except Ipswich) could make. Brockman also scored 18. After the match we dined together and were very convivial. In the evening we proceeded to the play.

TO THE HON. AUGUSTA BYRON   *Trin. Coll.*
                            [*Wednesday*], *Novr. 6th, 1805*

MY DEAR AUGUSTA,—As might be supposed I like a College Life extremely, especially as I have escaped the Trammels or rather *Fetters* of my domestic Tyrant Mrs. Byron, who continued to plague me during my visit in July and September. I am now most pleasantly situated in *Super*excellent Rooms, flanked on one side by my Tutor, on the other by an old Fellow, both of whom are rather checks upon my *vivacity*. I am allowed 500 a year, a Servant and Horse, so Feel as independent as a German Prince who coins his own Cash, or a Cherokee Chief who coins no Cash at all, but enjoys what is more precious, Liberty. I talk in raptures of that *Goddess* because my amiable Mama was so despotic. I am afraid the Specimens I have lately given her of my Spirit, and determination to submit to no more unreasonable demands, (or the insults which follow a refusal to obey her implicitly whether right or wrong,) have given high offence, as I had a most *fiery* Letter from the *Court* at *Southwell* on Tuesday, because I would not turn off my Servant, (whom I had not the least reason to distrust, and who had an excellent Character from his last Master) at her suggestion, from some caprice she had taken into her head. I sent back to the Epistle, which was couched in *elegant* terms, a severe answer, which so nettled her Ladyship, that after reading it, she returned it in a Cover without deigning a Syllable in return.

The Letter and my answer you shall behold when you next see me, that you may judge of the Comparative merits of Each. I shall let her go on in the *Heroics*, till she cools, without taking the least notice. Her Behaviour to me for the last two Years neither merits my respect, nor deserves my affection. I am comfortable here, and having one of the best allowances in College, go on Gaily, but not extravagantly. I need scarcely inform you that I am not the least obliged to Mrs. B. for it, as it comes off my property, and She refused to fit out a single thing for me from her own pocket; my Furniture is paid for, and she has moreover a handsome addition made to her own income, which I do not in the least regret, as I would wish her to be happy, but by *no means* to live with me in *person*. The sweets of her society I have already drunk to the last dregs, I hope we shall meet on more affectionate Terms, or meet no more.

But why do I say *meet*? her temper precludes every idea of happiness, and therefore in future I shall avoid her *hospitable* mansion, though she has the folly to suppose She is to be mistress of my house when I come of [age].[1] I must apologize to you for the [dullness?][1] of this letter, but to tell you the [truth][1] [the effects][1] of last nights Claret have no[t gone][1] out of my head, as I supped with a large party. I suppose that Fool Hanson in his *vulgar* Idiom, by the word Jolly did not mean Fat, but High Spirits, for so far from increasing I have lost one pound in a fortnight as I find by being regularly weighed.

Adieu, Dearest Augusta. [Signature cut out.]

TO JOHN HANSON *Trinity College, Cambridge, Novr. 30, 1805*

SIR,—After the contents of your epistle, you will probably be less surprized at my answer, than I have been at many points

[1] Words torn out with the seal.

of yours ; never was I more astonished than at the perusal, for I confess I expected very different treatment. Your *indirect* charge of Dissipation does not affect me, nor do I fear the strictest inquiry into my conduct; neither here nor at *Harrow* have I disgraced myself, the " Metropolis " and the " Cloisters " are alike unconscious of my debauchery, and on the plains of *merry Sherwood* I have experienced *Misery* alone ; in July I visited them for the last time. Mrs. Byron and myself are now totally separated, injured by her, I sought refuge with Strangers, too late I see my error, for how was kindness to be expected from *others*, when denied by a *parent*? In you, Sir, I imagined I had found an Instructor; for your advice I thank you ; the Hospitality of yourself and Mrs. H. on many occasions I shall always gratefully remember, for I am not of opinion that even present injustice can cancel past obligations. Before I proceed, it will be necessary to say a few words concerning Mrs. Byron ; you hinted a probability of her appearance at Trinity ; the instant I hear of her arrival I quit Cambridge, though *Rustication* or *Expulsion* be the consequence. Many a weary week of *torment* have I passed with her, nor have I forgot the insulting *Epithets* with which myself, my *Sister*, my *father* and my *Family* have been repeatedly reviled.

To return to you, Sir, though I feel obliged by your hospitality, etc., etc., in the present instance I have been completely deceived. When I came down to College, and even previous to that period I stipulated that not only my Furniture, but even my Gowns and Books, should be paid for that I might set out free from *Debt*. Now with all the *Sang Froid* of your profession you tell me, that not only I shall not be permitted to repair my rooms (which was at first agreed to) but that I shall not even be indemnified for my present expence. In one word, hear my determination. I will *never* pay for them out of my allowance, and the Disgrace will not attach to me but to *those* by whom I have been deceived. Still, Sir, not even the Shadow of dishonour shall reflect on *my* Name, for I will see that the Bills are discharged ; whether by you or not is to me indifferent, so that the men I employ are not the victims of my Imprudence or your Duplicity. I have ordered nothing extravagant ; every man in College is allowed to fit up his rooms; mine are secured to me during my residence which will probably be some time, and in rendering them decent I am more praiseworthy than culpable. The money I requested was but a secondary consideration; as a *Lawyer* you were not obliged to advance it till due; as a *Friend* the request might have been complied with. When it is required at Xmas I shall expect the demand will be answered. In the course of my letter I perhaps have expressed more asperity than I intended, it is my nature to feel warmly, nor shall any consideration of interest or Fear ever deter me from giving vent to my Sentiments, when injured, whether by a Sovereign or a Subject.

I remain, etc., etc., BYRON

TO THE HON. AUGUSTA BYRON *16, Piccadilly,*
Decr. 27th, 1805

MY DEAR AUGUSTA,—You will doubtless be surprised to see a second epistle so close upon the arrival of the first, (especially as it is not my custom) but the Business I mentioned rather mysteriously in my last compels me again to proceed. But before I disclose it, I must require the most inviolable Secrecy, for if ever I find that it has transpired, all confidence, all Friendship between us has concluded. I do not mean this exordium as a threat to induce you to comply with my request but merely (whether you accede or not) to keep it a Secret. And although your compliance would essentially oblige me, yet, believe me, my esteem will not be diminished by your Refusal; nor shall I suffer a complaint to escape. The Affair is briefly thus; like all other young men just let loose, and especially one as I am, freed from the worse than bondage of my maternal home, I have been extravagant, and consequently am in want of Money. You will probably now imagine that I am going to apply to you for some. No, if you would offer me thousands, I declare solemnly that I would without hesitation refuse, nor would I accept them were I in danger of Starvation. All I expect or wish is, that you will be joint Security with me for a few Hundreds a person (one of the money lending tribe) has offered to advance in case I can bring forward any collateral guarantee that he will not be a loser, the reason of this requisition is my being a Minor, and might refuse to discharge a debt contracted in my nonage. If I live till the period of my minority expires, you cannot doubt my paying, as I have property to the amount of 100 times the sum I am about to raise; if, as I think rather probable, a pistol or a Fever cuts short the thread of my existence, you will receive half the *Dross* saved since I was ten years old, and can be no great loser by discharging a debt of 7 or £800 from as many thousands. It is far from my Breast to exact any promise from you that would be detrimental, or tend to lower me in your opinion. If you suppose this leads to either of those consequences, forgive my impertinence and bury it in oblivion. I have many Friends, most of them in the same predicament with myself; to those who are not, I am too proud to apply, for I hate obligation; my Relations you know I *detest*; who then is there that I can address on the subject but yourself? to you therefore I appeal, and if I am disappointed, at least let me not be tormented by the advice of Guardians, and let silence rule your Resolution. I know you will think me foolish, if not criminal; but tell me so yourself, and do not rehearse my failings to others, no, not even to that proud Grandee the Earl, who, whatever his qualities may be, is certainly not amiable, and that Chattering puppy Hanson would make still less allowance for the foibles of a Boy. I am now trying the experiment, whether a woman can retain a secret; let me not be deceived. If you have the least doubt of my integrity, or that you run too great a Risk, do not hesitate in your refusal. Adieu. I expect an answer with impatience, believe me, whether you accede or not,

[Signature cut out.]

P.S.—I apologize for the numerous errors probably enveloped in this cover; the temper of my mind at present, and the hurry I have written in, must plead for pardon. Adieu.

TO JOHN M. B. PIGOT [1]   *16 Piccadilly, August 9, 1806*

My dear Pigot,—Many thanks for your amusing narrative of the last proceedings of my amiable Alecto, who now begins to feel the effects of her folly. I have just received a penitential epistle, to which, apprehensive of pursuit, I have despatched a moderate answer, with a *kind* of promise to return in a fort-night;—this, however (*entre nous*), I never mean to fulfil. Her soft warblings must have delighted her auditors, her higher notes being particularly musical, and on a calm moonlight evening would be heard to great advantage. Had I been present as a spectator, nothing would have pleased me more; but to have come forward as one of the *dramatis personæ*—St. Dominic defend me from such a scene! Seriously, your mother has laid me under great obligations, and you, with the rest of your family, merit my warmest thanks for your kind connivance at my escape from " Mrs. Byron *furiosa* ".

Oh! for the pen of Ariosto to rehearse, in epic, the scolding of that momentous eve,—or rather, let me invoke the shade of Dante to inspire me, for none but the author of the Inferno could properly preside over such an attempt. But, perhaps, where the pen might fail, the pencil would succeed. What a group!—Mrs. B. the principal figure; you cramming your ears with cotton, as the only antidote to total deafness; Mrs. —— in vain endeavouring to mitigate the wrath of the lioness robbed of her whelp; and last, though not least, Elizabeth and *Wousky*,—wonderful to relate!—both deprived of their parts of speech, and bringing up the rear in mute astonishment. How did S. B. receive the intelligence? How many *puns* did he utter on so *facetious* an event? In your next inform me on this point, and what excuse you made to A. You are probably, by this time, tired of deciphering this hieroglyphical letter;—like Tony Lumpkin, you will pronounce mine to be " a damned up and down hand." All Southwell, without doubt, is involved in amazement. *Apropos*, how does my blue-eyed nun, the fair * *? Is she " *robed in sable garb of woe* "?

Here I remain at least a week or ten days; previous to

---

[1] His friendship with the Pigot family, which included John Pigot and his sister, Elizabeth Bridget, was one of the few agreeable features of Byron's life at Southwell. Miss Pigot, who survived till 1866, remembered him as a " fat, bashful boy, with his hair combed straight over his forehead. . . ."

my departure you shall receive my address, but what it will be I have not determined. My lodgings must be kept secret from Mrs. B. You may present my compliments to her, and say any attempt to pursue me will fail, as I have taken measures to retreat immediately to Portsmouth, on the first intimation of her removal from Southwell. You may add, I have proceeded to a friend's house in the country, there to remain a fortnight.

I have now *blotted* (I must not say written) a complete double letter, and in return shall expect a *monstrous budget*. Without doubt, the dames of Southwell reprobate the pernicious example I have shown, and tremble lest their *babes* should disobey their mandates, and quit, in dudgeon, their mammas on any grievance. Adieu. When you begin your next, drop the " lordship ", and put " Byron " in its place.

Believe me yours, etc., BYRON

TO THE EARL OF CLARE[1]   *Southwell, Notts, February 6, 1807*

MY DEAREST CLARE,—Were I to make all the apologies necessary to atone for my late negligence, you would justly say you had received a petition instead of a letter, as it would be filled with prayers for forgiveness ; but instead of this, I will acknowledge my *sins* at once, and I trust to your friendship and generosity rather than to my own excuses. Though my health is not perfectly re-established, I am out of all danger, and have recovered every thing but my spirits, which are subject to depression. You will be astonished to hear I have lately written to Delawarr, for the purpose of explaining (as far as possible without involving some *old friends* of mine in the business) the cause of my behaviour to him during my last residence at Harrow (nearly two years ago), which you will recollect was rather " *en cavalier* ". Since that period, I have discovered he was treated with injustice both by those who misrepresented his conduct, and by me in consequence of their suggestions. I have therefore made all the reparation

---

[1] Of all his Harrow friendships, that with Lord Clare lasted longest, and was remembered by Byron with most tenderness and gratitude.

in my power, by apologizing for my mistake, though with very faint hopes of success; indeed I never expected any answer, but desired one for form's sake; *that* has not yet arrived, and most probably never will. However, I have *eased* my own *conscience* by the atonement, which is humiliating enough to one of my disposition; yet I could not have slept satisfied with the reflection of having, *even unintentionally*, injured any individual. I have done all that could be done to repair the injury, and there the affair must end. Whether we renew our intimacy or not is of very trivial consequence.

My time has lately been much occupied with very different pursuits. I have been *transporting* a servant, who cheated me,—rather a disagreeable event;—performing in private theatricals;—publishing a volume of poems (at the request of my friends, for their perusal);—making love,—and taking physic. The two last amusements have not had the best effect in the world; for my attentions have been divided amongst so many fair damsels, and the drugs I swallow are of such variety in their composition, that between Venus and Æsculapius I am harassed to death. However, I have still leisure to devote some hours to the recollections of past, regretted friendships, and in the interval to take the advantage of the moment, to assure you how much I am, and ever will be, my dearest Clare,

Your truly attached and sincere BYRON

TO JOHN HANSON   Southwell, April 2nd, 1807

DEAR SIR,—Before I proceed in Reply to the other parts of your Epistle, allow me to congratulate you on the *Accession* of *Dignity* and *profit*, which will doubtless accrue, from your official appointment.

You was fortunate in obtaining possession at so critical a period; your patrons " exeunt omnes ". I trust they will soon supersede the Cyphers, their successors. The Reestablishment of your health is another happy event, and, though *secondary* in my *Statement*, is by no means so in my *Wishes*. As to our Feuds, they are purely *official*, the natural consequence of our relative Situations, but as little connected with *personal animosity*, as the *Florid Declamations* of *parliamentary Demagogues*. I return you my thanks for your favorable opinion of my muse; I have lately been honoured with many very flattering literary critiques, from men of high Reputation in the Sciences, particularly Lord Woodhous[lee] and Henry Mackenzie, both *Scots* and of great Eminence as *Authors* themselves. I have received also some most favorable Testimonies from *Cambridge*. This you will *marvel* at, as indeed I did myself. Encouraged by these and several other Encomiums, I am about to publish a volume at large; this will be very different from the present; the amatory effusions (not to be wondered at from the *dissipated* Life I have led) will be cut out, and others substituted. I coincide with you in opinion that the *Poet* yields to the *orator*; but as nothing can be done in the latter capacity till the expiration of my *Minority*, the former occupies my present attention, and both *ancients* and *moderns* have declared that the two pursuits are so nearly similar as to require in a great measure the same Talents, and he who excels in the one, would on application succeed in the other. Lyttelton, Glover, and Young (who was a celebrated Preacher and a Bard) are instances of the kind. *Sheridan* and *Fox* also; *these* are *great Names*. I may imitate, I can never equal them.

You speak of the *Charms* of Southwell; the *place* I *abhor*. The Fact is I remain here because I can appear no where else, being *completely done* up. *Wine* and *Women* have *dished* your *humble Servant*, not a *Sou* to be *had*; all *over*; condemned to exist (I cannot say live) at this *Crater* of Dullness till my *Lease* of *Infancy* expires. To appear at Cambridge is impossible; no money even to pay my College expences. You will be surprized to hear I am grown *very thin*; however it is the *Fact*, so much so, that the people here think I am *going*. I have lost 18 LB in my weight, that is one Stone and 4 pounds since January, this was ascertained last Wednesday, on account of a *Bet* with an acquaintance. However don't be alarmed; I have taken every means to accomplish the end, by violent exercise and Fasting, as I found myself too plump. I shall continue my Exertions, having no other amusement; I wear *seven* Waistcoats and a great Coat, run, and play at cricket in this Dress, till quite exhausted by excessive perspiration, use the hot Bath daily; eat only a quarter of a pound of Butcher's Meat in

24 hours, no Suppers or Breakfast, only one Meal a Day; drink no malt liquor, but a little Wine, and take Physic occasionally. By these means my *Ribs* display Skin of no great Thickness, and my Clothes have been taken in nearly *half a yard*. Do you believe me now?

Adieu. Remembrance to Spouse and the Acorns.

Yours ever, BYRON

TO ELIZABETH BRIDGET PIGOT   *Cambridge, June 30, 1807*

" Better late than never, Pal " is a saying of which you know the origin, and as it is applicable on the present occasion, you will excuse its conspicuous place in the front of my epistle. I am almost superannuated here. My old friends (with the exception of a very few) all departed, and I am preparing to follow them, but remain till Monday to be present at three *Oratorios*, two *Concerts*, a *Fair*, and a *Ball*. I find I am not only *thinner* but *taller* by an inch since my last visit. I was obliged to tell every body my *name*, nobody having the least recollection of my *visage*, or person. Even the hero of *my Cornelian* [1] (who is now sitting *vis-à-vis* reading a volume of my *Poetics*) passed me in Trinity walks without recognising me in the least, and was thunderstruck at the alteration which had taken place in my countenance, etc., etc. Some say I look *better*, others *worse*, but all agree I am *thinner*,—more I do not require. I have lost two pounds in my weight since I left your *cursed, detestable*, and *abhorred* abode of *scandal*, where, excepting yourself and John Becher,[2] I care not if the whole race were consigned to the *Pit* of *Acheron*, which I would visit in person rather than contaminate my *sandals* with the polluted dust of Southwell. *Seriously*, unless obliged by the *emptiness* of my purse to revisit Mrs. B., you will see me no more.

On Monday I depart for London. I quit Cambridge with little regret, because our *set* are *vanished*, and my *musical protégé* before mentioned has left the choir, and is stationed in a mer-

[1] John Edleston, a Cambridge chorister, whom Byron adopted as his protégé, and to whom he presented a Cornelian heart.

[2] The Reverend John Becher, another Southwell friend and an intimate of the Pigot family.

cantile house of considerable eminence in the metropolis.
You may have heard me observe he is exactly to an hour two
years younger than myself. I found him grown considerably,
and as you will suppose, very glad to see his former *Patron*.
He is nearly my height, very *thin*, very fair complexion, dark
eyes, and light locks. My opinion of his mind you already
know ;—I hope I shall never have occasion to change it. Every
body here conceives me to be an *invalid*. The University at
present is very gay from the fêtes of divers kinds. I supped out
last night, but eat (or ate) nothing, sipped a bottle of claret,
went to bed at two, and rose at eight. I have commenced early
rising, and find it agrees with me. The Masters and the
Fellows all very *polite*, but look a little *askance*—don't much
admire *lampoons*—truth always disagreeable.

Write, and tell me how the inhabitants of your *Menagerie*
go *on*, and if my publication goes *off* well : do the quadrupeds
growl? Apropos, my bull-dog is deceased—" Flesh both of cur
and man is grass ". Address your answer to Cambridge. If
I am gone, it will be forwarded. Sad news just arrived—
Russians beat—a bad set, eat nothing but *oil*, consequently
must melt before a *hard fire*. I get awkward in my academic
habiliments for want of practice. Got up in a window to hear
the oratorio at St. Mary's, popped down in the middle of the
Messiah, tore a *woeful* rent in the back of my best black silk
gown, and damaged an egregious pair of breeches. Mem.—
never tumble from a church window during service. Adieu,
dear * * * *! do not remember me to any body :—to *forget*
and be forgotten by the people of Southwell is all I aspire to.

TO ELIZABETH BRIDGET PIGOT   *Trin. Coll. Camb.*
                                                    July 5, 1807

Since my last letter I have determined to reside *another
year* at Granta, as my rooms, etc., etc., are finished in great
style, several old friends come up again, and many new acquaintances made ; consequently my inclination leads me
forward, and I shall return to college in October if still *alive*.
My life here has been one continued routine of dissipation—

out at different places every day, engaged to more dinners, etc., etc., than my *stay* would permit me to fulfil. At this moment I write with a bottle of claret in my *head* and *tears* in my *eyes*; for I have just parted with my " *Cornelian* ", who spent the evening with me. As it was our last interview, I postponed my engagement to devote the hours of the *Sabbath* to friendship :—Edleston and I have separated for the present, and my mind is a chaos of hope and sorrow. To-morrow I set out for London : you will address your answer to " Gordon's Hotel, Albemarle Street ", where I *sojourn* during my visit to the metropolis.

I rejoice to hear you are interested in my *protégé*; he has been my *almost constant* associate since October, 1805, when I entered Trinity College. His *voice* first attracted my attention, his *countenance* fixed it, and his *manners* attached me to him for ever. He departs for a *mercantile house* in *town* in October, and we shall probably not meet till the expiration of my minority, when I shall leave to his decision either entering as a *partner* through my interest, or residing with me altogether. Of course he would in his present frame of mind prefer the *latter*, but he may alter his opinion previous to that period ;—however, he shall have his choice. I certainly love him more than any human being, and neither time nor distance have had the least effect on my (in general) changeable disposition. In short, we shall put *Lady E. Butler* and *Miss Ponsonby* [1] to the blush, *Pylades* and *Orestes* out of countenance, and want nothing but a catastrophe like *Nisus* and *Euryalus*, to give *Jonathan* and *David* the " go by ". He certainly is perhaps more attached to *me* than even I am in return. During the whole of my residence at Cambridge we met every day, summer and winter, without passing *one* tiresome moment, and separated each time with increasing reluctance. I hope you will one day see us together. He is the only being I esteem, though I *like* many.

The Marquis of Tavistock was down the other day; I supped with him at his tutor's—entirely a Whig party. The opposition muster strong here now, and Lord Hartington, the Duke of Leinster, etc., etc., are to join us in October, so every thing will be *splendid*. The *music* is all over at present. Met

---

[1] Those " two dear inseparable inimitables ", the celebrated " Ladies of Llangollen ".

with another " *accidency* "—upset a butter-boat in the lap of
a lady—look'd very *blue*—*spectators* grinned—" curse 'em ! "
Apropos, sorry to say, been *drunk* every day, and not quite
sober yet—however, touch no meat, nothing but fish, soup, and
vegetables, consequently it does me no harm—sad dogs all
the *Cantabs*. Mem.—*we mean* to reform next January. This
place is a *monotony of endless variety*—like it—hate Southwell.
Has Ridge sold well? or do the ancients demur? What ladies
have bought?

Saw a girl at St. Mary's the image of Anne * * *, thought
it was her—all in the wrong—the lady stared, so did I—I
blushed, so did *not* the lady,—sad thing—wish women had *more
modesty*. Talking of women, puts me in mind of my terrier
Fanny—how is she? Got a headache, must go to bed, up early
in the morning to travel. My *protégé* breakfasts with me ;
parting spoils my appetite—excepting from Southwell. Mem.
I hate Southwell.

Yours, etc.

TO ELIZABETH BRIDGET PIGOT *Gordon's Hotel,*
July 13, 1807

You write most excellent epistles—a fig for other correspondents, with their nonsensical apologies for " *knowing nought about
it* ",—you send me a delightful budget. I am here in a perpetual vortex of dissipation (very pleasant for all that), and,
strange to tell, I get thinner, being now below eleven stone
considerably. Stay in town a *month*, perhaps six weeks, trip
into Essex, and then, as a favour, *irradiate* Southwell for three
days with the light of my countenance ; but nothing shall ever
make me *reside* there again. I positively return to Cambridge
in October ; we are to be uncommonly gay, or in truth I
should *cut* the University. An extraordinary circumstance
occurred to me at Cambridge ; a girl so very like * * made her
appearance, that nothing but the most *minute inspection* could
have undeceived me. I wish I had asked if *she* had ever been
at H * * *

What the devil would Ridge [1] have? is not fifty in a fortnight, before the advertisements, a sufficient sale? I hear many of the London booksellers have them, and Crosby has sent copies to the principal watering places. Are they liked or not in Southwell? * * * * * I wish Boatswain [2] had *swallowed* Damon! How is Bran? by the immortal gods, Bran ought to be a *Count* of the *Holy Roman Empire*.

The intelligence of London cannot be interesting to you, who have rusticated all your life—the annals of routs, riots, balls and boxing-matches, cards and crim. cons., parliamentary discussion, political details, masquerades, mechanics, Argyle Street Institution and aquatic races, love and lotteries, Brookes's and Buonaparte, opera-singers and oratorios, wine, women, wax-work, and weathercocks, can't accord with your *insulated* ideas of decorum and other *silly expressions* not inserted in *our vocabulary*.

Oh! Southwell, Southwell, how I rejoice to have left thee, and how I curse the heavy hours I dragged along, for so many months, among the Mohawks who inhabit your kraals!—However, one thing I do not regret, which is having *pared off* a sufficient quantity of flesh to enable me to slip into " an eel-skin ", and vie with the *slim* beaux of modern times; though I am sorry to say, it seems to be the mode amongst *gentlemen* to grow *fat*, and I am told I am at least fourteen pound below the fashion. However, I *decrease* instead of enlarging, which is extraordinary, as *violent* exercise in London is impracticable; but I attribute the *phenomenon* to our *evening squeezes* at public and private parties. I heard from Ridge this morning (the 14th, my letter was begun yesterday): he says the poems go on as well as can be wished; the seventy-five sent to town are circulated, and a demand for fifty more complied with, the day he dated his epistle, though the advertisements are not yet half published. Adieu.

[1] Byron's first collection of juvenile verses, published in 1806 and entitled *Fugitive Pieces*, had been suppressed on the advice of the Reverend John Becher. During the next year it was followed by a second, *Poems on Various Occasions*, issued anonymously, and during the summer months by a third, *Hours of Idleness*, which received considerable notice. All three were published by S. & J. Ridge of Newark.

[2] Boatswain, Byron's big black-and-white Newfoundland dog, died during the following year and was buried in the garden vault at Newstead, where the poet afterwards directed that he was himself to lie.

P.S.—Lord Carlisle, on receiving my poems, sent, before he opened the book, a tolerably handsome letter:—I have not heard from him since. His opinions I neither know nor care about: if he is the least insolent, I shall enrol him with *Butler* and the other worthies. He is in Yorkshire, poor man! and very ill! He said he had not had time to read the contents, but thought it necessary to acknowledge the receipt of the volume immediately. Perhaps the Earl " *bears no brother near the throne* ",—*if so*, I will make his *sceptre* totter *in his hands.*— Adieu!

TO ELIZABETH BRIDGET PIGOT   *August 2, 1807*

London begins to disgorge its contents—town is empty— consequently I can scribble at leisure, as occupations are less numerous. In a fortnight I shall depart to fulfil a country engagement; but expect two epistles from you previous to that period. Ridge does not proceed rapidly in Notts—very possible. In town things wear a more promising aspect, and a man whose works are praised by *reviewers*, admired by *duchesses*, and sold by every bookseller of the metropolis, does not dedicate much consideration to *rustic readers*. I have now a review before me, entitled *Literary Recreations* where my *bardship* is applauded far beyond my deserts. I know nothing of the critic, but think *him* a very discerning gentleman, and *myself* a devilish *clever* fellow. His critique pleases me particularly, because it is of great length, and a proper quantum of censure is administered, just to give an agreeable *relish* to the praise. You know I hate insipid, unqualified, common-place compliment. If you would wish to see it, order the 13th Number of *Literary Recreations* for the last month. I assure you I have not the most distant idea of the writer of the article—it is printed in a periodical publication—and though I have written a paper (a review of Wordsworth), which appears in the same work, I am ignorant of every other person concerned in it—even the editor, whose name I have not heard. My cousin, Lord Alexander Gordon, who resided in the same hotel, told me his mother, her Grace of Gordon, requested he would introduce my *Poetical* Lordship to her *Highness*, as she had bought my volume, admired it exceedingly, in common with the rest of the fashionable world, and wished to claim her relationship with the author. I was unluckily engaged on an excursion for some days afterwards; and, as the Duchess was on the eve of departing for Scotland, I have postponed my introduction till the winter, when I shall favour the lady, *whose taste I shall not dispute*, with my most sublime and edifying conversation. She is now in the Highlands, and Alexander took his departure, a few days ago, for the same *blessed* seat of " *dark rolling winds* ".

Crosby, my London publisher, has disposed of his second importation, and has sent to Ridge for a *third*—at least so he says. In every bookseller's window I see my *own name*, and *say nothing*, but enjoy my fame in secret. My last reviewer kindly requests me to alter my determination of writing no more: and " A Friend to the Cause of Literature " begs I will *gratify* the *public* with some new work " at no very distant period ". Who would not be a bard?—that is to say, if all critics would be so polite. However, the others will pay me off, I doubt not, for this *gentle* encouragement. If so, have at 'em? By the by, I have written at my intervals of leisure, after two in the morning, 380 lines in blank verse, of Bosworth Field. I have luckily got Hutton's account. I shall extend the poem to eight or ten books, and shall have finished it in a year. Whether it will be published or not must depend on circumstances. So much for *egotism*! My *laurels* have turned my brain, but the *cooling acids* of forthcoming criticism will probably restore me to *modesty*.

Southwell is a damned place—I have done with it—at least in all probability; excepting yourself, I esteem no one within its precincts. You were my only *rational* companion; and in plain truth, I had more respect for you than the whole *bevy*, with whose foibles I amused myself in compliance with their prevailing propensities. You gave yourself more trouble with me and my manuscripts than a thousand *dolls* would have done. Believe me, I have not forgotten your good nature in *this circle* of *sin*, and one day I trust I shall be able to evince my gratitude. Adieu.

Yours, etc.

P.S.—Remember me to Dr. P.

TO ELIZABETH BRIDGET PIGOT   *London, August 11, 1807*

On Sunday next I set off for the Highlands. A friend of mine accompanies me in my carriage to Edinburgh. There we shall leave it, and proceed in a *tandem* (a species of open carriage) through the western passes to Inverary, where we shall purchase *shelties*, to enable us to view places inaccessible to *vehicular conveyances*. On the coast we shall hire a vessel, and visit the most remarkable of the Hebrides; and, if we have time and favourable weather, mean to sail as far as Iceland, only 300 miles from the northern extremity of Caledonia, to peep at *Hecla*. This last intention you will keep a secret, as my nice *mamma* would imagine I was on a Voyage of *Discovery*, and raise the accustomed *maternal warwhoop*.

Last week I swam in the Thames from Lambeth through the two bridges, Westminster and Blackfriars, a distance, including the different turns and tracks made on the way, of three miles! You see I am in excellent training in case of a *squall* at sea. I mean to collect all the Erse traditions, poems, etc., etc., and translate, or expand the subject to fill a volume, which may appear next spring under the denomination of " *The Highland Harp* ", or some title equally *picturesque*. Of Bosworth Field, one book is finished, another just began. It will be a work of three or four years, and most probably never *conclude*. What would you say to some stanzas on Mount Hecla? they would be written at least with *fire*. How is the immortal Bran? and the Phœnix of canine quadrupeds, Boatswain? I have lately purchased a thorough-bred bull-dog, worthy to be the coadjutor of the aforesaid celestials—his name is *Smut*!—" Bear it, ye breezes, on your *balmy* wings ".

Write to me before I set off, I conjure you, by the fifth rib of your grandfather. Ridge goes on well with the books—I thought that worthy had not done much in the country. In town they have been very successful; Carpenter (Moore's publisher) told me a few days ago they sold all their's immediately, and had several enquiries made since, which, from the books being gone, they could not supply. The Duke of York, the Marchioness of Headfort, the Duchess of Gordon, etc., etc., were among the purchasers; and Crosby says the circulation will be still more extensive in the winter, the summer season being very bad for a sale, as most people are absent from London. However, they have gone off extremely well altogether. I shall pass very near you on my journey through Newark, but cannot approach. Don't tell this to Mrs. B, who supposes I travel a different road. If you have a letter, order it to be left at Ridge's shop, where I shall call, or the post-office, Newark, about six or eight in the evening. If your brother would ride over, I should be devilish glad to see him—he can return the same night, or sup with us and go home the next morning—the Kingston Arms is my inn. Adieu.

Yours ever, BYRON

TO LORD CLARE *   *Cambridge, August 20th, 1807*

MY DEAR CLARE,—What apology will be adequate to atone for my offence I know not. I can only say your letters would not have remained so long unnoticed, had I received them previous to my arrival at this place after an absence of 10 months when your kind epistles were diligently perused. Here they had waited for 6 months, and from them I received the first intimation of your departure from Harrow. Since *we* met, they tell me I am grown taller and so much thinner from illness and violent exercise that many who had lived with me in habits of intimacy, even old *school fellows*, found great difficulty in acknowledging me to be the *same person*. Indeed I ought to be *thin* for I weigh less by *three stone* and 9 *pounds* than I did 6 months ago. My weight was then 14 stone and 6 lbs. It is now 10 *stone* 11 lbs !!!

I believe I saw you and your brother a few weeks since passing through Bond Street in a lady's carriage. I was *only* a pedestrian and escaped your notice. The Poems you were pleased to mention have been published about 6 weeks. My bookseller tells me he has sold a great number. When we meet I shall be happy to present a copy for your inspection. The present volume differs very materially from the one printed privately last winter ; several poems published in the former are withheld from the latter, which however contains many more pieces, original and translated, and is of considerably larger size. When you answer this (if I can expect so much after my apparent, yet unintentional, neglect) address the reply to Trinity College, where I remain another year. Illness prevented my residence for the last twelve months. I have heard 3 times from Delawarr, that is to say, *twice* more often than I expected, or indeed desired, for, though I formerly liked him, long absence and our serious quarrel entirely destroyed the seeds of affection once *deeply* sown. I addressed him merely to explain the mistaken grounds on which he had acted, without (as I plainly told him) any view to a reconciliation. This produced a reply, etc., etc. In short the affair was compromised and we are what the World commonly call *friends*. Long may we be so, but never so intimate as before. Indeed, I shall take care we are not much together, and I doubt not D's inclinations are not more violently bent on a renewal of our acquaintance than my own. All things considered, how should it be otherwise?

I have never seen Harrow since the last day I spent there with your Lordship; next summer, *we old Harrow men* will favour the *little* Boys, our successors, with a visit. I hope this letter will find you *safe*. I saw in the morning paper a long account of robbery etc. etc. committed on the persons of *sundry Majors, Colonels* and Esquires, passing from *Lady Clare's* to *Limerick*. From such banditti the *Lord* deliver your *carcase* and *habitation*, you may exclaim with Pope in his Imitation of Spenser " Bad Neighbourhood I ween ". I am now setting off for the Highlands of Scotland [1] and expect your answer on my return to Cambridge. Have we any chance of meeting next winter? I shall pass some time in Town, where you will probably spend your vacation. Present my remembrances to Brother Richard and believe me, dearest Clare, yours ever affectly

BYRON

[1] Byron's often postponed journey to Scotland became, we are told, a joke among his friends.

TO ELIZABETH BRIDGET PIGOT   *Trinity College, Cambridge,*
October 26, 1807

MY DEAR ELIZABETH,—Fatigued with sitting up till four in
the morning for the last two days at hazard, I take up my
pen to inquire how your highness and the rest of my female
acquaintance at the seat of archiepiscopal grandeur go on. I
know I deserve a scolding for my negligence in not writing
more frequently; but racing up and down the country for
these last three months, how was it possible to fulfil the duties
of a correspondent? Fixed at last for six months, I write, as
thin as ever (not having gained an ounce since my reduction),
and rather in better humour;—but, after all, Southwell was
a detestable residence. Thank St. Dominica, I have done
with it: I have been twice within eight miles of it, but could
not prevail on myself to *suffocate* in its heavy atmosphere. This
place is wretched enough—a villainous chaos of din and
drunkenness, nothing but hazard and burgundy, hunting,
mathematics, and Newmarket, riot and racing. Yet it is a
paradise compared with the eternal dulness of Southwell.
Oh! the misery of doing nothing but make *love, enemies,* and
verses.

Next January (but this is *entre nous only,* and pray let it be
so, or my maternal persecutor will be throwing her tomahawk
at any of my curious projects), I am going to *sea* for four or
five months, with my cousin Captain Bettesworth, who commands the *Tartar,* the finest frigate in the navy. I have seen
most scenes, and wish to look at a naval life. We are going
probably to the Mediterranean, or to the West Indies, or—to
the devil; and if there is a possibility of taking me to the latter,
Bettesworth will do it; for he has received four and twenty
wounds in different places, and at this moment possesses a
letter from the late Lord Nelson, stating Bettesworth as the
only officer in the navy who had more wounds than himself.

I have got a new friend, the finest in the world, a *tame bear.*
When I brought him here, they asked me what I meant to do
with him, and my reply was, "he should *sit* for a *fellowship*".
Sherard will explain the meaning of the sentence, if it is
ambiguous. This answer delighted them not. We have
several parties here, and this evening a large assortment of

jockeys, gamblers, boxers, authors, parsons, and poets, sup with me,—a precious mixture, but they go on well together; and for me, I am a *spice* of every thing except a jockey; by the bye, I was dismounted again the other day.

Thank your brother in my name for his treatise. I have written 214 pages of a novel—one poem of 380 lines,[1] to be published (without my name) in a few weeks, with notes,—560 lines of Bosworth Field, and 250 lines of another poem in rhyme, besides half a dozen smaller pieces. The poem to be published is a Satire. *Apropos*, I have been praised to the skies in the *Critical Review*, and abused greatly in another publication. So much the better, they tell me, for the sale of the book: it keeps up controversy, and prevents it being forgotten. Besides, the first men of all ages have had their share, nor do the humblest escape;—so I bear it like a philosopher. It is odd two opposite critiques came out on the same day, and out of five pages of abuse, my censor only quotes *two lines* from different poems, in support of his opinion. Now, the proper way to *cut up*, it to quote long passages, and make them appear absurd, because simple allegation is no proof. On the other hand, there are seven pages of praise, and more than *my modesty* will allow said on the subject. Adieu.

P.S.—Write, write, write!!!

TO JOHN CAM HOBHOUSE †   *Dorant's, February 27th, 1808*

DEAR HOBHOUSE,—I write to you to explain a foolish circumstance, which has arisen from some words uttered by me before Pearce and Brown, when I was devoured with Chagrin, and almost insane with the fumes of, not " last night's Punch " but that evening's wine. In consequence of a misconception of something on my part, I mentioned an intention of withdrawing my name from the Whig Club. This I hear has been broached, and perhaps in a moment of Intoxication and passion such might be my idea, but *soberly* I have no such design, particularly as I could not abandon my principles,

---

[1] *English Bards*, printed but not published, which subsequently formed the basis of *English Bards and Scotch Reviewers*.

even if I renounced the society with whom I have the honour to be united in sentiments which I never will disavow. This I beg you will explain to the members as publicly as possible, but should not this be sufficient, and they think proper to erase my name, be it so. I only request that in this case they will recollect I shall become a *Tory* of *their own making*. I shall expect your answer on this point with some impatience. Now a few words on the subject of my own conduct.

*   *   *   *   *   *   *

As an author, I am cut to atoms by the E—— Review. It is just out, and has completely demolished my little fabric of fame. This is rather scurvy treatment from a Whig Review, but politics and poetry are different things, and I am no adept in either. I therefore submit in Silence.

Scrope Davies is meandering about London, feeding upon Leg of Beef Soup, and frequenting the British Forum. He has given up hazard, as also a considerable sum at the same time. Altamont is a good deal with me. Last night at the Opera Masquerade, we supped with seven whores, a *Bawd* and a *Ballet master*, in Madame Catalani's apartment behind the Scenes, (of course Catalani was *not* there). I have some thoughts of purchasing d'Egville's pupils: they would fill a glorious Haram.

I do not write often, but I like to receive letters. When therefore you are disposed to philosophize, no one standeth more in need of precepts of all sorts than

Yours very truly BYRON

TO JOHN CAM HOBHOUSE *   *Dorant's, March 26th 1808*

DEAR HOBHOUSE,—I have sent Fletcher to Cambridge for various purposes, and he has this *dispatch* for you. I am still living with my Dalilah, who has only two faults, unpardonable in a woman—she can read and write. Greet in my name the Bilious Birdmore. If you journey this way, I shall be glad to furnish you with Bread and Salt.

The university still chew the Cud of my degree. Please

God they shall swallow it, though Inflammation be the consequence.

I am leading a quiet though debauched life.

Yours very truly, BYRON

TO THE REV. JOHN BECHER   *Dorant's, March 28, 1808*

I have lately received a copy of the new edition from Ridge, and it is high time for me to return my best thanks to you for the trouble you have taken in the superintendence. This I do most sincerely, and only regret that Ridge has not seconded you as I could wish,—at least, in the bindings, paper, etc., of the copy he sent to me. Perhaps those for the public may be more respectable in such articles.

You have seen the *Edinburgh Review*, of course. I regret that Mrs. Byron is so much annoyed. For my own part, these " paper bullets of the brain " have only taught me to stand fire ; and, as I have been lucky enough upon the whole, my repose and appetite are not discomposed. Pratt, the gleaner, author, poet, etc., etc., addressed a long rhyming epistle to me on the subject, by way of consolation ; but it was not well done, so I do not send it, though the name of the man might make it go down. The E. R^s have not performed their task well ; at least the literati tell me this ; and I think *I* could write a more sarcastic critique on *myself* than any yet published. For instance, instead of the remark,—ill-natured enough, but not keen,—about Macpherson, I (quoad reviewers) could have said, " Alas, this imitation only proves the assertion of Dr. Johnson, that many men, women, and *children*, could write such poetry as Ossian's ".

I am *thin* and in exercise. During the spring or summer I trust we shall meet. I hear Lord Ruthyn leaves Newstead in April. As soon as he quits it for ever, I wish much you would take a ride over, survey the mansion, and give me your candid opinion on the most advisable mode of proceeding with regard to the *house*. *Entre nous*, I am cursedly dipped ; my debts, *every* thing inclusive, will be nine or ten thousand before I am twenty-one. But I have reason to think my property will turn

out better than general expectation may conceive. Of Newstead I have little hope or care; but Hanson, my agent,
intimated my Lancashire property was worth three Newsteads.
I believe we have it hollow; though the defendants are pro-
tracting the surrender, if possible, till after my majority, for
the purpose of forming some arrangement with me, thinking
I shall probably prefer a sum in hand to a reversion. Newstead
I may *sell*;—perhaps I will not,—though of that more anon.
I will come down in May or June.

Yours most truly, etc.

TO JOHN CAM HOBHOUSE *   *Dorant's, April 15th 1808*

MY DEAR HOBHOUSE,—I proceed as usual turning the
twenty four hours to the best account, particularly the nocturnal
moiety. My Belles would probably differ, were they together.
But one is *with* me, and the other *for* me—or any body else,
I dare say, in my absence. * * * * * * I have been well about
a fortnight, and I trust shall continue so, but I am sadly meagre,
and vigilant. Alas! for the Shepherd and his Lambkin!
How cursedly absurd such proceedings appear compared with
your chastity and my Carnality.

I shall be in Cambridge next month to graduate. The first
night I went out after my illness I got into a Row and gave a
fellow at the theatre my address and a black eye, after pugilising
with him and his friend, on their refusing to name their place
of Residence; they were kicked out into the Piazzas. I was
very weak and languid, but managed to keep these youths
at Bay, till a person whom I don't know engaged one, and I
then contended singly with the other, till the above consequence
ensued. Scrope Davies is at Portsmouth. I form one of a very
sad set, consisting of Capt. Wallace, Sir Godfrey, Sir B.
Graham, and other sensual Sinners. We have kept it up with
the most laudable systematic profligacy. Sir G. is with his
regiment at present, to the sorrow of his Confederates. I have
given up *play* altogether. I saw Mahon last night. He made
one of a party of ten * * * * *.

When do you come to town? I long to see you. Adieu.

Yours very truly, BYRON

TO FRANCIS HODGSON   *Newstead Abbey, Notts, Nov. 3, 1808*

MY DEAR HODGSON,—I expected to have heard ere this the event of your interview with the mysterious Mr. Haynes, my volunteer correspondent; however, as I had no business to trouble you with the adjustment of my concerns with that illustrious stranger, I have no right to complain of your silence.

You have of course seen Drury, in all the pleasing palpitations of anticipated wedlock. Well! he has still something to look forward to, and his present extacies are certainly enviable. " Peace be with him and with his spirit ", and his flesh also, at least just now. . . .

Hobhouse and your humble are still here. Hobhouse hunts, etc., and I do nothing; we dined the other day with a neighbouring Esquire (not Collet of Staines), and regretted your absence, as the Bouquet of Staines was scarcely to be compared to our last " feast of reason ". You know, laughing is the sign of a rational animal; so says Dr. Smollett. I think so, too, but unluckily my spirits don't always keep pace with my opinions. I had not so much scope for risibility the other day as I could have wished, for I was seated near a woman, to whom, when a boy, I was as much attached as boys generally are, and more than a man should be. I knew this before I went, and was determined to be valiant, and converse with *sang froid*; but instead I forgot my valour and my nonchalance, and never opened my lips even to laugh, far less to speak, and the lady was almost as absurd as myself, which made both the object of more observation than if we had conducted ourselves with easy indifference. You will think all this great nonsense; if you had seen it, you would have thought it still more ridiculous. What fools we are! We cry for a plaything, which, like children, we are never satisfied with till we break open, though like them we cannot get rid of it by putting it in the fire.

I have tried for Gifford's *Epistle to Pindar*, and the bookseller says the copies were cut up for *waste paper*; if you can procure me a copy I shall be much obliged. Adieu!

Believe me, my dear Sir, yours ever sincerely, BYRON

TO FRANCIS HODGSON
Newstead Abbey, Notts.,
Nov. 18th, 1808

MY DEAR HODGSON,—Boatswain is dead! He expired in a state of madness on the 10th after suffering much, yet retaining all the gentleness of his nature to the last, never attempting to do the least injury to any one near him. I have now lost every thing except old Murray. . . .

I sent some game to Drury lately, which I hope escaped the scrutiny of the mutineers. I trust the letter to Claridge [1] was equally fortunate (after being put in the post by you at London) as it contained some cash, which my correspondent, notwithstanding the patriotic fervour of the moment, might not chuse to submit to the inspection of the William Tells and Gracchi of the day.

If my songs have produced the *glorious* effects you mention, I shall be a complete Tyrtaeus, though I am sorry to say I resemble that interesting Harper more in his person than Poesy. I only lament that Drury's conjecture should be more facetious than well founded. Nothing could give me greater glee than to suppose it was perfectly correct. It is singular enough that Wingfield and Keynis [?] were both my fags at Harrow, and they have now obtained that honour to which their master aspired in vain. I have written to Government for letters etc. Won't you come and broach a farewell batch at Xmas? Can't you " tice Drury into the woods and afterwards devour him "? This day twelvemonth, Deo favente, I shall be crossing Mount Caucasus. Is your information of Jeffrey's proposal to Southey well authenticated? If so, pray favour both with a few couplets in your satire. I should be too happy to think Gifford had troubled . . . [sentence missing] . . . could discover if he really wrote the " exposé " in your possession. My Rhymes on the Bards are forthcoming. Tell Drury he must purchase a copy. I can't afford to give away. Hobhouse and myself nearly suffocated a person in the Bath yesterday, by way of ascertaining the soundings. I was obliged to jump in and extricate the Drownee. Drury will find a letter from me at Harrow, which I hope he will answer. If still at Cambridge, greet him with an embrace. Hobhouse

[1] John Claridge, a former Harrow favourite.

presents all sorts of remembrances to both. But, the words of Gaffer Thumb, " I can no more ".

      Believe me, dear H. yours [Signature missing.]

TO JOHN HANSON   *Newstead Abbey, Notts.,*
                                  November 18ᵗʰ, 1808

DEAR SIR,—I am truly glad to hear your health is re-instated. As for my affairs I am sure you will do your best, and, though I should be glad to get rid of my Lancashire property for an equivalent in money, I shall not take any steps of that nature without good advice and mature consideration.

I am (as I have already told you) going abroad in the spring; for this I have many reasons. In the first place, I wish to study India and Asiatic policy and manners. I am young, tolerably vigorous, abstemious in my way of living; I have no pleasure in fashionable dissipation, and I am deter-mined to take a wider field than is customary with travellers. If I return, my judgment will be more mature, and I shall still be young enough for politics. With regard to expence, travelling through the East is rather inconvenient than ex-pensive : it is not like the tour of Europe, you undergo hardship, but incur little hazard of spending money. If I live here I must have my house in town, a separate house for Mrs. Byron ; I must keep horses, etc., etc. When I go abroad I place Mrs. Byron at Newstead (there is one great expence saved), I have no horses to keep. A voyage to India will take me six months, and if I had a dozen attendants cannot cost me five hundred pounds ; and you will agree with me that a like term of months in England would lead me into four times that expenditure. I have written to Government for letters and permission of the Company, so you see I am *serious.*

You honour my debts ; they amount to perhaps twelve thousand pounds, and I shall require perhaps three or four thousand at setting out, with credit on a Bengal agent. This you must manage for me. If my resources are not adequate to the supply I must *sell*, but *not Newstead.* I will at least transmit that to the next Lord. My debts must be paid, if possible, in February. I shall leave my affairs to the care of *trustees*, of whom, with your acquiescence, I shall *name you* one, Mr. Parker another, and two more, on whom I am not yet determined.

Pray let me hear from you soon. Remember me to Mrs. Hanson, whom I hope to see on her return. Present my best respects to the young lady, and believe me, etc.,

BYRON

TO FRANCIS HODGSON   *Newstead Abbey, Notts.,*
Nov. 27, 1808

MY DEAR SIR,—Boatswain is to be buried in a vault waiting for myself. I have also written an epitaph, which I would send, were it not for two reasons : one is, that it is too long for a letter ; and the other, that I hope you will some day read it on the spot where it will be engraved.

You discomfort me with the intelligence of the real orthodoxy of the Arch-fiend's name, but alas ! it must stand with me at present ; if ever I have an opportunity of correcting, I shall liken him to Geoffrey of Monmouth, a noted liar in his way, and perhaps a more correct prototype than the Carnifex of James II.

I do not think the composition of your poem " a sufficing reason " for not keeping your promise of a Christmas visit. Why not come? I will never disturb you in your moments of inspiration ; and if you wish to collect any materials for the *scenery*, Hardwicke (where Mary was confined for several years) is not eight miles distant, and, independent of the interest you must take in it as her vindicator, is a most beautiful and venerable object of curiosity. I shall take it very ill if you do not come ; my mansion is improving in comfort, and, when you require solitude, I shall have an apartment devoted to the purpose of receiving your poetical reveries.

I have heard from our Drury ; he says little of the Row, which I regret : indeed I would have sacrificed much to have contributed in any way (as a schoolboy) to its consummation ; but Butler survives, and thirteen boys have been expelled in vain. Davies is not here, but Hobhouse hunts as usual, and your humble servant " drags at each remove a lengthened chain ". I have heard from his Grace of Portland on the subject of my expedition : he talks of difficulties ; by the gods ! if he throws any in my way I will next session ring such a peal in his ears,

> That he shall wish the fiery Dane
> Had rather been his guest again.

You do not tell me if Gifford is really my commentator : it is too good to be true, for I know nothing would gratify my vanity so much as the reality ; even the idea is too precious to part with.

I shall expect you here ; let me have no more excuses. Hobhouse desires his best remembrance. We are now lingering over our evening potations. I have extended my letter further than I ought, and beg you will excuse it ; on the opposite page I send you some stanzas I wrote off on being questioned by a former flame as to my motives for quitting this country. You are the first reader. Hobhouse hates everything of the kind, therefore I do not show them to him. Adieu !

> Believe me, yours very sincerely, BYRON

TO THE HON. AUGUSTA LEIGH   *Newstead Abbey, Notts.,*
Novr. 30th 1808

MY DEAREST AUGUSTA,—I return you my best thanks for making me an uncle, and forgive the sex this time ; but the next *must* be a nephew. You will be happy to hear my Lancashire property is likely to prove extremely valuable : indeed my pecuniary affairs are altogether far superior to my expectations or any other person's. If I would *sell*, my income would probably be six thousand per annum ; but I will not part at least with Newstead, or indeed with the other, which is of a nature to increase in value yearly. I am living here *alone*, which suits my inclinations better than society of any kind. Mrs. Byron I have shaken off for two years, and I shall not resume her yoke in future, I am afraid my disposition will suffer in your estimation; but I never can forgive that woman, or breathe in comfort under the same roof.

I am a very unlucky fellow, for I think I had naturally not a bad heart; but it has been so bent, twisted, and trampled on, that it has now become as hard as a Highlander's heelpiece.

I do not know that much alteration has taken place in my person, except that I am grown much thinner, and somewhat taller! I saw Col. Leigh at Brighton in July, where I should have been glad to have seen you; I only know your husband by sight, though I am acquainted with many of the Tenth. Indeed my relations are those whom I know the least, and in most instances, I am not very anxious to improve the acquaintance. I hope you are quite recovered, I shall be in town in January to take my seat, and will call, if convenient; let me hear from you before.

[Signature cut off]

TO WILLIAM HARNESS [1]   *8 St. James's Street,*
                                          March 18, 1809

There was no necessity for your excuses; if you have time and inclination to write, " for what we receive, the " Lord make us thankful ",—if I do not hear from you, I console myself with the idea that you are much more agreeably employed.

I send down to you by this post a certain Satire lately published, and in return for the three and sixpence expenditure upon it, only beg that if you should guess the author, you will keep his name secret; at least for the present. London is full of the Duke's business.[2] The Commons have been at it these last three nights, and are not yet come to a decision. I do not know if the affair will be brought before our House, unless in the shape of an impeachment. If it makes its appearance in a debatable form, I believe I shall be tempted to say

---

[1] " A *Harrow* man ", one of several friends whom Byron described at different periods as ' earliest ' and ' dearest '.

[2] The inquiry into charges of corruption brought against the Duke of York, as Commander-in-Chief, and his mistress, Mary Ann Clarke. See also note on letter to Lady Melbourne, Sept. 13th, 1812.

something on the subject.—I am glad to hear you like Cambridge : firstly, because, to know that you are happy is pleasant to one who wishes you all possible sublunary enjoyment ; and, secondly, I admire the morality of the sentiment. *Alma mater* was to me *injusta noverca* ; and the old beldam only gave me my M.A. degree because she could not avoid it.—You know what a farce a noble Cantab. must perform.

I am going abroad, if possible, in the spring, and before I depart I am collecting the pictures of my most intimate schoolfellows ; I have already a few, and shall want yours, or my cabinet will be incomplete. I have employed one of the first miniature painters of the day to take them, of course, at my own expense, as I never allow my acquaintance to incur the least expenditure to gratify a whim of mine. To mention this may seem indelicate ; but when I tell you a friend of ours first refused to sit, under the idea that he was to disburse on the occasion, you will see that it is necessary to state these preliminaries to prevent the recurrence of any similar mistake. I shall see you in time, and will carry you to the *limner*. It will be a tax on your patience for a week ; but pray excuse it, as it is possible the resemblance may be the sole trace I shall be able to preserve of our past friendship and acquaintance. Just now it seems foolish enough ; but in a few years, when some of us are dead, and others are separated by inevitable circumstances, it will be a kind of satisfaction to retain in these images of the living the idea of our former selves, and, to contemplate, in the resemblances of the dead, all that remains of judgment, feeling and a host of passions. But all this will be dull enough for you, and so good night ; and, to end my chapter, or rather my homily,

Believe me, my dear H., yours most affectionately.

TO HIS MOTHER   *Falmouth, June 22, 1809*

DEAR MOTHER,—I am about to sail in a few days ; probably before this reaches you. Fletcher begged so hard, that I have continued him in my service. If he does not behave well abroad, I will send him back in a *transport*. I have a

German servant (who has been with Mr. Wilbraham in Persia before, and was strongly recommended to me by Dr. Butler, of Harrow), Robert [1] and William ; they constitute my whole suite. I have letters in plenty :—you shall hear from me at the different ports I touch upon ; but you must not be alarmed if my letters miscarry. The Continent is in a fine state—an insurrection has broken out at Paris, and the Austrians are beating Buonaparte—the Tyrolese have risen.

There is a picture of me in oil, to be sent down to Newstead soon.—I wish the Miss Pigots had something better to do than carry my miniatures to Nottingham to copy. Now they have done it, you may ask them to copy the others, which are greater favourites than my own. As to money matters, I am ruined—at least till Rochdale is sold ; and if that does not turn out well, I shall enter into the Austrian or Russian service—perhaps the Turkish, if I like their manners. The world is all before me, and I leave England without regret, and without a wish to revisit any thing it contains, except *yourself*, and your present residence.

Believe me, yours ever sincerely

P.S.—Pray tell Mr. Rushton his son is well, and doing well; so is Murray, indeed better than I ever saw him; he will be back in about a month. I ought to add the leaving Murray to my few regrets, as his age perhaps will prevent my seeing him again. Robert I take with me ; I like him, because, like myself, he seems a friendless animal.

TO EDWARD ELLICE * *Falmouth, June 25th, 1809*

DEAR ELLICE,[2]—You will think me a very sad dog for not having written a long acknowledgment of what I really feel viz. a sincere sense of the many favours I have received at your hands concerning my coming Tour. But if you knew the hurry I have been in and the natural laziness of my disposition, you would excuse an omission which cannot be attributed to neglect or ingratitude.

---

[1] Robert Rushton, Byron's servant and sparring-partner.
[2] Edward (" Bear ") Ellice afterwards sat as Member for Coventry.

I beg you will now accept my very hearty thanks for the divers troubles you have had on my account, which I am sure no person but yourself would have taken for so worthless an animal. I am afraid I shall never have any opportunity of repaying them, except by a promise that they shall not be repeated.

We are waiting here for a wind and other necessaries. Nothing of moment has occurred in the town save the castigation of one of the fair sex at a Cart's tail yesterday morn, whose hands had been guilty of " picking and stealing " and whose tongue of " evil speaking " for she stole a Cock and *damned* the corporation. She was much whipped, but exceeding impenitent. I shall say nothing of Falmouth because I know it, and you don't, a very good reason for being silent as I can say nothing in its favour, or you hear anything that would be agreeable. The Inhabitants both female and male, at least the young ones, are remarkably handsome, and how the devil they come to be so is the marvel! for the place is apparently not favourable to Beauty. The Claret is good, and Quakers [?] plentiful, so are Herrings salt and fresh. There is a port called St. Mawes off the harbour, which we were nearly taken up on a suspicion of having carried by storm. It is well defended by one able-bodied man of eighty years old, six ancient demi-culverins that would exceedingly annoy anybody except an enemy, and parapet walls which would withstand at least half a dozen kicks of any given grenadier in the kingdom of France.

Adieu, believe me your obliged and sincere BYRON

TO FRANCIS HODGSON   *Lisbon, July 16, 1809*

Thus far have we pursued our route, and seen all sorts of marvellous sights, palaces, convents, etc.;—which, being to be heard in my friend Hobhouse's forthcoming Book of Travels, I shall not anticipate by smuggling any account whatsoever to you in a private and clandestine manner. I must just observe, that the village of Cintra in Estremadura is the most beautiful, perhaps, in the world.

I am very happy here, because I loves oranges, and talks bad Latin to the monks, who understand it, as it is like their own,—and I goes into society (with my pocket-pistols), and I swims in the Tagus all across at once, and I rides on an ass or a mule, and swears Portuguese, and have got a diarrhœa and bites from the mosquitoes. But what of that? Comfort must not be expected by folks that go a pleasuring.

When the Portuguese are pertinacious, I say *Carracho!*—the great oath of the grandees, that very well supplies the place of " Damme ",—and, when dissatisfied with my neighbour, I pronounce him *Ambra di merdo*. With these two phrases, and a third, *Avra bouro*, which signifieth " Get an ass ", I am universally understood to be a person of degree and a master of languages. How merrily we lives that travellers be!—if we had food and raiment. But, in sober sadness, any thing is better than England, and I am infinitely amused with my pilgrimage as far as it has gone.

To-morrow we start to ride post near 400 miles as far as Gibraltar, where we embark for Melita and Byzantium. A letter to Malta will find me, or to be forwarded, if I am absent. Pray embrace the Drury and Dwyer, and all the Ephesians you encounter. I am writing with Butler's donative pencil, which makes my bad hand worse. Excuse illegibility.

Hodgson! send me the news, and the deaths and defeats and capital crimes and the misfortunes of one's friends; and let us hear of literary matters, and the controversies and the criticisms. All this will be pleasant—*Suave mari magno*, etc. Talking of that, I have been sea-sick, and sick of the sea. Adieu.

Yours faithfully, etc.

TO HIS MOTHER   *Gibraltar, August 11th, 1809*

DEAR MOTHER,—I have been so much occupied since my departure from England, that till I could address you at length I have forborne writing altogether. As I have now passed through Portugal, and a considerable part of Spain, and have leisure at this place, I shall endeavour to give you a short detail of my movements.

We sailed from Falmouth on the 2nd of July, reached Lisbon after a very favourable passage of four days and a half, and took up our abode in that city. It has been often described without being worthy of description; for, except the view from the Tagus, which is beautiful, and some fine churches and convents, it contains little but filthy streets, and more filthy inhabitants. To make amends for this, the village of Cintra, about fifteen miles from the capital, is, perhaps in every respect, the most delightful in Europe; it contains beauties of every description, natural and artificial. Palaces and gardens rising in the midst of rocks, cataracts, and precipices; convents on stupendous heights—a distant view of the sea and the Tagus; and, besides (though that is a secondary consideration), is remarkable as the scene of Sir Hew Dalrymple's Convention.[1] It unites in itself all the wildness of the western highlands, with the verdure of the south of France. Near this place, about ten miles to the right, is the palace of Mafra, the boast of Portugal, as it might be of any other country, in point of magnificence without elegance. There is a convent annexed; the monks, who possess large revenues, are courteous enough, and understand Latin, so that we had a long conversation: they have a large library, and asked me if the *English* had *any books* in their country?

I sent my baggage, and part of the servants, by sea to Gibraltar, and travelled on horseback from Aldea Galbega (the first stage from Lisbon, which is only accessible by water) to Seville (one of the most famous cities in Spain) where the Government called the Junta is now held. The distance to Seville is nearly four hundred miles, and to Cadiz almost ninety farther towards the coast. I had orders from the governments, and every possible accommodation on the road, as an English nobleman, in an English uniform, is a very respectable personage in Spain at present. The horses are remarkably good, and the roads (I assure you upon my honour, for you will hardly believe it) very far superior to the best English roads, without the smallest toll or turnpike. You will suppose this when I rode post to Seville, in four days, through this parching country in the midst of summer, without fatigue or annoyance.

[1] The Convention of Cintra, by which Junot evacuated Portugal, had been signed on August 31st, 1808.

Seville is a beautiful town; though the streets are narrow, they are clean. We lodged in the house of two Spanish unmarried ladies, who possess *six* houses in Seville, and gave me a curious specimen of Spanish manners. They are women of character, and the eldest a fine woman, the youngest pretty, but not so good a figure as Donna Josepha. The freedom of manner, which is general here, astonished me not a little; and in the course of further observation, I find that reserve is not the characteristic of the Spanish belles, who are, in general, very handsome, with large black eyes, and very fine forms. The eldest honoured your *unworthy* son with very particular attention, embracing him with great tenderness at parting (I was there but three days), after cutting off a lock of his hair, and presenting him with one of her own, about three feet in length,[1] which I send, and beg you will retain till my return. Her last words were, *Adios, tu hermoso! me gusto mucho*—" Adieu, you pretty fellow! you please me much ". She offered me a share of her apartment, which my *virtue* induced me to decline; she laughed, and said I had some English *amante* (lover), and added that she was going to be married to an officer in the Spanish Army.

I left Seville, and rode on to Cadiz, through a beautiful country. At *Xeres*, where the sherry we drink is made, I met a great merchant—a Mr. Gordon of Scotland—who was extremely polite, and favoured me with the inspection of his vaults and cellars, so that I quaffed at the fountain head.

Cadiz, sweet Cadiz, is the most delightful town I ever beheld, very different from our English cities in every respect except cleanliness (and it is as clean as London), but still beautiful, and full of the finest women in Spain, the Cadiz belles being the Lancashire witches of their land. Just as I was introduced and began to like the grandees, I was forced to leave it for this cursed place; but before I return to England I will visit it again. The night before I left it, I sat in the box at the opera with Admiral Cordova's family; he is the commander whom Lord St. Vincent defeated in 1797, and has an aged wife and a fine daughter, Sennorita Cordova. The girl is very pretty, in the Spanish style; in my opinion, by no means

[1] This relic is still preserved among Byronic archives by the poet's publisher at 50 Albemarle Street.

54

inferior to the English in charms, and certainly superior in fascination. Long black hair, dark languishing eyes, *clear* olive complexions, and forms more graceful in motion than can be conceived by an Englishman used to the drowsy, listless air of his countrywomen, added to the most becoming dress, and, at the same time, the most decent in the world, render a Spanish beauty irresistible.

I beg leave to observe that intrigue here is the business of life; when a woman marries she throws off all restraint, but I believe their conduct is chaste enough before. If you make a proposal, which in England will bring a box on the ear from the meekest of virgins, to a Spanish girl, she thanks you for the honour you intend her, and replies, " Wait till I am married, and I shall be too happy ". This is literally and strictly true.

Miss Cordova and her little brother understood a little French, and, after regretting my ignorance of the Spanish, she proposed to become my preceptress in that language. I could only reply by a low bow, and express my regret that I quitted Cadiz too soon to permit me to make the progress which would doubtless attend my studies under so charming a directress. I was standing at the back of the box, which resembles our Opera boxes, (the theatre is large and finely decorated, the music admirable,) in the manner which Englishmen generally adopt, for fear of incommoding the ladies in front, when this fair Spaniard dispossessed an old woman (an aunt or a duenna) of her chair, and commanded me to be seated next herself, at a tolerable distance from her mamma. At the close of the performance I withdrew, and was lounging with a party of men in the passage, when, *en passant*, the lady turned round and called me, and I had the honour of attending her to the admiral's mansion. I have an invitation on my return to Cadiz, which I shall accept if I repass through the country on my return from Asia.

I have met Sir John Carr, Knight Errant, at Seville and Cadiz. He is a pleasant man. I like the Spaniards much. You have heard of the battle near Madrid, and in England they would call it a victory—a pretty victory ! Two hundred officers and five thousand men killed, all English, and the French in as great force as ever. I should have joined the army, but we have no time to lose before we get up the Mediterranean and Archipelago. I am going over to Africa tomorrow; it is only six miles from this fortress. My next stage is Cagliari in Sardinia, where I shall be presented to His Majesty. I have a most superb uniform as a court dress, indispensable in travelling.

August 13.—I have not yet been to Africa—the wind is contrary—but I dined yesterday at Algesiras, with Lady Westmorland, where I met General Castanos, the celebrated Spanish leader in the late and present war. To-day I dine with him. He has offered me letters to Tetuan in Barbary, for the principal Moors, and I am to have the house for a few days of one of the great men, which was intended for Lady W., whose health will not permit her to cross the Straits.

August 15.—I could not dine with Castanos yesterday, but this afternoon I had that honour. He is pleasant and, for aught I know to the contrary, clever. I cannot go to Barbary. The Malta packet sails to-morrow, and myself in it. Admiral Purvis, with whom I dined at Cadiz, gave me a passage in a frigate to Gibraltar, but we have no ship of war destined for Malta at present. The packets sail fast, and have good accommodation. You shall hear from me on our route.

Joe Murray delivers this; I have sent him and the boy back. Pray show the lad kindness, as he is my great favourite; I would have taken him on, * * * Say this to his father, who may otherwise think he has behaved ill.

I hope this will find you well. Believe me,

Yours ever sincerely, BYRON

P.S.—So Lord G[rey de Ruthyn] is married to a rustic. Well done! If I wed, I will bring home a Sultana, with half a dozen cities for a dowry, and reconcile you to an Ottoman daughter-in-law, with a bushel of pearls not larger than ostrich eggs, or smaller than walnuts.

TO HIS MOTHER   *Malta, September 15, 1809*

DEAR MOTHER,—Though I have a very short time to spare, being to sail immediately for Greece, I cannot avoid taking an opportunity of telling you that I am well. I have been in Malta a short time, and have found the inhabitants hospitable and pleasant.

This letter is committed to the charge of a very extra-ordinary woman, whom you have doubtless heard of, Mrs. Spencer Smith,[1] of whose escape the Marquis de Salvo published a narrative a few years ago. She has since been shipwrecked, and her life has been from its commencement so fertile in remarkable incidents, that in a romance they would appear improbable. She was born at Constantinople, where her father, Baron Herbert, was Austrian Ambassador; married unhappily, yet has never been impeached in point of character; excited the vengeance of Buonaparte by a part in some conspiracy; several times risked her life; and is not yet twenty-five. She is here on her way to England, to join her husband, being obliged to leave Trieste, where she was paying a visit to her mother, by the approach of the French, and embarks soon in a ship of war. Since my arrival here, I have had scarcely any other companion. I have found her very pretty, very accomplished, and extremely eccentric. Buonaparte is even now so incensed against her, that her life would be in some danger if she were taken prisoner a second time.

You have seen Murray and Robert by this time, and received my letter. Little has happened since that date. I have touched at Cagliari in Sardinia, and at Girgenti in Sicily, and embark to-morrow for Patras, from whence I proceed to Yanina, where Ali Pacha holds his court. So I shall soon be among the Mussulmans. Adieu.

Believe me, with sincerity, yours ever, BYRON

TO CAPTAIN CARY, A.D.C.   *3, Strada di Torni [Malta],*
September 18th 1809

SIR,—The marked insolence of your behaviour to me the first time I had the honour of meeting you at table, I should

---

[1] The adventurous Mrs. Spencer Smith, wife of the British Minister at Stuttgart and the " Florence " of *Childe Harold,* caused Byron some emotional perturbation during his stay in Malta. According to Galt, " he affected a passion for her, but it was only Platonic. She, however, beguiled him of his valuable yellow diamond ring."

have passed over from respect to the General, had I not been informed that you have since mentioned my name in a public company with comments not to be tolerated, more particularly after the circumstance to which I allude. I have only just heard this, or I should not have postponed this letter to so late a period. As the vessel in which I am to embark must sail the first change of wind, the sooner our business is arranged the better. To-morrow morning at 6 will be the best hour, at any place you think proper, as I do not know where the officers and *gentlemen* settle these affairs in your island.

The favour of an immediate answer will oblige

Your obedient servant, BYRON

TO HIS MOTHER   *Prevesa, November 12, 1809*

MY DEAR MOTHER,—I have now been some time in Turkey: this place is on the coast, but I have traversed the interior of the province of Albania on a visit to the Pacha. I left Malta in the *Spider*, a brig of war, on the 21st of September, and arrived in eight days at Prevesa. I thence have been about 150 miles, as far as Tepaleen, his Highness's country palace, where I stayed three days. The name of the Pacha is *Ali*, and he is considered a man of the first abilities: he governs the whole of Albania (the ancient Illyricum), Epirus, and part of Macedonia. His son, Vely Pacha, to whom he has given me letters, governs the Morea, and has great influence in Egypt; in short, he is one of the most powerful men in the Ottoman empire. When I reached Yanina, the capital, after a journey of three days over the mountains, through a country of the most picturesque beauty, I found that Ali Pacha was with his army in Illyricum, besieging Ibrahim Pacha in the castle of Berat. He had heard that an Englishman of rank was in his dominions, and had left orders in Yanina with the commandant to provide a house, and supply me with every kind of necessary *gratis*; and, though I have been allowed to make presents to the slaves, etc., I have not been permitted to pay for a single article of household consumption.

I rode out on the vizier's horses, and saw the palaces of

himself and grandsons: they are splendid, but too much ornamented with silk and gold. I then went over the mountains through Zitza, a village with a Greek monastery (where I slept on my return), in the most beautiful situation (always excepting Cintra, in Portugal) I ever beheld. In nine days I reached Tepaleen. Our journey was much prolonged by the torrents that had fallen from the mountains, and intersected the roads. I shall never forget the singular scene on entering Tepaleen at five in the afternoon, as the sun was going down. It brought to my mind (with some change of *dress*, however) Scott's description of Branksome Castle in his *Lay*, and the feudal system. The Albanians, in their dresses, (the most magnificent in the world, consisting of a long *white kilt*, gold-worked cloak, crimson velvet gold-laced jacket and waistcoat, silver-mounted pistols and daggers,) the Tartars with their high caps, the Turks in their vast pelisses and turbans, the soldiers and black slaves with the horses, the former in groups in an immense large open gallery in front of the palace, the latter placed in a kind of cloister below it, two hundred steeds ready caparisoned to move in a moment, couriers entering or passing out with the despatches, the kettle-drums beating, boys calling the hour from the minaret of the mosque, altogether, with the singular appearance of the building itself, formed a new and delightful spectacle to a stranger. I was conducted to a very handsome apartment, and my health inquired after by the vizier's secretary, *à-la-mode Turque*!

The next day I was introduced to Ali Pacha. I was dressed in a full suit of staff uniform, with a very magnificent sabre, etc. The vizier received me in a large room paved with marble; a fountain was playing in the centre; the apartment was surrounded by scarlet ottomans. He received me standing, a wonderful compliment from a Mussulman, and made me sit down on his right hand. I have a Greek interpreter for general use, but a physician of Ali's named Femlario, who understands Latin, acted for me on this occasion. His first question was, why, at so early an age, I left my country?—(the Turks have no idea of travelling for amusement). He then said, the English minister, Captain Leake, had told him I was of a great family, and desired his respects to my mother; which I now, in the name of Ali Pacha, present to you. He said he was certain I was a man of birth, because I had small ears, curling hair, and little white hands, and expressed himself pleased with my appearance and garb. He told me to consider him as a father whilst I was in Turkey, and said he looked on me as his son. Indeed, he treated me like a child, sending me almonds and sugared sherbet, fruit and sweetmeats, twenty times a day. He begged me to visit him often, and at night, when he was at leisure. I then, after coffee and pipes, retired for the first time. I saw him thrice afterwards. It is singular that the Turks, who have no hereditary dignities, and few great families, except the Sultans, pay so much respect to birth; for I found my pedigree more regarded than my title.

To-day I saw the remains of the town of Actium, near which Antony lost the world, in a small bay, where two frigates could hardly manœuvre: a broken wall is the sole remnant. On another part of the gulf stand the ruins of Nicopolis, built by Augustus in honour of his victory. Last night I was at a Greek marriage; but this and a thousand things more I have neither time nor *space* to describe.

His highness is sixty years old, very fat, and not tall, but with a fine face, light blue eyes, and a white beard; his manner is very kind, and at the same time he possesses that dignity which I find universal amongst the Turks. He has the appearance of anything but his real character, for he is a remorseless tyrant, guilty of the most horrible cruelties, very brave, and so good a general that they call him the Mahometan Buonaparte. Napoleon has twice offered to make him King of Epirus, but he prefers the English interest, and abhors the French, as he himself told me. He is of so much consequence, that he is much courted by both, the Albanians being the most warlike subjects of the Sultan, though Ali is only nominally dependent on the Porte; he has been a mighty warrior, but is as barbarous as he is successful, roasting rebels, etc., etc. Buonaparte sent him a snuff-box with his picture. He said the snuff-box was very well, but the picture he could excuse, as he neither liked it nor the original. His ideas of judging of a man's birth from ears, hands, etc., were curious enough. To me he was, indeed, a father, giving me letters, guards, and every possible accommodation. Our next conversations were of war and travelling, politics and England. He called my

Albanian soldier, who attends me, and told him to protect me
at all hazard; his name is Viscillie, and, like all the Albanians,
he is brave, rigidly honest, and faithful; but they are cruel,
though not treacherous, and have several vices but no mean-
nesses. They are, perhaps, the most beautiful race, in point of
countenance, in the world; their women are sometimes handsome also, but they are treated like slaves, *beaten*, and, in short,
complete beasts of burden; they plough, dig, and sow. I
found them carrying wood, and actually repairing the highways.
The men are all soldiers, and war and the chase their sole
occupations. The women are the labourers, which after all
is no great hardship in so delightful a climate. Yesterday, the
11th of November, I bathed in the sea; to-day is so hot that
I am writing in a shady room of the English consul's, with
three doors wide open, no fire, or even *fireplace*, in the house,
except for culinary purposes.

I am going to-morrow, with a guard of fifty men, to Patras
in the Morea, and thence to Athens, where I shall winter.
Two days ago I was nearly lost in a Turkish ship of war, owing
to the ignorance of the captain and crew, though the storm was
not violent. Fletcher yelled after his wife, the Greeks called
on all the saints, the Mussulmans on Alla; the captain burst
into tears and ran below deck, telling us to call on God; the
sails were split, the main-yard shivered, the wind blowing
fresh, the night setting in, and all our chance was to make
Corfu, which is in possession of the French, or (as Fletcher
pathetically termed it) " a watery grave ". I did what I
could to console Fletcher, but finding him incorrigible,
wrapped myself up in my Albanian capote (an immense
cloak), and lay down on deck to wait the worst. I have learnt
to philosophise in my travels; and if I had not, complaint was
useless. Luckily the wind abated, and only drove us on the
coast of Suli, on the main land, where we landed, and proceeded, by the help of the natives, to Prevesa again; but I
shall not trust Turkish sailors in future, though the Pacha had
ordered one of his own galliots to take me to Patras. I am
therefore going as far as Missolonghi by land, and there have
only to cross a small gulf to get to Patras.

Fletcher's next epistle will be full of marvels. We were one
night lost for nine hours in the mountains in a thunder-storm,

and since nearly wrecked. In both cases Fletcher was sorely bewildered, from apprehensions of famine and banditti in the first, and drowning in the second instance. His eyes were a little hurt by the lightning, or crying (I don't know which), but are now recovered. When you write, address to me at Mr. Strané's, English consul, Patras, Morea.

I could tell you I know not how many incidents that I think would amuse you, but they crowd on my mind as much as they would swell my paper, and I can neither arrange them in the one, nor put them down on the other, except in the greatest confusion. I like the Albanians much; they are not all Turks; some tribes are Christians. But their religion makes little difference in their manner or conduct. They are esteemed the best troops in the Turkish service. I lived on my route, two days at once, and three days again, in a barrack at Salora, and never found soldiers so tolerable, though I have been in the garrisons of Gibraltar and Malta, and seen Spanish, French, Sicilian, and British troops in abundance. I have had nothing stolen, and was always welcome to their provision and milk. Not a week ago an Albanian chief, (every village has its chief, who is called Primate,) after helping us out of the Turkish galley in her distress, feeding us, and lodging my suite, consisting of Fletcher, a Greek, two Athenians, a Greek priest, and my companion, Mr. Hobhouse, refused any compensation but a written paper stating that I was well received; and when I pressed him to accept a few sequins, " No," he replied; " I wish you to love me, not to pay me ". These are his words.

It is astonishing how far money goes in this country. While I was in the capital I had nothing to pay by the vizier's order; but since, though I have generally had sixteen horses, and generally six or seven men, the expense has not been *half* as much as staying only three weeks in Malta, though Sir A. Ball, the governor, gave me a house for nothing, and I had only *one servant*. By the by, I expect Hanson to remit regularly; for I am not about to stay in this province for ever. Let him write to me at Mr. Strané's, English consul, Patras. The fact is, the fertility of the plains is wonderful, and specie is scarce, which makes this remarkable cheapness. I am going to Athens, to study modern Greek, which differs much from the ancient, though radically similar. I have no desire to return to England, nor shall I, unless compelled by absolute want, and Hanson's neglect; but I shall not enter into Asia for a year or two, as I have much to see in Greece, and I may perhaps cross into Africa, at least the Egyptian part. Fletcher, like all Englishmen, is very much dissatisfied, though a little reconciled to the Turks by a present of eighty piastres from the vizier, which, if you consider every thing, and the value of specie here, is nearly worth ten guineas English. He has suffered nothing but from cold, heat, and vermin, which those who lie in cottages and cross mountains in a cold country must undergo, and of which I have equally partaken with himself; but he is not valiant, and is afraid of robbers and tempests. I have no one to be remembered to in England, and wish to hear nothing from it, but that you are well, and a letter or two on business from Hanson, whom you may tell to write. I will write when I can, and beg you to believe me,

Your affectionate son, BYRON

P.S.—I have some very " magnifiques " Albanian dresses, the only expensive articles in this country. They cost fifty guineas each, and have so much gold, they would cost in England two hundred.

I have been introduced to Hussein Bey, and Mahmout Pacha, both little boys, grandchildren of Ali, at Yanina; they are totally unlike our lads, have painted complexions like rouged dowagers, large black eyes, and features perfectly regular. They are the prettiest little animals I ever saw, and are broken into the court ceremonies already. The Turkish salute is a slight inclination of the head, with the hand on the heart; intimates always kiss. Mahmout is ten years old, and hopes to see me again; we are friends without understanding each other, like many other folks, though from a different cause. He has given me a letter to his father in the Morea, to whom I have also letters from Ali Pacha.

TO HENRY DRURY   Salsette *frigate, May 3, 1810*

MY DEAR DRURY,—When I left England, nearly a year ago, you requested me to write to you—I will do so. I have crossed Portugal, traversed the south of Spain, visited Sardinia, Sicily, Malta, and thence passed into Turkey, where I am still wandering. I first landed in Albania, the ancient Epirus, where we penetrated as far as Mount Tomarit—excellently treated by the chief Ali Pacha,—and, after journeying through Illyria, Chaonia, etc., crossed the Gulf of Actium, with a guard of fifty Albanians, and passed the Achelous in our route through Acarnania and Ætolia. We stopped a short time in the Morea, crossed the Gulf of Lepanto, and landed at the foot of Parnassus;—saw all that Delphi retains, and so on to Thebes and Athens, at which last we remained ten weeks.

His Majesty's ship, *Pylades*, brought us to Smyrna; but not before we had topographised Attica, including, of course, Marathon and the Sunian promontory. From Smyrna to the Troad (which we visited when at anchor, for a fortnight, off the tomb of Antilochus) was our next stage; and now we are in the Dardanelles, waiting for a wind to proceed to Constantinople.

This morning I *swam* from *Sestos* to *Abydos*. The immediate distance is not above a mile, but the current renders it hazardous;—so much so that I doubt whether Leander's conjugal affection must not have been a little chilled in his passage to Paradise. I attempted it a week ago, and failed,—owing to the north wind, and the wonderful rapidity of the tide,— though I have been from my childhood a strong swimmer. But, this morning being calmer, I succeeded, and crossed the " broad Hellespont " in an hour and ten minutes.

Well, my dear sir, I have left my home, and seen part of Africa and Asia, and a tolerable portion of Europe. I have been with generals and admirals, princes and pashas, governors and ungovernables,—but I have not time or paper to expatiate. I wish to let you know that I live with a friendly remembrance of you, and a hope to meet you again; and if I do this as shortly as possible, attribute it to any thing but forgetfulness.

Greece, ancient and modern, you know too well to require description. Albania, indeed, I have seen more of than any Englishman (except a Mr. Leake), for it is a country rarely visited, from the savage character of the natives, though abounding in more natural beauties than the classical regions of Greece,—which, however, are still eminently beautiful, particularly Delphi and Cape Colonna in Attica. Yet these are nothing to parts of Illyria and Epirus, where places without a name, and rivers not laid down in maps, may, one day, when more known, be justly esteemed superior subjects, for the pencil and the pen, to the dry ditch of the Ilissus and the bogs of Bœotia.

The Troad is a fine field for conjecture and snipe-shooting, and a good sportsman and an ingenious scholar may exercise their feet and faculties to great advantage upon the spot;— or, if they prefer riding, lose their way (as I did) in a cursed quagmire of the Scamander, who wriggles about as if the Dardan virgins still offered their wonted tribute. The only vestige of Troy, or her destroyers, are the barrows supposed to contain the carcasses of Achilles, Antilochus, Ajax, etc.;— but Mount Ida is still in high feather, though the shepherds are now-a-days not much like Ganymede. But why should I say more of these things? are they not written in the *Boke* of *Gell*?[1] and has not Hobhouse got a journal? I keep none, as I have renounced scribbling.

I see not much difference between ourselves and the Turks, save that we have * * and they have none—that they have long dresses, and we short, and that we talk much, and they little. They are sensible people. Ali Pacha told me he was sure I was a man of rank, because I had *small ears* and *hands*, and *curling hair*. By the by, I speak the Romaic, or modern Greek, tolerably. It does not differ from the ancient dialects so much as you would conceive; but the pronunciation is diametrically opposite. Of verse, except in rhyme, they have no idea.

I like the Greeks, who are plausible rascals,—with all the Turkish vices, without their courage. However, some are brave, and all are beautiful, very much resembling the busts of Alcibiades;—the women not quite so handsome. I can swear in Turkish; but, except one horrible oath, and " pimp ", and " bread ", and " water ", I have got no great vocabulary in that language. They are extremely polite to strangers of any rank, properly protected; and as I have two servants and two soldiers, we get on with great *éclat*. We have been occasion-

[1] Sir William Gell was the author of *Topography of Troy, Geography and Antiquities of Ithaca*, etc.

ally in danger of thieves, and once of shipwreck,—but always escaped.

Of Spain I sent some account to our Hodgson, but have subsequently written to no one, save notes to relations and lawyers, to keep them out of my premises. I mean to give up all connection, on my return, with many of my best friends— as I supposed them—and to snarl all my life. But I hope to have one good-humoured laugh with you, and to embrace Dwyer, and pledge Hodgson, before I commence cynicism.

Tell Dr. Butler I am now writing with the gold pen he gave me before I left England, which is the reason my scrawl is more unintelligible than usual. I have been at Athens, and seen plenty of these reeds for scribbling, some of which he refused to bestow upon me, because topographic Gell had brought them from Attica. But I will not describe,—no—you must be satisfied with simple detail till my return, and then we will unfold the flood-gates of colloquy. I am in a thirty-six gun frigate, going up to fetch Bob Adair from Constantinople, who will have the honour to carry this letter.

And so Hobhouse's *boke* [1] is out, with some sentimental sing-song of my own to fill up,—and how does it take, eh? and where the devil is the second edition of my Satire,[2] with additions? and my name on the title page? and more lines tagged to the end, with a new exordium and what not, hot from my anvil before I cleared the Channel? The Mediterranean and the Atlantic roll between me and criticism; and the thunders of the Hyperborean Review are deafened by the roar of the Hellespont.

Remember me to Claridge, if not translated to college, and present to Hodgson assurances of my high consideration. Now, you will ask, what shall I do next? and I answer, I do not know. I may return in a few months, but I have intents and projects after visiting Constantinople.—Hobhouse, how- ever, will probably be back in September.

On the 2d of July we have left Albion one year—*oblitus meorum obliviscendus et illis*. I was sick of my own country, and not much prepossessed in favour of any other; but I

---

[1] *Imitations and Translations from the Ancient and Modern Classics* contained sixty- five pieces, nine by Byron's hand.

[2] *English Bards and Scotch Reviewers*, published by James Cawthorn.

" drag on my chain " without " lengthening it at each remove."
I am like the Jolly Miller, caring for nobody, and not cared for.
All countries are much the same in my eyes. I smoke, and
stare at mountains, and twirl my mustachios very independently.
I miss no comforts, and the musquitoes that rack the morbid
frame of H. have, luckily for me, little effect on mine, because
I live more temperately.

I omitted Ephesus in my catalogue, which I visited during
my sojourn at Smyrna ; but the Temple has almost perished,
and St. Paul need not trouble himself to epistolise the present
brood of Ephesians, who have converted a large church built
entirely of marble into a mosque, and I don't know that the
edifice looks the worse for it.

My paper is full, and my ink ebbing—good afternoon !
If you address to me at Malta, the letter will be forwarded
wherever I may be. H. greets you ; he pines for his poetry,—
at least, some tidings of it. I almost forgot to tell you that I
am dying for love of three Greek girls at Athens, sisters. I
lived in the same house. Teresa,[1] Mariana, and Katinka,
are the names of these divinities,—all of them under fifteen.

Your ταπεινοτατος δουλος, BYRON

TO FRANCIS HODGSON   Salsette *frigate, in the Dardanelles,*
                              off Abydos, May 5, 1810

I am on my way to Constantinople, after a tour through
Greece, Epirus, etc., and part of Asia Minor, some particulars
of which I have just communicated to our friend and host,
H. Drury. With these, then, I shall not trouble you ; but as
you will perhaps be pleased to hear that I am well, etc., I take
the opportunity of our ambassador's return to forward the
few lines I have time to despatch. We have undergone some
inconveniences, and incurred partial perils, but no events
worthy of communication, unless you will deem it one that two
days ago I swam from Sestos to Abydos. This, with a few
alarms from robbers, and some danger of shipwreck in a Turkish
galliot six months ago, a visit to a Pacha, a passion for a married

---

[1] Teresa Macri was, of course, the " Maid of Athens ".

woman at Malta, a challenge to an officer, an attachment to three Greek girls at Athens, with a great deal of buffoonery and fine prospects, form all that has distinguished my progress since my departure from Spain.

Hobhouse rhymes and journalises; I stare and do nothing —unless smoking can be deemed an active amusement. The Turks take too much care of their women to permit them to be scrutinised; but I have lived a good deal with the Greeks, whose modern dialect I can converse in enough for my purposes. With the Turks I have also some male acquaintances—female society is out of the question. I have been very well treated by the Pachas and Governors, and have no complaint to make of any kind. Hobhouse will one day inform you of all our adventures—were I to attempt the recital, neither *my* paper nor *your* patience would hold out during the operation.

Nobody, save yourself, has written to me since I left England; but indeed I did not request it. I except my relations, who write quite as often as I wish. Of Hobhouse's volume I know nothing, except that it is out; and of my second edition I do not even know *that*, and certainly do not, at this distance, interest myself in the matter. I hope you and Bland roll down the stream of sale with rapidity.

Of my return I cannot positively speak, but think it probable Hobhouse will precede me in that respect. We have been very nearly one year abroad. I should wish to gaze away another, at least, in these evergreen climates; but I fear business, law business, the worst of employments, will recall me previous to that period, if not very quickly. If so, you shall have due notice.

I hope you will find me an altered personage,—I do not mean in body, but in manner, for I begin to find out that nothing but virtue will do in this damned world. I am tolerably sick of vice, which I have tried in its agreeable varieties, and mean, on my return, to cut all my dissolute acquaintance, leave off wine and carnal company, and betake myself to politics and decorum. I am very serious and cynical, and a good deal disposed to moralise; but fortunately for you the coming homily is cut off by default of pen and defection of paper.

Good morrow! If you write, address to me at Malta,

whence your letters will be forwarded. You need not remember me to any body, but believe me,

Yours with all faith, BYRON

Constantinople, May 15, 1810

P.S.—MY DEAR H.,—The date of my postscript " will prate to you of my whereabouts ". We anchored between the Seven Towers and the Seraglio on the 13th, and yesterday settled ashore. The ambassador is laid up; but the secretary does the honours of the palace, and we have a general invitation to his palace. In a short time he has his leave of audience, and we accompany him in our uniforms to the Sultan, etc., and in a few days I am to visit the Captain Pacha with the commander of our frigate. I have seen enough of their Pashas already; but I wish to have a view of the Sultan, the last of the Ottoman race.

Of Constantinople you have Gibbon's description, very correct as far as I have seen. The mosques I shall have a firman to visit. I shall most probably (*Deo volente*), after a full inspection of Stamboul, bend my course homewards; but this is uncertain. I have seen the most interesting parts, particularly Albania, where few Franks have ever been, and all the most celebrated ruins of Greece and Ionia.

Of England I know nothing, hear nothing, and can find no person better informed on the subject than myself. I this moment drink your health in a bumper of hock; Hobhouse fills and empties to the same; do you and Drury pledge us in a pint of any liquid you please—vinegar will bear the nearest resemblance to that which I have just swallowed to your name; but when we meet again the draught shall be mended and the wine also.

Yours ever, B.

TO HIS MOTHER †   *Constantinople, June 28, 1810*

MY DEAR MOTHER,—I regret to perceive by your last letter that several of mine have not arrived, particularly a very long one written in November last from Albania, where

I was on a visit to the Pacha of that province. Fletcher has also written to his spouse perpetually.

Mr. Hobhouse, who will forward or deliver this, and is on his return to England, can inform you of our different movements, but I am very uncertain as to my own return. He will probably be down in Notts. some time or other; but Fletcher, whom I send back as an incumbrance (English servants are sad travellers), will supply his place in the interim, and describe our travels, which have been tolerably extensive.

I have written twice briefly from this capital, from Smyrna, from Athens and other parts of Greece; from Albania, the Pacha of which province desired his respects to my mother, and said he was sure I was a man of high birth because I had small ears, curling hair, and white hands!!! He was very kind to me, begged me to consider him as a father, and gave me a guard of forty soldiers through the forests of Acarnania. But of this and other circumstances I have written to you at large, and yet hope you will receive my letters.

I remember Mahmout Pacha, the grandson of Ali Pacha, at Yanina, (a little fellow of ten years of age, with large black eyes, which our ladies would purchase at any price, and those regular features which distinguish the Turks,) asked me how I came to travel so young, without anybody to take care of me. This question was put by the little man with all the gravity of threescore. I cannot now write copiously; I have only time to tell you that I have passed many a fatiguing, but never a tedious moment; and all that I am afraid of is that I shall contract a gypsylike wandering disposition, which will make home tiresome to me: this, I am told, is very common with men in the habit of peregrination, and, indeed, I feel it so. On the 3d of May I swam from *Sestos* to *Abydos*. You know the story of Leander, but I had no *Hero* to receive me at landing.

I also passed a fortnight on the Troad. The tombs of Achilles and Æsyetes still exist in large barrows, similar to those you have doubtless seen in the North. The other day I was at Belgrade (a village in these environs), to see the house built on the same site as Lady Mary Wortley's. By-the-by, her ladyship, as far as I can judge, has lied, but not half so much as any other woman would have done in the same situation.

I have been in all the principal mosques by the virtue of a firman : this is a favour rarely permitted to Infidels, but the ambassador's departure obtained it for us. I have been up the Bosphorus into the Black Sea, round the walls of the city, and, indeed, I know more of it by sight than I do of London. I hope to amuse you some winter's evening with the details, but at present you must excuse me ;—I am not able to write long letters in June. I return to spend my summer in Greece. I shall not proceed further into Asia, as I have visited Smyrna, Ephesus and the Troad. I write often, but you must not be alarmed when you do not receive my letters ; consider we have no regular post farther than Malta, where I beg you will in future send your letters, and not to this city.

Fletcher is a poor creature, and requires comforts that I can dispense with. He is very sick of his travels, but you must not believe his account of the country. He sighs for ale, and idleness, and a wife, and the devil knows what besides. I have not been disappointed or disgusted. I have lived with the highest and the lowest. I have been for days in a Pacha's palace, and have passed many a night in a cowhouse, and I find the people inoffensive and kind. I have also passed some time with the principal Greeks in the Morea and Livadia, and, though inferior to the Turks, they are better than the Spaniards, who, in their turn, excel the Portuguese. Of Constantinople you will find many descriptions in different travels ; but Lady Mary Wortley errs strangely when she says, " St. Paul's would cut a strange figure by St. Sophia's ". I have been in both, surveyed them inside and out attentively. St. Sophia's is undoubtedly the most interesting from its immense antiquity, and the circumstance of all the Greek emperors, from Justinian, having been crowned there, and several murdered at the altar, besides the Turkish Sultans who attend it regularly. But it is inferior in beauty and size to some of the mosques, particularly " Soleyman ", etc., and not to be mentioned in the same page with St. Paul's (I speak like a *Cockney*). However, I prefer the Gothic cathedral of Seville to St. Paul's, St. Sophia's, and any religious building I have ever seen.

The walls of the Seraglio are like the walls of Newstead gardens, only higher, and much in the same *order* ; but the ride by the walls of the city, on the land side, is beautiful.

Imagine four miles of immense triple battlements, covered with ivy, surmounted with 218 towers, and, on the other side of the road, Turkish burying-grounds (the loveliest spots on earth), full of enormous cypresses. I have seen the ruins of Athens, of Ephesus, and Delphi. I have traversed great part of Turkey, and many other parts of Europe, and some of Asia ; but I never beheld a work of nature or art which yielded an impression like the prospect on each side from the Seven Towers to the end of the Golden Horn.

Now for England. You have not received my friend Hobhouse's volume of poesy : it has been published several months ; you ought to read it. I am glad to hear of the progress of *English Bards*, etc. Of course, you observed I have made great additions to the new edition. Have you received my picture from Sanders, Vigo Lane, London ? It was finished and paid for long before I left England : pray, send for it. You seem to be a mighty reader of magazines : where do you pick up all this intelligence, quotations, etc., etc. ? Though I was happy to obtain my seat without the assistance of Lord Carlisle, I had no measures to keep with a man who declined interfering as my relation on that occasion, and I have done with him, though I regret distressing Mrs. Leigh, poor thing !—I hope she is happy.

It is my opinion that Mr. B * * ought to marry Miss R * *. Our first duty is not to do evil ; but, alas ! that is impossible : our next is to repair it, if in our power. The girl is his equal : if she were his inferior, a sum of money and provision for the child would be some, though a poor, compensation : as it is, he should marry her. I will have no gay deceivers on my estate, and I shall not allow my tenants a privilege I do not permit myself—*that* of debauching each other's daughters. God knows, I have been guilty of many excesses ; but, as I have laid down a resolution to reform, and lately kept it, I expect this Lothario to follow the example, and begin by restoring this girl to society, or, by the beard of my father ! he shall hear of it. Pray take some notice of Robert, who will miss his master ; poor boy, he was very unwilling to return. I trust you are well and happy. It will be a pleasure to hear from you.

Believe me, yours very sincerely, BYRON

P.S.—How is Joe Murray?

P.S.—I open my letter again to tell you that Fletcher having petitioned to accompany me into the Morea, I have taken him with me, contrary to the intention expressed in my letter.

TO EDWARD ELLICE *   *Constantinople, July, 4th, 1810*

MY DEAR ELLICE,—I seize the occasion of Mr. Adair's return to convey my congratulations on your marriage, (for I hear you have taken unto yourself a wife) these, though somewhat of the latest, will arrive at a time when you must be more sensible of their value, as having full experience of matrimony and its concomitant blessings. Hobhouse is returning, but I am going back to Greece. To that loquacious traveller I refer you for all our adventures, but I must beg leave to mention to you as a feat that I have swum from Sestos to Abydos.

I hear your friend Brougham is in the lower house mouthing at the ministry. Notwithstanding my enmity against him and the dogs without faith with whom he is critically connected, I wish him success. You remember, he would not believe that *I* had written my pestilent Satire. Now that was very cruel and unlike me, for the moment I read his speech I believed it to be *his* entire from Exordium to Peroration. My fellow traveller Hobby, who is posting to your country full of marvels, has, as you no doubt know, put forth a volume of Poesy, which I do exhort you and all your acquaintance who may be possessed of a dormant half-guinea to purchase, and he himself (when he is worth so much money) will in return buy rhyme at the same rate from any of the said persons who shall please to be poetical. *My* work, it seems, has frisked through another edition with my name prefixed to it, despite of the advice of all my friends, who were fearful I should be cut off in the flower of my youth by an Insurrection in Grub street. Now I mean to live a long time in defiance of pens or penknives.

I suppose by this time you have become a bitter politician. I hope in no very long time to be amongst you, but I have one or two little things to adjust in the Morea before I sail. We have been in Portugal, Spain, Sardinia, Sicily, Malta, Albania, Greece, Asia Minor, and seen the Troad, Athens, Ephesus and sundry cities with names that would choak you, but I spare you. I shall not proceed into Persia, as I prophesied in rather too great a hurry, but having satiated my curiosity in this metropolis quietly repair home—and then—I hope you will be glad to see me, and I will have a speech ready for your spouse, and marry myself, seeing I have such excellent encouragement. Present my humble service to your brethren, and my cousin Trunnion. I am sorry to hear that my sister Mrs. Leigh is annoyed at my attack on the Earl of C[arlisle], though I had motives enough to justify any measures against that silly old man. Had I been aware that she would have laid it to heart, I would have cast my pen and poem both into the flames, and, in good truth (if she knew the feelings of us scribblers) no small sacrifice. But the mischief is done, Lord forgive me! This it is to have tender-hearted she-relations. If I had been lucky enough to be a bastard, I might have abused everybody to my dying-day, and *nobody never* the *worser*. I have sent no descriptions to you of these parts, because you know the Mackenzies and other vagrant people who have told you all . . . about them. I address this to Brookes's, supposing marriage to have driven you from Park Street. I have nothing left to wish you but an heir, of whose Papa I remain

the obliged and very sincere friend, BYRON

TO JOHN CAM HOBHOUSE†   *Patras, July 29th, 1810*

DEAR HOBHOUSE,—The same day which saw me ashore at Zea, set me forth once more upon the high seas, where I had the pleasure of seeing the frigate in the *Doldrums* by the light of sun and moon. Before daybreak I got into the Attics at Thaskalio, hence I dispatched men to Keratia for horses, and in ten hours from landing I was at Athens. There I was greeted by my Lord Sligo, and next day Messrs. North, Knight, and Fazakerly paid me formal visits. Sligo has a brig with

50 men who won't work, 12 guns that refuse to go off, and
sails that have cut every wind except a contrary one, and then
they are as willing as may be. He is sick of the concern, but
an engagement of six months prevents him from parting with
this precious ark. He *would* travel with me to Corinth, though
as you may suppose I was already heartily disgusted with
travelling in company. He has " en suite " a painter, a
captain, a gentleman misinterpreter (who boxes with the
painter), besides sundry idle English varlets. We were obliged
to have twenty-nine horses in all. The captain and the
Drogueman were left at Athens to kill bullocks for the crew, and
the Marquis and the limner, with a ragged Turk by way of
Tartar, and the ship's carpenter in the capacity of linguist,
with two servants (one of whom had the gripes) clothed both
in leather breeches (the thermometer 125°!!), followed over
the hills and far away. On our route, the poor limner in these
gentle latitudes was ever and anon condemned to bask for
half-an-hour, that he might produce what he himself termed a
" bellissimo sketche " (pardon the orthography of the last
word) of the surrounding country. You may also suppose that
a man of the Marchese's kidney was not very easy in his seat.
As for the *servants*, they and their *leather breeches* were equally
immovable at the end of the first stage. Fletcher, too, with
his usual acuteness, contrived at Megara to ram his damned
clumsy foot into a boiling tea-kettle. At Corinth we separated,
the M[arquis] for Tripolitza, I for Patras. Thus far the
ridiculous part of my narrative belongs to others, now comes
my turn. At Vostitza I found my dearly-beloved Eustathius,
ready to follow me not only to England, but to Terra Incognita, if so be my compass pointed that way. This was *four*
days ago : at present affairs are a little changed. The next
morning I found the dear soul upon horseback clothed very
sprucely in Greek Garments, with those ambrosial curls
hanging down his amiable back, and to my utter astonishment,
and the great abomination of Fletcher, a *parasol* in his hand
to save his complexion from the heat. However, in spite of
the *Parasol* on we travelled very much enamoured, as it should
seem, till we got to Patras, where Strané received us into his
new house where I now scribble. Next day he went to visit
some accursed cousin and the day after we had a grand quarrel.

Strané said I spoilt him. I said nothing; the child was as froward as an unbroken colt, and Strané's Janizary said I must not be surprised, for he was too *true* a *Greek* not to be disagreeable. I think I never in my life took so much pains to please any one, or succeeded so ill. I particularly avoided every thing which *could possibly give* the *least offence* in *any manner*. Somebody says, that those who try to please will please. This I know not; but I am sure that no one likes to fail in the attempt. At present he goes back to his father, though he is now become more tractable. Our *parting* was vastly pathetic, as many kisses as would have sufficed for a boarding school, and embraces enough to have ruined the character of a county in England, besides tears (not on *my* part) and expressions of " Tenerezza " to a vast amount. All this and the warmth of the weather has quite overcome me. Tomorrow I will continue. At present, " to bed ", " to bed ", " to bed ". The youth insists on seeing me tomorrow, the issue of which interview you shall hear. I wish you a pleasant sleep.

July 30th, 1810

I hope you have slept well. I have only dozed. For this last six days I have slept little and eaten less. The heat has burnt me brown, and as for Fletcher he is a walking Cinder. My new Greek acquaintance has called thrice, and we improve vastly. In good truth, so it ought to be, for I have quite exhausted my poor powers of pleasing, which God knows are little enough, Lord help me ! We are to go on to Tripolitza and Athens together. I do not know what has put him into such good humour unless it is some Sal Volatile I administered for his headache, and a green shade instead of that effeminate parasol. But so it is. We have *redintegrated* (a new *word* for you) our affections at a great rate. Now is not all this very ridiculous? Pray tell Matthews. It would do his heart good to see me travelling with my Tartar, Albanians, Buffo, Fletcher and this amiable παιδη prancing by my side. Strané hath got a steed which I have bought, full of spirit, I assure you, and very handsome accoutrements. My *account* with him was as I stated on board the Salsette. Here hath just arrived the Chirugeon of the Spider from Zante, who will take this letter

76

to Malta. I hope it will find you warm. You cannot conceive what a delightful companion you are now you are gone. Sligo has told me some things that ought to set you and me by the ears, but they shan't; and as a proof of it, I won't tell you what they are till we meet, but in the meantime I exhort you to behave well in polite society. His Lordship has been very kind, and as I crossed the Isthmus of Corinth, offered if I chose to take me to that of Darien, but I liked it not, for you have cured me of "villainous company".

I am about—after a Giro of the Morea—to move to Athens again, and thence I know not where; perhaps to Englonde, Malta, Sicily, Ægypt, or the Low Countries. I suppose you are at Malta or Palermo. I amuse myself alone very much to my satisfaction, riding, bathing, sweating, hearing Mr. Paul's musical clock, looking at his red breeches; we visit him every evening. There he is, playing at stopper with the old Cogia Bachi. When these amusements fail, there is my Greek to quarrel with, and a sopha to tumble upon. Nourse and Dacres had been at Athens scribbling all sorts of ribaldry over my old apartment, where Sligo, before my arrival, had added to your B.A. an A.S.S., and scrawled the compliments of Jackson, Deville, Miss Cameron, and "*I am very unappy Sam Jennings*". Wallace is incarcerated, and wanted Sligo to bail him, at the "Bell and Savage", Fleet Rules. The news are not surprising. What think you? Write to me from Malta, the Mediterranean, or Ingleterra, to care of ὁ μονόλοο Στράνε.

Have you cleansed my pistols? and dined with the "*Gineral*"? My compliments to the church of St. John's, and peace to the ashes of Ball. How is the Skipper? I have drank his cherry-brandy, and his rum has floated over half the Morea. Plaudite et valete.

Yours ever, BYRON

TO JOHN CAM HOBHOUSE †   *Tripolitza, August 16th, 1810*

DEAR HOBHOUSE,—I am on the rack of setting off for Argos amidst the usual creaking, swearing, loading, and neighing of sixteen horses and as many men, serrugees included. You have probably received one letter dated Patras, and I send this at a venture. Vely Pasha received me even better than his father did, though he is to join the Sultan, and the city is full of troops and confusion, which, as he said, prevented him from paying proper attention. He has given me a very pretty horse, and a most particular invitation to meet him at Larissa, which last is singular enough, as he recommended a different route to Lord Sligo, who asked leave to accompany him to the Danube. I asked no such thing, but on his enquiry where I meant to go, and receiving for answer that I was about to return to Albania, for the purpose of penetrating higher up the country, he replied, " No, you must not take that route, but go round by Larissa, where I shall remain some time, on my way. I will send to Athens, and you shall join me ; we will eat and drink and go a hunting." He said he wished all the old men (specifying under that epithet North, Forresti, and Strané,) to go to his father, but the young ones to come to him, to use his own expression, " Vecchio con Vecchio, Giovane con Giovane ". He honoured me with the appellations of his *friend* and *brother*, and hoped that we should be on good terms, not for a few days but for life. All this is very well, but he has an awkward manner of throwing his arm round one's waist, and squeezing one's hand in *public* which is a high compliment, but very much embarrasses " *ingenuous youth* ".

The first time I saw him he received me *standing*, accompanied me at my departure to the door of the audience chamber, and told me I was a παλικαρι and an εὔμορφω παίδι. He asked if I did not think it very proper that as *young* men (he has a *beard* down to his middle) we should live together, with a variety of other sayings, which made Strané stare, and puzzled me in my replies. He was very facetious with Andreas and Viscillie, and recommended that my Albanians' heads should be cut off if they behaved ill. I shall write to you from Larissa, and inform you of our proceedings in that city. In the meantime I sojourn at Athens. I have sent Eustathius back to his home ; he plagued my soul out with his whims, and is besides subject to *epileptic* fits (tell *M.* this) which made him a perplexing companion ; in *other* matters he was very tolerable,

I mean as to his learning, being well versed in the Ellenics. You remember Nicolo at Athens, Lusieri's wife's brother. Give my *compliments* to *Matthews*, from whom I expect a congratulatory letter. I have a thousand anecdotes for him and you, but at present, τί να κάμω ? I have neither time nor space, but in the words of Dawes, " I have things in store ". I have scribbled thus much. Where shall I send it? Why, to Malta or Paternoster Row. Hobby, you wretch, how is the Miscellany? that damned and damnable work. What has the learned world said to your Paradoxes? I hope you did not forget the importance of Monogamy. Strané has just arrived with bags of piastres, so that I must conclude by the usual phrase of

Yours, etc. etc., BYRON

P.S.—You knew young Bossari at Yanina ; he is a piece of Ali Pacha's ! ! Well did Horace write " Nil Admirari ".

TO JOHN CAM HOBHOUSE †   *The Convent, Athens,*
August 23rd, 1810

MY DEAR HOBHOUSE,—Lord Sligo's unmanageable brig being remanded to Malta, with a large quantity of vases, amounting in value (according to the depreciation of Fauriel) to one hundred and fifty piastres, I cannot resist the temptation of assailing you in this third letter, which I trust will find you better than your deserts, and no worse than my wishes can make you. I have girated the Morea, and was presented with a very fine horse (a stallion), and honoured with a number of squeezes and speeches by Velly Pasha, besides a most pressing invitation to meet him at Larissa in his way to the wars. But of these things I have written already. I returned to Athens by Argos, where I found Lord Sligo with a painter, who has got a fever with sketching at midday, and a dragoman who has actually lied himself into a lockjaw. I grieve to say the Marchese has done a number of young things, because I believe him to be a clever, and I am sure he is a good man. I am most auspiciously settled in the Convent, which is more commodious than any tenement I have yet occupied, with room for my *suite*; and it is by no means solitary, seeing there is not only " il Padre Abbate ", but his " schuola ", consisting of six " Ragazzi ", all my most particular allies. These gentle-men being almost (saving Fauvel and Lusieri) my only associates, it is but proper their character, religion, and morals, should be described. Of this goodly company three are Catho-lics, and three are Greeks, which schismatics I have already set a boxing to the great amusement of the Father, who rejoices to see the Catholics conquer. Their names are Barthelemi, Giuseppè, *Nicolo*, Yani, and two anonymous, at least in my memory. Of these, Barthelemi is a " simplice Fanciullo ", according to the account of the Father, whose favourite is Giuseppè, who sleeps in the lantern of Demosthenes. We have nothing but riot from noon to night.

The first time I mingled with these sylphs, after about two minutes' reconnoitring, the amiable Signor Barthelemi, without any previous notice, seated himself by me, and after observing by way of compliment that my " Signoria " was the " piu bello " of his English acquaintance, saluted me on the left cheek, for which freedom being reproved by Giuseppè, who very properly informed him that I was " μεγάλος "; he told him I was his " φίλος ", and " by his beard " he would do so again, adding, in reply to the question " διὰ τὶ ἀσπάσετε?" " you see he laughs ", as in good truth I did heartily. But my friend, as you may easily imagine, is Nicolo, who, by-the-by, is my Italian master, and we are already very philosophical. I am his " Padrone " and his " amico ", and the Lord knows what besides. It is about two hours since, that, after informing me he was most desirous to follow *him* (that is me) over the world, he concluded by telling me it was proper for us not only to live, but " morire insieme ". The latter I hope to avoid—as much of the former as he pleases. I am awakened in the morning by those imps shouting " Venite abasso ", and the friar gravely observes it is " bisogno bastonare " everybody before the studies can possibly commence. Besides these lads, my suite,—to which I have added a Tartar and a youth to look after my two new saddle horses,—my suite, I say, are very obstreperous, and drink skinfuls of Zean wine at eight paras the olne daily. Then we have several Albanian women washing in the " giardino ", whose hours of relaxation are spent in running pins into Fletcher's backside. " *Damnata di mi, if I have seen such a spectaculo in my way from Viterbo*." In short, what with the *women*, and the *boys*, and the *suite*, we are very disorderly. But I am vastly happy and childish, and shall have a world of anecdotes for you and the "citoyen".

Intrigue flourishes: the old woman, Theresa's mother, was mad enough to imagine I was going to marry the girl; but I have better amusement. Andreas is fooling with Dudu, as usual, and Mariana has made a conquest of Dervise Tahiri; Vircillie, Fletcher and Sullee, my new Tartar, have each a mistress—" Vive l'Amour ".

I am learning Italian, and this day translated an ode of Horace, " Exegi monumentum ", into that language. I chatter with everybody, good or bad, and tradute prayers out of the mass ritual; but my lessons, though very long, are sadly interrupted by scamperings, and eating fruit, and peltings and playings; and I am in fact at school again, and make as little improvement now as I did then, my time being wasted in the same way.

However, it is too good to last; I am going to make a second tour of Attica with Lusieri, who is a new ally of mine, and Nicolo goes with me at his own most pressing solicitation, " per mare per terras ". " Forse " you may see us in Inghilterra, but " non so, come, etc." For the present, good-even, Buona sera a vos signoria. Bacio le mani :—August 24th, 1810.

I am about to take my daily ride to the Piræus, where I swim for an hour despite of the heat; here hath been an Englishman ycleped Watson, who died and is buried in the Tempio of Theseus. I knew him not, but I am told that the surgeon of Lord Sligo's brig slew him with an improper potion, and a cold bath.

Lord Sligo's crew are sadly addicted to liquor. He is in some apprehension of a scrape with the Navy concerning certain mariners of the King's ships.

He himself is now at Argos with his hospital, but intends to winter in Athens. I think he will be sick of it, poor soul, he has all the indecision of your humble servant, without the relish for the ridiculous which makes my life supportable.

I wish you were here to partake of a number of waggeries, which you can hardly find in the gun-room or in Grub Street, but then you are so very crabbed and disagreeable, that when the laugh is over I rejoice in your absence. After all, I do love thee, Hobby, thou hast so many good qualities, and so many bad ones, it is impossible to live with or without thee.

Nine in the Evening.

I have, as usual, swum across the Piræus, the Signor Nicolo also laved, but he makes as bad a hand in the water as L'Abbé Hyacinth at Falmouth; it is a curious thing that the Turks when they bathe wear their lower garments, as your humble servant always doth, but the Greeks not; however, questo Giovane e vergognó [*sic*].

Lord Sligo's surgeon has assisted very materially the malignant fever now fashionable here; another man *dead* to-day, two men a week, like fighting Bob Acres in the country. Fauriel says he is like the surgeon whom the Venetians fitted out against the Turks, with whom they were then at war.

I have been employed the greater part of today in conjugating the verb " ασπαζω " (which word being Ellenic as well as Romaic may find a place in the *Citoyen's* Lexicon). I assure you my progress is rapid, but like Caesar " nil actum reputans dum quid superesset agendum ", I must arrive at the [indecipherable], and then I will write to ——. I hope to escape the fever, at least till I finish this affair, and then it is welcome to try. I don't think without its friend the drunken Pothecary it has any chance. Take a quotation:—" Et Lycam *nigris* oculis, nigroque *crine* decorum ".

yours and the Sieur's ever, B.

TO JOHN CAM HOBHOUSE†   *Patras, September 25th, 1810*

My dear Hobhouse,—I am at present in a very ridiculous situation, under the hands of Dr. Romanelli, and a fever which hath confined me to my bed for these three days past, but by the blessing of God and two glysters, I am now able to sit up, but much debilitated. I will describe my situation in a parody on Pope's lines on the Duke of Buckingham, the which I composed during an interval for your edification.

> On a cold room's cold floor, within a bed
> Of iron, with three coverlids like lead,

A coat and breeches dangling o'er a nook,
Where sits a doctor and prescribes a puke,
Poor B—r—n sweats,—alas! how changed from him,
So plump in feature, and so round in limb,
Grinning and gay in Newstead's monkish fane,
The scene of profanation, and champagne,
Or just as gay with scribblers in a ring
Of twenty hungry authors banqueting.
No whore to fondle left of half a score,
Yet one thing left him, which he values more,
Here victor of a fever, and its friends,
Physicians and their art, his lordship *mends*.

I have been vomited and purged according to rule, and as my
fever has almost subsided, I hope to weather this bout, which
has been pretty tight, I assure you. Yet if I do fall by the
Glyster pipe of Romanelli, recollect my injunction.

Odious! in boards, 'twould any Bard provoke
(Were the last words that dying Byron spoke);
No, let some charming cuts and frontispiece
Adorn my volume, and the sale increase.
One would not be unpublished when one's dead,
And, Hobhouse, let my works be bound in *Red*.

TO JOHN CAM HOBHOUSE †   *Patras, October 2nd, 1810*

DEAR YANI,—By this second date you will perceive that
I have been again ill. Indeed I have had this fever very
violently, and five days bed-riding with Emetics, glysters,
Bark, and all the host of Physic shewed how vain were my
former hopes of complete recovery. But being well toasted
and watered etc., I shall endeavour to conclude this letter of
two beginnings, which I must do quickly and attend poor
Nicolo who has waited on me day and night till he is worse than
I was and is now undergoing the same process for his recovery.
I believe you recollect him. He is the brother of Lusieri's
spouse, and has been with me nearly two months, at his
particular request. He is now my sole dragoman (I have
commenced Italian), for the moment I received yours Andreas

was dismissed at the instance of Dominus Magelli. I have made a tolerable tour of the Morea, and visited Vely Pasha, who gave me a very pretty horse.

The other day I went to Olympia. Argos, Napoli, and Mantinea I saw in my route to and from Tripolitza.

I have seen a good deal of Lord Sligo; by the bye, there is a silly report all over the Morea, that he and I quarrelled, fought, and were wounded at Argos, there is not a word of truth in it from beginning to end.

If I kept any journal your request would be immediately complied with, but I have none.

Vely is gone to the Danube. I have been here on business with Strané, but the moment Nicolo and myself are enough recovered to set out, I shall proceed again to Athens. I lodge in the convent.

Perhaps I am in possession of anecdotes that would amuse you and the Citoyen, but I must defer the detail till we meet, I have written to you three times since I left you in Zea, and direct my letters to Ridgways, where I presume you will be found on Sundays. You are now in England. What you tell me of the Miscellany grieves me (in spite of Rochefoucault); I commend your design of not letting the public off so easily; come out as a tourist, prose must go down.

But don't ask half a guinea for your next book. Consider, half a guinea carries a man to the Opera, and if he goes to Hookham's, 'tis odds but he buys more tickets than books, aye, and cheaper too; try seven shillings, Mr. Hobhouse, seven shillings, sir, stick to that, and let me tell you, when you have received seven hundred seven shilling pieces, they will cut a figure on your little deal writing-table. I have a regard for you, sir, and out of it, I beg you to strike off the odd three and sixpence.

I have nothing to request in England; everybody with whom I am at all connected seems asleep; as far as regards me, I shan't awake them. Hanson you may just fillup on the nose, and ask him from me if he is insane, not to have answered my letters. As to the others, their conduct is optional, and I have nothing to say. I shall certainly be in England in a few months, perhaps before, but I do not wish this to go forth, as it will only make Hanson more dilatory. If you hear anything you will write, and I will apprise you of my intentions as they rise and subside, for it would be very absurd in me to pretend to any regular plan. You have no doubt, a deal to do and say and hear and reply ; wishing you well through it,

I am yours very sincerely etc., BYRON

TO JOHN CAM HOBHOUSE†   *Patras, Morea, October 4th, 1810*

MY DEAR HOBHOUSE,—I wrote to you two days ago, but the weather and my friend Strané's conversation being much the same, and my ally Nicolo in bed with a fever, I think I may as well talk to you, the rather, as you can't answer me; and excite my wrath with impertinent observations, at least for three months to come. I will try not to say the same things I have set down in my other letter of the 2nd, but I can't promise, as my poor head is still giddy with my late fever. I saw the Lady Hesther Stanhope ¹ at Athens, and do not admire " that dangerous thing a female wit ". She told me (take her own words) that she had given you a good set-down at Malta, in some disputation about the Navy ; from this, of course, I readily inferred the contrary, or in the words of an *acquaintance* of ours, that " you had the best of it ". She evinced a similar disposition to *argufy* with me, which I avoided by either laughing or yielding. I despise the sex too much to squabble with them, and I rather wonder you should allow a woman to draw you into a contest, in which, however, I am sure you had the advantage, she abuses you so bitterly. I have seen too little of the Lady to form any decisive opinion, but I have discovered nothing different from other she-things, except a great disregard of received notions in her conversation as well as conduct. I don't know whether this will recommend her to our sex, but I am sure it won't to her own. She is going on to Constantinople. Ali Pacha is in a scrape. Ibrahim Pacha and the Pacha of Scutari have come down upon him with 20,000 Gegdes and Albanians, retaken Berat, and threaten Tepaleni. Adam Bey

¹ The celebrated Lady Hester Stanhope was at this time travelling through European Turkey. The impression that Byron made upon her was not entirely favourable. " One time [she remarked] he was mopish, and nobody was to speak to him ; another, he was for being jocular with everybody. . . . He had a great deal of vice in his looks. . . ."

is dead, Vely Pacha was on his way to the Danube, but has gone off suddenly to Yanina, and all Albania is in an uproar. The mountains we crossed last year are the scene of warfare, and there is nothing but carnage and cutting of throats. In my other letter I mentioned that Vely had given me a fine horse. On my late visit he received me with great pomp, standing, conducted me to the door with his arm round my waist, and a variety of civilities, invited me to meet him at Larissa and see his army, which I should have accepted, had not this rupture with Ibrahim taken place. Sultan Mahmout is in a phrenzy because Vely has not joined the army. We have a report here, that the Russians have beaten the Turks and taken Muchtar Pacha prisoner, but it is a Greek Bazaar rumour and not to be believed. I have now treated you with a dish of Turkish politics. You have by this time gotten into England, and your ears and mouth are full of " Reform Burdett, Gale Jones, minority, last night's division, dissolution of Parliament, battle in Portugal ", and all the cream of forty newspapers.

In my t'other letter, to which I am perpetually obliged to refer, I have offered some moving topics on the head of your *Miscellany*, the neglect of which I attribute to the half guinea annexed as the indispensable equivalent for the said volume. Now I do hope, notwithstanding that exorbitant demand, that on your return you will find it selling, or, what is better, sold, in consequence of which you will be able to face the public with your new volume, if that intention still subsists. My journal, did I keep one, should be yours. As it is I can only offer my sincere wishes for your success, if you will believe it possible for a brother scribbler to be sincere on such an occasion. Will you execute a commission for me? Lord Sligo tells me it was the intention of Miller in Albemarle Street to send by him a letter to me, which he stated to be of consequence. Now I have no concern with Mr. M. except a bill which I hope is paid before this time; will you visit the said M. and if it be a pecuniary matter, refer him to Hanson, and if not, tell me what he means, or forward his letter. I have just received an epistle from Galt, with a Candist poem, which it seems I am to forward to you. This I would willingly do, but it is too large for a letter, and too small for a parcel, and besides appears to be damned nonsense, from all which considerations

I will deliver it in person. It is entitled the " Fair Shepherd-ess ", or rather " Herdswoman " ; if you don't like the transla-tion take the original title ' ἡ βοσκοπούλα ". Galt also writes something not very intelligible about a " Spartan State paper " which by his account is everything but Laconic. Now the said Sparta having some years ceased to be a state, what the devil does he mean by a paper? he also adds mysteriously that the *affair* not being concluded, he cannot at present apply for it. Now, Hobhouse, are you mad? or is he? Are these documents for Longman and Co.? Spartan state papers! and Cretan rhymes! indeed these circumstances superadded to his house at Mycene (whither I am invited) and his Levant wines, make me suspect his sanity.

Athens is at present infested with English people, but they are moving, *Dio bendetto!* I am returning to pass a month or two ; I think the spring will see me in England, but do not let this transpire, nor cease to urge the most dilatory of mortals, Hanson. I have some idea of purchasing the Island of Ithaca ; I suppose you will add me to the Levant lunatics. I shall be glad to hear from your Signoria of your welfare, politics, and literature. Tell M. that I have obtained above two hundred [word indecipherable] and am almost tired of them ; for the history of these he must wait my return, as after many attempts I have given up the idea of conveying information on paper. You know the monastery of Mendele ; it was there I made myself master of the first. Your last letter closes pathetically with a postscript about a nosegay ; I advise you to introduce that into your next sentimental novel. I am sure I did not suspect you of any fine feelings, and I believe you were laughing, but you are welcome. *Vale* ; " I can no more ", like Lord Grizzle.

Yours, Μπαίρων

TO JOHN CAM HOBHOUSE　　　*Capuchin Convent, Athens,*
January 10th, 1811

DEAR HOBHOUSE,—I have written at intervals several letters, some of which it is probable you have received. Two have arrived of yours, dated Malta and Cagliari, and I con-ceive there be others *on* the sea, or *in* it, for you must have been months in England. Since your departure from the Cyclades I have been principally in Attica, which I have traversed more than once, besides two tours in the Morea, of the particulars of which Mr. Fletcher, now on his voyage with despatches, will apprise you. Here be many English, and there have been more, with all of whom I have been and *am* on dining terms, and we have had balls and a variety of fooleries with the females of Athens. I am very undecided in my intentions, though stationary enough, as you perceive by my date. I sometimes think of moving homewards in spring, and sometimes of not moving at all till I have worn out my shoes, which are all as good as new. Hanson has at last written, and wants me to sell Newstead. I *will not*; and though I have in more than one letter to you requested you to corroborate and assist this *negative*, I beg in this and all subsequent communications, to entreat you to tell him and all whom it may concern, that I will not sell my patrimony. I suppose, however, the adjustment of that, and other damned affairs will drag me to England. Well, sir, and I suppose you are holding forth to your acquaintance, on the subject of your travels, and they are all very glad to see you, and you have been tipsy and loquacious as usual on such occasions, and are just beginning to subside into the old track of living, after shaking about sixty pairs of hands, and seeing the play and such like, all of which must be very new to a voyager from the Levant. You will present my respects to Matthews and Davies, who is I hear about to throw himself away on a rich wife, and none of the seemliest, according to my reporter. Pray what profits make ye of the Miscellany? Eh, eh! I warrant you now, you are preparing a tome of travel for the press. I have no journal, or you should have it to abet your design. I am now tolerable in Italian, and am studying the Romaic under a master, being obliged to cashier my Latin with my last dragoman, and betake myself to the moderns. I have sent a bark to Smyrna in the faint hope of letters, and shall not fill up this sheet till its return.

January 14th, 1811

My boat is returned with some newspapers, and duplicates of letters already arrived. None from you, but all in good time. I shall certainly not (without something very novel occurs), move towards your Island till spring, nor even then if I receive any further remittances, a business which I hope you did not fail to urge to my agent. You have, I humbly presume, forwarded all my epistles to their respective destinations. I certainly wish to hear how you go on, and what plan you have chalked out. Five and twenty is almost too late in life for anything but the Senate, or the Church. I wish you was a parson, or a counsellor-at-law; by the bye Lord Erskine did not commence till nearly thirty. I do not think your sire so blameable; the fault lies of course with the stepdame; the old story; Baillie has got rid of his " injusta noverca ", see what it is to have luck! As you are fond of scribbling, and are said to have a talent that way, why don't you, and *Matthews*, and some other wits, undertake some periodical, hebdomadal or diurnal concern, I leave you to find out what, but I think you might bring such a scheme to bear. Fyott is this day arrived from Mount Athos (" ἅγιον ὄρος "), he has discovered nothing to signify in the manuscript way; Graham and Haygarth are to depart shortly, one for Stamboul, Haygarth for Sicily. I shall send this by the latter. Galt is in Pera, full of his Sour Wine Company speculation. I shall look at him in Mycenæ, in the " Prima Vera ". He sent me a Candiot poem for you, but being the worst Romaic, and the vilest nonsense ever seen, it was not worth the carriage. As you know Athens and all its peculiarities, I shall not afflict you with description. I have three horses (one a gift of Vely Pasha), and live rather better and cheaper than last winter. I see a good deal of the English, and Lusieri, chiefly of late, and have had no disputes with anyone. I am tranquil, and as contented as I suppose one can be in any situation. I have also a Bavarian Baron and celebrated painter, taking views for me.

Yours very affectionately and truly, B——

[Written inside the wrapper]   *January 17th, 1811*

P.S.—This goes by Haygarth, who moves in a few days to Malta, by way of the Morea and Zante. Graham is off too.

I stay till spring, at all events till I receive letters, which as usual take their time on the way. Good-night, you port-drinking fellow. I am just returned from dining with Haygarth.

TO HIS MOTHER   *Athens, January 14, 1811*

MY DEAR MADAM,—I seize an occasion to write as usual, shortly, but frequently, as the arrival of letters, where there exists no regular communication, is, of course, very precarious. I have received, at different intervals, several of yours, but generally six months after date ; some sooner, some later, and, though lately tolerably stationary, the delays appear just the same. I have lately made several small tours of some hundred or two miles about the Morea, Attica, etc., as I have finished my grand giro by the Troad, Constantinople, etc., and am returned down again to Athens. I believe I have mentioned to you more than once that I swam (in imitation of Leander, though without his lady) across the Hellespont, from Sestos to Abydos. Of this, and all other particulars, Fletcher, whom I have sent home with papers, etc., will apprise you. I cannot find that he is any loss ; being tolerably master of the Italian and modern Greek languages, which last I am also studying with a master, I can order and discourse more than enough for a reasonable man. Besides, the perpetual lamentations after beef and beer, the stupid, bigoted contempt for every thing foreign, and insurmountable incapacity of acquiring even a few words of any language, rendered him, like all other English servants, an incumbrance. I do assure you, the plague of speaking for him, the comforts he required (more than myself by far), the pilaws (a Turkish dish of rice and meat) which he could not eat, the wines which he could not drink, the beds where he could not sleep, and the long list of calamities, such as stumbling horses, want of *tea!!!* etc., which assailed him, would have made a lasting source of laughter to a spectator, and inconvenience to a master. After all, the man is honest enough, and, in Christendom, capable enough ; but in Turkey, Lord forgive me ! my Albanian soldiers, my Tartars and Jannissary, worked for him and us too, as my friend Hobhouse can testify.

It is probable I may steer homewards in spring; but to enable me to do that, I must have remittances. My own funds would have lasted me very well; but I was obliged to assist a friend, who, I know, will pay me; but, in the mean time, I am out of pocket. At present, I do not care to venture a winter's voyage, even if I were otherwise tired of travelling; but I am so convinced of the advantages of looking at mankind instead of reading about them, and the bitter effects of staying at home with all the narrow prejudices of an islander, that I think there should be a law amongst us, to set our young men abroad, for a term, among the few allies our wars have left us.

Here I see and have conversed with French, Italians, Germans, Danes, Greeks, Turks, Americans, etc., etc., etc.; and without losing sight of my own, I can judge of the countries and manners of others. Where I see the superiority of England (which, by the by, we are a good deal mistaken about in many things), I am pleased, and where I find her inferior, I am at least enlightened. Now, I might have stayed, smoked in your towns, or fogged in your country, a century, without being sure of this, and without acquiring any thing more useful or amusing at home. I keep no journal, nor have I any intention of scribbling my travels. I have done with authorship, and if, in my last production, I have convinced the critics or the world I was something more than they took me for, I am satisfied; nor will I hazard *that reputation* by a future effort. It is true I have some others in manuscript, but I leave them for those who come after me; and, if deemed worth publishing, they may serve to prolong my memory when I myself shall cease to remember. I have a famous Bavarian artist taking some views of Athens, etc., etc., for me. This will be better than scribbling, a disease I hope myself cured of. I hope, on my return, to lead a quiet, recluse life, but God knows and does best for us all; at least, so they say, and I have nothing to object, as, on the whole, I have no reason to complain of my lot. I am convinced, however, that men do more harm to themselves than ever the devil could do to them. I trust this will find you well, and as happy as we can be; you will, at least, be pleased to hear I am so, and

Yours ever

TO JOHN CAM HOBHOUSE*   *Athens, March 5th, 1811*

DEAR HOBHOUSE,—Two English gentlemen after 7 years captivity in France having made their escape through Bosnia, and having arrived here in their way home, I shall follow up my last letter with the present which will be conveyed by these runaways whose names are Cazenove [?].

I am this moment come out of the Turkish Bath, which is an immense luxury to me, though I am afraid it would not suit you at all, there being a great deal of rubbing, sweating, and *washing* (your aversion) to go through, which I indulge in every other day. . . . I cannot sufficiently admire the punctuality and success with which you have written to me in reward for my numerous communications, the last of which must have arrived with the nincompoop Fletcher. Since my last letter, 27 ult, I have begun an Imitation of the " De Arte Poetica " of Horace (in rhyme of course) and have translated or rather varied about 200 lines and shall probably finish it for lack of other argument. The Horace I found in the convent where I have sojourned some months.

Ever since my fever in the Morea in Septr. of which I wrote you an account, my health has been changing in the most tramontane way. I have been fat, and thin (as I am at present) and had a cough and a catarrh and the piles and be damned to them, and I have had pains in my side and left off animal food, which last has done me some service. But I expect great things from the coming summer and if well and wealthy shall go to Jerusalem, for which I have a firman.

Dun Hanson, and tell him, he won't persuade me to sell Newstead, unless something particular occurs. If I sell it, I live abroad; if not, I come home; and I have no intention of selling it, but the contrary. The English here and myself are on very good terms. We have balls and dinners frequently. As I told you before, no letters have arrived from anybody. Consequently I know nothing of you, or Matthews, or the Miscellany. I have seen English papers of October, which say little or nothing; but I have lately sent a Battello [?] to Smyrna in hopes of hearing from my vagabond connections. I don't think you will see me before July, and if things go on to my wish, not for another year. I take it for granted all this time that you are arrived in England, as the Salsette has returned these six months to Smyrna, but your silence makes me rather doubt it. You see, you were mistaken in your conjectures on the subject of my return, and I have remanded Fletcher, whom I by no means miss, unless it be by having less confusion than usual in my wardrobe and household. I got your Malta and Cagliari letters, but I expected you would have written from England, though I can excuse a little delay and drunkenness on your first arrival. I feel also interested in your plans. I want to know what you are doing, saying, and writing, whether your domestic affairs go on to your satisfaction, and having heard all this, I should be glad to be informed of Matthieu, who I suppose was pleased to see you again. As for my own affairs, I don't want to hear of them unless they shine a little brighter than in June last, when I received a jocose account of their inextricability from Mr. H., who might as well have kept his good things for a better opportunity. If he remits a round sum, I will take that and his wit in good part; but I can't allow any naggery from Temple Bar without an adequate remuneration, particularly as three thousand miles (according to Fletcher's invariable calculation from the moment he *cleared* the *channel*) are too long for a repartee. I am at present out of spirits, having just lost a particular friend; poor dear Dr. Bronstedt of Copenhagen (who lost half his rix dollars by our cursed bombardment) is lately gone to Constantinople. We used to tipple punch and talk politics; Sandford Graham is also gone. But then there are more coming.

Pray have you sent Mrs. Pigot a copy of the Miscellany? Have you sent my letters to their proper places? Have you fulfilled my commissions? And how d'ye do?

Yours ever very truly, BYRON

TO JOHN CAM HOBHOUSE †   Volage, *frigate, at Sea,*
June 19th, 1811

MY DEAR HOBHOUSE,—In the gentle dullness of a summer voyage I shall converse with you for half-an-hour.

We left Malta on the 2nd, with three other frigates, inclusive of the Lissa prizes, and we are on our way, they to glory, and I to what God pleases. I am recovered from my Tertian, but neither my health nor my hitherto hoydenish spirits are as rampant as usual. I received at Malta your letters, which I have answered; and I have succeeded in the discovery and embarkation of your memorable marbles; they shall be brought to town or left in proper care at Portsmouth, till you can arrange their removal.

I am accompanied by two Greek servants, both middle-aged men, and one is Demetrius your old mis-interpreter. I have letters for you from Cockerell, whom I left well with other Franks. My own antiquities consist of four *tortoises*, and four *Skulls*, all taken out of ancient sarcophagi. Our health is very lackadaisycal. I have a *, and Sr. Demetrius a * *, the fatal consequence of some forty " Sculamente ". I shall put off all account of my Winter in Athens, which was most social and fantastical, as also all my marchings and countermarchings, till our meeting, and indulge in speculation on my prospects in your Country. I shall first endeavour to repair my irreparable affairs, and it seems I must set out for Lancashire, for I shall neither have coals nor comfort till I visit Rochdale in person. I wish you would meet me or tell me where to meet you, as I wish to consult you on various subjects, besides the pleasure I shall experience in your society.

With regard to all *Dross* business between us, don't think of it till it is most perfectly convenient. I would rather you did not think of it at all, but as I know your sentiments on the subject, I shall not annoy you by such a proposition.

You tell me fine things—very fine things—on the *literary* " *lay* ", I suppose from your natural knowledge of our weak side, and with a view to set me *marble-hunting*, by dint of compliment. I have, as I told you before, completed an Imitation of Horace, " Ad Pisones ", addressed to you, and to be published forthwith, as you will readily conjecture.

I hope the Miscellany mends in sale. Its failure must be attributed to that accursed " Walsh-ean " preface, which the Citoyen M. would recommend, and you see what it has come to. M[atthe]ws has written to me; thank him, and say further I shall have great pleasure in gratifying his curiosity, which, however, he must not raise too high.

You talk of the militia—Santissimi Coglioni!—the militia at five-and-twenty; boys over your head, and brutes under you, mess, country-quarters, courts-martial, and quelling of riots. If you will be mad or martial ('tis the same thing) go to Portugal again, and I will go with you (for I have some serious thoughts of it, if matters are intricate at home), but don't waste your time in mere *holiday* soldiering, as Major Sturgeon would call it. I am writing all this time without knowing your address. However I shall send as usual to Ridgways, who will forward my present as he has done the other letters. Fletcher must have arrived some time. I sent him off in November. He was useless and in the way, and in every respect I did better without him. How goes on " La Bagatelle "? Have you met with any clubbable persons with a sufficient tincture of Literature for your purpose. You have not been in London, it should seem. I shall proceed there from Portsmouth to Reddish's or Dorant's for a few days, and afterwards to Newstead, and most probably abroad again as soon as my arrangements will admit. Ld. Sligo is on his way home; I left him at Malta in quarantine. Bruce is gone or going to Persia; he is a singular being; on the night he left Athens he made me a profession of friendship, on the extremity of the Piræus, the only one I ever received in my life, and certainly very unexpected, for I had done nothing to deserve it. Whitbread (in Peter Pindar's visit from George Guelph) says he is too old for a *knight*, and I am too old for a friend, at least a new one. Tell M[atthews] I have bade adieu to every species of affection, and may say with Horace, " Me jam nec fœmina ", etc., he will finish the lines. Seriously, I can't think, for the soul of me, what possessed Michael, for, like the Rovers, " a sudden thought struck him ". We had dined together, so I know he was not drunk; but the truth is, he is a little chivalrous and romantic, and is smitten with unimaginable fantasies ever since his connection with Lady H. Stanhope. However, both her ladyship and he were very polite, and asked me to go on with them a second time to Constantinople; but having been there once, and preferring *philosophy* at Athens, I staid in my convent. Matthews tells me that Jeffrey [1] means to review your book; if he does, it

---

[1] Lord Jeffrey, editor of the *Edinburgh Review*.

will do you good, one way or the other, but I think it probable he will praise you. Have you nothing new for the press? Don't be discouraged by the Miscellany, but throw the blame on your friends, and the preface, and Matthews, and me, and the damned trash of your auxiliaries. There is something very impudent in my offering this pert consolation, but I hope you will stand in no need of it, and begin to receive half-guineas at a rare rate; by-the-bye, would not seven-and-sixpence have sold and sounded better? Matthews has been advising you to philosophize at Cambridge—do, and I'll join you for a time, and we will tipple and talk Matthews to death with our travels, and jest and squabble, and be as insipid as the best of them.

Bold Webster [1] (by way of keeping up that epithet, I suppose) has married, and, *bolder* still, a sister of Ld. V^t Valentia, and, *boldest* of all, has published letters to the Commr. in Chief! Corpo di Caio Mario! what will the world come to? I take this to be one of the newest events " under the sun ".

Had he no friend, no relation, no pitying monitor to snatch the manuscript from one devil to save it from the other? Pray are the letters in prose or verse? I have gossiped away till we are off Cape St. Vincent, and I am puzzled what to say next, or rather to ask, for my letter is a string of questions, quite forgetting you can't answer my Catechism. I am dull, " dull as the last new comedy " (*vide* Goldsmith's " Good Natured Man "), though Capt. Hornby is a gentlemanly and pleasant man, and a Salamander in his profession, fight anything; but as I have got all the particulars of his late action out of him, I don't know what to ask *him* next any more than *you*. But we are infested in the cabin by another passenger, a teller of tough stories, all about himself. I could laugh at him were there anybody to laugh with; as it is, I yawn and swear to myself, and take refuge in the quarter gallery; thank God he is now asleep, or I should be worried with impertinence. His name is Thomas, and he is Staff- or Stuff- Apothecary to General Oakes, who has rammed him down our throats for the voyage, and a bitter Bolus he is, that's the truth on't. But I long for land, and then for a post-chaise, and I believe my

[1] James Wedderburn Webster, an irrepressibly foolish personage, whose wife, Lady Frances, was destined to play a part in Byron's later career.

enjoyments will end there, for I have no other pleasure to expect that I know of.

We have had a tedious passage, all except the Straits, where we had an easterly gale, and glided through the gut like an oil Glyster. Dear Hobby, you must excuse all this facetiousness, which I should not have let loose if I knew what the devil to do, but I am so out of spirits, and hopes, and humour, and pocket, and health, that you must bear with my merriment, my only resource against a Calentura. Write to me; I am now going to patrole the melancholy deck. God be wi' ye!

Yours always, B.

[On the envelope]

P.S.—Take a mouthful of Saltwater poetry, by a Tar on the late Lissa Victory.

> If I had an *ed*ication
> I'd sing your praise more large,
> But I'm only a common foremast Jack
> On board of *the le Volage!!!!!*

TO HIS MOTHER   *Volage frigate, at sea, June 25, 1811*

DEAR MOTHER,—This letter, which will be forwarded on our arrival at Portsmouth, probably about the 4th of July, is begun about twenty-three days after our departure from Malta. I have just been two years (to a day, on the 2d of July) absent from England, and I return to it with much the same feelings which prevailed on my departure, viz. indifference; but within that apathy I certainly do not comprise yourself, as I will prove by every means in my power. You will be good enough to get my apartments ready at Newstead; but don't disturb yourself, on any account, particularly mine, nor consider me in any other light than as a visiter. I must only inform you that for a long time I have been restricted to an entire vegetable diet, neither fish nor flesh coming within my regimen; so I expect a powerful stock of potatoes, greens, and biscuit; I drink no wine. I have two servants, middle-aged men, and both Greeks. It is my intention to proceed first to town, to see Mr. Hanson, and thence to Newstead, on my way to Rochdale. I have only to beg you will not forget my diet, which it is very necessary for me to observe. I am well in health, as I have generally been, with the exception of two agues, both of which I quickly got over.

My plans will so much depend on circumstances, that I shall not venture to lay down an opinion on the subject. My prospects are not very promising, but I suppose we shall wrestle through life like our neighbours; indeed, by Hanson's last advices, I have some apprehension of finding Newstead dismantled by Messrs. Brothers, etc., and he seems determined to force me into selling it, but he will be baffled. I don't suppose I shall be much pestered with visiters; but if I am, you must receive them, for I am determined to have nobody breaking in upon my retirement: you know that I never was fond of society, and I am less so than before. I have brought you a shawl, and a quantity of attar of roses, but these I must smuggle, if possible. I trust to find my library in tolerable order.

Fletcher is no doubt arrived. I shall separate the mill from Mr. B * *'s farm, for his son is too gay a deceiver to inherit both, and place Fletcher in it, who has served me faithfully, and whose wife is a good woman; besides, it is necessary to sober young Mr. B * *, or he will people the parish with bastards. In a word, if he had seduced a dairy-maid, he might have found something like an apology; but the girl is his equal, and in high life or low life reparation is made in such circumstances. But I shall not interfere further than (like Buonaparte) by dismembering Mr. B.'s *kingdom*, and erecting part of it into a principality for field-marshal Fletcher! I hope you govern my little *empire* and its sad load of national debt with a wary hand. To drop my metaphor, I beg leave to subscribe myself

Yours ever, BYRON

P.S. July 14.—This letter was written to be sent from Portsmouth, but, on arriving there, the squadron was ordered to the Nore, from whence I shall forward it. This I have not done before, supposing you might be alarmed by the interval mentioned in the letter being longer than expected between our arrival in port and my appearance at Newstead.

TO R. C. DALLAS   Volage *Frigate, at sea, June 28, 1811*

After two years' absence (to a day, on the 2d of July, before which we shall not arrive at Portsmouth), I am retracing my way to England. I have, as you know, spent the greater part of that period in Turkey, except two months in Spain and Portugal, which were then accessible. I have seen every thing most remarkable in Turkey, particularly the Troad, Greece, Constantinople, and Albania, into which last region very few have penetrated so high as Hobhouse and myself. I don't know that I have done anything to distinguish me from other voyagers, unless you will reckon my swimming from Sestos to Abydos, on May 3d, 1810, a tolerable feat for a *modern*.

I am coming back with little prospect of pleasure at home, and with a body a little shaken by one or two smart fevers, but a spirit I hope yet unbroken. My affairs, it seems, are considerably involved, and much business must be done with lawyers, colliers, farmers, and creditors. Now this, to a man who hates bustle as he hates a bishop, is a serious concern. But enough of my home department.

I find I have been scolding Cawthorn without a cause, as I found two parcels with two letters from you on my return to Malta. By these it appears you have not received a letter from Constantinople, addressed to Longman's, but it was of no consequence.

My Satire, it seems, is in a fourth edition, a success rather above the middling run, but not much for a production which, from its topics, must be temporary, and of course be successful at first, or not at all. At this period, when I can think and act more coolly, I regret that I have written it, though I shall probably find it forgotten by all except those whom it has offended. My friend Hobhouse's *Miscellany* has not succeeded; but he himself writes so good-humouredly on the subject, I don't know whether to laugh or cry with him. He met with your son at Cadiz, of whom he speaks highly.

Yours and Pratt's *protégé*, Blacket, the cobbler, is dead, in spite of his rhymes, and is probably one of the instances where death has saved a man from damnation. You were the ruin of that poor fellow amongst you: had it not been for his patrons, he might now have been in very good plight, shoe- (not verse-) making; but you have made him immortal with a vengeance. I write this, supposing poetry, patronage, and strong waters, to have been the death of him. If you are in town in or about the beginning of July, you will find me at Dorant's, in Albemarle Street, glad to see you. I have an imitation of Horace's *Art of Poetry* ready for Cawthorn, but don't let that deter you, for I sha'n't inflict it upon you. You know I never read my rhymes to visiters. I shall quit town in a few days for Notts., and thence to Rochdale. I shall send this the moment we arrive in harbour, that is a week hence.

Yours ever sincerely, BYRON

TO HENRY DRURY   *Volage frigate, off Ushant, July 17, 1811*

MY DEAR DRURY,—After two years' absence (on the 2d) and some odd days, I am approaching your country. The day of our arrival you will see by the outside date of my letter. At present, we are becalmed comfortably, close to Brest Harbour;—I have never been so near it since I left Duck Puddle. We left Malta thirty-four days ago, and have had a tedious passage of it. You will either see or hear from or of me, soon after the receipt of this, as I pass through town to repair my irreparable affairs; and thence I want to go to Notts. and raise rents, and to Lancs. and sell collieries, and back to London and pay debts,—for it seems I shall neither have coals nor comfort till I go down to Rochdale in person.

I have brought home some marbles for Hobhouse;—for myself, four ancient Athenian skulls, dug out of sarcophagi— a phial of Attic hemlock—four live tortoises—a greyhound (died on the passage)—two live Greek servants, one an Athen- ian, t'other a *Yaniote*, who can speak nothing but Romaic and Italian—and *myself*, as Moses in the *Vicar of Wakefield* says, *slily*, and I may say it too, for I have as little cause to boast of my expedition as he had of his to the fair.

I wrote to you from the Cyanean Rocks to tell you I had swam from Sestos to Abydos—have you received my letter? Hobhouse went to England to fish up his *Miscellany*, which foundered (so he tells me) in the Gulph of Lethe. I daresay it capsized with the vile goods of his contributory friends, for his own share was very portable. However, I hope he will either weigh up or set sail with a fresh cargo, and a luckier vessel. Hodgson, I suppose, is four deep by this time. What would he have given to have seen, like me, the *real Parnassus*, where I robbed the Bishop of Chrisso of a book of geography! —but this I only call plagiarism, as it was done within an hour's ride of Delphi.

2

The Years of Fame

August 1811 to January 1815

B yron returned to England in a mood of deep despondency. He regretted the past and dreaded the future: the friends he had loved were scattered, and the prospect he had to face was decidedly unpromising. Very soon his fears were justified. News reached him that his mother was seriously ill: before he could gain Newstead, he learned that on August 1st, 1811, her violent, unhappy, foolish life had ended. Though he had never loved her, he was exceedingly shocked by her death. Then, before her funeral procession had left the Abbey, he received a letter telling him that his great friend, Charles Skinner Matthews, had been drowned while bathing near Cambridge. In desperation, he appealed to another Cambridge friend, Scrope Davies: " Some curse ", he declared, " hangs over me and mine. My mother lies a corpse in this house; one of my best friends is drowned in a ditch. . . . Come to me, Scrope, I am almost desolate—left almost alone in the world. . . ."

He was not long to remain uncomforted; for the poem which he had brought back with him from Greece, and had handed to a serviceable admirer and remote family connection, Robert Charles Dallas, was going through the printing-press. Byron attached no special importance to these Spenserian stanzas; but Dallas had praised them warmly and, once entrusted with the manuscript, after trying in vain a less enterprising publisher, had submitted them to John Murray who presently accepted them. Childe Harold's Pilgrimage was published at the end of February or the beginning of March 1812—a few days after the poet had delivered his vigorous maiden speech in the House of Lords—and proved immediately successful. The author became the lion of the season, the hero of every drawing-room and the talk of every dinner-table. From loneliness, poverty and obscurity, he was raised overnight to the height of fame and fashion.

Byron's letters give a vivid and detailed account of the adventures of this period : his entanglement with Lady Caroline Lamb, for which he was in some measure consoled by his friendship with her mother-in-law, Lady Melbourne ; his escape from Lady Caroline's furious infatuation into the maternal arms of Lady Oxford ; his inconclusive passage with Lady Frances Webster, which was reported at length for Lady Melbourne's benefit ; finally, that " strange summer adventure ", as to the nature of which the student of Byron's biography must form his own conclusions.   Whatever it was, this " new scrape " caused his well-wishers, particularly Lady Melbourne and his half-sister, Augusta Leigh, many anxious moments.   An unusually grave scandal seemed to be impending ; Byron's state of mind was volcanic ; and they agreed that the sooner he was married off—to a suitable, sensible and well-endowed young woman—the better for their peace of mind.   Byron himself-was prepared to admit that they were right.   The candidate eventually selected was Anne Isabella (or Annabella) Milbanke, the daughter of Lady Melbourne's brother, Sir Ralph Milbanke of Seaham, a highly educated girl of very decided views and rigid moral principles. Byron's first proposal was refused ; a second proposal was accepted.   He was married at Seaham on January 2nd, 1815.

TO JOHN M. B. PIGOT   *Newport Pagnell, August 2, 1811*

MY DEAR DOCTOR,—My poor mother died yesterday ! and I am on my way from town to attend her to the family vault. I heard *one* day of her illness, the *next* of her death.   Thank God her last moments were most tranquil.   I am told she was in little pain, and not aware of her situation.   I now feel the truth of Mr. Gray's observation, " That we can only have *one* mother ".   Peace be with her !   I have to thank you for your expressions of regard; and as in six weeks I shall be in Lancashire on business, I may extend to Liverpool and Chester, —at least I shall endeavour.

If it will be any satisfaction, I have to inform you that in November next the Editor of the *Scourge* [1] will be tried for two different libels on the late Mrs. B. and myself (the decease of Mrs. B. makes no difference in the proceedings); and as he is guilty, by his very foolish and unfounded assertion of a breach of privilege, he will be prosecuted with the utmost rigour.

I inform you of this, as you seem interested in the affair, which is now in the hands of the Attorney-general.

I shall remain at Newstead the greater part of this month, where I shall be happy to hear from you, after my two years' absence in the East.

I am, dear Pigot, yours very truly, BYRON

TO SCROPE BERDMORE DAVIES *Newstead Abbey,*
August 7, 1811

MY DEAREST DAVIES,—Some curse hangs over me and mine. My mother lies a corpse in this house; one of my best friends is drowned in a ditch. What can I say, or think, or do? I received a letter from him the day before yesterday. My dear Scrope, if you can spare a moment, do come down to me— I want a friend. Matthews's last letter was written on *Friday* —on Saturday he was not. In ability, who was like Matthews? How did we all shrink before him? You do me but justice in saying, I would have risked my paltry existence to have preserved his. This very evening did I mean to write, inviting him, as I invite you, my very dear friend, to visit me. God forgive —— for his apathy! What will our poor Hobhouse feel? His letters breathe but of Matthews. Come to me, Scrope, I am almost desolate—left almost alone in the world— I had but you, and H., and M., and let me enjoy the survivors

---

[1] The attack on Byron in the *Scourge* was the work of a journalist named Hewson Clarke, who had been mentioned abusively in *English Bards*. Clarke retaliated by describing Byron as the " illegitimate descendant of a murderer " and asserting that Mrs. Byron passed her " days and nights . . . in the delirium of drunkenness ".

whilst I can. Poor M., in his letter of Friday, speaks of his intended contest for Cambridge, and a speedy journey to London. Write or come, but come if you can, or one or both.

Yours ever.

TO JOHN CAM HOBHOUSE   *Newstead Abbey, August 10th, 1811*

My DEAR HOBHOUSE,—From Davies I had already received the death of Matthews, and from *M. a letter* dated the *day* before his *death*. In that letter he mentions you, and as it was perhaps the last he ever wrote, you will derive a poor consolation from hearing that he spoke of you with that affectionate familiarity, so much more pleasing from those we love, than the highest encomiums of the world.

My dwelling you already know is the house of mourning, and I am really so much bewildered with the different shocks I have sustained, that I can hardly reduce myself to reason by the most frivolous occupations. My poor friend, J. Wing-field, my mother, and your best friend (and surely not the worst of mine), C. S. M., have disappeared in one little month, since *my return*, and without my seeing *either*, though I have *heard* from *all*. There is to me something so incomprehensible in death, that I can neither speak nor think on the subject. Indeed, when I looked on the mass of corruption which was the being from whence I sprung, I doubted within myself whether I *was*, or she *was not*. I have lost her who gave me being, and some of those who made that being a blessing. I have neither hopes nor fears beyond the grave, yet if there is within us " a spark of that Celestial fire ", M[atthews] has already " mingled with the gods ".

In the room where I now write (flanked by the *skulls* you have seen so often) did you and Matthews and myself pass some joyous unprofitable evenings, and here we will drink to his memory, which though it cannot reach the dead, will soothe the survivors, and to them only death can be an evil. I can neither receive nor administer consolation ; time will do it for us ; in the interim let me see or hear from you, if possible both. I am very lonely, and should think myself miserable were it not for a kind of hysterical merriment, which I can neither account for nor conquer; but strange as it is, I do laugh, and heartily, wondering at myself while I sustain it. I have tried reading, and boxing, and swimming, and writing, and rising early, and sitting late, and water, and wine, with a number of ineffectual remedies, and here I am, wretched, but not " melancholy or gentleman-like ".

My dear " *Cam of the Cornish* " (Matthews's last expression!!) may man or God give you the happiness which I wish rather than expect you may attain; believe me, none living are more sincerely yours than

BYRON

TO R. C. DALLAS   *Newstead Abbey, Notts., August 12, 1811*

Peace be with the dead! Regret cannot wake them. With a sigh to the departed, let us resume the dull business of life, in the certainty that we also shall have our repose. Besides her who gave me being, I have lost more than one who made that being tolerable.—The best friend of my friend Hobhouse, Matthews, a man of the first talents, and also not the worst of my narrow circle, has perished miserably in the muddy waves of the Cam, always fatal to genius:—my poor school-fellow, Wingfield, at Coimbra—within a month; and whilst I had heard from *all three*, but not seen *one*. Matthews wrote to me the very day before his death; and though I feel for his fate, I am still more anxious for Hobhouse, who, I very much fear, will hardly retain his senses: his letters to me since the event have been most incoherent. But let this pass; we shall all one day pass along with the rest—the world is too full of such things, and our very sorrow is selfish.

I received a letter from you, which my late occupations prevented me from duly noticing.—I hope your friends and family will long hold together. I shall be glad to hear from you, on business, on commonplace, or any thing, or nothing— but death—I am already too familiar with the dead. It is strange that I look on the skulls which stand beside me (I have always had *four* in my study) without emotion, but I cannot strip the features of those I have known of their fleshy covering, even in idea, without a hideous sensation; but the worms are less ceremonious.—Surely, the Romans did well when they burned the dead.—I shall be happy to hear from you, and am,

Yours, etc.

TO JOHN CAM HOBHOUSE   *Newstead Abbey, August 30th, 1811*

My dear Hobhouse,—Scrope Davies has been here and seemed as much affected by late events as could be expected, from one who has lived so much in the world.   His society was (as it always wont to be) very reviving, but now he is gone, and I am solitary and sullen.

Not a scrap of paper has been found at Cambridge, which is singular.   I can hardly agree with you in a wish to forget, I love to remember the dead, for we see only the virtues, and when our best friends are thus removed, we become reconciled to our own prospects, and " long to be with them, and at rest ".

I think when your mind is more calm you ought to write his epitaph, and we will erect to his memory a monument in some appropriate place.   I do not know any other who would do him justice; indeed, it is *your right*, and perhaps your *duty*.

Then " give his fame to the winds, and let the harp sigh over his narrow house "; you are now in the land of Ossian.

In the poem which I wrote abroad, and is now in the hands of Murray the bookseller for publication, at the close of the first canto, which treats of Spain, I have two stanzas in commemoration of W[ingfield], who died at Coimbra; and in a note to those, having occasion to mention the loss of three persons very dear to me, in so very short a time, I have added a very short sentence or two on the subject of our friend; which, though they can neither add to his credit or satisfaction, will at least show my own pride in the acquaintance of such a man.

Your book goes on well, and I trust will answer your purpose and my expectations.   Demetrius has made out a most formidable vocabulary, on which I wait for further orders.

I do not know who is your deputy in town; perhaps Baillie, or Shepherd. I have had a letter from Bankes, of the patronising kind, where I am invited to "*one* of *my places in Wales!!*"

I am going to Lancs., and am in daily expectation of Hanson to back me; and I mean to marry, prudently if possible; that is, wealthily; I can't afford anything to Love.

I wish you were here; but you *will* be *here*, and we shall laugh again as usual, and be very miserable dogs for all that.

My sister writes me melancholy letters; things are not going on well there, but mismanagement is the hereditary epidemic of our brood.

Hodgson is battening on "Laver Moor, Herefordshire", Davies at Harrowgate.

I am to visit him in October at King's Coll.

Dallas is running to and from Mortlake, with his pocket full of proofs of *all* his *friends*, who are all scribblers and make him a packhorse.

I am here boxing in a Turkish pelisse to prevent obesity, and as usual very much yours,

BYRON

TO THE HON. AUGUSTA LEIGH   *Newstead Abbey,*
                                             August 30th, 1811

MY DEAR AUGUSTA,—The embarrassments you mention in your last letter I never heard of before, but that disease is epidemic in our family. Neither have I been apprised of any of the changes at which you hint, indeed how should I? On the borders of the Black Sea, we heard only of the Russians. So you have much to tell, and all will be novelty.

I don't know what Scrope Davies meant by telling you I liked Children. I abominate the sight of them so much that I have always had the greatest respect for the character of Herod. But, as my house here is large enough for us all, we should go on very well, and I need not tell you that I long to see *you*. I really do not perceive any thing so formidable in a Journey hither of two days, but all this comes of Matrimony, you have a Nurse and all the etcæteras of a family. Well, I must marry to repair the ravages of myself and prodigal ancestry, but if I am ever so unfortunate as to be presented with an Heir, instead of a *Rattle* he shall be provided with a *Gag*.

I shall perhaps be able to accept D's invitation to Cambridge, but I fear my stay in Lancashire will be prolonged, I proceed there in the 2ᵈ week in Sepᵗʳ to arrange my coal concerns, and then if I can't persuade some wealthy dowdy to ennoble the dirty puddle of her mercantile Blood,—why—I shall leave England and all its clouds for the East again; I am very sick of it already. Joe has been getting well of a disease that would have killed a troop of horse; he promises to bear away the palm of longevity from old Parr. As you won't come, you will write; I long to hear all those unutterable things, being utterly unable to guess at any of them, unless they concern *your* relative the Thane of Carlisle,—though I had great hopes we had done with him.

I have little to add that you do not already know, and being quite alone, have no great variety of incident to gossip with; I am but rarely pestered with visiters, and the few I have I get rid of as soon as possible. I will now take leave of you in the Jargon of 1794. " Health and *Fraternity!* "

Yours alway, B.

TO THE HON. AUGUSTA LEIGH   *Newstead Abbey,*
                                        Sept. 2ᵈ, 1811

MY DEAR AUGUSTA,—I wrote you a vastly dutiful letter since my answer to your second epistle, and I now write you a third, for which you have to thank Silence and Solitude. Mr. Hanson comes hither on the 14ᵗʰ, and I am going to Rochdale on business, but that need not prevent you from coming here, you will find Joe, and the house and the cellar and all therein very much at your Service.

As to Lady B., when I discover one rich enough to suit

me and foolish enough to have me, I will give her leave to make me miserable if she can. Money is the magnet ; as to Women, one is as well as another, the older the better, we have then a chance of getting her to Heaven. So, your Spouse does not like brats better than myself; now those who beget them have no right to find fault, but *I* may rail with great propriety.

My " Satire ! "—I am glad it made you laugh for Somebody told me in Greece that you was angry, and I was sorry, as you were perhaps the only person whom I did *not* want to *make angry*.

But how you will make *me laugh* I don't know, for it is a vastly *serious* subject to me I assure you ; therefore take care, or I shall hitch *you* into the next Edition to make up our family party. Nothing so fretful, so despicable as a Scribbler, see what *I* am, and what a parcel of Scoundrels I have brought about my ears, and what language I have been obliged to treat them with to deal with them in their own way ;—all this comes of Authorship, but now I am in for it, and shall be at war with Grubstreet, till I find some better amusement.

You will write to me your Intentions and may almost depend on my being at Cambridge in October. You say you mean to be etc. in the *Autumn* ; I should be glad to know what you call this present Season, it would be Winter in every other Country which I have seen. If we meet in October we will travel in my *Vis.* and can have a cage for the children and a cart for the Nurse. Or perhaps we can forward them by the Canal. Do let us know all about it, your " *bright thought* " is a little clouded, like the Moon in this preposterous climate. Good even, Child.

Yours ever, B.

TO FRANCIS HODGSON   *Newstead Abbey, Sept. 3, 1811*

MY DEAR HODGSON,—I will have nothing to do with your immortality; we are miserable enough in this life, without the absurdity of speculating upon another. If men are to live, why die at all? and if they die, why disturb the sweet and sound sleep that " knows no waking "? " Post Mortem nihil est, ipsaque Mors nihil . . . quæris quo jaceas post obitum loco? Quo *non* Nata jacent."

As to revealed religion, Christ came to save men; but a good Pagan will go to heaven, and a bad Nazarene to hell; " Argal " (I argue like the gravedigger) why are not all men Christians? or why are any? If mankind may be saved who never heard or dreamt, at Timbuctoo, Otaheite, Terra Incognita, etc., of Galilee and its Prophet, Christianity is of no avail: if they cannot be saved without, why are not all orthodox? It is a little hard to send a man preaching to Judæa, and leave the rest of the world—Negers and what not—*dark* as their complexions, without a ray of light for so many years to lead them on high; and who will believe that God will damn men for not knowing what they were never taught? I hope I am sincere; I was so at least on a bed of sickness in a far-distant country, when I had neither friend, nor comforter, nor hope, to sustain me. I looked to death as a relief from pain, without a wish for an after-life, but a confidence that the God who punishes in this existence had left that last asylum for the weary.

$$\text{Ὃν ὁ θεὸς ἀγαπάει ἀποθνήσκει νέος.}$$

I am no Platonist, I am nothing at all; but I would sooner be a Paulician, Manichean, Spinozist, Gentile, Pyrrhonian, Zoroastrian, than one of the seventy-two villainous sects who are tearing each other to pieces for the love of the Lord and hatred of each other. Talk of Galileeism? Show me the effects —are you better, wiser, kinder by your precepts? I will bring you ten Mussulmans shall shame you in all goodwill towards men, prayer to God, and duty to their neighbours. And is there a Talapoin, or a Bonze, who is not superior to a fox-hunting curate? But I will say no more on this endless theme; let me live, well if possible, and die without pain. The rest is with God, who assuredly, had He *come* or *sent*, would have made Himself manifest to nations, and intelligible to all.

I shall rejoice to see you. My present intention is to accept Scrope Davies's invitation; and then, if you accept mine, we shall meet *here* and *there*. Did you know poor Matthews? I shall miss him much at Cambridge.

TO JOHN MURRAY *Newstead Abbey, Notts., Sept. 5, 1811*

SIR,—The time seems to be past when (as Dr. Johnson said) a man was certain to "hear the truth from his bookseller", for you have paid me so many compliments, that, if I was not the veriest scribbler on earth, I should feel affronted. As I accept your compliments, it is but fair I should give equal or greater credit to your objections, the more so as I believe them to be well founded. With regard to the political and meta-physical parts, I am afraid I can alter nothing; but I have high authority for my Errors in that point, for even the *Æneid* was a *political* poem, and written for a *political* purpose; and as to my unlucky opinions on Subjects of more importance, I am too sincere in them for recantation. On Spanish affairs I have said what I saw, and every day confirms me in that notion of the result formed on the Spot; and I rather think honest John Bull is beginning to come round again to that Sobriety which Massena's retreat had begun to reel from its centre—the usual consequence of *un*usual success. So you per-ceive I cannot alter the Sentiments; but if there are any altera-tions in the structure of the versification you would wish to be made, I will tag rhymes and turn stanzas as much as you please. As for the "*Orthodox*", let us hope they will buy, on purpose to abuse—you will forgive the one, if they will do the other. You are aware that any thing from my pen must expect no quarter, on many accounts; and as the present publication is of a nature very different from the former, we must not be sanguine.

You have given me no answer to my question—tell me fairly, did you show the M.S. to some of your corps?—I sent an introductory stanza to Mr. Dallas, that it might be for-warded to you; the poem else will open too abruptly. The Stanzas had better be numbered in Roman characters, there is a disquisition on the literature of the modern Greeks, and some smaller poems to come in at the close. These are now at Newstead, but will be sent in time. If Mr. D. has lost the Stanza and note annexed to it, write, and I will send it myself. —You tell me to add two cantos, but I am about to visit my *Collieries* in Lancashire on the 15th instant, which is so *unpoetical* an employment that I need say no more.

I am, sir, your most obedient, etc., etc., BYRON

TO R. C. DALLAS   *Newstead Abbey, September 7, 1811*

As Gifford[1] has been ever my " Magnus Apollo ", any approbation, such as you mention, would, of course, be more welcome than " all Bocara's vaunted gold, than all the gems of Samarcand ". But I am sorry the MS. was shown to him in such a manner, and had written to Murray to say as much, before I was aware that it was too late.

Your objection to the expression " central line " I can only meet by saying that, before Childe Harold left England, it was his full intention to traverse Persia, and return by India, which he could not have done without passing the equinoctial.

The other errors you mention, I must correct in the progress through the press. I feel honoured by the wish of such men that the poem should be continued, but to do that I must return to Greece and Asia; I must have a warm sun, a blue sky; I cannot describe scenes so dear to me by a sea-coal fire. I had projected an additional canto when I was in the Troad and Constantinople, and if I saw them again, it would go on; but under existing circumstances and *sensations*, I have neither harp, " heart, nor voice " to proceed. I feel that *you are all right* as to the metaphysical part; but I also feel that I am sincere, and that if I am only to write " *ad captandum vulgus* ", I might as well edit a magazine at once, or spin canzonettas for Vauxhall.

My work must make its way as well as it can; I know I have every thing against me, angry poets and prejudices; but if the poem is a *poem*, it will surmount these obstacles, and if *not*, it deserves its fate. Your friend's Ode I have read— it is no great compliment to pronounce it far superior to Smythe's on the same subject, or to the merits of the new Chancellor. It is evidently the production of a man of taste, and a poet, though I should not be willing to say it was fully equal to what might be expected from the author of " *Horæ Ionicæ* ". I thank you for it, and that is more than I would do for any other Ode of the present day.

I am very sensible of your good wishes, and, indeed, I have need of them. My whole life has been at variance with propriety, not to say decency; my circumstances are become

[1] William Gifford, editor of the *Quarterly Review* and *Anti-Jacobin*.

involved ; my friends are dead or estranged, and my existence
a dreary void. In Matthews I have lost my " guide, philosopher, and friend " ; in Wingfield a friend only, but one
whom I could have wished to have preceded in his long
journey.

Matthews was indeed an extraordinary man ; it has not
entered into the heart of a stranger to conceive such a man :
there was the stamp of immortality in all he said or did ;—
and now what is he? When we see such men pass away and
be no more—men, who seem created to display what the
Creator *could make* his creatures, gathered into corruption,
before the maturity of minds that might have been the pride of
posterity, what are we to conclude? For my own part, I am
bewildered. To me he was much, to Hobhouse every thing.
My poor Hobhouse doted on Matthews. For me, I did not
love quite so much as I honoured him ; I was indeed so sensible
of his infinite superiority, that though I did not envy, I stood
in awe of it. He, Hobhouse, Davies, and myself, formed a
coterie of our own at Cambridge and elsewhere. Davies is a
wit and man of the world, and feels as much as such a character
can do ; but not as Hobhouse has been affected. Davies, who
is not a scribbler, has always beaten us all in the war of words,
and by his colloquial powers at once delighted and kept us in
order. Hobhouse and myself always had the worst of it with
the other two ; and even Matthews yielded to the dashing
vivacity of Scrope Davies. But I am talking to you of men,
or boys, as if you cared about such beings.

I expect mine agent down on the 14th to proceed to
Lancashire, where I hear from all quarters that I have a very
valuable property in coals, etc. I then intend to accept an
invitation to Cambridge in October, and shall, perhaps, run
up to town. I have four invitations—to Wales, Dorset, Cambridge, and Chester ; but I must be a man of business. I am
quite alone, as these long letters sadly testify. I perceive, by
referring to your letter, that the Ode is from the author ;
make my thanks acceptable to him. His muse is worthy a
nobler theme. You will write as usual, I hope. I wish you
good evening, and am, etc.

TO JOHN CAM HOBHOUSE

Newstead Abbey,
September 20th, 1811

My dear Hᴱ,—Our friend Scrope is a pleasant person, a " facetious companion ", and well " respected by all who know him " ; he laughs with the living, though he don't weep with the dead, yet I believe he would do that also, could it do them good service, but good or bad we must endeavour to follow his example, and return to the dull routine of business or pleasure, though I fear the more we see of life, the more we shall regret those who have ceased to live—we will speak of them no more.

Demetrius has completed a copious specimen of the Arnaut dialect, which shall be sent to-morrow ; the print might perhaps be improved by an elongation of the ὑποκάμισον— as the drawers don't appear to advantage below it ; altogether it is very characteristic.

I had a visit lately from Major (Capt.) Leake " *en passant* ". He talks of returning to Ali Pacha, and says the E[dinburgh] R[eview] knows nothing of Romaic ; he is grown less taciturn, better dressed, and more like an (English) man of this world than he was at Yanina. Jⁿ Claridge is here, improved in person a good deal, and amiable, but not amusing. Now he is a good man, a handsome man, an honourable man, a most inoffensive man, a well informed man, and a—*dull* man, and this last damned epithet undoes all the rest ; there is Scrope B. Davies, with perhaps no better intellects, and certainly not half his sterling qualities, is the life and soul of me, and everybody else, but my old friend, with the soul of honour and the zeal of friendship, and a vast variety of insipid virtues, can't keep me or himself awake.—Alas, " *Motley's the only wear* ". As for Claridge you can't ever quarrel with him, and my life is as still as the Lake before the Abbey, till the North wind disturbs the one, and Fletcher and my learned Thebans break my pottery, or my tenants, or Mr. Hanson ruffle the other.

I expect Hanson down daily to proceed to Rochdale, or nothing will ever be settled.

You are coming out in quarto, but I wish you to be out first, or at any rate *one* before the other ; I am going to use you

very shabbily, for I fear *that* Note is a " sine quâ non " to
" C^e Harold " ; had it been the Horace, you should have had
it all to yourself. As it is, you shall have it to extract the essence,
long before it is published, and the information will be all the
better for being in your own words, and if you are out first
(as you must probably will be) I trust we shall answer both
our purposes. In my notes to the poem I have assigned your
publication as my excuse for saying very little about the Greeks,
and referred my readers to *your* work for more interesting
particulars of that people. You *must* have six plates at the
least, indeed ten or twelve would be better. Of course they
are all at your service, and the Romaic MSS. such as they are.

I must contrive to meet you in the spring or summer, and
will bring Hodgson or Davies with me. I am invited to
Cambridge in Octr to meet them and Dr. Clarke. I don't
know whether to be glad or sorry that you will not be *there* ;
if I am *glad*, you will conceive it is on YOUR account. I shall
write with Demetrius' Vocabulary.

> Dear H, Yours ever, B.

TO FRANCIS HODGSON   *Newstead Abbey, Sept. 25, 1811*

MY DEAR HODGSON,—I fear that before the latest of
October or the first of November, I shall hardly be able to
make Cambridge. My everlasting agent puts off his coming
like the accomplishment of a prophecy. However, finding
me growing serious he hath promised to be here on Thursday,
and about Monday we shall remove to Rochdale. I have only
to give discharges to the tenantry here (it seems the poor
creatures must be raised, though I wish it was not necessary),
and arrange the receipt of sums, and the liquidation of some
debts, and I shall be ready to enter upon new subjects of
vexation. I intend to visit you in Granta, and hope to prevail
on you to accompany me here or there or anywhere.

I am plucking up my spirits, and have begun to gather my
little sensual comforts together. Lucy is extracted from War-
wickshire ; some very bad faces have been warned off the
premises, and more promising substituted in their stead ;

the partridges are plentiful, hares fairish, pheasants not quite so good, and the Girls on the Manor * * * * Just as I had formed a tolerable establishment my travels commenced, and on my return I find all to do over again; my former flock were all scattered; some married, not before it was needful. As I am a great disciplinarian, I have just issued an edict for the abolition of caps; no hair to be cut on any pretext; stays permitted, but not too low before; full uniform always in the evening; Lucinda to be commander—*vice* the present, about to be wedded (*mem*, she is 35 with a flat face and a squeaking voice), of all the makers and unmakers of beds in the household.

My tortoises (all Athenians), my hedgehog, my mastiff and the other live Greek, are all purely. The tortoises lay eggs, and I have hired a hen to hatch them. I am writing notes for *my* quarto (Murray would have it a *quarto*), and Hobhouse is writing text for *his* quarto; if you call on Murray or Cawthorn you will hear news of either. I have attacked De Pauw, Thornton, Lord Elgin, Spain, Portugal, the *Edinburgh Review*, travellers, Painters, Antiquarians, and others, so you see what a dish of Sour Crout Controversy I shall prepare for myself. It would not answer for me to give way, now; as I was forced into bitterness at the beginning, I will go through to the last. *Væ Victis!* If I fall, I shall fall gloriously, fighting against a host.

Felicissima Notte a Voss. Signoria, B.

TO R. C. DALLAS   *Newstead Abbey, Oct. 11, 1811*

I have returned from Lancashire, and ascertained that my property there may be made very valuable, but various circumstances very much circumscribe my exertions at present. I shall be in town on business in the beginning of November, and perhaps at Cambridge before the end of this month; but of my movements you shall be regularly apprised. Your objections I have in part done away by alterations, which I hope will suffice; and I have sent two or three additional stanzas for both " *Fyttes* ". I have been again shocked with a *death*, and have lost one very dear to me in happier times;

but " I have almost forgot the taste of grief ", and " supped full of horrors " till I have become callous, nor have I a tear left for an event which, five years ago, would have bowed down my head to the earth. It seems as though I were to experience in my youth the greatest misery of age. My friends fall around me, and I shall be left a lonely tree before I am withered. Other men can always take refuge in their families ; I have no resource but my own reflections, and they present no prospect here or hereafter, except the selfish satisfaction of surviving my betters. I am indeed very wretched, and you will excuse my saying so, as you know I am not apt to cant of sensibility.

Instead of tiring yourself with *my* concerns, I should be glad to hear *your* plans of retirement. I suppose you would not like to be wholly shut out of society? Now I know a large village, or small town, about twelve miles off, where your family would have the advantage of very genteel society, without the hazard of being annoyed by mercantile affluence ; where *you* would meet with men of information and independence ; and where I have friends to whom I should be proud to introduce you. There are, besides, a coffee-room, assemblies, etc., etc., which bring people together. My mother had a house there some years, and I am well acquainted with the economy of Southwell, the name of this little commonwealth. Lastly, you will not be very remote from me ; and though I am the very worst companion for young people in the world, this objection would not apply to *you*, whom I could see frequently. Your expenses, too, would be such as best suit your inclinations, more or less, as you thought proper ; but very little would be requisite to enable you to enter into all the gaieties of a country life. You could be as quiet or bustling as you liked, and certainly as well situated as on the lakes of Cumberland, unless you have a particular wish to be *picturesque*.

Pray, is your Ionian friend in town? You have promised me an introduction. You mention having consulted some friend on the MSS. Is not this contrary to our usual way? Instruct Mr. Murray not to allow his shopman to call the work *Child of Harrow's Pilgrimage* ! ! ! ! ! as he has done to some of my astonished friends, who wrote to inquire after my *sanity* on the occasion, as well they might. I have heard nothing of Murray, whom I scolded heartily. Must I write more notes?

Are there not enough? Cawthorn must be kept back with the *Hints*. I hope he is getting on with Hobhouse's quarto. Good evening.

Yours ever, etc.

TO FRANCIS HODGSON   *Newstead Abbey, Oct. 13, 1811*

You will begin to deem me a most liberal correspondent; but as my letters are free, you will overlook their frequency. I have sent you answers in prose and verse to all your late communications; and though I am invading your ease again, I don't know why, or what to put down that you are not acquainted with already. I am growing *nervous* (how you will laugh!)—but it is true,—really, wretchedly, ridiculously, fine-ladically *nervous*. Your climate kills me; I can neither read, write, nor amuse myself, or any one else. My days are listless, and my nights restless; I have very seldom any society, and when I have, I run out of it. At " this present writing ", there are in the next room three *ladies*, and I have stolen away to write this grumbling letter.—I don't know that I sha'n't end with insanity, for I find a want of method in arranging my thoughts that perplexes me strangely; but this looks more like silliness than madness, as Scrope Davies would facetiously remark in his consoling manner. I must try the hartshorn of your company; and a session of Parliament would suit me well,—any thing to cure me of conjugating the accursed verb " *ennuyer* ".

When shall you be at Cambridge? You have hinted, I think, that your friend Bland is returned from Holland. I have always had a great respect for his talents, and for all that I have heard of his character; but of me, I believe he knows nothing, except that he heard my sixth form repetitions ten months together at the average of two lines a morning, and those never perfect. I remembered him and his *Slaves* as I passed between Capes Matapan, St. Angelo, and his Isle of Ceriga, and I always bewailed the absence of the *Anthology*. I suppose he will now translate Vondel, the Dutch Shakspeare, and *Gysbert van Amstel* will easily be accommodated to our stage in its present state; and I presume he saw the Dutch poem, where the love of Pyramus and Thisbe is compared to the *passion* of *Christ*; also the love of *Lucifer* for Eve, and other varieties of Low Country literature. No doubt you will think me crazed to talk of such things, but they are all in black and white and good repute on the banks of every canal from Amsterdam to Alkmaar.

Yours ever, B.

My poesy is in the hands of its various publishers; but the *Hints from Horace* (to which I have subjoined some savage lines on Methodism, and ferocious notes on the vanity of the triple Editory of the *Edin. Annual Register*), my *Hints*, I say, stand still, and why?—I have not a friend in the world (but you and Drury) who can construe Horace's Latin or my English well enough to adjust them for the press, or to correct the proofs in a grammatical way. So that, unless you have bowels when you return to town (I am too far off to do it for myself), this ineffable work will be lost to the world for—I don't know how many *weeks*.

Childe Harold's Pilgrimage must wait till *Murray's* is finished. He is making a tour in Middlesex, and is to return soon, when high matter may be expected. He wants to have it in quarto, which is a cursed unsaleable size; but it is pestilent long, and one must obey one's bookseller. I trust Murray will pass the Paddington Canal without being seduced by Payne and Mackinlay's example,[1]—I say Payne and Mackinlay, supposing that the partnership held good. Drury, the villain, has not written to me; " I am never (as Mrs. Lumpkin says to Tony) to be gratified with the monster's dear wild notes ".

So you are going (going indeed!) into orders. You must make your peace with the Eclectic Reviewers—they accuse you of impiety, I fear, with injustice. Demetrius, the " Sieger of Cities ", is here, with " Gilpin Horner ". The painter is not necessary, as the portraits he already painted are (by anticipation) very like the new animals.—Write, and send me your " Love Song "—but I want *paulo majora* from you. Make a dash before you are a deacon, and try a *dry* publisher.

Yours always, B.

---

[1] Mr. Payne of the firm of Payne & Mackinlay, Hodgson's publishers, had committed suicide by drowning in the Paddington Canal.

TO JOHN CAM HOBHOUSE   *Newstead Abbey, October 14th, 1811*

DEAR HOBHOUSE,—In my last I answered your queries, and now I shall acquaint you with my movements, according to your former request. I have been down to Rochdale with Hanson; the property there, if I work the mines myself, will produce about £4000 pr. ann.; but to do this I must lay out at least £10,000 in etceteras, or if I chance to *let* it without incurring such expenditure, it will produce a rental of half the above sum, so we are to work the collieries ourselves, of course. Newstead is to be advanced immediately to £2100 pr. ann., so that my income might be made about £6000 pr. ann. But here comes at least £20,000 of debt, and I must mortgage for that and other expenses, so that altogether my situation is perplexing. I believe the above statement to be nearly correct, and so ends the chapter. If I chose to turn out my old bad tenants, and take monied men, they say Newstead would bear a few hundreds more from its great extent; but this I shall hardly do. It contains 3800 acres, including the Forest land, the Rochdale manor, 8256 acres of Lancashire, which are larger than ours. So there you have my territories on the earth, and in " the waters under the earth "; but I must marry some heiress, or I shall always be involved.

Now for higher matters. My Boke is in yᵉ press, and proceeds leisurely; I have lately been sweating notes, which I don't mean to make very voluminous,—some remarks written at Athens, and the flourish on Romaic which you have seen will constitute most of them. The essence of that " *valuable information* ", as you call it, is at your service, and shall be sent in time for your purpose. I had also by accident detected in Athens a blunder of Thornton, of a ludicrous nature, in the *Turkish language*, of which I mean to make some " pleasaunt mirth ", in return for his abuse of the Greeks. It is the passage about Pouqueville's story of the " Eater of Corrosive Sublimate ". By-the-bye, I rather suspect we shall be at right angles in our opinion of the Greeks; I have not quite made up my mind about them, but you I know are decisively inimical.

I will write to you from Cambridge, or elsewhere. Address to Newstead. Claridge is gone, after a lethargic visit of three perennial weeks. How dull he is! I wish the dog had any *bad* qualities that one might not be ashamed of disliking him.

Adio! D. V. E. Umilissimo Servitore.

B.

TO JOHN CAM HOBHOUSE †
King's College Ce.,
October 22nd, 1811

MY DEAR HOBHOUSE,—I write from Scrope's rooms, whom I have just assisted to put to bed in a state of *outrageous* intoxication. I think I never saw him so bad before. We dined at Mr. Caldwell's, of Jesus Coll., where we met Dr. Clarke and others of the gown, and Scrope finished himself as usual. He has been in a similar state every evening since my arrival here a few days ago. We are to dine at Dr. Clarke's on Thursday. I find he knows little of Romaic, so we shall have *that* department entirely to ourselves. I tell you this that you need not fear any competitor, particularly so formidable a one as Dr. Clarke would probably have been. I like him much, though Scrope says *we* talked so bitterly, that he (the said Scrope) lost his listeners.

I proceed hence to town, where I shall enquire after your work, which I am sorry to say stands still for " *want of copy* ", to talk in technicals.

I am very low spirited on many accounts, and wine, which, however, I do not quaff as formerly, has lost its power over me. We all wish you here, and well, wherever you are, but surely better with us. If you don't soon return, Scrope and I mean to visit you in quarters.

The event I mentioned in my last [1] has had an effect on me, I am ashamed to think of. But there is no arguing on these points. I could " have better spared a better being ". Wherever I turn, particularly in this place, the idea goes with me. I say all this at the risk of incurring your contempt; but you cannot despise me more than I do myself. I am indeed very wretched, and like all complaining persons I can't help telling you so.

[1] The death of his Cambridge protégé, John Edleston, of whose death during the previous May Byron had recently heard.

The Marquis Sligo is in a great scrape about his kidnapping
the seamen; I, who know him, do not think him so culpable
as the Navy are determined to make him. He is a good man.
I have been in Lancashire, Notts, but all places are alike;
I cannot live under my present feelings; I have lost my
appetite, my rest, and can neither read, write, or act in comfort. Everybody here is very polite and hospitable, my friend
Scrope particularly; I wish to God he would grow sober, as
I much fear no constitution can long support his excesses.
If I lose him and you, what am I? Hodgson is not here, but
expected soon; Newstead is my regular address. Demetrius
is here, much pleased with yᵉ place, Lord Sligo is about to
send back his Arnaouts. Excuse this dirty paper, it is of
Scrope's best. Good night.

Ever yours, BYRON

TO THOMAS MOORE   *Cambridge, October 27, 1811*

SIR,[1]—Your letter followed me from Notts. to this place,
which will account for the delay of my reply. Your former
letter I never had the honour to receive;—be assured in
whatever part of the world it had found me, I should have
deemed it my duty to return and answer it in person.

The advertisement you mention, I know nothing of.—
At the time of your meeting with Mr. Jeffrey, I had recently
entered College, and remember to have heard and read a
number of squibs on the occasion; and from the recollection
of these I derived all my knowledge on the subject, without
the slightest idea of " giving the lie " to an address which I
never beheld. When I put my name to the production, which
has occasioned this correspondence, I became responsible to
all whom it might concern,—to explain where it requires
explanation, and, where insufficiently or too sufficiently
explicit, at all events to satisfy. My situation leaves me no

---

[1] Moore had taken resentful notice of a joke at his expense in *English Bards*.
He had at one moment challenged Byron; but the challenge had miscarried;
and by 1811, having during the interval married, he was prepared to adopt a
more conciliatory attitude, with results that appear in Byron's letter of November
1st. The party at Samuel Rogers's house helped to launch a life-long friendship.

choice; it rests with the injured and the angry to obtain reparation in their own way.

With regard to the passage in question, *you* were certainly *not* the person towards whom I felt personally hostile. On the contrary, my whole thoughts were engrossed by one, whom I had reason to consider as my worst literary enemy, nor could I foresee that his former antagonist was about to become his champion. You do not specify what you would wish to have done: I can neither retract nor apologise for a charge of falsehood which I never advanced.

In the beginning of the week, I shall be at No. 8, St. James's Street.—Neither the letter nor the friend to whom you stated your intention ever made their appearance.

Your friend, Mr. Rogers, or any other gentleman delegated by you, will find me most ready to adopt any conciliatory proposition which shall not compromise my own honour,—or, failing in that, to make the atonement you deem it necessary to require.

I have the honour to be, Sir,

Your most obedient, humble servant, BYRON

TO THOMAS MOORE   *8, St. James's Street, November 1, 1811*

SIR,—As I should be very sorry to interrupt your Sunday's engagement, if Monday, or any other day of the ensuing week, would be equally convenient to yourself and friend, I will then have the honour of accepting his invitation. Of the professions of esteem with which Mr. Rogers has honoured me, I cannot but feel proud, though undeserving. I should be wanting to myself, if insensible to the praise of such a man; and, should my approaching interview with him and his friend lead to any degree of intimacy with both or either, I shall regard our past correspondence as one of the happiest events of my life. I have the honour to be,

Your very sincere and obedient servant, BYRON

TO JOHN CAM HOBHOUSE   *8, St. James's Street,*
                                        December 9th, 1811

MY DEAR HOBHOUSE,—At length I am your rival in good
fortune. I, this night, saw *Robert Coates*[1] perform Lothario
at the Haymarket, the house crammed, but bribery (a bank
token) procured an excellent place near the stage. Before
the curtain drew up, a performer (all gemmen) came forward
and thus addressed the house, Ladies, etc., " A melancholy
accident has happened to the gentleman who undertook the
part of Altamont——" (here a dead stop—then—) " this
accident has *happened* to *his brother*, who fell this afternoon
through a *loop-hole* into the *London Dock*, and was taken up dead,
Altamont has just entered the house, distractedly, is—now
dressing ! ! ! and will appear in five minutes ! ! ! " Such were
verbatim the words of the apologist; they were followed by a
roar of laughter, and Altamont himself, who did not fall short
of Coates in absurdity. Damn me, if I ever saw such a scene
in my life; the play was closed in 3rd act; after Bob's demise,
nobody would hear a syllable, he was interrupted several
times before, and made speeches, every soul was in hysterics,
and all the actors on his own model. You can't conceive how
I longed for *you*; your taste for the ridiculous would have been
gratified to surfeit. A farce followed in dumb-show, after Bob
had been hooted from the stage, for a bawdy address he
attempted to deliver between play and farce. " Love à la
mode " was damned, Coates was damned, everything was
damned, and damnable. His enacting I need not describe,
you have seen him at Bath. But never did you see the *others*,
never did you hear the *apology*, never did you behold the
" distracted " survivor of a " brother neck-broken through
a *loop-hole* in yᵉ *London Docks* ". Like George Faulkner these
fellows defied burlesque. Oh, Captain ! eye hath not seen,
ear hath not heard, nor can the heart of man conceive to-
night's performance. Baron Geramb was in the stage box,
and Coates in his address *nailed* the *Baron* to the infinite amusement of the audience, and the discomfiture of *Geramb*, who
grew very wroth indeed.

[1] " Romeo " Coates, a wealthy and hapless eccentric, fancied himself a great
tragic actor.

I meant to write on other topics, but I must postpone. I can think, and talk, and dream only of these buffoons. " 'Tis done, 'tis numbered with the things that were, would, would it were to come " and you by my side to see it.

Heigh ho! Good-night.

Yours ever, B.

TO WILLIAM HARNESS[1] *8, St. James's Street, Dec. 15, 1811*

MY DEAREST WILLIAM,—I wrote you an answer to your last, which, on reflection, pleases me as little as it probably has pleased yourself. I shall not wait for your rejoinder; but proceed to tell you, that I had just then been greeted with an epistle of Hodgson's full of his petty grievances, and this at the moment when (from circumstances it is not necessary to enter upon) I was bearing up against recollections to which *his* imaginary sufferings are as a scratch to a cancer. These things combined, put me out of humour with him and all mankind. The latter part of my life has been a perpetual struggle against affections which embittered the earliest portion; and though I flatter myself I have in a great measure conquered them, yet there are moments (and this was one) when I am as foolish as formerly. I never said so much before, nor had I said this now, if I did not suspect myself of having been rather savage in my letter, and wish to inform you this much of the cause. You know I am not one of your dolorous gentlemen: so now let us laugh again.

Yesterday I went with Moore to Sydenham to visit your " costive " Campbell (as you call him). He was not visible. Moore said he was probably within, but " nefariously dirty " and did not like to be seen in so poetical a plight. So we jogged homeward merrily enough. To-morrow I dine with Rogers, and am to hear Coleridge, who is a kind of rage at present. Last night I saw Kemble in Coriolanus;—he *was glorious*, and exerted himself wonderfully. By good luck I got an excellent place in the best part of the house, which was more than overflowing. Clare and Delawarr, who were there on the same speculation, were less fortunate. I saw them by accident,—we were not together. I wished for you, to gratify

---

[1] The Reverend William Harness, " a *Harrow* man ", one of several friends whom Byron at different periods claimed as earliest and dearest.

your dramatic propensities in their fullest extent. Last week I saw an exhibition of a different kind in a Mr. Coates, at the Haymarket, who performed Lothario in a *damned* and damnable manner. * * * So much for these sentimentalites, who console themselves in the stews for the loss—the never to be recovered loss—the despair of the refined attachment of a brace of drabs! When I compare myself with these men, my elders and my betters, I really begin to conceive myself a monument of prudence—a walking statue—without feeling or failing; and yet the world in general hath given me a proud pre-eminence over them in profligacy. Yet I like the men, and, God knows, ought not to condemn their aberrations. But I own I feel provoked when they dignify all this with the name of *love* and deify their common strumpets. Romantic attachments for things marketable at a dollar! Their ladies may be averaged at a token each, I believe they have been bought cheaper.

Dec. 16th.—I have just received your letter;—I feel your kindness very deeply. The foregoing part of my letter, written yesterday, will, I hope, account for the tone of my former, though it cannot excuse it. I do *like* to hear from you—more than *like*. Next to seeing you, I have no greater satisfaction. But you have other duties, and greater pleasures, and I should regret to take a moment from either. Hodgson was to call to-day, but I have not seen him. The circumstance you mention at the close of your letter is another proof in favour of my opinion of mankind. Such you will always find them—selfish and distrustful. I except none. The cause of this is the state of society. In the world, every one is to stir for himself—it is useless, perhaps selfish, to expect any thing from his neighbour. But I do not think we are born of this disposition; for you find *friendship* as a schoolboy, and *love* enough before twenty.

I went to see Hodgson; he keeps me in town, where I don't wish to be at present. He is a good man, but totally without conduct. And now, my dearest William, I must wish you good morrow. Notwithstanding your veto, I must still sign myself
" sincerely " but ever most affectionately BYRON

P.S. I shall write the moment I have been able to fix the day. φίλτατε χαῖρε.

TO ROBERT RUSHTON   *8, St. James's Street, Jan. 21, 1812*

Though I have no objection to your refusal to carry *letters*
to Mealey's, you will take care that the letters are taken by
Spero at the proper time.   I have also to observe, that Susan [1]
is to be treated with civility, and not *insulted* by any person
over whom I have the smallest control, or, indeed, by any
one whatever, while I have the power to protect her.   I am
truly sorry to have any subject of complaint against *you*; I
have too good an opinion of you to think I shall have occasion
to repeat it, after the care I have taken of you, and my favourable intentions in your behalf.   I see no occasion for any
communication whatever between *you* and the *women*, and
wish you to occupy yourself in preparing for the situation in
which you will be placed.   If a common sense of decency
cannot prevent you from conducting yourself towards them
with rudeness, I should at least hope that your *own interest*,
and regard for a master who has *never* treated you with unkindness, will have some weight.

Yours, etc., BYRON

P.S.—I wish you to attend to your arithmetic, to occupy
yourself in surveying, measuring, and making yourself acquainted with every particular relative to the *land* of Newstead,
and you will *write* to me *one letter every week*, that I may know
how you go on.

TO ROBERT RUSHTON   *8, St. James's Street, January 25, 1812*

Your refusal to carry the letter was not a subject of remonstrance : it was not a part of your business ; but the
language you used to the girl was (as *she* stated it) highly
improper.

You say, that you also have something to complain of;
then state it to me immediately : it would be very unfair, and
very contrary to my disposition, not to hear both sides of the
question.

---

[1] For further information regarding Susan Vaughan, apparently one of the
Newstead housemaids whom Byron was inclined to favour, see *To Lord Byron*,
by Paston and Quennell (John Murray).

If any thing has passed between you *before* or since my last visit to Newstead, do not be afraid to mention it. I am sure *you* would not deceive me, though *she* would. Whatever it is, *you* shall be forgiven. I have not been without some suspicions on the subject, and am certain that, at your time of life, the blame could not attach to you. You will not *consult* any one as to your answer, but write to me immediately. I shall be more ready to hear what you have to advance, as I do not remember ever to have heard a word from you before *against* any human being, which convinces me you would not maliciously assert an untruth. There is not any one who can do the least injury to you, while you conduct yourself properly. I shall expect your answer immediately.

Yours, etc., BYRON

TO THOMAS MOORE   *January 29, 1812*

MY DEAR MOORE,—I wish very much I could have seen you; I am in a state of ludicrous tribulation. * * *

Why do you say that I dislike your poesy? I have expressed no such opinion, either in *print* or elsewhere. In scribbling myself, it was necessary for me to find fault, and I fixed upon the trite charge of immorality, because I could discover no other, and was so perfectly qualified in the innocence of my heart, to " pluck that mote from my neighbour's eye ".

I feel very, very much obliged by your approbation; but, at *this moment*, praise, even *your* praise, passes by me like " the idle wind ". I meant and mean to send you a copy the moment of publication; but now I can think of nothing but damned, deceitful,—delightful woman, as Mr. Liston says in the *Knight of Snowdon*. Believe me, my dear Moore,

Ever yours, most affectionately, BYRON

TO JOHN CAM HOBHOUSE*   *8 St. James's Street, February 10th, 1812*

DEAR HOBHOUSE,—I have just recovered from an attack of the *Stone* in the *kidney*, an agreeable disease which promises to be periodically permanent. The very unpromising state of my worldly affairs compels me to recur to a subject upon which I have not often touched, and which I shall now dispatch as quickly as possible. In case of any accident befalling yourself or me, you are aware that I possess no *document*, *note* or *memorial* of the money transactions between us beyond the mention of the sum in one or two of your letters, and I should, if you have no particular objection, like to have your note of hand for the amount. Of this you will hardly suspect that I shall take any advantage. I wish it merely as an acknowledgment in case of accidents. Now to change the theme—your MSS are found. I have been most painfully ill, cupped on the loin, glystered, purged and vomited secundum artem, and am condemned to the strictest regimen, and the most durable of disorders for the residue of my life. I have been voting for the Catholics. I am about to sell off my furniture etc. at Newstead. I have almost arranged the annuity business with Scrope Davies, who has behaved very well indeed, much better than he has been treated, though that was not my fault. I have dismissed my Seraglio for squabbles and infidelities. Now for you—I regret that your work has met with so many obstructions. I have told Demo to write 150 times, but he either don't or won't understand me; if you were on the spot, all this could be easily arranged; as it is, I see no remedy. Your letters have all been put into his hands. God knows I wish you every success that a man in great bodily pain and mortal uneasiness can wish anything of anybody's. I assure you I have lately suffered very severely from kidneys within and creditors without. My two great *bodily* comfiters are Wm Bankes and Mr. Hanson; one tells me that his Grandfather died of a *Stone*, and the other that his father was killed by the *Gravel*! For my part I am *kilt* (you will understand that phrase by this time) by what a methodist would call a congregation, a bookseller compilation and a quack a complication of disorders.

Yrs. ever, B.

TO FRANCIS HODGSON   *8, St. James's Street, February 16, 1812*

DEAR HODGSON,—I send you a proof. Last week I was very ill and confined to bed with stone in the kidney, but I am now quite recovered. The women are gone to their relatives, after many attempts to explain what was already too clear. If the stone had got into my heart instead of my kidneys, it would have been all the better. However, I have quite recovered *that* also, and only wonder at my folly in excepting my own strumpets from the general corruption,—albeit a two months' weakness is better than ten years. I have one request to make, which is, never mention a woman again in any letter to me, or even allude to the existence of the sex. I won't even read a word of the feminine gender;—it must all be *propria quæ maribus.*

In the spring of 1813 I shall leave England for ever. Every thing in my affairs tends to this, and my inclinations and health do not discourage it. Neither my habits nor constitution are improved by your customs or your climate. I shall find employment in making myself a good Oriental scholar. I shall retain a mansion in one of the fairest islands, and retrace, at intervals, the most interesting portions of the East. In the mean time, I am adjusting my concerns, which will (when arranged) leave me with wealth sufficient even for home, but enough for a principality in Turkey. At present they are involved, but I hope, by taking some necessary but unpleasant steps, to clear every thing. Hobhouse is expected daily in London: we shall be very glad to see him; and, perhaps, you will come up and " drink deep ere he depart ", if not, " Mahomet must go to the mountain ";—but Cambridge will bring sad recollections to him, and worse to me, though for very different reasons. I believe the only human being, that ever loved me in truth and entirely, was of, or belonging to, Cambridge, and, in that, no change can now take place. There is one consolation in death—where he sets his seal, the impression can neither be melted nor broken, but endureth for ever.

Yours always, B.

P.S.—I almost rejoice when one I love dies young, for I could never bear to see them old or altered.

TO LORD HOLLAND   *8, St. James's Street, February 25, 1812*

MY LORD,[1]—With my best thanks, I have the honour to return the Notts. letter to your Lordship. I have read it with attention, but do not think I shall venture to avail myself of its contents, as my view of the question differs in some measure from Mr. Coldham's. I hope I do not wrong him, but *his* objections to the bill appear to me to be founded on certain apprehensions that he and his coadjutors might be mistaken for the " *original advisers* " (to quote him) of the measure. For my own part, I consider the manufacturers as a much injured body of men, sacrificed to the views of certain individuals who have enriched themselves by those practices which have deprived the frame-workers of employment. For instance ;— by the adoption of a certain kind of frame, one man performs the work of seven—six are thus thrown out of business. But it is to be observed that the work thus done is far inferior in quality, hardly marketable at home, and hurried over with a view to exportation. Surely, my Lord, however we may rejoice in any improvement in the arts which may be beneficial to mankind, we must not allow mankind to be sacrificed to improvements in mechanism. The maintenance and well-doing of the industrious poor is an object of greater consequence to the community than the enrichment of a few monopolists by any improvement in the implements of trade, which deprives the workman of his bread, and renders the labourer " unworthy of his hire ".

My own motive for opposing the bill is founded on its palpable injustice, and its certain inefficacy. I have seen the state of these miserable men, and it is a disgrace to a civilised country. Their excesses may be condemned, but cannot be subject of wonder. The effect of the present bill would be to drive them into actual rebellion. The few words I shall venture to offer on Thursday will be founded upon these opinions formed from my own observations on the spot. By

[1] Lord Holland, the nephew of Charles James Fox, was at this time Recorder of Nottingham. Byron's maiden speech, delivered on February 27th, was an attack on the oppressive Frame-Breaking Bill, introduced by Lord Liverpool. The Holland House coterie had been satirized by Byron in *English Bards*. Anxious to make amends, he presented Lord Holland with an advance copy of *Childe Harold* on March 5th.

previous inquiry, I am convinced these men would have been restored to employment, and the county to tranquillity. It is, perhaps, not yet too láte, and is surely worth the trial. It can never be too late to employ force in such circumstances. I believe your Lordship does not coincide with me entirely on this subject, and most cheerfully and sincerely shall I submit to your superior judgment and experience, and take some other line of argument against the bill, or be silent altogether, should you deem it more advisable. Condemning, as every one must condemn, the conduct of these wretches, I believe in the existence of grievances which call rather for pity than punishment. I have the honour to be, with great respect, my Lord, your Lordship's

Most obedient and obliged servant, BYRON

P.S.—I am a little apprehensive that your Lordship will think me too lenient towards these men, and half a *framebreaker myself*.

TO FRANCIS HODGSON   *8, St. James's Street, March 5, 1812*

MY DEAR HODGSON,—*We* are not answerable for reports of speeches in the papers; they are always given incorrectly, and on this occasion more so than usual, from the debate in the Commons on the same night. The *Morning Post* should have said *eighteen years*. However, you will find the speech, as spoken, in the Parliamentary Register, when it comes out. Lords Holland and Grenville, particularly the latter, paid me some high compliments in the course of their speeches, as you may have seen in the papers, and Lords Eldon and Harrowby answered me. I have had many marvellous eulogies repeated to me since, in person and by proxy, from divers persons *ministerial*—yea, *ministerial!*—as well as oppositionists; of them I shall only mention Sir F. Burdett. *He* says it is the best speech by a *lord* since the " *Lord* knows when ", probably from a fellow-feeling in the sentiments. Lord H. tells me I shall beat them all if I persevere; and Lord G. remarked that the construction of some of my periods are very like *Burke's!!* And so much for vanity. I spoke very violent sentences with a sort of modest impudence, abused every thing and every body, put the Lord Chancellor very much out of humour : and if I may believe what I hear, have not lost any character by the experiment. As to my delivery, loud and fluent enough, perhaps a little theatrical. I could not recognize myself or any one else in the newspapers.

I hire myself unto Griffiths, and my poesy comes out on Saturday. Hobhouse is here; I shall tell him to write. My stone is gone for the present, but I fear is part of my habit. We *all* talk of a visit to Cambridge.

Yours ever, B.

TO LADY CAROLINE LAMB †   *Sy Evening*

I never supposed you artful : we are all selfish, nature did that for us. But even when you attempt deceit occasionally, you cannot maintain it, which is all the better ; want of success will curb the tendency. Every word you utter, every line you write, proves you to be either *sincere* or a *fool*. Now as I know you are not the one, I must believe you the other. I never knew a woman with greater or more pleasing talents, *general* as in a woman they should be, something of everything, and too much of nothing. But these are unfortunately coupled with a total want of common conduct. For instance, the *note* to your *page*—do you suppose I delivered it? or did you mean that I should? I did not of course. Then your heart, my poor Caro (what a little volcano !), that pours *lava* through your veins ; and yet I cannot wish it a bit colder, to make a *marble slab* of, as you sometimes see (to understand my foolish metaphor) brought in vases, tables, etc., from Vesuvius, when hardened after an eruption. To drop my detestable tropes and figures, you know I have always thought you the cleverest, most agreeable, absurd, amiable, perplexing, dangerous, fascinating little being that lives now, or ought to have lived 2000 years ago. I won't talk to you of beauty ; I am no judge. But our beauties cease to be so when near you, and therefore you have either some, or something better. And now, Caro, this nonsense is the first and last compliment (if it be such) I ever paid you. You have often reproached me as wanting in that respect; but others will make up the deficiency. Come to Lord Grey's; at least do not let me keep you away. All that you so often *say*, I *feel*. Can more be said or felt? This same prudence is tiresome enough; but one *must* maintain it, or what *can* one do to be saved? Keep to it.

[On a covering sheet]

If you write at all, write as usual, but do as you please. Only as I never see you—Basta!

TO LADY CAROLINE LAMB   *May 1st, 1812*

My dear Lady Caroline,—I have read over the few poems of Miss Milbank with attention. They display fancy, feeling, and a little practice would very soon induce facility of expression. Though I have an abhorrence of Blank Verse, I like the lines on Dermody so much that I wish they were in rhyme. The lines in the Cave at Seaham have a turn of thought which I cannot sufficiently commend, and here I am at least candid as my own opinions differ upon such subjects. The first stanza is very good indeed, and the others, with a few slight alterations, might be rendered equally excellent. The last are smooth and pretty. But these are all, has she no others? She certainly is a very extraordinary girl; who would imagine so much strength and variety of thought under that placid Countenance? It is not necessary for Miss M. to be an authoress, indeed I do not think publishing at all creditable either to men or women, and (though you will not believe me) very often feel ashamed of it myself; but I have no hesitation in saying that she has talents which, were it proper or requisite to indulge, would have led to distinction.

A friend of mine (fifty years old, and an author, but not *Rogers*) has just been here. As there is no name to the MSS. I shewed them to him, and he was much more enthusiastic in his praises than I have been. He thinks them beautiful; I shall content myself with observing that they are better, much better, than anything of Miss M.'s protegee [*sic*] Blacket.[1]

----

[1] Joseph Blackett, " Cobbler Joe ", was a shoe-making bard whom Miss Milbanke had befriended.

You will say as much of this to Miss M. as you think proper.
I say all this very sincerely. I have no desire to be better
acquainted with Miss Milbank; she is too good for a fallen
spirit to know, and I should like her more if she were less
perfect.

Believe me, yours ever most truly, B.

TO THOMAS MOORE   *May 20, 1812*

On Monday, after sitting up all night, I saw Bellingham [1]
launched into eternity, and at three the same day I saw * * *
launched into the country.

I believe, in the beginning of June, I shall be down for a
few days in Notts. If so, I shall beat you up *en passant* with
Hobhouse, who is endeavouring, like you and every body else,
to keep me out of scrapes.

I meant to have written you a long letter, but I find I
cannot. If any thing remarkable occurs, you will hear it from
me—if good; if *bad*, there are plenty to tell it. In the mean
time, do you be happy.

Ever yours, etc.

P.S.—My best wishes and respects to Mrs. Moore;—she
is beautiful. I may say so even to you, for I was never more
struck with a countenance.

TO LORD HOLLAND   *June 25, 1812*

MY DEAR LORD,—I must appear very ungrateful, and
have, indeed, been very negligent, but till last night I was not
apprised of Lady Holland's restoration, and I shall call to-
morrow to have the satisfaction, I trust, of hearing that she is
well.—I hope that neither politics nor gout have assailed your
Lordship since I last saw you, and that you also are " as well
as could be expected ".

---

[1] John Bellingham, a crazy timber-merchant with a grievance, was executed
for the murder of the Prime Minister, Spencer Perceval. The asterisks evidently
stand for Lady Caroline Lamb. The original of this letter has been lost.

The other night, at a ball, I was presented by order to our gracious Regent, who honoured me with some conversation, and professed a predilection for poetry.—I confess it was a most unexpected honour, and I thought of poor Brummell's adventure, with some apprehension of a similar blunder. I have now great hope, in the event of Mr. Pye's decease, of " warbling truth at court ", like Mr. Mallet of indifferent memory.—Consider, one hundred marks a year! besides the wine and the disgrace; but then remorse would make me drown myself in my own butt before the year's end, or the finishing of my first dithyrambic.—So that, after all, I shall not meditate our laureate's death by pen or poison.

Will you present my best respects to Lady Holland? and believe me, hers and yours very sincerely

TO MISS MERCER ELPHINSTONE*   *St. James's Street,*
                                        29 July 1812

DEAR MISS MERCER,[1]—In compliance with your request, I send the Frank which you will find on the outside; and in compliance with no request at all—but I believe in defiance of the etiquette established between single ladies and all gentlemen whatsoever, plural or singular—I annex a few lines to keep the cover in countenance.

London is very dull, and I am still duller than London. Now I am at a stand still—what shall I say next? I must have recourse to hoping! This then " comes hoping " that you survived the dust of your journey and the fatigue of not dancing at Lady Clonmell's the night before; that Mrs. Lamb bears her widowhood like the Matron of Ephesus, and that all Tunbridge is at this moment waltzing or warbling its best in honour of you both. I hope moreover that you will not gladden the eyes and break the hearts of the Royal Corps of Marines at Plymouth for sometime to come, and that . . . that . . . I am come to an end of all I can say upon nothing.

[1] Miss Margaret Mercer Elphinstone, Baroness Keith in her own right, was a young woman of great wealth and considerable character. She married the Comte de Flahault in 1817. For her correspondence with Byron, see *To Lord Byron*, by Paston and Quennell.

Pray forgive the inside of this for the sake of the *out*, and believe me, if you had done me the honour to require the one, I would never have troubled you with the other. I am (to talk diplomatically) with the very highest consideration, yr sincere and most obed^t serv^t.

B.

P.S.—I am not sure that I have not been guilty of considerable impertinence in sending a word beyond the superscription. If so, let my offence and apology go together with my best respects to Mrs. Lamb and tell her I wish the circuit well over.

TO LADY MELBOURNE * [*Aug. 12th, 1812*]

DEAR LY. M.,—I trust that Ly. C[aroline] has by this time reappeared or that her mother is better acquainted than I am: God knows where she is. If this be the case I hope you will favour me with a line, because in the interim my situation is by no means a *sinecure*, although I did not chuse to add to *your* perplexities this morning by joining in a *duet* with Ly. B.[1] As I am one of the principal performers in this unfortunate drama, I should be glad to know what my part requires next? Mainly I am extremely uneasy on account of Ly. C. and others. As for myself, it is of little consequence. I shall bear and forbear as much as I can. But I must not shrink now from anything.

6 o'clock.

Thus much I had written when I receive yours. Not a word *of* or *from* her. What is the cause of all this—I mean, the *immediate* circumstances which has led to it? I thought everything was well and quiet in the morning till the apparition of Ly. B. If I should hear from her, Ly. B. shall be informed: if *you*, pray tell me. I am apprehensive for her personal safety, for her state of mind. Here I sit alone, and however I might *appear* to you, in the most painful suspense.

Ever yours, B.

[1] Lady Caroline's anxious mother, Lady Bessborough, subsequently nicknamed by Byron " Lady Blarney ". This letter evidently refers to Lady Caroline's famous flight from Melbourne House, when she had temporarily disappeared, much to the confusion of her intimates.

TO LADY CAROLINE LAMB   [*August, 1812?*]

MY DEAREST CAROLINE,—If tears which you saw and know
I am not apt to shed,—if the agitation in which I parted from
you,—agitation which you must have perceived through the
whole of this most *nervous* affair, did not commence until the
moment of leaving you approached,—if all I have said and
done, and am still but too ready to say and do, have not
sufficiently proved what my real feelings are, and must ever be
towards you, my love, I have no other proof to offer. God
knows, I wish you happy, and when I quit you, or rather you,
from a sense of duty to your husband and mother, quit me,
you shall acknowledge the truth of what I again promise and
vow, that no other in word or deed, shall ever hold the place
in my affections, which is, and shall be, most sacred to you,
till I am nothing. I never knew till *that moment* the *madness*
of my dearest and most beloved friend; I cannot express
myself; this is no time for words, but I shall have a pride, a
melancholy pleasure, in suffering what you yourself can scarcely
conceive, for you do not know me. I am about to go out with
a heavy heart, because my appearing this evening will stop
any absurd story which the event of the day might give rise
to. Do you think *now* I am *cold* and *stern* and *artful*? Will even
others think so? Will your *mother* ever—that mother to whom
we must indeed sacrifice much, more, much more on my part
than she shall ever know or can imagine? " Promise not to
love you! " ah, Caroline, it is past promising. But I shall
attribute all concessions to the proper motive, and never cease to
feel all that you have already witnessed, and more than can
ever be known but to my own heart,—perhaps to yours.
May God protect, forgive, and bless you. Ever, and even more
than ever,

> Your most attached, BYRON

P.S.—These taunts which have driven you to this, my
dearest Caroline, were it not for your mother and the kindness
of your connections, is there anything on earth or heaven
that would have made me so happy as to have made you mine
long ago? and not less *now* than *then*, but *more* than ever at
this time. You know I would with pleasure give up all here
and all beyond the grave for you, and in refraining from this,

must my motives be misunderstood? I care not who knows this, what use is made of it,—it is to *you* and to *you* only that they are *yourself* [*sic*]. I was and am yours freely and most entirely, to obey, to honour, love,—and fly with you when, where, and how you yourself *might* and *may* determine.

TO LADY MELBOURNE   *Cheltenham, September 10th, 1812*

DEAR LADY MELBOURNE,—I presume you have heard and will not be sorry to hear *again*, that *they* are safely deposited in Ireland, and that the sea rolls between you and *one* of your torments; the other you see is still at your elbow. Now (if you are as sincere as I sometimes almost dream) you will not regret to hear, that I wish this to end, and it certainly shall not be renewed on my part. It is not that I love another, but loving at all is quite out of my way; I am tired of being a fool, and when I look back on the waste of time, and the destruction of all my plans last winter by this last romance, I am—what I ought to have been long ago. It is true from early habit, one must make love mechanically, as one swims. I was once very fond of both, but now as I never swim, unless I tumble into the water, I don't make love till almost obliged, though I fear *that* is not the shortest way out of the troubled waves with which in such accidents we must struggle. But I will say no more on this topic, as I am not sure of my ground, and you can easily outwit me, as you always hitherto have done.

To-day I have had a letter from Lord Holland, wishing me to write for the opening theatre, but as all Grub Street seems engaged in the contest, I have no ambition to enter the lists, and have thrown my few ideas into the fire. I never risk *rivalry* in anything, you see the very *lowest*, as in this case, discourages me, from a sort of mixed feeling, I don't know if it be *pride*, but *you* will say it certainly is not *modesty*. I suppose your friend Twiss will be *one*. I hear there are five hundred, and I wish him success. I really think he would do it well, but few men who have any character to lose, would risk it in an anonymous scramble, for the sake of their own feelings. I have written to Lord H. to thank him and decline the chance.

Betty¹ is performing here, I fear very ill. His figure is that of a hippopotamus, his face like the bull and mouth on the panels of a heavy coach, his arms like fins fattened out of shape, his voice the gargling of an alderman with the quinsy, and his acting altogether ought to be natural, for it certainly is like nothing that *Art* has ever yet exhibited on the stage.

Will you honour me with a line at your leisure? On the most *indifferent* subjects you please, and believe me ever,

Yours very affectionately, B.

TO LADY MELBOURNE   *Cheltenham, September 13th, 1812*

MY DEAR LADY M.,—The end of Lady B[essborough]'s letter shall be the beginning of mine. " For Heaven's sake do not lose your hold on him." Pray don't, *I* repeat, and assure you it is a very firm one, " but the yoke is easy, and the burthen is light ", to use one of my scriptural phrases.

So far from being ashamed of being governed like Lord Delacour or any *other Lord* or *master*, I am always but too happy to find one to regulate or misregulate me, and I am as docile as a dromedary, and can bear almost as much. Will you undertake me? If you are sincere (which I still a little hesitate in believing), give me but time, let *hers* retain her in Ireland— the " gayer " the better. I want her just to be sufficiently gay that I may have enough to bear me out on my own part. Grant me but till December, and if I do not disenchant the Dulcinea and Don Quichotte, both, then I must attack the windmills, and leave the land in quest of adventures. In the meantime I must, and do write the greatest absurdities to keep her " gay ", and the more so because the last epistle informed me that " eight guineas, a mail, and a packet could soon bring her to London ", a threat which immediately called forth a letter worthy of the Grand Cyrus or the Duke of York, or any other hero of Madame Scudery or Mrs. Clarke.²

¹ William Henry West Betty, the " Young Roscius ", was an infant prodigy whose accomplishments were widely celebrated. In 1812, he had come of age. He retired from the theatre, having amassed a large fortune, in 1824.

² Mary Anne Clarke, mistress of the Duke of York, while he was Commander-in-Chief. In 1809 her sale of commissions had provoked a resounding parliamentary scandal. The Duke of York's love-letters, during the resultant investigation, became public property.

Poor Lady B.! with her hopes and her fears. In fact it is no jest for her, or indeed any of us. I must let you into one little secret—*her* folly half did this. At the commencement she piqued that " vanity " (which it would be the vainest thing in the world to deny) by telling me she was certain I was not beloved, " that I was only led on for the sake of etc., etc." This raised a devil between us, which now will only be laid, I really do believe, in the *Red* Sea; I made no answer, but determined, not to *pursue*, for pursuit it was not, but to sit still, and in a week after I was convinced—not that [Caroline] loved me, for I do not believe in the existence of what is called Love—but that any other man in my situation would have believed that he was loved. Now, my dear Lady M., you are all out as to my real sentiments. I was, am, and shall be, I fear, attached to another, one to whom I have never said much, but have never lost sight of, and the whole of this interlude has been the result of circumstances which it may be too late to regret. Do you suppose that at my *time* of *life*, were I so very *far* gone, that I should not be in Ireland, or at least have followed into Wales, as it was hinted was *expected*. Now they have crossed the Channel, I feel anything but regret. I told you in my two last, that I did not " like any other, etc., etc." I deceived you and myself in saying so; there was, and is one whom I wished to marry, had not this affair intervened, or had not some occurrences rather discouraged me. When our drama was " rising " (" I'll be d—d if it falls off," I may say with Sir Fretful), in the 5th Act, it was no time to hesitate. I had made up my mind to bear the consequences of my own folly; honour, pity, and a kind of affection all forbade me to shrink, but now if I can *honorably* be off, if *you* are not deceiving me, and if she does not take some accursed step to precipitate her own inevitable fall (if not with me, with some less lucky successor)—if these impossibilities can be got over, all will be well. If not—she will travel.

As I have said so much, I may as well say all. The woman I mean is Miss Milbanke; I know nothing of her fortune, and I am told that her father is ruined, but my own will, when my Rochdale arrangements are closed, be sufficient for both. My debts are not £25,000, and the deuce is in it, if with R[ochdale] and the surplus of N[ewstead], I could not contrive to be as independent as half the peerage. I know little of her, and have not the most distant reason to suppose that I am at all a favourite in that quarter. But I never saw a woman whom I *esteemed* so much. But that chance is gone, and there's an end. Now, my dear Lady M., I am completely in your power. I have not deceived you as to —— [C. L.]. I hope you will not deem it vanity, when I soberly say that it would have been want of gallantry, though the acme of virtue, if I had played the Scipio on this occasion. If through your means, or any means, I can be free, or at least change my fetters, my regard and admiration would not be increased, but my gratitude would. In the meantime, it is by no means unfelt for what you have already done. To Lady B[ess-borough] I could not say all this, for she would with the best intentions make the most absurd use of it. What a miserable picture does her letter present of this daughter! She seems afraid to know her, and, blind herself, writes in such a manner as to open the eyes of all others.

I am still here in Holland's house, quiet and alone, without any wish to add to my acquaintances. Your departure was, I assure you, much more regretted than that of any of your lineals or collaterals, so do not you go to Ireland, or I shall follow you o'er " flood and fen ", a complete Ignis fatuus— that is *I*, the epithet will not apply to you, so we will divide the expression ; you would be the *light*, and I the *fool*.

I send you back the letter, and this fearful ream of my own. C. is suspicious about our counterplots, and I am obliged to be as treacherous as Talleyrand, but remember *that treachery* is *truth* to you ; I write as rarely as I can, but when I do, I must lie like George Rose. Your name, I never mention when I can help it ; and all my amatory tropes and figures are exhausted. I have a glimmering of hope. I *had* lost it—it is renewed—all depends on it ; her worst enemy could not wish her such a fate as *now* to be thrown back upon me.

Yours ever most truly, B.

P.S.—DEAR LADY M.,—Don't think me careless. My correspondence since I was sixteen has not been of a nature to allow of any trust except to a lock and key, and I have of late been doubly guarded. The few letters of yours, and all others in case of the worst, shall be sent back or burnt. Surely after returning the one with *Mr. L.'s message*, you will hardly suspect me of wishing to take any advantage; *that* was the only important one in behalf of my own interests. Think me bad if you please, but not *meanly* so. Lady B.'s under another cover accompanies this.

TO LADY MELBOURNE   *Cheltenham, September 15th, 1812*

MY DEAR LADY M.,—" If I were looking in your face, entre les deux yeux ", I know not whether I should find " frankness or truth ", but certainly something which looks quite as well if not better than either, and whatever it may be, I would not have it changed for any other expression; as it has defied time, no wonder it should perplex *me*.—" Manage her ! " it is impossible, and as to friendship—no—it must be broken off at once, and all I have left is to take some step which will make her hate me effectually, for she must be in extremes. What you state however is to be dreaded; besides, she presumes upon the weakness and affection of all about her, and the very confidence and kindness which would break or reclaim a good heart, merely lead her own farther from deserving them. Were this but secure, you would find yourself mistaken in me. I speak from experience; except in one solitary instance, three months have ever cured me. Take an example: in the autumn of 1809 in the Mediterranean I was seized with an *everlasting* passion, considerably more violent on my part than this has ever been—everything was settled— and we (the *we* of that day) were to set off for the Friuli: but, lo ! the Peace spoilt everything, by putting this in possession of the French, and some particular occurrences in the interim, determined me to go to Constantinople. However we were to meet next year at a certain time; though I told my *amica* there was no time like the present, and that I could not answer for the future. She trusted to her power, and I at the moment had certainly much greater doubts of her than myself. A year sped, and on my return downwards I found at Smyrna and Athens despatches, requiring the performance of this

" bon billet qu' à la Chatre " [*sic*], and telling me that one of us had returned to the spot on purpose. But things had altered, as I foresaw, and I proceeded very leisurely, not arriving till some months after, pretty sure that in the interim my idol was in no want of worshippers. But she *was* there, and we met at the Palace. The Governor (the most accommodating of all possible chief magistrates) was kind enough to leave us to come to the most diabolical of explanations. It was in the dog-days, during a sirocco (I almost perspire now with the thoughts of it), during the intervals of an intermittent fever (my love had also intermitted with my malady), and I certainly feared the ague and my passion would both return in full force. I however got the better of both, and she sailed up the Adriatic and I down to the Straits. I had, *certes*, a good deal to contend against, for the lady (who was a *select* friend of the Queen of Naples) had something to gain in a few points and nothing to lose in *reputation*, and was a woman perfectly mistress of herself and every art of intrigue, personal or political —not at all in love, but very able to persuade me that she was so, and sure that I should make a most *convenient* and complaisant fellow-traveller. She is now, I am told, writing her memoirs at Vienna, in which I shall cut a very indifferent figure ; and nothing survives of this most ambrosial amour, which made me on one occasion risk my life, and on another almost drove me mad, but a few Duke of York*ish* letters and certain baubles, which I dare swear by this time have decorated the hands of half Hungary and all Bohemia. Cosi finiva la musica.

TO LADY MELBOURNE   *Cheltenham, September 18th, 1812*

MY DEAR LY. MELBOURNE,—I only wish you thought your influence worth a " *boast* ", I should ask, when it is the highest compliment paid to myself. To you it would be none, for (besides the little value of the thing) you have seen enough to convince you how easily I am governed by anyone's *presence*, but *you* would be obeyed even in absence. All persons in this situation are so, from having too much *heart*, or too little head, one or both. Set mine down according to your calculations. You and yours seem to me much the same as the Ottoman family to the faithful; they frequently change their rulers, but never the reigning race. I am perfectly convinced if I fell in love with a woman of Thibet, she would turn out an *emigrée cousine* of some of you.

You ask, " Am I sure of myself? " and I answer no, but *you* are, which I take to be a much better thing. Miss M[il-banke] I admire because she is a clever woman, an amiable woman, and of high blood, for I have still a few Norman and Scotch inherited prejudices on the last score, were I to marry. As to *love*, that is done in a week (provided the lady has a reason-able share) ; besides, marriage goes on better with esteem and confidence than romance, and she is quite pretty enough to be loved by her husband, without being so glaringly beautiful as to attract too many rivals. She always reminds me of " Emma " in the modern Griselda, and whomever I *may* marry, that is the woman I would wish to *have married*. It is odd enough that my acquaintance with Caroline commenced with a confidence on my part about your niece; C. herself (as I have often told her) was *then* not at all to my taste, nor I (and I may believe her) to hers, and we shall end probably as we began. However, if after all " it is decreed on high ", that, like James the fatalist, I *must* be hers, she shall be *mine* as long as it pleases her, and the circumstances under which she be-comes so, will at least make me devote my life to the vain attempt of reconciling her to herself. Wretched as it would render me, she should never know it; the sentence once past, I could never restore that which she had lost, but all the reparation I could make should be made, and the cup drained to the very dregs by myself, so that its bitterness passed from her.

In the meantime, till it *is* irrevocable, I must and may fairly endeavour to extricate both from a situation which, from our total want of all but selfish considerations, has brought us to the brink of the gulf. Before I sink I will at least have a *swim* for it, though I wish with all my heart it was the Helles-pont instead, or that I could cross *this* as easily as I did ye other. One reproach I cannot escape. Whatever happens hereafter, *she* will charge it on me, and so shall I, and I fear that

> " The first step or error none e'er could recall,
> And the woman once fallen for ever must fall;
> Pursue to the last the career she begun,
> And be *false* unto *many*, as *faithless* to *one*."

Forgive one stanza of my own sad rhymes; you know I never did inflict any upon you before, nor will again. What think you of Lady B.'s last? She is losing those brilliant hopes expressed in the former epistle. I have written three letters to Ireland and cannot compass more, the last to Lady B. herself, in which I never mentioned Lady C.'s name nor yours (if I recollect aright), nor alluded to either. It is an odd thing to say, but I am sure Lady B. will be a little provoked, if *I* am the first to change, for, like the Governor of Tilbury Fort, although " the Countess is resolved ", the mother *intenerisce un poco*, and doubtless will expect her daughter to be adored (like an Irish lease) for a term of 99 years. I say it again, that happy as she must and will be to have it broken off *anyhow*, she will hate me if *I* don't break my heart; now is it not so? Laugh—but answer me truly.

I am not sorry that C. sends you extracts from my epistles. I deserve it for the passage I showed once to you, but remember that was in the *outset*, and when everything said or sung was exculpatory and innocent and what not. Moreover, recollect what absurdities a man must write to his idol, and that " garbled extracts " prove nothing without the context; for my own part I declare that I recollect no such proposal of an *epistolary truce*, and the gambols at divers houses of entertainment with ye express, etc., tend ye rather to confirm my statement. But I cannot be sure, or answerable for all I have said or unsaid, since " Jove " himself (some with Mrs. Malaprop would read *Job*) has forgotten to " laugh at our perjuries ". I am certain that I tremble for the trunkfuls of my contradictions, since, like a minister or a woman, she may one day exhibit them in some magazine or some quartos of villainous memories written in her 7000th love-fit.

Now, dear Lady M., my *paper* spares you.

Believe me, with great regard, Yours ever, B.

P.S.—In your last you say you are " surrounded by fools " ;
Why then " motley's the only wear " :

> " Oh that I were a fool, a motley fool ;
> I am ambitious of a motley coat."

Well, will you answer, " Thou shalt have one ".

> Chi va piano va sano,
> E chi va sano va lontano.

My progress has been " lontano ", but alas ! y^e " sano "
and " piano " are past praying for.

TO LADY MELBOURNE   *September 25th, 1812*

My dear Lady M.,—It would answer no purpose to
write a syllable on any subject whatever, and neither accelerate
nor retard what we wish to prevent. She must be left to chance ;
conjugal affection and the Kilkenny theatricals are equally
in your favour. For my part it is an accursed business, *towards*
nor *from* which I shall not move a single step ; if she throws
herself upon me, " cosi finiva " ; if not, the sooner it is over
the better. From this moment I have done with it ; only
before she returns allow me to know, that I may act accordingly.
But there will be nothing to fear before that time, as if a woman,
and a selfish woman also, would not fill up the vacancy with
the first comer ! As to Annabella, she requires time and all
the cardinal virtues, and in the interim I am a little verging
towards one who demands neither, and saves me besides the
trouble of marrying, by being married already. She besides
does not speak English, and to me nothing but Italian—a great
point, for from certain coincidences the very sound of that
language is music to me, and she has black eyes, and *not* a
very white skin, and reminds me of many in the Archipelago
I wished to forget, and makes me forget what I ought to
remember, all which are against me. I only wish she did not
swallow so much supper—chicken wings, sweetbreads, custards,
peaches and port wine ; a woman should never be seen eating

or drinking, unless it be *lobster salad* and *champagne*, the only truly feminine and becoming viands. I recollect imploring one lady not to eat more than a fowl at a sitting, without effect, and I have never yet made a single proselyte to Pythagoras.

Now a word to yourself—a much more pleasing topic than any of the preceding. I have no very high opinion of your sex, but when I do see a woman superior not only to all her own but to most of ours, I worship her in proportion as I despise the rest. And when I know that men of the first judgment and the most distinguished abilities have entertained and do entertain an opinion which my own humble observation, without any great effort of discernment, has enabled me to confirm on the same subject, you will not blame me for following the example of my elders and betters, and admiring you certainly as much as you ever were admired. My only regret is that the very awkward circumstances in which we are placed prevent and will prevent the improvement of an acquaintance which I now almost regret having made, but recollect, whatever happens, that the loss of it must give me more pain than even the *precious acquisition* (and this is saying *much*) which will occasion that loss.

Ld Jersey has reinvited me to M[iddleton] for the 4th Oct., and I will be there if possible ; in the meantime, whatever step you take to break off this affair has my full concurrence. But *what* you wished me to write, would be a little too indifferent ; and *that* now would be an insult, and I am much more unwilling to hurt her feelings now than ever (not from the mere apprehension of a disclosure in her wrath), but I have always felt that one who has given up much has a claim upon *me* (at least—whatever she deserves from others) for every respect that she may not feel her own degradation, and this is the reason that I have not written at all lately lest some expression might be misconstrued by her. When the lady herself begins the quarrel, and adopts a new " *Cortejo* ", then my conscience is comforted. She has not written to me for some days, which is either a very bad or very good omen.

Y^rs ever, B.

TO LADY MELBOURNE *October 18th, 1812*

MY DEAR LADY M.,—Of A[nnabella] I have little to add, but I do not regret what has passed ; the report alluded to had hurt her feelings, and she has now regained her tranquillity by the refutation to her own satisfaction without disturbing mine. This was but fair, and was not unexpected by me ; all things considered, perhaps it could not have been better. I think of her nearly as I did. The specimen [1] you send me is more favourable to her talents than her discernment, and much *too indulgent* to the subject she has chosen ; in some points the resemblance is very exact, but you have not sent me the whole (I imagine) by the abruptness of both beginning and end. I am glad that your opinion coincides with mine on the subject of her abilities and her excellent qualities ; in both these points she is singularly fortunate. Still there is something of the *woman* about her ; her *preferring* that the letter to you should be sent forward to me, *per essémpio*, appears as if, though she would not encourage, she was not disgusted with being admired. I also may hazard a conjecture that an *answer* addressed to *herself* might not have been displeasing, but of this you are the best judge from actual observation. I cannot, however, see the necessity of its being forwarded, unless I was either to admire the composition, or reply to ye contents. *One* I certainly do, the other would merely lead to mutual compliments, very sincere but somewhat *tedious*.

By the bye, what two famous letters *your own* are ! I never saw such traits of discernment, observation of character, knowledge of your *own sex* and sly concealment of your *knowledge* of the *foibles* of *ours*, than [*sic*] in these epistles ; and so that I preserve you *always* as a friend, and *sometimes* as a correspondent (the oftener the better), believe me, my dear L^dy M., I shall regret nothing but—the week we passed at Middleton, till I can enjoy such another.

Now for C[aroline]. Your name was never mentioned or hinted at. The passage was nearly as follows :—" I know

---

[1] In reply to a proposal of marriage, forwarded by her aunt, Annabella Milbanke had not only set forth her views on marriage, but had composed a literary portrait of her suitor. In this effusion, among other characteristic statements, she observed that Byron's " love of goodness in its chastest form, and his abhorrence of all that degrades human nature, prove the uncorrupted purity of his moral sense ".

from the *best* authority, your *own*, that your time has passed in a very different manner, nor do I object to it; amuse yourself, but leave me *quiet*. What would you have? I go nowhere, I see no one, I mix with no society, I write when it is proper; these perpetual causeless caprices are equally selfish and absurd, etc. etc." and so on in answer to her description of her *lonely lovelorn condition!!!* much in the same sever*er* style. And now this must end. If she persists I will leave the country. I shall enter into no explanations, write no epistles, softening or reverse, nor will I meet her if it can be avoided, and certainly never but in society. The sooner she is apprised of this the better; but with one so totally devoid of all conduct it is difficult to decide. I have no objection to her knowing what passed about A[nnabella], if it would have any good effect; nor do I wish it to be concealed, even from others, or the world in general; my vanity will not be piqued by its development, and though it was not accepted, I am not at all ashamed of my admiration of the amiable *Mathematician*.

I did not reproach C. for "*her behaviour*", but the misrepresentation of it, and her suspicions of mine. Why tell me she was *dying* instead of *dancing*, when I had much rather hear she was acting, as she in fact acted—viz. like any other person in good health, tolerable society and high spirits? In short I am not her lover, and would rather not be her friend, though I never can, nor will be her enemy. If it can be ended, let it be without my interference. I will have nothing more to do with it. Her letters (all but one about *Ld Clare* unanswered, and the answer to *that* strictly confined to his concerns, except a hint on vanity at the close) are filled with the most ridiculous egotism: "*how* the Duke's mob observed her, *how* the boys followed her, the women caressed and the men admired, and *how* many lovers were all sacrificed to this brilliant fit of constancy". Who wants it forsooth, or expects it, after sixteen? Can't she take example from me? Do I embarrass myself about A.? or the fifty B., C., D., E., F., G., H.'s, etc. etc., that have preceded her in cruelty, or kindness (the latter always the greater plague)? Not I; and really, *sans phrase*, I think *my loss* is the most *considerable*.

I hear L^{dy} Holland is ill, I hope *not seriously*. Ld O. went to-day, and I am still here with some idea of proceeding either to Herefordshire or to Ld Harrowby's, and one notion of being obliged to go to London to meet my agent.

Pray let me hear from you ; I am so provoked at the thought that our acquaintance may be interrupted by the old phantasy. I had and have twenty thousand things to say, and I trust as many to hear, but somehow our conversations never come to a clear conclusion.

I thank you again for your efforts with my Princess of Parallelograms, who has puzzled you more than the Hypothenuse ; in her character she has not forgotten " *Mathematics* ", wherein I used to praise her cunning. Her proceedings are quite rectangular, or rather we are two parallel lines prolonged to infinity side by side, but never to meet. Say what you please for, or of me, and I will swear it.

Good even, my dear L^{dy} Melbourne,

Ever y^{rs} most affectionately, B.

TO LADY MELBOURNE   *October 24th, 1812*

My dear L^{dy} Melbourne,—I am just setting off through detestable roads for—[Eywood]. You can make such use of the incident of our acquaintance as you please with C., only do not say that I am *there*, because she will possibly write, or do some absurd thing in that quarter, which will spoil everything, and I think there are enough of persons embroiled already, without the addition of ——, who has besides enough to manage already without these additions. This I know also to be *her* wish, and certainly it is mine. You may say that we met at C[heltenham] or elsewhere—anything but that we are *now* together. By all means confide in L^{dy} " Blarney " or the " Morning Post ". Seriously, if anything requires a little *hyperbole*, let her have it ; I have left off writing entirely, and will have nothing more to do with it. " If you mention anything to me " *she* is sure to have it ! How ? I have not written these two months but *twice*, nor was your name mentioned in either. The last was entirely about Ld Clare, between whom and me she has been intermeddling and conveying notes from L^{dy} C[lar]e on the subject of a foolish difference between Clare and myself, in which I believe I am wrong as usual. But that is over. Her last letters to me are full of complaints against *you*, for I know not what disrespectful expressions about the " letter opened." etc. etc. I have not answered them nor shall.

They talk of going to Sicily. On that head I have nothing to say, you and Mr. L[amb] are the best judges; to me it must be a matter of perfect indifference; and though I am written to professedly to be consulted on the subject, what possible answer could I give that would not be impertinent? It would be the *best* place for *her* and the worst for him (in all points of view) on earth, unless he was in some official capacity.

As I have said before, do as you will. In my next I will answer your questions as to the three persons you speak of; at present I have not time, though I am *tempted* by the *theme*. As to A[nnabella] that must take its chance—I mean the *acquaintance*; for it never will be anything more, depend upon it, even if she *revoked*. I have still the same opinion, but I never was *enamoured*; and as I very soon shall be in some other quarter, *Cossi finiva* [*sic*].

Do not fear about C[aroline] even if we meet, but allow me to keep out of the way if I can, merely for the sake of peace and quietness. You were never more *groundlessly* alarmed; for I am not what you imagine, in one respect. I have gone through the experiment before; more than once, and I never was separated three months without a perfect *cure*; even though yᵉ acquaintance was renewed. I have even stood as much *violence* as could be brought into the field in yᵉ present occasion. In the first vol. of Marmontel's Memoirs, towards the end, you will find my opinion on the subject of women in *general* in the mouth of Madame de *Tencin*, should you deign to think it worth a moment's notice.

Evers yours most affectionately, B.

P.S.—If you write to Cheltenham my letters will be forwarded. And *do* write. I have very few correspondents, and none but this which give me much pleasure.

TO LADY MELBOURNE   *November 9th, 1812*

MY DEAR L^DY M.,—With y^r letter I have received an *Irish* Epistle, foolish, headstrong, and vainly threatening *herself*, etc. etc. To this I shall return no answer; and though it is of very great importance to me to be in London at this time, I shall if possible delay it till I hear from you that there is no chance of any scenes. Mr. D. could hardly avoid guessing but too correctly, for not a servant in the house but was afraid to awaken me, and *he* was called home from a club for that purpose; his first and natural question to the man, was whence he came, from whom, and why? the answer to all which is obvious, but D. ought not to have mentioned it, and so I shall tell him.

Why he placed me in Notts at this moment I cannot say, except that he knew no better. Mr. C[laughton] [1] may repent of his bargain for aught I know to the contrary, but he has paid part of the money. If he fails, the Law will decide between us; and if he acts in an ungentlemanly manner, the remedy is still more simple.

With regard to L^dy B[essborough] and L^dy C[aroline], I have little more to say, and I hope nothing to do.—She has hurt and disgusted me by her latter conduct beyond expression, and even if I did not love another, I would never speak to her again while I existed, and this you have my full consent to state to those whom it may concern. I have passed my time since her departure *always* quietly and partly delightfully, nor will I submit to caprice and injustice. This *was* to *be* broken off—it is broken off. I had neither the hope nor the inclination to satisfy L^dy B[essborough] on all points; if it is unfair to comply with her own express wishes, let her complain till she is tired, but I trust a little reflection will convince even her that she is wrong to be dissatisfied. C. threatens to revenge herself upon *herself*, by all kinds of perverseness; this is her concern. All I desire is to have nothing more to do with them—no explanations, no interviews; in short I neither can nor will bear it any longer. As long as there was a necessity for supporting her I did not *shrink* from any consequences,

---

[1] A prospective purchaser of Newstead, who eventually failed to complete his bargain.

but when all was adjusted and you agreed to overlook the past, in the hope of the future, my resolution was taken, and to that I have adhered, and will adhere. I cannot exist without some object of love. I have found one with whom I am perfectly satisfied, and who as far as I can judge is no less so with me; our mutual wish is *quiet*, and for this reason I find a double pleasure (after all the ridiculous display of last season) in repose. I have engaged myself too far to recede, nor do I regret it. Are *you* at least satisfied with what I have done to comply with your wishes, if L^{dy} B[essborough] is not? If L^{dy} C[aroline] wishes any interview pray explain for me that *I* WILL NOT meet her; if she has either pride or feeling this will be sufficient. All letters, etc. etc., may be easily destroyed without it.

TO JOHN MURRAY   *Eywood, Presteign, January 8, 1813*

DEAR SIR,—You have been imposed upon by a letter forged in my name to obtain the picture left in your possession. This I know by the confession of the culprit, and as she is a woman (and of rank), with whom I have unfortunately been too much connected, you will for the present say very little about it; but if you have the letter *retain* it—write to me the particulars. You will also be more cautious in future, and not allow anything of mine to pass from your hands without my *Seal* as well as Signature.

I have not been in town, nor have written to you since I left it. So I presume the forgery was a skilful performance. —I shall endeavour to get back the picture by fair means, if possible.

Yours ever, BYRON

P.S.—Keep the letter if you have it. I did not receive your parcel, and it is now too late to send it on, as I shall be in town on the 17th. The *delinquent* is one of the first families in this kingdom; but, as Dogberry says, this is " flat burglary ". Favour me with an answer. I hear I am scolded in the *Quarterly*; but you and it are already forgiven. I suppose that made you bashful about sending it.

TO LADY CAROLINE LAMB*   *January [?], 1813*
[This letter was found enclosed in a letter to Lady Melbourne of Jan. 10th, 1813.]

You should answer the note for the writer seems unhappy. And when we are so a slight is doubly felt.

I shall go at 12; but you must send me a ticket, which I shall religiously pay for. I shall not call because I do not see that we are at all improved by it. Why did you send your boy? I was out, and am always so occupied in a morning that I could not have seen him as I wished had I been at home. I have seen Moore's wife, who is beautiful, with the darkest eyes. They have left town. M. is in great distress about us, and indeed people talk as if there were no other pair of absurdities in London. It is hard to bear all this without cause,

but worse to give cause for it. Our folly has had the effect
of a fault. I conformed and could conform, if you would lend
your aid, but I can't bear to see you look unhappy, and am
always on the watch to observe if you are trying to make me
so. We must make an effort. This dream, this delirium of
two months must pass away. We in fact do not know one
another. A month's absence would make us rational. You
do not think so. I know it. We have both had 1000 previous
fancies of the same kind, and shall get the better of this and
be ashamed of it according to the maxim of Rochefoucault.
But it is better that I should leave town than you, and I will
make a turn [?], or go to Cambridge or Edinburgh. Now
don't abuse me, or think me altered. It is because I am not,
cannot alter, that I shall do this, and cease to make fools talk,
friends grieve, and the wise pity.

Ever most affectionately and truly Yrs, B.

TO JOHN CAM HOBHOUSE*   *January 17th, 1813*

DEAR H.,—I am on my way to town, writing from my
sordid Inn. Many thanks for your successful diplomacy with
Ma-Mee. And now " Grant him one favour and he'll ask you
two "—I have written to Batt for rooms. Would it hurt your
dignity to order me some at any other hotel (by a note) in
case he should not have them?—for I have no opportunity of
receiving your or his answer before I reach London, and if
he has not any to spare and I arrive late I shall be as bewildered as Whittington.

I rejoice in your good understanding with Murray. Through
him you will become a " *staple author* ". D. is a *damned* nincom.
assuredly. He has bored me into getting young Fox to recommend his further *damnation* to the Manager Whitbread. God
(and the Gods) knows and know what will become of his " 25
acts and some odd scenes ".

I am at Ledbury. Ly. O. and famille I left at Hereford,
as I hate travelling with Children unless they have gotten a
Stranguary. However I wait here for her tomorrow like a
dutiful Cortejo. O[xford] has been in town these ten days.
Car. L. has been *forging letters* in my name and hath thereby

pilfered the best picture of *me*, the Newstead Miniature!!!
Murray was the imposed upon. The Devil, and Medea, and
her Dragons to boot, are possessed of that little maniac. Bankes
is gone or going to tourify. I gave him a few letters.

I expect and hope you will have a marvellous run and
trust you have not forgotten " *monogamy* my dr. boy ". If
the " learned world are not in arms against your paradoxes "
I shall despise these coster-monger days when Merit availeth
not.

Excuse my buffoonery, for I write under the influence of
a solitary nipperkin of Grog, such as the Salsette afforded " us
youth " in the Arches [?]

Ever yrs. dr. H., B.

TO FRANCIS HODGSON   *February 3, 1813*

MY DEAR HODGSON,—I will join you in any bond for the
money you require, be it that or a larger sum. With regard
to security, as Newstead is in a sort of abeyance between sale
and purchase, and my Lancashire property very unsettled,
I do not know how far I can give more than personal security,
but what I can I will. At any rate you can try, and as the sum
is not very considerable, the chances are favourable. I hear
nothing of my own concerns, but expect a letter daily. Let
me hear from you where you are and will be this month.
I am a great admirer of the *R.A.* [*Rejected Addresses*], though
I have had so great a share in the cause of their publication,
and I like the *C.H.* [*Childe Harold*] imitation one of the best.
Lady Oxford has heard me talk much of you as a relative of the
Cokes, etc., and desires me to say she would be happy to have
the pleasure of your acquaintance. You must come and see
me at K[insham].[1] I am sure you would like *all* here if you
knew them.

The " Agnus " is furious. You can have no idea of the
horrible and absurd things she has said and done since (really
from the best motives) I withdrew my homage. " Great
pleasure " is, certes, my object, but " *why brief*, Mr. Wild? "

---

[1] Kinsham Court, a dower house belonging to Lord Oxford, of which Byron
was for a time the tenant.

I cannot answer for the future, but the past is pretty secure; and in it I can number the last two months as worthy of the gods in *Lucretius*. I cannot review in the " *Monthly* " ; in fact I can just now do nothing, at least with a pen ; and I really think the days of Authorship are over with me altogether. I hear and rejoice in Bland's and Merivale's intentions. Murray has grown great, and has got him new premises in the fashionable part of the town. We live here so shut out of the *monde* that I have nothing of general import to communicate, and fill this up with a " happy new year ", and drink to you and Drury.

Ever yours, dear H., B.

I have no intention of continuing " *Childe Harold* ". There are a few additions in the " body of the book " of description, which will merely add to the number of pages in the next edition. I have taken Kinsham Court. The business of last summer I broke off, and now the amusement of the gentle fair is writing letters literally threatening my life, and much in the style of " Miss Mathews " in " *Amelia* ", or " Lucy " in the " *Beggar's Opera* ". Such is the reward of restoring a woman to her family, who are treating her with the greatest kindness, and with whom I am on good terms. I am still in *palatia Circes*, and, being no Ulysses, cannot tell into what animal I may be converted ; as you are aware of the turn of both parties, your conjectures will be very correct, I daresay, and, seriously, I am very much *attached*. She has had her share of the denunciations of the brilliant Phryne, and regards them as much as I do. I hope you will visit me at K. which will not be ready before spring, and I am very sure you would like my neighbours if you knew them. If you come down now to Kington, pray come and see me.

TO THE HON. AUGUSTA LEIGH   *4, Bennet Street, St. James's,*
March 26th, 1813

MY DEAREST AUGUSTA,—I did not answer your letter, because I could not answer as I wished, but expected that every week would bring me some tidings that might enable me to reply better than by apologies. But Claughton has not, will not, and, I think, cannot pay his money, and though, luckily, it was stipulated that he should never have possession till the whole was paid, the estate is still on my hands, and your brother consequently not less embarrassed than ever. This is the truth, and is all the excuse I can offer for inability, but not unwillingness, to serve you.

I am going abroad again in June,[1] but should wish to see you before my departure. You have perhaps heard that I have been fooling away my time with different " *regnantes* " ; but what better can be expected from me? I have but one *relative*, and her I never see. I have no connections to domesticate with, and for marriage I have neither the talent nor the inclination. I cannot fortune-hunt, nor afford to marry without a fortune. My parliamentary schemes are not much to my taste—I spoke twice last Session, and was told it was well enough ; but I hate the thing altogether, and have no intention to " strut another hour " on that stage. I am thus wasting the best part of life, daily repenting and never amending.

On Sunday, I set off for a fortnight for Eywood, near Presteign, in Herefordshire—with the *Oxfords*. I see you put on a *demure* look at the name, which is very becoming and matronly in you ; but you won't be sorry to hear that I am quite out of a more serious scrape with another singular personage which threatened me last year, and trouble enough I had to steer clear of it I assure you. I hope all my nieces are well, and increasing in growth and number ; but I wish you were not always buried in that bleak common near Newmarket.

I am very well in health, but not happy, nor even comfortable ; but I will not bore you with complaints. I am a fool, and deserve all the ills I have met, or may meet with, but nevertheless very *sensibly*, dearest Augusta,

Your most affectionate brother, BYRON

TO THE HON. AUGUSTA LEIGH *4, Bennet Street,*
June 26th, 1813

MY DEAREST AUGUSTA,—Let me know when you arrive, and when, and where, and how, you would like to see me,

Byron planned at this moment to go abroad with the Oxfords.

—any where in short but at *dinner*. I have put off going into
yᵉ country on purpose to *waylay* you.

Ever yours, Bᴺ

TO THE HON. AUGUSTA LEIGH   [*June, 1813*]

My dearest Augusta,—And if you knew *whom* I had put
off besides my journey—you would think me grown strangely
fraternal. However I won't overwhelm you with my *own
praises*.

Between one and two be it—I shall, in course, prefer
seeing you all to myself without the incumbrance of third
persons, even of *your* (for I won't own the relationship) fair
cousin of *eleven page* memory, who, by the bye, makes one of
the finest busts I have seen in the Exhibition, or out of it.
Good night!

Ever yours, Byron

P.S.—Your writing is grown like my Attorney's, and gave
me a qualm, till I found the remedy in your signature.

TO LADY MELBOURNE   *July 6th, 1813*

Dear Lʸ M,—Since I wrote yᵉ enclosed I have heard a
strange story of C.'s scratching herself with glass, and I know
not what besides; of all this I was ignorant till this evening.
What I did, or said to provoke her I know not. I told her
it was better to *waltz*; " because she danced well, and it
would be imputed to *me*, if she did not "—but I see nothing
in this to produce cutting and maiming; besides, before
supper I saw her, and though she said, and did even then
a foolish thing, I could not suppose her so frantic as to be in
earnest. She took hold of my hand as I passed, and pressed
it against some sharp instrument, and said, " I mean to use
this ". I answered, " Against me, I presume ? " and passed
on with Lʸ R[ancliffe], trembling lest Lᵈ Y. or Lʸ R. should
overhear her; though not believing it possible that this was

more than one of her, not uncommon, *bravadoes*, for *real feeling* does not disclose its intentions, and always shuns display. I thought little more of this, and leaving the table in search of her would have appeared more particular than proper—though, of course, had I guessed her to be serious, or had I been conscious of offending I should have done everything to pacify or prevent her. I know not what to say, or do. I am quite unaware of what I did to displease; and useless regret is all I can feel on the subject. Can she be in her senses? Yet I would rather think myself to blame—than that she were so silly without cause.

I really remained at L^y H[eathcote's] till 5, totally ignorant of all that passed. Nor do I now know where this cursed scarification took place, nor when—I mean the room—and the hour.

TO LADY MELBOURNE   *July 6th, 1813*

My dear Lady M.,—God knows what has happened, but at four in the morning L^y Ossulstone looking angry (and at that moment, ugly), delivered to me a confused kind of message from you of some scene—this is all I know, except that with laudable logic she drew the usual feminine deduction that I " *must* have behaved very ill ". If L^y C. is offended, it really must be anger at my *not* affronting her—for one of the few things I said, was a request to know her will and pleasure, if there was anything I could say, do, or not do to give her the least gratification. She walked away without answering, and after leaving me in this not very dignified situation, and showing her independence to twenty people near, I only saw her dancing and in the doorway for a moment, where she said something so very violent that I was in distress lest Ld Y. or L^y Rancliffe overheard her. I went to supper, and saw and heard no more till L^y Ossulstone told me your words and her own opinion, and here I am in stupid innocence and ignorance of my offence or her proceedings. If I am to be haunted with hysterics wherever I go, and whatever I do, I think she is not the only person to be pitied. I should have returned to her after her *doorway whisper*, but I could not with any kind of politeness leave L^y Rancliffe to drown herself in wine and water, or be suffocated in a jelly dish, without a spoon, or a hand to help her; besides if there was, and I foresaw there would be something ridiculous, surely I was better absent than present.

This is really insanity, and everybody seems inoculated with the same distemper. L^y W[estmoreland] says, "You must have done something; you know between people in your situation, a word or a look goes a great way", etc. etc. So it seems indeed—but I never knew that *neither* words nor looks—in short down-right, innocent, vacant, undefinable *nothing*, had the same precious power of producing this perpetual worry.

I wait to hear from you, in case I have to answer you. I trust nothing has occurred to spoil your breakfast, for which the Regent has got a fine day.

TO THOMAS MOORE   *4, Benedictine Street, St. James's,*
                                        July 8, 1813

I presume by your silence that I have blundered into something noxious in my reply to your letter, for the which I beg leave to send beforehand a sweeping apology which you may apply to any, or all, parts of that unfortunate epistle. If I err in my conjecture, I expect the like from you in putting our correspondence so long in quarantine. God he knows what I have said; but he also knows (if he is not as indifferent to mortals as the *nonchalant* deities of Lucretius), that you are the last person I want to offend. So, if I have,—why the devil don't you say it at once, and expectorate your spleen?

Rogers is out of town with Madame de Stael,[1] who hath published an Essay against Suicide, which, I presume, will make somebody shoot himself;—as a sermon by Blenkinsop, in *proof* of Christianity, sent a hitherto most orthodox acquaintance of mine out of a chapel of ease a perfect atheist. Have you found or founded a residence yet? and have you begun

---

[1] Madame de Staël had recently arrived in London, accompanied by her eldest son, her daughter and her unacknowledged second husband, M. de Rocca.

or finished a poem? If you won't tell me what *I* have done, pray say what you have done, or left undone, yourself. I am still in equipment for voyaging, and anxious to hear from, or of, you *before* I go, which anxiety you should remove more readily, as you think I sha'n't cogitate about you afterwards. I shall give the lie to that calumny by fifty foreign letters, particularly from any place where the plague is rife,—without a drop of vinegar or a whiff of sulphur to save you from infection.

The Oxfords have sailed almost a fortnight, and my sister is in town, which is a great comfort,—for, never having been much together, we are naturally more attached to each other. I presume the illuminations have conflagrated to Derby (or wherever you are) by this time. We are just recovering from tumult and train oil, and transparent fripperies, and all the noise and nonsense of victory. Drury Lane had a large *M.W.*, which some thought was Marshal Wellington; others, that it might be translated into Manager Whitbread; while the ladies of the vicinity of the saloon conceived the last letter to be complimentary to themselves. I leave this to the commentators to illustrate. If you don't answer this, I sha'n't say what *you* deserve, but I think *I* deserve a reply. Do you conceive there is no Post-Bag but the Twopenny? Sunburn me, if you are not too bad.

TO THOMAS MOORE *July 13, 1813*

Your letter set me at ease; for I really thought (as I hear of your susceptibility) that I had said—I know not what—something I should have been very sorry for, had it, or I, offended you;—though I don't see how a man with a beautiful wife—*his own* children,—quiet—fame—competency and friends, (I will vouch for a thousand, which is more than I will for a unit in my own behalf,) can be offended with any thing.

Do you know, Moore, I am amazingly inclined—remember I say but *inclined*—to be seriously enamoured with Lady A[delaide] F[orbes]—but this * * has ruined all my prospects. However, you know her; is she *clever*, or sensible, or good-tempered? either *would* do—I scratch out the *will*. I don't ask as to her beauty—that I see; but my circumstances are mending, and were not my other prospects blackening, I would take a wife, and that should be the woman, had I a chance. I do not yet know her much, but better than I did.

I want to get away, but find difficulty in compassing a passage in a ship of war. They had better let me go; if I cannot, patriotism is the word—" nay, an they'll mouth, I'll rant as well as they ". Now, what are you doing?—writing, we all hope, for own sakes. Remember you must edit my posthumous works, with a Life of the Author, for which I will send you Confessions, dated " Lazaretto ", Smyrna, Malta, or Palermo—one can die any where.

There is to be a thing on Tuesday ycleped a national fête. The Regent and * * * are to be there, and every body else, who has shillings enough for what was once a guinea. Vauxhall is the scene—there are six tickets issued for the modest women, and it is supposed there will be three to spare. The passports for the lax are beyond my arithmetic.

P.S.—The Stael last night attacked me most furiously—said that I had " no right to make love—that I had used * * barbarously—that I had no feeling, and was totally *in*sensible to *la belle passion*, and *had* been all my life ". I am very glad to hear it, but did not know it before. Let me hear from you anon.

TO THOMAS MOORE   *July 25, 1813*

I am not well versed enough in the ways of single woman to make much matrimonial progress.

I have been dining like the dragon of Wantley for this last week. My head aches with the vintage of various cellars, and my brains are muddled as their dregs. I met your friends the Daltons :—she sang one of your best songs so well, that, but for the appearance of affectation, I could have cried; he reminds me of Hunt, but handsomer, and more musical in soul, perhaps. I wish to God he may conquer his horrible anomalous complaint. The upper part of her face is beautiful, and she seems much attached to her husband. He is right, nevertheless, in leaving this nauseous town. The first winter would infallibly destroy her complexion,—and the second, very probably, every thing else.

I must tell you a story. Morris (of indifferent memory) was dining out the other day, and complaining of the Prince's coldness to his old wassailers. D'Israeli (a learned Jew) bored him with questions—why this? and why that? "Why did the Prince act thus? "—" Why, sir, on account of Lord * *, who ought to be ashamed of himself."—" And why ought Lord * * to be ashamed of himself? "—" Because the Prince, sir, * * * * * * * *."—" And why, sir, did the Prince cut *you*? "—" Because, G—d d—mme, sir, I stuck to my principles."—" And *why* did you stick to your principles? "

Is not this last question the best that was ever put, when you consider to whom? It nearly killed Morris. Perhaps you may think it stupid, but, as Goldsmith said about the peas, it was a very good joke when I heard it—as I did from an ear-witness—and is only spoilt in my narration.

The season has closed with a dandy ball;—but I have dinners with the Harrowbys, Rogers, and Frere and Mackintosh, where I shall drink your health in a silent bumper, and regret your absence till " too much canaries " wash away my memory, or render it superfluous by a vision of you at the opposite side of the table. Canning has disbanded his party by a speech from his * * * *—the true throne of a Tory. Conceive his turning them off in a formal harangue, and bidding them think for themselves. " I have led my ragamuffins where they are well peppered. There are but three of the 150 left alive ", and they are for the *Townsend* (*query*, might not Falstaff mean the Bow Street officer? I dare say Malone's posthumous edition will have it so) for life.

Since I wrote last, I have been into the country. I journeyed by night—no incident, or accident, but an alarm on the part of my valet on the outside, who, in crossing Epping Forest, actually, I believe, flung down his purse before a mile-stone, with a glow-worm in the second figure of number XIX—mistaking it for a footpad and dark lantern. I can only attribute his fears to a pair of new pistols wherewith I had armed him ; and he thought it necessary to display his vigilance by calling out to me whenever we passed any thing—no matter

whether moving or stationary. Conceive ten miles, with a
tremor every furlong. I have scribbled you a fearfully long
letter. This sheet must be blank, and is merely a wrapper,
to preclude the tabellarians of the post from peeping. You
once complained of my *not* writing ;—I will " heap coals of fire
upon your head " by *not* complaining of your *not* reading.
Ever, my dear Moore, your'n (isn't that the Staffordshire
termination?),

BYRON

TO THOMAS MOORE   *Bennet Street, August 22, 1813*

As our late—I might say, deceased—correspondence had
too much of the town-life leaven in it, we will now, *paulo
majora*, prattle a little of literature in all its branches ; and
first of the first—criticism. The Prince is at Brighton, and
Jackson, the boxer, gone to Margate, having, I believe, de-
coyed Yarmouth to see a milling in that polite neighbourhood.
Made de Stael Holstein has lost one of her young barons,
who has been carbonadoed by a vile Teutonic adjutant,—
kilt and killed in a coffee-house at Scrawsenhawsen. Corinne
is, of course, what all mothers must be,—but will, I venture
to prophesy, do what few mothers could—write an Essay
upon it. She cannot exist without a grievance—and somebody
to see, or read, how much grief becomes her. I have not seen
her since the event ; but merely judge (not very charitably)
from prior observation.

In a " mail-coach copy " of the *Edinburgh*, I perceive
The Giaour is second article. The numbers are still in the Leith
smack—*pray which way is the wind?* The said article is so very
mild and sentimental, that it must be written by Jeffrey *in
love* ;—you know he is gone to America to marry some fair
one, of whom he has been, for several *quarters*, *éperdument
amoureux*. Seriously—as Winifred Jenkins says of Lismahago
—Mr. Jeffrey (or his deputy) " has done the handsome thing
by me ", and I say *nothing*. But this I will say, if you and I had
knocked one another on the head in this quarrel, how he
would have laughed, and what a mighty bad figure we should
have cut in our posthumous works. By the by, I was call'd

in the other day to mediate between two gentlemen bent upon carnage, and—after a long struggle between the natural desire of destroying one's fellow-creatures, and the dislike of seeing men play the fool for nothing,—I got one to make an apology, and the other to take it, and left them to live happy ever after. One was a peer, the other a friend untitled, and both fond of high play;—and one, I can swear for, though very mild, " not fearful ", and so dead a shot, that, though the other is the thinnest of men, he would have split him like a cane. They both conducted themselves very well, and I put them out of *pain* as soon as I could.

There is an American *Life* of G. F. Cooke, *Scurra* deceased, lately published. Such a book!—I believe, since *Drunken Barnaby's Journal*, nothing like it has drenched the press. All green-room and tap-room—drams and the drama—brandy, whisky-punch, and, *latterly*, toddy, overflow every page. Two things are rather marvellous,—first, that a man should live so long drunk, and, next, that he should have found a sober biographer. There are some very laughable things in it, nevertheless;—but the pints he swallowed, and the parts he performed, are too regularly registered.

All this time you wonder I am not gone; so do I; but the accounts of the plague are very perplexing—not so much for the thing itself as the quarantine established in all ports, and from all places, even from England. It is true, the forty or sixty days would, in all probability, be as foolishly spent on shore as in the ship; but one likes to have one's choice, nevertheless. Town is awfully empty; but not the worse for that. I am really puzzled with my perfect ignorance of what I mean to do;—not stay, if I can help it, but where to go? Sligo is for the North;—a pleasant place, Petersburgh, in September, with one's ears and nose in a muff, or else tumbling into one's neckcloth or pocket-handkerchief! If the winter treated Buonaparte with so little ceremony, what would it inflict upon your solitary traveller?—Give me a *sun*, I care not how hot, and sherbet, I care not how cool, and *my* Heaven is as easily made as your Persian's. *The Giaour* is now a thousand and odd lines. " Lord Fanny spins a thousand such a day ", eh, Moore?—thou wilt needs be a wag, but I forgive it.

Yours ever, BYRON

P.S.—I perceive I have written a flippant and rather cold-hearted letter! let it go, however. I have said nothing, either, of the brilliant sex; but the fact is, I am at this moment in a far more serious, and entirely new, scrape than any of the last twelve months,—and that is saying a good deal. It is unlucky we can neither live with nor without these women.

I am now thinking of regretting that, just as I have left Newstead, you reside near it. Did you ever see it? *do*—but don't tell me that you like it. If I had known of such intellectual neighbourhood, I don't think I should have quitted it. You could have come over so often, as a bachelor,—for it was a thorough bachelor's mansion—plenty of wine and such sordid sensualities—with books enough, room enough, and an air of antiquity about all (except the lasses) that would have suited you, when pensive, and served you to laugh at when in glee. I had built myself a bath and a *vault*—and now I sha'n't even be buried in it. It is odd that we can't even be certain of a *grave*, at least a particular one. I remember, when about fifteen, reading your poems there, which I can repeat almost now,—and asking all kinds of questions about the author, when I heard that he was not dead according to the preface; wondering if I should ever see him—and though, at that time, without the smallest poetical propensity myself, very much taken, as you may imagine, with that volume. Adieu—I commit you to the care of the gods—Hindoo, Scandinavian, and Hellenic!

P.S. 2d.—There is an excellent review of Grimm's *Correspondence* and Made de Stael in this No of the *E[dinburgh] R[eview]*. Jeffrey, himself, was my critic last year; but this is, I believe, by another hand. I hope you are going on with your *grand coup*—pray do—or that damned Lucien Buonaparte will beat us all. I have seen much of his poem in MS., and he really surpasses every thing beneath Tasso. Hodgson is translating him *against* another bard. You and (I believe Rogers,) Scott, Gifford, and myself, are to be referred to as judges between the twain,—that is, if you accept the office. Conceive our different opinions! I think we, most of us (I am talking very impudently, you will think—*us*, indeed!) have a way of our own,—at least, you and Scott certainly have.

TO LADY MELBOURNE   *September 5th, 1813.*

DEAR LADY MELBOURNE,—I return you the plan of
A[nnabella]'s spouse elect,[1] of which I shall say nothing
because I do not understand it; though I dare say it is exactly
what it ought to be. Neither do I know why I am writing this
note, as I mean to call on you, unless it be to try your " new
patent pens " which delight me infinitely with their colours.
I have pitched upon a yellow one to begin with. Very likely
you will be out, and I must return all the annexed epistles.
I would rather have seen your answer. She seems to have been
spoiled—not as children usually are—but systematically
Clarissa Harlowed into an awkward kind of correctness, with
a dependence upon her own infallibility which will or may lead
her into some egregious blunder. I don't mean the usual
error of young gentlewomen, but she will find exactly what
she wants, and then discover that it is much more dignified
than entertaining. [*The second page of this letter has been torn
off.*]

TO MISS MILBANKE [EXTRACT]   *Sep^{tr} 6th, 1813*

I look upon myself as a very facetious personage and may
appeal to most of my acquaintance (L^y M. for instance) in
proof of my assertion. Nobody laughs more, and though
your friend Joanna Baillie says somewhere that " Laughter
is the child of misery ", I do not believe her (unless indeed in a
hysteric), tho' I think it is sometimes the parent. Nothing
could do me more honor than the acquaintance of that Lady,
who does not possess a more enthusiastic admirer than myself.
She is our only dramatist since Otway and Southerne; I don't
except Home. With all my presumed prejudice against your
sex, or rather the perversion of manners and principle in many,
which you admit in some circles, I think the worst woman
that ever existed would have made a man of very passable
reputation. They are all better than us, and their faults,
such as they are, must originate with ourselves. Your sweeping

---

[1] Besides her sketch of Byron's character, Annabella Milbanke had produced
an imaginary portrait of her ideal husband.

sentence " on the circles where we have met " amuses me much when I recollect some of those who constituted that society. After all, bad as it is, it has its *agrémens*. The great object of life is sensation—to feel that we exist, even though in pain. It is this " craving void " which drives us to gaming —to battle—to travel—to intemperate, but keenly felt pursuits of any description, whose principal attraction is the agitation inseparable from their accomplishment. I am but an awkward dissembler; as my friend you will bear with my faults. I shall have the less constraint in what I say to you—firstly because I may derive some benefit from your observations—and next because I am very sure you can never be perverted by any paradoxes of mine. You have said a good deal and very well too on the subject of Benevolence systematically exerted; two lines of Pope will explain mine (if I have any) and that of half mankind—

" Perhaps prosperity becalmed his breast,
Perhaps the Wind just shifted from the East ".

By the bye you are a *bard* also—have you quite given up that pursuit? Is your friend Pratt one of your critics? or merely one of your systematic benevolents? You were very kind to poor Blackett which he requited by falling in love, rather presumptuously to be sure—like Metastasio with the Empress Maria Theresa. When you can spare an instant, I shall of course be delighted to hear from you—but do not let me encroach a moment on better avocations—— Adieu.

Ever yours, B.

TO THE HON. AUGUSTA LEIGH   [*Wednesday*],
                                                  Septr 15th, 1813

MY DEAR AUGUSTA,—I joined my friend Scrope about 8, and before eleven we had swallowed six bottles of his burgundy and Claret, which left him very unwell and me rather feverish; we were *tête à tête*. I remained with him next day and set off last night for London, which I reached at three in the morning.

Tonight I shall leave it again, perhaps for Aston or Newstead. I have not yet determined, nor does it much matter. As you perhaps care more on the subject than I do, I will tell you when I know myself.

When my departure is arranged, and I can get this long-evaded passage, you will be able to tell me whether I am to expect a visit or not, and I can come for or meet you as you think best. If you write, address to Bennet Street.

Yours very truly, B.

TO LADY MELBOURNE †   *Aston Hall, Rotherham,*
September 21st, 1813

MY DEAR Lᵧ Mᴇ,—My stay at Cambridge was very short, but feeling feverish and restless in town I flew off, and here I am on a visit to my friend Webster, now married, and (according to yᵉ Duke of Buckingham's curse) " settled in yᵉ country ". His bride, Lady Frances, is a pretty, pleasing woman, but in delicate health, and, I fear, going—if not gone—into a decline. Stanhope and his wife—pretty and pleasant too, but not at all consumptive—left us to-day, leaving only yᵉ family, another single gentleman, and your slave. The sister, Lᵧ Catherine, is here too, and looks very pale from a *cross* in her love for Lord Bury (Lᵈ Alb[emarl]e's son) ; in short, we are a society of happy wives and unfortunate maidens. The place is very well, and quiet, and the children only scream in a low voice, so that I am not much disturbed, and shall stay a few days in tolerable repose. W[ebster] don't want sense, nor good nature, but both are occasionally obscured by his suspicions, and absurdities of all descriptions ; he is passionately fond of having his wife admired, and at the same time jealous to jaundice of everything and everybody. I have hit upon the medium of praising her to him perpetually behind her back, and never looking at her before his face ; as for her, I believe she is disposed to be very faithful, and I don't think anyone now here is inclined to put her to the test. W[ebster] himself is, with all his jealousy and admiration, a little tired ; he has been lately at Newstead, and wants to go again. I suspected this sudden

penchant, and soon discovered that a foolish nymph of the
Abbey, about whom fortunately I care not, was the attraction.
Now if I wanted to make mischief I could extract much good
perplexity from a proper management of such events; but I
am grown so good, or so indolent, that I shall not avail myself
of so pleasant an opportunity of tormenting mine host, though
he deserves it for poaching. I believe he has hitherto been
unsuccessful, or rather it is too astonishing to be believed.
He proposed to me, with great gravity, to carry him over
there, and I replied with equal candour, that *he* might set
out when he pleased, but that I should remain here to take
care of his household in the interim—a proposition which I
thought very much to the purpose, but which did not seem at
all to his satisfaction. By way of opiate he preached me a
sermon on his wife's good qualities, concluding by an assertion
that in all moral and mortal qualities, she was very like
" Christ!!! " I think the Virgin Mary would have been a more
appropriate typification; but it was the first comparison of
the kind I ever heard, and made me laugh till he was angry,
and then I got out of humour too, which pacified him, and
shortened the panegyric.

Ld Petersham is coming here in a day or two, who will
certainly flirt furiously with L^y F[rances], and I shall have
some comic Iagoism with our little Othello. I should have no
chance with his Desdemona myself, but a more lively and better
dressed and formed personage might, in an innocent way, for
I really believe the girl is a very good, well-disposed wife, and
will do very well if she lives, and he himself don't tease her
into some dislike of her lawful owner.

I passed through Hatfield the night of your *ball*. Suppose
we had jostled at a turnpike!! At Bugden I blundered on a
Bishop; the Bishop put me in mind of ye Government—the
Government of the Governed—and the governed of their
indifference towards their governors, which you must have
remarked as to all *parties*. These reflections expectorated as
follows—you know I *never* send you my scribblings—and when
you read these, you will wish I never may:

" 'Tis said *Indifference* marks the present time,
      Then hear the reason—though 'tis told in rhyme—

A king who *can't*, a Prince of Wales who *don't*,
Patriots who *sha'n't*, and Ministers who *won't*,
What matters who are *in* or *out* of place,
The *Mad*, the *Bad*, the *Useless*, or the *Base*? "

You may read the 2nd couplet *so*, if you like,

" A King who *cannot*, and a Prince who don't,
Patriots who would not, ministers who won't."

I am asked to stay for the Doncaster races, but I am not in plight, and am a miserable beau at the best of times; so I shall even return to town, or elsewhere; and in the meantime ever am

Yours, dear L^y M^e, B.

P.S.—If you write, address to *B[enne]t Street*; were I once gone, I should not wish my letters to travel *here* after me, for fear of *accidents*.

There is a delightful epitaph on Voltaire in Grimm. I read it coming down. The French I should probably misspell, so take it only in bad English—" Here lies the spoilt child of the a world which he spoiled ". This is good, short and true.

TO LADY MELBOURNE   [*London*] *October 1st, 1813*

M^Y DEAR L^Y M.,—You will have received two letters of mine, to atone for my late portentous silence, and this is intended as a further expiation. I have just been dining at Holland House. The Queen is grown thin and gracious, both of which become her royalty. I met Curran [1] there, who electrified me with his imagination, and delighted me with his humour. He is a man of a million. The Irish *when* good are perfect; the little I have seen of him has less *leaven* than any mortal compound I have lately looked into.

---

[1] John Philpot Curran, the Irish patriot, one of the most accomplished orators of his time and a brilliant frequenter of the Holland House coterie. For further impressions of Curran, see *Detached Thoughts*.

To-day I heard from my friend W[ebster] again; his *Countess* is, he says, " inexorable ". What a lucky fellow— happy in his obstacles. In his case I should think them very pleasant; but I don't lay this down as a general proposition. All my prospect of amusement is clouded, for Petersham has sent an excuse; and there will be no one to make him jealous of but the curate and the butler—and I have no thoughts of setting up for myself. I am not exactly cut out for the lady of the mansion; but I think a stray dandy would have a chance of preferment. She evidently expects to be attacked, and seems prepared for a brilliant defence; my character as a roué has gone before me, and my careless and quiet behaviour astonished her so much that I believe she began to think herself ugly, or me blind—if not worse. They seemed surprised at my declining the races in particular; but for this I had good reasons; firstly: I wanted to go elsewhere; secondly: if I had gone, I must have paid some attention to some of them; which is troublesome, unless one has something in memory, or hope to induce it; and then mine host is so marvellous green-eyed that he might have included me in his calenture —which I don't deserve—and probably should not like it a bit better if I did.

I have also reasons for returning there on Sunday, with which they have nothing to do; but if C. takes a suspicious twist that way, let her—it will keep her in darkness; but I hope, however, she won't take a fit of scribbling, as she did to L^y Oxford last year—though Webster's face on the occasion would be quite a comet, and delight me infinitely more than O[xford]'s, which was comic enough.

Friday morn.—Yours arrived. I will answer on the next page.

So—L^dy H[olland] says I am *fattening*, and you say I talk " *nonsense* ". Well—I must fast and unfool again, if possible. But, as Curran told me last night that he had been assured upon oath by half the Court, that " the Prince was *not* at all *corpulent*, that he was stout certainly, but by no means pro-tuberant, or obese ", " there's comfort yet ". As to folly, that's incurable.

" See C.! *if* I should see C.! " I hope not, though I am not sure a visit would be so disagreeable as it ought to be.

" I pique myself on constancy ", but it is but a sensitive plant ,and thrives best by itself. Then there is the story of L^y B[essborough]'s novelty, which I am sure she longs to unravel. How your passage on " the kneeling in the *middle* of the room " made me laugh this morning; it certainly was not the centre of gravity—pardon a wretched quibble which I don't often hazard. I did not kneel in the middle of the room; but the first time I saw her this year, she thought proper to fix herself there and turn away her head: and, as one does not kneel exactly for one's own convenience, my genuflexions would have been all lost upon her if she did not perceive them.

To return to the W[ebster]s. I am glad they amaze you; anything that confirms, or extends one's observations on life and character delights me, even when I don't know people— for this reason I would give the world to pass a month with Sheridan, or any lady or gentleman of the old school, and hear them talk every day, and all day of themselves, and acquaintance, and all they have heard and seen in their lives. W[ebster] seems in no present peril. I believe the woman is mercenary; and I happen to know that he can't at present bribe her. I told him that it would be known, and that he must expect reprisals—and what do you think was his answer? " I think any woman fair game, because I can *depend* upon L^y F.'s principles—she can't go wrong, and therefore I may." " Then, why are you jealous of her? " " Because—because—zounds ! I am not jealous. Why the devil do you suppose I am? " I then enumerated some very gross symptoms which he had displayed, even before her face, and his servants, which he could not deny; but persisted in his determination to add to his " bonnes fortunes ";—it is a strange being! When I came home in 1811, he was always saying, " B., do marry— it is the happiest ", etc. The first thing he said on my arrival at A[ston] was, " B., whatever you do, *don't marry* "; which, considering he had an unmarried sister-in-law in the house, was a very *un*necessary precaution.

Every now and then he has a fit of fondness, and kisses her hand before his guests; which she receives with the most lifeless indifference, which struck me more than if she had appeared pleased, or annoyed. Her brother told me last year that she married to get rid of her family (who are ill-tempered), and had not been *out* two months; so that, to use a fox-hunting phrase, she was " killed in covert ".

You have enough of them, and me for yᵉ present.

Yʳˢ ever, B.

P.S.   I do not wish to know yᵉ person's name, but to whom is the likeness—to *me* or to *her*?

TO THOMAS MOORE   *October 2, 1813*

You have not answered some six letters of mine.   This, therefore, is my penultimate.   I will write to you once more, but, after that—I swear by all the saints—I am silent and super-cilious.   I have met Curran at Holland House—he beats every body;—his imagination is beyond human, and his humour (it is difficult to define what is wit) perfect.   Then he has fifty faces, and twice as many voices, when he mimics—I never met his equal.   Now, were I a woman, and eke a virgin, that is the man I should make my Scamander.   He is quite fascinating.   Remember, I have met him but once; and you, who have known him long, may probably deduct from my panegyric.   I almost fear to meet him again, lest the im-pression should be lowered.   He talked a great deal about you—a theme never tiresome to me, nor any body else that I know.   What a variety of expression he conjures into that naturally not very fine countenance of his!   He absolutely changes it entirely.   I have done—for I can't describe him, and you know him.   On Sunday I return to Aston, where I shall not be far from you.   Perhaps I shall hear from you in the mean time.   Good night.

Saturday morn.—Your letter has cancelled all my anxieties. I did *not suspect* you in *earnest*.   Modest again!   Because I don't do a very shabby thing, it seems, I " don't fear your competition ".   If it were reduced to an alternative of prefer-ence, I *should* dread you, as much as Satan does Michael. But is there not room enough in our respective regions?   Go on—it will soon be my turn to forgive.   To-day I dine with Mackintosh and Mrs. *Stale*—as John Bull may be pleased to denominate Corinne—whom I saw last night, at Covent Garden, yawning over the humour of Falstaff.

The reputation of " gloom ", if one's friends are not included in the *reputants*, is of great service; as it saves one from a legion of impertinents, in the shape of common-place acquaintance. But thou know'st I can be a right merry and conceited fellow, and rarely *larmoyant*. Murray shall reinstate your line forthwith. I believe the blunder in the motto was mine;—and yet I have, in general, a memory for *you*, and am sure it was rightly printed at first.

I do " blush " very often, if I may believe Ladies H. and M.;—but luckily, at present, no one sees me. Adieu.

TO LADY MELBOURNE   *Aston Hall, Rotherham,*
                                           October 5th, 1813

MY DEAR Lʸ M.,—W. has lost his Countess, his time and his temper (I would advise anyone who finds the *last* to return it immediately; it is of no use to any but the owner). Lʸ F[rances] has lost Petersham, for the present at least; the other sister, as I have said before, has lost Lᵈ Bury; and I have nobody to lose—*here*, at least—and am not very anxious to find one. Here be two friends of the family, besides your slave: a Mr. Westcombe—very handsome, but silly—and a Mr. Agar—frightful, but facetious. The whole party are out in carriages—a species of amusement from which I always *avert*; and, consequently, declined it to-day; it is very well with two, but not beyond a *duet*. I think, being bumped about between two or more of one's acquaintance intolerable. W[ebster] grows rather intolerable, too. He is out of humour with my *Italian* books (Dante and Alfieri, and some others as harmless as ever wrote), and requests that sa femme may not see them, because, forsooth, it is a language which doth infinite damage!! and because I enquired after the Stanhopes, our mutual acquaintance, he *answers* me by another *question*, " Pray, do you enquire after *my* wife of others in the same way?" so that you see my Virtue is its own reward—for never, in word or deed, did I speculate upon his spouse; nor did I ever

see much in her to encourage either hope, or much fulfilment
of hope, supposing I had any. She is pretty, but not surpassing
—too thin, and not very animated; but good-tempered—
and a something interesting enough in her manner and figure;
but I never should think of her, nor anyone else, if left to my
own cogitations, as I have neither the patience nor presumption
to advance till met half-way. The other two pay her ten
times more attention, and, of course, are more attended to.
I really believe he is bilious, and suspects something extraordinary from my nonchalance; at all events, he has hit
upon the wrong person. I can't help laughing to you, but he
will soon make me very serious with him, and then he will
come to his senses again. The oddest thing is, that he wants
me to stay with him some time; which I am not much inclined
to do, unless the gentleman transfers his fretfulness to someone
else. I have written to you so much lately, you will be glad to
be spared from any further account of the " Blunderhead
family ".

Ever yʳˢ, my dear Lʸ Mᵉ, B.

TO LADY MELBOURNE   *October 8th, 1813*

My dear Lʸ M.,—I have volumes, but neither time nor
space. I have already trusted too deeply to hesitate now;
besides, for certain reasons, you will not be sorry to hear that
I am anything but what I was. Well then, to begin, and first,
a word of mine host.—He has lately been talking *at*, rather
than *to*, me before the party (with the exception of the women)
in a tone, which as I never use it myself, I am not particularly
disposed to tolerate in others. What *he* may do with impunity,
it seems, but not suffer, till at last I told him that the whole of
his argument involved the interesting contradiction that " he
might love where he liked, but that no one else might like
what he ever thought proper to love ", a doctrine which, as
the learned Partridge observed, contains a " non sequitur "
from which I, for one, begged leave as a general proposition
to dissent. This nearly produced a scene with me, as well as
another guest, who seemed to admire my sophistry the most
of the two; and as it was after dinner, and debating time,

might have ended in more than wineshed, but that the devil, for some wise purpose of his own, thought proper to restore good humour, which has not as yet been further infringed.

In these last few days I have had a good deal of conversation with an amiable person, whom (as we deal in *letters* and initials only) we will denominate *Ph*.[1] Well, these things are dull in detail. Take it once, I have made love, and if I am to believe mere *words* (for there we have hitherto stopped), it is returned. I must tell you the place of declaration, however, a billiard room. I did not, as C. says : " kneel in the middle of the room ", but, like Corporal Trim to the Nun, " I made a speech ", which, as you might not listen to it with the same patience, I shall not transcribe. We were before on very amicable terms, and I remembered being asked an odd question, " how a woman who liked a man could inform him of it when he did not perceive it ". I also observed that we went on with our game (of billiards) without *counting the hazards*; and supposed that, as mine certainly were not, the thoughts of the other party also were not exactly occupied by what was our ostensible pursuit. Not quite, though pretty well satisfied with my progress, I took a very imprudent step with pen and paper, in tender and tolerably turned *prose* periods (no poetry even when in earnest). Here were risks, certainly : first, how to convey, then how would it be received? It was received, however, and deposited not very far from the heart which I wished it to reach when, who should enter the room but the person who ought at that moment to have been in the Red Sea, if Satan had any civility. But *she* kept her countenance, and the paper; and I my composure as well as I could. It was a risk, and *all* had been lost by failure; but then recollect how much more I had to gain by the reception, if not declined, and how much one always hazards to obtain anything worth having. My billet prospered, it did more, it even (I am this moment interrupted by the *Marito*, and write this before him, he has brought me a political pamphlet in MS. to decypher and applaud, I shall content myself with the last; oh, he is gone again), my billet produced an *answer*, a very unequivocal one too, but a little too much about virtue, and indulgence of attachment in some sort of

[1] Lady Frances Webster.

etherial process, in which the soul is principally concerned, which I don't very well understand, being a bad metaphysician ; but one generally *ends* and *begins* with platonism, and, as my proselyte is only twenty, there is time enough to materialize. I hope nevertheless this spiritual system won't last long, and at any rate must make the experiment. I remember my last case was the reverse, as Major O'Flaherty recommends, " we fought first and explained afterwards ".

This is the present state of things : much mutual profession, a good deal of melancholy, which, I am sorry to say, was remarked by " the Moor ", and as much love as could well be made, considering the time, place and circumstances.

I need not say that the folly and petulance of [Webster] has tended to all this. If a man is not contented with a pretty woman, and not only runs after any little country girl he meets with, but absolutely boasts of it ; he must not be surprised if others admire that which he knows not how to value. Besides, he literally provoked, and goaded me into it, by something not unlike bullying, *indirect* to be sure, but tolerably obvious : " he *would* do this, and he would do that ", " if any man ", etc., etc., and *he* thought that every " woman " was *his* lawful prize, nevertheless. Oons ! who is this strange monopolist ? It is odd enough, but on other subjects he is like other people, on this he seems infatuated. If he had been rational, and not prated of his pursuits, I should have gone on very well, as I did at Middleton. Even now, I shan't quarrel with him if I can help it ; but one or two of his speeches have blackened the blood about my heart, and curdled the milk of kindness. If put to the proof, I shall behave like other people, I presume.

I have heard from A[nnabella], but her letter to me is *melancholy*, about her old friend Miss My's departure, etc., etc. I wonder who will have her at last ; her letter to you is *gay* you say ; that to me must have been written at the same time ; the little demure nonjuror !

I wrote to C[aroline] the other day, for I was afraid she might repeat last year's epistle, and make it *circular* among my friends.

Good evening, I am now going to *billiards*.

Ever y^{rs}, B.

P.S. 6 o'clock.—This business is growing serious, and I think *Platonism* in some peril. There has been very nearly a scene, almost an *hysteric*, and really without cause, for I was conducting myself with (to me) very irksome decorum. Her expressions astonish me, so young and cold as she appeared. But these professions must end as usual, and *would* I think *now*, had " l'occasion " been *not* wanting. Had anyone come in during the *tears*, and consequent consolation, all had been spoiled ; we must be more cautious, or ¹ess larmoyante.

P.S. second, 10 o'clock.—I write to you, just escaped from claret and vocification on G—d knows what paper. My landlord is a rare gentleman. He has just proposed to me a bet that *he*, for a certain sum, " wins any given *woman*, against any given *homme* including *all friends* present ", which I de-clined with becoming deference to him, and the rest of the company. Is not this, at the moment, a perfect comedy? I forgot to mention that on his entrance yesterday during the letter scene, it reminded me so much of an awkward passage in " The Way to Keep Him " between Lovemore, Sir Bashful, and my Lady, that, embarrassing as it was, I could hardly help laughing. I hear his voice in the passage ; he wants me to go to a ball at Sheffield, and is talking to me as I write. Good night. I am in the act of praising his pamphlet.

I don't half like your story of *Corinne*, some day I will tell you why, if I can, but at present, good night.

TO LADY MELBOURNE *Newstead Abbey, October 10th, 1813*

MY DEAR L^Y M.,—I write to you from the melancholy mansion of my fathers, where I am dull as the longest deceased of my progenitors. I hate reflection on irrevocable things, and won't now turn sentimentalist. W[ebster] alone accom-panied me here (I return to-morrow to [Aston]). He is now sitting opposite ; and between us are red and white Cham-[pagn]e, Burgundy, two sorts of Claret, and lighter vintages, the relics of my youthful cellar, which is yet in formidable number and famous order. But I leave the wine to him, and prefer conversing soberly with you.

Ah! if you knew what a quiet Mussulman life (except in wine) I led here for a few years. But no matter.

Yesterday I sent you a long letter, and must recur to the same subject which is uppermost in my thoughts. I am as much astonished, but I hope not so much mistaken, as Lord Ogleby at the dénouement or rather commencement of the last week. It has changed my views, my wishes, my hopes, my everything, and will furnish you with additional proof of my weakness. Mine guest (late host) has just been congratulating himself on possessing a partner without *passion*. I don't know, and cannot yet speak with certainty, but I never yet saw more decisive preliminary symptoms.

As I am apt to take people at their word, on receiving my answer, that whatever the weakness of her heart might be, I should never derive further proof of it than the confession, instead of pressing the point, I told her that I was willing to be hers on her own terms, and should never attempt to infringe upon the conditions. I said this without pique, and believing her perfectly in earnest for the time; but in the midst of our mutual professions, or, to use her own expression, " more than mutual ", she bursts into an agony of crying, and at such a time, and in such a place, as rendered such a scene particularly perilous to both—her sister in the next room, and ——— not far off. Of course I said and did almost everything proper on the occasion, and fortunately we restored sunshine in time to prevent anyone from perceiving the cloud that had darkened our horizon. She says she is convinced that my own declaration was produced solely because I perceived her previous penchant, which by-the-bye, as I think I said to you before, I neither perceived nor expected. I really did not suspect her of a predilection for anyone, and even now in public, with the exception of those little indirect, yet mutually understood—I don't know how and it is unnecessary to name, or describe them—her conduct is as coldly correct as her still, fair, Mrs. L[amb]-like [1] aspect. She, however, managed to give me a note and to receive another, and a ring before [Webster]'s very face, and yet she is a thorough devotee, and takes prayers, morning and evening, besides being measured for a new Bible once a quarter.

[1] Mrs. George Lamb, Lady Caroline's sister-in-law.

The only alarming thing is that [Webster] complains of her aversion from being beneficial to population and posterity. If this is an invariable maxim, I shall lose my labour. Be this as it may, she owns to more than I ever heard from any woman within the time, and I shan't take [Webster]'s word any more for her feelings than I did for that celestial comparison, which I once mentioned. I think her eye, her change of colour, and the trembling of her hand, and above all her devotion, tell a different tale.

Good night. We return to-morrow, and now I drink your health; you are my only correspondent, and I believe friend.

Ever yours, B.

TO LADY MELBOURNE *[Aston] October 11th, 1813*

MY DEAR L*ᴰʸ* M.,—C[aroline] is angry with me for having written by the *post* not a *very cold* letter, but below (it seems) her freezing point; pray say something—anything to prevent any of the old absurdities. Her letter arrived during my absence at N[ewstead] with a never sufficiently to be confounded seal, with C. at full length on the malignant wax; this must have been to answer the purpose it effected; at any rate, the person who opened the *bag* was the last I wished to see the *impression*, and it is not yet *effaced*, but it shall be—this is not to be endured. That my " chienne of a star ", as Captain Raggado says, should have produced such an incident, and at such a time !

I have written to you so much, and so frequently, that you must be sick of the sight of my scrawls. I believe all the *stars* are no better than they should be. [Webster] is on the verge of a precious scrape, his quondam *tutor !* and ally, who has done him some not very reputable services since his marriage, writing, I believe his billets, and assisting him to those to whom they were addressed, being now discarded, threatens a development, etc. [Webster] consults me on the subject ! Of this I shall take no advantage in another quarter, however convenient; if I gain my point it shall be as fairly as such things will admit. It is odd enough that his name has never hitherto been taken in vain by her or me. I have told him that if the discovery is inevitable, his best way is to antici-pate it, and sue for an act of indemnity: if she likes him she will forgive, and if she don't like him, it don't matter whether she does or no.

From me she shall never hear of it.

It is three in the morning, and I cannot rest, but I must try. I have been at N[ewstead] and between that and this my mind is in a state of chaotic inaction; but you won't pity me, and I don't deserve it. Was there ever such a slave to impulse.

As y^{rs} ever, B.

Monday Afternoon

I am better to-day, but not much advanced. I began the week so well that I thought the conclusion would have been more decisive. But the topography of this house is not the most favourable. I wonder how my father managed; but he had it not till L^y Carmarthen[1] came with it too. We shall be at Newstead again, the whole party for a week, in a few days, and there the genii of the place will be perhaps more propitious. *He* haunts me—here he is again, and here are a party of purple stockings come to dine. Oh, that accursed pamphlet! I have not read it; what shall I say to the author, now in the room? Thank the stars which I yesterday abused, he is diverted by the mirror opposite, and is now surveying with great complacency himself—he is gone!

Your letter has arrived, but it is evidently written before my last three have been delivered. Adieu, for the present. I must dress, and have got to *sheer* one of those precious curls on which you say I set so high a value; and I cannot, and *would* not, play the same pass you may laughingly remember on a similar occasion with C. My proselyte is so young a beginner that you won't wonder at these exchanges and mummeries. You are right, she is " very pretty ", and not so inanimate as I imagined, and must at least be allowed an excellent taste ! !

---

[1] Captain John Byron's first wife. Divorced by Lord Carmarthen, she married Captain Byron and became the mother of Augusta.

10 o'clock

Nearly a scene (always *nearly*) at dinner. There is a Lady Sitwell, a wit and blue; and, what is more to the purpose, a dark, tall, fierce-looking, conversable personage. As it is usual to separate the women at table, I was under the necessity of placing myself between her and the sister, and was seated, and in the agonies of conjecture whether the dish before me required carving, when my little Platonist exclaimed, " Ld Byron, *this* is your place ". I stared, and before I had time to reply, she repeated, looking like C. when *gentle* (for she is very unlike that fair creature when angry), " Ld Byron, change places with Catherine ". I did, and very willingly, though awkwardly; but " the Moor " (mine host) roared out, " B[yron], that is the most ungallant thing I ever beheld ". Lady Catherine by way of mending matters, answered, " Did you not hear Frances ask him? " *He* has looked like the Board of *Green* Cloth ever since, and is now mustering wine and spirits for a lecture to her, and a squabble with me; he had better let it alone, for I am in a pestilent humour at this present writing, and shall certainly disparage his eternal " *pamphlet* ".

Good even. I solicit your good wishes in all good deeds, and your occasional remembrance.

TO LADY MELBOURNE *October 13th, 1813*

My dear L^y M.,—You must pardon the quantity of my letters, and much of the *quality* also, but I have really no other *confidential* correspondent on earth, and much to say which may call forth the advice which has so often been to me of essential service. Anything, you will allow, is better than the *last*; and I cannot exist without some object of attachment. You will laugh at my perpetual *changes*, but recollect, the circumstances which have broken off the last three and don't exactly attribute their conclusion to caprice. I think you will at least admit, whatever C[aroline] may assert, that I did not use her ill, though I find *her own* story, even in this part of the world, to be the *genuine* narrative; as to L^y O[xford], that I did to please you, and luckily, finding it pleasant to myself also, and very useful to C., it might have lasted longer, but for the voyage. I spare you the third.

I am so spoilt by intellectual *drams* that I begin to believe that *danger* and *difficulty* render these things more piquant to my taste. As far as the *former* goes, C. might have suited me very well, but though we may admire *drams*, nobody is particularly fond of aqua fortis; at least, I should have liked it a *little diluted*, the liquid I believe which is now slowly mingling in my cup. In the meantime, let us laugh while we can, for I see no reason why you should be tormented with sentimental or solid sorrows of your acquaintance. I think you will allow that I have as little of that affectation as any person of similar pursuits.

I mentioned to you yesterday a laughable occurrence at dinner. This morning *he* burst forth with a homily upon the subject to the *two* and myself, instead of taking us separately (like the last of the *Horatii* with the *Curiatii*). You will easily suppose with such odds he had the worst of it, and the satisfaction of being laughed at into the bargain. Serious as I am—or seem,—I really cannot frequently keep my countenance: yesterday, *before my face*, they disputed about their apartments at N[ewstead], *she* insisting that her sister should share her room, and he very properly, but heinously out of place, maintaining, and proving to his own satisfaction, that none but husbands have any legal claim to divide their spouse's pillow. You may suppose, notwithstanding the ludicrous effect of the scene, I felt and looked a little uncomfortable; this she must have seen—for, of course, I said not a word—and turning round at the close of the dialogue, she whispered, " N'importe, this is all nothing ", an ambiguous sentence which I am puzzled to translate; but, as it was meant to console me, I was very glad to hear it, though quite unintelligible.

As far as I can pretend to judge of her disposition and character—I will say, of course, I am partial—she is, you know, very handsome, and very gentle, though sometimes decisive; fearfully romantic, and singularly warm in her *affections*; but I should think of a *cold* temperament, yet I have my doubts on that point, too; accomplished (as all decently educated women are), and clever, though her style a little too *German*;

no dashing nor desperate talker, but never—and I have watched in *mixed* conversation—saying a silly thing (*duet dialogues* in course between young and Platonic people must be varied with a little chequered absurdity); good tempered (always excepting L^y O[xford], which was, outwardly, the *best* I ever beheld), and jealous as *myself*—the ne plus ultra of green-eyed monstrosity; seldom abusing other people, but listening to it with great patience. These qualifications, with an unassuming and sweet voice, and very soft manner, constitute the *bust* (all I can yet pretend to model) of my present idol.

You, who know me and my weakness so well, will not be surprised when I say that I am totally absorbed in this passion —that I am even ready to take a *flight* if necessary, and as she says, " We cannot part ", it is no impossible dénouement— though as yet *one* of us at least does not think of it. W. will probably want to cut my throat, which would not be a difficult task, for I trust I should not return the fire of a man I had injured, though I could not refuse him the pleasure of trying me as a target. But I am not sure I shall not have more work in that way. There is a friend in the house who looks a little suspicious; he can only conjecture, but if he *Iagonizes*, or finds, or makes mischief, let him look to it. To W[ebster] I am decidedly wrong, yet he almost provoked me into it—*he* loves other women; at least he follows them; *she* evidently did not love him, even before. I came here with no plan, no intention of the kind as my former letters will prove to *you* (the only person to whom I care about proving it) and have not yet been here *ten* days—a week yesterday, on recollection: you cannot be more astonished than I am how, and why all this has happened.

All my correspondences, and every other business, are at a standstill; I have not answered A., no, nor B., nor C., nor any *initial* except your own, you will wish me to be less troublesome to *that one*, and I shall now begin to draw at longer dates upon y^r patience.

Ever yours, B.

P.S.—*always P.S.* I begged you to pacify C[aroline], who is pettish about what she calls a *cold* letter; it was not so, but she evidently has been too long quiet; she threatens me with grow-

ing very bad, and says that if so, " I am the sole cause ".   This I
should regret, but she is in no danger ; no one in his senses will
run the risk, till her late exploits are forgotten.   Her last I
shall not answer ; it was very silly in me to write at all ; but
I did it with the best intention, like the Wiseacre in " The
Rovers ",—" Let us by a song conceal our purposes ", you
remember in the " Anti-Jacobin ".   I have gone through a
catechism about her, without abusing or betraying her ; this
is not exactly the way to recommend myself ; I have generally
found that the *successor* likes to hear both of the last regnante.
But I really did not, notwithstanding the temptation.

TO LADY MELBOURNE   *October 14th, 1813*

But this is " le premier pas ", my dear L^y M., at least I
think so, and perhaps you will be of my opinion when you
consider the *age*, the *country*, and the short time since such *pas*
became probable ; I believe little but " l'occasion manque ",
and to that many things are tending.   He [Webster] is a little
indirect blusterer who neither knows what he would have, nor
what he deserves.   To-day at breakfast (I was too late for the
scene) he attacked *both* the girls in such a manner, no one
knew why, or wherefore, that one had left the room, and the
other. had half a mind to leave the house ; this too before
servants, and the other guest!   On my appearance the storm
blew over, but the narrative was detailed to me subsequently
by one of the sufferers.   You may be sure that I shall not
" consider *self* ", nor create a squabble while it can be avoided ;
on the contrary I have been endeavouring to serve him essentially (except on the *one* point, and there I was goaded into
it by his own absurdities), and to extricate him from some
difficulties of various descriptions.   Of course all obligations
are cancelled between two persons in our circumstances, but
that I shall not dwell upon ; of the other I shall try to make an
" affaire réglée " ; if that don't succeed we shall probably go
off together ; but *she* only shall make me resign the hope.   As
for him he may convert his antlers into *powder-horns* and
welcome, and such he has announced as his intention when

"*any* man at *any* time, etc. etc. ", " he would not give *him* a chance, but exterminate *him* without suffering defence ". Do you know I was fool enough to lose my temper at this circuitous specimen of Bobadil jealousy, and tell him and the other (there are a brace, lion and jackal) that *I*, not their roundabout *he*, desired no better than to put these " epithets of war ", with which their sentences were " horribly stuffed ", to the proof. This was silly and suspicious, but my liver could bear it no longer. My poor little *Helen* tells me that there never was such a *temper* and *talents*, that the marriage was *not* one of attachment, that—in short, *my* descriptions fade before hers, all foolish fellows are alike, but this has a patent for his cap and bells.

The scene between Sir B. and Lovemore I remember, but the one I alluded to was the letter of Lovemore to L^y Constant —there is no comedy after all like real life. We have progressively improved into a less spiritual species of tenderness, but the seal is not yet fixed, though the wax is preparing for the impression. There *ought* to be an excellent *occasion* to-morrow ; but who can command circumstances? The most we can do is to avail ourselves of them.

Publicly I have been cautious enough, and actually declined a dinner where they went, because I thought something *intelligible* might be seen or suspected. I regretted, but regret it less, for I hear one of the Fosters was there, and they be cousins and gossips of our good friends the D.'s. Good-night. Do *you fear* to write to *me*? Are *these* epistles, or your answers in any peril *here*? I must remember, however, the advice of a sage personage to me while abroad—take it in their English— " Remember, milor, that *delicaci* ensure every succès."

Y^{rs} ever, B.

TO LADY MELBOURNE   *Newstead Abbey, October 17th, 1813*

MY DEAR LADY M.,—The whole party are here—and now to my narrative. But first I must tell you that I am rather unwell, owing to a folly of last night. About midnight, after deep and drowsy potations, I took it into my head to empty my *skull cup*, which holds rather better than a bottle of claret, at *one draught*, and nearly died the death of Alexander—which I shall be content to do when I have achieved his conquests. I had just sense enough left to feel that I was not fit to join the ladies, and went to bed, where, my valet tells me, that I was first convulsed, and afterwards so motionless, that he thought, " Good night to Marmion ". I don't know how I came to do so very silly a thing; but I believe my guests were boasting, and " company, villainous company, hath been the spoil of me ". I detest drinking in general, and beg your pardon for this excess. I *can't* do so any more.

To my theme. You were right. I have been a little too sanguine as to the *conclusion*—but hear. One day, left entirely to ourselves, was nearly fatal—another such *victory*, and with Pyrrhus we were lost—it came to this. " I am entirely at your *mercy*. I own it. I give myself up to you. I am not *cold*— whatever I seem to others; but I know that I cannot bear the reflection hereafter. Do not imagine that these are mere words. I tell you the truth—now act as you will." Was I wrong? I spared her. There was a something so very peculiar in her manner—a kind of mild decision—no scene—not even a struggle; but still I know not what, that convinced me that she was serious. It was not the mere " *No* ", which one has heard forty times before, and always with the same accent; but the *tone*, and the aspect—yet I sacrificed much—the hour *two* in the morning—away—the Devil whispering that it was mere *verbiage*, etc. And yet I know not whether I can regret it—she seems so very thankful for my forbearance—a proof, at least, that she was not playing merely the usual decorous reluctance, which is sometimes so tiresome on these occasions.

You ask if I am prepared to go " all lengths ". If you mean by " all lengths " anything including duel, or divorce? I answer, *Yes*. I love her. If I did not, and much too, I should have been more selfish on the occasion before mentioned. I have offered to go away with her, and her answer, whether sincere or not, is " that on *my account* she declines it ". In the meantime we are all as wretched as possible; he scolding on *account* of *unaccountable* melancholy; the sister very suspicious, but rather amused—the friend very suspicious too (why I know not), not at all amused—il Marito something like Lord

Chesterfield in De Grammont, putting on a martial physiognomy, prating with his worthy ally; swearing at servants, sermonizing both sisters; and buying sheep; but never quitting her side now; so that we are in despair. *I* am very feverish, restless, and silent, as indeed seems to be the tacit agreement of everyone else. In short I can foresee nothing—it may end in nothing; but here are half a dozen persons very much occupied, and two, if not three, in great perplexity; and, as far as I can judge, so we must continue.

She *don't* and *won't* live with him, and they have been so far separate for a long time; therefore I have nothing to answer for on that point. Poor thing—she is either the most *artful* or *artless* of her age (20) I ever encountered. She *owns* to so much, and perpetually says, " Rather than you should be angry ", or " Rather than you should like anyone else, I will do whatever you please "; " I won't speak to this, that, or the other if you dislike it ", and throws, or seems to throw, herself so entirely upon my discretion in every respect, that it disarms me quite; but I am really wretched with the perpetual conflict with myself. Her health is so very delicate; she is so thin and pale, and seems to have lost her appetite so entirely, that I doubt her living much longer. This is also her own opinion. But these fancies are common to all who are not very happy; if she were once my wife, or likely to be so, a warm climate should be the first resort, nevertheless, for her recovery.

The most perplexing—and yet I can't prevail upon myself to give it up—is the caressing system. In her it appears perfectly childish, and I do think innocent; but it really puzzles all the Scipio about me to confine myself to the laudable portion of these endearments.

What a cursed situation I have thrust myself into! Potiphar (it used to be O[xford]'s name) putting some stupid question to me the other day, I told him that I rather admired the *sister*, and what does he? but tell her this; and his *wife* too, who a little too hastily asked him " if he was mad? " which put him to demonstration that a man ought not to be asked if he was mad, for relating that a friend thought his wife's sister a pretty woman. Upon this topic he held forth with great fervour for a customary period. I wish he had a quinsey.

Tell L[or]d H[ollan]d that Clarke is the name, and Craven

Street (No. forgotten) the residence—may be heard of at
Trin. Coll.—excellent man—able physician—shot a friend in
a duel (about his sister) and I believe killed him professionally
afterwards. L⁴ H. may have him for self or friends. I don't
know where I am going—my mind is a chaos. I always am
setting all upon single stakes, and this is one. Your story of the
Frenchman Matta, in "Grammont," and the Marquis.
Heigh ho! Good night. Address to Aston.

Ever yrs., B.

P.S.—My stay is quite uncertain—a moment may overturn
everything; but you shall hear—happen what may—nothing
or something.

TO LADY MELBOURNE   *Northampton, October 19th, 1813*

MY DEAR LADY M.,—[Webster] and I are thus far on our
way to town—he was seized with a sudden fit of friendship, and
would accompany me—or rather, finding that some business
could not conveniently be done without me, he thought proper
to assume yᵉ appearance of it. He is not exactly the companion
I wished to take; it is really laughable when you think of the
other—a kind of pig in a poke. Nothing but squabbles between
them for the last three days, and at last he rose up with a solemn
and mysterious air, and spake, "Lʸ [Frances], you have at
last rendered an explanation necessary between me and Ld.
B[yron], which must take place". I stared, and knowing that
it is the custom of country gentlemen (if Farquhar is correct)
to apprize their moieties of such intentions, and being also a
little out of humour and conscience, I thought a crisis must
ensue, and answered very quietly that "he would find me in
such a room at his leisure ready to hear, and reply". "Oh!"
says he, "I shall choose my own time." I wondered that he
did not choose his *own* house, too, but walked away, and
waited for him. All this mighty prelude led only to what he
called an explanation for *my satisfaction*, that whatever appearances were, *he* and *she* were on the very best terms, that she
loved him so much, and he her, it was impossible not to dis-
agree upon *tender* points, and for fear a man who, etc., etc.,

should suppose that marriage was not the happiest of all possible estates, he had taken this resolution of never quarrelling without letting me know that he was the best husband, and most fortunate person in existence. I told him he had fully convinced me, that it was utterly impossible people who liked each other could behave with more interesting suavity—and so on. Yesterday morning, on our going (I pass over the scene, which shook me, I assure you), " B.," quoth he, " I owe to you the most unhappy moments of my life ". I begged him to tell me how, that I might either sympathize, or put him out of his pain. " Don't you see how the poor girl *doats* on me " (he replied) ; " when I quit her but for a week, as you perceive, she is absolutely overwhelmed, and you stayed so long, and I necessarily for you, that she is in a worse state than I ever saw her in before, even before we married ! "

Here we are—I could not return to A[ston] unless he had asked me—it is true he did, but in such a manner as I should not accept. What will be the end, I know not. I have left everything to *her*, and would have rendered all further *plots* superfluous by the most conclusive step ; but she wavered, and escaped. Perhaps so have I—at least it is as well to think so— yet it is not over.

Whatever I may feel, you know me too well to think I shall plague my friends with long faces or elegies.

My dear Lady M., Ever Yours, B.

TO LADY MELBOURNE *October 21st, 1813*

My dear L*y* M.,—You may well be surprised, but I had more reasons than one or two. Either [Webster] had taken it into his notable head, or wished to put it into mine, aye, and worse still, into y*e* girls, also ; that I was a pretendant to the *hand* of the sister of " the Lady " whom I had nearly—but no matter—(to continue Archer's speech with the variation of one word) " 'tis a cursed *fortnight's* piece of work, and there's an end ". This brilliant notion, besides widening y*e* breach between him and me, did not add to the harmony of the two females ; at least my idol was not pleased with the prospect of any transfer of incense to another altar. She was so unguarded, after telling me too fifty times to "take care of Catherine", "that she could conceal nothing, etc., etc.", as to give me a very unequivocal proof of her own imprudence, in a carriage —(dusk to be sure) before her face—and yet with all this, and much more, she was the most tenacious personage either from fear, or weakness, or delicate health, or G—d knows what, that with the vigilance of no less than three Arguses in addition, it was utterly impossible, save once, to be decisive—and then— tears and tremors and prayers, which I am not yet old enough to find piquant in such cases, prevented me from making her wretched. I do detest everything which is not perfectly mutual, and any subsequent reproaches (as I know by one former long ago bitter experience) would heap coals of fire upon my head. Do you remember what Rousseau says to somebody, "If you would know that you are beloved, watch your lover when he leaves you"—to me the most pleasing moments have generally been, when there is nothing more to be required; in short, the subsequent repose without satiety— which Lewis never dreamed of in that poem of his, "Desire and Pleasure"—when you are secure of the past, yet without regret or disappointment; of this there was no prospect with her, she had so much more dread of the d—l, than gratitude for his kindness; and I am not yet sufficiently in his good graces to indulge my own passions at the certain misery of another. Perhaps after all, I was her dupe—if so—I am the dupe also of the few good feelings I could ever boast of, but here perhaps I am my own dupe too, in attributing to a good motive what may be quite otherwise.

[Webster] is a most extraordinary person; he has just left me, and a snuff-box with a flaming inscription, after squabbling with me for these last ten days! and I too, have been of some real service to *him*,[1] which I merely mention to mark the in- consistency of human nature. I have brought off a variety of foolish trophies (foolish indeed without victory), such as epistles, and lockets, which look as if she were in earnest; but she would not go off *now*, nor render going off unnecessary. Am I not candid to own my want of success, when I might have assumed the airs of an "aimable Vainqueur"? but that

---

[1] Byron had lent Webster £1000.

is so paltry and so common—without cause, too; and what I hear, and see every day, that I would not, even to gain the point I have missed. I assure you no one knows but you one particle of this business, and you always must know everything concerning me. It is hard if I may not have one friend. Believe me, none will ever be so valued, and none ever was so trusted, by

> Yours ever, B.

TO LADY MELBOURNE   *November 22nd, 1813*

My dear L^y M.,—C[aroline] has at last done a very good-natured thing; she sent me Holmes's picture for a *friend leaving England*, to which friend it is now making the best of its way. You do not go to M[iddleton] till 28th, and I shall procrastinate accordingly. Yesterday the Lady Ossulstone sent for me to complain of you *all*. We had met at Ld Holland's the night before, and she asserted that the " extreme gravity of my countenance " made her and Ld O. believe that I had some whim about that slip of the pen-*knife* of *C.'s* and the consequent rumours, etc., etc., and some resentment about her in particular; to all of which I pleaded ignorance and innocence. She says Lady Blarney is a very noxious person, and hates her, and that none of you have taken the least notice of her since; that she is the most *discreet* of women, to prove which she produced an epistle of L^y Somebody's, *wondering* (it was but *three* hours after) she had not *already* written a full and true account of it to her!! I thought I should have laughed in her pretty black face—and, in short, we are all very repulsive sort of persons, and have not behaved well to her, nor anybody else. Remember all *this* (like all our *this*-es) is *entre nous*; and so there is an end of the matter. We had had a kind of squabble at the Argyle, which I could not help tormenting her a little by reminding her, not of *that*, but that evening, when we were all wrong-paired. *She* wanted to sit by Mildmay at supper, and I wanted to have been next that Kashmeer Butterfly of the " Blues "—Lady Charlemont—or in short, anybody but a person who had serious concerns to think of. Everybody else was coupled much in the same way; in short, Noah's ark *upset* had been but a type of the *pairing* of our supper-table. L^y Holland and I go on very well; her *unqualified* praises of you, proving their *sincerity!* She is the first woman I ever heard praise another *entirely.* L^y B[essborough] had better let us remain undisturbed, for if L^y H[olland] thinks that it annoys her there will be no end to ye intimacy. I have taken the half-weeks (3 days in each) of Lord Salisbury's box at Covent Garden, and there, when C. is in town, we can always talk for an hour on emergency.

The occasional oddity of Ph.'s letters has amused me much. The simplicity of her cunning, and her exquisite reasons. She vindicates her treachery to [Webster] thus : after condemning deceit in general, and hers in particular, she says : " but then remember it is to deceive ' un marito ', and to prevent all the unpleasant consequences, etc., etc."; and she says this in perfect persuasion that she has a full conception of the " fitness of things ", and the " beauty of virtue ", and " the social compact ", as Philosopher Square has it. Again, she desires me to write to *him kindly,* for she believes he cares for nobody but *me!* Besides, she will then hear *of* when she can't hear *from* me. Is not all this a comedy? Next to Ld Ossulstone's *voucher* for her discretion, it has enlivened my ethical studies on the human mind beyond 50 volumes. How admirably we accommodate our reasons to our wishes !

She concludes by denominating that respectable man *Argus,* a very irreverent appellation. If we can both hold out till spring, perhaps he may have occasion for his optics. After all " it is to deceive un marito ". Does not this expression convey to you the strongest mixture of right and wrong? A really guilty person could not have used it, or rather they would, *but* in different words. I find she has not the *but,* and that makes much difference if you consider it. The experienced would have said it is " *only* deceiving *him* ", thinking of themselves. She makes a *merit* of it on his account and mine.

The Dutch have taken Holland, and got Bernadotte and Orange, the Stork and King Log at once, in their froggery.[1]

Ever y^rs, B.

---

[1] In 1813 the Dutch revolted against Napoleon and declared their independence, electing the Prince of Orange as their constitutional sovereign. Bernadotte, King of Sweden, also joined the allies.

I must quote to you correctly—" How easily mankind are deceived. *May he be always deceived!* and I, alas, am the base instrument of deception ; but in this instance *concealment* is not a *crime*, for it preserves the Peace of ' d'un marito ' : the contrary would ", etc. I have been arguing on wrong premises ; but no matter, the *marked* lines are quite as good.

TO LADY MELBOURNE   *Monday Even.* [*Nov. 1813*]

A " person of the least consequence " ! You wrong yourself there, my dear L^dy M.—and so far she is right—you know very well, and so do I, that you can make me do whatever you please without reluctance—I am sure there exists no one to whom I feel half so much obliged—and for whom (gratitude apart) I entertain a greater regard. With regard to her, I certainly love—and in that case it has always been my lot to be entirely at the disposal of " la regnante " ; their caprices I cannot reason upon—and only obey them. In favour of my acquaintance with you there is however a special clause, and nothing shall make me cancel it, I promise you. I meant to have paid you a visit on Saturday in your box—but I thought it possible C[aroline] might be there—from her I find two epistles—in the last the old story of the interview, to which if she still harps upon it I have no objection—she desires me not to go to L^dy Ossulstone's—I was not asked—she was there, I presume, for she talks of going away if I came. But I can't help laughing at the coincidence of objections in the late and present to my going there—both unnecessary—for the presence of the one or the absence of the other would operate sufficiently as a dissuasive. I am just returned from Harrow, where I managed to get a headache, which that I may not communicate I will close this sheet—ever, L^dy M.,

Yours most truly, B.

P.S.—C.'s letter is half in rhyme—an additional proof that she is not in earnest—at least I know from experience one may begin with it—or end—when the subject is dead or changed and indifferent, but during the meridian it is improbable—all is happiness and nonsense.

TO THOMAS MOORE   *November 30, 1813*

Since I last wrote to you, much has occurred, good, bad, and indifferent,—not to make me forget you, but to prevent me from reminding you of one who, nevertheless, has often thought of you, and to whom *your* thoughts, in many a measure, have frequently been a consolation. We were once very near neighbours this autumn; and a good and bad neighbourhood it has proved to me. Suffice it to say, that your French quotation was confoundedly to the purpose,—though very *unexpectedly* pertinent, as you may imagine by what I *said* before, and my silence since. However, " Richard's himself again ", and except all night and some part of the morning, I don't think very much about the matter.

All convulsions end with me in rhyme; and to solace my midnights, I have scribbled another Turkish story—not a Fragment—which you will receive soon after this. It does not trench upon your kingdom in the least, and if it did, you would soon reduce me to my proper boundaries. You will think, and justly, that I run some risk of losing the little I have gained in fame, by this further experiment on public patience; but I have really ceased to care on that head. I have written this, and published it, for the sake of the *employment*,—to wring my thoughts from reality, and take refuge in " imaginings ", however " horrible "; 'and, as to success! those who succeed will console me for a failure—excepting yourself and one or two more, whom luckily I love too well to wish one leaf of their laurels a tint yellower. This is the work of a week, and will be the reading of an hour to you, or even less,—and so, let it go * * * *.

P.S.—Ward and I *talk* of going to Holland. I want to see how a Dutch canal looks after the Bosphorus. Pray respond.

TO THOMAS MOORE   *December 8, 1813*

Your letter, like all the best, and even kindest things in this world, is both painful and pleasing. But, first, to what sits nearest. Do you know I was actually about to dedicate to you,—not in a formal inscription, as to one's *elders*,—but through a short prefatory letter, in which I boasted myself your intimate, and held forth the prospect of *your* poem; when, lo! the recollection of your strict injunctions of secrecy as to the said poem, more than *once* repeated by word and letter, flashed upon me, and marred my intents. I could have no motive for repressing my own desire of alluding to you (and not a day passes that I do not think and talk of you), but an idea that you might, yourself, dislike it. You cannot doubt my sincere admiration, waving personal friendship for the present, which, by the by, is not less sincere and deep rooted. I have you by rote and by heart; of which *ecce signum!* When I was at Aston, on my first visit, I have a habit, in passing my time a good deal alone, of—I won't call it singing, for that I never attempt except to myself—but of uttering, to what I think tunes, your "Oh breathe not", "When the last glimpse", and "When he who adores thee", with others of the same minstrel;—they are my matins and vespers. I assuredly did not intend them to be overheard, but, one morning, in comes, not *La Donna*, but *Il Marito*, with a very grave face, saying, "Byron, I must request you won't sing any more, at least of *those* songs". I stared, and said, "Certainly, but why?"— "To tell you the truth," quoth he, "they make my wife *cry*, and so melancholy, that I wish her to hear no more of them."

Now, my dear M., the effect must have been from your words, and certainly not my music. I merely mention this foolish story to show you how much I am indebted to you for even my pastimes. A man may praise and praise, but no one recollects but that which pleases—at least, in composition. Though I think no one equal to you in that department, or in satire,—and surely no one was ever so popular in both,—I certainly am of opinion that you have not yet done all *you* can do, though more than enough for any one else. I want, and the world expects, a longer work from you; and I see in you what I never saw in poet before, a strange diffidence of your own powers, which I cannot account for, and which must be unaccountable, when a *Cossac* like me can appal a *cuirassier*. Your story I did not, could not, know,—I thought only of a Peri. I wish you had confided in me, not for your sake, but mine, and to prevent the world from losing a much better poem than my own, but which, I yet hope, this *clashing* will not even now deprive them of. Mine is the work of a week, written, *why* I have partly told you, and partly I cannot tell you by letter—some day I will.

Go on—I shall really be very unhappy if I at all interfere with you. The success of mine is yet problematical; though the public will probably purchase a certain quantity, on the presumption of their own propensity for *The Giaour* and such " horrid mysteries ". The only advantage I have is being on the spot; and that merely amounts to saving me the trouble of turning over books which I had better read again. If *your chamber* was furnished in the same way, you have no need to *go there* to describe—I mean only as to *accuracy*—because I drew it from recollection.

This last thing of mine *may* have the same fate, and I assure you I have great doubts about it. But, even if not, its little day will be over before you are ready and willing. Come out— " screw your courage to the sticking-place ". Except the *Post Bag* (and surely you cannot complain of a want of success there), you have not been *regularly* out for some years. No man stands higher,—whatever you may think on a rainy day, in your provincial retreat. " Aucun homme, dans aucune langue, n'a été, peut-être, plus complètement le poëte du cœur et le poëte des femmes. Les critiques lui reprochent de n'avoir représenté le monde ni tel qu'il est, ni tel qu'il doit être ; *mais les femmes répondent qu'il l'a représenté tel qu'elles le désirent.*"—I should have thought Sismondi had written this for you instead of Metastasio.

Write to me, and tell me of *yourself*. Do you remember what Rousseau said to some one—" Have we quarrelled? you have talked to me often, and never once mentioned yourself ".

P.S.—The last sentence is an indirect apology for my egotism,—but I believe in letters it is allowed. I wish it was *mutual*. I have met with an odd reflection in Grimm ; it shall not—at least the bad part—be applied to you or me, though *one* of us has certainly an indifferent name—but this it is :— " Many people have the reputation of being wicked, with whom we should be too happy to pass our lives ". I need not add it is a woman's saying—a Mademoiselle de Sommery's.

TO E. D. CLARKE   *Decr. 15th, 1813*

My DEAR SIR,[1]—Your very kind letter is the more agreeable because, setting aside talents, judgement and the " laudari a laudato " &c, *you* have been on the spot. *You* have seen and described more of the East than any of your predecessors— I need not say how ably and successfully—and (excuse the *Bathos*) *you* are of the very few who can pronounce how far my *costume* (to use an affected but expressive word) is correct. As to poesy, *that* is, as " Men, Gods and Columns " please to decide upon it ; but I am sure that I am anxious to have an observer's, particularly a *famous* observer's, testimony on the fidelity of my *manners* and *dresses* ; and as far as memory and an Oriental twist in my imagination have permitted, it has been my endeavour to present to the Franks a sketch of that with which you *have* and will present them a complete picture [*sic*]. It was with this notion that I felt compelled to make my hero and heroine *relatives*, as you well know that none else could *there* obtain that degree of intercourse leading to genuine affection. I had nearly made them rather too much akin to each other ; and, though the wild passions of the East, and some great examples in Alfieri, Ford and Schiller (to stop short of Anti- quity) might have pleaded in favour of a copyist, yet the times and the *North* (*not* Frederic but our climate) inclined me to alter their consanguinity and confine them to cousinship. I also wished to try my hand on a female character in Zuleika, and have endeavoured, as far as the grossness of our masculine ideas will allow, to preserve her purity without impairing the ardour of her attachment. As to *criticism*, I have been reviewed about 150 times, praised and abused. I will not say that I am become indifferent to either eulogy or condemnation ; but for some years at least I have felt grateful for the former and have never attempted to answer the latter. For success equal to the first efforts I had and have no hope. The novelty was over, and the " Bride ", like all other brides, must suffer or rejoice for and with her husband. By the bye, I have used Bride

---

[1] Edward Daniel Clarke, Professor of Mineralogy at Cambridge and well- known traveller. He was the author of *Travels in Various Countries of Europe, Asia and Africa*, in six volumes. Byron had met and discussed Greece with him during 1811. The poem to which Byron refers is *The Bride of Abydos*.

Turkishly as *affianced*, not married; and so far it is an English *bull*, which I trust will be at least a comfort to all Hibernians not bigotted to monopoly. You are good enough to mention your *quotations* in your 3rd vol. I shall not only be indebted to it for the renewal of the high gratification received from the 2 first but for presenting my relics embalmed in your own spices, and ensuring me readers to whom I could not otherwise have aspired.

I called on you as bounden by duty and inclination when last in your neighbourhood; but I shall always take my *chance* —you surely would not have me inflict upon a formal annunciation. I am proud of your friendship, but not so proud as to break in upon your better avocations.

I trust that Mrs. Clarke is well. I have never had the honour of presentation; but I have heard so much of her in many quarters that any notice she is pleased to take of my productions is not less gratifying than my thanks are sincere both to her and you. By all accounts I may safely congratulate you on the possession of a " Bride " whose personal and mental accomplishments are more than poetical.

Ever yrs. mostly truly, BYRON.

P.S.—Murray has sent, or will send, a double copy of the Bride and Giaour. In the last are some lengthy additions. Pray accept these according to old custom " from the Author " to one of his better brethren. Your *Persian* or any memorial will be a most agreeable, and it is my fault if not a useful, present.

JOURNAL: NOVEMBER 14, 1813–APRIL 19, 1814

IF this had been begun ten years ago, and faithfully kept ! ! !— heigho ! there are too many things I wish never to have remembered, as it is. Well,—I have had my share of what are called the pleasures of this life, and have seen more of the European and Asiatic world than I have made a good use of. They say " Virtue is its own reward ",—it certainly should be paid well for its trouble. At five-and-twenty, when the better part of life is over, one should be *something* ;—and what am I? nothing but five-and-twenty—and the odd months. What have I seen? the same man all over the world,—ay, and woman too. Give *me* a Mussulman who never asks questions, and a she of the same race who saves one the trouble of putting them. But for this same plague—yellow fever—and Newstead delay, I should have been by this time a second time close to the Euxine. If I can overcome the last, I don't so much mind your pestilence ; and, at any rate, the spring shall see me there, —provided I neither marry myself, nor unmarry any one else in the interval. I wish one was—I don't know what I wish. It is odd I never set myself seriously to wishing without attaining it—and repenting. I begin to believe with the good old Magi, that one should only pray for the nation, and not for the individual ;—but, on my principle, this would not be very patriotic.

No more reflections.—Let me see—last night I finished " Zuleika ",[1] my second Turkish Tale. I believe the composition of it kept me alive—for it was written to drive my thoughts from the recollection of—

" Dear sacred name, rest ever unreveal'd."

At least, even here, my hand would tremble to write it. This afternoon I have burnt the scenes of my commenced comedy. I have some idea of expectorating a romance, or rather a tale in prose ;—but what romance could equal the events—

" quæque ipse . . . . . . vidi,
Et quorum pars magna fui."

To-day Henry Byron called on me with my little cousin Eliza. She will grow up a beauty and a plague ; but, in the mean time, it is the prettiest child ! dark eyes and eyelashes, black and long as the wing of a raven. I think she is prettier even than my niece, Georgina,—yet I don't like to think so neither : and though older, she is not so clever.

Dallas called before I was up, so we did not meet. Lewis, too,—who seems out of humour with every thing. What can

---

[1] *The Bride of Abydos*, Byron's first Turkish Tale being *The Giaour*.

be the matter? he is not married—has he lost his own mistress or any other person's wife? Hodgson, too, came. He is going to be married, and he is the kind of man who will be the happier. He has talent, cheerfulness, every thing that can make him a pleasing companion ; and his intended is handsome and young, and all that. But I never see any one much improved by matrimony. All my coupled contemporaries are bald and discontented. W[ordsworth] and S[outhey] have both lost their hair and good humour ; and the last of the two had a good deal to lose. But it don't much signify what falls *off* a man's temples in that state.

Mem. I must get a toy to-morrow for Eliza, and send the device for the seals of myself and * * * * * Mem. too, to call on the Stael and Lady Holland to-morrow, and on * *, who has advised me (without seeing it, by the by) not to publish " Zuleika " ; I believe he is right, but experience might have taught him that not to print is *physically* impossible. No one has seen it but Hodgson and Mr. Gifford. I never in my life *read* a composition, save to Hodgson, as he pays me in kind. It is a horrible thing to do too frequently ;—better print, and they who like may read, and if they don't like, you have the satisfaction of knowing that they have, at least, *purchased* the right of saying so.

I have declined presenting the Debtors' Petition, being sick of parliamentary mummeries. I have spoken thrice ; but I doubt my ever becoming an orator. My first was liked ; the second and third—I don't know whether they succeeded or not. I have never yet set to it *con amore* ;—one must have some excuse to one's self for laziness, or inability, or both, and this is mine. " Company, villanous company, hath been the spoil of me " ;—and then, I have drunk medicines ", not to make me love others, but certainly enough to hate myself.

Two nights ago I saw the tigers sup at Exeter 'Change. Except Veli Pacha's lion in the Morea,—who followed the Arab keeper like a dog,—the fondness of the hyæna for her keeper amused me most. Such a conversazione !—There was a " hippopotamus ", like Lord Liverpool in the face ; and the " Ursine Sloth " had the very voice and manner of my valet— but the tiger talked too much. The elephant took and gave me my money again—took off my hat—opened a door—

trunked a whip—and behaved so well, that I wish he was my butler. The handsomest animal on earth is one of the panthers ; but the poor antelopes were dead. I should hate to see one *here* :—the sight of the *camel* made me pine again for Asia Minor. " *Oh quando te aspiciam ?* "

November 16

Went last night with Lewis [1] to see the first of *Antony and Cleopatra*. It was admirably got up, and well acted—a salad of Shakspeare and Dryden. Cleopatra strikes me as the epitome of her sex—fond, lively, sad, tender, teasing, humble, haughty, beautiful, the devil !—coquettish to the last, as well with the " asp " as with Antony. After doing all she can to persuade him that—but why do they abuse him for cutting off that poltroon Cicero's head ? Did not Tully tell Brutus it was a pity to have spared Antony ? and did he not speak the Philippics ? and are not " *words things* "? and such " *words* " very pestilent " *things* " too ? If he had had a hundred heads, they deserved (from Antony) a rostrum (his was stuck up there) apiece—though, after all, he might as well have pardoned him, for the credit of the thing. But to resume—Cleopatra, after securing him, says, " yet go—it is your interest ", etc.—how like the sex ! and the questions about Octavia—it is woman all over.

To-day received Lord Jersey's invitation to Middleton—to travel sixty miles to meet Madame De Stael ! I once travelled three thousand to get among silent people ; and this same lady writes octavos, and *talks* folios. I have read her books—like most of them, and delight in the last ; so I won't hear it, as well as read.

Read Burns to-day. What would he have been, if a patrician ? We should have had more polish—less force—just as much verse, but no immortality—a divorce and a duel or two, the which had he survived, as his potations must have been less spirituous, he might have lived as long as Sheridan, and out-lived as much as poor Brinsley. What a wreck is that man ! and all from bad pilotage ; for no one had ever better gales, though now and then a little too squally. Poor dear Sherry !

[1] Matthew Gregory (" Monk ") Lewis, frequenter of Holland House and celebrated author of macabre and sadistic tales : elsewhere voted by Byron " a damned bore ".

I shall never forget the day he and Rogers and Moore and I passed together; when *he* talked, and *we* listened, without one yawn, from six till one in the morning.

Got my seals * * * * * *. Have again forgot a plaything for *ma petite cousine* Eliza; but I must send for it to-morrow. I hope Harry will bring her to me. I sent Lord Holland the proofs of the last " *Giaour* ", and " *The Bride of Abydos* ". He won't like the latter, and I don't think that I shall long. It was written in four nights to distract my dreams from * *. Were it not thus, it had never been composed; and had I not done something at that time, I must have gone mad, by eating my own heart,—bitter diet;—Hodgson likes it better than " *The Giaour* ", but nobody else will,—and he never liked the Fragment. I am sure, had it not been for Murray, *that* would never have been published, though the circumstances which are the ground-work make it * * * heigh-ho!

To-night I saw both the sisters of * *; my God! the youngest so like! I thought I should have sprung across the house, and am so glad no one was with me in Lady H.'s box. I hate those likenesses—the mock-bird, but not the nightingale —so like as to remind, so different as to be painful. One quarrels equally with the points of resemblance and of dis- tinction.

Nov. 17

No letter from * *; but I must not complain. The re- spectable Job says, " Why should a *living man* complain? " I really don't know, except it be that a *dead man* can't; and he, the said patriarch, *did* complain, nevertheless, till his friends were tired and his wife recommended that pious prologue, " Curse—and die "; the only time, I suppose, when but little relief is to be found in swearing. I have had a most kind letter from Lord Holland on " *The Bride of Abydos* ", which he likes, and so does Lady H. This is very good-natured in both, from whom I don't deserve any quarter. Yet I *did* think, at the time, that my cause of enmity proceeded from Holland House, and am glad I was wrong, and wish I had not been in such a hurry with that confounded satire, of which I would suppress even the memory;—but people, now they can't get it, make a fuss, I verily believe, out of contradiction.

George Ellis and Murray have been talking something about Scott and me, George *pro Scoto*,—and very right too. If they want to depose him, I only wish they would not set me up as a competitor. Even if I had my choice, I would rather be the Earl of Warwick than all the *kings* he ever made! Jeffrey and Gifford I take to be the monarch-makers in poetry and prose. The *British Critic*, in their Rokeby Review, have presupposed a comparison which I am sure my friends never thought of, and W. Scott's subjects are injudicious in descending to. I like the man—and admire his works to what Mr. Braham calls *Entusymusy*. All such stuff can only vex him, and do me no good. Many hate his politics—(I hate all politics); and, here, a man's politics are like the Greek *soul*—an εἰδωλον, besides God knows what *other soul*; but their estimate of the two generally go together.

Harry has not brought *ma petite cousine*. I want us to go to the play together;—she has been but once. Another short note from Jersey, inviting Rogers and me on the 23d. I must see my agent to-night. I wonder when that Newstead business will be finished. It cost me more than words to part with it— and to *have* parted with it! What matters it what I do? or what becomes of me?—but let me remember Job's saying, and console myself with being " a living man ".

I wish I could settle to reading again,—my life is monotonous, and yet desultory. I take up books, and fling them down again. I began a comedy, and burnt it because the scene ran into *reality*;—a novel, for the same reason. In rhyme, I can keep more away from facts; but the thought always runs through, through . . . yes, yes, through. I have had a letter from Lady Melbourne—the best friend I ever had in my life, and the cleverest of women.

Not a word from * * [Lady F. W. Webster]. Have they set out from * *? or has my last precious epistle fallen into the lion's jaws? If so—and this silence looks suspicious—I must clap on my " musty morion " and " hold out my iron ". I am out of practice—but I won't begin again at Manton's now. Besides, I would not return his shot. I was once a famous wafer-splitter; but then the bullies of society made it necessary. Ever since I began to feel that I had a bad cause to support, I have left off the exercise.

What strange tidings from that Anakim of anarchy— Buonaparte! Ever since I defended my bust of him at Harrow against the rascally time-servers, when the war broke out in 1803, he has been a *Héros de Roman* of mine—on the Continent; I don't want him here. But I don't like those same flights— leaving of armies, etc., etc. I am sure when I fought for his bust at school, I did not think he would run away from himself. But I should not wonder if he banged them yet. To be beat by men would be something; but by three stupid, legitimate- old-dynasty boobies of regular-bred sovereigns—O-hone-a-rie! —O-hone-a-rie! It must be, as Cobbett says, his marriage with the thick-lipped and thick-headed *Autrichienne* brood. He had better have kept to her who was kept by Barras. I never knew any good come of your young wife, and legal espousals, to any but your " sober-blooded boy " who " eats fish " and drinketh " no sack ". Had he not the whole opera? all Paris? all France? But a mistress is just as perplexing—that is, *one*— two or more are manageable by division.

I have begun, or had begun, a song, and flung it into the fire. It was in remembrance of Mary Duff,[1] my first of flames, before most people begin to burn. I wonder what the devil is the matter with me! I can do nothing, and—fortunately there is nothing to do. It has lately been in my power to make two persons (and their connections) comfortable, *pro tempore*, and one happy, *ex tempore*,—I rejoice in the last particularly, as it is an excellent man. I wish there had been more inconvenience and less gratification to my self-love in it, for then there had been more merit. We are all selfish—and I believe, ye gods of Epicurus! I believe in Rochefoucault about *men*, and in Lucretius (not Busby's translation) about yourselves. Your bard has made you very *nonchalant* and blest; but as he has excused *us* from damnation, I don't envy you your blessedness *much*—a little, to be sure. I remember, last year, * * [Lady Oxford] said to me, at * * [Eywood], " Have we not passed our last month like the gods of Lucretius? " And so we had. She is an adept in the text of the original (which I like too); and when that booby Bus. sent his translating prospectus, she subscribed. But, the devil prompting him to add a specimen, she transmitted him a subsequent answer, saying, that " after

---

[1]   A distant cousin whom Byron had loved in childhood.

perusing it, her conscience would not permit her to allow her name to remain on the list of subscribblers ". Last night, at Lord H.'s—Mackintosh, the Ossulstones, Puységur, etc., there—I was trying to recollect a quotation (as *I* think) of Stael's, from some Teutonic sophist about architecture. " Architecture ", says this Macoronico Tedescho, " reminds me of frozen music." It is somewhere—but where?—the demon of perplexity must know and won't tell. I asked M., and he said it was not in her : but Puységur said it must be *hers*, it was so *like*. H. laughed, as he does at all " *De l'Allemagne* " —in which, however, I think he goes a little too far. B., I hear, contemns it too. But there are fine passages ;—and, after all, what is a work—any—or every work—but a desert with fountains, and, perhaps, a grove or two, every day's journey? To be sure, in Madame, what we often mistake, and " pant for ", as the " cooling stream ", turns out to be the " *mirage* " (criticè *verbiage*) ; but we do, at last, get to something like the temple of Jove Ammon, and then the waste we have passed is only remembered to gladden the contrast.

Called on C * *, to explain * * *. She is very beautiful, to my taste, at least ; for on coming home from abroad, I recollect being unable to look at any woman but her—they were so fair, and unmeaning, and *blonde*. The darkness and regularity of her features reminded me of my " Jannat al Aden ". But this impression wore off ; and now I can look at a fair woman, without longing for a Houri. She was very good-tempered, and every thing was explained.

To-day, great news—" the Dutch have taken Holland ", —which, I suppose, will be succeeded by the actual explosion of the Thames. Five provinces have declared for young Stadt, and there will be inundation, conflagration, constupration, consternation, and every sort of nation and nations, fighting away, up to their knees, in the damnable quags of this will-o'-the-wisp abode of Boors. It is said Bernadotte is amongst them, too ; and, as Orange will be there soon, they will have (Crown) Prince Stork and King Log in their Loggery at the same time. Two to one on the new dynasty !

Mr. Murray has offered me one thousand guineas for *The Giaour* and *The Bride of Abydos*. I won't—it is too much, though I am strongly tempted, merely for the *say* of it. No bad price for a fortnight's (a week each) what?—the gods know—it was intended to be called poetry.

I have dined regularly to-day, for the first time since Sunday last—this being Sabbath, too. All the rest, tea and dry biscuits —six *per diem*. I wish to God I had not dined now!—It kills me with heaviness, stupor, and horrible dreams; and yet it was but a pint of Bucellas, and fish. Meat I never touch,— nor much vegetable diet. I wish I were in the country, to take exercise,—instead of being obliged to *cool* by abstinence, in lieu of it. I should not so much mind a little accession of flesh, —my bones can well bear it. But the worst is, the devil always came with it,—till I starved him out,—and I will *not* be the slave of *any* appetite. If I do err, it shall be my heart, at least, that heralds the way. Oh, my head—how it aches?—the horrors of digestion! I wonder how Buonaparte's dinner agrees with him?

Mem. I must write to-morrow to " Master Shallow, who owes me a thousand pounds ", and seems, in his letter, afraid I should ask him for it;—as if I would!—I don't want it (just now, at least,) to begin with; and though I have often wanted that sum I never asked for the repayment of 10*l.* in my life— from a friend. His bond is not due this year, and I told him when it was, I should not enforce it. How often must he make me say the same thing?

I am wrong—I did once ask * * * to repay me. But it was under circumstances that excused me *to him*, and would to any one. I took no interest, nor required security. He paid me soon,—at least, his *padre*. My head! I believe it was given me to ache with. Good even.

Nov. 22, 1813

" Orange Boven! " So the bees have expelled the bear that broke open their hive. Well,—if we are to have new De Witts and De Ruyters, God speed the little republic! I should like to see the Hague and the village of Brock, where they have such primitive habits. Yet, I don't know,—their canals would cut a poor figure by the memory of the Bosphorus; and the Zuyder Zee look awkwardly after " Ak-Denizi ". No matter, —the bluff burghers, puffing freedom out of their short tobacco- pipes, might be worth seeing; though I prefer a cigar or a hooka, with the rose-leaf mixed with the milder herb of the Levant. I don't know what liberty means,—never having seen it,—but wealth is power all over the world; and as a shilling performs the duty of a pound (besides sun and sky and beauty for nothing) in the East,—*that* is the country. How I envy Herodes Atticus!—more than Pomponius. And yet a little *tumult*, now and then, is an agreeable quickener of sensation; such as a revolution, a battle, or an *aventure* of any lively description. I think I rather would have been Bonneval, Ripperda, Alberoni, Hayreddin, or Horuc Barbarossa, or even Wortley Montague, than Mahomet himself.

Rogers will be in town soon?—the 23d is fixed for our Middleton visit. Shall I go? umph!—In this island, where one can't ride out without overtaking the sea, it don't much matter where one goes.

I remember the effect of the *first Edinburgh Review* on me. I heard of it six weeks before,—read it the day of its denunciation,—dined and drank three bottles of claret, (with S. B. Davies, I think,) neither ate nor slept the less, but, nevertheless, was not easy till I had vented my wrath and my rhyme, in the same pages, against every thing and every body. Like George in the *Vicar of Wakefield*, "the fate of my paradoxes" would allow me to perceive no merit in another. I remembered only the maxim of my boxing-master, which, in my youth, was found useful in all general riots,—"Whoever is not for you is against you—*mill* away right and left," and so I did;—like Ishmael, my hand was against all men, and all men's anent me. I did wonder, to be sure, at my own success—

"And marvels so much wit is all his own",

as Hobhouse sarcastically says of somebody (not unlikely myself, as we are old friends);—but were it to come over again, I would *not*. I have since redde the cause of my couplets, and it is not adequate to the effect. C * * told me that it was believed I alluded to poor Lord Carlisle's nervous disorder in one of the lines.[1] I thank Heaven I did not know

---

[1] " Roscommon! Sheffield! with your spirits fled
No future laurels deck a noble head;
No Muse will cheer, with renovating smile,
The paralytic puling of Carlisle."

it—and would not, could not, if I had. I must naturally be the last person to be pointed on defects or maladies.

Rogers is silent,—and, it is said, severe. When he does talk, he talks well; and, on all subjects of taste, his delicacy of expression is pure as his poetry. If you enter his house—his drawing-room—his library—you of yourself say, this is not the dwelling of a common mind. There is not a gem, a coin, a book thrown aside on his chimney-piece, his sofa, his table, that does not bespeak an almost fastidious elegance in the possessor. But this very delicacy must be the misery of his existence. Oh the jarrings his disposition must have encountered through life!

Southey, I have not seen much of. His appearance is *Epic*; and he is the only existing entire man of letters. All the others have some pursuit annexed to their authorship. His manners are mild, but not those of a man of the world, and his talents of the first order. His prose is perfect. Of his poetry there are various opinions: there is, perhaps, too much of it for the present generation; posterity will probably select. He has *passages* equal to any thing. At present, he has *a party*, but no *public*—except for his prose writings. The life of Nelson is beautiful.

Sotheby [1] is a *Littérateur*, the Oracle of the Coteries, of the * * s, Lydia White (Sydney Smith's " Tory Virgin "), Mrs. Wilmot (she, at least, is a swan, and might frequent a purer stream), Lady Beaumont, and all the Blues, with Lady Charlemont at their head—but I say nothing of *her*—" look in her face and you forget them all ", and every thing else. Oh that face!—by *te, Diva potens Cypri*, I would, to be beloved by that woman, build and burn another Troy.

Moore has a peculiarity of talent, or rather talents,—poetry, music, voice, all his own; and an expression in each, which never was, nor will be, possessed by another. But he is capable of still higher flights in poetry. By the by, what humour, what—every thing, in the " *Post-Bag!* " There is nothing Moore may not do, if he will but seriously set about it. In society, he is gentlemanly, gentle, and, altogether, more pleasing than any individual with whom I am acquainted.

---

[1] William Sotheby, cavalry officer turned man of letters. See also *Detached Thoughts*: " A good man; rhymes well (if not wisely), but is a bore ".

For his honour, principle, and independence, his conduct to
* * * * speaks " trumpet-tongued ". He has but one fault—
and that one I daily regret—he is not *here*.

Nov. 23

Ward [1]—I like Ward. By Mahomet! I begin to think I like
every body;—a disposition not to be encouraged;—a sort of
social gluttony that swallows every thing set before it. But I
like Ward. He is *piquant*; and, in my opinion, will stand *very*
high in the House, and every where else, if he applies *regularly*.
By the by, I dine with him to-morrow, which may have some
influence on my opinion. It is as well not to trust one's gratitude *after* dinner. I have heard many a host libelled by his
guests, with his burgundy yet reeking on their rascally lips.

I have taken Lord Salisbury's box at Covent Garden for
the season; and now I must go and prepare to join Lady
Holland and party, in theirs, at Drury Lane, *questa sera*.

Holland doesn't think the man *is Junius*; but that the yet
unpublished journal throws great light on the obscurities of
that part of George the Second's reign.—What is this to
George the Third's? I don't know what to think. Why
should Junius be yet dead? If suddenly apoplexed, would he
rest in his grave without sending his εἰδωλον to shout in the
ears of posterity, " Junius was X. Y. Z., Esq., buried in the
parish of * * *. Repair his monument, ye churchwardens!
Print a new edition of his Letters, ye booksellers! " Impossible,
—the man must be alive, and will never die without the disclosure. I like him;—he was a good hater.

Came home unwell and went to bed,—not so sleepy as
might be desirable.

Tuesday morning

I awoke from a dream!—well! and have not others
dreamed?—Such a dream!—but she did not overtake me. I
wish the dead would rest, however. Ugh! how my blood
chilled,—and I could not wake—and—and—heigho!

> " Shadows to-night
> Have struck more terror to the soul of Richard,
> Than could the substance of ten thousand * * s,
> Arm'd all in proof, and led by shallow * *."

[1] The Hon. John William Ward, afterwards Lord Dudley, journalist and orator.

I do not like this dream,—I hate its " foregone conclusion ". And am I to be shaken by shadows? Ay, when they remind us of—no matter—but, if I dream thus again, I will try whether *all* sleep has the like visions. Since I rose, I've been in considerable bodily pain also; but it is gone, and now, like Lord Ogleby, I am wound up for the day.

A note from Mountnorris—I dine with Ward;—Canning is to be there, Frere [1] and Sharpe,[2] perhaps Gifford. I am to be one of " the five " (or rather six), as Lady * * said a little sneeringly yesterday. They are all good to meet, particularly Canning, and—Ward, when he likes. I wish I may be well enough to listen to these intellectuals.

No letters to-day;—so much the better,—there are no answers. I must not dream again;—it spoils even reality. I will go out of doors, and see what the fog will do for me. Jackson has been here: the boxing world much as usual;— but the club increases. I shall dine at Crib's [3] to-morrow. I like energy—even animal energy—of all kinds; and I have need of both mental and corporeal. I have not dined out, nor, indeed, *at all*, lately: have heard no music—have seen nobody. Now for a *plunge*—high life and low life. *Amant* alterna *Camœnæ!*

I have burnt my *Roman*—as I did the first scenes and sketch of my comedy—and, for aught I see, the pleasure of burning is quite as great as that of printing. These two last would not have done. I ran into *realities* more than ever; and some would have been recognised and others guessed at.

Redde the *Ruminator*—a collection of Essays, by a strange, but able, old man (Sir Egerton Brydges), and a half-wild young one, author of a poem on the Highlands, called *Childe Alarique.* The word " sensibility " (always my aversion) occurs a thousand times in these Essays; and, it seems, is to be an excuse for all kinds of discontent. This young man can know nothing of life; and, if he cherishes the disposition which runs through his papers, will become useless, and, perhaps, not even a poet,

---

[1] John Hookham Frere, a distinguished member of the Holland House circle.

[2] Richard (" Conversation ") Sharp, the wealthy Radical, another ornament of Holland House parties.

[3] Tom Cribb, the retired pugilist, who kept a public house in Duke Street, St. James's.

after all, which he seems determined to be. God help him! no one should be a rhymer who could be any thing better. And this is what annoys one, to see Scott and Moore, and Campbell and Rogers, who might have all been agents and leaders, now mere spectators. For, though they may have other ostensible avocations, these last are reduced to a secondary consideration. * *, too, frittering away his time among dowagers and unmarried girls. If it advanced any *serious* affair, it were some excuse; but, with the unmarried, that is a hazardous speculation, and tiresome enough, too; and, with the veterans, it is not much worth trying, unless, perhaps, one in a thousand.

If I had any views in this country, they would probably be parliamentary. But I have no ambition; at least, if any, it would be *aut Cæsar aut nihil*. My hopes are limited to the arrangement of my affairs, and settling either in Italy or the East (rather the last), and drinking deep of the languages and literature of both. Past events have unnerved me; and all I can now do is to make life an amusement, and look on while others play. After all, even the highest game of crowns and sceptres, what is it? *Vide* Napoleon's last twelvemonth. It has completely upset my system of fatalism. I thought, if crushed, he would have fallen, when *fractus illabitur orbis*, and not have been pared away to gradual insignificance; that all this was not a mere *jeu* of the gods, but a prelude to greater changes and mightier events. But men never advance beyond a certain point; and here we are, retrograding, to the dull, stupid old system,—balance of Europe—poising straws upon kings' noses, instead of wringing them off! Give me a republic, or a despotism of one, rather than the mixed government of one, two, three. A republic!—look in the history of the Earth—Rome, Greece, Venice, France, Holland, America, our short (*eheu!*) Commonwealth, and compare it with what they did under masters. The Asiatics are not qualified to be republicans, but they have the liberty of demolishing despots, which is the next thing to it. To be the first man—not the Dictator—not the Sylla, but the Washington or the Aristides— the leader in talent and truth—is next to the Divinity! Franklin, Penn, and, next to these, either Brutus or Cassius—even Mirabeau—or St. Just. I shall never be any thing, or rather

always be nothing. The most I can hope is, that some will say,
" He might, perhaps, if he would ".

12, midnight

Here are two confounded proofs from the printer. I have
looked at the one, but for the soul of me, I can't look over that
Giaour again,—at least, just now, and at this hour—and yet
there is no moon.

Ward talks of going to Holland, and we have partly discussed an *ensemble* expedition. It must be in ten days, if at all,
if we wish to be in at the Revolution. And why not? * * is
distant, and will be at * *, still more distant, till spring. No
one else, except Augusta, cares for me ; no ties—no trammels
—*andiamo dunque—se torniamo, bene—se non, ch' importa?* Old
William of Orange talked of dying in " the last ditch " of his
dingy country. It is lucky I can swim, or I suppose I should
not well weather the first. But let us see. I have heard
hyænas and jackalls in the ruins of Asia ; and bull-frogs in
the marshes ; besides wolves and angry Mussulmans. Now,
I should like to listen to the shout of a free Dutchman.

Alla ! Viva ! For ever ! Hourra ! Huzza !—which is
the most rational or musical of these cries? " Orange Boven ",
according to the *Morning Post*.

Wednesday, 24

No dreams last night of the dead, nor the living ; so—I
am " firm as the marble, founded as the rock ", till the next
earthquake.

Ward's dinner went off well. There was not a disagreeable
person there—unless *I* offended any body, which I am sure I
could not by contradiction, for I said little, and opposed
nothing. Sharpe (a man of elegant mind, and who has lived
much with the best—Fox, Horne Tooke, Windham, Fitzpatrick, and all the agitators of other times and tongues,) told
us the particulars of his last interview with Windham, a few
days before the fatal operation which sent " that gallant spirit
to aspire the skies ". Windham,—the first in one department
of oratory and talent, whose only fault was his refinement
beyond the intellect of half his hearers,—Windham, half his
life an active participator in the events of the earth, and one of
those who governed nations,—*he* regretted,—and dwelt much

on that regret, that " he had not entirely devoted himself to literature and science !!! " His mind certainly would have carried him to eminence there, as elsewhere ;—but I cannot comprehend what debility of that mind could suggest such a wish. I, who have heard him, cannot regret any thing but that I shall never hear him again. What! would he have been a plodder? a metaphysician?—perhaps a rhymer? a scribbler? Such an exchange must have been suggested by illness. But he is gone, and Time " shall not look upon his like again ".

I am tremendously in arrear with my letters,—except to * *, and to her my thoughts overpower me :—my words never compass them. To Lady Melbourne I write with most pleasure —and her answers, so sensible, so *tactique*—I never met with half her talent. If she had been a few years younger, what a fool she would have made of me, had she thought it worth her while,—and I should have lost a valuable and most agreeable *friend*. Mem.—a mistress never is nor can be a friend. While you agree, you are lovers ; and, when it is over, any thing but friends.

I have not answered W. Scott's last letter,—but I will. I regret to hear from others, that he has lately been unfortunate in pecuniary involvements. He is undoubtedly the Monarch of Parnassus, and the most *English* of bards. I should place Rogers next in the living list (I value him more as the last of the *best* school)—Moore and Campbell both *third*—Southey and Wordsworth and Coleridge—the rest, οἱ πολλοι—thus :— There is a triangular *Gradus ad Parnassum*!—the names are too numerous for the base of the triangle. Poor Thurlow has gone wild about the poetry of Queen Bess's reign—*c'est dommage*. I have ranked the names upon my triangle more upon what I believe popular opinion, than any decided opinion of my own. For, to me, some of Moore's last *Erin* sparks—" As a beam o'er the face of the waters "—" When he who adores thee "— " Oh blame not "—and " Oh breathe not his name "—are worth all the Epics that ever were composed.

Rogers thinks the *Quarterly* will attack me next. Let them. I have been " peppered so highly " in my time, *both* ways, that it must be cayenne or aloes to make me taste. I can sincerely say, that I am not very much alive *now* to criticism. But—in tracing this—I rather believe that it proceeds from my not attaching that importance to authorship which many do, and which, when young, I did also. "One gets tired of every thing, my angel", says Valmont. The "angels" are the only things of which I am not a little sick—but I do think the preference of *writers* to *agents*—the mighty stir made about scribbling and scribes, by themselves and others—a sign of

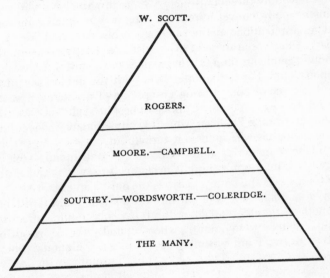

effeminacy, degeneracy, and weakness. Who would write, who had any thing better to do? "Action—action—action" —said Demosthenes: "Action*s*—action*s*", I say, and not writing,—least of all, rhyme. Look at the querulous and monotonous lives of the "genus";—except Cervantes, Tasso, Dante, Ariosto, Kleist (who were brave and active citizens), Æschylus, Sophocles, and some other of the antiques also— what a worthless, idle brood it is!

12, Mezza Notte

Just returned from dinner with Jackson (the Emperor of Pugilism) and another of the select, at Crib's,[1] the champion's. I drank more than I like, and have brought away some three

[1] Tom Cribb had won his championship by defeating Molineaux, the coloured boxer, in 1810 and 1811.

bottles of very fair claret—for I have no headach. We had
Tom Crib up after dinner ;—very facetious, though somewhat
prolix. He don't like his situation—wants to fight again—pray
Pollux (or Castor, if he was the *miller*) he may ! Tom has been
a sailor—a coal-heaver—and some other genteel profession,
before he took to the cestus. Tom has been in action at sea,
and is now only three-and-thirty. A great man ! has a wife and
a mistress, and conversations well—bating some sad omissions
and misapplications of the aspirate. Tom is an old friend of
mine ; I have seen some of his best battles in my nonage. He
is now a publican, and, I fear, a sinner ;—for Mrs. Crib is on
alimony, and Tom's daughter lives with the champion. *This*
Tom told me,—Tom, having an opinion of my morals, passed
her off as a legal spouse. Talking of her, he said, " she was the
truest of women "—from which I immediately inferred she
could *not* be his wife, and so it turned out.

These panegyrics don't belong to matrimony ;—for, if
" true ", a man don't think it necessary to say so ; and if not,
the less he says the better. Crib is the only man except * * * *,
I ever heard harangue upon his wife's virtue ; and I listened
to both with great credence and patience, and stuffed my
handkerchief into my mouth, when I found yawning irresistible
—By the by, I am yawning now—so, good night to thee.—
Μπαῖρων.

Thursday, November 26

Awoke a little feverish, but no headach—no dreams
neither, thanks to stupor ! Two letters ; one from [? Frances
Webster], the other from Lady Melbourne—both excellent in
their respective styles. [? Frances Webster]'s contained also a
very pretty lyric on " concealed griefs " ; if not her own, yet
very like her. Why did she not say that the stanzas were, or
were not, of her own composition ? I do not know whether
to wish them *hers* or not. I have no great esteem for poetical
persons, particularly women ; they have so much of the " ideal "
in *practics*, as well as *ethics*.

I have been thinking lately a good deal of Mary Duff.[1]

---

[1] Hobhouse declined to accept Moore's account of this precocious passion,
remarking in his pencil notes on a copy of the *Life* that he was " acquainted with
a singular fact, scarcely fit for narration but much less romantic and more satisfactory than the amour with Mary Duff ".

How very odd that I should have been so utterly, devotedly fond of that girl, at an age when I could neither feel passion, nor know the meaning of the word. And the effect! My mother used always to rally me about this childish amour; and, at last, many years after, when I was sixteen, she told me one day, " Oh, Byron, I have had a letter from Edinburgh, from Miss Abercromby, and your old sweetheart Mary Duff is married to a Mr. Coe ". And what was my answer? I really cannot explain or account for my feelings at that moment; but they nearly threw me into convulsions, and alarmed my mother so much, that after I grew better, she generally avoided the subject—to *me*—and contented herself with telling it to all her acquaintance. Now, what could this be? I had never seen her since her mother's *faux pas* at Aberdeen had been the cause of her removal to her grandmother's at Banff; we were both the merest children. I had and have been attached fifty times since that period; yet I recollect all we said to each other, all our caresses, her features, my restlessness, sleeplessness, my tormenting my mother's maid to write for me to her, which she at last did, to quiet me. Poor Nancy thought I was wild, and, as I could not write for myself, became my secretary. I remember, too, our walks, and the happiness of sitting by Mary, in the children's apartment, at their house not far from the Plain-stanes at Aberdeen, while her lesser sister Helen played with the doll, and we sat gravely making love, in our way.

How the deuce did all this occur so early? where could it originate? I certainly had no sexual ideas for years afterwards; and yet my misery, my love for that girl were so violent, that I sometimes doubt if I have ever been really attached since. Be that as it may, hearing of her marriage several years after was like a thunder-stroke—it nearly choked me—to the horror of my mother and the astonishment and almost incredulity of every body. And it is a phenomenon in my existence (for I was not eight years old) which has puzzled, and will puzzle me to the latest hour of it; and lately, I know not why, the *recollection* (*not* the attachment) has recurred as forcibly as ever. I wonder if she can have the least remembrance of it or me? or remember pitying her sister Helen for not having an admirer too? How very pretty is the perfect image of her in my memory —her brown, dark hair, and hazel eyes; her very dress! I

should be quite grieved to see *her now*; the reality, however
beautiful, would destroy, or at least confuse, the features of the
lovely Peri which then existed in her, and still lives in my
imagination, at the distance of more than sixteen years. I
am now twenty-five and odd months. . . .

I think my mother told the circumstances (on my hearing
of her marriage) to the Parkynses, and certainly to the Pigot
family, and probably mentioned it in her answer to Miss A.,
who was well acquainted with my childish *penchant*, and had
sent the news on purpose for *me*,—and thanks to her!

Next to the beginning, the conclusion has often occupied
my reflections, in the way of investigation. That the facts are
thus, others know as well as I, and my memory yet tells me
so, in more than a whisper. But, the more I reflect, the
more I am bewildered to assign any cause for this precocity of
affection.

Lord Holland invited me to dinner to-day; but three
days' dining would destroy me. So, without eating at all since
yesterday, I went to my box at Covent Garden.

Saw * * * * looking very pretty, though quite a different
style of beauty from the other two. She has the finest eyes in
the world, out of which she pretends *not* to see, and the longest
eyelashes I ever saw, since Leila's and Phannio's Moslem
curtains of the light. She has much beauty,—just enough,—
but is, I think, *méchante*.

I have been pondering on the miseries of separation, that—
oh how seldom we see those we love! yet we live ages in
moments, *when met*. The only thing that consoles me during
absence is the reflection that no mental or personal estrange-
ment, from ennui or disagreement, can take place; and when
people meet hereafter, even though many changes may have
taken place, in the mean time, still, unless they are *tired* of
each other, they are ready to reunite, and do not blame each
other for the circumstances that severed them.

> *Saturday* 27—(I believe or rather am in *doubt*, which
>   is the *ne plus ultra* of mortal faith)

I have missed a day; and, as the Irishman said, or Joe
Miller says for him, " have gained a loss ", or *by* the loss.
Every thing is settled for Holland, and nothing but a cough, or

a caprice of my fellow-traveller's, can stop us. Carriage ordered, funds prepared, and, probably, a gale of wind into the bargain. *N'importe*—I believe, with Clym o' the Clow, or Robin Hood, " By our Mary, (dear name!) thou art both Mother and May, I think it never was a man's lot to die before his day ". Heigh for Helvoetsluys, and so forth!

To-night I went with young Henry Fox[1] to see *Nourjahad*, a drama, which the *Morning Post* hath laid to my charge, but of which I cannot even guess the author. I wonder what they will next inflict upon me. They cannot well sink below a melodrama; but that is better than a satire, (at least, a personal one,) with which I stand truly arraigned, and in atonement of which I am resolved to bear silently all criticisms, abuses, and even praises, for bad pantomimes never composed by me, without even a contradictory aspect. I suppose the root of this report is my loan to the manager of my Turkish drawings for his dresses, to which he was more welcome than to my name. I suppose the real author will soon own it, as it has succeeded; if not, Job be my model, and Lethe my beverage!

* * * * has received the portrait safe; and, in answer, the only remark she makes upon it is, " indeed it is like "—and again, " indeed it is like ". With her the likeness " covered a multitude of sins "; for I happen to know that this portrait was not a flatterer, but dark and stern,—even black as the mood in which my mind was scorching last July, when I sat for it. All the others of me, like most portraits whatsoever, are, of course, more agreeable than nature.

Redde the *Edinburgh Review* of Rogers. He is ranked highly; but where he should be. There is a summary view of us all—*Moore* and *me* among the rest; and both (the *first* justly) praised—though, by implication (justly again) placed beneath our memorable friend. Mackintosh is the writer, and also of the critique on the Stael. His grand essay on Burke, I hear, is for the next number. But I know nothing of the *Edinburgh*, or of any other *Review*, but from rumour; and I have long ceased; indeed, I could not, in justice, complain of

---

[1] Lord and Lady Holland's eldest legitimate son. Byron had a particular sympathy for him since he, too, was lame. Fox subsequently became the author of an interesting journal, and one of Byron's numerous successors in the affections of the Countess Guiccioli.

any, even though I were to rate poetry, in general, and my rhymes in particular, more highly than I really do. To withdraw *myself* from *myself* (oh that cursed selfishness!) has ever been my sole, my entire, my sincere motive in scribbling at all; and publishing is also the continuance of the same object, by the action it affords to the mind, which else recoils upon itself. If I valued fame, I should flatter received opinions, which have gathered strength by time, and will yet wear longer than any living works to the contrary. But, for the soul of me, I cannot and will not give the lie to my own thoughts and doubts, come what may. If I am a fool, it is, at least, a doubting one; and I envy no one the certainty of his self-approved wisdom.

All are inclined to believe what they covet, from a lottery-ticket up to a passport to Paradise,—in which, from the description, I see nothing very tempting. My restlessness tells me I have something " within that passeth show ". It is for Him, who made it, to prolong that spark of celestial fire which illuminates, yet burns, this frail tenement; but I see no such horror in a " dreamless sleep ", and I have no conception of any existence which duration would not render tiresome. How else " fell the angels ", even according to your creed? They were immortal, heavenly, and happy, as their *apostate Abdiel* is now by his treachery. Time must decide; and eternity won't be the less agreeable or more horrible because one did not expect it. In the mean time, I am grateful for some good, and tolerably patient under certain evils—*grace à Dieu et mon bon tempérament.*

Tuesday, 30th

Two days missed in my log-book;—*hiatus* haud *deflendus*. They were as little worth recollection as the rest; and, luckily, laziness or society prevented me from *notching* them.

Sunday, I dined with the Lord Holland in St. James's Square. Large party—among them Sir S. Romilly and Lady Rᵧ—General Sir Somebody Bentham, a man of science and talent, I am told—Horner—*the* Horner, an Edinburgh Reviewer, an excellent speaker in the " Honourable House ", very pleasing, too, and gentlemanly in company, as far as I have seen—Sharpe—Philips of Lancashire—Lord John Russell,

and others, " good men and true ". Holland's society is very
good ; you always see some one or other in it worth knowing.
Stuffed myself with sturgeon, and exceeded in champagne and
wine in general, but not to confusion of head. When I *do*
dine, I gorge like an Arab or a Boa snake, on fish and vegetables,
but no meat. I am always better, however, on my tea and
biscuit than any other regimen, and even *that* sparingly.

Why does Lady H. always have that damned screen
between the whole room and the fire ? I, who bear cold no
better than an antelope, and never yet found a sun quite *done*
to my taste, was absolutely petrified, and could not even shiver.
All the rest, too, looked as if they were just unpacked, like
salmon from an ice-basket, and set down to table for that day
only. When she retired, I watched their looks as I dismissed
the screen, and every cheek thawed, and every nose reddened
with the anticipated glow.

Saturday, I went with Harry Fox to *Nourjahad*; and, I
believe, convinced him, by incessant yawning, that it was not
mine. I wish the precious author would own it, and release
me from his fame. The dresses are pretty, but not in costume ;
—Mrs. Horn's, all but the turban, and the want of a small
dagger (if she is a sultana), *perfect*. I never saw a Turkish
woman with a turban in my life—nor did any one else. The
sultanas have a small poniard at the waist. The dialogue is
drowsy—the action heavy—the scenery fine—the actors
tolerable. I can't say much for their seraglio—Teresa, Phannio,
or * * * *, were worth them all.

Sunday, a very handsome note from Mackintosh, who is a
rare instance of the union of very transcendent talent and great
good nature. To-day (Tuesday) a very pretty billet from M. la
Baronne de Stael Holstein. She is pleased to be much pleased
with my mention of her and her last work in my notes. I
spoke as I thought. Her works are my delight, and so is she
herself, for—half an hour. I don't like her politics—at least,
her *having changed* them ; had she been *qualis ab incepto*, it were
nothing. But she is a woman by herself, and has done more
than all the rest of them together, intellectually ;—she ought to
have been a man. She *flatters* me very prettily in her note ;—
but I *know* it. The reason that adulation is not displeasing is,
that, though untrue, it shows one to be of consequence enough,

in one way or other, to induce people to lie, to make us their friend :—that is their concern.

* * is, I hear, thriving on the repute of a *pun* which was *mine* (at Mackintosh's dinner some time back), on Ward, who was asking, " how much it would take to *re-whig* him? " I answered that, probably, " he must first, before he was *re-whigged*, be re-*warded* ". This foolish quibble, before the Stael and Mackintosh, and a number of conversationers, has been mouthed about, and at last settled on the head of * *, where long may it remain !

George [1] is returned from afloat to get a new ship. He looks thin, but better than I expected. I like George much more than most people like their heirs. He is a fine fellow, and every nch a sailor. I would do any thing, *but apostatise*, to get him on n his profession.

Lewis called. It is a good and good-humoured man, but pestilently prolix and paradoxical and *personal*. If he would but talk half, and reduce his visits to an hour, he would add to his popularity. As an author he is very good, and his vanity is *uverte*, like Erskine's, and yet not offending.

Yesterday, a very pretty letter from Annabella, which I answered. What an odd situation and friendship is ours !— without one spark of love on either side, and produced by circumstances which in general lead to coldness on one side, and aversion on the other. She is a very superior woman, and very little spoiled, which is strange in an heiress—a girl of twenty—a peeress that is to be, in her own right—an only child, and a *savante*, who has always had her own way. She is a poetess—a mathematician—a metaphysician, and yet, withal, very kind, generous, and gentle, with very little pretension. Any other head would be turned with half her acquisitions, and a tenth of her advantages.

Wednesday, December 1, 1813

To-day responded to La Baronne de Stael Holstein, and sent to Leigh Hunt [2] (an acquisition to my acquaintance—

---

[1] The poet's cousin and heir presumptive, who succeeded him as the seventh Lord Byron in 1824.

[2] Leigh Hunt and his brother had been fined and sentenced to two years' imprisonment for a savage personal attack on the Prince Regent in the *Examiner* of March 1812.

through Moore—of last summer) a copy of the two Turkish
tales. Hunt is an extraordinary character, and not exactly
of the present age. He reminds me more of the Pym and
Hampden times—much talent, great independence of spirit,
and an austere, yet not repulsive, aspect. If he goes on *qualis
ab incepto*, I know few men who will deserve more praise or
obtain it. I must go and see him again;—the rapid succession
of adventure, since last summer, added to some serious uneasiness and business, have interrupted our acquaintance;
but he is a man worth knowing; and though, for his own sake,
I wish him out of prison, I like to study character in such
situations. He has been unshaken, and will continue so. I
don't think him deeply versed in life;—he is the bigot of virtue
(not religion), and enamoured of the beauty of that " empty
name ", as the last breath of Brutus pronounced, and every
day proves it. He is, perhaps, a little opinionated, as all men
who are the *centre* of *circles*, wide or narrow—the Sir Oracles,
in whose name two or three are gathered together—must be,
and as even Johnson was; but, withal, a valuable man, and
less vain than success and even the consciousness of preferring
" the right to the expedient " might excuse.

To-morrow there is a party of *purple* at the " blue " Miss
Berry's. Shall I go? um!—I don't much affect your blue-
bottles;—but one ought to be civil. There will be, " I guess
now " (as the Americans say), the Staels and Mackintoshes—
good—the * * * s and * * * s—not so good—the * * * s, etc.,
etc.—good for nothing. Perhaps that blue-winged Kashmirian
butterfly of book-learning, Lady Charlemont, will be there.
I hope so; it is a pleasure to look upon that most beautiful of
faces.

Wrote to H. :—he has been telling that I —— I am sure,
at least, *I* did not mention it, and I wish he had not. He is a
good fellow, and I obliged myself ten times more by being of
use than I did him,—and there's an end on't.

Baldwin is boring me to present their King's Bench petition.
I presented Cartwright's last year; and Stanhope and I stood
against the whole House, and mouthed it valiantly—and had
some fun and a little abuse for our opposition. But " I am not
i' th' vein " for this business. Now, had * * been here, she
would have *made* me do it. *There* is a woman, who, amid all

her fascination, always urged a man to usefulness or glory. Had she remained, she had been my tutelar genius.

Baldwin is very importunate—but, poor fellow, " I can't get out, I can't get out—said the starling ". Ah, I am as bad as that dog Sterne, who preferred whining over " a dead ass to relieving a living mother "—villain—hypocrite—slave—sycophant! but *I* am no better. Here I cannot stimulate myself to a speech for the sake of these unfortunates, and three words and half a smile of * * had she been here to urge it (and urge it she infallibly would—at least she always pressed me on senatorial duties, and particularly in the cause of weakness) would have made me an advocate, if not an orator. Curse on Rochefoucault for being always right! In him a lie were virtue,—or, at least, a comfort to his readers.

George Byron has not called to-day; I hope he will be an admiral, and, perhaps, Lord Byron into the bargain. If he would but marry, I would engage never to marry myself, or cut him out of the heirship. He would be happier, and I should like nephews better than sons.

I shall soon be six-and-twenty (January 22d, 1814). Is there any thing in the future that can possibly console us for not being always *twenty-five*?

> " Oh Gioventu !
> Oh Primavera ! gioventu dell' anno.
> Oh Gioventu ! primavera della vita."

Sunday, December 5

Dallas's nephew (son to the American Attorney-general) is arrived in this country, and tells Dallas that my rhymes are very popular in the United States. These are the first tidings that have ever sounded like *Fame* to my ears—to be redde on the banks of the Ohio ! The greatest pleasure I ever derived, of this kind, was from an extract, in Cooke the actor's life, from his journal, stating that in the reading-room at Albany, near Washington, he perused *English Bards, and Scotch Reviewers*. To be popular in a rising and far country has a kind of *posthumous feel*, very different from the ephemeral *éclat* and fête-ing, buzzing and party-ing compliments of the well-dressed multitude. I can safely say that, during my *reign* in the spring of

1812, I regretted nothing but its duration of six weeks instead of a fortnight, and was heartily glad to resign.

Last night I supped with Lewis; and, as usual, though I neither exceeded in solids nor fluids, have been half dead ever since. My stomach is entirely destroyed by long abstinence, and the rest will probably follow. Let it—I only wish the *pain* over. The " leap in the dark " is the least to be dreaded.

The Duke of * * called. I have told them forty times that, except to half-a-dozen old and specified acquaintances, I am invisible. His Grace is a good, noble, ducal person; but I am content to think so at a distance, and so—I was not at home.

Galt [1] called.—Mem.—to ask some one to speak to Raymond in favour of his play. We are old fellow-travellers, and, with all his eccentricities, he has much strong sense, experience of the world, and is, as far as I have seen, a good-natured philosophical fellow. I showed him Sligo's letter on the reports of the Turkish girl's *aventure* at Athens soon after it happened. He and Lord Holland, Lewis, and Moore, and Rogers, and Lady Melbourne have seen it. Murray has a copy. I thought it had been *unknown*, and wish it were; but Sligo arrived only some days after, and the *rumours* are the subject of his letter. That I shall preserve,—*it is as well.* Lewis and Galt were both *horrified*; and L. wondered I did not introduce the situation into *The Giaour*. He *may* wonder;—he might wonder more at that production's being written at all. But to describe the *feelings* of *that situation* were impossible—it is *icy* even to recollect them.

The *Bride of Abydos* was published on Thursday the second of December; but how it is liked or disliked, I know not. Whether it succeeds or not is no fault of the public, against whom I can have no complaint. But I am much more indebted to the tale than I can ever be to the most partial reader; as it wrung my thoughts from reality to imagination—from selfish regrets to vivid recollections—and recalled me to a country replete with the *brightest* and *darkest*, but always most *lively* colours of my memory. Sharpe called, but was not let in, which I regret.

---

[1] John Galt, author of *The Annals of the Parish*, met Byron at Gibraltar during the year 1809 and afterwards travelled with him from Gibraltar to Malta. His impressions of that journey are the most interesting part of his fragmentary *Life of Byron*.

Saw [Rogers] yesterday. I have not kept my appointment at Middleton, which has not pleased him, perhaps; and my projected voyage with [Ward] will, perhaps, please him less. But I wish to keep well with both. They are instruments that don't do in concert; but, surely, their separate tones are very musical, and I won't give up either.

It is well if I don't jar between these great discords. At present I stand tolerably well with all, but I cannot adopt their *dislikes*;—so many *sets*. Holland's is the first;—every thing *distingué* is welcome there, and certainly the *ton* of his society is the best. Then there is Madame de Staël's—there I never go, though I might, had I courted it. It is composed of the * * s and the * * family, with a strange sprinkling,—orators, dandies, and all kinds of *Blue*, from the regular Grub Street uniform, down to the azure jacket of the *Littérateur*. To see * * and * * sitting together, at dinner, always reminds me of the grave, where all distinctions of friend and foe are levelled; and they —the Reviewer and the Reviewée—the Rhinoceros and Elephant—the Mammoth and Megalonyx—all will lie quietly together. They now *sit* together, as silent, but not so quiet, as if they were already immured.

I did not go to the Berrys' the other night. The elder is a woman of much talent, and both are handsome, and must have been beautiful. To-night asked to Lord H.'s—shall I go? um!—perhaps.

Morning, two o'clock

Went to Lord H.'s—party numerous—milady in perfect good humour, and consequently *perfect*. No one more agreeable, or perhaps so much so, when she will. Asked for Wednesday to dine and meet the Stael—asked particularly, I believe, out of mischief to see the first interview after the *note*, with which Corinne professes herself to be so much taken. I don't much like it; she always talks of *my*self or *her*self, and I am not (except in soliloquy, as now,) much enamoured of either subject—especially one's works. What the devil shall I say about *De l'Allemagne*? I like it prodigiously; but unless I can twist my admiration into some fantastical expression, she won't believe me; and I know, by experience, I shall be overwhelmed with fine things about rhyme, etc., etc. The lover,

Mr. * * [Rocca], was there to-night, and C * * said " it was the only proof *he* had seen of her good taste ". Monsieur L'Amant is remarkably handsome ; but *I* don't think more so than her book.

C * * [Campbell] looks well,—seems pleased, and dressed to *sprucery*. A blue coat becomes him,—so does his new wig. He really looked as if Apollo had sent him a birthday suit, or a wedding-garment, and was witty and lively. He abused Corinne's book, which I regret ; because, firstly, he understands German, and is consequently a fair judge ; and, secondly, he is *first-rate*, and, consequently, the best of judges. I reverence and admire him ; but I won't give up my opinion—why should I? I read *her* again and again, and there can be no affectation in this. I cannot be mistaken (except in taste) in a book I read and lay down, and take up again ; and no book can be totally bad which finds *one*, even *one* reader, who can say as much sincerely.

Campbell talks of lecturing next spring ; his last lectures were eminently successful. Moore thought of it, but gave it up,—I don't know why. * * had been prating *dignity* to him, and such stuff ; as if a man disgraced himself by instructing and pleasing at the same time.

Introduced to Marquis Buckingham—saw Lord Gower— he is going to Holland ; Sir J. and Lady Mackintosh and Horner, G. Lamb, with I know not how many (Richard Wellesley, one—a clever man), grouped about the room. Little Henry Fox, a very fine boy, and very promising in mind and manner,—he went away to bed, before I had time to talk to him. I am sure I had rather hear him than all the *savans*.

Monday, Dec. 6

Murray tells me that Croker asked him why the thing was called the *Bride* of Abydos? It is a cursed awkward question, being unanswerable. *She* is not a *bride*, only about to be one ; but for, etc., etc., etc.

I don't wonder at his finding out the *Bull* ; but the detection * * * is too late to do any good. I was a great fool to make it, and am ashamed of not being an Irishman.

Campbell last night seemed a little nettled at something or

other—I know not what. We were standing in the ante-saloon, when Lord H. brought out of the other room a vessel of some composition similar to that which is used in Catholic churches, and, seeing us, he exclaimed, " Here is some *incense* for you ". Campbell answered—" Carry it to Lord Byron, *he is used to it* ".

Now, this comes of " bearing no brother near the throne ". I, who have no throne, nor wish to have one *now*, whatever I may have done, am at perfect peace with all the poetical fraternity; or, at least, if I dislike any, it is not *poetically*, but *personally*. Surely the field of thought is infinite; what does it signify who is before or behind in a race where there is no *goal*? The temple of fame is like that of the Persians, the universe; our altar, the tops of mountains. I should be equally content with Mount Caucasus, or Mount Anything; and those who like it, may have Mount Blanc or Chimborazo, without my envy of their elevation.

I think I may *now* speak thus; for I have just published a poem, and am quite ignorant whether it is *likely* to be *liked* or not. I have hitherto heard little in its commendation, and no one can *downright* abuse it to one's face, except in print. It can't be good, or I should not have stumbled over the threshold, and blundered in my very title. But I began it with my heart full of * * *, and my head of orienta*lities* (I can't call them *isms*), and wrote on rapidly.

This journal is a relief. When I am tired—as I generally am—out comes this, and down goes every thing. But I can't read it over; and God knows what contradictions it may contain. If I am sincere with myself (but I fear one lies more to one's self than to any one else), every page should confute, refute, and utterly abjure its predecessor.

Another scribble from Martin Baldwin the petitioner; I have neither head nor nerves to present it. That confounded supper at Lewis's has spoiled my digestion and my philanthropy. I have no more charity than a cruet of vinegar. Would I were an ostrich, and dieted on fire-irons,—or any thing that my gizzard could get the better of.

To-day saw Ward. His uncle is dying, and W. don't much affect our Dutch determinations. I dine with him on Thursday, provided *l'oncle* is not dined upon, or peremptorily bespoke by

the posthumous epicures before that day. I wish he may
recover—not for *our* dinner's sake, but to disappoint the under-
taker, and the rascally reptiles that may well wait, since they
will dine at last.

Gell called—he of Troy—after I was out. Mem.—to
return his visit. But my Mems. are the very landmarks of
forgetfulness;—something like a light-house, with a ship
wrecked under the nose of its lantern. I never look at a Mem.
without seeing that I have remembered to forget. Mem.—
I have forgotten to pay Pitt's taxes, and suppose I shall be
surcharged. "An I do not turn rebel when thou art king"—
oons! I believe my very biscuit is leavened with that impostor's
imposts.

Lady Melbourne returns from Jersey's to-morrow;—I must
call. A Mr. Thomson has sent a song, which I must applaud.
I hate annoying them with censure or silence;—and yet I hate
lettering.

Saw Lord Glenbervie and his Prospectus, at Murray's,
of a new Treatise on Timber. Now here is a man more useful
than all the historians and rhymers ever planted. For, by
preserving our woods and forests, he furnishes materials for all
the history of Britain worth reading, and all the odes worth
nothing.

Redde a good deal, but desultorily. My head is crammed
with the most useless lumber. It is odd that when I do read,
I can only bear the chicken broth of—*any thing* but Novels. It
is many a year since I looked into one, (though they are sometimes ordered, by way of experiment, but never taken,) till I
looked yesterday at the worst parts of the *Monk*. These descriptions ought to have been written by Tiberius at Caprea—
they are forced—the *philtered* ideas of a jaded voluptuary. It is
to me inconceivable how they could have been composed by a
man of only twenty—his age when he wrote them. They
have no nature—all the sour cream of cantharides. I should
have suspected Buffon of writing them on the death-bed of his
detestable dotage. I had never redde this edition, and merely
looked at them from curiosity and recollection of the noise they
made, and the name they had left to Lewis. But they could do
no harm, except * * * *.

Called this evening on my agent—my business as usual.

Our strange adventures are the only inheritances of our family that have not diminished.

I shall now smoke two cigars, and get me to bed. The cigars don't keep well here. They get as old as a *donna di quaranti anni* in the sun of Africa. The Havannah are the best; —but neither are so pleasant as a hooka or chiboque. The Turkish tobacco is mild, and their horses entire—two things as they should be. I am so far obliged to this Journal, that it preserves me from verse,—at least from keeping it. I have just thrown a poem into the fire (which it has relighted to my great comfort), and have smoked out of my head the plan of another. I wish I could as easily get rid of thinking, or, at least, the confusion of thought.

Tuesday, December 7

Went to bed, and slept dreamlessly, but not refreshingly. Awoke, and up an hour before being called; but dawdled three hours in dressing. When one subtracts from life infancy (which is vegetation),—sleep, eating, and swilling—buttoning and unbuttoning—how much remains of downright existence? The summer of a dormouse.

Redde the papers and *tea*-ed and soda-watered, and found out that the fire was badly lighted. Lord Glenbervie wants me to go to Brighton—um!

This morning, a very pretty billet from the Stael about meeting her at Ld. H.'s to-morrow. She has written, I dare say, twenty such this morning to different people, all equally flattering to each. So much the better for her and those who believe all she wishes them, or they wish to believe. She has been pleased to be pleased with my slight eulogy in the note annexed to *The Bride*. This is to be accounted for in several ways,—firstly, all women like all, or any, praise; secondly, this was unexpected, because I have never courted her; and, thirdly, as Scrub says, those who have been all their lives regularly praised, by regular critics, like a little variety, and are glad when any one goes out of his way to say a civil thing; and, fourthly, she is a very good-natured creature, which is the best reason, after all, and, perhaps, the only one.

A knock—knocks single and double. Bland called. He says Dutch society (he has been in Holland) is second-hand

French; but the women are like women every where else. This is a bore: I should like to see them a little *un*like; but that can't be expected.

Went out—came home—this, that, and the other—and " all is vanity, saith the preacher ", and so say I, as part of his congregation. Talking of vanity, whose praise do I prefer? Why, Mrs. Inchbald's, and that of the Americans. The first, because her *Simple Story* and *Nature and Art* are, to me, *true* to their *titles*; and, consequently, her short note to Rogers about *The Giaour* delighted me more than any thing, except the *Edinburgh Review*. I like the Americans, because *I* happened to be in *Asia*, while the *English Bards, and Scotch Reviewers* were redde in *America*. If I could have had a speech against the *Slave Trade in Africa*, and an epitaph on a dog in *Europe* (i.e. in the *Morning Post*), my *vertex sublimis* would certainly have displaced stars enough to overthrow the Newtonian system.

Friday, December 10, 1813

I am *ennuyé* beyond my usual tense of that yawning verb, which I am always conjugating; and I don't find that society much mends the matter. I am too lazy to shoot myself—and it would annoy Augusta, and perhaps * *; but it would be a good thing for George, on the other side, and no bad one for me; but I won't be tempted.

I have had the kindest letter from Moore. I *do* think that man is the best-hearted, the only *hearted* being I ever encountered; and, then, his talents are equal to his feelings.

Dined on Wednesday at Lord H.'s—the Staffords, Staels, Cowpers, Ossulstones, Melbournes, Mackintoshes, etc., etc.— and was introduced to the Marquis and Marchioness of Stafford, —an unexpected event. My quarrel with Lord Carlisle (their or his brother-in-law) having rendered it improper, I suppose, brought it about. But, if it was to happen at all, I wonder it did not occur before. She is handsome, and must have been beautiful—and her manners are *princessly*.

The Stael was at the other end of the table, and less loquacious than heretofore. We are now very good friends; though she asked Lady Melbourne whether I had really any *bon-hommie*. She might as well have asked that question before she told C. L. "*c'est un démon*". True enough, but rather premature, for *she* could not have found it out, and so—she wants me to dine there next Sunday.

Murray prospers, as far as circulation. For my part, I adhere (in liking) to my Fragment. It is no wonder that I wrote one—my mind is a fragment.

Saw Lord Gower, Tierney, etc., in the square. Took leave of Lord Gower, who is going to Holland and Germany. He tells me that he carries with him a parcel of *Harolds* and *Giaours*, etc., for the readers of Berlin, who, it seems, read English, and have taken a caprice for mine. Um!—have I been *German* all this time, when I thought myself *Oriental*?

Lent Tierney my box for to-morrow; and received a new comedy sent by Lady C. A.—but *not hers*. I must read it, and endeavour not to displease the author. I hate annoying them with cavil; but a comedy I take to be the most difficult of compositions, more so than tragedy.

Galt says there is a coincidence between the first part of *The Bride* and some story of his—whether published or not, I know not, never having seen it. He is almost the last person on whom any one would commit literary larceny, and I am not conscious of any *witting* thefts on any of the genus. As to originality, all pretensions are ludicrous,—" there is nothing new under the sun ".

Went last night to the play. Invited out to a party, but did not go;—right. Refused to go to Lady * *'s on Monday;—right again. If I must fritter away my life, I would rather do it alone. I was much tempted;—C * * looked so Turkish with her red turban, and her regular, dark, and clear features. Not that *she* and *I* ever were, or could be, any thing; but I love any aspect that reminds me of the " children of the sun ".

To dine to-day with Rogers and Sharpe, for which I have some appetite, not having tasted food for the preceding forty-eight hours. I wish I could leave off eating altogether.

Saturday, December 11

238

Sunday, December 12

By Galt's answer, I find it is some story in *real life*, and not any work with which my late composition coincides. It is still more singular, for mine is drawn from *existence* also.

I have sent an excuse to Madame de Stael. I do not feel sociable enough for dinner to-day;—and I will not go to Sheridan's on Wednesday. Not that I do not admire and prefer his unequalled conversation; but—that "*but*" must only be intelligible to thoughts I cannot write. Sheridan was in good talk at Rogers's the other night, but I only stayed till *nine*. All the world are to be at the Stael's to-night, and I am not sorry to escape any part of it. I only go out to get me a fresh appetite for being alone. Went out—did not go to the Stael's but to Ld. Holland's. Party numerous—conversation general. Stayed late—made a blunder—got over it—came home and went to bed, not having eaten. Rather empty, but *fresco*, which is the great point with me.

Monday, December 13, 1813

Called at three places—read, and got ready to leave town to-morrow. Murray has had a letter from his brother bibliopole of Edinburgh, who says, " he is lucky in having such a *poet* "— something as if one was a pack-horse, or " ass, or any thing that is his "; or, like Mrs. Packwood, who replied to some inquiry after the Odes on Razors,—" Laws, sir, we keeps a poet ". The same illustrious Edinburgh bookseller once sent an order for books, poesy, and cookery, with this agreeable postscript—" The *Harold* and *Cookery* are much wanted ". Such is fame, and, after all, quite as good as any other " life in others' breath ". 'Tis much the same to divide purchasers with Hannah Glasse [1] or Hannah More.

Some editor of some magazine has *announced* to Murray his intention of abusing the thing " *without reading it* ". So much the better; if he redde it first, he would abuse it more.

Allen [2] (Lord Holland's Allen—the best informed and one of the ablest men I know—a perfect Magliabecchi—a devourer,

---

[1] Authoress of *The Art of Cookery Made Easy*.

[2] John Allen was for many years the Hollands's librarian, confidential friend and general *factotum*.

a *Helluo* of books, and an observer of men,) has lent me a quantity of Burns's unpublished and never-to-be-published Letters. They are full of oaths and obscene songs. What an antithetical mind!—tenderness, roughness—delicacy, coarseness—sentiment, sensuality—soaring and grovelling, dirt and deity—all mixed up in that one compound of inspired clay!

It seems strange; a true voluptuary will never abandon his mind to the grossness of reality. It is by exalting the earthly, the material, the *physique* of our pleasures, by veiling these ideas, by forgetting them altogether, or, at least, never naming them hardly to one's self, that we alone can prevent them from disgusting.

December 14, 15, 16

Much done, but nothing to record. It is quite enough to set down my thoughts,—my actions will rarely bear retrospection.

December 17, 18

Lord Holland told me a curious piece of sentimentality in Sheridan. The other night we were all delivering our respective and various opinions on him and other *hommes marquans*, and mine was this :—" Whatever Sheridan has done or chosen to do has been, *par excellence*, always the *best* of its kind. He has written the *best* comedy (*School for Scandal*), the *best* drama (in my mind, far before that St. Giles's lampoon, the *Beggar's Opera*), the best farce (the *Critic*—it is only too good for a farce), and the best Address (Monologue on Garrick), and, to crown all, delivered the very best Oration (the famous Begum Speech) ever conceived or heard in this country." Somebody told S. this the next day, and on hearing it he burst into tears!

Poor Brinsley! if they were tears of pleasure, I would rather have said these few, but most sincere, words than have written the Iliad or made his own celebrated Philippic. Nay, his own comedy never gratified me more than to hear that he had derived a moment's gratification from any praise of mine, humble as it must appear to " my elders and my betters ".

Went to my box at Covent Garden to-night; and my delicacy felt a little shocked at seeing S * * *'s mistress (who, to my certain knowledge, was actually educated, from her birth, for her profession) sitting with her mother, " a three-piled b——d, b——d-Major to the army ", in a private box opposite. I felt rather indignant; but, casting my eyes round the house, in the next box to me, and the next, and the next, were the most distinguished old and young Babylonians of quality;—so I burst out a laughing. It was really odd; Lady * * *divorced*—Lady * * and her daughter, Lady * *, both *divorceable*—Mrs. * *, in the next the *like*, and still nearer * * * * * * ! What an assemblage to *me*, who know all their histories. It was as if the house had been divided between your public and your *understood* courtesans;—but the intriguantes much outnumbered the regular mercenaries. On the other side were only Pauline and *her* mother, and, next box to her, three of inferior note. Now, where lay the difference between *her* and *mamma*, and Lady * * and daughter? except that the two last may enter Carleton and any *other house*, and the two first are limited to the opera and b—— house. How I do delight in observing life as it really is!—and myself, after all, the worst of any. But no matter—I must avoid egotism, which, just now, would be no vanity.

I have lately written a wild, rambling, unfinished rhapsody, called " *The Devil's Drive* ", the notion of which I took from Porson's " *Devil's Walk* ".

Redde some Italian, and wrote two Sonnets on * * *. I never wrote but one sonnet before, and that was not in earnest, and many years ago, as an exercise—and I will never write another. They are the most puling, petrifying, stupidly platonic compositions. I detest the Petrarch so much, that I would not be the man even to have obtained his Laura, which the metaphysical, whining dotard never could.

January 16, 1814

To-morrow I leave town for a few days. I saw Lewis to-day, who is just returned from Oatlands, where he has been squabbling with Mad. de Stael about himself, Clarissa Harlowe, Mackintosh, and me. My homage has never been paid in that quarter, or we would have agreed still worse. I don't talk—I can't flatter, and won't listen, except to a pretty or a foolish woman. She bored Lewis with praises of himself till he sickened —found out that Clarissa was perfection, and Mackintosh the first man in England. There I agree, at least *one* of the first— but Lewis did not. As to Clarissa, I leave to those who can read it to judge and dispute. I could not do the one, and am, consequently, not qualified for the other. She told Lewis wisely, he being my friend, that I was affected, in the first place ; and that, in the next place, I committed the heinous offence of sitting at dinner with my *eyes* shut, or half shut. I wonder if I really have this trick. I must cure myself of it, if true. One insensibly acquires awkward habits, which should be broken in time. If this is one, I wish I had been told of it before. It would not so much signify if one was always to be checkmated by a plain woman, but one may as well see some of one's neighbours, as well as the plate upon the table.

I should like, of all things, to have heard the Amabæan eclogue between her and Lewis—both obstinate, clever, odd, garrulous, and shrill. In fact, one could have heard nothing else. But they fell out, alas !—and now they will never quarrel again. Could not one reconcile them for the " nonce "? Poor Corinne—she will find that some of her fine sayings won't suit our fine ladies and gentlemen.

I am getting rather into admiration of [Lady C. Annesley] the youngest sister of [Lady F. Webster]. A wife would be my salvation. I am sure the wives of my acquaintances have hitherto done me little good. Catherine is beautiful, but very young, and, I think, a fool. But I have not seen enough to judge ; besides, I hate an *esprit* in petticoats. That she won't love me is very probable, nor shall I love her. But, on my system, and the modern system in general, that don't signify. The business (if it came to business) would probably be arranged between papa and me. She would have her own way ;

I am good-humoured to women, and docile; and, if I did not fall in love with her, which I should try to prevent, we should be a very comfortable couple. As to conduct, *that* she must look to. But *if* I love, I shall be jealous;—and for that reason I will not be in love. Though, after all, I doubt my temper, and fear I should not be so patient as becomes the *bienséance* of a married man in my station. Divorce ruins the poor *femme*, and damages are a paltry compensation. I do fear my temper would lead me into some of our oriental tricks of vengeance, or, at any rate, into a summary appeal to the court of twelve paces. So " I'll none on't ", but e'en remain single and solitary;— though I should like to have somebody now and then to yawn with one.

Ward, and, after him, * *, has stolen one of my buffooneries about Mde de Stael's Metaphysics and the Fog, and passed it, by speech and letter, as their own. As Gibbet says, " they are the most of a gentleman of any on the road ". W. is in sad enmity with the Whigs about this Review of Fox (if he *did* review him);—all the epigrammatists and essayists are at him. I hate *odds*, and wish he may beat them. As for me, by the blessing of indifference, I have simplified my politics into an utter detestation of all existing governments; and, as it is the shortest and most agreeable and summary feeling imaginable, the first moment of an universal republic would convert me into an advocate for single and uncontradicted despotism. The fact is, riches are power, and poverty is slavery all over the earth, and one sort of establishment is no better nor worse for a *people* than another. I shall adhere to my party, because it would not be honourable to act otherwise; but, as to *opinions*, I don't think politics *worth* an *opinion*. *Conduct* is another thing : —if you begin with a party, go on with them. I have no consistency, except in politics; and *that* probably arises from my indifference on the subject altogether.

Feb. 18

Better than a month since I last journalised :—most of it out of London and at Notts., but a busy one and a pleasant, at least three weeks of it. On my return, I find all the news-papers in hysterics, and town in an uproar, on the avowal and republication of two stanzas on Princess Charlotte's weeping

at Regency's speech to Lauderdale in 1812.[1] They are daily
at it still;—some of the abuse good, all of it hearty. They talk
of a motion in our House upon it—be it so.

Got up—redde the *Morning Post* containing the battle of
Buonaparte, the destruction of the Custom-house, and a paragraph on me as long as my pedigree, and vituperative, as usual.

Hobhouse is returned to England. He is my best friend,
the most lively, and a man of the most sterling talents extant.

The Corsair has been conceived, written, published, etc.,
since I last took up this journal. They tell me it has great
success;—it was written *con amore*, and much from *existence*.
Murray is satisfied with its progress; and if the public are
equally so with the perusal, there's an end of the matter.

Nine o'clock

Been to Hanson's on business. Saw Rogers, and had a
note from Lady Melbourne, who says, it is said I am " much
out of spirits ". I wonder if I really am or not? I have
certainly enough of " that perilous stuff which weighs upon the
heart ", and it is better they should believe it to be the result of
these attacks than of the real cause; but—ay, ay, always *but*,
to the end of the chapter.

Hobhouse has told me ten thousand anecdotes of Napoleon,
all good and true. My friend H. is the most entertaining of
companions, and a fine fellow to boot.

Redde a little—wrote notes and letters, and am alone,
which Locke says is bad company. " Be not solitary, be not
idle."—Um !—the idleness is troublesome; but I can't see so
much to regret in the solitude. The more I see of men, the less
I like them. If I could but say so of women too, all would be
well. Why can't I? I am now six-and-twenty; my passions
have had enough to cool them; my affections more than
enough to wither them,—and yet—and yet—always *yet* and
but—" Excellent well, you are a fishmonger—get thee to a
nunnery ". " They fool me to the top of my bent."

---

[1] Byron's *Stanzas to a Lady Weeping*—occasioned by the report that Princess
Charlotte had burst into tears at a Carlton House banquet on hearing her father,
the Prince Regent, attack his former friends, the Whigs—had originally appeared
anonymously in the *Morning Chronicle* during March 1812. Byron's avowal of
authorship caused a considerable commotion.

Midnight

Began a letter, which I threw into the fire. Redde—but to little purpose. Did not visit Hobhouse, as I promised and ought. No matter, the loss is mine. Smoked cigars.

Napoleon!—this week will decide his fate. All seems against him; but I believe and hope he will win—at least, beat back the invaders. What right have we to prescribe sovereigns to France? Oh for a Republic! " Brutus, thou sleepest." Hobhouse abounds in continental anecdotes of this extraordinary man; all in favour of his intellect and courage, but against his *bonhommie*. No wonder;—how should he, who knows mankind well, do other than despise and abhor them?

The greater the equality, the more impartially evil is distributed, and becomes lighter by the division among so many—therefore, a Republic!

More notes from Madame de Stael unanswered—and so they shall remain. I admire her abilities, but really her society is overwhelming—an avalanche that buries one in glittering nonsense—all snow and sophistry.

Shall I go to Mackintosh's on Tuesday? um!—I did not go to Marquis Lansdowne's nor to Miss Berry's, though both are pleasant. So is Sir James's,—but I don't know—I believe one is not the better for parties; at least, unless some *regnante* is there.

I wonder how the deuce any body could make such a world; for what purpose dandies, for instance, were ordained —and kings—and fellows of colleges—and women of " a certain age "—and many men of any age—and myself, most of all!

> " Divesne prisco natus ab Inacho
> Nil interest, an pauper et infimâ
> De gente, sub dio [*sic*] moreris,
> Victima nil miserantis Orci.
> Omnes eodem cogimur ", etc.

Is there any thing beyond?—*who* knows? *He* that can't tell. Who tells that there *is*? He who don't know. And when shall he know? perhaps, when he don't expect, and generally when he don't wish it. In this last respect, however, all are not alike: it depends a good deal upon education,—something upon nerves and habits—but most upon digestion.

Saturday, Feb. 19

Just returned from seeing Kean in Richard. By Jove, he is a soul! Life—nature—truth without exaggeration or diminution. Kemble's Hamlet is perfect; but Hamlet is not Nature. Richard is a man; and Kean is Richard. Now to my own concerns.

Went to Waite's. Teeth are all right and white; but he says that I grind them in my sleep and chip the edges. That same sleep is no friend of mine, though I court him sometimes for half the twenty-four.

February 20

Got up and tore out two leaves of this Journal—I don't know why. Hodgson just called and gone. He has much *bonhommie* with his other good qualities, and more talent than he has yet had credit for beyond his circle.

An invitation to dine at Holland House to meet Kean. He is worth meeting; and I hope, by getting into good society, he will be prevented from falling like Cooke. He is greater now on the stage, and off he should never be less. There is a stupid and underrating criticism upon him in one of the newspapers. I thought that, last night, though great, he rather under-acted more than the first time. This may be the effect of these cavils; but I hope he has more sense than to mind them. He cannot expect to maintain his present eminence, or to advance still higher, without the envy of his green-room fellows, and the nibbling of their admirers. But, if he don't beat them all, why then—merit hath no purchase in " these coster-monger days ".

I wish that I had a talent for the drama; I would write a tragedy *now*. But no,—it is gone. Hodgson talks of one,—he will do it well;—and I think M—e [Moore] should try. He has wonderful powers, and much variety; besides, he has lived and felt. To write so as to bring home to the heart, the heart must have been tried,—but, perhaps, ceased to be so. While you are under the influence of passions, you only feel, but cannot describe them,—any more than, when in action, you could turn round and tell the story to your next neighbour! When all is over,—all, all, and irrevocable,—trust to memory— she is then but too faithful.

Went out, and answered some letters, yawned now and then, and redde the *Robbers*. Fine,—but *Fiesco* is better; and Alfieri, and Monti's *Aristodemo best*. They are more equal than the Tedeschi dramatists.

Answered—or rather acknowledged—the receipt of young Reynolds's poem, *Safie*. The lad is clever, but much of his thoughts are borrowed,—*whence*, the Reviewers may find out. I hate discouraging a young one; and I think,—though wild and more oriental than he would be, had he seen the scenes where he has placed his tale,—that he has much talent, and, certainly fire enough.

Received a very singular epistle; and the mode of its conveyance, through Lord H.'s hands, as curious as the letter itself. But it was gratifying and pretty.

Sunday, February 27

Here I am, alone, instead of dining at Lord H.'s, where I was asked,—but not inclined to go any where. Hobhouse says I am growing a *loup garou*,—a solitary hobgoblin. True;—" I am myself alone ". The last week has been passed in reading —seeing plays—now and then visitors—sometimes yawning and sometimes sighing, but no writing,—save of letters. If I could always read, I should never feel the want of society. Do I regret it?—um!—" Man delights not me ", and only one woman—at a time.

There is something to me very softening in the presence of a woman,—some strange influence, even if one is not in love with them—which I cannot at all account for, having no very high opinion of the sex. But yet,—I always feel in better humour with myself and every thing else, if there is a woman within ken. Even Mrs. Mule, my firelighter,—the most ancient and withered of her kind,—and (except to myself) not the best-tempered—always makes me laugh,—no difficult task when I am " i' the vein ".

Heigho! I would I were in mine island!—I am not well; and yet I look in good health. At times I fear, " I am not in my perfect mind ";—and yet my heart and head have stood many a crash, and what should ail them now? They prey upon themselves, and I am sick—sick—" Prithee, undo this button—why should a cat, a rat, a dog have life—and *thou* no life at all? " Six-and-twenty years, as they call them, why, I might and should have been a Pasha by this time. " I 'gin to be a-weary of the sun."

Buonaparte is not yet beaten; but has rebutted Blucher, and repiqued Schwartzenburg. This it is to have a head. If he again wins, *Væ victis!*

Sunday, March 6

On Tuesday last dined with Rogers,—Madame de Staël, Mackintosh, Sheridan, Erskine, and Payne Knight, Lady Donegal, and Miss R. there. Sheridan told a very good story of himself and Madame de Recamier's handkerchief; Erskine a few stories of himself only. *She* is going to write a big book about England, she says;—I believe her. Asked by her how I liked Miss Edgeworth's thing, called *Patronage*, and answered (very sincerely) that I thought it very bad for *her*, and worse than any of the others. Afterwards thought it possible Lady Donegal, being Irish, might be a patroness of Miss Edgeworth, and was rather sorry for my opinion, as I hate putting people into fusses, either with themselves or their favourites; it looks as if one did it on purpose. The party went off very well, and the fish was very much to my gusto. But we got up too soon after the women; and Mrs. Corinne always lingers so long after dinner that we wish her in—the drawing-room.

To-day Campbell called, and while sitting here in came Merivale. During our colloquy, C. (ignorant that Merivale was the writer) abused the " mawkishness of the *Quarterly Review* of Grimm's *Correspondence* ". I (knowing the secret) changed the conversation as soon as I could; and C. went away, quite convinced of having made the most favourable impression on his new acquaintance. Merivale is luckily a very good-natured fellow, or God he knows what might have been engendered from such a malaprop. I did not look at him while this was going on, but I felt like a coal—for I like Merivale, as well as the article in question.

Asked to Lady Keith's to-morrow evening—I think I will go; but it is the first party invitation I have accepted this " season ", as the learned Fletcher called it, when that youngest brat of Lady * *'s cut my eye and cheek open with a misdirected pebble—" Never mind, my Lord, the scar will be gone before the *season* "; as if one's eye was of no importance in the mean time.

Lord Erskine called, and gave me his famous pamphlet,[1] with a marginal note and corrections in his handwriting. Sent it to be bound superbly, and shall treasure it.

Sent my fine print of Napoleon to be framed. It *is* framed; and the Emperor becomes his robes as if he had been hatched in them.

March 7

Rose at seven—ready by half-past eight—went to Mr. Hanson's, Bloomsbury Square—went to church with his eldest daughter, Mary Anne (a good girl), and gave her away to the Earl of Portsmouth.[2] Saw her fairly a countess—congratulated the family and groom (bride)—drank a bumper of wine (wholesome sherris) to their felicity, and all that—and came home. Asked to stay to dinner, but could not. At three sat to Phillips for faces. Called on Lady M. [Melbourne]—I like her so well, that I always stay too long. (Mem.—to mend of that.)

Passed the evening with Hobhouse, who has begun a poem, which promises highly;—wish he would go on with it. Heard some curious extracts from a life of Morosini, the blundering Venetian, who blew up the Acropolis at Athens with a bomb, and be damned to him! Waxed sleepy—just come home— must go to bed, and am engaged to meet Sheridan to-morrow at Rogers's.

Queer ceremony that same of marriage—saw many abroad, Greek and Catholic—one, at *home*, many years ago. There be some strange phrases in the prologue (the exhortation), which made me turn away, not to laugh in the face of the surpliceman. Made one blunder, when I joined the hands of the happy—rammed their left hands, by mistake, into one another. Corrected it—bustled back to the altar-rail, and said " Amen ". Portsmouth responded as if he had got the whole by heart; and, if any thing, was rather before the priest. It is now midnight and * * *.

March 10, Thor's Day

On Tuesday dined with Rogers,—Mackintosh, Sheridan, Sharpe,—much talk, and good,—all, except my own little

---

[1] Lord Erskine, Lord Chancellor in 1806, was a Whig and sympathizer with the principles of the French Revolution. The pamphlet to which Byron alludes was published in 1797, *On the Causes and Consequences of the War with France*.

[2] Mary Anne Hanson's marriage to Lord Portsmouth eventually led to an embittered law-suit, during which the bridegroom's sanity at the time of their marriage was called in question.

prattlement. Much of old times—Horne Tooke—the Trials—
evidence of Sheridan, and anecdotes of those times, when *I*,
alas! was an infant. If I had been a man, I would have made
an English Lord Edward Fitzgerald.

Set down Sheridan at Brookes's,—where, by the by, he
could not have well set down himself, as he and I were the only
drinkers. Sherry means to stand for Westminster, as Cochrane
(the stock-jobbing hoaxer) must vacate. Brougham is a candidate. I fear for poor dear Sherry. Both have talents of the
highest order, but the youngster has *yet* a character. We shall
see, if he lives to Sherry's age, how he will pass over the redhot
ploughshares of public life. I don't know why, but I hate to
see the *old* ones lose; particularly Sheridan, notwithstanding
all his *méchanceté*.

Received many, and the kindest, thanks from Lady
Portsmouth, *père* and *mère*, for my match-making. I don't
regret it, as she looks the countess well, and is a very good girl.
It is odd how well she carries her new honours. She looks a
different woman, and high-bred, too. I had no idea that I
could make so good a peeress.

Went to the play with Hobhouse. Mrs. Jordan superlative
in Hoyden, and Jones well enough in Foppington. *What
plays!* what wit!—*hélas!* Congreve and Vanbrugh are your
only comedy. Our society is too insipid now for the like copy.
Would *not* go to Lady Keith's. Hobhouse thought it odd. I
wonder *he* should like parties. If one is in love, and wants to
break a commandment and covet any thing that is there, they
do very well. But to go out amongst the mere herd, without a
motive, pleasure, or pursuit—'sdeath! " I'll none of it." He
told me an odd report,—that *I* am the actual Conrad, the
veritable Corsair, and that part of my travels are supposed to
have passed in privacy. Um!—people sometimes hit near the
truth; but never the whole truth. H. don't know what I was
about the year after he left the Levant; nor does any one—
nor —— nor —— nor —— however, it is a lie—but, " I doubt
the equivocation of the fiend that lies like truth! "

I shall have letters of importance to-morrow. Which, * *,
* *, or * *? heigho!—* * is in my heart, * * in my head, * * in
my eye, and the *single* one, Heaven knows where. All write,
and will be answered. " Since I have crept in favour with

myself, I must maintain it " ; but I never " mistook my person ",
though I think others have.

* * called to-day in great despair about his mistress, who
has taken a freak of * * *. He began a letter to her, but was
obliged to stop short—I finished it for him, and he copied and
sent it. If *he* holds out, and keeps to my instructions of affected
indifference, she will lower her colours. If she don't, he will,
at least, get rid of her, and she don't seem much worth keeping.
But the poor lad is in love—if that is the case, she will win.
When they once discover their power, *finita è la musica*.

Sleepy, and must go to bed.

Tuesday, March 15

Dined yesterday with Rogers, Mackintosh, and Sharpe.
Sheridan could not come. Sharpe told several very amusing
anecdotes of Henderson, the actor. Stayed till late, and came
home, having drunk so much *tea*, that I did not get to sleep till
six this morning. R. says I am to be in *this Quarterly*—cut up,
I presume, as they " hate us youth ". *N'importe*. As Sharpe
was passing by the doors of some debating society (the Westminster Forum), in his way to dinner, he saw rubricked on the
wall *Scott's* name and *mine*—" Which the best poet? " being
the question of the evening; and I suppose all the Templars
and *would-bes* took our rhymes in vain in the course of the
controversy. Which had the greater show of hands, I neither
know nor care; but I feel the coupling of the names as a
compliment—though I think Scott deserves better company.

Wedderburn Webster called—Lord Erskine, Lord Holland,
etc., etc. Wrote to * * *The Corsair* report. She says she don't
wonder, since " Conrad is so *like* ". It is odd that one, who
knows me so thoroughly, should tell me this to my face. However, if she don't know, nobody can.

Mackintosh is, it seems, the writer of the defensive letter in
the *Morning Chronicle*. If so, it is very kind, and more than I
did for myself.

Told Murray to secure for me Bandello's Italian Novels at
the sale to-morrow. To me they will be *nuts*. Redde a satire
on myself, called " Anti-Byron ", and told Murray to publish
it if he liked. The object of the author is to prove me an
atheist and a systematic conspirator against law and govern-

ment. Some of the verse is good; the prose I don't quite understand. He asserts that my " deleterious works " have had " an effect upon civil society, which requires ", etc., etc., etc., and his own poetry. It is a lengthy poem, and a long preface, with an harmonious title-page. Like the fly in the fable, I seem to have got upon a wheel which makes much dust; but, unlike the said fly, I do not take it all for my own raising.

A letter from *Bella*, which I answered. I shall be in love with her again if I don't take care.

I shall begin a more regular system of reading soon.

Thursday, March 17

I have been sparring with Jackson for exercise this morning; and mean to continue and renew my acquaintance with the muffles. My chest, and arms, and wind are in very good plight, and I am not in flesh. I used to be a hard hitter, and my arms are very long for my height (5 feet 8½ inches). At any rate, exercise is good, and this the severest of all; fencing and the broadsword never fatigued me half so much.

Redde the *Quarrels of Authors* (another sort of *sparring*)—a new work, by that most entertaining and researching writer, Israeli. They seem to be an irritable set, and I wish myself well out of it. " I'll not march through Coventry with them, that's flat." What the devil had I to do with scribbling? It is too late to inquire, and all regret is useless. But, an it were to do again,—I should write again, I suppose. Such is human nature, at least my share of it;—though I shall think better of myself, if I have sense to stop now. If I have a wife, and that wife has a son—by any body—I will bring up mine heir in the most anti-poetical way—make him a lawyer, or a pirate, or—any thing. But, if he writes too, I shall be sure he is none of mine, and cut him off with a Bank token. Must write a letter—three o'clock.

Sunday, March 20

I intended to go to Lady Hardwicke's, but won't. I always begin the day with a bias towards going to parties; but, as the evening advances, my stimulus fails, and I hardly ever go out—and, when I do, always regret it. This might have been a pleasant one ;—at least, the hostess is a very superior woman. Lady Lansdowne's to-morrow—Lady Heathcote's Wednesday. Um !—I must spur myself into going to some of them, or it will look like rudeness, and it is better to do as other people do—confound them !

Redde Machiavel, parts of Chardin, and Sismondi, and Bandello—by starts. Redde the *Edinburgh*, 44, just come out. In the beginning of the article on Edgeworth's *Patronage*, I have gotten a high compliment, I perceive. Whether this is creditable to me, I know not ; but it does honour to the editor, because he once abused me. Many a man will retract praise ; none but a high-spirited mind will revoke its censure, or *can* praise the man it has once attacked. I have often, since my return to England, heard Jeffrey most highly commended by those who know him for things independent of his talents. I admire him for *this*—not because he has *praised me* (I have been so praised elsewhere and abused, alternately, that mere habit has rendered me as indifferent to both as a man at twenty-six can be to any thing), but because he is, perhaps, the *only man* who, under the relations in which he and I stand, or stood, with regard to each other, would have had the liberality to act thus ; none but a great soul dared hazard it. The height on which he stands has not made him giddy ;—a little scribbler would have gone on cavilling to the end of the chapter. As to the justice of his panegyric, that is matter of taste. There are plenty to question it, and glad, too, of the opportunity.

Lord Erskine called to-day. He means to carry down his reflections on the war—or rather wars—to the present day. I trust that he will. Must send to Mr. Murray to get the binding of my copy of his pamphlet finished, as Lord E. has promised me to correct it, and add some marginal notes to it. Any thing in his handwriting will be a treasure, which will gather compound interest from years. Erskine has high expectations of Mackintosh's promised History. Undoubtedly it must be a classic, when finished.

Sparred with Jackson again yesterday morning, and shall to-morrow. I feel all the better for it, in spirits, though my arms and shoulders are very stiff from it. Mem.—to attend the pugilistic dinner :—Marquess Huntley is in the chair.

Lord Erskine thinks that ministers must be in peril of going

out. So much the better for him. To me it is the same who
are in or out;—we want something more than a change of
ministers, and someday we will have it.

I remember, in riding from Chrisso to Castri (Delphos),
along the sides of Parnassus, I saw six eagles in the air. It is
uncommon to see so many together; and it was the number—
not the species, which is common enough—that excited my
attention.

The last bird I ever fired at was an *eaglet*, on the shore of
the Gulf of Lepanto, near Vostitza. It was only wounded,
and I tried to save it, the eye was so bright; but it pined, and
died in a few days; and I never did since, and never will,
attempt the death of another bird. I wonder what put these
two things into my head just now? I have been reading
Sismondi, and there is nothing there that could induce the
recollection.

I am mightily taken with Braccio di Montone, Giovanni
Galeazzo, and Eccelino. But the last is *not* Bracciaferro (of
the same name), Count of Ravenna, whose history I want to
trace. There is a fine engraving in Lavater, from a picture by
Fuseli, of *that* Ezzelin, over the body of Meduna, punished by
him for a *hitch* in her constancy during his absence in the
Crusades. He was right—but I want to know the story.

Tuesday, March 22

Last night, *party* at Lansdowne House. To-night, *party*
at Lady Charlotte Greville's—deplorable waste of time, and
something of temper. Nothing imparted—nothing acquired—
talking without ideas :—if any thing like *thought* in my mind,
it was not on the subjects on which we were gabbling. Heigho!
—and in this way half London pass what is called life. To-
morrow there is Lady Heathcote's—shall I go? yes—to punish
myself for not having a pursuit.

Let me see—what did I see? The only person who much
struck me was Lady S[taffor]d's eldest daughter, Lady C[har-
lotte] L[eveson]. They say she is *not* pretty. I don't know—
every thing is pretty that pleases; but there is an air of *soul*
about her—and her colour changes—and there is that shyness
of the antelope (which I delight in) in her manner so much,

that I observed her more than I did any other woman in the rooms, and only looked at any thing else when I thought she might perceive and feel embarrassed by my scrutiny. After all, there may be something of association in this. She is a friend of Augusta's, and whatever she loves I can't help liking.

Her mother, the Marchioness, talked to me a little; and I was twenty times on the point of asking her to introduce me to *sa fille*, but I stopped short. This comes of that affray with the Carlisles.

Earl Grey told me laughingly of a paragraph in the last *Moniteur*, which has stated, among other symptoms of rebellion, some particulars of the *sensation* occasioned in all our government gazettes by the " tear " lines,—*only* amplifying, in its re-statement, an epigram (by the by, no epigram except in the *Greek* acceptation of the word) into a *roman*. I wonder the *Couriers*, etc., etc., have not translated that part of the *Moniteur*, with additional comments.

The Princess of Wales has requested Fuseli to paint from *The Corsair*—leaving to him the choice of any passage for the subject : so Mr. Locke tells me. Tired, jaded, selfish, and supine—must go to bed.

Roman, at least *Romance*, means a song sometimes, as in the Spanish. I suppose this is the *Moniteur's* meaning, unless he has confused it with *The Corsair*.

Albany, March 28

This night got into my new apartments, rented of Lord Althorpe, on a lease of seven years. Spacious, and room for my books and sabres. *In* the *house*, too, another advantage. The last few days, or whole week, have been very abstemious, regular in exercise, and yet very *un*well.

Yesterday, dined *tête-à-tête* at the Cocoa with Scrope Davies—sat from six till midnight—drank between us one bottle of champagne and six of claret, neither of which wines ever affect me. Offered to take Scrope home in my carriage ; but he was tipsy and pious, and I was obliged to leave him on his knees praying to I know not what purpose or pagod. No headach, nor sickness, that night nor to-day. Got up, if any thing, earlier than usual—sparred with Jackson *ad sudorem*, and have been much better in health than for many days. I have heard nothing more from Scrope. Yesterday paid him four thousand eight hundred pounds, a debt of some standing, and which I wished to have paid before. My mind is much relieved by the removal of that *debit*.

Augusta wants me to make it up with Carlisle. I have refused *every* body else, but I can't deny her any thing;—so I must e'en do it, though I had as lief " drink up Eisel—eat a crocodile ". Let me see—Ward, the Hollands, the Lambs, Rogers, etc., etc.,—every body, more or less, have been trying for the last two years to accommodate this *couplet* quarrel, to no purpose. I shall laugh if Augusta succeeds.

Redde a little of many things—shall get in all my books to-morrow. Luckily this room will hold them—with " ample room and verge, etc., the characters of hell to trace ". I must set about some employment soon; my heart begins to eat *itself* again.

April 8

Out of town six days. On my return, found my poor little pagod, Napoleon, pushed off his pedestal;—the thieves are in Paris. It is his own fault. Like Milo, he would rend the oak; but it closed again, wedged his hands, and now the beasts— lion, bear, down to the dirtiest jackal—may all tear him. That Muscovite winter *wedged* his arms;—ever since, he has fought with his feet and teeth. The last may still leave their marks; and " I guess now " (as the Yankees say) that he will yet play them a pass. He is in their rear—between them and their homes. Query—will they ever reach them?

Saturday, April 9, 1814

I mark this day!

Napoleon Buonaparte has abdicated the throne of the world. " Excellent well." Methinks Sylla did better; for he revenged and resigned in the height of his sway, red with the slaughter of his foes—the finest instance of glorious contempt of the rascals upon record. Dioclesian did well too—Amurath not amiss, had he become aught except a dervise—Charles the Fifth but so so—but Napoleon, worst of all. What! wait till they were in his capital, and then talk of his readiness to give up what is already gone !! " What whining monk art thou—what holy cheat? " 'Sdeath!—Dionysius at Corinth was yet a king to this. The " Isle of Elba " to retire to !—Well—if it had been Caprea, I should have marvelled less. " I see men's minds are but a parcel of their fortunes." I am utterly bewildered and confounded.

I don't know—but I think *I*, even *I* (an insect compared with this creature), have set my life on casts not a millionth part of this man's. But, after all, a crown may be not worth dying for. Yet, to outlive *Lodi* for this !!! Oh that Juvenal or Johnson could rise from the dead ! *Expende—quot libras in duce summo invenies?* I knew they were light in the balance of mortality; but I thought their living dust weighed more *carats*. Alas! this imperial diamond hath a flaw in it, and is now hardly fit to stick in a glazier's pencil :—the pen of the historian won't rate it worth a ducat.

Psha ! " something too much of this ". But I won't give him up even now; though all his admirers have, " like the thanes, fallen from him ".

April 10

I do not know that I am happiest when alone ; but this I am sure of, that I never am long in the society even of *her* I love, (God knows too well, and the devil probably too,) without a yearning for the company of my lamp and my utterly confused and tumbled-over library. Even in the day, I send away my carriage oftener than I use or abuse it. *Per esempio*,—I have not stirred out of these rooms for these four days past : but I have sparred for exercise (windows open) with Jackson an hour daily, to attenuate and keep up the ethereal part of me. The more violent the fatigue, the better my spirits for the rest of the day ; and then, my evenings have that calm nothingness of languor, which I most delight in. To-day I have boxed an hour—written an ode to Napoleon Buonaparte—copied it—eaten six biscuits—drunk four bottles of soda water—redde away the rest of my time—besides giving poor [? Webster] a world of advice about this mistress of his, who is plaguing him into a phthisic and intolerable tediousness. I am a pretty fellow truly to lecture about " the sect ". No matter, my counsels are all thrown away.

April 19, 1814

There is ice at both poles, north and south—all extremes are the same—misery belongs to the highest and the lowest only, to the emperor and the beggar, when unsixpenced and unthroned. There is, to be sure, a damned insipid medium—an equinoctial line—no one knows where, except upon maps and measurement.

> " And all our *yesterdays* have lighted fools
>   The way to dusty death."

I will keep no further journal of that same hesternal torch-light ; and, to prevent me from returning, like a dog, to the vomit of memory, I tear out the remaining leaves of this volume, and write, in *Ipecacuanha*,—" that the Bourbons are re-stored ! ! ! "—" Hang up philosophy." To be sure, I have long despised myself and man, but I never spat in the face of my species before—" O fool ! I shall go mad ".

TO THOMAS MOORE *January 6, 1814*

I have got a devil of a long story in the press, entitled " *The Corsair* ", in the regular heroic measure. It is a pirate's isle, peopled with my own creatures, and you may easily suppose they do a world of mischief through the three cantos. Now for your dedication—if you will accept it. This is positively my last experiment on public *literary* opinion, till I turn my thirtieth year,—if so be I flourish until that downhill period. I have a confidence for you—a perplexing one to me, and, just at present, in a state of abeyance in itself. * * * * * * However, we shall see. In the mean time, you may amuse yourself with my suspense, and put all the justices of peace in requisition, in case I come into your county with " hackbut bent ".

Seriously, whether I am to hear from her or him, it is a *pause*, which I shall fill up with as few thoughts of my own as I can borrow from other people. Any thing is better than stagnation; and now, in the interregnum of my autumn and a strange summer adventure, which I don't like to think of, (I don't mean * *'s, however, which is laughable only), the antithetical state of my lucubrations makes me alive, and Macbeth can " sleep no more " :—he was lucky in getting rid of the drowsy sensation of waking again.

Pray write to me. I must send you a copy of the letter of dedication. When do you come out? I am sure we don't *clash* this time, for I am all at sea, and in action,—and a wife, and a mistress, etc.

Thomas, thou art a happy fellow; but if you wish us to be so, you must come up to town, as you did last year; and we shall have a world to say, and to see, and to hear. Let me hear from you.

P.S.—Of course you will keep my secret, and don't even talk in your sleep of it. Happen what may, your dedication is ensured, being already written; and I shall copy it out fair to-night, in case business or amusement—*Amant alterna Camœnæ.*

TO LADY MELBOURNE *January 8th, 1814*

MY DEAR L^Y M^E,—I have had too much in my head to write; but don't think my silence capricious.

C. is quite out—in yᵉ first place *she* [1] was not under the same roof, but first with my old friends the H[arrowby]'s in B[erkele]y Square, and afterwards at her friends the V[illiers]'s, nearer me. The separation and the express are utterly false, and without even a shadow of foundation; so you see her spies are ill paid, or badly informed. But if she had been in yᵉ same house, it is less singular than C.'s *coming* to it; the house was a very decent house, till that illustrious person thought proper to render it otherwise.

As to Mᵉ de Staël, I never go near her; her books are very delightful, but in society I see nothing but a plain woman forcing one to listen, and look at her, with her pen behind her ear, and her mouth full of ink—so much for her.

Now for a confidence—my old love of all loves—Mrs. ——[2] (whom somebody told you knew nothing about me) has written to me *twice*—no *love*, but she wants to see me; and though it will be a melancholy interview, I shall go; we have hardly met, and never been on any intimate terms since her marriage. *He* has been playing the Devil with all kinds of vulgar mistresses; and behaving ill enough, in every respect. I enclose you the *last*, which pray return immediately with your *opinion*, whether I *ought* to see her, or not—you see she is unhappy; she was a spoilt heiress; but has seen little or nothing of the world—very pretty, and once simple in character, and clever, but with no peculiar accomplishments, but endeared to me by a thousand childish, and singular recollections—you know her estate joined mine; and we were as children very much together; but no matter; *this* was a love match, they are *separated*.

I have heard from Ph.[3] who seems embarrassed with constancy. Her *date* is the *Grampian* hills, to be sure. With that latitude, and her precious *époux*, it must be a shuddering kind of existence.

C. may do as she pleases, thanks to your good-nature, rather than my merits, or prudence; there is little to dread from her love, and I forgive her hatred.

[1] Augusta Leigh. Caroline Lamb, " C.", had recently made an incursion into Byron's lodgings.

[2] Mary Anne Chaworth, the object of Byron's schoolboy passion, had married John Musters in 1805.

[3] Lady Frances Webster.

L^y H.'s second son is in Notts, and *she* has been guessing, and asking about Mrs. C.; no matter; so that I keep her from all other conjectures. I wrote to you in a tone which nothing but hurry can excuse. Don't think me impertinent, or peevish, but merely confused; *consider* one moment *all things*, and do not wonder. By-the-bye, I lately passed my time very *happily*.

By-the-bye, this letter will prove to you that we were at least friends, and that the mother-in-law erred when she told you that it was quite a *dream*. You will believe me another time. Adieu, ever y^{rs} Pray write and believe me

Most affect^y y^{rs}, B.

TO LADY MELBOURNE   *January 13th, 1814*

My DEAR L^y M^e,—I do not see how you could well have said less, and that I am not angry may be proved by my saying a word more on ye subject.

You are quite mistaken, however, as to *her*, and it must be from some misrepresentation of mine, that you throw the blame so completely on the side least deserving, and least able to bear it. I dare say I made the best of my own story, as one always does from natural selfishness without intending it, but it was not her fault, but my own *folly* (give it what name may suit it better) and her weakness, for the intentions of both were very different, and for some time adhered to, and when not, it was entirely my own—in short, I know no name for my conduct. Pray do not speak so harshly of her to me—the cause of all.

I wrote to you yesterday on other subjects, and particularly C. As to *manner*, mine is the same to anyone I know and like, and I am almost sure less marked to her than to *you*, besides any constraint, or reserve would appear much more extraordinary than the reverse, until something more than manner is ascertainable. Nevertheless, I heartily wish Me de Staël at the devil with her observations. I am certain I did not see her, and she might as well have had something else to do with her eyes than to observe people at so respectful a distance.

So " *Ph.* is out of my thoughts "—in the first place, if she were out of them, she had probably not found a place in my words, and in the next, she has no *claim*. If people will stop at the first tense of the verb " aimer ", they must not be surprised if one finishes the conjugation with somebody else—" How soon I get the better of—" in the name of St. Francis and his wife of snow, and Pygmalion and his statue—what was there here to get the better of? A few kisses, for which she was no worse, and I no better. Had the event been different, so would my subsequent resolutions, and feelings—for I am neither ungrateful, nor at all disposed to be disappointed ; on the contrary, I do firmly believe that I have often begun to *love*, at the very time I have heard people say that some dispositions become indifferent. Besides, her fool of a husband, and my own recent good resolutions, and a mixture of different piques and mental stimulants, together with something not unlike encouragement on her part, led me into that foolish business, out of which the way is quite easy ; and I really do not see that I have much to reproach myself with on her account. If you think differently pray say so.

As to Mrs. C[haworth-Musters], I will go ; but I don't see any good that can result from it, certainly none to me—but I have no right to consider myself. When I say this, I merely allude to uncomfortable *feelings*, for there is neither chance, nor fear of anything else ; for she is a very good girl, and I am too much dispirited to rise, even to admiration. I do verily believe *you* hope otherwise, as a means of improving me ; but I am sunk in my own estimation, and care of course very little for that of others.

As to *Ph.* she will end as all women in her situation do. It is impossible she can care about a man who acted so weakly as I did, with regard to herself.

What a fool I am—I have been interrupted by a visitor who is just gone, and have been laughing this half hour at a thousand absurdities, as if I had nothing serious to think about.

Y^rs ever, B.

P.S.—Another epistle from M[ary]. My answer must be under cover to " dear friend ", who is doing or suffering a folly —what can *she*, Miss R[adford], be about ?—the only thing that could make it look ill, is *mystery*. I wrote to her and *franked*, thinking there was no need of concealment; and indeed conceiving the affectation of it in an impertinence—but she desires me not—and I obey. I suspect R[adford] of wishing to make a scene between *him* and *me*, out of dislike to both, but that shall not prevent me from going, a moment.

I shall leave town on Sunday.

FRAGMENT OF A LETTER TO LADY MELBOURNE
                                    [*Undated*]

. . . pantomime. I don't think I laughed once, save in soliloquy, for ten days, which *you*, who know me, won't believe (everyone else thinks me the most gloomy of existences). We used to sit and look at one another, except in *duetto*, and then even our serious nonsense was not fluent; to be sure our gestures were rather more sensible. The most amusing part was the interchange of notes, for we sat up all night scribbling to each other, and came down like ghosts in the morning. I shall never forget the quiet manner in which she would pass her epistles in a music-book, or any book, looking in [Webster's] face with great tranquillity the whole time, and taking mine in the same way. One she offered me as I was leading her to dinner at N[ewstead], all the servants before, and W[ebster] and sister close behind. To take it was impossible, and how she was to retain it, without *pockets*, was equally perplexing. I had the cover of a letter from Claughton in mine, and gave it to her, saying, " There is the frank for L^y Water^d you asked for "; she returned it with the note beneath, with " it is dated wrong, alter it to-morrow ", and W[ebster] complaining that women did nothing but scribble—wondered how people could have the patience to frank and alter franks, and then happily digressed to the day of the month—fish sauce—good wine— and bad weather.

Your " matrimonial ladder " wants but one more descend-ing step—" d—nation ". I wonder how the carpenter omitted it—it concerned me much. I wish I were married, and don't care about beauty, nor *subsequent* virtue—nor much about fortune. I have made up my mind to share the decorations of

my betters—but I should like—let me see—liveliness, gentleness, cleanliness, and something of comeliness—and *my own*
first born. Was ever man more moderate? what do you think
of my " Bachelor's wife "? What a letter have I written !

TO LADY MELBOURNE *January 16th, 1814*

MY DEAR LADY M[ELBOURN]E,—Lewis is just returned from
Oatlands, where he has been quarrelling with Stael about
everything and everybody. She has not even let poor quiet
me alone, but has discovered, first, that I am affected ; and
2ndly, that I " *shut* my *eyes* during dinner ! " What this last
can mean I don't know, unless *she* is opposite. If I then do, she
is very much obliged to me ; and if at the same time I could
contrive to shut my ears, she would be still more so. If I really
have so ludicrous a habit, will *you* tell me so—and I will try
and break myself of it. In the meantime, I think the charge
will amuse you. I have worse faults to find with *her* than
" *shutting* her eyes "—one of which is opening her mouth too
frequently.

Do not you think people are very naught[y]? What do
you think I have this very day heard said of poor M[ary]. ? It
provoked me beyond anything, as *he* was named as authority—
why the abominable stories they circulate about Lady *W.*, of
which I can say no more. All this is owing to " dear friend " ;
and yet, as far as it regards " dear friend ", I must say I have
·very sufficing suspicions for believing them totally false ; at
least, she must have altered strangely within these nine years—
but this is the age of revolutions. Her ascendancy always
appeared to me that of a cunning mind over a weak one. But
—but—why the woman is a fright, which, after all, is the best
reason for not believing it.

I still mean to set off to-morrow, unless this snow adds so
much to the impracticability of the roads as to render it useless.
I don't mind anything but delay ; and I might as well be in
London as at a sordid inn, waiting for a thaw, or the subsiding
of a flood and the clearing of snow. I wonder what *your*
answer will be on *Ph.'s letter*. I am growing rather partial to

her younger sister; who is very pretty, but fearfully young—
and I think a *fool*. A wife, you say, would be my salvation.
Now I could have but one motive for marrying into that family
—and even *that* might possibly only produce a scene, and spoil
everything; but at all events it would in some degree be a
revenge, and in the very face of your compliment (*ironical*, I
believe) on the want of *selfishness*, I must say that I never can
quite get over the " *not* " of last summer—no—though it were
to become " yea " to-morrow.

I do believe that to marry would be my wisest step—but
whom? I might manage *this* easily with " le Père ", but I
don't admire the connection—and I have not committed myself by any attentions hitherto. But all wives would be much
the same. I have no *heart* to spare and expect none in return;
but, as Moore says, " A pretty wife is something for the fastidious vanity of a roué to *retire* upon ". And mine might do
as she pleased, so that she had a fair temper, and a *quiet* way of
conducting herself, leaving me the same liberty of conscience.
What I want is a companion—a friend rather than a sentimentalist. I have seen enough of love matches—and of all
matches—to make up my mind to the common lot of happy
couples. The only misery would be if I fell in love afterwards—
which is not unlikely, for habit has a strange power over my
affections. In that case I should be jealous, and then you do
not know what a devil any bad passion makes me. I should
very likely *do* all that *C. threatens* in her paroxysms; and I have
more reasons than you are aware of, for mistrusting myself on
this point.

Heigh-ho! Good night.

Ever y^rs most truly, B.

P.S.—The enclosed was written last night, and I am just
setting off. You shall hear from Newstead—if one ever gets
there in a coach really as large as the cabin of a " 74 ", and, I
believe, meant for the Atlantic instead of the Continent.

1,000 thanks for yours of this morn; " never loved so
before ". Well, then, I hope never to be loved *so* again—for
what is it to the *purpose*? You wonder how I answered it?
To tell you the *truth* (which I could not tell *her*), I have not
answered it at all—nor *shall*. I feel so much inclined to believe

her sincere, that I cannot sit down and coolly repay her truth with fifty falsehoods. I do not believe her for the same *reason* you *believe*, but because by writing she *commits* herself—and that is seldom done unless in earnest.

I shall be delighted to hear your *defence* against my insinuations, but you will make nothing of it—and he *is* very much to be envied. But you mistake me, for I do not mean in *general*; on the contrary, I coincide with him in taste but upon *one* instance.

C. was right about the poem. I have scribbled a longer one than either of the last, and it is in the press, but you know I never hold forth to you on such topics—why should I? Now you will think this a piece of conceit, but, really, it is a relief to the fever of my mind to *write*; and as at present I am what they call popular as an author—it enables me to serve one or two people without embarrassing anything but my brains—for I never have, nor shall avail myself of the *lucre*. And yet it would be folly merely to make presents to a bookseller, whose accounts *to* me last year are just 1,500 guineas, *without* including C[hild]e H[arol]d. Now the odd part is, that if I were a regular stipendiary, and wanted it, probably I should not be offered *one half*. But such are mankind—always offering or denying in the wrong place. But I have written more than enough already; and this is my last experiment on *public* patience—and just at present I won't try *yours* any further.

Ever, my dear L^{dy} M^e, etc., B.

TO LADY MELBOURNE *Newark, February 6th, 1814*

MY DEAR L^Y M^E,—I am thus far on my return to town, and having passed the Trent (which threatens a flood on ye first opportunity), I hope to reach town in tolerable plight.

Mr. Claughton has been with us during the last two days at N[ewstea]d, and this day set off for Cheshire, and I for the south, to prepare for a final and amicable arrangement.

M[ary Chaworth] I have not seen. Business and the weather, and badness of roads, and partly a late slight illness of her own, have interfered to prevent our meeting for the present, but I have heard a good deal from and of her. Him I have not heard from nor of; nor have I seen him; nor do I know exactly where he is; but somewhere in the country, I believe. You will very probably say that I ought to have gone over at all events, and Augusta has also been trying her rhetoric to the same purpose, and urging me repeatedly to call before I left the county. But I have been one day too busy, and another too lazy, and altogether so sluggish upon the subject, that I am thus far on my return without making this important visit on my way. She seems in her letters very undecided whether to return to —— or no, and I have always avoided both sides of the topic, or, if I touched on it at all, it was on the *rational* bearing of the question.

I have written to you two long letters from the Abbey, and, as I hope to see you soon, I will not try your eye-glass and patience further at present.

Ever y^{rs}, B.

FRAGMENT OF A LETTER TO LADY MELBOURNE
[Undated]

. . . prospect. I never shall. One of my great induce-ments to that brilliant negociation with the Princess of Parallelo-grams, was the vision of our *family party*, and the quantity of domestic lectures I should faithfully detail, without mutual comments thereupon.

You seem to think I am in some scrape at present by my unequal spirits. Perhaps I am, but you shan't be shocked, so you shan't. I won't draw further upon you for sympathy. You will be in town so soon, and I have scribbled so much, that you will be glad to see a letter shorter than usual.

I wish you would *lengthen* yours.

Ever my dear L^y M^e, B.

TO LADY MELBOURNE   *February 11th, 1814*

MY DEAR LADY M.,—On my arrival in town on Wednesday, I found myself in what the learned call a dilemma, and the vulgar a scrape.[1] Such a clash of paragraphs, and a conflict of newspapers, lampoons of all description, some good, and all hearty, the Regent (as reported) wroth ; Ld Carlisle in a fury ; the *Morning Post* in hysterics ; and the *Courier* in convulsions of criticism and contention. To complete the farce, the Morning Papers this day announce the intention of some zealous Rosencrantz or Guildenstern to " play upon this pipe " in our house of hereditaries. This last seems a little too ludicrous to be true, but, even if so—and nothing is too ridiculous for some of them to attempt—all the motions, censures, sayings, doings and ordinances of that august body, shall never make me even endeavour to explain, or soften a syllable of the twenty words which have excited, *what* I really do not yet exactly know, as the accounts are contradictory, but be it what it may, " as the wine is tapped it shall be drunk to the lees ". You tell me not to be " violent ", and not to " answer ". I *have not* and shall *not* answer, and although the consequences may be, for aught I know to the contrary, exclusion from society, and all sorts of disagreeables, the " Demon whom I still have served, has not yet cowed my better part of man " ; and whatever I may, and have, or shall feel, I have that within me, that bounds against opposition. I have *quick feelings*, and not very *good nerves* ; but somehow they have more than once served me pretty well, when I most wanted them, and may again. At any rate I shall try.

Did you ever know anything like this? At a time when peace and war, and Emperors and Napoleons, and the destinies of the things they have made of mankind, are trembling in the balance, the Government Gazettes can devote half their attention and columns, day after day, to 8 *lines*, written two years ago and now *republished only* (by an individual), and suggest them for the consideration of Parliament, probably about the same period with the treaty of peace.

I really begin to think myself a most important personage ; what would poor Pope have given to have brought down this upon his " epistle to Augustus "?

I think you must allow, considering all things, public and private, that mine has been an odd destiny. But I prate, and will spare you.

[1] Caused by Byron's acknowledgment of *Stanzas to a Lady Weeping*, which had appeared bound up with *The Corsair*.

Pray when are you most visible? or will any of your " predilections " interfere between you and me?

How is C[aroline]. ? It is a considerable compensation for all other disturbances, that she has left us in peace, and I do not think you will ever be further troubled with her anniversary scenes. I am glad you like the Corsair, and was afraid he might be too larmoyant a gentleman for your favour. But all these externals are nothing to *that within*, on a subject to which I have not alluded.

Ever y^{rs} most affec^{ly}, B.

P.S.—Murray took fright and shuffled in my absence, as you say, but I made him instantly replace the lines as before. It was not time to shrink now, and if it were otherwise, they should never be expunged and never shall. All the edicts on earth could not suppress their circulation, after the foolish fuss of these journalists who merely extend the demands of curiosity by the importance they attach to two " doggerel stanzas ", as they repeatedly call them.

TO MISS ANNE ISABELLA MILBANKE   *Fy. 12th, 1814*

I am just returned to London after a month's absence and am indeed sorry to hear that your own will be so much longer—and the cause is not of a description to reconcile your friends to it entirely, although the benefit you will derive to your health will prevent us from regretting anything but the time—if the effect is accomplished. All expressions of my good wishes to you and for you would be superfluous.

Mr. Ward postponed our Dutch expedition ; but as I have now nearly arranged my domestic concerns—or at least have put them in train—and the Newstead business is set at rest in my favour, " the world is all before me " and all parts of it as much a country to me as it was to Adam—perhaps more so ; for Eve as an atonement for tempting him out of one habitation might probably assist him in selecting another, and persuade him into some " Valley of Sweet Waters " on the banks of Euphrates.

In thanking you for your letter will you allow me to say

that there is one sentence I do not understand. As you may have forgotten it I will copy it. . . .

This I believe is word for word from your letter now before me. I do not see in what you have deceived yourself; and you have certainly never been otherwise than candid with me —and I have endeavoured to act accordingly. In regard to your kind observations on my adoption of my conduct to your wishes—I trust I should have been able to do so even without your suggestion. The moment I sunk into your friend, I tried to regard you in no other light. Our affections are not in our own power; but it would seem strange indeed because you could not like me that I should repine at the better fortune of another. If I had ever possessed a preference, the case would have been altered—and I might not have been so patient in resigning my pretensions. But you never did— never for an instant—trifle with me nor amuse me with what is called encouragement—a thing, by-the-bye, which men are continually supposing they receive without sufficient grounds; but of which I am no great judge—as except in this instance I never had an opportunity. When I say " this instance ", I mean of course any advance on my part towards that con- nexion which requires duty as well as attachment; and I begin to entertain an opinion that though they do not always go together, their separate existence is very precarious. I have lately seen a singular instance of ill-fortune. You have perhaps heard that in my childhood I was extremely intimate with the family of my nearest neighbours—an inheritor of the estate of a very old house and her mother. She is two years older than me; and consequently at so early a period any proposal on my part was out of the question—although from the continuity of our lands and other circumstances of no great importance, it was supposed that our union was within the probabilities of human life. I never did propose to her, and if I had it would have answered very little purpose—for she married another. From that period we met rarely—and I do not know very well why—but when we did meet, it was with coldness on both sides. To cut short a tale which is growing tedious: eight years have now elapsed, and she is separated from her husband at last after frequent dissensions arising entirely from *his* neglect, and (I fear) injuries still more serious.

At eight-and-twenty, still in the prime of life, beautiful (at least she was so), with a large fortune, of an ancient family, unimpeached and unimpeachable in her own conduct—this woman's destiny is bitter.   For the first time for many years I heard from her desiring to see me.   There could be nothing improper in this request.   I was the friend of her youth ; and I have every reason to believe—to be certain—that a being of better principle never breathed.   But she was once deep in my heart ; and though she had long ceased to be so, and I had no doubts of her, yet I had many of myself—at least of my own feelings if revived rather than of any consequence that might arise from them ; and as we had not met since I was 21 . . . to be brief, I did not see her.   There is the whole history of circumstances to which you may have possibly heard some allusion from those who knew me in the earlier part of my life. I *confide* them to you, and shall dwell upon them no further except to state that they bear no relation whatever to what I hinted at in a former letter as having occurred to prevent my reviving the topic discussed between us—at least with a view to renewal.

I have to ask for an answer, when you have leisure, and to thank you for your description, which brings the scene fully before me.   Are you aware of an amplified coincidence of thought with Burns ?

> " Or like the snowflake on the river
>   A moment shines—then melts forever."

The verses are very graceful and pleasing.   My opinion of your powers in that way I long ago mentioned to another person—who perhaps transmitted it to you.   I am glad you like *The Corsair*, which they tell me is popular.   God bless you. Ever yours

                                                             B.

P.S.—I am not perhaps an impartial judge of Lady M.— as amongst other obligations I am indebted to her for my acquaintance with yourself ; but she is doubtless in talent a superior—a *supreme* woman—and her heart I know to be of the kindest, in the best sense of the word.   Her defects I never could perceive—as her society makes me forget them and everything else for the time. I do love that woman (*filially or fraternally*) better than any being on earth; and you see that I am therefore unqualified to give an opinion.

TO THOMAS MOORE   *March 3, 1814*

MY DEAR FRIEND,—I have a great mind to tell you that I *am* "uncomfortable", if only to make you come to town; where no one ever more delighted in seeing you, nor is there any one to whom I would sooner turn for consolation in my most vapourish moments. The truth is, I have "no lack of argument" to ponder upon of the most gloomy description, but this arises from *other* causes. Some day or other, when we are *veterans*, I may tell you a tale of present and past times; and it is not from want of confidence that I do not now,—but—but—always a *but* to the end of the chapter.

There is nothing, however, upon the *spot* either to love or hate;—but I certainly have subjects for both at no very great distance, and am besides embarrassed between *three* whom I know, and one (whose name, at least) I do not know. All this would be very well if I had no heart; but, unluckily, I have found that there is such a thing still about me, though in no very good repair, and, also, that it has a habit of attaching itself to *one* whether I will or no. *Divide et impera*, I begin to think, will only do for politics.

If I discover the "toad", as you call him, I shall "tread", —and put spikes in my shoes to do it more effectually. The effect of all these fine things I do not inquire much nor perceive. I believe * * felt them more than either of us. People are civil enough, and I have had no dearth of invitations,—none of which, however, I have accepted. I went out very little last year, and mean to go about still less. I have no passion for circles, and have long regretted that I ever gave way to what is called a town life;—which, of all the lives I ever saw (and they are nearly as many as Plutarch's), seems to me to leave the least for the past and future.

How proceeds the poem? Do not neglect it, and I have no fears. I need not say to you that your fame is dear to me,—

I really might say *dearer* than my own; for I have lately begun to think my things have been strangely over-rated; and, at any rate, whether or not, I have done with them for ever. I may say to you what I would not say to every body, that the last two were written, *The Bride* in four, and *The Corsair* in ten days,—which I take to be a most humiliating confession, as it proves my own want of judgment in publishing, and the public's in reading things, which cannot have stamina for permanent attention. "So much for Buckingham."

I have no dread of your being too hasty, and I have still less of your failing. But I think a *year* a very fair allotment of time to a composition which is not to be Epic; and even Horace's "*Nonum prematur*" must have been intended for the Millennium, or some longer-lived generation than ours. I wonder how much we should have had of *him*, had he observed his own doctrines to the letter. Peace be with you! Remember that I am always and most truly yours, etc.

P.S.—I never heard the "report" you mention, nor, I dare say, many others. But, in course, you, as well as others, have "damned good-natured friends", who do their duty in the usual way. One thing will make you laugh. * * * *

TO LADY MELBOURNE   *April 8th, 1814*

I have been out of town since Saturday, and only returned last night from my visit to Augusta.

I swallowed the D—l in ye shape of a collar of brawn one evening for supper (after an enormous dinner, too), and it required all kinds of brandies, and I don't know what besides, to put me again in health and good humour; but I am now quite restored, and it is to avoid your congratulations upon *fatness* (which I abhor and you always inflict upon me after a return from the country) that I don't pay my respects to you to-day. Besides which, I dislike to see L^d M^e standing by the chimney-piece, all horror and astonishment at my appearance while C. is within reach of the twopenny postman. To-day I have been very sulky; but an hour's exercise with Mr. Jackson, of pugilistic memory, has given me spirits, and fatigued me into that state of languid laziness, which I prefer to all other.

I left all my relations—at least my niece and her mamma—very well. L[eigh] was in Yorkshire; and I regret not having seen him of course very much. My intention was to have joined a party at Cambridge; but somehow I overstaid my time, and the inclination to visit the University went off, and here I am alone, and not overpleased with being so.

You don't think the " Q[uarterly] R[eview] so very complimentary "; most people do. I have no great opinion on the subject, and (except in the E[dinburg]h) am not much interested in any criticisms, favourable or otherwise. I have had my day, have done with all that stuff; and must try something new—politics—or rebellion—or Methodism—or gaming. Of the two last I have serious thoughts, as one can't travel till we see how long Paris is to be the quarter of the Allies. I can't help suspecting that my little Pagod will play them some trick still. If Wellington, or one hero had beaten another, it would be nothing; but to be worried by brutes, and conquered by recruiting sergeants—why there is not a *character* amongst them.

Ever yrs. most affect^{ly}, B.

TO THOMAS MOORE   *2, Albany, April 9, 1814*

Viscount Althorpe is about to be married, and I have gotten his spacious bachelor apartments in Albany, to which you will, I hope, address a speedy answer to this mine epistle.

I am but just returned to town, from which you may infer that I have been out of it; and I have been boxing, for exercise, with Jackson for this last month daily. I have also been drinking, and, on one occasion, with three other friends at the Cocoa Tree, from six till four, yea, unto five in the matin. We clareted and champagned till two—then supped, and finished with a kind of regency punch composed of madeira, brandy, and *green* tea, no *real* water being admitted therein. There was a night for you! without once quitting the table, except to ambulate home, which I did alone, and in utter contempt of a

hackney-coach and my own *vis*, both of which were deemed
necessary for our conveyance. And so,—I am very well, and
they say it will hurt my constitution.

I have also, more or less, been breaking a few of the favourite
commandments; but I mean to pull up and marry, if any one
will have me. In the mean time, the other day I nearly killed
myself with a collar of brawn, which I swallowed for supper,
and *in*digested for I don't know how long; but that is by the
by. All this gourmandise was in honour of Lent; for I am
forbidden meat all the rest of the year, but it is strictly enjoined
me during your solemn fast. I have been, and am, in very
tolerable love; but of that hereafter as it may be.

My dear Moore, say what you will in your preface; and
quiz any thing or any body,—me if you like it. Oons! dost
thou think me of the *old,* or rather *elderly* school? If one can't
jest with one's friends, with whom can we be facetious? You
have nothing to fear from * *, whom I have not seen, being out
of town when he called. He will be very correct, smooth, and
all that, but I doubt whether there will be any " grace beyond
the reach of art " ;—and, whether there is or not, how long
will you be so damned modest? As for Jeffrey, it is a very
handsome thing of him to speak well of an old antagonist,—
and what a mean mind dared not do. Any one will revoke
praise ; but—were it not partly my own case—I should say
that very few have strength of mind to unsay their censure, or
follow it up with praise of other things.

What think you of the review of *Levis*?[1] It beats the *Bag*
and my hand-grenade hollow, as an invective, and hath thrown
the Court into hysterics, as I hear from very good authority.
Have you heard from * * * * * *

No more rhyme for—or rather, *from*—me. I have taken
my leave of that stage, and henceforth will mountebank it no
longer. I have had my day, and there's an end. The utmost
I expect, or even wish, is to have it said in the *Biographia
Britannica*, that I might perhaps have been a poet, had I gone
on and amended. My great comfort is, that the temporary
celebrity I have wrung from the world has been in the very
teeth of all opinions and prejudices. I have flattered no ruling

[1] A criticism of *Souvenirs et portraits, par M. de Levis* had recently appeared in
the *Edinburgh Review.*

powers; I have never concealed a single thought that tempted me. They can't say I have truckled to the times, nor to popular topics, (as Johnson, or somebody, said of Cleveland,) and whatever I have gained has been at the expenditure of as much *personal* favour as possible; for I do believe never was a bard more unpopular, *quoad homo*, than myself. And now I have done;—*ludite nunc alios*. Every body may be damned, as they seem fond of it, and resolve to stickle lustily for endless brimstone.

Oh—by the by, I had nearly forgot. There is a long poem, an *Anti-Byron*, coming out, to prove that I have formed a conspiracy to overthrow, by *rhyme*, all religion and government, and have already made great progress! It is not very scurrilous, but serious and ethereal. I never felt myself important, till I saw and heard of my being such a little Voltaire as to induce such a production. Murray would not publish it, for which he was a fool, and so I told him; but some one else will, doubtless. "Something too much of this."

Your French scheme is good, but let it be *Italian*; all the Angles will be at Paris. Let it be Rome, Milan, Naples, Florence, Turin, Venice, or Switzerland, and "egad!" (as Bayes saith,) I will connubiate and join you; and we will write a new *Inferno* in our Paradise. Pray think of this—and I will really buy a wife and a ring, and say the ceremony, and settle near you in a summer-house upon the Arno, or the Po, or the Adriatic.

Ah! my poor little pagod, Napoleon, has walked off his pedestal. He has abdicated, they say. This would draw molten brass from the eyes of Zatanai. What! "kiss the ground before young Malcolm's feet and then be baited by the rabble's curse!" I cannot bear such a crouching catastrophe. I must stick to Sylla, for my modern favourites don't do,—their resignations are of a different kind. All health and prosperity, my dear Moore. Excuse this lengthy letter.

Ever, etc.

P.S.—The *Quarterly* quotes you frequently in an article on America; and every body I know asks perpetually after you and yours. When will you answer them in person?

TO LADY MELBOURNE   *April 25th, 1814*

My dear L^y M^e,—Thanks as to C—— though the task will be difficult; if she is to determine as to kindness or unkindness, the best way will be to avoid each other *without appearing* to do so, or if we jostle, at any rate *not* to *bite*.

Oh! but it is " worth while ", I can't tell you why, and it is *not* an " *Ape* ", and if it is, that must be my fault; however, I will positively reform. You must however allow that it is utterly impossible I can ever be half so well liked elsewhere, and I have been all my life trying to make someone love me, and never got the sort that I preferred before. But positively she and I will grow good and all that, and so we are *now* and shall be these three weeks and more too.

Yesterday I dined at the Princess's,[1] where I deported myself like a white stick; till, as the Devil would have it, a man with a flute played a solemn and somewhat tedious piece of music. Well, I got through that, but down sate Lady Anne H. to give evidence at the pianoforte with a Miss Somebody (the " privy purse ", in a pair of spectacles—dark green) these, and the flute man, and the " damnable faces " (as Hamlet says) of the whole party, threw me into a convulsion of uncourtly laughter, which Gell and Lady Crewe encouraged; at least the *last* joined in it so heartily that the hooping-cough would have been an Æolian harp in comparison to us both. At last I half strangled it, and myself, with my kerchief; and here I am grave and sedate again.

You will be sorry to hear that I have got a physician just in time for an old complaint, " troublesome, but not dangerous ", like Lord Stair and L^y Stair's, of which I am promised an eventual removal. It is very odd; he is a staid grave man, and puts so many questions to me about *my mind*, and the state of it, that I begin to think he half suspects my senses. He asked me how I felt " when anything weighed upon my mind? " and I answered him by a question, why he should suppose that anything did? I was laughing and sitting quietly in my chair the whole time of his visits, and yet he thinks me horribly restless and irritable, and talks about my having lived *excessively* " out of all compass " some time or other; which has no more to do

—————
[1] The Princess of Wales.

with the malady he has to deal with than I have with the Wisdom of Solomon.

To-morrow I go to the Berrys; on Wednesday to the Jerseys; on Thursday I dine at Ld Grey's, and there is L^y Hard[wick]e in the evening; and on Friday I am asked to a Lady Charleville's, whom I don't know, and where I shan't go. We shall meet, I hope, at one or two of these places.

I don't often bore you with rhyme—but as a wrapper [1] to this note I send you some upon a *brunette*, which I have shown to no one else. If you think them not much beneath the common places you may give them to any of your " album " acquaintances.

Ever y^{rs} most truly, B.

TO LADY MELBOURNE   *April 29th, 1814*

I delivered " mamma's message " with anatomical precision; [2] the *knee* was the refractory limb was it not? Injured I presume at prayers, for I cannot conjecture by what other possible attitude a female knee could become so perverse. Having given an account of my embassy, I enclose you a note which will only repeat what you already know, but to obviate a possible *Pharisaical* charge, I must observe that the first part of her epistle alludes to an answer of mine, in which, talking about that eternal Liturgy, I said that I had no great opinions one way or the other, assuredly no decided unbelief, and that the *clamour* had wrung from me many of the objectionable passages in the pure quintessence of the spirit of contradiction, etc., etc. She talks of " talking " over the same metaphysics. To shorten the conversation, I shall propose the Litany— " from the crafts and assau——" aye, that will do very well; what comes next, " deliver us ", an't it? Seriously, if she imagines that I particularly delight in canvassing the creed of St. Athanasius, or prattling of rhyme, I think she will be mistaken; but *you* know best. I don't suspect myself of often talking about poets, or clergymen, of rhyme or the rubrick; but very likely I am wrong; for assuredly no one knows *itself*, and for aught I know, I may for these last two years have

---

[1] Not preserved with the original letter.

[2] Byron was now in sentimental correspondence with Lady Melbourne's niece, Annabella Milbanke.

inflicted upon you a world of theology, and the greater part of Walker's rhyming dictionary.

I don't know what to say or do about going. Sometimes I wish it, at other times I think it foolish, as assuredly my design will be imputed to a motive, which, by-the-bye, if once fairly there, is very likely to come into my head, and *failing*, to put me into no very good humour with myself. I am not now in love with her; but I can't at all foresee that I should not be so, if it came " a warm June " (as Falstaff observes), and, seriously, I do admire her as a very superior woman, a little encumbered with Virtue, though perhaps your opinion and mine, from the laughing turn of " our philosophy ", may be less exalted upon her merits than that of the more zealous, though in fact less benevolent advocates, of charity schools and Lying-in Hospitals.

By the close of her note you will perceive that she has been " frowning " occasionally, and has written some pretty lines upon it to a friend (he or she is not said). As for rhyme I am naturally no fair judge, and can like it no better than a grocer does figs.

I am quite irresolute and undecided. If I were sure of *myself* (not of her) I would go; but I am not, and never can be, and what is still worse, I have no judgement and less common sense than an infant. This is *not affected* humility; with *you* I have no affectation; with the world I have a part to play; to be diffident there, is to wear a drag-chain, and luckily I do so thoroughly despise half the people in it, that my insolence is almost natural.

I enclose you also a letter written some time ago, and of which I do not remember the precise contents; most likely they contradict every syllable of this, no matter. Don't plague yourself to write; we shall meet at Mrs. Hope's I trust.

Ever yours, B.

TO LADY MELBOURNE   *April, 30th, 1814*

MY DEAR LADY Mᴱ,—*You*—or rather *I*—have done *my A* [1] much injustice. The expression which you recollect as

[1] Augusta Leigh, so called to distinguish her from "*your* A ", Annabella Milbanke.

objectionable meant only "loving" in the *senseless* sense of that wide word, and it must be some selfish stupidity of mine in telling my own story, but really and truly—as I hope mercy and happiness for her—by that God who made me for my own misery, and not much for the good of others, *she* was not to blame, one thousandth part in comparison. She was not aware of her own peril till it was too late, and I can only account for her subsequent "*abandon*" by an observation which I think is not unjust, that women are much more *attached* than men if they are treated with anything like fairness or tenderness.

As for *your* A, I don't know what to make of her. I enclose her last but one, and *my* A's last but one, from which you may form your own conclusions on *both*. I think you will allow *mine* to be a very extraordinary person in point of *talent*, but I won't say more, only do not allow your good nature to lean to my side of *this* question; on all others I shall be glad to avail myself of your partiality.

Now for *common* life. There *is* a party at Lady J[erse]y's on Monday and on Wednesday. I am asked to both, and excused myself out of Tuesday's dinner because I want to see Kean in Richard again. Pray *why* did you say I am getting into a *scrape* with R.'s moiety?[1] One must talk to somebody. I always give you the preference when you are disposed to listen, and when you seem fidgetted, as you do now and then (and no wonder, for latterly I do but repeat), I turn to anyone, and she was the first that I stumbled upon. As for anything more, I have not even advanced to the tip of her little finger, and never shall unless she gives it. You won't believe me, and won't care if you do, but I really believe that I have more true regard and affection for yourself than for any other existence. As for my A, my feelings towards her are a mixture of good and diabolical. I hardly know one passion which has not some share in them, but I won't run into the subject.

Your niece has committed herself perhaps, but it can be of no consequence; if I pursued and succeeded in that quarter, of course I must give up all other pursuits, and the fact is that my wife, if she had common sense, would have more power over me than any other whatsoever, for my heart always

[1] Probably Milbanke.

alights on the nearest *perch*—if it is withdrawn it goes God knows where—but one must like something.

Ever yrs., B.

TO LADY MELBOURNE   *April—May 1st, 1814*

My dear Lady M*ᴱ*,—She says " if la tante " ; neither did she imagine nor did I assert that you did have an opinion of what Philosopher Square calls " the fitness of things ".

You are very kind in allowing us the few merits we can claim : *she* surely is very clever, and not only so but in some things of good judgement : her expressions about Aᵃ are exactly your *own*, and these most certainly without being aware of the coincidence, and excepting our one *tremendous* fault. I know her to be in point of temper and goodness of heart almost unequalled ; now grant me this, that she is in truth a very *loveable* woman and I will try and not love any longer. If you don't believe me, ask those who know her *better*. I say *better*, for a man in love is blind as that deity.

You yourself soften a little in the P.S., and say the letters " make you melancholy ". It is indeed a very triste and extraordinary business, and what is to become of us I know not, and I won't think just now.

Did you observe that she says, " *if* la tante approved she should " ? She is little aware how much " la tante " has to *dis*approve, but you perceive that, without intending it, she pays me a compliment by supposing you to be my friend and a sincere one, whose *approval* could alter even *her* opinions.

To-morrow I am asked to Lady Jersey's in the evening, and on Wednesday again. Tuesday I go to Kean and dine after the play with Lord Rancliffe, and on Friday there is Mrs. Hope's : we shall clash at some of them.

What on earth can plague you? I won't ask, but am very sorry for it, it is very hard that one who feels so much for others should suffer pain herself. God bless you. Good night.

Ever yours most truly, B.

P.S.—A thousand loves and excuses to Mrs. Damer with whom I weep *not* to dine.

P.S. *ad.*—It, indeed, puzzles me to account for ——: it is true she married a fool, but she *would* have him; they agreed, and agree very well, and I never heard a complaint, but many vindications, of him. As for me, brought up as I was, and sent into the world as I was, both physically and morally, nothing better could be expected, and it is odd that I always had a foreboding and I remember when a child reading the Roman history about a *marriage* I will tell you of when we meet, asking ma mère why I should not marry X.

Since writing this I have received yᵉ enclosed. I will not trouble you with another, but *this* will, I think, enable you to appreciate *her* better. She seems very triste, and I need hardly add that the reflection does not enliven me.

TO MISS MERCER ELPHINSTONE*   *2 Albany, May 3ᵈ, 1814*

I send you the Arnaout garments which will make an admirable costume for a Dutch Dragoon. The Camesa or Kilt (to speak Scottishly) you will find very long. It is the custom with the Beys, and a sign of rank, to wear it to the ancle—I know not why, but it is so. The million shorten it to the knee, which is more antique—and becoming, at least to those who have legs and a propensity to show them. I have sent but one camesa, the other I will dispatch when it has undergone the Musselman process of ablution.

There are greaves for the legs—2 waistcoats, one beneath, one over the Jacket—the cloak—a sash—a short shawl and cap —and a pair of garters (something of the Highland order) with an Ataghan wherewithal to cut your fingers if you don't take care. Over the sash there is a small leather girdle with a buckle in the centre.

It is put off and on in a few minutes. If you like the dress, keep it. I shall be very glad to get rid of it, as it reminds me of one or two things I don't wish to remember. To make it more acceptable, I have worn this very little and never in England except for half an hour at Phillips, I had more of the same description but parted with them when my Arnaouts went back to Tepalen and I returned to England. It will do for a masquerade.

One word about " caprice ". I know you were merely in jest and that my *caprices*, supposing such to exist, must be a subject of laughter or indifference ; but I am not unconscious of something not unlike them in the course of our acquaintance. Yet you must recollect that from your situation you can never be *sure* you have a friend (as somebody has said of Sovereigns I believe) and that any apparent anxiety on my part to cultivate your acquaintance might have appeared to yourself like importunity, and—as I happen to know—would have been attributed by others to a motive *not* very creditable to me and agreeable to neither.

This is quite enough, and more than I have a right to trouble you with on this or any other subject.

Ever yrs very sincerely, B.

TO THOMAS MOORE   *May 4, 1814*

" Last night we supp'd at R—fe's board ", etc.

* * * * * * * I wish people would not shirk their *dinners*—ought it not to have been a dinner?—and that damned anchovy sandwich !

That plaguy voice of yours made me sentimental, and almost fall in love with a girl who was recommending herself, during your song, by *hating* music. But the song is past, and my passion can wait, till the *pucelle* is more harmonious.

Do you go to Lady Jersey's to-night? It is a large party, and you won't be bored into " softening rocks ", and all that. *Othello* is to-morrow and Saturday too. Which day shall we go? When shall I see you? If you call, let it be after three, and as near four as you please.

Ever, etc.

TO THOMAS MOORE   *May 5, 1814*

Do you go to the Lady Cahir's this even? If you do go—and whenever we are bound to the same follies let us embark in the same *Shippe of Fooles*. I have been up till five, and up at nine; and feel heavy with only winking for the last three or four nights.

I lost my party and place at supper trying to keep out of the way of * * * *. I would have gone away altogether, but that would have appeared a worse affectation than t'other. You are of course engaged to dinner, or we may go quietly together to my box at Covent Garden, and afterwards to this assemblage. Why did you go away so soon?

Ever, etc.

P.S.—*Ought not* Rancliffe's supper to have been a dinner? Jackson is here, and I must fatigue myself into spirits.

TO LADY MELBOURNE   *May 16th, 1814*

My dear Lᵞ Mᴱ,—Your letter is not without effect when I tell you that I have *not written* to-day and shall weigh my words when I write to —— to-morrow. I *do* thank you, and as somebody says—I hope *not* Iago—" I think you know I love you well ".

As for C., we both know her for a foolish wicked woman. I am sorry to hear that she is still fermenting her weak head and cold heart to an *ice cream* which will only sicken everyone about her: as I heard a girl say the other night at *Othello*, when I asked her how she liked it, " I shall like it much better when that woman (a bad actress in Desdemona) is fairly smothered ". So—if C. were fairly shut up, and bread and watered into common sense and some regard to truth, no one would be the worse, and she herself much the better for the process.

By-the-bye (*entre nous*, remember) she has sent for Moore on some mysterious concern, which he will tell me probably, at least if it regards the old eternal, and never sufficiently to be bored with, story.

I dine at Lord Jersey's to-morrow—that is, I am asked, and (to please you) I am trying to fall in love, which I suppose will end in falling *out* with somebody, for I am perplexed about two and would rather have both. I don't see any use in one without a chance at least of the other.

But all this is nonsense. I won't say a word more about your grievance, though I cannot at all conceive what there can be more *now* than ever to plague you anywhere, particularly as C. has nothing to do with it.

Horace Twiss has sent me his melodies, which I perceive are inscribed to you; don't you think yourself lucky to have escaped one of *my* dedications? I am going to dine at Wm. Spencer's to-day. I believe I told you the *claret* story at Mrs. Hope's last ball but one.

Ever yours most affectionately, B.

P.S. I am just elected into Watier's. Shall I resume *play*? That will be a change, and for the better.

TO LADY MELBOURNE　　　　　　　　　　　*May 28th, 1814*

DEAR LADY M^E,—I have just received a wrathful epistle from C[aroline] demanding letters, pictures, and all kinds of gifts which I never requested, and am ready to resign as soon as they can be gathered together; at the same signal it might be as well for her to restore *my* letters, as everybody has read them by this time, and they can no longer be of use to herself and her five hundred sympathizing friends. She also complains of some barbarous usage, of which I know nothing, except that I was told of an *inroad* which occurred when I was fortunately out; and am not at all disposed to regret the circumstance of my absence, either for her sake or my own. I am also menaced in her letter with immediate *marriage*, of which I am equally unconscious; at least *I* have not proposed to anybody, and if anyone has to me I have quite forgotten it. If she alludes to L[ad]y A[delaide] F[orbes] she has made a sad mistake; for not a syllable of love ever passed between us, but a good deal of heraldry, and mutual hatred of music; the merits of Mr. Kean, and the excellence of white soup and plovers' eggs for a light supper. Besides, Lady R., who is good authority, says that *I* do not care about L^y A., nor L^y A. about me, and that if such an impossibility did occur, she could not possibly approve of it, nor anyone else; in all which I quite acquiesce with ye said Lady R., with whom, however, I never had a moment's conversation on the subject; but hear this from a friend, who is in very bad humour with her, and not much better with me; why, I can't divine, being as innocent and ill-used as C. herself in her very best story. If you can *pare* her down to good humour, do. I am really at this moment thinking as little of the person with whom she commits me to matrimony, as of herself; and I mean to leave London next week if I can. In the meantime, I hope we shall meet at Lady Grey's, or Clare's this evening.

Ever y^rs, most affectionately, B.

TO HENRIETTA D'USSIÈRES[1]*   *June 8th, 1814*

Excepting your compliments (which are only excusable because you don't know me) you write like a clever woman, for which reason I hope you *look* as *un*like one as possible. I never knew but one of your country—Me de Stael—and she is frightful as a precipice. As it seems impracticable my visiting you, cannot you contrive to visit me? telling me the time previously that I may be in ye way—and if this same interview leads to the " leap into the Serpentine " you mention, we can take the jump together, and shall be very good company, for I swim like a Duck (one of the few things I can do well) and you say that your Sire taught you the same useful acquirement. I like your education of all things. It in some degree resembles my own, for the first ten years of my life were passed much amongst mountains, and I had also a tender and peremptory parent who indulged me sometimes with holidays and now and then with a box on the ear. If you will become acquainted with me, I will promise not to make love to you unless you like it—and even if I did there is no occasion for you to receive more of it than you please. You must, however, do me two favours—the first is not to mistake me for *S.*, who is an excellent

---

[1] A young woman of Swiss descent, domiciled in London, who had written to Byron, claiming advice and sympathy. For further information on this unsolicited correspondent, see *To Lord Byron*, by Paston and Quennell.

man, but to whom I have not the honour to bear the smallest (I won't say *slightest*, for he has the circumference of an Alderman) resemblance; and the next is to recollect that as " no man is a hero to his Valet " so I am a hero to no person whatsoever, and not treat me with such outrageous respect and awe, which makes me feel as if I was in a strait waistcoat. You shall be a *heroine*, however, if you prefer it and I will be and am y^r very humble Servt

B.

P.S.—" Surprized " oh ! no !—I am surprized at nothing, except at your taking so much trouble about one who is not worth it. . . .

You say—what would " my servants think "? 1^{stly} they seldom think at all. 2^{ndly} they are generally out of the way— particularly when most wanted. 3^{rdly} *I* do not know you—and I humbly imagine that they are no wiser than their Master.

TO SAMUEL ROGERS   *June 9, 1814*

I am always obliged to trouble you with my awkwardnesses, and now I have a fresh one. Mr. W.[1] called on me several times, and I have missed the honour of making his acquaintance, which I regret, but which *you*, who know my desultory and uncertain habits, will not wonder at, and will, I am sure, attribute to any thing but a wish to offend a person who has shown me much kindness, and possesses character and talents entitled to general respect. My mornings are late, and passed in fencing and boxing, and a variety of most unpoetical exercises, very wholesome, etc., but would be very disagreeable to my friends, whom I am obliged to exclude during their operation. I never go out till the evening, and I have not been fortunate enough to meet Mr. W. at Lord Lansdowne's or Lord Jersey's, where I had hoped to pay him my respects.

I would have written to him, but a few words from you will go further than all the apologetical sesquipedalities I could muster on the occasion. It is only to say that, without intend-

---

[1] Francis Wrangham, cleric and man of letters.

ing it, I contrive to behave very ill to every body, and am very
sorry for it.

Ever, dear R., etc.

TO LADY MELBOURNE   *June 10th, 1814*

DEAR LADY Mᴱ,—I don't remember one syllable of such
a request; but the truth is that I do not always read yᵉ letters
through. She has no more variety than my maccaw; and her
note is not much more musical. Judge then, whether (being
also in yᵉ delectable situation which winds up the moral of your
note) I can attend the yᵉ same tones if there is a nightingale,
or a canary bird to be got by love, or money.

All you say is exceeding true; but who ever said, or
supposed that you were not shocked, and all that? You *have*
done everything in your power; and more than any other
person breathing would have done for *me*, to make me act
rationally; but there is an old saying (excuse the Latin, which
I won't quote, but translate), " Whom the gods wish to
destroy they first madden ". I am as mad as C. on a different
topic, and in a different way; for I never break out into scenes,
but am not a whit more in my senses. I will, however, not
persuade *her* into any *fugitive* piece of absurdity, but more I
cannot promise. I love no one else (in a proper manner),
and, whatever you may imagine, I cannot, or at least do not,
put myself in the way of—let me see—Annabella is the most
prudish and correct person I know, so I refer you to the last
emphatic substantive, in her last letter to you.

There is that little Lady R. tells me that C. has taken a
sudden fancy to *her*—what can that be for? C. has also taken
some offence at Lady G. Sloane's frigid appearance; and
supposes that Augusta, who never troubles her head about her,
has said something or other on my authority—*this* I remember
is in *C.'s* last letter—one of her twaddling questions I presume—
she seems puzzled about me, and not at all near the truth.
The Devil, who ought to be civil on such occasions, will
probably keep her from it still; if he should not, I must invent
some flirtation, to lead her from approaching it.

I am sorry to hear of your *tristesse*, and conceive that I have at last guessed or perceived the real cause; it won't trouble you long; besides, what is it or anything else compared with our melodrame? *Take* comfort, you very often give it.

Ever y^{rs}, B.

TO SAMUEL ROGERS   *Tuesday*

MY DEAR ROGERS,—Sheridan was yesterday, at first, too sober to remember your invitation, but in the dregs of the third bottle he fished up his memory, and found that he had a party at home. I left and leave any other day to him and you, save Monday, and some yet undefined dinner at Burdett's. Do you go to-night to Lord Eardley's, and if you do, shall I call for you (anywhere)? it will give me great pleasure.

Ever yours entire, B.

P.S.—The Staël out-talked Whitbread, overwhelmed his spouse, was *ironed* by Sheridan, confounded Sir Humphry, and utterly perplexed your slave. The rest (great names in the Red-book, nevertheless,) were mere segments of the circle. Ma'mselle danced a Russ saraband with great vigour, grace, and expression.

TO THOMAS MOORE   *June 14, 1814*

I *could* be very sentimental now, but I won't. The truth is, that I have been all my life trying to harden my heart, and have not yet quite succeeded—though there are great hopes—and you do not know how it sunk with your departure. What adds to my regret is having seen so little of you during your stay in this crowded desert, where one ought to be able to bear thirst like a camel,—the springs are so few, and most of them so muddy.

The newspapers will tell you all that is to be told of emperors,[1]

[1] The Allied sovereigns, headed by the Emperor of Russia, visited London in state during June 1814.

etc. They have dined, and supped, and shown their flat faces in all thoroughfares, and several saloons. Their uniforms are very becoming, but rather short in the skirts; and their conversation is a catechism, for which and the answers I refer you to those who have heard it.

I think of leaving town for Newstead soon. If so, I shall not be remote from your recess, and (unless Mrs. M. detains you at home over the caudle-cup and a new cradle) we will meet. You shall come to me, or I to you, as you like it;—but *meet* we will. An invitation from Aston has reached me, but I do not think I shall go. I have also heard of * * *—I should like to see her again, for I have not met her for years; and though " the light that ne'er can shine again " is set, I do not know that " one dear smile like those of old " might not make me for a moment forget the " dulness " of " life's stream ".

I am going to R[ancliffe]'s to-night—to one of those suppers which " *ought* to be dinners ". I have hardly seen her, and never *him*, since you set out. I told you, you were the last link of that chain. As for * *, we have not syllabled one another's names since. The post will not permit me to continue my scrawl. More anon.

Ever, dear Moore, etc.

P.S.—Keep the Journal; I care not what becomes of it; and if it has amused you, I am glad that I kept it. *Lara* is finished, and I am copying him for my third vol., now collecting;—but *no separate* publication.

TO THE HON. AUGUSTA LEIGH　　　　*June 18th, 1814*

DEAREST A.,—Well, I *can* " judge for myself ", and a pretty piece of judgement it is! You shall hear. Last night at Earl Grey's, or rather this *morning* (about 2 by the account of the said Aurora), in one of the cooler rooms, sitting in the corner of a great chair wherein was deposited Lady M., *she* talking Platonics and listening to a different doctrine, I observed Mr. Rogers not far off colloquizing with your friend.[1] Presently he came up and interrupted our duet, and, after different remarks, began upon her and her's. What seized me I know not, but I

[1] Lady Charlotte Leveson-Gower.

desired him to introduce me, at which he expressed much good
humour.

I stopped him, and said he had better ask her first, and in
the mean time, to give her entire option, I walked away to
another part of the room separated by a great Screen, so that
she had the best opportunity of getting off without the awkward-
ness of being overheard or seen, etc., etc.; all which I duly
considered.

My Goddess of the Arm-chair in the mean time was left to
a soliloquy, as she afterwards told me, wondering what Rogers
and I were about. To my astonishment, in a minute up comes
R. with *your* ch^e at the *pas de charge* of introduction; the bow
was made, the curtsey returned, and so far " excellent well ",
all except the disappearance of the said Rogers, who immediately marched off, leaving us in the middle of a huge apartment with about 20 scattered pairs all employed in their own
concerns. While I was thinking of a *nothing* to say, the Lady
began—" a friend of mine,—a great friend of yours ", and
stopped. Wondering what the Devil was coming next, I
said, " perhaps you mean a relation "—" Oh yes—a relation
——" and stopped *again*. Finding this would never do, and
being myself beginning to break down into shyness,—she too
confused,—I uttered your respectable name, and prattled I
know not what syllables, and so on for about 3 minutes; and
then how we parted I know not, for never did two people seem
to know less what they said or did. Well! we met again 2 or 3
times in passages, etc., where I endeavoured to improve this
dialogue into something like sense, still taking you and people
she knew (and the dead Marquis of Granby, I believe) for the
topics. In this interval she lost her party, and seemed in an
agony. " Shall I get your shawl? " " I have got it " (they
were going; by the bye, *La Mère* was not there). " Is it your
brother that you want? he is not gone." " No—but have you
seen Lady or Mrs. Somebody? Oh! there she is "—and away
she went!

She is shy as an Antelope, and unluckily as pretty, or we
should not remark it. By the bye, I must say that it looked
more like *dislike* than shyness; and I do not much wonder—
for her first confusion in calling you a *friend*, forgetting the
relationship, set me off—not laughing—but in one of our

glows and stammers, and then all I had heard from you and others of *her* diffidence brought our own similar malady upon me in a double degree.

The only thing is that she might have not been introduced, unless she had liked, as I did not stand near as people usually do, so that the introdu*cee* can't get off, but was out of sight and hearing. Then I must say that *till* the first sentence, there was a deal of valour on both sides; but after that—Oh Dear! this is all your fault. The Duchess of Somerset also, to mend matters, insisted on presenting me to a Princess *Biron*, Duchess of Hohen—God-know's-what, and another person to her two isters, Birons too. But I flew off, and *would* not, saying I had enough of introductions for that night at least.

Devonshire asked me *twice* (last night) to come to Chiswick on Sunday!—is not *that* a little odd? I have seen Blucher, etc., etc., and was surprized into an introduction, after all, to a Prince Radzivil, a Pole and a Potentate, a good and great man but very like a Butler. God bless you, my dear.

Ever yours most affectionately, BYRON.

TO LADY MELBOURNE *June 21st,* 1814

Since I wrote last night I have received the two enclosed. What shall I do about Ph. and her epistles? since by her own account they run great hazard in their way to her. I am willing to give them up, but she says not a syllable about mine; no matter.

The other is from A., and prim and pretty as usual. Somebody or other has been seized with a fit of amazement at her correspondence with so naughty a personage, and this has naturally given a fillup of contradiction in my favour which was much wanted.

Ever y^{rs}, B.

TO LADY MELBOURNE *June 26th, 1814*

MY DEAR L^y M^e,—To continue the conversation which Lord C^r has broken off by falling asleep (and his wife by keeping awake) I know nothing of C.'s last night adventures;

to prove it there is her letter which I have not read through, nor answered nor written these two months, and then only by *desire* to keep her quiet.

You talked to me about keeping her out. It is impossible; she comes at all times, at any time, and the moment the door is open in she walks. I can't throw her out of the window: as to getting rid of her, that is rational and probable, but *I* will not receive her.

The Bessboroughs may take her if they please—or any steps they please; I have no hesitation in saying that I have made up my mind as to the alternative, and would sooner, much sooner, be with the dead in purgatory, than with her, *Caroline* (I put the name at length as I am not jesting), upon earth. She may hunt me down—it is the power of any mad or bad woman to do so by any man—but *snare* me she shall not: torment me she may; how am I to bar myself from her! I am already almost a prisoner; she has no shame, no feeling, no one estimable or redeemable quality. These are strong words, but I know what I am writing; they will avail nothing but to convince you of my own determination. My first object in such a dilemma would be to take —— with me; that might fail, so much the better, but even if it did—I would lose a hundred souls rather than be bound to C. If there is one human being whom I do utterly *detest* and *abhor* it is she, and, all things considered, I feel to myself justified in so doing. She has been an adder in my path ever since my return to this country; she has often belied and sometimes betrayed me; she has crossed me everywhere; she has watched and worried and *guessed* and been a curse to me and mine.

You may show *her* this if you please—or to anyone you please; if these were the last words I were to write upon earth I would not revoke one letter except to make it more legible.

Ever yours most sincerely, BYRON.

TO LADY MELBOURNE   *July 2nd, 1814*

DEAR LADY M.,—I leave town to-morrow for two or three days, and as I shall probably be occupied at Cambridge, I

may as well " say my say " with regard to C. " Conquer."
Oh no—*crush*—if you please, and not unlikely whether she goes
or stays. She perplexed me very much with questions and
guesses—and as I verily believe her growing actually and
seriously disordered in her intellects, there is no conjecturing
what she may assert or do, as far as I can judge from observation, not less towards myself than others (though in a different
way to the last), she cannot be in her senses.[1] I was obliged to
talk to her, for she laid hold of Hobhouse, and passed before
where another person and myself were discussing points of
Platonism, so frequently and remarkably, as to make us
anticipate a scene; and as she was masked, and dominoed,
and it was daylight, there could be little harm, and there was
at least a probability of more quiet. Not all I could say could
prevent her from displaying her green *pantaloons* every now and
then; though I scolded like her grandfather upon these very
uncalled for, and unnecessary gesticulations. Why do you say
that I was mistaken about another mask with you? I never
even pretended to guess at so pious a person, nor supposed
they were in so profane an assembly, and now I am convinced
they were not there at all; since you tell me of the illness of the
little boy, who so happily recovered, by the timely devotion of
her staying away to take care of him.

To be sure, I thought I saw somebody very like; but there
is no trusting to likenesses, and it is not easy to unmask anybody,
even without their pasteboard.

I don't wonder at your dislike to C., etc., and whatever
absurdity, or enormity, her madness may plunge me into, I
do think you have already done at least tenfold more than
anyone on earth would have done; and if you were to do more,
I should conceive you no less mad than herself. I thank you
for the past, for the thousandth time, and as to the present and
future I shall parry her off as well as I can, and if foiled, I
must abide by the consequence : so there's an end. After all,
it is not much your concern (except as far as good nature went),
and rests between me and the Blarneys, whom I regard not.
To *yourself* I own that I am anxious to appear as having done

---

[1] The events to which Byron refers took place at the celebrated Watier's
Masquerade, held by the members of Watier's Club in honour of the return of the
Duke of Wellington

all that could be done to second your wishes in breaking off the connection, which would have been effectual with any, or every other person.

I am glad you were amused with ——'s correspondent. —— is very much astonished, but in very good humour, and I too—on account of my *theory*, of which, by-the-bye, I despaired very much at first in the present instance. I think I should make a good Tartuffe; it was by paring down my demeanour to a very quiet and hesitating deportment, which however my natural shyness (though that goes off at times) helped to forward, that I ensured the three days' recollection of ——'s amiable ally.

Good-bye, for the present. I am still sadly sleepy with the wear and tear of the last two nights, and have had nothing for my trouble. I wanted very much to talk to you, but you preferred Robinson. The next time he breaks a leg I shall be less sorry, and send you to nurse him.

I am in amity (the purest, and of course most insipid) with a person; and one condition is, that I am to tell her her faults without reserve. How long do you think such a treaty, fully observed, would endure? I will tell you—five minutes. I was assailed by a Mask for some time, teazing enough, but with a sweet voice, and someone of whom all I could learn was that " I had said of her, she *had been* very beautiful ". This quite cured my desire of discovery, as such a speech could never be forgiven, so I told her, and got away.

Good-bye again.

Ever most affectionately, your servitor, B.

TO THOMAS MOORE   *Hastings, August 3, 1814*

By the time this reaches your dwelling, I shall (God wot) be in town again probably. I have been here renewing my acquaintance with my old friend Ocean; and I find his bosom as pleasant a pillow for an hour in the morning as his daughters of Paphos could be in the twilight. I have been swimming and eating turbot, and smuggling neat brandies and silk handkerchiefs,—and listening to my friend Hodgson's raptures about a pretty wife-elect of his,—and walking on cliffs, and tumbling down hills and making the most of the *dolce far-niente* for the last fortnight. I met a son of Lord Erskine's, who says he has been married a year, and is the " happiest of men " ; and I have met the aforesaid H., who is also the " happiest of men " ; so, it is worth while being here, if only to witness the superlative felicity of these foxes, who have cut off their tails, and would persuade the rest to part with their brushes to keep them in countenance.

It rejoiceth me that you like *Lara*. Jeffrey is out with his 45th Number, which I suppose you have got. He is only too kind to me, in my share of it, and I begin to fancy myself a golden pheasant, upon the strength of the plumage wherewith he hath bedecked me. But then, " *surgit amari* ", etc.—the gentlemen of the *Champion*, and Perry, have got hold (I know not how) of the condolatory address to Lady Jersey on the picture-abduction by our Regent, and have published them—with my name, too, smack—without even asking leave, or inquiring whether or no! Damn their impudence, and damn every thing. It has put me out of patience, and so, I shall say no more about it.

You shall have *Lara* and *Jacque* [1] (both with some additions) when out; but I am still demurring and delaying, and in a fuss, and so is Rogers in his way.

Newstead is to be mine again. Claughton forfeits twenty-five thousand pounds; but that don't prevent me from being very prettily ruined. I mean to bury myself there—and let my beard grow—and hate you all.

Oh! I have had the most amusing letter from Hogg, the Ettrick minstrel and shepherd. He wants me to recommend him to Murray; and, speaking of his present bookseller, whose " bills " are never " lifted ", he adds, *totidem verbis*, " God damn him and them both ". I laughed, and so would you too, at the way in which this execration is introduced. The said Hogg is a strange being, but of great, though uncouth, powers. I think very highly of him, as a poet; but he, and half of these Scotch and Lake troubadours, are spoilt by living in little circles and petty societies. London and the world is the only place to take the conceit out of a man—in the milling phrase.

[1] Rogers' poem, *Jacqueline*, was first circulated in combination with Byron's *Lara*.

Scott, he says, is gone to the Orkneys in a gale of wind;—during which wind, he affirms, the said Scott, " he is sure, is not at his ease,—to say the best of it ".   Lord, Lord, if these home-keeping minstrels had crossed your Atlantic or my Mediterranean, and tasted a little open boating in a white squall—or a gale in " the Gut "—or the " Bay of Biscay ", with no gale at all—how it would enliven and introduce them to a few of the sensations !—to say nothing of an illicit amour or two upon shore, in the way of essay upon the Passions, beginning with simple adultery, and compounding it as they went along.

I have forwarded your letter to Murray,—by the way, you had addressed it to *Miller*.   Pray write to me, and say what art thou doing?   " Not finished? "—Oons! how is this?—these " flaws and starts " must be " authorised by your grandam ", and are unbecoming of any other author.   I was sorry to hear of your discrepancy with the * * s, or rather your abjuration of agreement.   I don't want to be impertinent, or buffoon on a serious subject, and am therefore at a loss what to say.

I hope nothing will induce you to abate from the proper price of your poem, as long as there is a prospect of getting it. For my own part, I have *seriously* and *not whiningly* (for that is not my way—at least, it used not to be) neither hopes, nor prospects, and scarcely even wishes.   I am, in some respects, happy, but not in a manner that can or ought to last,—but enough of that.   The worst of it is, I feel quite enervated and indifferent.   I really do not know, if Jupiter were to offer me my choice of the contents of his benevolent cask, what I would pick out of it.   If I was born, as the nurses say, with a " silver spoon in my mouth ", it has stuck in my throat, and spoiled my palate, so that nothing put into it is swallowed with much relish,—unless it be cayenne.   However, I have grievances enough to occupy me that way too;—but for fear of adding to yours by this pestilent long diatribe, I postpone the reading of them, *sine die*.

> Ever, dear M., yours, etc.

P.S.—Don't forget my godson.   You could not have fixed on a fitter porter for his sins than me, being used to carry double without inconvenience. * * *

TO MISS ANNE ISABELLA MILBANKE   *August 10th, 1814*

I will answer your question as openly as I can. I did—do —and always shall love you; and as this feeling is not exactly an act of will, I know no remedy, and at all events should never find one in the sacrifice of your comfort. When our acquaintance commenced, it appeared to me from all that I saw and heard that you were the woman most adapted to render any man (who was neither inveterately foolish nor wicked) happy; but I was informed that you were attached, if not engaged—and very luckily—to a person for whose success all the females of the family where I received my intelligence were much interested. Before such powerful interest—and your supposed inclinations—I had too much humility or pride to hazard importunity or even attention; till I at last learned— almost by accident—that I was misinformed as to the engagement. The rest you know; and I will not trouble you with " a twice told tale ", " signifying nothing ".

What your own feelings and objections were and are I have not the right and scarcely the wish to enquire. It is enough for me that they exist; they excite neither astonishment nor displeasure. It would be a very hard case if a woman were obliged to account for her repugnance. You would probably like me if you could; and as you cannot I am not quite coxcomb enough to be surprised at a very natural occurrence. You ask me how far my peace is, or may be, affected by those feelings towards you. I do not know—not quite enough to invade yours, or request from your pity what I cannot owe to your affection.

I am interrupted—perhaps it is as well upon such a subject.

TO THOMAS MOORE   *August 12, 1814*

I was *not* alone, nor will be while I can help it. Newstead is not yet decided. Claughton is to make a grand effort by Saturday week to complete,—if not, he must give up twenty-five thousand pounds and the estate, with expenses, etc., etc. If I resume the Abbacy, you shall have due notice, and a cell set apart for your reception, with a pious welcome. Rogers I have not seen, but Larry and Jacky came out a few days ago. Of their effect I know nothing. * * *

There is something very amusing in *your* being an *Edinburgh Reviewer*. You know, I suppose, that Thurlow is none of the placidest, and may possibly enact some tragedy on being told that he is only a fool. If, now, Jeffrey were to be slain on account of an article of yours, there would be a fine conclusion. For my part, as Mrs. Winifred Jenkins says, " he has done the handsome thing by me ", particularly in his last number ; so, he is the best of men and the ablest of critics, and I won't have him killed—though I dare say many wish he were, for being so good-humoured.

Before I left Hastings I got in a passion with an ink-bottle, which I flung out of the window one night with a vengeance ;— and what then? Why, next morning I was horrified by seeing that it had struck, and split upon, the petticoat of Euterpe's graven image in the garden, and grimed her as if it were on purpose. Only think of my distress,—and the epigrams that might be engendered on the Muse and her misadventure.

I had an adventure almost as ridiculous, at some private theatricals near Cambridge—though of a different description —since I saw you last. I quarrelled with a man in the dark for asking me who I was (insolently enough to be sure), and followed him into the green-room (a *stable*) in a rage, amongst a set of people I never saw before. He turned out to be a low comedian, engaged to act with the amateurs, and to be a civil-spoken man enough, when he found out that nothing very pleasant was to be got by rudeness. But you would have been amused with the row, and the dialogue, and the dress— or rather the undress—of the party, where I had introduced myself in a devil of a hurry, and the astonishment that ensued. I had gone out of the theatre, for coolness, into the garden ;— there I had tumbled over some dogs, and, coming away from them in very ill humour, encountered the man in a worse, which produced all this confusion.

Well—and why don't you " launch "?—Now is your time. The people are tolerably tired with me, and not very much enamoured of Wordsworth, who has just spawned a quarto of metaphysical blank verse, which is nevertheless only a part of a poem.

Murray talks of divorcing Larry and Jacky—a bad sign for the authors, who, I suppose, will be divorced too, and throw the blame upon one another. Seriously, I don't care a cigar about it, and I don't see why Sam should.

Let me hear from and of you and my godson. If a daughter, the name will do quite as well.

> Ever, etc.

TO LADY MELBOURNE　　　　　　　*Newstead Abbey,*
　　　　　　　　　　　　　　[Sunday] September 18th, 1814

MY DEAR LADY M^E,—Miss Milbanke has accepted me; and her answer was accompanied by a very kind letter from your brother. May I hope for your consent, too? Without it I should be unhappy, even were it not for many reasons important in other points of view; and with it I shall have nothing to require, except your good wishes now, and your friendship always.

I lose no time in telling you how things are at present. Many circumstances may doubtless occur in this, as in other cases, to prevent its completion, but I will hope otherwise. I shall be in town by Thursday, and beg one line to Albany, to say you will see me at your own day, hour, and place.

In course I mean to reform most thoroughly, and become " a good man and true ", in all the various senses of these respective and respectable appellations. Seriously, I will endeavour to make your niece happy; not by " my deserts, but what I will deserve ". Of my deportment you may reasonably doubt; of her merits you can have none. I need not say that this must be a *secret*. Do let me find a few words from you in Albany, and believe me ever

> Most affec^{tly} y^{rs}, B.

TO MISS ANNE ISABELLA MILBANKE　　　　*Septr. 18th 1814*

Your letter has given me a new existence [1]—it was unexpected—I need not say welcome—but *that* is a poor word to express my present feelings—and yet equal to any other—for express them adequately I cannot. I have ever regarded you

[1] Byron refers to Miss Milbanke's letter, finally accepting his proposal of marriage.

as one of the first of human beings—not merely from my own observation but that of others—as one whom it was as difficult *not* to love—as scarcely possible to deserve; —I know your worth—and revere your virtues as I love yourself and if every proof in my power of my full sense of what is due to you will contribute to *your* happiness—I shall have secured my own.— It *is* in your power to render me happy—you have made me so already.—I wish to answer your letter immediately—but am at present scarcely collected enough to do it rationally—I was upon the point of leaving England without hope without fear —almost without feeling—but wished to make one effort to discover—not if I could pretend to your present affections—for to those I had given over all presumption—but whether time —and my most sincere endeavour to adopt any mode of conduct that might lead you to think well of me—might not eventually in securing your approbation awaken your regard.— These hopes are now dearer to me than ever; dear as they have ever been; —from the moment I became acquainted my attachment has been increasing and the very follies—give them a harsher name—with which I was beset and bewildered the conduct to which I had recourse for forgetfulness only made recollection more lively and bitter by the comparisons it forced on me in spite of Pride—and of Passions—which might have destroyed but never deceived me.—

I am going to London on some business which once over— I hope to be permitted to visit Seaham; your father I will answer immediately and in the mean time beg you will present my best thanks and respects to him and Lady Milbanke.   Will you write to me? and permit me to assure you how faithfully I shall ever be

> yr. most attached and obliged Sert.[1]

TO THOMAS MOORE   *Newstead Abbey, Sept. 20, 1814*

> Here's to her who long
>   Hath waked the poet's sigh!
> The girl who gave to song
>   What gold could never buy.

[1] In this letter the characteristically wild punctuation is left unchanged, since it well conveys his agitation.

MY DEAR MOORE,—I am going to be married—that is, I am accepted, and one usually hopes the rest will follow. My mother of the Gracchi (that *are* to be), *you* think too strait-laced for me, although the paragon of only children, and invested with " golden opinions of all sorts of men ", and full of " most blest conditions " as Desdemona herself. Miss Milbanke is the lady, and I have her father's invitation to proceed there in my elect capacity,—which, however, I cannot do till I have settled some business in London, and got a blue coat.

She is said to be an heiress, but of that I really know nothing certainly, and shall not enquire. But I do know, that she has talents and excellent qualities ; and you will not deny her judgment, after having refused six suitors and taken me.

Now, if you have anything to say against this, pray do ; my mind's made up, positively fixed, determined, and there-fore I will listen to reason, because now it can do no harm. Things may occur to break it off, but I will hope not. In the mean time, I tell you (a *secret*, by the by,—at least, till I know she wishes it to be public) that I have proposed and am accepted. You need not be in a hurry to wish me joy, for one mayn't be married for months. I am going to town to-morrow : but expect to be here, on my way there, within a fortnight.

If this had not happened, I should have gone to Italy. In my way down, perhaps, you will meet me at Nottingham, and come over with me here. I need not say that nothing will give me greater pleasure. I must, of course, reform thoroughly ; and, seriously, if I can contribute to her happiness, I shall secure my own. She is so good a person, that—that—in short, I wish I was a better.

Ever, etc.

TO MISS MILBANKE [FRAGMENT] *14 Oc^{tr} 1814*

I have not seen the paragraph you mention ; but it cannot speak more humbly of me in the comparison than I think. This is one of the lesser evils to which notoriety and a carelessness of fame,—in the only good sense of the word,—has rendered me liable,—a carelessness which I do not now feel since I have obtained something worth caring for. The truth is that could I have foreseen that your life was to be linked to mine,—had I even possessed a distinct hope however distant,— I would have been a different and better being. As it is, I have sometimes doubts, even if I should not disappoint the future nor act hereafter unworthily of you, whether the past ought not to make you still regret me—even that portion of it with which you are not unacquainted.

I did not believe such a woman existed—at least for me,— and I sometimes fear I ought to wish that she had not. I must turn from the subject.

My love, do forgive me if I have written in a spirit that renders you uncomfortable. I cannot embody my feelings in words. I have nothing to desire—nothing I would see altered in *you*—but so much in myself. I can conceive no misery equal to mine, if I failed in making you happy,—and yet how can I hope to do justice to those merits from whose praise there is not a dissentient voice?

TO THOMAS MOORE   *October 14, 1814*

An there were any thing in marriage that would make a difference between my friends and me, particularly in your case, I would " none on't ". My agent sets off for Durham next week, and I shall follow him, taking Newstead and you in my way. I certainly did not address Miss Milbanke with these views, but it is likely she may prove a considerable *parti*. All her father can give, or leave her, he will; and from her childless uncle, Lord Wentworth, whose barony, it is supposed, will devolve on Ly. Milbanke (*his* sister), she has expectations. But these will depend upon his own disposition, which seems very partial towards her. She is an only child, and Sir R.'s estates, though dipped by electioneering, are considerable. Part of them are settled on her; but whether *that* will be *dowered* now, I do not know,—though, from what has been intimated to me, it probably will. The lawyers are to settle this among them, and I am getting my property into matrimonial array, and myself ready for the journey to Seaham, which I must make in a week or ten days.

I certainly did not dream that she was attached to me, which it seems she has been for some time. I also thought her of a very cold disposition, in which I was also mistaken—it is a long story, and I won't trouble you with it. As to her virtues etc., etc., you will hear enough of them (for she is a kind of *pattern* in the north), without my running into a display on the subject. It is well that *one* of us is of such fame, since there is sad deficit in the *morale* of that article upon my part,—all owing to my " bitch of a star ", as Captain Tranchemont says of his planet.

Don't think you have not said enough of me in your article on T[hurlow]; what more could or need be said?

* * Your long-delayed and expected work—I suppose you will take fright at *The Lord of the Isles* and Scott now. You must do as you like,—I have said my say. You ought to fear comparison with none, and any one would stare, who heard you were so tremulous,—though, after all, I believe it is the surest sign of talent. Good morning. I hope we shall meet soon, but I will write again, and perhaps you will meet me at Nottingham. Pray say so.

P.S.—If this union is productive, you shall name the first fruits.

TO JOHN CAM HOBHOUSE   *October 17th, 1814*

MY DEAR HOBHOUSE,—If I have not answered your very kind letter immediately, do not impute it to neglect. I have expected you would be in town or near it, and waited to thank you in person. Believe me, no change of time or circumstance short of insanity, can make any difference in my feelings, and I hope, in my conduct towards you. I have known you too long, and tried you too deeply; a new mistress is nothing to an old friend, the latter can't be replaced in this world, nor, I very much fear, in the next, and neither in this nor the other

could I meet with one so deserving of my respect and regard.
Well, H.—I am engaged, and we wait only for settlements
" and all that " to be married. My intended, it seems, has
liked me very well for a long time, which, I am sure, her
encouragement gave me no reason to suspect; but so it is, according to her account. The circumstances which led to the
renewal of my proposal I will acquaint you with when we
meet, if you think such material concerns worth your enquiry.
Hanson is going down next week to Durham, to confabulate
with Sir R.'s agents on the score of temporalities, and I suppose
I must soon follow to my sire-in-law's that is to be. I confess
that the character of wooer in this regular way does not sit
easy upon me. I wish I could wake some morning, and find
myself fairly married. I do hate (out of Turkey) all fuss, and
bustle, and ceremony so much; and one can't be married,
according to what I hear, without *some*. I wish, whenever this
same form is muttered over us, that you could make it convenient to be present. I will give you due notice:—if you
would but take a wife and be coupled then also, like people
electrified in company through the same chain, it would be
still further comfort.

Good even.

Ever yours most truly, B.

TO MISS MILBANKE [FRAGMENT]   *20ᵗʰ Octʳ 1814*

I have been so much amused with your " extracts ", though
I had no idea what an evil spirit I then appeared in your eyes.
You were quite right however, as far as appearances, but that
was not my natural character. I was just returned from a far
country where everything was different, and felt bewildered
and not very happy in my own, which I had left without
regret and returned to without interest. I found myself, I did
not very well know why, an object of curiosity which I never
wished to excite—and about a poem which I had no conception was to make such a fuss. My mind and my feelings were
moreover occupied with considerations which had nothing in
common with the circle where I was whirling, so that no

wonder I was repulsive and cold. I never could conquer my disposition to be both in a crowd from which I was always wishing myself away.

Those who know me most intimately can tell you that I am if anything too *childish*, with a greater turn for the ridiculous than for anything serious,—and, I could hope, not very ill natured *off the stage*, and, if angry, never loud. I can't say much for these qualifications, but I have such a regard for yours, that I am sure we shall be a very happy couple. I wish you had a greater passion for governing, for I don't shine in conducting myself, and am very docile with a gentle guide.

TO LADY MELBOURNE   *Seaham, November 4th, 1814*

MY DEAR LADY Mᵉ,—I have been here these two days; but waited to observe before I imparted to you—" my confidential counsel ", as Master Hoar would say—my remarks.

Your brother pleases me much. To be sure his stories are long; but I believe he has told most of them, and he is to my mind the perfect gentleman; but I don't like Lady M[ilbanke] at all. I can't tell why, for we don't differ, but so it is; she seems to be everything here, which is all very well; and I am, and mean to be, very conformable, and dutiful, but nevertheless I wish she and mine aunt could change places, as far as regards me and mine. A[nnabella]'s meeting and mine made a kind of scene; though there was no acting, nor even speaking, but the pantomime was very expressive. She seems to have more feeling than we imagined; but is the most *silent* woman I ever encountered; which perplexes me extremely. I like them to talk, because then they *think* less. Much cogitation will not be in my favour; besides, I can form my judgments better, since, unless the countenance is flexible, it is difficult to steer by mere looks. I am studying her, but can't boast of my progress in getting at her disposition; and if the conversation is to be all on one side I fear committing myself; and those who only listen, must have their thoughts so much about them as to seize any weak point at once. However, the die is cast; neither party can recede; the lawyers are here—mine and all—and I presume, the parchment once scribbled, I shall become Lord Annabella.

I can't yet tell whether we are to be happy or not. I have every disposition to do her all possible justice, but I fear she won't govern me; and if she don't it will not do at all; but perhaps she may mend of that fault. I have always thought— first, that she did not like me at all; and next, that her supposed after-liking was *imagination*. This last I conceive that my presence would—perhaps has removed—if so, I shall soon discover it, but mean to take it with great philosophy, and to behave attentively and well, though I never could love but that which *loves*; and this I must say for myself, that my attachment always increases in due proportion to the return it meets with, and never changes in the presence of its object; to be sure, like Mrs. Damer, I have " an opinion of absence ".

Pray write. I think you need not fear that the *answer* to *this* will run any of the risks you apprehend. It will be a great comfort to me, in all events, to call you aunt, and to know that you are sure of my being

Ever y^rs, B.

TO MISS ANNE ISABELLA MILBANKE   *Novr. 23rd 1814*

My Love—While I write this letter I have desired my very old and kind friend Mr. Hodgson to send you a note, which I will enclose, as it contains a piece of information that will come better from him than me—and yet not give you less pleasure. I think of setting off for London to-morrow— where I will write again. I am quite confused and bewildered here with the voting and the fuss and the crowd—to say nothing of yesterday's dinner and meeting all one's old acquaintances, the consequence of which is that infallible next-day's headache ever attendant upon sincere Friendship. Here are Hobhouse and our cousin George Lamb—who called on me ; and we have all voted the same way, but they say nevertheless our man won't win—but have many votes howbeit. To-day I dine with Clarke the traveller—one of the best and most goodnatured of souls—and uniformly kind to me. When we meet I think and hope I shall make you laugh at the scene I went through—or rather which went through me; for I was quite unprepared, and am not at the best of times sufficiently master of " the family shyness " to acquit myself otherwise than awkwardly on such an occasion.

Well but—sweet Heart—do write and love me—and regard me as thine

ever and most

P.S.—Love to parents.   I have not and am not to see H's note, so I hope it is all very correct.

3

Marriage

January 1815 to October 1816

Byron had not been averse from the prospect of marriage; but, when the prospect began to materialize, he had shown many signs of hesitation. *Never was lover less in haste*, observed Hobhouse, noting the lack of enthusiasm with which he prepared to join the Milbankes. Almost from the first day the marriage was unfortunate: Byron was in one of his darkest moods; and his attitude towards the young woman he had married, even allowing for his love of exaggeration and an element of romantic bravado, was neither kindly nor considerate. After an over-clouded honeymoon, the married couple returned to London and took up residence at an expensive house in Piccadilly Terrace. Byron's creditors, excited by the report that he had married an heiress, became extremely troublesome; and incessant financial difficulties added to the depression of spirits from which he was already suffering. Nor was the anxious solemnity with which Lady Byron watched her husband's movements calculated to soothe him. She did not approve of his choice of friends, who encouraged him, she believed, to sit up drinking brandy, and she mistrusted his connection with Drury Lane Theatre, where Byron and Douglas Kinnaird both served on the Committee. Despite the intervention of Augusta Leigh, who did what she could to comfort her sister-in-law and calm her brother's tantrums, the relationship between Byron and his wife became rapidly more painful. It was not improved by the birth of their only child, Augusta Ada Byron, on December 10th, 1815. During January bailiffs entered the house; and on the 15th, at Byron's request, Annabella and her child set out from London and took refuge with her parents. En route she wrote him an affectionate message; but, during the first week of February 1816, Sir Ralph Milbanke informed the poet that Lady Byron's parents " could not feel themselves justified in permitting her return ", and proposed a separation. Byron

refused indignantly, but eventually agreed, though he professed
that he still could not understand why his wife should wish to
leave him.   On April 25th, 1816, he sailed from England for
the last time and, having travelled across the Low Countries
with Dr. Polidori, his personal physician, settled beside the Lake
of Geneva at the Villa Diodati.   There his associates were Percy
Bysshe Shelley (a connection much regretted by Mrs. Leigh and
by her confidant, Byron's old acquaintance, the Reverend Francis
Hodgson), Shelley's youthful mistress, Mary Godwin, and her
turbulent step-sister, Claire Clairmont, who had previously
encountered Byron in London and who after a time returned to
England to give birth to his natural child, Allegra.

TO LADY MELBOURNE   *Halnaby, January 3rd, 1815*

MY DEAREST AUNT,—We were married yesterday at ten
upon yᵉ clock, so there's an end of that matter, and the beginning of many others.   Bell has gone through all the ceremonies with great fortitude, and I am much as usual, and your
dutiful nephew.   All those who are disposed to make presents
may as well send them forthwith, and pray let them be handsome, and we wait your congrats besides, as I am sure your
benediction is very essential to all our undertakings.

Lady M[ilbanke] was a little hysterical, and fine-feeling;
and the kneeling was rather tedious, and the cushions hard;
but upon the whole it did vastly well.   The drawing-room at
Seaham was the scene of our conjunction, and then we set off,
according to approved custom, to be shut up by ourselves.

You would think we had been married these fifty years.
Bell is fast asleep on a corner of the sopha, and I am keeping
myself awake with this epistle—she desires her love, and mine
you have had ever since we were acquainted.   Pray, how
many of our new relations (at least, of mine) mean to own us?
I reckon upon George and you, and Lord M[elbourne] and

the Countess and Count of the Holy Roman Empire; as for *Caro* and Caro George, and *William*, I don't know what to think, do you?

I shall write to you again anon; at present, receive this as an apology for that silence of which you were kind enough to complain; and believe me ever most affectionately thine,

BYRON

P.S.—I enclose you an order for the box; it was not at liberty before. The week after next will be mine, and so on alternately. I have lent it, for the present week only, to another person; the next is yours.

TO THOMAS MOORE   *January 19, 1815*

Egad! I don't think he is "down"; and my prophecy—like most auguries, sacred and profane—is not annulled, but inverted. * * *

To your question about the "dog"—Umph!—my "mother", I won't say any thing against—that is, about her: but how long a "mistress" or friend may recollect paramours or competitors (lust and thirst being the two great and only bonds between the amatory or the amicable), I can't say,—or, rather, you know, as well as I could tell you. But as for canine recollections, as far as I could judge by a cur of mine own, (always bating Boatswain, the dearest, and, alas! the maddest of dogs,) I had one (half a *wolf* by the she side) that doted on me at ten years old, and very nearly ate me at twenty. When I thought he was going to enact Argus, he bit away the backside of my breeches, and never would consent to any kind of recognition, in despite of all kinds of bones which I offered him. So, let Southey blush and Homer too, as far as I can decide upon quadruped memories.

I humbly take it, the mother knows the son that pays her jointure—a mistress her mate, till he * * and refuses salary—a friend his fellow, till he loses cash and character—and a dog his master, till he changes him.

So, you want to know about milady and me? But let me not, as Roderick Random says, " profane the chaste mysteries of Hymen "—damn the word, I had nearly spelt it with a small *h*. I like Bell as well as you do (or did, you villain!) Bessy—and that is (or was) saying a great deal.

Address your next to Seaham, Stockton-on-Tees, where we are going on Saturday (a bore, by the way,) to see father-in-law, Sir Jacob, and my lady's lady-mother. Write—and write more at length—both to the public and

Yours ever most affectionately, B.

TO THOMAS MOORE   *Seaham, Stockton-on-Tees, February 2, 1815*

I have heard from London that you have left Chatsworth and all the women full of " entusymusy " about you, personally and poetically; and, in particular, that " When first I met thee " has been quite overwhelming in its effect. I told you it was one of the best things you ever wrote, though that dog Power wanted you to omit part of it. They are all regretting your absence at Chatsworth, according to my informant— " all the ladies quite ", etc., etc., etc. Stap my vitals!

Well, now you have got home again—which I dare say is as agreeable as a " draught of cool small beer to the scorched palate of a waking sot "—now you have got home again, I say, probably I shall hear from you. Since I wrote last, I have been transferred to my father-in-law's, with my lady and my lady's maid, etc., etc., etc., and the treacle-moon is over, and I am awake, and find myself married. My spouse and I agree to—and in—admiration. Swift says " no *wise* man ever married "; but, for a fool, I think it the most ambrosial of all possible future states. I still think one ought to marry upon *lease*; but am very sure I should renew mine at the expiration, though next term were for ninety and nine years.

I wish you would respond, for I am here *oblitusque meorum obliviscendus et illis*. Pray tell me what is going on in the way of intriguery, and how the w——s and rogues of the upper Beggar's Opera go on—or rather go off—in or after marriage; or who are going to break any particular commandment. Upon this dreary coast, we have nothing but county meetings and shipwrecks: and I have this day dined upon fish, which probably dined upon the crews of several colliers lost in the late gales. But I saw the sea once more in all the glories of surf and foam,—almost equal to the Bay of Biscay, and the interesting white squalls and short seas of Archipelago memory.

My papa, Sir Ralpho, hath recently made a speech at a Durham tax-meeting; and not only at Durham, but here, several times since after dinner. He is now, I believe, speaking it to himself (I left him in the middle) over various decanters, which can neither interrupt him nor fall asleep,—as might possibly have been the case with some of his audience.

Ever thine, B.

I must go to tea—damn tea. I wish it was Kinnaird's brandy, and with you to lecture me about it.

TO LADY MELBOURNE   *Seaham, February 2nd, 1815*

MY DEAR AUNT,—Sans letter paper, I have co-opted awkwardly enough a sheet of foolscap whereupon to answer your epistle. I cannot " laugh " at anything which gave you pain, and therefore will say nothing about your nervous head-ache, except that I am glad that it is gone; one may see a " double face " without being *delirious* though; but I must cease talking of your complaint for fear of growing as senti-mental as Bob Adair, your larmoyant admirer. Had you seen Lord Stair? If so the disorder, as far as the *ache* (the face is too dull to be double) is accounted for.

It rejoices me to hear of Moore's success; he is an excellent companion as well as poet, though I cannot recollect that I " wept " at the song you mention. I ought to have done so; but whether I did or not, it is one of the most beautiful and touching compositions that ever he penned, and much better than ever was compounded by anyone else.

The *moon* is over; but Bell and I are as lunatic as hereto-fore; she does as she likes, and don't bore me, and we may win the Dunmow flitch of bacon for anything I know. Mamma and Sir Ralph are also very good, but I wish the last would not speak his speech at the Durham meeting above once a week after its first delivery.

I won't betray you, if you will only write me something worth betraying. I suppose your " C— noir " is **X**, but if **X** were a raven, or a griffin, I must still take omens from her flight.

I can't help loving her, though I have quite enough at home to prevent me from loving anyone essentially for some time to come.

We have two visitors here, a Mrs. and Miss Somebody; the latter plain, and both humdrum, they have made me so sleepy that I must say Good night.

Ever yours most nepotically, B.

TO THOMAS MOORE   *July 7, 1815*

Grata superveniet, etc., etc. I had written to you again, but burnt the letter, because I began to think you seriously hurt at my indolence, and did not know how the buffoonery it contained might be taken. In the mean time, I have yours, and all is well.

I had given over all hopes of yours. By-the-by, my *grata superveniet* should be in this present tense; for I perceive it looks now as if it applied to this present scrawl reaching you, whereas it is to the receipt of thy Kilkenny epistle that I have tacked that venerable sentiment.

Poor Whitbread died yesterday morning,—a sudden and severe loss. His health had been wavering, but so fatal an attack was not apprehended. He dropped down, and I believe never spoke afterwards. I perceive Perry attributes his death to Drury Lane,—a consolatory encouragement to the new Committee. I have no doubt that * *, who is of a plethoric habit, will be bled immediately; as I have, since my marriage, lost much of my paleness, and—*horresco referens* (for I hate even *moderate* fat)—that happy slenderness, to which when I first knew you, I had attained, I by no means sit easy under this dispensation of the *Morning Chronicle*. Every one must regret the loss of Whitbread; he was surely a great and very good man.

Paris is taken for the second time. I presume it, for the future, will have an anniversary capture. In the late battles, like all the world, I have lost a connexion,—poor Frederic Howard, the best of his race. I had little intercourse, of late years, with his family, but I never saw or heard but good of him. Hobhouse's brother is killed. In short, the havoc has not left a family out of its tender mercies.

Every hope of a republic is over, and we must go on under the old system. But I am sick at heart of politics and slaughters; and the luck which Providence is pleased to lavish on Lord Castlereagh is only a proof of the little value the gods set upon prosperity, when they permit such * * *s as he and that drunken corporal, old Blucher, to bully their betters. From this, however, Wellington should be excepted. He *is* a man,— and the Scipio of our Hannibal. However, he may thank the Russian frosts, which destroyed the *real élite* of the French army, for the successes of Waterloo.

La! Moore—how you blasphemes about " Parnassus " and " Moses! " I am ashamed for you. Won't you do any thing for the drama? We beseech an Opera. Kinnaird's blunder was partly mine. I wanted you of all things in the Committee, and so did he. But we are now glad you were wiser; for it is, I doubt, a bitter business.

When shall we see you in England? Sir Ralph Noel (*late* Milbanke—he don't promise to be *late* Noel in a hurry), finding that one man can't inhabit two houses, has given his place in the north to me for a habitation; and there Lady B. threatens to be brought to bed in November. Sir R. and my Lady Mother are to quarter at Kirby—Lord Wentworth's that was. Perhaps you and Mrs. Moore will pay us a visit at Seaham in the course of the autumn. If so, you and I (*without our wives*) will take a *lark* to Edinburgh and embrace Jeffrey. It is not much above one hundred miles from us. But all this, and other high matters, we will discuss at meeting, which I hope will be on your return. We don't leave town till August.

Ever yours, etc., B.

TO S. T. COLERIDGE *   *13 Terrace, Piccadilly, October 18th, 1815*

DEAR SIR,—Your letter I have just received. I will willingly do whatever you direct about the volumes in question—the

sooner the better : it shall not be for want of endeavour on
my part, as a negotiator with the " Trade " (to talk technically)
that you are not enabled to do yourself justice. Last spring I
saw Wr. Scott. He repeated to me a considerable portion of
an unpublished poem of yours—the wildest and finest I ever
heard in that kind of composition. The title he did not
mention, but I think the heroine's name was Geraldine. At all
events, the " toothless mastiff bitch " and the " witch Lady ",
the description of the hall, the lamp suspended from the image,
and more particularly of the girl herself as she went forth in
the evening—all took a hold on my imagination which I never
shall wish to shake off. I mention this, not for the sake of
boring you with compliments, but as a prelude to the hope that
this poem is or is to be in the volumes you are now about to
publish. I do not know that even " Love " or the " Antient
Mariner " are so impressive—and to me there are few things
in our tongue beyond these two productions.

Wr. Scott is a staunch and sturdy admirer of yours, and
with a just appreciation of your capacity deplored to me the
want of inclination and exertion which prevented you from
giving full scope to your mind. I will answer your question
as to the " Beggar's Bush " tomorrow or next day. I shall see
Rae and Dibdin (the acting Mrs.) tonight for that purpose.

Oh—your tragedy—I do not wish to hurry you, but I am
indeed very anxious to have it under consideration. It is a
field in which there are none living to contend against you
and in which I should take a pride and pleasure in seeing you
compared with the dead. I say this *not* disinterestedly, but as
a *Committee*man. We have nothing even tolerable, except a
tragedy of Sotheby's, which shall not interfere with yours when
ready. You can have no idea what trash there is in the four
hundred *fallow* dramas now lying on the shelves of D[rury]
L[ane]. I never thought so highly of good writers as lately,
since I have had an opportunity of comparing them with the
bad.

Ever yours truly,

BYRON

MY DEAR HUNT,—Many thanks for your books, of which you already know my opinion. Their external splendour should not disturb you as inappropriate—they have still more within than without. I take leave to differ with you on Wordsworth, as freely as I once agreed with you; at that time I gave him credit for a promise, which is unfulfilled. I still think his capacity warrants all you say of *it* only, but that his performances since *Lyrical Ballads* are miserably inadequate to the ability which lurks within him: there is undoubtedly much natural talent spilt over the *Excursion*; but it is rain upon rocks—where it stands and stagnates, or rain upon sands —where it falls without fertilizing. Who can understand him? Let those who do, make him intelligible. Jacob Behmen, Swedenborg, and Joanna Southcote, are mere types of this arch-apostle of mystery and mysticism. But I have done,— no, I have not done, for I have two petty, and perhaps unworthy objections in small matters to make to him, which, with his pretensions to accurate observation, and fury against Pope's false translation of " the Moonlight scene in Homer ", I wonder he should have fallen into;—these be they:—He says of Greece in the body of his book—that it is a land of

> " *Rivers, fertile plains,* and *sounding* shores,
>   Under a cope of *variegated* sky ".

The rivers are dry half the year, the plains are barren, and the shores *still* and *tideless* as the Mediterranean can make them; the sky is any thing but variegated, being for months and months but " darkly, deeply, beautifully blue ".—The next is in his notes, where he talks of our " Monuments crowded together in the busy, etc., of a large town ", as compared with the " still seclusion of a Turkish cemetery in some *remote* place ". This is pure stuff; for *one* monument in our church-yards there are *ten* in the Turkish, and so crowded, that you cannot walk between them; that is, divided merely by a path or road; and as to " *remote* places ", men never take the trouble in a barbarous country, to carry their dead very far; they must have lived near to where they were buried. There are no cemeteries in " remote places ", except such as have the cypress and the tombstone still left, where the olive and the habitation of the living have perished. . . .

These things I was struck with, as coming peculiarly in my own way; and in both of these he is wrong; yet I should have noticed neither, but for his attack on Pope for a like blunder, and a peevish affectation about him of despising a popularity which he will never obtain. I write in great haste, and, I doubt, *not* much to the purpose; but you have it hot and hot, just as it comes, and so let it go. By-the-way, both he and you go too far against Pope's " So when the moon ", etc.; it is no translation, I know; but it is not such false description as asserted. I have read it on the spot; there is a burst, and a lightness, and a glow about the night in the Troad, which makes the " planets vivid ", and the " pole glowing ". The moon is—at least the sky is, clearness itself; and I know no more appropriate expression for the expansion of such a heaven —o'er the scene—the plain—the sky—Ida—the—Hellespont —Simois—Scamander—and the Isles—than that of a " flood of glory ". I am getting horribly lengthy, and must stop: to the whole of your letter " I say ditto to Mr. Burke ", as the Bristol candidate cried by way of electioneering harangue. You need not speak of morbid feelings and vexations to me; I have plenty; but I must blame partly the times, and chiefly myself: but let us forget them. *I* shall be very apt to do so when I see you next. Will you come to the theatre and see our new management? You shall cut it up to your heart's content, root and branch, afterwards, if you like; but come and see it! If not, I must come and see you.

Ever yours, very truly and affectionately, Byron

P.S.—Not a word from Moore for these two months. Pray let me have the rest of *Rimini*. You have two excellent points in that poem—originality and Italianism. I will back you as a bard against half the fellows on whom you have thrown away much good criticism and eulogy; but don't let your bookseller publish in *quarto*; it is the worst size possible for circulation. I say this on bibliopolical authority.

Again, yours ever, B.

TO THOMAS MOORE   *Terrace, Piccadilly, October 31, 1815*

I have not been able to ascertain precisely the time of
duration of the stock market; but I believe it is a good time
for selling out, and I hope so. First, because I shall see you;
and, next, because I shall receive certain monies on behalf of
Lady B., the which will materially conduce to my comfort,—
I wanting (as the duns say) " to make up a sum ".

Yesterday, I dined out with a large-ish party, where were
Sheridan and Colman,[1] Harry Harris of C[ovent] G[arden],
and his brother, Sir Gilbert Heathcote, Douglas Kinnaird,
and others, of note and notoriety. Like other parties of the
kind, it was first silent, then talky, then argumentative, then
disputatious, then unintelligible, then altogethery, then in-
articulate, and then drunk. When we had reached the last
step of this glorious ladder, it was difficult to get down again
without stumbling; and, to crown all, Kinnaird and I had to
conduct Sheridan down a damned corkscrew staircase, which
had certainly been constructed before the discovery of fer-
mented liquors, and to which no legs, however crooked, could
possibly accommodate themselves. We deposited him safe
at home, where his man, evidently used to the business, waited
to receive him in the hall.

Both he and Colman were, as usual, very good; but I
carried away much wine, and the wine had previously carried
away my memory; so that all was hiccup and happiness for
the last hour or so, and I am not impregnated with any of the
conversation. Perhaps you heard of a late answer of Sheridan
to the watchman who found him bereft of that " divine particle
of air ", called reason, * * *. He, the watchman, who found
Sherry in the street, fuddled and bewildered, and almost
insensible, " Who are *you*, sir? "—no answer. " What's your
name? "—a hiccup. " What's your name? "—Answer, in a
slow, deliberate, and impassive tone—" Wilberforce!!! "
Is not that Sherry all over?—and, to my mind, excellent. Poor
fellow, *his* very dregs are better than the " first sprightly run-
nings " of others.

My paper is full, and I have a grievous head-ach.

[1] George Colman the Younger, the popular dramatist, a favourite at Drury
Lane, where Byron, somewhat to his wife's distress, served on the Committee.

P.S.—Lady B. is in full progress. Next month will bring to light (with the aid of " Juno Lucina, *fer opem* ", or rather *opes*, for the last are most wanted,) the tenth wonder of the world—Gil Blas being the eighth, and he (my son's father) the ninth.

TO THOMAS MOORE   *January 5, 1816*

I hope Mrs. M. is quite re-established. The little girl was born on the 10th of December last; her name is Augusta *Ada* (the second a very antique family name,—I believe not used since the reign of King John). She was, and is, very flourishing and fat, and reckoned very large for her days—squalls and sucks incessantly. Are you answered? Her mother is doing very well, and up again.

I have now been married a year on the second of this month—heigh-ho! I have seen nobody lately much worth noting, except Sebastiani and another general of the Gauls once or twice at dinners out of doors. Sebastiani is a fine, foreign, villanous-looking, intelligent, and very agreeable man; his compatriot is more of the *petit-maître* and younger, but I should think not at all of the same intellectual calibre with the Corsican—which Sebastiani, you know, is, and a cousin of Napoleon's.

Are you never to be expected in town again? To be sure, there is no one here of the fifteen hundred fillers of hot rooms, called the fashionable world. My approaching papa-ship detained us for advice, etc., etc., though I would as soon be here as any where else on this side of the Straits of Gibraltar.

I would gladly—or, rather, sorrowfully—comply with your request of a dirge for the poor girl you mention. But how can I write on one I have never seen or known? Besides, you will do it much better yourself. I could not write upon any thing, without some personal experience and foundation: far less on a theme so peculiar. Now, you have both in this case; and, if you had neither, you have more imagination, and would never fail.

This is but a dull scrawl, and I am but a dull fellow. Just at present, I am absorbed in 500 contradictory contemplations, though with but one object in view—which will probably end in nothing, as most things we wish do. But never mind,—as somebody says, " for the blue sky bends over all ". I only could be glad, if it bent over me where it is a little bluer; like the " skyish top of blue Olympus ", which, by the way, looked very white when I last saw it.

                                                   Ever, etc.

TO SIR RALPH NOEL   *February 2, 1816*

SIR,[1] I have received your letter. To the vague and general charge contained in it I must naturally be at a loss how to answer it—I shall therefore confine myself to the tangible fact which you are pleased to alledge as one of the motives for your present proposition. Lady Byron received no dismissal from my house in the sense you have attached to the word. She left London by medical advice. She parted from me in apparent and, on my part, real harmony, though at that particular time, rather against my inclination, for I begged her to remain with the intention of myself accompanying her : when some business necessary to be arranged prevented my departure.

It is true that previous to this period I had suggested to her the expediency of a temporary residence with her parents. My reason for this was very simple and shortly stated, viz. the embarrassment of my circumstances, and my inability to maintain our present establishment. The truth of what is thus stated may be easily ascertained by reference to Lady B.—who is truth itself. If she denies it, I abide by that denial.

My intention of going abroad originated in the same painful motive and was postponed from a regard to her supposed feelings on that subject. During the last year I have had to contend with distress without and disease within. Upon the former I have little to say—except that I have endeavoured to remove it by every sacrifice in my power ; and the latter I should not mention if I had not professional authority for saying that the disorder that I have to combat, without much impairing my apparent health, is such as to induce a morbid irritability of temper, which without recurring to external causes may have rendered me little less disagreeable to others than I am to myself. I am, however, ignorant of any particular ill-treatment which your daughter has encountered. She may have seen me gloomy, and at times violent ; but she knows the causes too well to attribute such inequalities of disposition to herself, or even to me, if all things be fairly considered. And now, Sir, not for your satisfaction—for I owe you none—but for my own, and in justice to Lady Byron, it is

---

[1] Byron's reply to Sir Ralph Noel's letter of the same date, announcing that Lady Byron and her parents wished for a separation.

my duty to say that there is no part of her conduct, character, temper, talents, or disposition, which could in my opinion have been changed for the better. Neither in word or deed, nor (as far as thought can be dived into) thought, can I bring to my recollection a fault on her part, or hardly even a failing. She has ever appeared to me as one of the most amiable of human beings, and nearer to perfection than I had conceived could belong to humanity in its present state of existence. Having said thus much, though more in words, less in substance, than I wished to express, I come to the point—on which subject I must for a few days decline giving a decisive answer. I will not, however, detain you longer than I can help, and as it is of some importance to your family as well as to mine, and a step which cannot be recalled when taken, you will not attribute my pause to any wish to inflict farther pain on you or yours— although there are parts of your letter which, I must be permitted to say, arrogate a right which you do not now possess; for the present at least, your daughter is my wife; she is the mother of my child; and till I have her express sanction of your proceedings, I shall take leave to doubt the propriety of your interference. This will be soon ascertained, and when it is, I will submit to you my determination, which will depend very materially on hers.

I have the honour to be,

Your most obed. and very humble servt., BYRON.

TO LADY BYRON *February 5, 1816*

DEAREST BELL, No answer from you yet; but perhaps it is as well; only do recollect that all is at stake, the present, the future, and even the colouring of the past. My errors, or by whatever harsher name you choose to call them, you know; but I loved you, and will not part from you without your express and expressed refusal to return to, or receive me. Only say the word that you are still mine in your heart, and

" Kate, I will buckler thee against a million."

Ever, dearest, yours most, etc., B.

TO SIR RALPH NOEL   *February 7, 1816*

SIR, I have read Lady Byron's letter, inclosed by you to Mrs. Leigh, with much surprise and more sorrow. Lady B. left London without a single hint of such feelings or intentions— neither did they transpire in her letters on the road, nor subsequent to her arrival at Kirkby. In these letters Lady Byron expresses herself to me with that playful confidence and affectionate liveliness which is perhaps a greater proof of attachment than more serious professions; she speaks to her husband of his child, like a wife and a mother. I am therefore reduced to the melancholy alternative of either believing her capable of a duplicity very foreign to my opinion of her character, or that she has lately sunk under influence, the admission of which, however respected and respectable heretofore, is not recognised in her vows at the altar.

My house, while I have one, is open to her, and my heart always—even though I should have no other shelter to offer her. I cannot suspect Lady Byron of making the grounds stated the pretext for dissolving our connection with a view to escape from my scattered fortunes; although the time chosen for this proposition, and the manner in which it was made—without inquiry, without appeal, without even a doubt, or an attempt at reconciliation—might almost excuse such a supposition. If I address you in strong language, Sir, I still wish to temper it with that respect which is required by the very duties you would persuade me to abandon, and request your candid interpretation of such expressions as circumstances have compelled me to use. I may not debase myself to implore as a suppliant the restoration of a reluctant wife, but I will not compromise my rights as a husband and as a father; I invite Lady Byron's return—I am ready to go to her should she desire or require it—and I deprecate all attempts which have been made or may be made to part us.

I have the honour to be, Sir, with great respect,
        Your most obed. and very humble servant, BYRON.

TO LADY BYRON   *February 8, 1816*

All I can say seems useless—and all I could say might be
no less unavailing—yet I still cling to the wreck of my hopes,
before they sink for ever.   Were you, then, *never* happy with
me ?   Did you never at any time or times express yourself so ?
Have no marks of affection of the warmest and most reciprocal
attachment passed between us ?   or did in fact hardly a day
go down without some such on one side, and generally on both ?
Do not mistake me : I have not denied my state of mind—but
you know its causes—and were those deviations from calm-
ness never followed by acknowledgments and repentance ?
Was not the last that recurred more particularly so ? and had
I not—had we not the days before and on the day we parted—
every reason to believe that we loved each other ? that we
were to meet again ?   Were not your letters kind ?   Had I not
acknowledged to you all my faults and follies—and assured
you that some had not and could not be repeated ?   I do not
require these questions to be answered to me, but to your own
heart.   The day before I received your father's letter I had
fixed a day for rejoining you.   If I did not write lately,
Augusta did ; and as you had been my proxy in correspondence
with her, so did I imagine she might be the same from me to
you.

Upon your letter to me this day I surely may remark that
its expressions imply a treatment which I am incapable of
inflicting, and you of imputing to me, if aware of their latitude,
and the extent of the inference to be drawn from them.   This
is not just, but I have no reproaches nor the wish to find cause
for them.   Will you see me ?—when and where you please—
in whose presence you please.   The interview shall pledge you
to nothing, and I will say and do nothing to agitate either.   It
is torture to correspond thus, and there are things to be settled
and said which cannot be written.

You say it is my disposition to deem what I have worthless.
Did I deem *you* so ?   Did I ever so express myself to you, or of
you to others ?   You are much changed within these twenty
days or you would never have thus poisoned your own better
feelings and trampled on mine.

Ever your most truly and affecty.

TO LADY BYRON   *February 15, 1816*

I know not what to say, every step taken appears to bear you farther from me, and to widen " the great gulf between thee and me ". If it cannot be crossed I will perish in its depth.

Two letters have been written by me to you, but I have not sent them, and I know not well why I write this, or whether I shall send it or no.   How far your conduct is reconcilable to your duties and affections as a wife and a mother, must be a question for your own reflection.   The trial has not been very long—a year, I grant you—of distress, distemper, and misfortune ; but these fell chiefly on me, and bitter as the recollection is to me of what I have felt, it is much more so to have made you a partner of my desolation.   On the charges to be preferred against me I have *twice* been refused any information by your father and his advisers.   It is now a fortnight, which has been passed in suspense, in humiliation, in obloquy, exposed to the most black and blighting calumnies of every kind, without even the power of contradicting conjecture and vulgar assertion as to the accusations, because I am denied the knowledge of all, or any, particulars from the only quarter than can afford them.   In the meantime I hope your ears are gratified by the general rumours.

I have invited your return ; it has been refused.   I have requested to know with what I am charged ; it is refused.   Is this mercy or justice ?   We shall see.   And now, Bell, dearest Bell, whatever may be the event of this calamitous difference, whether you are returned to or torn from me, I can only say in the truth of affliction, and without hope, motive, or end in again saying what I have lately but vainly repeated, that I love you, bad or good, mad or rational, miserable or content, I love you, and shall do, to the dregs of my memory and existence.   If I can feel thus for you now under every possible aggravation and exasperating circumstance that can corrode the heart and inflame the brain, perhaps you may one day know, or think at least, that I was not all you have persuaded yourself to believe me ; but that nothing, nothing can touch me farther.

I have hitherto avoided naming my child, but this was a

feeling you never doubted in me. I must ask of its welfare. I have heard of its beauty and playfulness, and I request, not from you, but through any other channel—Augusta, if you please—some occasional news of its wellbeing.

I am, yours, etc., B.

TO THOMAS MOORE   *February 29, 1816*

I have not answered your letter for a time ; and, at present, the reply to part of it might extend to such a length, that I shall delay it till it can be made in person, and then I will shorten it as much as I can.

In the mean time, I am at war " with all the world and his wife " ; or rather, " all the world and *my* wife " are at war with me, and have not yet crushed me,—whatever they *may* do. I don't know that in the course of a hair-breadth existence I was ever, at home or abroad, in a situation so completely up-rooting of present pleasure, or rational hope for the future, as this same. I say this, because I think so, and feel it. But I shall not sink under it the more for that mode of considering the question—I have made up my mind.

By the way, however, you must not believe all you hear on the subject ; and don't attempt to defend me. If you succeeded in that, it would be a mortal, or an immortal, offence—who can bear refutation? I have but a very short answer for those whom it concerns ; and all the activity of myself and some vigorous friends have not yet fixed on any tangible ground or personage, on which or with whom I can discuss matters, in a summary way, with a fair pretext ;—though I nearly had *nailed one* yesterday, but he evaded by—what was judged by others—a satisfactory explanation. I speak of *circulators*—against whom I have no enmity, though I must act according to the common code of usage, when I hit upon those of the serious order.

Now for other matters—poesy, for instance. Leigh Hunt's poem is a devilish good one—quaint, here and there, but with the substratum of originality, and with poetry about it, that will stand the test. I do not say this because he has inscribed it to me, which I am sorry for, as I should otherwise have begged you to review it in the *Edinburgh*. It is really deserving of much praise, and a favourable critique in the *E. R.* would but do it justice, and set it up before the public eye, where it ought to be.

How are you? and where? I have not the most distant idea what I am going to do myself—or with myself—or where—or what. I had a few weeks ago, some things to say that would have made you laugh; but they tell me now that I must not laugh, and so I have been very serious—and am.

I have not been very well—with a *liver* complaint—but am much better within the last fortnight, though still under Iatrical advice. I have latterly seen a little of * *. * * I must go and dress to dine. My little girl is in the country, and, they tell me, is a very fine child, and now nearly three months old. Lady Noel (my mother-in-law, or, rather, *at* law) is at present overlooking it. Her daughter (Miss Milbanke that was) is, I believe, in London with her father. A Mrs. C.[1] (now a kind of housekeeper and spy of Lady N.'s), who, in her better days, was a washerwoman, is supposed to be—by the learned—very much the occult cause of our late domestic discrepancies.

In all this business, I am the sorriest for Sir Ralph. He and I are equally punished, though *magis pares quam similes* in our affliction. Yet it is hard for both to suffer for the fault of one, and so it is—I shall be separated from my wife; he will retain his.

Ever, etc.

TO LADY BYRON   *March 4, 1816*

I know of no offence, not merely from man to wife, nor of one human being to another, but of any being almost to God Himself, which we are not taught to believe would be expiated by the repeated atonement which I have offered even for the *unknown* faults (for to me, till stated, they are unknown to any extent which can justify such persevering rejections) I may

---

[1] " The respectable Mrs. Clermont ", Annabella Byron's former governess, her mother's companion, whom Byron suspected of having played a sinister part in his differences with his wife.

have been supposed to commit, or can have committed, against you. But since all hope is over, and instead of the duties of a wife and the mother of my child, I am to encounter accusation and implacability, I have nothing more to say, but shall act according to circumstances, though not even injury can alter the love with which (though I shall do my best to repel attack) I must ever be yours,

B.

I am told that you say *you* drew up the proposal of separation ; if so, I regret I hear it ; it appeared to me to be a kind of appeal to the supposed mercenary feelings of the person to whom it was made—" if you part with, etc., you will gain *so much now*, and so much at the death of ", etc., a matter of pounds, shillings, and pence ! No allusion to my child ; a hard, dry, attorneys' paper. Oh, Bell ! to see you thus stifling and destroying all feeling, all affections, all duties (for they are your first duties, those of a wife and a mother), is far more bitter than any possible consequences to me.

TO THOMAS MOORE *March 8, 1816*

I rejoice in your promotion as Chairman and Charitable Steward, etc., etc. These be dignities which await only the virtuous. But then, recollect you are *six* and *thirty*, (I speak this enviously—not of your age, but the " honour—love—obedience—troops of friends ", which accompany it,) and I have eight years good to run before I arrive at such hoary perfection ; by which time,—if I *am* at all,—it will probably be in a state of grace or progressing merits.

I must set you right in one point, however. The fault was *not*—no, nor even the misfortune—in my " choice " (unless in *choosing at all*)—for I do not believe—and I must say it, in the very dregs of all this bitter business—that there ever was a better, or even a brighter, a kinder, or a more amiable and agreeable being than Lady B. I never had, nor can have, any reproach to make her, while with me. Where there is blame, it belongs to myself, and, if I cannot redeem, I must bear it.

Her nearest relatives are a * * * *—my circumstances have been and are in a state of great confusion—my health has been a good deal disordered, and my mind ill at ease for a considerable period. Such are the causes (I do not name them as excuses) which have frequently driven me into excess, and disqualified my temper for comfort. Something also may be attributed to the strange and desultory habits which, becoming my own master at an early age, and scrambling about, over and through the world, may have induced. I still, however, think that, if I had a fair chance, by being placed in even a tolerable situation, I might have gone on fairly. But that seems hopeless,—and there is nothing more to be said. At present—except my health, which is better (it is odd, but agitation or contest of any kind gives a rebound to my spirits and sets me up for the time)—I have to battle with all kinds of unpleasantnesses, including private and pecuniary difficulties, etc., etc.

I believe I may have said this before to you, but I risk repeating it. It is nothing to bear the *privations* of adversity, or, more properly, ill fortune; but my pride recoils from its *indignities*. However, I have no quarrel with that same pride, which will, I think, buckler me through every thing. If my heart could have been broken, it would have been so years ago, and by events more afflicting than these.

I agree with you (to turn from this topic to our shop), that I have written too much. The last things were, however, published very reluctantly by me, and for reasons I will explain when we meet. I know not why I have dwelt so much on the same scenes, except that I find them fading, or *confusing* (if such a word may be) in my memory, in the midst of present turbulence and pressure, and I felt anxious to stamp before the die was worn out. I now break it. With those countries, and events connected with them, all my really poetical feelings begin and end. Were I to try, I could make nothing of any other subject, and that I have apparently exhausted. " Wo to him ", says Voltaire, " who says all he could say on any subject." There are some on which, perhaps, I could have said still more : but I leave them all, and too soon.

Do you remember the lines I sent you early last year, which you still have? I don't wish (like Mr. Fitzgerald, in the *Morning*

Post) to claim the character of "Vates" in all its translations, but were they not a little prophetic? I mean those beginning, "There's not a joy the world can", etc., etc., on which I rather pique myself as being the truest, though the most melancholy, I ever wrote.

What a scrawl have I sent you! You say nothing of yourself, except that you are a Lancasterian churchwarden, and an encourager of mendicants. When are you out? and how is your family? My child is very well and flourishing, I hear; but I must see also. I feel no disposition to resign it to the contagion of its grandmother's society, though I am unwilling to take it from the mother. It is weaned, however, and something about it must be decided.

Ever, etc.

TO MISS MERCER ELPHINSTONE*   *April 11, 1816*

DEAR MISS MERCER,[1]—I thank you truly for yr kind acceptance of my memorial—more particularly as I felt a little apprehension that I was taking a liberty of which you might disapprove. A more useless friend you could not have, but still a very sincere and by no means a new one—altho' from circumstances you never knew (nor would it have pleased you to know) how much. These having long ceased to exist, I breathe more freely on this point, because *now* no motive can be attributed to me with regard to you of a selfish nature—at least I hope not.

I know not why I venture to talk thus, unless it be that the time is come when, whatever I may say, cannot be of importance enough to give offence; and that neither my vanity *nor my wishes* ever induced me at any time to suppose that I could by any chance have become more to you than I now am.

This may account to you for that which—however little worth accounting for—must otherwise appear inexplicable in our former acquaintance. I mean those "intermittents" at which you used to laugh, as I did too, although they caused me a serious reflection.

---

[1] At the disastrous party given by Lady Jersey after the separation, Miss Mercer Elphinstone was one of the few women who had consented to speak to Byron and his sister. Byron had expressed his gratitude by giving her a book.

But this is foolish, perhaps improper, yet it is (or rather was) the truth, and has been a silent one while it could have been supposed to proceed from hope or presumption. I am now as far removed from both by irrevocable circumstances as I always was by my own opinion and by yours, and soon shall be still further, if further be possible, by distance.

I cannot conclude without wishing you a much happier destiny not than *mine is,* for that is nothing, but than mine ever could have been, with a little common sense and prudence on my own part—no one else has been to blame. It may seem superfluous to wish *you* all this, and it would be so if our happiness always depended on ourselves; but it does not—a truth which I fear I have taught rather than learned, however unintentionally.

Ever most truly yrs, BYRON.

P.S.—This letter was intended as an answer to your note, which however required none. Will you excuse it for the sake of the paper on which it is written? It is part of the spoils of Malmaison and the Imperial bureau (as it was told me) and for this reason, you will perhaps have the kindness to accept the few sheets of it which accompany this. Their stamp is the Eagle. Adieu.

TO LADY BYRON [1]   *[April, 1816]*

More last words—not many—and such as you will attend to; answer I do not expect, nor does it import; but you will at least hear me.—I have just parted from Augusta, almost the last being whom you have left me to part with.

Wherever I may go,—and I am going far,—you and I can never meet in this world, nor in the next. Let this content or atone.—— If any accident occurs to me, be kind to Augusta; if she is then also nothing—to her children. You know that some time ago I made my will in her favour and her children, because any child of ours was provided for by other and better means. This could not be prejudice to you, for we had not

---

[1] From a copy made by Hobhouse, and endorsed by him, " Lord Byron's last letter to Lady B. on leaving England, 1816, given to Mrs. Leigh by Mr. Hobhouse ".

then differed, and even now is useless during your life by the terms of our settlements. Therefore,—be kind to her, for never has she acted or spoken towards you but as your friend. And recollect, that, though it may be an advantage to you to have lost a husband, it is sorrow to her to have the waters now, or the earth hereafter, between her and her brother. It may occur to your memory that you formerly promised me this much. I repeat it—for deep resentments have but *half* recollections. Do not deem this promise cancell'd, for it was not a vow.

I have received from Mr. Wharton a letter containing one question and two pieces of intelligence. The carriage is yours, and, as it only carried us to Halnaby, and London, and you to Kirkby, it will yet convey you many a more propitious journey.

The receipts can remain, unless you find them troublesome; if so, let them be sent to Augusta, through whom I would also receive occasional accounts of my child. My address will be left with Mrs. Leigh; the ring is of no lapidary value, but it contains the hair of a King and of an ancestor, and I wish it to be preserved to Miss Byron.

With regard to a subsequent letter from Mr. Wharton I have to observe that it is the " law's delay " not mine, and that, when the tenor of the bond is settled between him and Mr. H., I am ready to sign.

Yours truly, Byron

TO THE HON. AUGUSTA LEIGH *Bruxelles,*
[*Wednesday,*] *May 1st, 1816*

My Heart,—We are detained here for some petty carriage repairs, having come out of our way to the Rhine on purpose, after passing through Ghent, Antwerp, and Mechlin. I have written to you twice,—once from Ostend, and again from Ghent. I hope most truly that you will receive my letters, not as important in themselves, but because you wish it, and so do I. It would be difficult for me to write anything amusing; this country has been so frequently described, and has so little for description, though a good deal for observation, that I know not what to say of it, and one don't like talking only of oneself. We saw at Antwerp the famous basons of Bonaparte for his navy, which are very superb—as all his undertakings were, and as for churches, and pictures, I have stared at them till my brains are like a guide-book :—the last (though it is heresy to say so) don't please me at all. I think Rubens a very great dauber, and prefer Vandyke a hundred times over (but then I know nothing about the matter). Rubens' women have all red gums and red shoulders—to say nothing of necks, of which they are more liberal than charming ; it may all be very fine, and I suppose it may be Art, for 'tis not Nature.

As the low Countries did not make part of my plan (except as a route), I feel a little anxious to get out of them. Level roads don't suit me, as thou knowest ; it must be up hill or down, and then I am more *au fait*. Imagine to yourself a succession of avenues with a Dutch Spire at the end of each, and you see the road ;—an accompaniment of highly cultivated farms on each side, intersected with small canals or ditches, and sprinkled with very neat and clean cottages, a village every two miles,—and you see the country ; not a rise from Ostend to Antwerp—a molehill would make the inhabitants think that the Alps had come here on a visit ; it is a perpetuity of plain and an eternity of *pavement* (on the *road*), but it is a country of great apparent comfort, and of singular though *tame* beauty, and, were it not out of my way, I should like to survey it less cursorily. The towns are wonderfully fine. The approach to Brussels is beautiful, and there is a fine palace to the right in coming.

TO JOHN CAM HOBHOUSE †   *Bruxelles, May 1st, 1816*

MY DEAR H^E,—You will be surprised that we are not more " en avant ", and so am I, but Mr. Baxter's wheel and springs have not done their duty, for which I beg that you will abuse him like a pick-pocket (that is—*He*—the said Baxter being the *pick-pocket*) and say that I expect a deduction, having been obliged to come out of the way to this place, which was not in my route, for repairs, which however I hope to have accomplished, so as to put us in motion in a day or two.

We passed through Ghent, Antwerp, and Mechlin, and thence diverged here, having seen all the sights, pictures, docks, basins, and having climbed up steeples, etc., etc., and so forth. The first thing, after the flatness and fertility of the country, which struck me, was the beauty of the towns, Bruges first, where, you may tell Douglas Kinnaird, on entering at sunset, I overtook a crew of beggarly looking gentlemen, not unlike Oxberry, headed by a monarch with a staff, the very fac-simile, of King Clause in the said D. K.'s revived drama.

We lost our way in the dark, or rather twilight, not far from Ghent, by the stupidity of the postilion (*one* only, by the way, to four horses), which produced an alarm of intended robbery amongst the uninitiated, whom I could not convince that four or five well-armed people were not immediately to be plundered and anatomized by a single person, fortified with a horsewhip to be sure, but, nevertheless, a little encumbered with large jack boots, and a tight jacket that did not fit him. The way was found again without loss of life or limb. I thought the learned Fletcher at least would have known better after our Turkish expeditions, and defiles and banditti, and guards, etc., etc., than to have been so valorously alert, without at least a better pretext for his superfluous courage. I don't mean to say that they were frightened, but were vastly suspicious, without any cause.

At Ghent we stared at pictures ; and climbed up a steeple, 450 steps in altitude, from which I had a good view and notion of these " paese bassi ".

Next day we broke down, by a damned wheel (on which Baxter should be broken) pertinaciously refusing its stipulated rotation. This becalmed us at Lo-Kristy (2 leagues from Ghent) and obliged us to return for repairs ; at Lo-Kristy I came to anchor in the house of a Flemish blacksmith (who was ill of a fever for which Dr. Dori [1] physicked him—I daresay he is dead by now), and saw somewhat of Lo-Kristy ; Low-country low-life, which regaled me much ; besides, it being a Sunday, all the world were on their way to mass, and I had the

[1] Dr. John William Polidori, whom Byron took abroad with him as his personal physician.

pleasure of seeing a number of very ordinary women in extraordinary garments :—we found the " Contadini ", however,
very good-natured and obliging, though not at all useful.

At Antwerp we pictured—churched—and steepled again,
but the principal street and *bason* pleased me most—poor dear
Buonaparte !!! and the foundries, etc., etc. As for Rubens,
I was glad to see his tomb on account of that ridiculous description (in Smollett's P. Pickle) of Pallet's absurdity at his
monument—but as for his works, and his superb " tableaux ",
he seems to me (who by the way know nothing of the matter)
the most glaring—flaring—staring—harlotry impostor that
ever passed a trick upon the senses of mankind,—it is not nature
—it is not art—with the exception of some linen (which hangs
over the cross in one of his pictures) which, to do it justice,
looked like a very handsome table-cloth—I never saw such an
assemblage of florid nightmares as his canvas contains ; his
portraits seem clothed in pulpit cushions.

On the way to Mechlin, a wheel, and a *spring* too gave
way ; that is, the one went, and the other would not go ; so
we came off here to get into dock. I hope we shall sail shortly.
On to Geneva.

Will you have the goodness to get at my account with
Hoares (my bankers)? I believe there must be a balance in
my favour, as I did not draw a great deal previously to going :
—whatever there may be, over the two thousand five hundred,
they can send by you, to me in a further credit, when you come
out. I wish you to enquire (for fear any tricks might be
played with my drafts)—*my* banker's books, left with you, will
shew you exactly what I have drawn ; and you can let them
have the book, to make out the remainder of the account. All
I have to urge to Hanson, or to our friend Douglas K., is to
sell if possible.

All kind things to Scrope and the rest.
                    Ever yrs. most truly and obligedly, B.

P.S.—If you hear of my child let me know any good of
her health and well-doing. Will you bring out a παυσανιας
(Taylor's ditto) when you come. I shall bring to for you at
Geneva [*sic*]. Don't forget to urge Scrope into our crew. We
will buy females and found a colony—provided Scrope does

not find those ossified barriers to " the forefended place " which cost him such a siege at Brighthelmstone.

Write at your leisure, or "ipse veni ".

TO JOHN CAM HOBHOUSE   *Evian, June 23rd, 1816*

MY DEAR Hᴱ,—Despite of this date, address as usual to the Genevese Poste, which awaits your answers as I await your arrival, with that of Scrope, whose pocket appears (by your late letter of revolutions at the Union) to have become as " light " as his " wines ", though I suppose, on the whole, he is still worth at least £50,000 : being what is called here a " millionaire "—that is in francs, and such Lilliputian coinage.

I have taken a very pretty little villa in a vineyard, with the Alps behind, and Mount Jura and the lake before—it is called Diodati, from the name of the proprietor, who is a descendant of the critical and illustrissimi Diodati's, and has an agreeable house, which he lets at a reasonable rate per season or annum, as suits the lessee. When you come out don't go to an inn, not even to Secheron ; but come on to headquarters, where I have rooms ready for you and Scrope, and all " appliances and means to boot ". Bring with you also for me—some bottles of *Calcined Magnesia*, a new *Sword-cane*, procured by Jackson—he alone knows the sort (my last tumbled into this lake)—some of Waite's *red* tooth-powder and tooth-brushes—a Taylor's *Pawrsanias*—and I forget the other things.

Tell Murray I have a 3rd Canto of Childe Harold finished, it is the longest of the three, being one hundred and eleven stanzas. I shall send it by the first plausible conveyance. At the present writing I am on my way on a water-tour round the Lake Leman, and am thus far proceeded in a pretty open boat which I bought and navigate—it is an English one, and was brought lately from Bordeaux. I am on shore for the night, and have just had a row with the Syndic of this town, who wanted my passports, which I left at Diodati, not thinking they could be wanted, except in grande route—but it seems this is Savoy, and the dominion of his Cagliari Majesty whom we saw at his own Opera in his own city, in 1809 ; however, by dint of references to Geneva, and other corroborations—

together with being in a very ill-humour—truth has prevailed, wonderful to relate, and they actually take one's word for a fact, although it is credible and indubitable.

To-morrow we go to Meillerei, and Clarens, and Vevey, with Rousseau in hand, to see his scenery, according to his delineation in his Héloïse, now before me; the views have hitherto been very fine, but, I should conceive, less so than those of the remainder of the lake.

All your letters (that is *two*) have arrived—thanks, and greetings :—What—and who—and the devil is " Glenarvon "? I know nothing—nor ever heard of such a person ; and what do you mean by a brother in India? You have none in India ; it is Scrope who has a brother in India—my remembrances to Kinnaird—and Mrs. Kinnaird—to all and everybody, and Hunt in particular, and Scrope, and Mr. Murray, and believe me

Yours ever most truly, B.

P.S.—I left the Doctor at Diodati ; he sprained his ancle.

P.S.—Will you also particularly remember to bring me a largish bottle of the strongest *Pot Ash* as before—*Mr. Le Shan* will furnish it—that child and childish Dr. Pollydolly contrived to find it broken, or to break it at Carlsruhe—so that I am in a fuss—the Genevese make it badly—it effervesces in the sulphuric acid, and it ought not—bring me some of a more quiescent character.

TO JOHN MURRAY   *Ouchy, near Lausanne, June 27, 1816*

DEAR SIR,—I am thus far (kept by stress of weather) on my way back to Diodati (near Geneva) from a voyage in my boat round the Lake ; and I enclose you a sprig of *Gibbon's Acacia* and some rose-leaves from his garden, which, with part of his house, I have just seen. You will find honorable mention, in his *Life*, made of this " Acacia ", when he walked out on the night of concluding his history. The garden and *summer-house*, where he composed, are neglected, and the last utterly decayed ; but they still show it as his " Cabinet ", and seem perfectly aware of his memory.

My route through Flanders, and by the Rhine, to Switzerland, was all I expected, and more.

I have traversed all Rousseau's ground, with the *Héloise* before me; and am struck, to a degree, with the force and accuracy of his descriptions and the beauty of their reality. Meillerie, Clarens, and Vevay, and the Château de Chillon, are places of which I shall say little, because all I could say must fall short of the impressions they stamp.

Three days ago, we were most nearly wrecked in a Squall off Meillerie, and driven to shore. I ran no risk, being so near the rocks, and a good swimmer; but our party were wet, and incommoded a good deal, the wind was strong enough to blow down some trees, as we found at landing, however, all is righted and right, and we are thus far on return.

Dr. Polidori is not here, but at Diodati, left behind in hospital with a sprained ancle, acquired in tumbling from a wall—he can't jump.

I shall be glad to hear you are well, and have received for me certain helms and swords, sent from Waterloo, which I rode over with pain and pleasure.

I have finished a third canto of *Childe Harold* (consisting of one hundred and seventeen stanzas), longer than either of the two former, and in some parts, it may be, better; but of course on that *I* cannot determine. I shall send it by the first safe-looking opportunity.

Ever very truly yours, B.

TO THE HON. DOUGLAS KINNAIRD *   *Diodati nr. Geneva,*
July 20th 1816

DEAR KINNAIRD,—I send you, not what you want, but all I can give,[1] and such as it is I give it with good will. It may be too long and if so, whatever may be cut in speaking, at least let it be published *entire*, as it is written so as not very well to endure curtailment without the sense of suffering also. Let Miss *Somerville*, (and none else) deliver it, if she has *energy*, that's the woman I want, I mean for spouting. I protest against

[1] *Monody on the Death of Sheridan*, delivered at Drury Lane Theatre.

Mrs. Davison, I protest against the *temple* or anything but an *Urn* on the scene, and above all I protest against the " Comic Muse in Mourning." If she is *Comic*, she should not be in *Mourning*, if she is in *mourning*, she ought not to be in Mourning, but should she be *comic* and in *mourning* too, the verses and Sheridan's memory (for *that* occasion at least) will go to the devil together. No, I say, an *Urn* (not a tea urn) and Miss Somerville with a little teaching. As to " Energy " I have spiced it with Cayenne all through, except a small infusion of the pathetic at starting.

I send the lines (118 in number) in a separate sheet by this post, and will send a duplicate in a day or two, for fear of you not receiving this copy in time.

Tragedy—I have none, an act, a first act of one, I had nearly finished some time before my departure from England, when events occurred which furnished me with so many real passions for time to come, that I had no attention for fictitious ones. The scenes I had scrawled are thrown with other papers and sketches into one of my trunks now in England, but into which I know not—nor care not—except that I should have been glad to have done anything you wished in my power ; but I have no power nor will to recommence, and, surely, *Maturin* is your man, not I. Of what has passed in England I know but little, and have no desire to know more, except that you and my other friends are well.

I have written a third Canto of Childe Harold (of 118 Stanzas) and a (not long) poem on the Castle of Chillon, both of which I mean to send to England soon for publication, during which I could wish to ask you to *correct* the *proofs* and arrange with Murray for me. I merely wait a good opportunity to convey these to your care and if you can afford leisure and patience, perhaps G. Lamb, or some other good-natured fellow would halve it with you, though I have hardly the conscience to ask either them or you.

I have now answered you and arrived at my sheet's end— with my best remembrances to Mrs. K—— (whose silk kerchief is as precious as Othello's) believe me ever yours,

B.

TO JOHN MURRAY   *Diodati, near Geneva, July 22ᵈ, 1816*

DEAR SIR,—I wrote to you a few weeks ago, and Dr.
P[olidori] received your letter; but the packet has not made
its appearance, nor the epistle, of which you gave notice therein. I enclose you an advertisement, which was copied by Dr.
P[olidori], and which appears to be about the most impudent
imposition that ever issued from Grub Street. I need hardly
say that I know nothing of all this trash, nor whence it may
spring,—" Odes to St. Helena ",—" Farewells to England ",
etc., etc.; and if it can be disavowed, or is worth disavowing,
you have full authority to do so. I never wrote, nor conceived,
a line on any thing of the kind, any more than of two other
things with which I was saddled—something about " Gaul ",
and another about " Mrs. La Valette "; and as to the " Lily
of *France* ", I should as soon think of celebrating a turnip. On
the " Morning of my Daughter's Birth ", I had other things to
think of than verses; and should never have dreamed of such
an invention, till Mr. Johnston and his pamphlet's advertisement broke in upon me with a new light on the Crafts and
subtilties of the Demon of printing,—or rather publishing.

I did hope that some succeeding lie would have super-
seded the thousand and one which were accumulated during
last winter. I can forgive whatever may be said *of* or against
me,—but not what they make me say or sing for myself. It
is enough to answer for what I have written; but it were too
much for Job himself to bear what one has not. I suspect that
when the Arab Patriarch wished that his " Enemy had written
a book ", he did not anticipate his own name on the title-page.
I feel quite as much bored with this foolery as it deserves, and
more than I should be, if I had not a headache.

Of *Glenarvon*,[1] Madame de Stael told me (ten days ago, at
Copet) marvellous and grievous things; but I have seen
nothing of it but the Motto, which promises amiably " for us
and for our tragedy ". If such be the posy, what should the
ring be? " a name to all succeeding ", etc. The generous
moment selected for the publication is probably its kindest
accompaniment, and—truth to say—the time was well chosen.

[1] Lady Caroline Lamb's novel, which contained a romantic travesty of Byron
and caricatures of Lady Holland and other Friends.

I have not even a guess at the contents, except from the very vague accounts I have heard, and I know but one thing which a woman can say to the purpose on such occasions, and that she might as well for her own sake keep to herself, which by the way they very rarely can—the old reproach against their admirers of " *Kiss* and *tell* ", bad as it is, is surely somewhat less than—and publish.

I ought to be ashamed of the Egotism of this letter. It is not my fault altogether, and I shall be but too happy to drop the subject when others will allow me. I am in tolerable plight, and in my last letter told you what I had done in the way of all rhyme. I trust that you prosper, and that your authors are in good condition. I should suppose your Stud has received some increase, by what I hear. *Bertram* must be a good horse ; does he run next meeting? and does the *Quarterly* cover still at so much the mare and the groom? I hope you will beat the Row.

Yours always, very truly, B.

TO THE HON. AUGUSTA LEIGH   *Diodati, Geneva,*
Septr 8th, 1816

MY DEAREST AUGUSTA,—By two opportunities of private conveyance, I have sent answers to your letter, delivered by Mr. H. S—— is on his return to England and may possibly arrive before this. He is charged with a few packets of seals, necklaces, balls etc. and I know not what, formed of Chrystals, Agates and other stones—*all of* and *from Mont Blanc*, bought and brought by me on and from the Spot, expressly for you to divide among yourself and the children—including also your niece Ada, for whom I selected a ball (of Granite—a *soft* substance by the way—but the only one there) wherewithal to roll and play, when she is old enough, and mischievous enough, and moreover a Chrystal necklace, and anything else you may like to add for her—the Love ! The rest are for you, and the Nursery—but particularly Georgiana, who has sent me a very nice letter. I hope Scrope will carry them all safely, as he promised. There are seals and all kinds of fooleries. Pray like them, for they come from a very curious place (nothing like it hardly in all I ever saw)—to say nothing of the giver.

And so—Lady B. has been " kind to you ", you tell me—" very kind "—Umph—it is as well she should be kind to some of us—and I am glad she has the heart and the discernment to be still *your* friend—you was ever so to her. I heard the other day that she was very unwell. I was shocked enough, and sorry enough, God knows—but never mind. H. tells me, however, that she is *not* ill, that she *had* been indisposed, but is better and well to do. This is a relief. As for me, I am in good health and fair, though unequal, spirits. But, for all that, she—or rather the separation—has broken my heart : I feel as if an Elephant had trodden on it. I am convinced I shall never get over it, but I try. I had enough before I ever knew her, and more than enough. But time and agitation had done something for me. But this last wreck has affected me very differently. If it were *acutely*, it would not signify. But it is not that,—I breathe lead.

While the storm lasted and you were all piping and comforting me with condemnation in Piccadilly, it was bad enough, and violent enough. But it's worse now ; I have neither strength nor spirits, nor inclination to carry me through anything which will clear my brain or lighten my heart. I mean to cross the Alps at the end of this month, and go—God knows where—by Dalmatia, up to the Arnauts again, if nothing better can be done. I have still a world before me—this—or the next.

H. has told me all the strange stories in circulation of me and mine—*Not* true. I have been in some danger on the lake (near Meillerie), but nothing to speak of; and, as to all these " mistresses ", Lord help me—I have had but one.[1] Now don't scold ; but what could I do?—a foolish girl, in spite of all I could say or do, would come after me, or rather went before—for I found her here—and I have had all the plague possible to persuade her to go back again ; but at last she went. Now, dearest, I do most truly tell thee, that I could not help this, that I did all I could to prevent it, and have at last put an end to it. I was not in love, nor have any love left for any ; but I could not exactly play the Stoic with a woman, who had scrambled eight hundred miles to unphilosophize me.

[1] Claire Clairmont, who had previously made his acquaintance in London.

Besides, I had been regaled of late with so many "two courses and a *desert*" (Alas!) of aversion, that I was fain to take a little love (if pressed particularly) by way of novelty. And now you know all that I know of that matter, and it's over. Pray write. I have heard nothing since your last, at least a month or five weeks ago. I go out very little, except into the *air*, and on journeys, and on the water, and to Copet, where Mᵉ de Staël has been particularly kind and friendly towards me, and (I hear) fought battles without number in my very indifferent cause. It has (they say) made quite as much noise on this as the other side of *La Manche*. Heaven knows why—but I seem destined to set people by the ears.

Don't hate me, but believe me, ever yours most affectionately,

BYRON

TO THE HON. AUGUSTA LEIGH   *Ouchy, Sepᵗ 17, 1816*

MY DEAREST AUGUSTA,—I am thus far on my way to the Bernese Alps and the Grindenwald, and the *Yung frau* (that is the "Wild woman" being interpreted—as it is so perverse a mountain that no other sex would suit it), which journey may occupy me about eight days or so, and then it is my intention to return to Geneva, preparatory to passing the Simplon——

Continue you to direct as usual to Geneva. I have lately written to you several letters (3 or 4 by post and two by hand) and I have received all yours very safely. I rejoice to have heard that you are well. You have been in London too lately, and H. tells me that at your levée he generally found Lᵈ F. Bentinck—pray why is that fool so often a visitor? is he in love with you? I have recently broken through my resolution of not speaking to you of Lady B— but do not on that account name her to me. It is a relief—a partial relief to me to talk of her sometimes to you—but it would be none to hear of her. *Of* her you are to judge for yourself, but do not altogether forget that she has destroyed your brother. Whatever my faults might or may have been—*She*—was not the person marked out by providence to be their avenger. One day or another her

conduct will recoil on her own head ; *not* through *me*, for my
feelings towards her are not those of Vengeance, but—mark—
if she does not end miserably *tot ou tard*. She may think—talk
—or act as she will, and by any process of cold reasoning and
a jargon of " duty and acting for the best " etc., etc., impose
upon her own feelings and those of others for a time—but woe
unto her—the wretchedness she has brought upon the man to
whom she has been everything evil [except in one respect (effaced)] will flow
back into its fountain. I may thank the strength of my constitution that has enabled me to bear all this, but those who bear
the longest and the most do not suffer the least. I do not think
a human being could endure more mental torture than that
woman has directly and indirectly inflicted upon me—within
the present year.

She has (for a time at least) separated me from my child—
and from you—but I turn from the subject for the present.

To-morrow I repass Clarens and Vevey ; if in the new and
more extended tour I am making, anything that I think may
please you occurs, I will detail it.

Scrope has by this time arrived with my little presents for
you and yours and Ada. I still hope to be able to see you next
Spring, perhaps you and one or two of the children could be
spared some time next year for a little tour *here* or in France
with me of a month or two. I think I could make it pleasing
to you, and it should be no expense to L. or to yourself. Pray
think of this hint. You have no idea how very beautiful great
part of this country is—and *women* and *children* traverse it with
ease and expedition. I would return from any distance at any
time to see you, and come to England for you ; and when
you consider the chances against our—but I won't relapse into
the dismals and anticipate long absences——

The great obstacle would be that you are so admirably
yoked—and necessary as a housekeeper—and a letter writer—
and a place-hunter to that very helpless gentleman your
Cousin, that I suppose the usual self-love of an elderly person
would interfere between you and any scheme of recreation or
relaxation, for however short a period.

What a fool was I to marry—and *you* not very wise—my
dear—we might have lived so single and so happy—as old
maids and bachelors ; I shall never find any one like you—

nor you (vain as it may seem) like me.   We are just formed to pass our lives together, and therefore—we—at least—I—am by a crowd of circumstances removed from the only being who could ever have loved me, or whom I can unmixedly feel attached to.

Had you been a Nun—and I a Monk—that we might have talked through a grate instead of across the sea—no matter— my voice and my heart are

ever thine—B.

A JOURNAL

Clarens, Septr 18th 1816

Yesterday September 17th 1816—I set out (with H[obhouse]) on an excursion of some days to the Mountains.   I shall keep a short journal of each day's progress for my Sister Augusta.

Septr 17th

Rose at five; left Diodati about seven, in one of the country carriages (a Charaban), our servants on horseback : weather very fine ; the Lake calm and clear ; Mont Blanc and the Aiguille of Argentières both very distinct ; the borders of the Lake beautiful.   Reached Lausanne before Sunset ; stopped and slept at Ouchy.

H. went to dine with a Mr. Okeden.   I remained at our Caravansera (though invited to the house of H.'s friend—too lazy or tired, or something else, to go), and wrote a letter to Augusta.   Went to bed at nine—sheets damp : swore and stripped them off and flung them—Heaven knows where : wrapt myself up in the blankets, and slept like a child of a month's existence till 5 o'Clock of

Septr 18th

Called by Berger (my Courier who acts as Valet for a day or two, the learned Fletcher being left in charge of Chattels at Diodati) : got up.   H. walked on before.   A mile from Lausanne the road overflowed by the lake ; got on horseback and rode till within a mile of Vevay.   The Colt young, but went very well : overtook H., and resumed the carriage, which is an open one.   Stopped at Vevay two hours (the *second* time

I had visited it); walked to the church; view from the Churchyard superb; within it General Ludlow's (the Regicide's) monument—black marble—long inscription—Latin, but simple, particularly the latter part, in which his wife (Margaret de Thomas) records her long, her tried, and unshaken affection; he was an Exile *two and thirty years*—one of King's (Charles's) Judges—a fine fellow. I remember reading his memoirs in January 1815 (at Halnaby)—the first part of them very amusing, the latter less so: I little thought, at the time of their perusal by me, of seeing his tomb. Near him Broughton (who read King Charles's sentence to Charles Stuart) is buried, with a queer and rather canting, but still a Republican, epitaph. Ludlow's house shown; it retains still his inscription—*Omne Solum forti patria*. Walked down to the Lake side; servants, Carriage, saddle horses—all set off and left us *plantés là*, by some mistake; and we walked on after them towards Clarens: H. ran on before, and overtook them at last. Arrived the second time (1st time was by water) at Clarens, beautiful Clarens! Went to Chillon through Scenery worthy of I know not whom; went over the Castle of Chillon again. On our return met an English party in a carriage; a lady in it fast asleep!—fast asleep in the most anti-narcotic spot in the world—excellent! I remember, at Chamouni, in the very eyes of Mont Blanc, hearing another woman, English also, exclaim to her party " did you ever see any thing more *rural*? "—as if it was Highgate, or Hampstead, or Brompton, or Hayes,—" *Rural!* " quotha!—Rocks, pines, torrents, Glaciers, Clouds, and Summits of eternal snow far above them —and " *Rural!* " I did not know the thus exclaiming fair one, but she was a very good kind of a woman.

After a slight and short dinner, we visited the Chateau de Clarens; an English woman has rented it recently (it was not let when I saw it first): the roses are gone with their Summer; the family out, but the servants desired us to walk over the interior of the mansion. Saw on the table of the saloon Blair's sermons and somebody else's (I forget who's) sermons, and a set of noisy children. Saw all worth seeing, and then descended to the " Bosquet de Julie ", etc., etc.; our Guide full of *Rousseau*, whom he is eternally confounding with *St. Preux*, and mixing the man and the book. On the steps of a cottage in the village, I saw a young paysan*ne*, beautiful as Julie herself. Went again as far as Chillon to revisit the little torrent from the hill behind it. Sunset reflected in the lake. Have to get up at 5 tomorrow to cross the mountains on horseback—carriage to be sent round; lodged at my old Cottage—hospitable and comfortable; tired with a longish ride on the Colt, and the subsequent jolting of the Charaban, and my scramble in the hot sun. Shall go to bed, thinking of you, dearest Augusta.

Mem. The Corporal who showed the wonders of Chillon was as drunk as Blucher, and (to my mind) as great a man. He was *deaf* also, and thinking every one else so, roared out the legends of the Castle so fearfully that H. got out of humour. However, we saw all things from the Gallows to the Dungeons (the *Potence* and the *Cachots*), and returned to Clarens with more freedom than belonged to the 15th Century.

At Clarens—the only book (except the Bible), a translation of " *Cecilia* " (Miss Burney's *Cecilia*); and the owner of the Cottage had also called her dog (a fat Pug ten years old, and hideous as *Tip*) after Cecilia's (or rather Delville's) dog, Fidde.

Septr 19th

Rose at five: order the carriage round. Crossed the mountains to Montbovon on horseback, and on Mules, and, by dint of scrambling, on foot also; the whole route beautiful as a Dream, and now to me almost as indistinct. I am so tired; for though healthy, I have not the strength I possessed but a few years ago. At Mont Davant we breakfasted; afterwards, on a steep ascent dismounted, tumbled down, and cut a finger open; the baggage also got loose and fell down a ravine, till stopped by a large tree: swore; recovered baggage: horse tired and dropping; mounted Mule. At the approach of the summit of Dent Jamant dismounted again with H. and all the party. Arrived at a lake in the very nipple of the bosom of the Mountain; left our quadrupeds with a Shepherd, and ascended further; came to some snow in patches, upon which my forehead's perspiration fell like rain, making the same dints as in a sieve: the chill of the wind and the snow turned me giddy, but I scrambled on and upwards. *H.* went to the highest *pinnacle*; I did not, but paused within a few yards (at an opening of the Cliff). In coming down, the Guide tumbled three times; I fell a laughing, and tumbled too—the descent luckily soft, though steep and slippery: H. also fell, but nobody hurt. The whole of the Mountain superb. A Shepherd on a very steep and high cliff playing upon his *pipe*; very different from *Arcadia*, (where I saw the pastors with a long Musquet instead of a Crook, and pistols in their Girdles). Our Swiss Shepherd's pipe was sweet, and his tune agreeable. Saw a cow strayed; am told that they often break their necks on and over the crags. Descended to Montbovon; pretty scraggy village, with a wild river and a wooden bridge. H. went to fish—caught one. Our carriage not come; our horses, mules, etc., knocked up; ourselves fatigued; but so much the better—I shall sleep.

The view from the highest points of to-day's journey comprized on one side the greatest part of Lake Leman; on the other, the valleys and mountains of the Canton of Fribourg, and an immense plain, with the Lakes of Neuchâtel and Morat, and all which the borders of these and of the Lake of Geneva inherit: we had both sides of the Jura before us in one point of view, with Alps in plenty. In passing a ravine, the Guide recommended strenuously a quickening of pace, as the Stones fall with great rapidity and occasional damage: the advice is excellent, but, like most good advice, impracticable, the road being so rough in this precise point, that neither mules, nor mankind, nor horses, can make any violent progress. Passed without any fractures or menace thereof.

The music of the Cows' bells (for their wealth, like the Patriarchs', is cattle) in the pastures, (which reach to a height far above any mountains in Britain), and the Shepherds' shouting to us from crag to crag, and playing on their reeds where the steeps appeared almost inaccessible, with the surrounding scenery, realized all that I have ever heard or imagined of a pastoral existence :—much more so than Greece or Asia Minor, for there we are a little too much of the sabre and musquet order; and if there is a Crook in one hand, you are sure to see a gun in the other :—but this was pure and un-mixed—solitary, savage, and patriarchal : the effect I cannot describe. As we went, they played the " Ranz des Vaches " and other airs, by way of farewell. I have lately repeopled my mind with Nature.

Septr 20th

Up at 6. Off at 8. The whole of this day's journey at an average of between from two thousand seven hundred to three thousand feet above the level of the Sea. This valley, the longest, narrowest, and considered one of the finest of the Alps, little traversed by travellers. Saw the bridge of La Roche. The bed of the river very low and deep, between immense rocks, and rapid as anger;—a man and mule said to have tumbled over without damage (the mule was lucky at any rate: unless I knew the *man*, I should be loth to pronounce *him* fortunate). The people looked free, and happy, and *rich* (which last implies neither of the former): the cows superb; a Bull nearly leapt into the Charaban—" agreeable companion in a post-chaise "; Goats and Sheep very thriving. A mountain with enormous Glaciers to the right—the Kletsgerberg; further on, the Hockthorn—nice names—so soft!—Hockthorn, I believe, very lofty and craggy, patched with snow only; no Glaciers on it, but some good epaulettes of clouds.

Passed the boundaries, out of Vaud and into Bern Canton; French exchanged for a bad German; the district famous for Cheese, liberty, property, and no taxes. H. went to fish—caught none. Strolled to river: saw boy and kid; kid followed him like a dog; kid could not get over a fence, and bleated piteously; tried myself to help kid, but nearly overset both self and kid into the river. Arrived here about six in the evening. Nine o'clock—going to bed. H. in next room knocked his head against the door, and exclaimed of course against doors; not tired to-day, but hope to sleep nevertheless. Women gabbling below: read a French translation of Schiller. Good Night, Dearest Augusta.

Septr 21st

Off early. The valley of Simmenthal as before. Entrance to the plain of Thoun very narrow; high rocks, wooded to the top; river; new mountains, with fine Glaciers. Lake of Thoun; extensive plain with a girdle of Alps. Walked down to the Chateau de Schadau; view along the lake: crossed the river in a boat rowed by women: *women* went right for the first time in my recollection. Thoun a very pretty town. The whole day's journey Alpine and proud.

Septr 22^d

Left Thoun in a boat, which carried us the length of the lake in three hours. The lake small; but the banks fine: rocks down to the water's edge. Landed at Neuhause; passed Interlachen; entered upon a range of scenes beyond all description or previous conception. Passed a rock; inscription —2 brothers—one murdered the other; just the place for it. After a variety of windings came to an enormous rock. Girl with fruit—very pretty; blue eyes, good teeth, very fair: long but good features—reminded me rather of F^y Bought some of her pears, and patted her upon the cheek; the expression of her face very mild, but good, and not at all coquettish. Arrived at the foot of the Mountain (the Yung frau, *i.e.* the Maiden); Glaciers; torrents; one of these torrents *nine hundred feet* in height of visible descent. Lodge at the Curate's. Set out to see the Valley; heard an Avalanche fall, like thunder; saw Glacier—enormous. Storm came on, thunder, lightning, hail; all in perfection, and beautiful. I was on horseback; Guide wanted to carry my cane; I was going to give it him, when I recollected that it was a Swordstick, and I thought the lightning might be attracted towards him; kept it myself; a good deal encumbered with it, and my cloak, as it was too heavy for a whip, and the horse was stupid, and stood still with every other peal. Got in, not very wet; the Cloak being staunch. H. wet through; H. took refuge in cottage; sent man, umbrella, and cloak (from the Curate's when I arrived) after him. Swiss Curate's house very good indeed,—much better than most English Vicarages. It is immediately opposite the torrent I spoke of. The torrent is in shape curving over the rock, like the *tail* of a white horse streaming in the wind, such as it might be conceived would be that of the " *pale* horse " on which *Death* is mounted in the Apocalypse. It is neither mist nor water, but a something between both; it's immense height (nine hundred feet) gives it a wave, a curve, a spreading here, a condensation there, wonderful and indescribable. I think, upon the whole, that this day has been better than any of this present excursion.

Sept. 23^d

Before ascending the mountain, went to the torrent (7 in the morning) again; the Sun upon it forming a *rainbow* of

the lower part of all colours, but principally purple and gold ;
the bow moving as you move ; I never saw any thing like this ;
it is only in the Sunshine. Ascended the Wengen Mountain ;
at noon reached a valley on the summit ; left the horses, took
off my coat, and went to the summit, 7000 feet (English feet)
above the level of the *sea*, and about 5000 above the valley we
left in the morning. On one side, our view comprized the
Yung frau, with all her glaciers ; then the *Dent d'Argent*, shining
like truth ; then the *little Giant* (the Kleiner Eigher) ; and the
great Giant (the Grosser Eigher), and last, not least, the Wetterhorn. The height of Jungfrau is 13,000 feet above the sea,
11,000 above the valley ; she is the highest of this range. Heard
the Avalanches falling every five minutes nearly—as if God was
pelting the Devil down from Heaven with snow balls. From
where we stood, on the *Wengen* Alp, we had all these in view
on one side : on the other the clouds rose from the opposite
valley, curling up perpendicular precipices like the foam of the
Ocean of Hell, during a Springtide—it was white, and sul-
phury, and immeasurably deep in appearance. The side we
ascended was (of course) not of so precipitous a nature ; but
on arriving at the summit, we looked down the other side upon
a boiling sea of cloud, dashing against the crags on which we
stood (these crags on one side quite perpendicular). Staid a
quarter of an hour ; began to descend ; quite clear from cloud
on that side of the mountain. In passing the masses of snow,
I made a snowball and pelted H. with it.

Got down to our horses again ; eat something ; remounted ;
heard the Avalanches still ; came to a morass ; H. dismounted ;
H. got over well : I tried to pass my horse over ; the horse
sunk up [to] the chin, and of course he and I were in the mud
together ; bemired all over, but not hurt ; laughed, and rode
on. Arrived at the Grindenwald ; dined, mounted again, and
rode to the higher Glacier—twilight, but distinct—very fine
Glacier, like *a frozen hurricane*. Starlight, beautiful, but a devil
of a path ! Never mind, got safe in ; a little lightning ; but
the whole of the day as fine in point of weather as the day on
which Paradise was made. Passed *whole woods of withered pines,
all withered* ; trunks stripped and barkless, branches lifeless ;
done by a single winter,—their appearance reminded me of me
and my family.

Septr 24th.

Set out at seven; up at five. Passed the black Glacier, the Mountain Wetterhorn on the right; crossed the Scheideck mountain; came to the *Rose* Glacier, said to be the largest and finest in Switzerland. *I* think the Bossons Glacier at Chamouni as fine; H. does not. Came to the Reichenback waterfall, two hundred feet high; halted to rest the horses. Arrived in the valley of Oberhasli; rain came on; drenched a little; only 4 hours' rain, however, in 8 days. Came to Lake of Brientz, then to town of Brientz; changed. H. hurt his head against door. In the evening, four Swiss Peasant Girls of Oberhasli came and sang the airs of their country; two of the voices beautiful—the tunes also: they sing too that *Tyrolese air* and song which you love, Augusta, because I love it—and I love, because you love it; they are still singing. Dearest, you do not know how I should have liked this, were you with me. The airs are so wild and original, and at the same time of great sweetness. The singing is over: but below stairs I hear the notes of a Fiddle, which bode no good to my night's rest. The *Lard* help us—I shall go down and see the dancing.

Septr 25th

The whole town of Brientz were apparently gathered together in the rooms below; pretty music and excellent Waltzing; none but peasants; the dancing much better than in England; the English can't Waltz, never could, nor ever will. One man with his pipe in his mouth, but danced as well as the others; some other dances in pairs and in fours, and very good. I went to bed, but the revelry continued below late and early. Brientz but a village. Rose early. Embarked on the Lake of Brientz, rowed by the women in a long boat (one very young and very pretty—seated myself by her, and began to row also): presently we put to shore, and another woman jumped in. It seems it is the custom here for the boats to be *manned by women*: for of five men and three women in our bark, all the women took an oar, and but one man.

Got to Interlachen in three hours; pretty lake, not so large as that of Thoun. Dined at Interlachen. Girl gave me some flowers, and made me a speech in German, of which I know nothing: I do not know whether the speech was pretty, but as the woman was, I hope so. Saw another—very pretty too, and tall, which I prefer: I hate short women, for more reasons than one. Re-embarked on the Lake of Thoun; fell asleep part of the way: sent our horses round; found people on the shore, blowing up a rock with gunpowder: they blew it up near our boat, only telling us a minute before;—mere stupidity, but they might have broke our noddles. Got to Thoun in the Evening: the weather has been tolerable the whole day; but as the wild part of our tour is finished, it don't matter to us: in all the desirable part, we have been most lucky in warmth and clearness of Atmosphere, for which " Praise we the Lord!!"

Septr 26th

Being out of the mountains, my journal must be as flat as my journey. From Thoun to Bern, good road, hedges, villages, industry, property, and all sorts of tokens of insipid civilization. From Bern to Fribourg; different Canton—Catholics: passed a field of Battle; Swiss beat the French in one of the late wars against the French Republic. Bought a dog—a very ugly dog, but " *très méchant* "; this was his great recommendation in the owner's eyes and mine, for I mean him to watch the carriage. He hath no tail, and is called " *Mutz* ", which signifies " *Short-tail* ": he is apparently of the Shepherd dog genus! The greater part of this tour has been on horseback, on foot, and on mule.

The Filly (which is one of two young horses I bought of the Baron de Vincy), carried me very well: she is young and as quiet as any thing of her sex can be—very good tempered, and perpetually neighing when she wants any thing, which is every five minutes. I have called her *Biche*, because her manners are not unlike a little dog's; but she is a very tame pretty childish quadruped.

Septr 28th

Saw the tree planted in honour of the battle of Morat; 340 years old; a good deal decayed. Left Fribourg, but first saw the Cathedral; high tower. Overtook the baggage of the Nuns of La Trappe, who are removing to Normandy from their late abode in the Canton of Fribourg; afterwards a coach, with a quantity of Nuns in it—Nuns old. Proceeded along the banks of the Lake of Neufchatel; very pleasing and soft, but not so mountainous—at least, the Jura, not appearing so, after the Bernese Alps. Reached Yverdun in the dusk; a long line of large trees on the border of the lake—fine and sombre: the Auberge nearly full—a German—with princess and suite; got rooms.

We hope to reach Diodati the day after tomorrow, and I wish for a letter from you, my own dearest Sis. May your sleep be soft, and your dreams of me. I am going to bed—good night.

Septr 29th

Passed through a fine and flourishing country, but not mountainous. In the evening reached Aubonne (the entrance and bridge something like that of Durham), which commands by far the fairest view of the Lake of Geneva; twilight; the Moon on the Lake; a grove on the height, and of very noble trees. Here Tavernier (the Eastern traveller) bought (or built) the Chateau, because the site resembled and equalled that of *Erivan*, (a frontier city of Persia); here he finished his voyages, and I this little excursion,—for I am within a few hours of Diodati, and have little more to see, and no more to say.

In the weather for this tour (of 13 days), I have been very fortunate—fortunate in a companion (Mr. H^e)—fortunate in our prospects, and exempt from even the little petty accidents and delays which often render journeys in a less wild country disappointing. I was disposed to be pleased. I am a lover of Nature and an admirer of Beauty. I can bear fatigue and welcome privation, and have seen some of the noblest views in the world. But in all this—the recollections of bitterness, and more especially of recent and more home desolation, which must accompany me through life, have preyed upon me here; and neither the music of the Shepherd, the crashing of the Avalanche, nor the torrent, the mountain, the Glacier, the Forest, nor the Cloud, have for one moment lightened the weight upon my heart, nor enabled me to lose my own wretched identity in the majesty, and the power, and the Glory, around, above, and beneath me.

I am past reproaches; and there is a time for all things.

I am past the wish of vengeance, and I know of none like for what I have suffered ; but the hour will come, when what I feel must be felt, and the—but enough.

To you, dearest Augusta, I send, and *for* you I have kept this record of what I have seen and felt. Love me as you are beloved by me.

TO THE HON. AUGUSTA LEIGH   *Diodati, October 1ˢᵗ, 1816*

MY DEAREST AUGUSTA,—Two days ago I sent you in three letter-covers a journal of a mountain-excursion lately made by me and Mʳ H. in the Bernese Alps. I kept it on purpose for you thinking it might amuse you. Since my return here I have heard by an indirect Channel that Lady B. is better, or well. It is also said that she has some intention of passing the winter on the Continent. Upon this subject I want a word or two, and as you are—I understand—on terms of acquaintance with her again you will be the properest channel of com-munication from me to her. It regards my child. It is far from my intention now or at any future period (without misconduct on her part which I should be grieved to antici-pate), to attempt to withdraw my child from its mother. I think it would be harsh ; and though it is a very deep priva-tion to me to be withdrawn from the contemplation and com-pany of my little girl, still I would not purchase even this so very dearly ; but I must strongly protest against my daughter's leaving England, to be taken over the Continent at so early a time of life and subjected to many unavoidable risks of health and comfort ; more especially in so unsettled a state as we know the greater part of Europe to be in at this moment. I do not choose that my girl should be educated like Lord Yarmouth's son (or run the chance of it which a war would produce), and I make it my personal and particular request to Lady Byron that—in the event of her quitting England—the child should be left in the care of proper persons. I have no objection to its remaining with Lady Noel and Sir Ralph, (who would natur-ally be fond of it), but my distress of mind would be very much augmented if my daughter quitted England without my consent

or approbation. I beg that you will lose no time in making
this known to Lady B. and I hope you will say something to
enforce my request, I have no wish to trouble her more than
can be helped. My whole hope—and prospect of a quiet
evening (if I reach it), are wrapt up in that little creature—
Ada—and you must forgive my anxiety in all which regards
her even to minuteness. My journal will have told you all my
recent wanderings. I am very well though I had a little accident yesterday. Being in my boat in the evening the pole of
the mainsail slipped in veering round, and struck me on a
nerve of one of my legs so violently as to make me faint away.
Mr He and cold water brought me to myself, but there was no
damage done—no bone hurt—and I have now no pain whatever. Some nerve or tendon was jarred—for a moment and
that was all. To-day I dine at Coppet; the Jerseys are I
believe to be there. Believe me ever and truly my own dearest
Sis. most affectionately and entirely yours

B.

END OF VOL. I

4

Venice

October 1816 to December 1819

After a romantic tour in the Bernese Alps, Byron left Switzerland in October 1816, passed through Milan (where he encountered Henri Beyle and discarded Dr. Polidori) and came to rest in Venice on the 11th of November. The city delighted him; and, as a relief from remorse and introspection, he at once plunged into a series of highly stimulating love-affairs. Two of his earlier Venetian mistresses—Marianna Segati, with her " large, black, oriental eyes ", the wife of a draper in the Frezzeria, and Margarita Cogni, the baker's runaway wife, a magnificent amazon, who installed herself in his palace on the Grand Canal, where she ruled her good-humoured lover and terrorized his household—are graphically portrayed in a celebrated letter to John Murray. Their successors and rivals were unconscionably numerous; and Byron's debaucheries presently began to surprise and alarm even his Venetian intimates. His health suffered; his temper did not improve; and Shelley, who visited him in 1818, found him lamentably the worse for wear. " He says he disapproves ", wrote Shelley, " but he endures. He is heartily and deeply discontented with himself. . . ." Yet, although, following Shelley's example, it is customary to deplore Byron's existence at the Palazzo Mocenigo, we must not forget that throughout this period he was busily and profitably occupied, and had triumphantly launched Don Juan, beyond a doubt his finest long poem. Work and dissipation, nevertheless, had overtaxed his energies; and he had already resolved on reform when, at the beginning of April 1819, he was caught up in a quasi-domestic liaison with the Countess Guiccioli, an ardent and impulsive young woman, recently married to a rich and elderly Romagnol landowner. His new mistress was a determined sentimentalist; Byron, an easygoing and self-indulgent cynic. He soon accepted the rôle to which Teresa Guiccioli assigned him—that of an accredited *lover in the recognized Italian style. Returning home to Ravenna, she fell seriously ill; and Byron, though not without some grumbling, obeyed her urgent summons.*

TO THE HON. AUGUSTA LEIGH   *Milan, Oct. 13th, 1816*

MY DEAREST AUGUSTA,—You see I have got to Milan. We came by the Simplon, escaping all perils of precipices and robbers, of which last there was some talk and apprehension, a chain of English carriages having been stopped near Cesto a few weeks ago and handsomely pilfered of various chattels. We were not molested.

The Simplon, as you know, is the most superb of all possible routes;—so I shall not describe it. I also navigated the Lago Maggiore, and went over the Borromean Islands; the latter are fine but too artificial; the lake itself is beautiful, as indeed is the whole country from Geneva hither, and the Alpine part most magnificent.

Close to Milan is the beginning of an unfinished triumphal arch for Napoleon, so beautiful as to make one regret its non-completion. As we only reached Milan last night, I can say little about it, but will write again in a few days. The Jerseys are here; Made de Stael is gone to Paris (or going) from Coppet. I was more there than elsewhere during my stay at Diodati, and she has been particularly kind, and friendly towards me the whole time. When you write, address to *Geneva* still, Post *restante*, and my banker (Monsr Hentsch) will forward your letters. I have written to you so often lately that you will not regret the brevity of this. I hope that you received safely my presents for the children (by Scrope) and that you also have (by the post) a little journal of a journey in and on the Alps which I sent you early this month, having kept it on purpose for *you*—Ever my own dearest

Yrs. most B

TO THE HON. AUGUSTA LEIGH   *Milan Octr 15, 1816*

My dearest Augusta,—I have been at Churches, Theatres, libraries, and picture galleries. The Cathedral is noble, the theatre grand, the library excellent, and the galleries I know nothing about—except as far as liking one picture out of a thousand. What has delighted me most is a manuscript collection (preserved in the Ambrosian library), of original love-letters and verses of Lucretia de Borgia and Cardinal Bembo; and a lock of her hair—so long—and fair and beautiful —and the letters so pretty and so loving that it makes one wretched not to have been born sooner to have at least seen her. And pray what do you think is one of her *signatures?*—why this + a Cross—which she says " is to stand for her name etc." Is not this amusing? I suppose you know that she was a famous beauty, and famous for the use she made of it; and that she was the love of this same Cardinal Bembo (besides a story about her papa Pope Alexander and her brother Cæsar Borgia—which some people don't believe—and others do), and that after all she ended with being Duchess of Ferrara, and an excellent mother and wife also; so good as to be quite an example. All this may or may not be, but the hair and the letters are so beautiful that I have done nothing but pore over them, and have made the librarian promise me a copy of some of them; and I mean to get some of the hair if I can. The verses are Spanish—the letters Italian—some signed—others with a cross—but all in her own hand-writing.

I am so hurried, and so sleepy, but so anxious to send you even a few lines my dearest Augusta, that you will forgive me troubling you so often; and I shall write again soon; but I have sent you so much lately, that you will have too many perhaps. *A thousand loves* to *you* from *me*—which is very generous for I only ask *one* in return

Ever dearest thine B.

TO THE HON. AUGUSTA LEIGH   *Octr 28th, 1816*

My dearest Augusta,—Two days ago I wrote you the enclosed but the arrival of your letter of the 12th has revived me a little, so pray forgive the apparent " *humeur* " of the other, which I do not tear up—from lazyness—and the hurry of the post as I have hardly time to write another at present.

I really do not and cannot understand all the mysteries and alarms in your letters and more particularly in the last. All I know is—that no human power short of destruction— shall prevent me from seeing you when—where—and how— I may please—according to time and circumstance; that you are the only comfort (except the remote possibility of my daughter's being so) left me in prospect in existence, and that I can bear the rest—so that you remain; but anything which is to divide us would drive me quite out of my senses; Miss Milbanke appears in all respects to have been formed for my destruction; I have thus far—as you know—regarded her without feelings of personal bitterness towards her, but if directly or indirectly—but why do I say this?—You know she is the cause of all—whether intentionally or not is little to the purpose——You surely do not mean to say that if I come to England in Spring, that you and I shall not meet? If so I will never return to it—though I must for many reasons—business etc etc—But I quit this topic for the present.

My health is good, but I have now and then fits of giddi- ness, and deafness, which make me think like Swift—that I shall be like him and the *withered* tree he saw—which occasioned the reflection and " die at top " first. My hair is growing grey, and *not* thicker; and my teeth are sometimes *looseish* though still white and sound. Would not one think I was sixty instead of not quite nine and twenty? To talk thus— Never mind—either this must end—or I must end—but I repeat it again and again—*that woman* has destroyed me.

Milan has been made agreeable by much attention and kindness from many of the natives; but the whole tone of Italian society is so different from yours in England; that I have not time to describe it, tho' I am not sure that I do not prefer it. Direct as usual to Geneva—hope the best—and love me the most—as I ever must love you.

B.

TO THE HON. AUGUSTA LEIGH *Milan, Nov. 2nd, 1816*

MY DEAREST AUGUSTA,—I wrote to you the other day, and I now do so to send a few lines, and request you to take particular care that Lady B. receives a letter sent in another enclosure. I feel so miserable that I must write to her—however useless.

In a day or two we set off for Venice. I have seen a good deal of Milanese society but nothing to make me forget others —or forgive myself.

Dr. Polidori (whom I dismissed some time before I left Geneva, as I had no use for him and his temper and habits were not good) had been in Milan some time before but, getting into a scrape and quarrel with some Austrians, has been sent by the Government out of the territory.

I had nothing to do with his squabble, and was not even present, though, when he sent for me, I tried of course to get him out of it, as well as Mr. Hobhouse, who tried also for him, but to no purpose. I tell you all this because in England, by some kind mistake, his squabbles may be set down to *me*, and now (if this should be the case) you have it in your power to contradict it. It happened about a week ago.

I shall probably write to you on my road to Venice—from Verona or elsewhere.

Ever, my dearest, thine, B.

TO THOMAS MOORE *Verona, November 6, 1816*

MY DEAR MOORE,—Your letter, written before my departure from England, and addressed to me in London, only reached me recently. Since that period, I have been over a portion of that part of Europe which I had not already seen. About a month since, I crossed the Alps from Switzerland to Milan, which I left a few days ago, and am thus far on my way to Venice, where I shall probably winter. Yesterday I was on the shores of the Benacus, with his *fluctibus et fremitu.* Catullus's Sirmium has still its name and site, and is remembered for his sake : but the very heavy autumnal rains and mists prevented our quitting our route, (that is, Hobhouse and myself, who are at present voyaging together,) as it was better not to see it at all than to a great disadvantage.

I found on the Benacus the same tradition of a city, still visible in calm weather below the waters, which you have preserved of Lough Neagh, " When the clear, cold eve's declining ". I do not know that it is authorised by records; but they tell you such a story, and say that the city was swallowed up by an earthquake. We moved to-day over the frontier to Verona, by a road suspected of thieves,—" the wise *convey* it call ",—but without molestation. I shall remain here a day or two to gape at the usual marvels,—amphitheatre, paintings, and all that time-tax of travel,—though Catullus, Claudian, and Shakspeare have done more for Verona than it ever did for itself. They still pretend to show, I believe, the " tomb of all the Capulets "—we shall see.

Among many things at Milan, one pleased me particularly, viz. the correspondence (in the prettiest love-letters in the world) of Lucretia Borgia with Cardinal Bembo, (who, *you say*, made a very good cardinal,) and a lock of her hair, and some Spanish verses of hers,—the lock very fair and beautiful. I took one single hair of it as a relic, and wished sorely to get a copy of one or two of the letters; but it is prohibited : *that* I don't mind; but it was impracticable; and so I only got some of them by heart. They are kept in the Ambrosian Library, which I often visited to look them over—to the scandal of the librarian, who wanted to enlighten me with sundry valuable MSS., classical, philosophical, and pious. But I stick to the Pope's daughter, and wish myself a cardinal.

I have seen the finest parts of Switzerland, the Rhine, the Rhone, and the Swiss and Italian lakes; for the beauties of which, I refer you to the Guide-book. The north of Italy is tolerably free from the English; but the south swarms with them, I am told. Madame de Stael I saw frequently at Copet, which she renders remarkably pleasant. She has been particularly kind to me. I was for some months her neighbour, in a country-house called Diodati, which I had on the Lake of Geneva. My plans are very uncertain; but it is probable that you will see me in England in the spring. I have some business there. If you write to me, will you address to the care of Mons.

Hentsch, *Banquier*, Geneva, who receives and forwards my letters. Remember me to Rogers, who wrote to me lately, with a short account of your poem, which, I trust, is near the light. He speaks of it most highly.

My health is very endurable, except that I am subject to casual giddiness and faintness, which is so like a fine lady, that I am rather ashamed of the disorder. When I sailed, I had a physician with me, whom, after some months of patience, I found it expedient to part with, before I left Geneva some time. On arriving at Milan, I found this gentleman in very good society, where he prospered for some weeks; but, at length, at the theatre, he quarrelled with an Austrian officer, and was sent out by the government in twenty-four hours. I was not present at his squabble; but, on hearing that he was put under arrest, I went and got him out of his confinement, but could not prevent his being sent off, which, indeed, he partly deserved, being quite in the wrong, and having begun a row for row's sake. I had preceded the Austrian government some weeks myself, in giving him his congé from Geneva. He is not a bad fellow, but very young and hot-headed, and more likely to incur diseases than to cure them. Hobhouse and myself found it useless to intercede for him. This happened some time before we left Milan. He is gone to Florence.

At Milan I saw, and was visited by, Monti, the most celebrated of the living Italian poets. He seems near sixty; in face he is like the late Cooke the actor. His frequent changes in politics have made him very unpopular as a man. I saw many more of their literati; but none whose names are well known in England, except Acerbi. I lived much with the Italians, particularly with the Marquis of Breme's family, who are very able and intelligent men, especially the Abbate. There was a famous improvisatore who held forth while I was there. His fluency astonished me; but, although I understand Italian, and speak it (with more readiness than accuracy), I could only carry off a few very common-place mythological images, and one line about Artemisia, and another about Algiers, with sixty words of an entire tragedy about Eteocles and Polynices. Some of the Italians liked him—others called his performance " *seccatura* " (a devilish good word, by the way) and all Milan was in controversy about him.

The state of morals in these parts is in some sort lax. A mother and son were pointed out at the theatre, as being pronounced by the Milanese world to be of the Theban dynasty —but this was all. The narrator (one of the first men in Milan) seemed to be most sufficiently scandalised by the taste or the tie. All society in Milan is carried on at the opéra : they have private boxes, where they play at cards, or talk, or any thing else ; but (except at the Cassino) there are no open houses, or balls, etc., etc. * * * * *

The peasant girls have all very fine dark eyes, and many of them are beautiful. There are also two dead bodies in fine preservation—one Saint Carlo Boromeo, at Milan ; the other not a saint, but a chief, named Visconti, at Monza—both of which appeared very agreeable. In one of the Boromean isles (the Isola bella), there is a large laurel—the largest known—on which Buonaparte, staying there just before the battle of Marengo, carved with his knife the word " Battaglia ". I saw the letters, now half worn out and partly erased.

Excuse this tedious letter. To be tiresome is the privilege of old age and absence ; I avail myself of the latter, and the former I have anticipated. If I do not speak to you of my own affairs, it is not from want of confidence, but to spare you and myself. My day is over—what then?—I have had it. To be sure, I have shortened it ; and if I had done as much by this letter, it would have been as well. But you will forgive that, if not the other faults of

Yours ever and most affectionately, B.

P.S.—*November 7, 1816*

I have been over Verona. The amphitheatre is wonderful —beats even Greece. Of the truth of Juliet's story they seem tenacious to a degree, insisting on the fact—giving a date (1303), and showing a tomb. It is a plain, open, and partly decayed sarcophagus, with withered leaves in it, in a wild and desolate conventual garden, once a cemetery, now ruined to the very graves. The situation struck me as very appropriate to the legend, being blighted as their love. I have brought away a few pieces of the granite, to give to my daughter and my nieces. Of the other marvels of this city, paintings, antiquities, etc., excepting the tombs of the Scaliger princes, I have no pretensions to judge. The Gothic monuments of the Scaligers pleased me, but " a poor virtuoso am I ", and ever yours.

TO THE HON. AUGUSTA LEIGH † *Verona, Novr 6th 1816*

MY DEAREST AUGUSTA,—I am thus far on my way to Venice, and shall stay here a day to see the place, the paintings, the " tomb of all the Capulets " which they show (at least a tomb they call so after the story, from which Shakespeare drew the plot of his play), and all the sights and so forths at which it is usual to gape in passing.

I left Milan on Sunday, and have travelled but slowly over some celebrated ground; but Lombardy is not a beautiful country—at least in autumn, excepting however the Lago di Garda and its outlines which are mountainous on one side: and it is a very fine stormy lake throughout—never quiet; and I had the pleasure of seeing it in all its vexation, foaming like a little Sea, as Virgil has described it. But (thank God) you are not a blue-stocking, and I won't inflict the appropriate bit of Latin upon you.

I wrote to you a few scraps of *letterets* (I may call them they were so short) from Milan.

Dr. Polidori, whom I parted with before I left Geneva (not for any great harm, but because he was always in squabbles, and had no kind of conduct), contrived at Milan, which he reached before me, to get into a quarrel with an Austrian, and to be ordered out of the city by the government. *I did not even see his adventure*, nor had any thing to do with it, except getting him out of arrest, and trying to get him altogether out of the scrape. This I mention, because I know in England some one or other will probably transfer his adventures to me. After what has been said already, I have a right to suspect every thing and every body; so I state all this for your satisfaction, and that you may be able to contradict any such report. Mr. Hobhouse and Trevannion, and indeed every body—Italian and English—then at Milan, can corroborate this if necessary. It occurred several days before Mr. H. and myself left it. So much for this.

When we reach Venice I shall write to thee again. I had

received your acknowledgement of the journal etc. and the
trinkets by Scrope, of which I delight to hear the reception.

In health I am pretty well, except that the confounded
Lombardy rains of this season (the autumn) have given me a
flying rheumatism, which is troublesome at times, and makes
me feel ancient. I am also growing *grey* and *giddy*, and cannot
help thinking my head will decay ; I wish my memory would,
at least my remembrance—except a parenthesis for *ou*—my
dearest Augusta.

Ada—by the way *Ada's* name (which I found in our
pedigree under King John's reign) is the same with that of the
Sister of Charlemagne, as I read the other day in a book treating
of the Rhine.

Ever my own—thy own B.

P.S.—I forgot to tell you that my dog (Mutz by name and
Swiss by nation) shuts a door when he is told : there—that's
more than Tip can do.

Remember me to the child*er*, and to Georgiana, who I
suppose has grown a prodigious penwoman. I hope she likes
her seals and all her share of Mont Blanc.

I have had so much of mountains that I am not yet reconciled
to the plains—but they improve. Verona seems a fine city.

P.S.—Novr 7th I have been over Verona. The Amphitheatre is superb, and in high preservation. Of the *truth* of the
story of Juliet they seem very tenacious, giving the date (1303),
and shewing a tomb. It is an open granite sarcophagus in a
most desolate convent garden, which looks quite wild and
withered, and once was a Cimetery [*sic*] since ruined. I
brought away four small pieces of it for you and the babes (at
least the female part of them), and for Ada, and her mother,
if she will accept it from you. I thought the situation more
appropriate to the history than if it had been less blighted.
This struck me more than all the antiquities, more even than
the Amphitheatre.

TO THOMAS MOORE   *Venice, November 17, 1816*

I wrote to you from Verona the other day in my progress
hither, which letter I hope you will receive. Some three years

ago, or it may be more, I recollect your telling me that you had received a letter from our friend Sam, dated " On board his gondola ". *My* gondola is, at this present, waiting for me on the canal ; but I prefer writing to you in the house, it being autumn—and rather an English autumn than otherwise. It is my intention to remain at Venice during the winter, probably, as it has always been (next to the East) the greenest island of my imagination. It has not disappointed me ; though its evident decay would, perhaps, have that effect upon others. But I have been familiar with ruins too long to dislike desolation. Besides, I have fallen in love, which, next to falling into the canal, (which would be of no use, as I can swim,) is the best or the worst thing I could do. I have got some extremely good apartments in the house of a " Merchant of Venice ", who is a good deal occupied with business, and has a wife in her twenty-second year. Marianna [Segati] (that is her name) is in her appearance altogether like an antelope. She has the large, black, oriental eyes, with that peculiar expression in them which is seen rarely among *Europeans*—even the Italians— and which many of the Turkish women give themselves by tinging the eyelid,—an art not known out of that country, I believe. This expression she has *naturally*,—and something more than this. In short, I cannot describe the effect of this kind of eye,—at least upon me. Her features are regular, and rather aquiline—mouth small—skin clear and soft, with a kind of hectic colour—forehead remarkably good : her hair is of the dark gloss, curl, and colour of Lady J[ersey]'s : her figure is light and pretty, and she is a famous songstress—scientifically so ; her natural voice (in conversation, I mean) is very sweet ; and the naïveté of the Venetian dialect is always pleasing in the mouth of a woman.

November 23

You will perceive that my description, which was proceeding with the minuteness of a passport, has been interrupted for several days. In the mean time * * * *

December 5

Since my former dates, I do not know that I have much to add on the subject, and, luckily, nothing to take away ; for I am more pleased than ever with my Venetian, and begin to

feel very serious on that point—so much so, that I shall be
silent. * * * * *

By way of divertisement, I am studying daily, at an
Armenian monastery, the Armenian language. I found
that my mind wanted something craggy to break upon; and
this—as the most difficult thing I could discover here for an
amusement—I have chosen, to torture me into attention. It
is a rich language, however, and would amply repay any one
the trouble of learning it. I try, and shall go on;—but I
answer for nothing, least of all for my intentions or my success.
There are some very curious MSS. in the monastery, as well
as books; translations also from Greek originals, now lost, and
from Persian and Syriac, etc.; besides works of their own
people. Four years ago the French instituted an Armenian
professorship. Twenty pupils presented themselves on Monday
morning, full of noble ardour, ingenuous youth, and impreg-
nable industry. They persevered, with a courage worthy of
the nation and of universal conquest, till Thursday; when
fifteen of the *twenty* succumbed to the six-and-twentieth letter
of the alphabet. It is, to be sure, a Waterloo of an Alphabet—
that must be said for them. But it is so like these fellows, to
do by it as they did by their sovereigns—abandon both; to
parody the old rhymes, " Take a thing and give a thing "—
" Take a king and give a king ". They are the worst of
animals, except their conquerors.

I hear that Hodgson is your neighbour, having a living in
Derbyshire. You will find him an excellent-hearted fellow,
as well as one of the cleverest; a little, perhaps, too much
japanned by preferment in the church and the tuition of youth,
as well as inoculated with the disease of domestic felicity,
besides being over-run with fine feelings about woman and
constancy (that small change of Love, which people exact so
rigidly, receive in such counterfeit coin, and repay in baser
metal) ; but, otherwise, a very worthy man, who has lately
got a pretty wife, and (I suppose) a child by this time. Pray
remember me to him, and say that I know not which to envy
most his neighbourhood—him, or you.

Of Venice I shall say little. You must have seen many
descriptions; and they are most of them like. It is a poetical
place; and classical, to us, from Shakespeare and Otway. I

have not yet sinned against it in verse, nor do I know that I shall do so, having been tuneless since I crossed the Alps, and feeling, as yet, no renewal of the *estro*. By the way, I suppose you have seen *Glenarvon*. Madame de Stael lent it me to read from Copet last autumn. It seems to me, that if the authoress had written the *truth*, and nothing but the truth—the whole truth—the romance would not only have been more *romantic*, but more entertaining. As for the likeness, the picture can't be good—I did not sit long enough. When you have leisure, let me hear from and of you, believing me,

Ever and truly yours most affectionately, B.

P.S.—Oh! *your poem*—is it out? I hope Longman has paid his thousands; but don't you do as H—— T——'s father did, who, having made money by a quarto tour, became a vinegar merchant; when, lo! his vinegar turned sweet (and be damned to it) and ruined him. My last letter to you (from Verona) was enclosed to Murray—have you got it? Direct to me *here*, *poste restante*. There are no English here at present. There were several in Switzerland—some women; but, except Lady Dalrymple Hamilton, most of them as ugly as virtue—at least, those I saw.

TO THE HON. DOUGLAS KINNAIRD   *Venice,*
November 27th, 1816

MY DEAR KINNAIRD,—Before I left Switzerland, I answered your last letter, and feel a little anxious to know that you have received it, as it was partly on business—that is to say, on the disposition of Murray's proposed payment.

I fear there is little chance of an immediate sale of Newstead, which is to be wished for many reasons.

H[obhouse] and I have been some time in the north of Italy, and reached Venice about a fortnight ago, where I shall remain probably during the winter. It is a place which I like, and which I long anticipated that I should like—besides, I have fallen in love, and with a very pretty woman—so much so as to obtain the approbation of the not easily approving H., who is, in general, rather tardy in his applause of the fairer part of the creation.

She is married—so our arrangement was formed according to the incontinent continental system, which need not be described to you, an experienced voyager—and gifted withal with a modest self-confidence, which my bashful nature is not endowed with—but nevertheless I have got the woman—I do not very well know how, but we do exceedingly well together. She is not two-and-twenty, with great black eastern eyes, and a variety of subsidiary charms, etc., etc., and amongst her other accomplishments is a mighty and admirable singer—as most of the Italians are—(though not a public one) ; luckily I can speak the language fluently ; and luckily (if I did not), we could employ ourselves a little without talking.

I meant to have given up gallivanting altogether on leaving your country, where I had been tolerably sickened of that and everything else ; but, I know not how it is, my health growing better, and my spirits not worse, the " besoin d'aimer " came back upon my heart again, and, after all, there is nothing like it. So much for that matter.

I hear you are in a row with Dibdin and Fanny Kelly, and the devil knows whom—Humph !

I hear also that at the meeting or in the committee, you said that I was coming back in spring—it is probable—and if you have said so I *will* come, for sundry reasons—to see my daughter—my sister—and my friends—(and not least nor last —*yourself*,) to renew my proxy (if Parliament be dissolved) for the Whigs—to see Mr. Waite, and Mr. Blake—and the newest play—and the S[ub]-committee—and to sell Newstead (if I can), but not to reside in England again. It neither suits me, nor I it ; my greatest error was remaining there,—that is to say, my greatest error but one. My ambition, if ever I had much—is over—or at least limited. If I could but remain as I now am, I should not merely be happy, but *contented*, which in my mind is the strangest, and most difficult attainment of the two—for any one who will hazard enough may have moments of happiness. I have books—a decent establishment—a fine country—a language which I prefer—most of the amusements and conveniences of life—as much of society as I choose to take—and a handsome woman, who is not a bore—and does not annoy me with looking like a fool, setting up for a sage. Life has little left for my curiosity ; there are few things in it of which I have not had a sight, and a share—it would be silly to quarrel with my luck because it did not last—and even that was partly my own fault. If the present does—I should fall out with the past; and if I could but manage to arrange my pecuniary concerns in England, so as to pay my debts, and leave me what would be here a very fair income (though nothing remarkable at home), you might consider me as *posthumous*, for I would never willingly dwell in the " tight little Island ".

Pray write to me a line or two, addressed to Venice, *Poste Restante*. I hope to remain here the winter—remember me to Maria, and believe me,

Yours ever truly and affectionately, B.

P.S.—Colonel Finch, an English acquaintance of H[obhouse]'s and mine, has, I believe, written to you to complain of his banker (who is also mine), and has with our permission mentioned our names to you, as knowing him. I must, however, say that *I* have no complaint whatever against (Mr. Siri), the banker—who has, on the contrary, been remarkably civil and attentive to both H. and myself.

Of Col. Finch's row with him, I understand nothing but that he had one.

Pray let me hear from you, and tell me what Murray has done, and if you have received my letter from Geneva in answer to your former one.

P.S.—If you write pray do not refer to any *persons* or *events* except our own *theatrical — political —* personal — *attorneycal — poetical*—or *diabolical* concerns.

You see I give a pretty wide range still—but what I wish to put under Quarantine are (*my*) *family events*, and all allusion thereto past—present—or to come. It is what I have laid an embargo on, with all my other friends.

It will be better that the *Author* of these lines (if spoken), be *not avowed*—pray make it a secret and keep it so.

TO JOHN MURRAY   *Venice, December 4, 1816*

DEAR SIR,—I have written to you so frequently of late, that you will think me a bore; as I think you a very impolite person for not answering my letters from Switzerland, Milan, Verona, and Venice. There are some things I wanted, and want, to know; viz. whether Mr. Davies, of inaccurate memory, had or had not delivered the MS. as delivered to him; because, if he has not, you will find that he will bountifully bestow extracts and transcriptions on all the curious of his acquaintance, in which case you may probably find your publication anticipated by the "Cambridge" or other Chronicles. In the next place,—I forget what was next; but in the 3^d place, I want to hear whether you have yet published, or when you mean to do so, or why you have not done so, because in your last (Sept. 20th,—you may be ashamed of the date) you talked of this being done immediately.

From England I hear nothing, and know nothing of any thing or any body. I have but one correspondent (except Mr. Kinnaird on business now and then), and that one is a female;[1] and her letters are so full of mysteries and miseries,—such a quantity of the trivial and conjectural, and such a dearth of any useful or even amusing information, that I know no more of your island, or city, than the Italian version of the French papers chooses to tell me, or the advertisements of Mr. Colburn tagged to the end of your *Quarterly Review* for the year *ago*. I wrote to you at some length last week; so that I have little to add, except that I have begun, and am proceeding in, a study of the Armenian language, which I acquire, as well as I can, at the Armenian convent, where I go every day to take lessons of a learned Friar, and have gained some singular and not useless information with regard to the literature and customs of that oriental people. They have an establishment here—a church and convent of ninety monks, very learned and accomplished men, some of them. They have also a press, and make great efforts for the enlightening of their nation. I find the language (which is *twin*, the *literal* and the *vulgar*) difficult, but not invincible (at least I hope not). I shall go on. I found it necessary to twist my mind round some severer study; and this, as being the hardest I could devise here, will be a file for the serpent.

I mean to remain here till the Spring, so address to me *directly* to *Venice, poste restante*.—Mr. Hobhouse, for the present,

[1] Augusta Leigh.

is gone to Rome, with his brother, brother's wife, and Sister, who overtook him here : he returns in two months. I should have gone too, but I fell in love, and must stay that over. I should think that and the Armenian alphabet will last the winter. The lady has, luckily for me, been less obdurate than the language, or, between the two, I should have lost my remains of sanity. By the way, *she* is not Armenian, but a Venetian, as I believe I told you in my last. As for Italian, I am fluent enough, even in its Venetian modification, which is something like the Somersetshire version of English ; and as for the more classical dialects, I had not forgot my former practice during my voyaging.

Yours, ever and truly, B.

P.S.—Remember me to Mr. Gifford. And do not forget me to—— but I don't think I have any other friends of your acquaintance.

TO THE HON. AUGUSTA LEIGH   *Venice, Dec^r, 18th 1816*

MY DEAREST AUGUSTA,—I have received one letter dated 19th Novr I think (or rather earlier by a week or two perhaps), since my arrival in Venice, where it is my intention to remain probably till the Spring. The place pleases me. I have found some pleasing society—and the *romance* of the situation—and it's extraordinary appearance—together with all the associations we are accustomed to connect with Venice, have always had a charm for me, even before I arrived here ; and I have not been disappointed in what I have seen.

I go every morning to the Armenian Convent (of *friars not Nuns*—my child) to study the language, I mean the *Armenian* language, (for as you perhaps know—I am versed in the Italian which I speak with fluency rather than accuracy), and if you ask me my reason for studying this out of the way language—I can only answer that it is Oriental and difficult, and employs me—which are—as you know my Eastern and difficult way of thinking—reasons sufficient. Then I have fallen in love with a very pretty Venetian of two and twenty, with great black eyes. She is married—and so am I—which is very much to the purpose. We have formed and sworn an eternal attachment, which has already lasted a lunar month, and I am more in love than ever, and so is the lady—at least she says so. She does not plague me (which is a wonder) and I verily believe we are one of the happiest—unlawful couples on this side of the Alps. She is very handsome, very Italian or rather Venetian, with something more of the Oriental cast of countenance; accomplished and musical after the manner of her nation. Her spouse is a very good kind of man who occupies himself elsewhere, and thus the world goes on here as elsewhere. This adventure came very opportunely to console me, for I was beginning to be " like Sam Jennings very *unappy*" but at present—at least for a month past—I have been very tranquil, very loving, and have not so much embarassed myself with the tortures of the last two years and that virtuous monster Miss Milbanke, who had nearly driven me out of my senses.—

Hobhouse is gone to Rome with his brother and sister—but returns here in February: you will easily suppose that I was not disposed to stir from my present position.

I have not heard recently from England and wonder if Murray has published the po's sent to him; and I want to know if you don't think them very fine and all that—Goosey my love—don't they make you " put finger in eye "?

You can have no idea of my thorough wretchedness from the day of my parting from you till nearly a month ago though I struggled against it with some strength. At present I am better—thank Heaven above—and woman beneath—and I will be a very good boy. Pray remember me to the babes, and tell me of little *Da*—who by the way—is a year old and a few days over.

My love to you all and to Aunt *Sophy*: pray tell *her* in particular that I have consoled myself; and tell Hodgson that his prophecy is accomplished. He said—you remember—I should be in love with an Italian—so I am.—

ever dearest yrs.   B.

P.S.—I forgot to tell you—that the *Demoiselle*—who returned to England from Geneva—went there to produce a new baby B., who is now about to make his appearance. You wanted to hear some adventures—there are enough I think for one epistle.——Pray address direct to Venice—Poste Restante.

TO THE HON. AUGUSTA LEIGH†   *Venice, Decr 19th 1816*

MY DEAREST AUGUSTA,—I wrote to you a few days ago.
Your letter of the 1st is arrived, and you have " a *hope* " for
me, it seems : what " *hope* ", child? my dearest Sis.   I remember
a methodist preacher who, on perceiving a profane grin on the
faces of part of his congregation, exclaimed " no *hopes* for *them*
as *laughs* ".   And thus it is with us : we laugh too much for
hopes, and so even let them go.   I am sick of sorrow, and must
even content myself as well as I can : so here goes—I won't be
woeful again if I can help it.   My letter to my moral Clytemnestra required no answer, and I would rather have none.   I
was wretched enough when I wrote it, and had been so for
many a long day and month : at present I am less so, for reasons
explained in my late letter (a few days ago) ; and as I never
pretend to be what I am not, you may tell her if you please that
I am recovering, and the reason also if you like it.   I do not
agree with you about Ada : there was *equivocation* in the answer,
and it shall be settled one way or the other.   I wrote to Hanson
to take proper steps to prevent such a removal of my daughter,
and even the probability of it.   You do not know the woman
so well as I do, or you would perceive in her *very negative
answer* that she *does intend* to take Ada with her, if she should
go abroad.   I have heard of Murray's squabble with one of
his brethren, who is an impudent impostor, and should be
trounced.

You do not say whether the *true po's* are out : I hope you
like them.

You are right in saying that I like Venice : it is very much
what you would imagine it, but I have no time just now for
description.   The Carnival is to begin in a week, and with it
the mummery of masking.

I have not been out a great deal, but quite as much as I
like.   I am going out this evening in my *cloak* and *Gondola*—
there are two nice Mrs. Radcliffe words for you.   And then
there is the place of St. Mark, and conversaziones, and various
fooleries, besides many *nau* : indeed, every body is *nau*, so
much so, that a lady with only *one lover* is not reckoned to have
overstepped the modesty of marriage—that being a regular
thing.   Some have two, three, and so on to twenty, beyond

which they don't account; but they generally begin by one.
The husbands of course belong to any body's wives—but their
own. . . . . .

My present beloved is aged two and twenty—with remarkably fine black eyes, and very regular and pretty features,
figure light and pretty, hair dark, a mighty good singer, as they
all are. She is married (of course) and has one child, a girl.
Her temper very good (as you know it had need to be) and
lively. She is a Venetian by birth, and was never further from
Venice than Milan in her days. Her lord is about five years
older than me, an exceeding good kind of a man. That
amatory appendage called by us a lover is here denominated
variously—sometimes an " Amoroso " (which is the same thing)
and sometimes a Cavaliere Servente—which I need not tell
you is a serving Cavalier. I told my fair one, at setting out,
that as to the love and the Cavaliership I was quite of accord,
but as to the *servitude* it would not suit me at all : so I begged
to hear no more about it. You may easily suppose I should not
at all shine in the ceremonious department—so little so that,
instead of handing the Lady as in duty bound into the Gondola,
I as nearly as possible conveyed her into the Canal, and this at
midnight. To be sure it was as dark as possible—but if you
could have seen the gravity with which I was committing her
to the waves, thinking all the time of something or other not to
the purpose. I always forget that the streets are canals, and
was going to walk her over the water, if the servants and the
Gondoliers had not awakened me.

So much for love and all that. The music here is famous,
and there will be a whole tribe of singers and dancers during the
Carnival, besides the usual theatres.

The Society here is something like our own, except that the
women sit in a semicircle at one end of the room, and the men
stand at the other.

I pass my mornings at the Armenian convent studying
Armenian,—my evenings here and there. To-night I am going
to the Countess Albrizzi's, one of the *noblesse*. I have also been
at the Governor's, who is an Austrian, and whose wife, the
Countess Goetz, appears to me in the little I have seen of her
a very amiable and pleasing woman, with remarkably good
manners, as many of the German women have.

There are no English here, except birds of passage, who stay a day and then go on to Florence or Rome.

I mean to remain here till Spring. When you write address *directly* here, as in your present letter.

Ever, dearest, yours, B.

TO THOMAS MOORE   *Venice, December 24, 1816*

I have taken a fit of writing to you, which portends postage—once from Verona—once from Venice, and again from Venice—*thrice* that is. For this you may thank yourself; for I heard that you complained of my silence—so, here goes for garrulity.

I trust that you received my other twain of letters. My " way of life " (or " May of life ", which is it according to the commentators?)—my " way of life " is fallen into great regularity. In the mornings I go over in my gondola to babble Armenian with the friars of the convent of St. Lazarus, and to help one of them in correcting the English of an English and Armenian grammar which he is publishing. In the evenings I do one of many nothings—either at the theatres, or some of the conversaziones, which are like our routs, or rather worse, for the women sit in a semicircle by the lady of the mansion, and the men stand about the room. To be sure, there is one improvement upon ours—instead of lemonade with their ices, they hand about stiff *rum-punch—punch*, by my palate ; and this they think *English*. I would not disabuse them of so agreeable an error,—" no, not for Venice ".

Last night I was at the Count Governor's, which, of course, comprises the best society, and is very much like other gregarious meetings in every country,—as in ours,—except that, instead of the Bishop of Winchester, you have the Patriarch of Venice, and a motley crew of Austrians, Germans, noble Venetians, foreigners, and, if you see a quiz, you may be sure he is a Consul. Oh, by the way, I forgot, when I wrote from Verona, to tell you that at Milan I met with a countryman of yours—a Colonel [Fitzgerald], a very excellent, good-natured fellow, who knows and shows all about Milan, and is, as it were, a native there. He is particularly civil to strangers, and this is his history,—at least, an episode of it.

Six-and-twenty years ago, Col. [Fitzgerald], then an ensign, being in Italy, fell in love with the Marchesa [Castiglione], and she with him. The lady must be, at least, twenty years his senior. The war broke out; he returned to England, to serve—not his country, for that's Ireland—but England, which is a different thing; and *she*—heaven knows what she did. In the year 1814, the first annunciation of the Definitive Treaty of Peace (and tyranny) was developed to the astonished Milanese by the arrival of Col. [Fitzgerald], who, flinging himself full length at the feet of Mad. [Castiglione], murmured forth, in half-forgotten Irish Italian, eternal vows of indelible constancy. The lady screamed, and exclaimed, " Who are you? " The Colonel cried, " What! don't you know me? I am so and so ", etc., etc., etc.; till, at length, the Marchesa, mounting from reminiscence to reminiscence, through the lovers of the intermediate twenty-five years, arrived at last at the recollection of her *povero* sub-lieutenant. She then said, " Was there ever such virtue? " (that was her very word) and, being now a widow, gave him apartments in her palace, reinstated him in all the rights of wrong, and held him up to the admiring world as a miracle of incontinent fidelity, and the unshaken Abdiel of absence.

Methinks this is as pretty a moral tale as any of Marmontel's. Here is another. The same lady, several years ago, made an escapade with a Swede, Count Fersen (the same whom the Stockholm mob quartered and lapidated not very long since), and they arrived at an Osteria on the road to Rome or thereabouts. It was a summer evening, and, while they were at supper, they were suddenly regaled by a symphony of fiddles in an adjacent apartment, so prettily played, that, wishing to hear them more distinctly, the Count rose, and going into the musical society, said, " Gentlemen, I am sure that, as a company of gallant cavaliers, you will be delighted to show your skill to a lady, who feels anxious ", etc., etc. The men of harmony were all acquiescence—every instrument was tuned and toned, and, striking up one of their most ambrosial airs, the whole band followed the Count to the lady's apartment. At their head was the first fiddler, who, bowing and fiddling at the same moment, headed his troop and advanced up the room. Death and discord!—it was the Marquis himself, who was on a serenading party in the country, while his spouse had run away from town. The rest may be imagined—but, first of all, the lady tried to persuade him that she was there on purpose to meet him, and had chosen this method for an harmonic surprise. So much for this gossip, which amused me when I heard it, and I send it to you in the hope it may have the like effect. Now we'll return to Venice.

The day after to-morrow (to-morrow being Christmas-day) the Carnival begins. I dine with the Countess Albrizzi and a party, and go to the opera. On that day the Phenix, (not the Insurance Office, but) the theatre of that name, opens: I have got me a box there for the season, for two reasons, one of which is, that the music is remarkably good. The Contessa Albrizzi, of whom I have made mention, is the De Stael of Venice; not young, but a very learned, unaffected, good-natured woman; very polite to strangers, and, I believe, not at all dissolute, as most of the women are. She has written very well on the works of Canova, and also a volume of Characters, besides other printed matter. She is of Corfu, but married a dead Venetian—that is, dead since he married.

My flame (my *Donna* whom I spoke of in my former epistle, my Marianna) is still my Marianna, and I her—what she pleases. She is by far the prettiest woman I have seen here, and the most loveable I have met with any where—as well as one of the most singular. I believe I told you the rise and pro-gress of our *liaison* in my former letter. Lest that should not have reached you, I will merely repeat, that she is a Venetian, two-and-twenty years old, married to a merchant well to do in the world, and that she has great black oriental eyes, and all the qualities which her eyes promise. Whether being in love with her has steeled me or not, I do not know; but I have not seen many other women who seem pretty. The nobility, in particular, are a sad-looking race—the gentry rather better. And now, what art *thou* doing?

> What are you doing now,
>   Oh Thomas Moore?
> What are you doing now,
>   Oh Thomas Moore?

>   Sighing or suing now,
>   Rhyming or wooing now,
>   Billing or cooing now,
>   Which, Thomas Moore?

Are you not near the Luddites? By the Lord! if there's a row,
but I'll be among ye! How go on the weavers—the breakers
of frames—the Lutherans of politics—the reformers?

>   As the Liberty lads o'er the sea
>   Bought their freedom, and cheaply, with blood,
>   So we, boys, we
>   Will *die* fighting, or *live* free,
>   And down with all kings but King Ludd!

>   When the web that we weave is complete,
>   And the shuttle exchanged for the sword,
>   We will fling the winding-sheet
>   O'er the despot at our feet,
>   And dye it deep in the gore he has pour'd.

>   Though black as his heart its hue,
>   Since his veins are corrupted to mud,
>   Yet this is the dew
>   Which the tree shall renew
>   Of Liberty, planted by Ludd!

There's an amiable *chanson* for you—all impromptu. I
have written it principally to shock your neighbour * *
[Hodgson?], who is all clergy and loyalty—mirth and innocence—milk and water.

>   But the Carnival's coming,
>   Oh Thomas Moore,
>   The Carnival's coming,
>   Oh Thomas Moore;
>   Masking and mumming,
>   Fifing and drumming,
>   Guitarring and strumming,
>   Oh Thomas Moore.

The other night I saw a new play,—and the author. The
subject was the sacrifice of Isaac. The play succeeded, and they

called for the author—according to continental custom—and
he presented himself, a noble Venetian, Mali—or Malapiero,
by name.   Mala was his name, and *pessima* his production,—
at least, I thought so; and I ought to know, having read more
or less of five hundred Drury Lane offerings, during my co-
adjutorship with the sub-and-super Committee.

When does your poem of poems come out?   I hear that the
Edinburgh Review has cut up Coleridge's *Christabel*, and declared
against me for praising it.   I praised it, firstly, because I thought
well of it; secondly, because Coleridge was in great distress,
and after doing what little I could for him in essentials, I
thought that the public avowal of my good opinion might help
him further, at least with the booksellers.   I am very sorry that
Jeffrey has attacked him, because, poor fellow, it will hurt him
in mind and pocket.   As for me, he's welcome—I shall never
think less of Jeffrey for any thing he may say against me or mine
in future.

I suppose Murray has sent you, or will send (for I do not
know whether they are out or no) the poem, or poesies, of mine,
of last summer.   By the mass! they are sublime—*Ganion
Coheriza*—gainsay who dares!   Pray, let me hear from you, and
of you, and, at least, let me know that you have received these
three letters.   Direct right *here, poste restante.*

Ever and ever, etc.

P.S.—I heard the other day of a pretty trick of a bookseller, who has published some damned nonsense, swearing the
bastards to me, and saying he gave me five hundred guineas
for them.   He lies—I never wrote such stuff, never saw the
poems, nor the publisher of them, in my life, nor had any
communication, directly or indirectly, with the fellow.   Pray
say as much for me, if need be.   I have written to Murray, to
make him contradict the impostor.

TO JOHN MURRAY   *Venice, Dec. 27, 1816*

DEAR SIR,—As the Demon of silence seems to have possessed
you, I am determined to have my revenge in postage.   This is
my sixth or seventh letter since summer and Switzerland.

My last was an injunction to contradict and consign to confusion that Cheapside impostor, who (I heard by a letter from
your Island) had thought proper to append my name to his
spurious poesy, of which I know nothing, nor of his pretended
purchase or copyright. I hope you have, at least, received
that letter.

As the news of Venice must be very interesting to you, I
will regale you with it.

Yesterday being the feast of St. Stephen, every mouth was
put in motion. There was nothing but fiddling and playing on
the virginals, and all kinds of conceits and divertisements, on
every canal of this aquatic city. I dined with the Countess
Albrizzi and a Paduan and Venetian party, and afterwards
went to the opera, at the Fenice theatre (which opens for the
Carnival on that day),—the finest, by the way, I have ever
seen ; it beats *our* theatres hollow in beauty and scenery, and
those of Milan and Brescia bow before it. The opera and its
Syrens were much like all other operas and women, but the
subject of the said opera was something edifying ; it turned—
the plot and conduct thereof—upon a fact narrated by Livy
of a hundred and fifty married ladies having *poisoned* a hundred
and fifty husbands in the good old times. The bachelors of
Rome believed this extraordinary mortality to be merely the
common effect of matrimony or a pestilence ; but the surviving
Benedicts, being all seized with the cholic, examined into the
matter, and found that " their possets had been drugged " ;
the consequence of which was much scandal and several suits
at law. This is really and truly the subject of the Musical piece
at the Fenice ; and you can't conceive what pretty things are
sung and recitativoed about the *horrenda strage*. The conclusion
was a lady's head about to be chopped off by a Lictor, but (I
am sorry to say) he left it on, and she got up and sung a trio
with the two Consuls, the Senate in the back-ground being
chorus. The ballet was distinguished by nothing remarkable,
except that the principal she-dancer went into convulsions
because she was not applauded on her first appearance ; and
the manager came forward to ask if there was " ever a physician
in the theatre ". There was a Greek one in my box, whom I
wished very much to volunteer his services, being sure that in
this case these would have been the last convulsions which

would have troubled the *Ballerina*; but he would not. The crowd was enormous; and in coming out, having a lady under my arm, I was obliged, in making way, almost to " beat a Venetian and traduce the state ", being compelled to regale a person with an English punch in the guts, which sent him as far back as the squeeze and the passage would admit. He did not ask for another; but, with great signs of disapprobation and dismay, appealed to his compatriots, who laughed at him.

I am going on with my Armenian studies in a morning, and assisting and stimulating in the English portion of an English and Armenian grammar, now publishing at the convent of St. Lazarus.

The Superior of the Friars is a bishop, and a fine old fellow, with the beard of a meteor. My spiritual preceptor, pastor and master, Father Paschal, is also a learned and pious soul: he was two years in England.

I am still dreadfully in love with the Adriatic lady whom I spoke of in a former letter (and *not* in *this*—I add, for fear of mistakes; for the only one mentioned in the first part of this epistle is elderly and bookish, two things which I have ceased to admire), and love in this part of the world is no sinecure. This is also the season when every body make up their intrigues for the ensuing year, and cut for partners for the next deal.

And now, if you don't write, I don't know what I won't say or do, nor what I will: send me some news—good news.

Yours very truly, etc., etc., etc. B.

P.S.—Remember me to Mr. G[ifford], with all duty.

I hear that the E[dinburgh] R[eview] has cut up Coleridge's *Christabel*, and me for praising it, which omen, I think, bodes no great good to your forthcome or coming Canto and Castle (of Chillon): my run of luck within the last year seems to have taken a turn every way; but never mind, I will bring myself through in the end—if not, I can but be where I began: in the mean time, I am not displeased to be where I am—I mean, at Venice. My Adriatic nymph is this moment here, and I must therefore repose from this letter, " rocked by the beating of her heart ".

TO JOHN MURRAY †   *Venice, Jan. 2, 1817*

DEAR SIR,—Your letter has arrived. Pray, in publishing the 3ᵈ canto [of *Childe Harold*], have you *omitted* any passage or passages? I hope *not*; and indeed wrote to you on my way over the Alps to prevent such an accident—say in your next whether or not the *whole* of the canto (as sent to you) has been published. I wrote to you again the other day, (*twice*, I think,) and shall be glad to hear of the reception of those letters.

To-day is the 2d of January. On this day *3* years ago *The Corsair's* publication is dated, I think, in my letter to Moore. On this day *two* years I married—" Whom the Lord loveth he chasteneth—blessed be the name of the Lord ".—I sha'n't forget the day in a hurry; and will take care to keep the Anniversary before the Evening is over. It is odd enough that I this day received a letter from you announcing the publication of *Cd. Hd.*, etc., etc., on the day of the date of *The Corsair*; and that I also received one from my Sister, written on the 10th of Decr., my daughter's birth-day (and relative chiefly to my daughter), and arriving on the day of the date of my marriage, this present 2d of January, the month of my birth,— and various other Astrologous matters, which I have no time to enumerate.

By the way, you might as well write to Hentsch, my Genevese banker, and enquire whether the *two packets* consigned to his care were or were not delivered to Mr. St. Aubyn, or if they are still in his keeping. One contains papers, letters, and all the original MS. of your 3ᵈ canto, as first conceived; and the other, some bones from the field of Morat. Many thanks for your news, and the good spirits in which your letter is written.

Venice and I agree very well; but I do not know that I have any thing new to say, except of the last new opera, which I sent in my late letter. The Carnival is commencing, and there is a good deal of fun here and there—besides business; for all the world are making up their intrigues for the season— changing, or going on upon a renewed lease. I am very well off with Marianna, who is not at all a person to tire me; firstly, because I do not tire of a woman *personally*, but because they are generally bores in their disposition; and, secondly, because she is amiable, and has a tact which is not always the portion of the fair creation; and, thirdly, she is very pretty; and, fourthly—but there is no occasion for further specification. I have passed a great deal of my time with her since my arrival at Venice, and never a twenty-four hours without giving and receiving from one to three (and occasionally an extra or so) pretty unequivocal proofs of mutual good contentment. So far we have gone on very well; as to the future, I never anticipate—" *Carpe diem* "—the past at least is one's own, which is one reason for making sure of the present. So much for my proper liaison.

The general state of morals here is much the same as in the Doges' time; a woman is virtuous (according to the code) who limits herself to her husband and one lover; those who have two, three, or more, are a little *wild*; but it is only those who are indiscriminately diffuse, and form a low connection, such as the Princess of Wales with her courier, (who, by the way, is made a knight of Malta,) who are considered as overstepping the modesty of marriage. In Venice, the Nobility have a trick of marrying with dancers or singers: and, truth to say, the women of their own order are by no means handsome; but the general race—the women of the 2^d and other orders, the wives of the Advocates, merchants, and proprietors, and untitled gentry, are mostly *bel' sangue*, and it is with these that the more amatory connections are usually formed: there are also instances of stupendous constancy. I know a woman of fifty who never had but one lover, who dying early, she became devout, renouncing all but her husband: she piques herself, as may be presumed, upon this miraculous fidelity, talking of it occasionally with a species of misplaced morality, which is rather amusing. There is no convincing a woman here, that she is in the smallest degree deviating from the rule of right or the fitness of things, in having an *Amoroso*: the great sin seems to lie in concealing it, or in having more than one; that is, unless such an extension of the prerogative is understood and approved of by the prior claimant.

In my case, I do not know that I had any predecessor, and am pretty sure that there is no participator; and am inclined to think, from the youth of the party, and from the frank undisguised way in which every body avows everything in this part of the world, when there is anything to avow, as well as from some other circumstances, such as the marriage being recent, etc., etc., etc., that this is the *premier pas* : it does not much signify.

In another sheet, I send you some sheets of a grammar, English and Armenian, for the use of the Armenians, of which I promoted, and indeed induced, the publication : (it cost me but a thousand francs—French livres.) I still pursue my lessons in the language, without any rapid progress, but advancing a little daily. Padre Paschal, with some little help from me, as translator of his Italian into English, is also proceeding in an MS. Grammar for the *English* acquisition of Armenian, which will be printed also, when finished.

We want to know if there are any *Armenian types* or letterpress in England—at Oxford, Cambridge, or elsewhere? You know, I suppose, that, many years ago, the two Whistons published in England an original text of a history of Armenia, with their own Latin translation? Do those types still exist? and where? Pray enquire among your learned acquaintance.

When this grammar (I mean the one now printing) is done, will you have any objection to take 40 or fifty copies, which will not cost in all above five or ten guineas, and try the curiosity of the learned with a sale of them? Say yes or no, as you like. I can assure you that they have some very curious books and MS., chiefly translations from Greek originals now lost. They are, besides, a much respected and learned community, and the study of their language was taken up with great ardour by some literary Frenchmen in Buonaparte's time.

I have not done a stitch of poetry since I left Switzerland, and have not, at present, the *estro* upon me : the truth is, that you are *afraid* of having a *4*^{*th*} canto *before* September, and of another copyright; but I have at present no thoughts of resuming that poem nor of beginning any other. If I write, I think of trying prose ; but I dread introducing living people, or applications which might be made to living people : perhaps one day or other, I may attempt some work of fancy in prose, descriptive of Italian manners and of human passions ; but at present I am preoccupied. As for poesy, mine is the *dream* of my sleeping Passions ; when they are awake, I cannot speak their language, only in their Somnambulism, and just now they are not dormant.

If Mr. G[ifford] wants *Carte blanche* as to *The Siege of Corinth*, he has it, and may do as he likes with it.

I sent you a letter contradictory of the Cheapside man (who invented the story you speak of) the other day. My best respects to Mr. Gifford, and such of my friends as you may see at your house. I wish you all prosperity and new year's gratulation, and am

Yours, ever and truly, B.

TO THE HON. DOUGLAS KINNAIRD* *Venice, January 12th, 1817*

MY DEAR KINNAIRD,—Since my arrival in Venice I have written to you *twice*, to request that you would have the goodness to transmit as soon as convenient letters for the credit of such sum or sums as Murray may have paid " according to the tenor " concluded in Septr. last. Address to me here, either Poste restante, or to the care of Messrs Siri and Wilhalm, bankers of this city; it is my intention to remain here probably till Spring. Hobhouse is gone to Rome with his brother and sister but will return in March or so.

I hope that you have received at least one of my letters. In these I told you all the gossip I could think of, and should be glad to have a little in return. To my surprise Murray in a recent letter tells me that you are out of the committee,[1] an event which it requires no great sagacity to attribute to the illustrious Frances Kelly of comic memory. If you recollect (for I am a wonderful judge in all concerns but my own) I forboded long ago disasters to some of you—or us—or one or more, from the intervention of that worthy young woman, and you may also recollect, that for my own part, among the very few pieces of prudence which grace my graceless history, one was to steer very clear of any colloquy or communion with that fair favourite of elderly gentlemen. I don't mean in an immodest way, for she is a Vestal as is well known, but in the

[1] *The Drury Lane Committee*, on which Byron had himself served during his last year in England.

chaster attentions which my coadjutors, including yourself, were accustomed to pay to her. I kept to distant politeness, and verily I have my reward, as you it seems have for being her friend first, and her manager afterwards.

Seriously, if this vexes you I am very sorry for it, but I know nothing of the matter, though I can't help thinking that if I had been at your elbow, and had not lost my temper at the pretty speeches you would have made me in the course of our dialogues, I could have prevented this, at least I should have tried. I say no more. Where the Devil are the other Committed? George, and Mr. Peter Moore? And my locum tenens whosoever he be? You will tell me these matters in your next.

Murray tells me the poems are out, with what success I know not except from his letter, which is written in good spirits. I wonder if he published them as *sent*; if he has made alterations or omissions, I shall not pardon him. I suspect him as a *Tory* of softening my M.S. If he has, by the Ass of Balaam! he shall endure my indignation. He tells me of a row with an Impostor, a bookseller who has been *injunctioned*, by the aid of an *oath* from Scrope Davies. I would give a trifle to see Scrope's affidavit, and to have heard half the good things he has said upon that subject. "Hath he laid perjury upon his soul?" No doubt he will say so, as he always adds his sins to the other obligations he has conferred upon me. When he left Switzerland he was determined to see a " Boa-Constrictor ", God knows why, but whatever he saw, he always wished for the addition of that amiable reptile. I hope that fortune has had the good taste to stick to him, turf or table. Doth he drink as of old?

We were sadly sober all the autumn, but I hope some day or other to revive and quench our antient thirst in the way of our youth. He promised to write; I trust that his affidavit was of a different complexion from his promise.

TO THOMAS MOORE   *Venice, January 28, 1817*

Your letter of the 8th is before me. The remedy for your plethora is simple—abstinence. I was obliged to have recourse to the like some years ago, I mean in point of *diet*, and, with the exception of some convivial weeks and days, (it might be months, now and then), have kept to Pythagoras ever since. For all this, let me hear that you are better. You must not *indulge* in " filthy beer ", nor in porter, nor eat *suppers*—the last are the devil to those who swallow dinner. * * * *

I am truly sorry to hear of your father's misfortune—cruel at any time, but doubly cruel in advanced life. However, you will, at least, have the satisfaction of doing your part by him, and, depend upon it, it will not be in vain. Fortune, to be sure, is a female, but not such a b * * as the rest (always excepting your wife and my sister from such sweeping terms) ; for she generally has some justice in the long run. I have no spite against her, though between her and Nemesis I have had some sore gauntlets to run—but then I have done my best to deserve no better. But to *you*, she is a good deal in arrear, and she will come round—mind if she don't : you have the vigour of life, of independence, of talent, spirit, and character all with you. What you can do for yourself, you have done and will do ; and surely there are some others in the world who would not be sorry to be of use, if you would allow them to be useful, or at least attempt it.

I think of being in England in the spring. If there is a row, by the sceptre of King Ludd, but I'll be there ; and if there is none, and only a continuance of " this meek, piping time of peace ", I will take a cottage a hundred yards to the south of your abode, and become your neighbour ; and we will compose such canticles, and hold such dialogues, as shall be the terror of the *Times* (including the newspaper of that name), and the wonder, and honour, and praise, of the *Morning Chronicle* and posterity.

I rejoice to hear of your forthcoming in February—though I tremble for the " magnificence ", which you attribute to the new *Childe Harold*. I am glad you like it ; it is a fine indistinct piece of poetical desolation, and my favourite. I was half mad during the time of its composition, between metaphysics, mountains, lakes, love unextinguishable, thoughts unutterable, and the nightmare of my own delinquencies. I should, many a good day, have blown my brains out, but for the recollection that it would have given pleasure to my mother-in-law ; and, even *then*, if I could have been certain to haunt her —— but I won't dwell upon these trifling family matters.

Venice is in the *estro* of her carnival, and I have been up these last two nights at the ridotto and the opera, and all that kind of thing. Now for an adventure. A few days ago a gondolier brought me a billet without a subscription, intimating a wish on the part of the writer to meet me either in gondola or at the island of San Lazaro, or at a third rendezvous, indicated in the note. " I know the country's disposition well " —in Venice " they do let Heaven see those tricks they dare not show ", etc., etc.; so, for all response, I said that neither of the three places suited me ; but that I would either be at home at ten at night *alone*, or be at the ridotto at midnight, where the writer might meet me masked. At ten o'clock I was at home and alone (Marianna was gone with her husband to a conversazione), when the door of my apartment opened, and in walked a well-looking and (for an Italian) *bionda* girl of about nineteen, who informed me that she was married to the brother of my *amorosa*, and wished to have some conversation with me. I made a decent reply, and we had some talk in Italian and Romaic (her mother being a Greek of Corfu), when lo ! in a very few minutes, in marches, to my very great astonishment, Marianna Segati, *in propriâ personâ*, and after making a most polite courtesy to her sister-in-law and to me, without a single word seizes her said sister-in-law by the hair, and bestows upon her some sixteen slaps, which would have made your ear ache only to hear their echo. I need not describe the screaming which ensued. The luckless visitor took flight. I seized Marianna, who, after several vain efforts to get away in pursuit of the enemy, fairly went into fits in my arms ; and, in spite of reasoning, eau de Cologne, vinegar, half a pint of water, and God knows what other waters beside, continued so till past midnight.

After damning my servants for letting people in without apprizing me, I found that Marianna in the morning had seen her sister-in-law's gondolier on the stairs, and, suspecting that his apparition boded her no good, had either returned of her own accord, or been followed by her maids or some other spy of her people to the conversazione, from whence she returned to perpetrate this piece of pugilism. I had seen fits before, and also some small scenery of the same genus in and out of our island : but this was not all. After about an hour, in comes— who? why, Signor Segati, her lord and husband, and finds me with his wife fainting upon the sofa, and all the apparatus of confusion, dishevelled hair, hats, handkerchiefs, salts, smelling-bottles—and the lady as pale as ashes, without sense or motion. His first question was, " What is all this? " The lady could not reply—so I did. I told him the explanation was the easiest thing in the world ; but in the mean time it would be as well to recover his wife—at least, her senses. This came about in due time of suspiration and respiration.

You need not be alarmed—jealousy is not the order of the day in Venice, and daggers are out of fashion ; while duels, on love matters, are unknown—at least, with the husbands. But, for all this, it was an awkward affair ; and though he must have known that I made love to Marianna, yet I believe he was not, till that evening, aware of the extent to which it had gone. It is very well known that almost all the married women have a lover ; but it is usual to keep up the forms, as in other nations. I did not, therefore, know what the devil to say. I could not out with the truth, out of regard to her, and I did not choose to lie for my sake ;—besides, the thing told itself. I thought the best way would be to let her explain it as she chose (a woman being never at a loss—the devil always sticks by them)—only determining to protect and carry her off, in case of any ferocity on the part of the Signor. I saw that he was quite calm. She went to bed, and next day—how they settled it, I know not, but settle it they did. Well—then I had to explain to Marianna about this never-to-be-sufficiently-confounded sister-in-law ; which I did by swearing innocence, eternal constancy, etc., etc. * * * But the sister-in-law, very much discomposed with being treated in such wise, has (not having her own shame before her eyes) told the affair to half Venice, and the servants (who were summoned by the fight and the fainting) to the other half. But, here, nobody minds such trifles, except to be amused by them. I don't know whether you will be so, but I have scrawled a long letter out of these follies.

Believe me ever, etc.

TO THOMAS MOORE   *Venice, February 28, 1817*

You will, perhaps, complain as much of the frequency of my letters now, as you were wont to do of their rarity. I think this is the fourth within as many moons. I feel anxious to hear from you, even more than usual, because your last indicated that you were unwell. At present, I am on the invalid regimen myself. The Carnival—that is, the latter part of it, and sitting up late o' nights, had knocked me up a little. But it is over,—and it is now Lent, with all its abstinence and sacred music.

The mumming closed with a masked ball at the Fenice, where I went, as also to most of the ridottos, etc., etc.; and, though I did not dissipate much upon the whole, yet I find " the sword wearing out the scabbard ", though I have but just turned the corner of twenty-nine.

> So we'll go no more a roving
>   So late into the night,
> Though the heart be still as loving,
>   And the moon be still as bright.
>
> For the sword outwears its sheath,
>   And the soul wears out the breast,
> And the heart must pause to breathe,
>   And Love itself have rest.
>
> Though the night was made for loving,
>   And the day returns too soon,
> Yet we'll go no more a roving
>   By the light of the moon.

I have lately had some news of litter*atoor*, as I heard the editor of the *Monthly* pronounce it once upon a time. I hear that W. W.[1] has been publishing and responding to the attacks of the *Quarterly*, in the learned Perry's *Chronicle*. I read his poesies last autumn, and, amongst them found an epitaph on his bull-dog, and another on *myself*. But I beg leave to assure him (like the astrologer Partridge) that I am not only alive now, but was alive also at the time he wrote it. * * Hobhouse has (I hear, also) expectorated a letter against the *Quarterly*,

[1] Wedderburn Webster.

395

addressed to me. I feel awkwardly situated between him and Gifford, both being my friends.

And this is your month of going to press—by the body of Diana! (a Venetian oath,) I feel as anxious—but not fearful for you—as if it were myself coming out in a work of humour, which would, you know, be the antipodes of all my previous publications. I don't think you have any thing to dread but your own reputation. You must keep up to that. As you never showed me a line of your work, I do not even know your measure; but you must send me a copy by Murray forthwith, and then you shall hear what I think. I dare say you are in a pucker. Of all authors, you are the only really *modest* one I ever met with,—which would sound oddly enough to those who recollect your morals when you were young—that is, when you were *extremely* young—I don't mean to stigmatise you either with years or morality.

I believe I told you that the E[*dinburgh*] R[*eview*] had attacked me, in an article on Coleridge (I have not seen it)—" *Et tu*, Jeffrey? "—" there is nothing but roguery in villanous man ". But I absolve him of all attacks, present and future; for I think he had already pushed his clemency in my behoof to the utmost, and I shall always think well of him. I only wonder he did not begin before, as my domestic destruction was a fine opening for all the world, of which all who could did well to avail themselves.

If I live ten years longer, you will see, however, that it is not over with me—I don't mean in literature, for that is nothing; and it may seem odd enough to say, I do not think it my vocation. But you will see that I shall do something or other—the times and fortune permitting—that, " like the cosmogony, or creation of the world, will puzzle the philosophers of all ages ". But I doubt whether my constitution will hold out. I have, at intervals, ex*o*rcised it most devilishly.

I have not yet fixed a time of return, but I think of the spring. I shall have been away a year in April next. You never mention Rogers, nor Hodgson, your clerical neighbour, who has lately got a living near you. Has he also got a child yet?—his desideratum, when I saw him last. * * *

Pray let me hear from you, at your time and leisure, believing me ever and truly and affectionately, etc.

TO THOMAS MOORE   *Venice, March 10, 1817*

I wrote again to you lately, but I hope you won't be sorry to have another epistle. I have been unwell this last month, with a kind of slow and low fever, which fixes upon me at night, and goes off in the morning; but, however, I am now better. In spring it is probable we may meet; at least I intend for England, where I have business, and hope to meet you in *your* restored health and additional laurels.

Murray has sent me the *Quarterly* and the *Edinburgh*. When I tell you that Walter Scott is the author of the article in the former, you will agree with me that such an article is still more honourable to him than to myself. I am perfectly pleased with Jeffrey's also, which I wish you to tell him, with my remembrances—not that I suppose it is of any consequence to him, or ever could have been, whether I am pleased or not, but simply in my private relation to him, as his well-wisher, and it may be one day as his acquaintance. I wish you would also add, what you know, that I was not, and, indeed, am not even *now*, the misanthropical and gloomy gentleman he takes me for, but a facetious companion, well to do with those with whom I am intimate, and as loquacious and laughing as if I were a much cleverer fellow.

I suppose now I shall never be able to shake off my sables in public imagination, more particularly since my moral * * [Clytemnestra?] clove down my fame. However, nor that, nor more than that, has yet extinguished my spirit, which always rises with the rebound.

At Venice we are in Lent, and I have not lately moved out of doors, my feverishness requiring quiet, and—by way of being more quiet—here is the Signora Marianna just come in and seated at my elbow.

Have you seen * * *'s book of poesy? and, if you have seen it, are you not delighted with it? And have you—I really cannot go on : there is a pair of great black eyes looking over my shoulder, like the angel leaning over St. Matthew's, in the old frontispieces to the Evangelists,—so that I must turn and answer them instead of you.

                                              Ever, etc.

Venice, March 25, 1817

I have at last learned, in default of your own writing (or *not* writing—which should it be? for I am not very clear as to the application of the word *default*), from Murray two particulars of (or belonging to) you ; one, that you are removing to Hornsey, which is, I presume, to be nearer London ; and the other, that your poem is announced by the name of *Lalla Rookh*. I am glad of it,—first that we are to have it at last, and next, I like a tough title myself—witness *The Giaour* and *Childe Harold*, which choked half the Blues at starting. Besides, it is the tail of Alcibiades's dog,—not that I suppose you want either dog or tail. Talking of tail, I wish you had not called it a " *Persian Tale* ". Say a " Poem ", or " Romance ", but not " Tale ". I am very sorry that I called some of my own things " Tales ", because I think that they are something better. Besides, we have had Arabian, and Hindoo, and Turkish, and Assyrian Tales. But, after all, this is frivolous in me ; you won't, however, mind my nonsense.

Really and truly, I want you to make a great hit, if only out of self-love, because we happen to be old cronies ; and I have no doubt you will—I am sure you *can*. But you are, I'll be sworn, in a devil of a pucker ; and *I* am *not* at your elbow, and Rogers *is*. I envy him ; which is not fair, because he does not envy any body. Mind you send to me—that is, make Murray send—the moment you are forth.

I have been very ill with a slow fever, which at last took to flying, and became as quick as need be. But, at length, after a week of half-delirium, burning skin, thirst, hot headach, horrible pulsation, and no sleep, by the blessing of barley water, and refusing to see any physician, I recovered. It is an epidemic of the place, which is annual, and visits strangers. Here follow some versicles, which I made one sleepless night.

> I read the " Christabel ",
> Very well :
> I read the " Missionary " ;
> Pretty—very :
> I tried at " Ilderim " ;
> Ahem !

I read a sheet of " Marg'ret of *Anjou* " ;
    Can you ?
I turn'd a page of Webster's " Waterloo " ;
    Pooh ! pooh !
I look'd at Wordsworth's milk-white " Rylstone Doe " :
    Hillo !
I read " Glenarvon ", too, by Caro. Lamb—
    God damn !

    *   *   *   *   *   *   *

I have not the least idea where I am going, nor what I am to do. I wished to have gone to Rome; but at present it is pestilent with English,—a parcel of staring boobies, who go about gaping and wishing to be at once cheap and magnificent. A man is a fool who travels now in France or Italy, till this tribe of wretches is swept home again. In two or three years the first rush will be over, and the Continent will be roomy and agreeable.

I stayed at Venice chiefly because it is not one of their " dens of thieves " ; and here they but pause and pass. In Switzerland it was really noxious. Luckily, I was early, and had got the prettiest place on all the Lake before they were quickened into motion with the rest of the reptiles. But they crossed me every where. I met a family of children and old women half-way up the Wengen Alp (by the Jungfrau) upon mules, some of them too old and others too young to be the least aware of what they saw.

By the way, I think the Jungfrau, and all that region of Alps, which I traversed in September—going to the very top of the Wengen, which is not the highest (the Jungfrau itself is inaccessible) but the best point of view—much finer than Mont-Blanc and Chamouni, or the Simplon. I kept a journal of the whole for my sister Augusta, part of which she copied and let Murray see.

I wrote a sort of mad Drama,[1] for the sake of introducing the Alpine scenery in description : and this I sent lately to Murray. Almost all the *dram. pers.* are spirits, ghosts, or magicians, and the scene is in the Alps and the other world, so you may suppose what a Bedlam tragedy it must be : make him show it you. I

[1] *Manfred.*

sent him all three acts piecemeal, by the post, and suppose they have arrived.

I have now written to you at least six letters, or letter*ets*, and all I have received in return is a note about the length you used to write from Bury Street to St. James's Street, when we used to dine with Rogers, and talk laxly, and go to parties, and hear poor Sheridan now and then. Do you remember one night he was so tipsy, that I was forced to put his cocked hat on for him,—for he could not,—and I let him down at Brookes's, much as he must since have been let down into his grave. Heigh ho! I wish I was drunk—but I have nothing but this damned barley-water before me.

I am still in love,—which is a dreadful drawback in quitting a place, and I can't stay at Venice much longer. What I shall do on this point I don't know. The girl means to go with me, but I do not like this for her own sake. I have had so many conflicts in my own mind on this subject, that I am not at all sure they did not help me to the fever I mentioned above. I am certainly very much attached to her, and I have cause to be so, if you knew all. But she has a child; and though, like all the " children of the sun ", she consults nothing but passion, it is necessary I should think for both; and it is only the virtuous, like * * * *, who can afford to give up husband and child, and live happy ever after.

The Italian ethics are the most singular ever met with. The perversion, not only of action, but of reasoning, is singular in the women. It is not that they do not consider the thing itself as wrong, and very wrong, but *love* (the *sentiment* of love) is not merely an excuse for it, but makes it an *actual virtue*, provided it is disinterested, and not a *caprice*, and is confined to one object. They have awful notions of constancy; for I have seen some ancient figures of eighty pointed out as *Amorosi* of forty, fifty, and sixty years' standing. I can't say I have ever seen a husband and wife so coupled.

Ever, etc.

P.S.—Marianna, to whom I have just translated what I have written on our subject to you, says—" If you loved me thoroughly, you would not make so many fine reflections, which are only good *forbirsi i scarpi* ",—that is, " to clean shoes withal ",—a Venetian proverb of appreciation, which is applicable to reasoning of all kinds.

TO JOHN CAM HOBHOUSE †   *Venice, March 31st, 1817*

My dear Hobhouse,—In verity, the *malaria* was a pretext, as I knew it was a summer and not a spring production, but the English crowd of the Holy Week was as sincere an excuse as need to be.

Since I wrote to you I have had a fever, like one I had from the marshes of Elis, which nearly finished me at Patras, but this was milder, and of shorter duration; it, however, left me weakly. It had been approaching by slow degrees ever since the Carnival, and at last came on rather sharply. It was not, however, the low, vulgar typhus, which is at present decimating Venice, and has half unpeopled Milan; but a sharp, gentlemanly fever that went away in a few days. I saw no physician; they sent for one without telling me, and when I heard he was below I had him sent out of the house. And so I recovered. It was not Aglietti, I believe, but you may be sure if it had [been], that prig should never have had a fee of mine.

At present I am very well, with a monstrous appetite. I think of coming on to Rome this ensuing month; in case you should be gone, will you delegate some friend to get me in without custom-house research, and will you tell me what hostel or inn I am to lay down my wallet in, and how about lodgement? Truly wroth am I to hear the rumours you wot of, particularly the first, but one is as false as the other. The origin of the latter I take to be a lie which was rife here about the *Fabre* or *Fabri* (which is it?), the singer from Milan—the girl we saw there. She sang here, at the Fenice, during the Carnival; and was in high and magnificent maintenance by a Sig^r Papadopoli, a Venetian of great wealth and concupiscence. But a man in a cloak was seen coming out of her abode one very early morning, and this man they would have to be me (I never saw her in my life but on the stage), and not content with this, it was added that I had decamped with her for Naples; and I had as much difficulty in proving my presence here, as Partridge in re-establishing his existence. The origin of these unseemly reports I take to be a translation in some Venetian gazette of the Jena review of C. L.'s *Glenarvon*, and another of the last canto of C. H^d, the one stating the scratching attempt at canicide of that " two-handed whore " at Lady Heathcote's, and the other representing me as the most decided panegyrist of Buonaparte. I have, you may be sure, noticed neither one, nor the other of these matters.

The Quarterly I have read (which is written by Walter Scott, so M[urray] says). Both it and the " Edinburgh " are as favourable as the author could wish; and more so than could be wished by anybody else; the Edin^h is by Jeffrey himself: I am very glad that anybody likes the Canto, but particularly glad that Baillie does, because he is a very superior if not a *supreme* man; as for you and I, we are such old friends that " we have travelled over one another's minds long ago "; don't you remember what a pet that sentence used to put you into? But never mind, is it not true.

In case you should not have heard from England, I will tell you some news of litera*toor*. K[innaird] writes to me that Mrs. K., under the colours of Keppel, has become " *a* PUBLIC *character* ", at Drury Lane as well as at Covent Garden, with great success. I suppose he means, of course, as a singer, but it is as well to be distinct.

Maturin's second tragedy, he says, has not succeeded, and he gives some very good reasons why it should not, which sound remarkably well, particularly as his very last letter save this anticipated its " complete success."

For my part I say nothing; but this I will say, Did I *ever*? No, I *never*, etc., etc., etc., etc., etc., etc., etc. Do you understand me? No one else can.

I have heard of my daughter, who is very fine they say; but there is a dispute about her suscitated between me and my moral Clytemnestra. Some day or other Ada will become my Orestes, and Electra too, both in one.

This dispute will probably end in a lawsuit. Having heard that they thought of voyaging, I refused to allow the child to leave the country, and demanded an explicit declaration that on no account should the attempt be made; this was evaded, and at last a sort of half reluctant kind of paper signed, which I have refused to accept, and so we are all at, or about, law.

That old fool Noel,[1] last year, I hear for the first time, had filed a bill in Chancery against me, upon some remote question of property, purely to make my daughter a ward of the Court and circumscribe my right over her, or rather my authority. I can tell you, however, that Hanson has behaved very well, and briskly in this business, for I have copies of the correspondence.

They have begun, and, by the Lord, I must go on—pretty separation! We are as fast as ever, only pulling the chain different ways, till one of us tumbles. My star is sure to win in the long run.

You do not say a word of your " paradoxes ", or of the Pope—only think of Dr. Polidori coming too!—well! I'm sure! Is he any sager? I suppose you mean that despicable lisping old ox and charlatan, Frederic North, by the successor to Ld Guilford. Of all the perambulating humbuggerers, that aged nondescript is the principal.

I send you a catalogue of some books " of poeshie of the king, my master ", as Freytag said to Voltaire:

> I read the " Christabel ".
>   Very well.
> I read the " Missionary ",
>   Somewhat visionary.
> I tried at " Ilderim ",
>   Ahem!
> I read a sheet of " Margaret of *Anjou* ",
>   Can *you*?
> I skimmed a page of Webster's " Waterloo ",
>   Pooh! Pooh!
> I looked at Wordsworth's milkwhite " Rylstone Doe ",
>   Hillo!!
> I read " Glenarvon ", too, by Caro. Lamb,
>   God damn.

I have bought several books which must be left for my bankers to forward to England; amongst others a complete Voltaire, in ninety-two volumes, whom I have been reading; he is delightful, but dreadfully inaccurate frequently. One of

---

[1] Sir Ralph Milbanke. Lady Milbanke had assumed the name of Noel on the death of her brother, Lord Wentworth, whose heiress Annabella Byron was.

his paragraphs (in a letter) begins " *Jean Jacques* is a Jean *foutre* " which he seems to say with all his heart and soul. This is one of the things which make me laugh—being a " clever Tom Clinch " and perhaps will have the like effect on you.

Yours ever, and very truly and affectly., B.

My best respects to your brother. I congratulate him.

TO JOHN MURRAY †   *Venice, April 2, 1817*

DEAR SIR,—I sent you the whole of the Drama at *three several* times, act by act, in separate covers. I hope that you have, or will receive, some or the whole of it.

So Love has a conscience. By Diana! I shall make him take back the box,[1] though it were Pandora's. The discovery of its intrinsic silver occurred on sending it to have the lid adapted to admit Marianna's portrait. Of course I had the box remitted *in statu quo*, and had the picture set in another, which suits it (the picture) very well. The defaulting box is not touched, hardly,—it was not in the man's hands above an hour.

I am aware of what you say of Otway; and am a very great admirer of his,—all except of that maudlin bitch of chaste lewdness and blubbering curiosity, Belvidera, whom I utterly despise, abhor, and detest; but the story of Marino Falieri is different, and, I think, so much finer, that I wish Otway had taken it instead: the head conspiring against the body for refusal of redress for a real injury,—jealousy—treason, with the more fixed and inveterate passions (mixed with policy) of an old or elderly man—the devil himself could not have a finer subject, and he is your only tragic dramatist.

Voltaire has asked *why* no woman has ever written even a tolerable tragedy? " Ah (said the Patriarch) the composition of a tragedy requires * * *." If this be true, Lord knows what Joanna Baillie does; I suppose she borrows them.

There is still, in the Doge's Palace, the black veil painted over Falieri's picture, and the staircase whereon he was first crowned Doge, and subsequently decapitated. This was the thing that most struck my imagination in Venice—more than

---

[1] Byron had discovered that a box purchased from a London jeweller as gold was, in fact, of silver gilt.

the Rialto, which I visited for the sake of Shylock; and more, too, than Schiller's " Armenian ", a novel which took a great hold of me when a boy. It is also called the " Ghost Seer ", and I never walked down St. Mark's by moonlight without thinking of it, and " *at nine o'clock he died!* "—But I hate things *all fiction* ; and therefore the *Merchant* and *Othello* have no great associations to me : but *Pierre* has. There should always be some foundation of fact for the most airy fabric, and pure invention is but the talent of a liar.

Maturin's tragedy.—By your account of him last year to me, he seemed a bit of a coxcomb, personally. Poor fellow ! to be sure, he had had a long seasoning of adversity, which is not so hard to bear as t'other thing. I hope that this won't throw him back into the " slough of Despond ". Let him take heart—" whom the Lord loveth he chasteneth ; blessed be the name of the Lord ! " This sentence, by the way, is a contrast to the other one of *Quem Deus vult perdere prius dementat*, which may be thus done into English :—

" God maddens him whom 'tis his will to lose,
    And gives the choice of death or phrenzy—choose."

You talk of " marriage " ;—ever since my own funeral, the word makes me giddy, and throws me into a cold sweat. Pray, don't repeat it.

Tell me that Walter Scott is better ; I would not have him ill for the world. I suppose it was by sympathy that I had my fever at the same time. I joy in the success of your *Quarterly* ; but I must still stick by the *Edinburgh*. Jeffrey has done so by me, I must say, through everything, and this is more than I deserved from him. I have more than once acknowledged to you by letter the " Article " (and articles) ; say that you have received the said letters, as I do not otherwise know what letters arrive. Both reviews came, but nothing more. M[aturin]'s play, and the extract not yet come.

There have been two articles in the Venice papers, one a Review of C. Lamb's *Glenarvon* (whom may it please the bene-ficent Giver of all Good to damn in the next world ! as she has damned herself in this) with the account of her scratching attempt at *Canicide* (at Lady Heathcote's), and the other a Review of *Childe Harold*, in which it proclaims me the most rebellious and contumacious admirer of Buonaparte now surviving in Europe. Both these articles are translations from the Literary Gazette of German Jena. I forgot to mention them at the time; they are some weeks old. They actually mentioned Caro: Lamb and her *mother's* name at full length. I have conserved these papers as curiosities.

Write to say whether or no my Magician has arrived, with all his scenes, spells, etc.

Yours ever, B.

P.S.—Will you tell Mr. Kinnaird that the two recent letters I wrote to him were, owing to a mistake of a booby of a Partner of Siri and Wilhalm (the Bankers here), and that one of them called this morning to say all was right—and that there was no occasion for a further letter; however, heaven knows whether they are right or not. I hope I shall not have the same bother at Rome.

You should close with Madame de Stael. This will be her best work, and permanéntly historical; it is on her father, the Revolution, and Buonaparte, etc. Bonstetten told me in Switzerland it was *very great*. I have not seen it myself, but the author often. She was very kind to me at Copet.

I like your delicacy—*you* who print *Margaret*—and *Ilderim* and then demur at Corinne. The failure of poor M's play will be a cordial to the aged heart of Saul,[1] who has been " kicking against the pricks " of the managers so long and so vainly— they ought to act his *Ivan*; as for Kean he is an " *infidus Scurra* ", and his conduct on this occasion is of a piece with all one ever heard of him. Pray look after *Mr. St Aubin*. He is an Oxonian. It is very odd and something more than negligent that he has not consigned the letters, etc.; it was his own offer.

It is useless to send to the *Foreign Office*: nothing arrives to me by that conveyance. I suppose some zealous clerk thinks it a Tory duty to prevent it.

TO THE HON. AUGUSTA LEIGH   *Rome, May 10th 1817*

MY DEAREST AUGUSTA,—I have taken a flight down here see the Map), but shall return to Venice in fifteen days from

---

[1] Sotheby, whose *Saul* was published in 1807.

this date, so address all answers to my usual head- (or rather heart-) quarters—that is to Venice. I am very well, quite recovered, and as is always the case after all illness—particularly fever—got large, ruddy, and robustous to a degree which would please you—and shock me. I have been on horseback several hours a day for this last ten days, besides now and then on my journey; proof positive of high health, and curiosity, and exercise. Love me—and don't be afraid—I mean of my sicknesses. I get well, and shall always get so, and have luck enough still to beat most things; and whether I win or not—depend upon it—I will fight to the last.

Will you tell my wife " mine excellent Wife " that she is brewing a Cataract for herself and me in these foolish equivocations about *Ada*,—a job for lawyers—and more hatred for every body, for which—(God knows), there is no occasion. She is surrounded by people who detest me—Brougham the lawyer—who never forgave me for saying that Mrs G^e Lamb was a damned fool (by the way I did not then know he was in love with her) in 1814, and for a former savage note in my foolish satire, all which is good reason for *him*—but not for *Lady Bⁿ*; besides her mother—etc etc etc—so that what I may say or you may say is of no great use—however—*say it*. If she supposes that I want to hate or plague her (however wroth circumstances at times may make me in words and in temporary gusts or disgusts of feeling), she is quite out—I have no such wish—and never had, and if she imagines that I now wish to become united to her again she is still more out. *I never will*. I *would* to the end of the *year* succeeding our separation— (expired nearly a month ago, *Legal reckoning*), according to a resolution I had taken thereupon—but the day and the hour is gone by—and it is irrevocable. But all this is no reason for further misery and quarrel; Give me but a *fair share* of my daughter—the half—my natural right and authority, and I am content; otherwise I come to England, and " law and claw before they get it ", all which will vex and out live Sir R. & L^y N. besides making Mrs Clermont bilious—and plaguing Bell herself, which I really by the great God ! wish to avoid. Now pray see her and say so—it may do good—and if not—she and I are but what we are, and God knows that is wretched enough—at least to me.

Of Rome I say nothing—you can read the Guide-book—which is very accurate.

I found here an old letter of yours dated November 1816 —to which the best answer I can make—is none. You are sadly timid my child, but so you all shewed yourselves when you could have been useful—particularly ——— but never mind. I shall not forget *him*, though I do not rejoice in any ill which befalls him. Is the fool's spawn a *son* or a *daughter*? you say one —and others another; so Sykes works him—*let him*—I shall live to see him and W. destroyed, and more than them—and then—but let all that pass for the present.

yrs. ever B.

P.S.—Hobhouse is here. I travelled from V—— *quite alone* so do not fuss about women etc—I am not so rash as I have been.

TO JOHN MURRAY *Venice, May 30, 1817*

DEAR SIR,—I returned from Rome two days ago, and have received your letter; but no sign nor tidings of the parcel sent through Sir ——— Stuart, which you mention. After an interval of months, a packet of *Tales*, etc., found me at Rome; but this is all, and may be all that ever will find me. The post seems to be the only sane conveyance; and *that only for letters*. From Florence I sent you a poem on Tasso, and from Rome the new third act of *Manfred*, and by Dr. Polidori two pictures for my sister. I left Rome, and made a rapid journey home. You will continue to direct here as usual. Mr. Hobhouse is gone to Naples: I should have run down there too for a week, but for the quantity of English whom I heard of there. I prefer hating them at a distance; unless an earthquake, or a good real eruption of Vesuvius, were insured to reconcile me to their vicinity.

I know no other situation except Hell which I should feel inclined to participate with them—as a race, always excepting several individuals. There were few of them in Rome, and I believe none whom you know, except that old Blue-*bore* Sotheby, who will give a fine account of Italy, in which he will be greatly assisted by his total ignorance of Italian, and yet this is the translator of Tasso.

The day before I left Rome I saw three robbers guillotined. The ceremony—including the *masqued* priests; the half-naked executioners; the bandaged criminals; the black Christ and his banner; the scaffold; the soldiery; the slow procession, and the quick rattle and heavy fall of the axe; the splash of the blood, and the ghastliness of the exposed heads—is altogether more impressive than the vulgar and ungentlemanly dirty " new drop ", and dog-like agony of infliction upon the sufferers of the English sentence. Two of these men behaved calmly enough, but the first of the three died with great terror and reluctance, which was very horrible. He would not lie down; then his neck was too large for the aperture, and the priest was obliged to drown his exclamations by still louder exhortations. The head was off before the eye could trace the blow; but from an attempt to draw back the head, notwithstanding it was held forward by the hair, the first head was cut off close to the ears: the other two were taken off more cleanly. It is better than the oriental way, and (I should think) than the axe of our ancestors. The pain seems little; and yet the effect to the spectator, and the preparation to the criminal, are very striking and chilling. The first turned me quite hot and thirsty, and made me shake so that I could hardly hold the opera-glass (I was close, but determined to see, as one should see every thing, once, with attention); the second and third (which shows how dreadfully soon things grow indifferent), I am ashamed to say, had no effect on me as a horror, though I would have saved them if I could.

It is some time since I heard from you—the 12*th April* I believe.

Yours ever truly, B.

TO THE HON. AUGUSTA LEIGH   *Venice, June 3ᵈ 1817*

DEAREST AUGUSTA—I returned home a few days ago from Rome but wrote to you on the road; at Florence I believe, or Bologna. The last city you know—or do not know—is celebrated for the production of Popes—Cardinals—painters—and sausages—besides a female professor of anatomy, who has left there many models of the art in waxwork, some of them not the most decent.—I have received all your letters I believe, which are full of woes, as usual, megrims and mysteries; but my sympathies remain in suspense, for, for the life of me I can't make out whether your disorder is a broken heart or the earache—or whether it is *you* that have been ill or the children —or what your melancholy and mysterious apprehensions tend to, or refer to, whether to Caroline Lamb's novels—Mrs Clermont's evidence—Lady Byron's magnanimity—or any other piece of imposture; I know nothing of what you are in the doldrums about at present. I should think all that could affect *you* must have been over long ago; and as for me— leave me to take care of myself. I may be ill or well—in high or low spirits—in quick or obtuse state of feelings—like any body else, but I can battle my way through; better than your exquisite piece of helplessness G. L.[1] or that other poor creature George Byron, who will be finely helped up in a year or two with his new state of life—I should like to know what they would do in my situation, or in any situation. I wish well to your George, who is the best of the two a devilish deal—but as for the other I shan't forget him in a hurry, and if I ever forgive or allow an opportunity to escape of evincing my sense of his conduct (and of more than his) on a certain occasion—write me down—what you will, but do not suppose me asleep. " Let them look to their bond "—sooner or later time and Nemesis will give me the ascendant—and then " let them look to their bond ". I do not of course allude only to that poor wretch, but to all—to the 3ᵈ and 4ᵗʰ generation of these accursed Amalekites and the woman who has been the stumbling block of my——

June 4ᵗʰ 1817

I left off yesterday at the stumbling block of my Midianite marriage—but having received your letter of the 20ᵗʰ May I will be in good humour for the rest of this letter. I had hoped you would like the miniatures, at least one of them, which is in pretty good health; the other is thin enough to be sure—and

---

[1] Colonel Leigh, Augusta's husband.

so was I—and in the ebb of a fever when I sate for it.   By the
" man of fashion " I suppose you mean that poor piece of
affectation and imitation Wilmot—another disgrace to me
and mine—that fellow.   I regret not having shot him, which the
persuasions of others—and circumstances which at that time
would have rendered combats presumptions against my cause
—prevented.   I wish you well of your indispositions which I
hope are slight, or I should lose my senses.

Yours ever very and truly   B.

TO JOHN MURRAY   *La Mira,*[1] *near Venice, July 1, 1817*

DEAR SIR,—Since my former letter, I have been working
up my impressions into a 4th Canto of *Childe Harold*, of which I
have roughened off about rather better than thirty stanzas,
and mean to go on ; and probably to make this " Fytte " the
concluding one of the poem, so that you may propose against
the Autumn to draw out the Conscription for 1818.   You must
provide monies, as this new resumption bodes you certain
disbursements ;   somewhere about the end of September or
October, I propose to be under way (*i.e.* in the press) ; but I
have no idea yet of the probable length or calibre of the canto,
or what it will be good for ; but I mean to be as mercenary
as possible, an example (I do not mean of any individual in
particular, and least of all any person or persons of our mutual
acquaintance) which I should have followed in my youth, and
I might still have been a prosperous gentleman.

No tooth-powder, no packet of letters, no recent tidings of
you.

Mr. Lewis is at Venice, and I am going up to stay a week
with him there—as it is one of his enthusiasms also to like the
city.

> I stood in Venice, on the " Bridge of Sighs " ;
>   A palace and a prison on each hand :
>   I saw from out the wave her structures rise
>
> As from the stroke of $\left\{{an \atop the}\right\}$ Enchanter's wand :

[1] Byron's summer residence on the Brenta.

A thousand Years their cloudy wings expand
Around me, and a dying Glory smiles
O'er the far times when many a subject land
Looked to the winged Lion's marble piles,
  Where Venice sate in state, throned on her Seventy Isles.

The " Bridge of Sighs " (*i.e. Ponte dei sospiri*) is that which
divides, or rather joins, the palace of the Doge to the prison of
the state. It has two passages : the criminal went by the one
to judgement, and returned by the other to death, being
strangled in a chamber adjoining, where there was a mechanical
process for the purpose.

This is the first stanza of the new canto ; and now for a line
of the second :—

In Venice, Tasso's echo is no more,
  And silent rows the songless gondolier,
    Her palaces, etc., etc.

You know that formerly the gondoliers sang always, and
Tasso's *Gerusalemme* was their ballad. Venice is built on seventy-
two islands.

There ! there's a brick of your new Babel ! and now, sirrah !
what say you to the sample?

Yours most sincerely, B^N

P.S.—I shall write again by and bye.

TO THOMAS MOORE   *La Mira, Venice, July 10, 1817*

Murray, the Mokanna of booksellers, has contrived to
send me extracts from *Lalla Rookh* by the post. They are taken
from some magazine, and contain a short outline and quotations
from the two first Poems. I am very much delighted with
what is before me, and very thirsty for the rest. You have
caught the colours as if you had been in the rainbow, and the
tone of the East is perfectly preserved : so that * * * and its
author must be somewhat in the background, and learn that it
requires something more than to have been upon the hunch
of a dromedary to compose a good oriental story. I am glad
you have changed the title from " Persian Tale ". * * * *

I suspect you have written a devilish fine composition, and I rejoice in it from my heart; because " the Douglas and the Percy both together are confident against a world in arms ". I hope you won't be affronted at my looking on us as " birds of a feather "; though, on whatever subject you had written, I should have been very happy in your success.

There is a simile of an orange-tree's " flowers and fruits ", which I should have liked better if I did not believe it to be a reflection on * * *.

Do you remember Thurlow's poem to Sam—" *When* Rogers "; and that damned supper at Rancliffe's that ought to have been a *dinner*? " Ah, Master Shallow, we have heard the chimes at midnight." But,

> My boat is on the shore,
>   And my bark is on the sea;
> But, before I go, Tom Moore,
>   Here's a double health to thee!
>
> Here's a sigh to those who love me,
>   And a smile to those who hate;
> And whatever sky's above me,
>   Here's a heart for every fate.
>
> Though the ocean roar around me,
>   Yet it still shall bear me on;
> Though a desert should surround me,
>   It hath springs that may be won.
>
> Were't the last drop in the well,
>   As I gasp'd upon the brink,
> Ere my fainting spirit fell,
>   'Tis to thee that I would drink.
>
> With that water, as this wine,
>   The libation I would pour
> Should be—peace with thine and mine,
>   And a health to thee, Tom Moore.

This should have been written fifteen moons ago—the first stanza was. I am just come out from an hour's swim in the Adriatic; and I write to you with a black-eyed Venetian girl before me, reading Boccaccio. * * *

Last week I had a row on the road (I came up to Venice from my casino, a few miles on the Paduan road, this blessed day, to bathe) with a fellow in a carriage, who was impudent to my horse. I gave him a swingeing box on the ear, which sent him to the police, who dismissed his complaint. Witnesses had seen the transaction. He first shouted, in an unseemly way, to frighten my palfry. I wheeled round, rode up to the window, and asked him what he meant. He grinned, and said some foolery, which produced him an immediate slap in the face, to his utter discomfiture. Much blasphemy ensued, and some menace, which I stopped by dismounting and opening the carriage door, and intimating an intention of mending the road with his immediate remains, if he did not hold his tongue. He held it.

Monk Lewis is here—" how pleasant ! " He is a very good fellow, and very much yours. So is Sam—so is every body— and amongst the number,

Yours ever, B.

P.S.—What think you of *Manfred* ? * * * *

TO JOHN MURRAY †   *La Mira, near Venice, August 21, 1817*

DEAR SIR,—I take you at your word about Mr. Hanson, and will feel obliged if you will *go* to him, and request Mr. Davies also to visit him by my desire, and repeat that I trust that neither Mr. Kinnaird's absence nor mine will prevent his taking all proper steps to accelerate and promote the sales of Newstead and Rochdale, upon which the whole of my future personal comfort depends. It is impossible for me to express how much any delays upon these points would inconvenience me ; and I do not know a greater obligation that can be con-ferred upon me than the pressing these things upon Hanson, and making him act according to my wishes. I wish you would *speak out*, at least to *me*, and tell me what you allude to by your odd way of mentioning him. All mysteries at such a distance are not merely tormenting but mischievous, and may be pre-judicial to my interests ; so, pray expound, that I may consult with Mr. Kinnaird when he arrives ; and remember that I

prefer the most disagreeable certainties to hints and inuendos.
The devil take every body : I never can get any person to
be explicit about any thing or any body, and my whole life is
passed in conjectures of what people mean : you all talk in the
style of Caroline Lamb's novels.

It is not Mr. St. John, but *Mr. St. Aubyn*, son of Sir John
St. Aubyn. *Polidori* knows him, and introduced him to me.
He is of Oxford, and has got my parcel. The Doctor will
ferret him out, or ought. The parcel contains many letters,
some of Madame de Stael's, and other people's, besides MSS.,
etc. By G—d, if I find the gentleman, and he don't find the
parcel, I will say something he won't like to hear.

You want a " civil and delicate declension " for the medical
tragedy? [1]   Take it—

> Dear Doctor,—I have read your play,
> Which is a good one in its way,
> Purges the eyes, and moves the bowels,
> And drenches handkerchiefs like towels
> With tears, that, in a flux of grief,
> Afford hysterical relief
> To shatter'd nerves and quicken'd pulses,
> Which your catastrophe convulses.
> I like your moral and machinery ;
> Your plot, too, has such scope for Scenery !
> Your dialogue is apt and smart ;
> The play's concoction full of art ;
> Your hero raves, your heroine cries,
> All stab, and every body dies ;
> In short, your tragedy would be
> The very thing to hear and see ;
> And for a piece of publication,
> If I decline on this occasion,
> It is not that I am not sensible
> To merits in themselves ostensible,
> But—and I grieve to speak it—plays
> Are drugs—mere drugs, Sir, nowadays.

[1] Dr. Polidori's latest freak had been to compose a tragedy, which he submitted
to Murray.

I had a heavy loss by *Manuel*,—
Too lucky if it prove not annual,—
And Sotheby, with his damned *Orestes*,
(Which, by the way, the old Bore's best is,)
Has lain so very long on hand
That I despair of all demand ;
I've advertized,—but see my books,
Or only watch my Shopman's looks ;—
Still *Ivan*, *Ina*, and such lumber,
My back-shop glut,—my shelves encumber.
There's Byron too, who once did better,
Has sent me—folded in a letter—
A sort of—it's no more a drama
Than *Darnley*, *Ivan*, or *Kehama* :
So altered since last year his pen is,
I think he's lost his wits at Venice,
Or drained his brains away as stallion
To some dark-eyed and warm Italian ;
In short, sir, what with one and t'other,
I dare not venture on another.
I write in haste ; excuse each blunder ;
The Coaches through the street so thunder !
My Room's so full ; we've Gifford here
Reading MSS., with Hookham Frere,
Pronouncing on the nouns and particles
Of some of our forthcoming articles,
The *Quarterly*—Ah, sir, if you
Had but the Genius to review !—
A smart Critique upon St. Helena,
Or if you only would but tell in a
Short compass what——but, to resume ;
As I was saying, Sir, the Room—
The Room's so full of wits and bards,
Crabbes, Campbells, Crokers, Freres, and Wards,
And others, neither bards nor wits :—
My humble tenement admits
All persons in the dress of Gent.,
From Mr. Hammond to Dog Dent.
A party dines with me today,
All clever men who make their way :

Crabbe, Malcolm, Hamilton, and Chantrey,
Are all partakers of my pantry.
They're at this moment in discussion
On poor De Staël's late dissolution.
Her book, they say, was in advance—
Pray Heaven! she tell the truth of France!
'Tis said she certainly was married
To Rocca, and had twice miscarried,
No—not miscarried, I opine,—
But brought to bed at forty-nine.
Some say she died a Papist; Some
Are of opinion *that's* a Hum;
I don't know that—the fellow, Schlegel,
Was very likely to inveigle
A dying person in compunction
To try the extremity of Unction.
But peace be with her! for a woman
Her talents surely were uncommon.
Her Publisher (and Public too)
The hour of her demise may rue—
For never more within his shop he—
Pray—was not she interred at Coppet?
Thus run our time and tongues away;—
But, to return, Sir, to your play;
Sorry, Sir, but I cannot deal,
Unless 'twere acted by O'Neill.
My hands are full—my head so busy,
I'm almost dead—and always dizzy;
And so, with endless truth and hurry,
Dear Doctor, I am yours,

JOHN MURRAY.

August, 1817.

P.S.—I've done the 4th and last Canto, which mounts to
133 stanzas. I desire you to name a price; if you don't, *I* will;
so I advise you in time.

Yours, etc.

There will be a good many notes.

TO JOHN MURRAY   *September 15, 1817*

DEAR SIR,—I enclose a sheet for correction, if ever you get to another edition. You will observe that the blunder in printing makes it appear as if the Château was *over* St. Gingo, instead of being on the opposite shore of the Lake, over Clarens. So, separate the paragraphs, otherwise my *to*pography will seem as inaccurate as your *ty*pography on this occasion.

The other day I wrote to convey my proposition with regard to the 4th and concluding canto. I have gone over and extended it to one hundred and fifty stanzas, which is almost as long as the two first were originally, and longer by itself than any of the smaller poems except *The Corsair*. Mr. Hobhouse has made some very valuable and accurate notes of considerable length, and you may be sure I will do for the text all that I can to finish with decency. I look upon *Childe Harold* as my best; and as I begun, I think of concluding with it. But I make no resolutions on that head, as I broke my former intention with regard to *The Corsair*. However, I fear that I shall never do better; and yet, not being thirty years of age, for some moons to come, one ought to be progressive as far as Intellect goes for many a good year. But I have had a devilish deal of wear and tear of mind and body in my time, besides having published too often and much already. God grant me some judgement! to do what may be most fitting in that and every thing else, for I doubt my own exceedingly.

I have read *Lallah Rookh*, but not with sufficient attention yet, for I ride about, and lounge, and ponder, and—two or three other things; so that my reading is very desultory, and not so attentive as it used to be. I am very glad to hear of its popularity, for Moore is a very noble fellow in all respects, and will enjoy it without any of the bad feeling which success—good or evil—sometimes engenders in the men of rhyme. Of the poem itself, I will tell you my opinion when I have mastered it : I say of the *poem*, for I don't like the *prose* at all—at all; and in the mean time, the " Fire worshippers " is the best, and the " Veiled Prophet " the worst, of the volume.

With regard to poetry in general, I am convinced, the more I think of it, that he and *all* of us—Scott, Southey, Wordsworth, Moore, Cambell, I,—are all in the wrong, one as much as another; that we are upon a wrong revolutionary poetical system, or systems, not worth a damn in itself, and from which none but Rogers and Crabbe are free; and that the present and next generations will finally be of this opinion. I am the more confirmed in this by having lately gone over some of our classics, particularly *Pope*, whom I tried in this way, —I took Moore's poems and my own and some others, and went over them side by side with Pope's, and I was really astonished (I ought not to have been so) and mortified at the ineffable distance in point of sense, harmony, effect, and even *Imagination*, passion, and *Invention*, between the little Queen Anne's man, and us of the Lower Empire. Depend upon it, it is all Horace then, and Claudian now, among us; and if I had to begin again, I would model myself accordingly. Crabbe's the man, but he has got a coarse and impracticable subject, and Rogers, the Grandfather of living Poetry, is retired upon half-pay, (I don't mean as a Banker),—

> Since pretty Miss Jaqueline,
> With her nose aquiline,

and has done enough, unless he were to do as he did formerly.

TO JOHN MURRAY † *Venice, January 27, 1818*

DEAR SIR,—My father—that is, not God the Father, but my father in God, my Armenian father, Padre Pasquali—in the name of all the other fathers of our convent, sends you the inclosed greeting.

Inasmuch as it has pleased the translators of the long-lost and lately-found portions of the text of Eusebius to put forth the inclosed prospectus, of which I send six copies, you are hereby implored to obtain Subscribers in the two Universities, and among the learned, and the unlearned who would unlearn their ignorance.—This *they* (the Convent) request, *I* request, and *do you* request.

I sent you *Beppo* some weeks agone. You had best publish it alone; it has politics and ferocity, and won't do for your Isthmus of a Journal.

Mr. Hobhouse, if the Alps have not broken his neck, is, or ought to be, swimming with my Commentaries and his own coat of Mail in his teeth and right hand, in a cork jacket, between Calais and Dover.

It is the height of the Carnival, and I am in the *estrum* and agonies of a new intrigue with I don't exactly know whom or what, except that she is insatiate of love, and won't take money, and has light hair and blue eyes, which are not common here, and that I met her at the Masque, and that when her mask is off, I am as wise as ever. I shall make what I can of the remainder of my youth, and confess, that, like Augustus, I would rather die *standing*.

B.

TO JOHN MURRAY *Venice, Feb. 20, 1818*

DEAR SIR,—I have to thank Mr. Croker for the arrival, and you for the Continents, of the parcel which came last week, much quicker than any before, owing to Mr. C.'s kind attention, and the official exterior of the bags; and all safe, except much fraction amongst the magnesia, of which only two bottles came entire; but it is all very well, and I am exceedingly obliged to you.

The books I have read, or rather am reading. Pray, who may be the Sexagenarian, whose gossip is very amusing? Many of his sketches I recognise, particularly Gifford, Mackintosh, Drummond, Dutens, H. Walpole, Mrs. Inchbald, Opie, etc., with the Scotts, Loughborough, and most of the divines and lawyers, besides a few shorter hints of authors, and a few lines about a certain " *Noble Author*", characterised as Malignant and Sceptical, according to the good old story " as it was in the beginning, is now, but *not* always shall be " : do you know such a person, Master Murray? eh?—And pray, of the Booksellers, which be *you*? the dry, the dirty, the honest, the opulent, the finical, the splendid, or the Coxcomb Bookseller? " Stap my vitals ", but the author grows scurrilous in his grand Climacteric !

I remember to have seen Porson [1] at Cambridge, in the Hall of our College, and in private parties, but not frequently : and I never can recollect him except as drunk or brutal, and generally both : I mean in an evening, for in the hall he dined at the Dean's table, and I at the Vice-master's, so that I was not near him ; and he then and there appeared sober in his demeanour, nor did I ever hear of excess or outrage on his part in public,—Commons, college, or Chapel ; but I have seen him in a private party of undergraduates, many of them freshmen and strangers—take up a poker to one of them, and heard him use language as blackguard as his action. I have seen Sheridan drunk, too, with all the world ; but his intoxication was that of Bacchus, and Porson's that of Silenus. Of all the disgusting brutes, sulky, abusive, and intolerable, Porson was the most bestial, as far as the few times that I saw him went, which were only at William Bankes's (the Nubian Discoverer's) rooms. I saw him once go away in a rage, because nobody knew the name of the " Cobbler of Messina ", insulting their ignorance with the most vulgar terms of reprobation. He was tolerated in this state amongst the young men for his talents—as the Turks think a Madman inspired, and bear with him. He used to recite, or rather vomit, pages of all languages, and could hiccup Greek like a Helot ; and certainly Sparta never shocked her children with a grosser exhibition than this man's intoxication.

[1] Professor Richard Porson, the celebrated classical scholar, 1759–1808.

I perceive, in the book you sent me, a long account of him; of Gilbert Wakefield's account of him, which is very savage, I cannot judge, as I never saw him sober, except in *Hall* or Combination-room; and then I was never near enough to hear, and hardly to see him. Of his drunken deportment I can be sure, because I saw it.

With the Reviews I have been much entertained. It requires to be as far from England as I am to relish a periodical paper properly: it is like Soda-water in an Italian Summer. But what cruel work you make with Lady Morgan!—You should recollect that she is a woman; though, to be sure, they are now and then very provoking: still, as authoresses, they can do no great harm; and I think it a pity so much good invective should have been laid out upon her, when there is such a fine field of us Jacobin gentlemen for you to work upon. It is perhaps as bitter a Critique as ever was written, and enough to make sad work for Dr. Morgan, both as a husband and an Apothecary, unless she should say as Pope did, of some attack upon him, " that it is as good for *her* as a dose of *Hartshorn* ".

I heard from Moore lately, and was very sorry to be made aware of his domestic loss. Thus it is—*medio de fonte leporum*—in the acmé of his fame and of his happiness comes a drawback as usual.

His letter, somehow or other, was more than two months on the road, so that I could only answer it the other day. What you tell me of Rogers in your last letter is like him; but he had best let *us*, that is one of us, if not both, alone. He cannot say that I have not been a sincere and a warm friend to him, till the black drop of his liver oozed through, too palpably to be overlooked. Now, if I once catch him at any of his jugglery with me or mine, let him look to it, for, if I spare him then, write me down a good-natured gentleman; and the more that I have been deceived,—the more that I once relied upon him,—I don't mean his petty friendship (what is that to me?), but his *good* will, which I really tried to obtain, thinking him at first a good fellow,—the more will I pay off the balance; and so, if he values his quiet, let him look to it; in three months I could restore him to the Catacombs.

Mr. Hoppner, whom I saw this morning, has been made the father of a very fine boy.—Mother and child doing very well indeed. By this time Hobhouse should be with you, and also certain packets, letters, etc., of mine, sent since his departure.—I am not at all well in health within this last eight days.. My remembrances to Gifford and all friends.

Yours, B.

P.S.—In the course of a month or two, Hanson will have probably to send off a clerk with conveyances to sign (Newstead being sold in November last for ninety-four thousand and five hundred pounds), in which case I supplicate supplies of articles as usual, for which desire Mr. Kinnaird to settle from funds in their bank, and deduct from my account with him.

P.S.—To-morrow night I am going to see *Otello*, an opera from our *Othello*, and one of Rossini's best, it is said. It will be curious to see in Venice the Venetian story itself represented, besides to discover what they will make of Shakespeare in Music.

TO THOMAS MOORE   *Venice, March 16, 1818*

MY DEAR TOM,—Since my last, which I hope that you have received, I have had a letter from our friend Samuel. He talks of Italy this summer—won't you come with him? I don't know whether you would like our Italian way of life or not. * * * * *

They are an odd people. The other day I was telling a girl, " You must not come to-morrow, because Margueritta [Cogni] is coming at such a time ",—(they are both about five feet ten inches high, with great black eyes and fine figures—fit to breed gladiators from—and I had some difficulty to prevent a battle upon a rencontre once before)—" unless you promise to be friends, and "—the answer was an interruption, by a declaration of war against the other, which she said would be a *Guerra di Candia*. Is it not odd, that the lower order of Venetians should still allude proverbially to that famous contest, so glorious and so fatal to the Republic?

They have singular expressions, like all Italians. For example, *Viscere*—as we should say, " My love ", or " My heart ", as an expression of tenderness. Also, " I would go for you into the midst of a hundred *knives* ".—" *Mazza ben* ", excessive attachment,—literally, " I wish you well even to killing ". Then they say (instead of our way, " Do you think I would do you such harm? ") " Do you think I would *assassinate* you in such a manner? "—" *Tempo perfido* ", bad weather; " *Strade perfide* ", bad roads,—with a thousand other allusions and metaphors, taken from the state of society and habits in the middle ages.

I am not so sure about *mazza*, whether it don't mean *massa*, i.e. a great deal, a *mass*, instead of the interpretation I have given it. But of the other phrases I am sure.

Three o' th' clock—I must " to bed, to bed, to bed ", as mother Siddons, that tragical friend of the mathematical * * *, says. * * * * *

Have you ever seen—I forget what or whom—no matter. They tell me Lady Melbourne is very unwell. I shall be so sorry. She was my greatest *friend*, of the feminine gender :— when I say " friend ", I mean *not* mistress, for that's the antipode. Tell me all about you and every body—how Sam is— how you like your neighbours, the Marquis and Marchesa, etc., etc.

Ever, etc.

TO THE HON. DOUGLAS KINNAIRD *Venice, April 23rd, 1818*

DEAR DOUGLAS,—I will *not* go to Geneva, and I look upon the proposition as a very gross neglect on the part of Hanson, and an affront on that of my friends, including you, Davies, Hobhouse, and everybody else. The messenger must come here—is it not evident that the expense and trouble must be less for the man and papers to come to me, than for me to go to the man and papers? At any rate, and at any cost, I won't stir ; and if anything occurs, it is all *your* faults for not taking better care of my interests, besides wanting to drag me a mile nearer to your infernal country.

" Poor Maria "—um ! I do not understand the particulars, nor wish to hear them ; all I know is that she made your house very pleasant to your friends, and as far as I know, made no mischief (which is saying infinitely for a woman), and therefore whatever has, or may happen, she has my good will, go where she will. I understand that you have provided for her in the handsomest manner, which is in your nature, and don't surprise me:—as far as prudence goes, you are in the right to dissolve such a connection; and as to provocation, doubtless you had sufficient, but I can't help being sorry for the woman—although she did tell you that I made love to her—which, by the God of Scrope Davies! was not true—for I never dreamed of making love to anything of yours, except sixty pints of brandy, sixty years old—all, or the greater part of which, I consumed in your suppers. God help me, I was very sorry when they were no more.

Now to business—" Shylock! I must have monies ", so have at Spooney [1] for Noel's and Newstead arrears, and have at Murray for coming copyrights, and let me have a credit forthwith—I am in cash, but I don't like to break in upon my *circular* notes—in case of a journey—or changing my residence, but look to my finance department, and above all, *don't lecture me*, for I won't bear it, and will run savage.

Make the *messenger proceed* to Geneva; and send him a letter therefor, that we may conclude the Newstead sale, and if you can sell, or settle a sale for Rochdale—do. Newstead has done well so far.

Do not suppose that I will be induced to return towards England for less than the most imperious motives, but believe me always

Yrs. B.

P.S.—Don't mind Hobhouse, he would whistle me home—that is, to his home if he could; but " thaut's impossible " for the son and heir of Sir Wm Meadows. So look to it, and don't conspire against me or my quiet.

TO JOHN MURRAY   *April 23, 1818*

DEAR SIR,—The time is past in which I could feel for the dead,—or I should feel for the death of Lady Melbourne, the best, and kindest, and ablest female I ever knew—old or young. But " I have supped full of horrors ", and events of this kind leave only a kind of numbness worse than pain,—

---

[1] Byron's nickname for Hanson.

like a violent blow on the elbow, or on the head. There is one link the less between England and myself.

Now to business. I presented you with *Beppo*, as part of the contract for Canto 4th,—considering the price you are to pay for the same, and intending it to eke you out in case of public caprice or my own poetical failure. If you choose to suppress it entirely, at Mr. Sotheby's suggestion, you may do as you please. But recollect it is not to be published in a *garbled* or *mutilated* state. I reserve to my friends and myself the right of correcting the press;—if the publication continue, it is to continue in its present form.

If Mr. S. fancies, or feels, himself alluded to and injured by the allusion, he has his redress—by law—by reply—or by such other remedy personal or poetical as may seem good to himself, or any person or persons acting for, by, or at his suggestion.

My reasons for presuming Mr. S. to be the author of the anonymous note sent to me at Rome last Spring, with a copy of " Chillon ", etc., with marginal notes by the writer of the billet were—firstly, Similarity in the handwriting: of which I could form a recollection from correspondence between Mr. S. and myself on the subject of *Ivan* a play offered to D. L. Theatre; 2dly, the *Style*, more especially the word " *Effulgence* ", a phrase which clinched my conjecture as decisively as any coincidence between Francis and Junius: 3dly, the paucity of English *then* at Rome, and the circumstances of Mr. S.'s return from Naples, and the delivery of this note and book occurring at the same period, he having then and there arrived with a party of Blue-Stocking Bi—women, I would say, of the same complexion whom he afterwards conveyed to the Abbate Morelli's at Venice—to view his Cameo, where they so tormented the poor old man (nearly twenty in number, all with pencil and note book in hand and questions in infamous Italian and villainous French), that it became the talk of Venice, as you may find by asking my friend Mr. Hoppner or others who were then at Venice; 4^{thly}, my being aware of Mr. S.'s patronage and anxiety on such occasions, which led me to the belief that, with very good intentions, he might nevertheless blunder in his mode of giving as well as taking opinions; and 5^{thly}, the Devil who made Mr. S. one author and me another.

As Mr. Sotheby says that he did not write this letter, etc., I am ready to believe him; but for the firmness of my former persuasion, I refer to Mr. Hobhouse, who can inform you how sincerely I erred on this point. He has also the note—or, at least, *had* it, for I gave it to him with my verbal comments thereupon. As to *Beppo*, I will not alter or suppress a syllable for any man's pleasure but my own.

If there are resemblances between Botherby and Sotheby, or Sotheby and Botherby, the fault is not mine, but in the person who resembles,—or the persons who trace a resemblance. *Who* find out this resemblance? Mr. S.'s *friends*. *Who* go about moaning over him and laughing? Mr. S.'s *friends*. Whatever allusions Mr. S. may imagine, or whatever may or may not really exist, in the passages in question, I can assure him that there is not a literary man, or a pretender to Literature, or a reader of the day—in the World of London, who does not think and express more obnoxious opinions of his Blue-Stocking Mummeries than are to be found in print, and I for one think and say that, to the best of my knowledge and belief, from past experience and present information, Mr. Sotheby has made, and makes, himself highly ridiculous.

He may be an amiable man, a moral man, a good father, a good husband, a respectable and devout individual. I have nothing to say against all this; but I have something to say to Mr. S.'s literary foibles, and to the wretched affectations and systematized Sophistry of many men, women, and Children, now extant and absurd in and about London and elsewhere;— which and whom, in their false pretensions and nauseous attempts to make learning a nuisance and society a Bore, I consider as fair game—to be brought down on all fair occasions, and I doubt not, by the blessing of God on my honest purpose, and the former example of Mr. Gifford and others, my betters, before my eyes, to extirpate, extinguish and eradicate such as come within the compass of my intention. And this is my opinion, of which you will express as much or as little as you think proper.

Did you receive two additional stanzas, to be inserted towards the close of Canto 4th? Respond, that (if not) they may be sent.

Tell Mr. Hobhouse and Mr. Hanson that they may as well

expect Geneva to come to me, as that I should go to Geneva. The messenger may go on or return, as he pleases; I won't stir: and I look upon it as a piece of singular absurdity in those who know me imagining that I should;—not to say *Malice*, in attempting unnecessary torture. If, on the occasion, my interests should suffer, it is their neglect that is to blame; and they may all be damned together. You may tell them this, and add that nothing but force or necessity shall stir me one step towards the places to which they would wring me. I wonder particularly at Mr. Hobhouse's (who is in possession of my opinions) sanctioning such a conspiracy against my tranquillity.

If your literary matters prosper, let me know. If *Beppo* pleases, you shall have more in a year or two in the same mood. And so " Good morrow to you, good Master Lieutenant ".

Yours, B.

TO JOHN CAM HOBHOUSE [1]   *Venice, June, 1818*

SIR,—With great grief I inform you of the death of my late dear Master, my Lord, who died this morning at ten of the

[1] It is interesting to compare this letter which purports to be from Byron's valet, Fletcher, with the letter Fletcher actually wrote from Missolonghi in April, 1824:

TO JOHN MURRY ESQRE   *Missolonghi, April 21st, 1824*

SIR,—Forgive Me for this Intrusion which I now am under the Painfull Necessity of wrighting to you to Inform you of the Malloncolly News of My Lord Byron whom his no more he Departed This Miserable Life on the 19 of April after an Illness of onley 10 Days his Lordship Began by a Nervious Feavor and Terminated with an Inflammation on the Brains For want of being Bled in time which his Lordship Refused till it was Too Late I have sent The Honble. Mrs. Leighs Letter Inclosed in yours which I think would Be Better for you to open and Explain to Mrs. Leigh For I fear the Contents of the Letter will be too much For her and you will Please to Inform Lady Byron and the Honble. Miss Byron whom I am wished to see when I Return with My Lords Effects and his Dear and Noble Remains Sir you will Please Mannage in the most Mildest way Possable or I am much affraid of the Consequences Sir you will Please give my duty to Lady Byron Hoping she will allow me to see Her by My Lords Pertickeler wish and Miss Byron Likewise Please to Excuse all Deffects for I scearseley Now what I either Say or Do for after 20 Years Services To My Lord he was more to me than a father and I am too much Distressed to now give a Correct accompt of every Pertickeler which I hope to Do at my arrival in England Sir you will likewise have the Goodness to Forward the Letter To The Honble. Capt. George

Clock of a rapid decline and slow fever, caused by anxiety, sea-bathing, women, and riding in the Sun against my advice.

He is a dreadful loss to every body, mostly to me, who have lost a master and a place—also, I hope you, Sir, will give me a charakter.

I saved in his service as you know several hundred pounds. God knows how, for I don't, nor my late master neither; and if my wage was not always paid to the day, still it was or is to be paid sometime and somehow. You, Sir, who are his executioner won't see a poor Servant wronged of his little all.

My dear Master had several phisicians and a Priest: he died a Papish, but is to be buried among the Jews in the Jewish burying ground; for my part I don't see why—he could not abide them when living nor any other people, hating whores who asked him for money.

He suffered his illness with great patience, except that when in extremity he twice damned his friends and said they were selfish rascals—you, Sir, particularly and Mr. Kinnaird, who had never answered his letters nor complied with his repeated requests. He also said he hoped that your new tragedy would be damned—God forgive him—I hope that my master won't be damned like the tragedy.

His nine whores are already provided for, and the other servants; but what is to become of me? I have got his Cloathes and Carriages, and Cash, and everything; but the Consul quite against law has clapt his seal and taken an inventary and swears that *he* must account to my Lord's heirs—who they are, I don't know—but they ought to consider poor Servants and above all his Vally de Sham.

Byron whom has the Representative of the family and title I thought it my duty To send him a Line But you Sir will Please to Explain to him all Pertickelers has I have not time has the Express his now Ready to make his voyage Day and Night till he arrives in London I must Sir Praying forgiveness and Hopeing at the same time that you will so far oblige me has to Execute all my wishes which I am well Convinced you will not Refuse I Remain Sir

your Most Obt. and Verry Humble

Servant W Fletcher

valet to The Late

L.B. For 20 years

P.S.—I mention My Name and Capacity that you may Remember and forgive this when you Remember the Quantity of times I have been at your house in Albemarle Street.

My Lord never grudged me perquisites—my wage was the least I got by him; and if I did keep the Countess (she is, or ought to be, a Countess, although she is upon the town) Marietta Monetta Piretta, after passing my word to you and my Lord that I would not never no more—still he was an indulgent master, and only said I was a damned fool, and swore and forgot it again. What could I do? she said as how she should die, or kill herself if I did not go with her, and so I did— and kept her out of my Lord's washing and ironing—and nobody can deny that, although the charge was high, the linen was well got up.

Hope you are well, Sir—am, with tears in my eyes,
　　　　　　Yours faithfoolly to command, Wᴹ Fletcher

P.S.—If you know any Gentleman in want of a Wally— hope for a charakter. I saw your late Swiss Servant in the Galleys at Leghorn for robbing an Inn—he produced your recommendation at his triál.

TO THOMAS MOORE　　　　*Palazzo Mocenigo, Grande Canal, Venice,*
June 1, 1818

Your letter is almost the only news, as yet, of Canto fourth, and it has by no means settled its fate—at least, does not tell me how the " Poeshie " has been received by the public. But, I suspect, no great things,—firstly, from Murray's " horrid stillness "; secondly, from what you say about the stanzas running into each other, which I take *not* to be *yours*, but a notion you have been dinned with among the Blues. The fact is, that the *terza rima* of the Italians, which always *runs* on and in, may have lead me into experiments, and carelessness into conceit—or conceit into carelessness—in either of which events failure will be probable, and my fair woman, *superne*, end in a fish; so that *Childe Harold* will be like the mermaid, my family crest, with the fourth Canto for a tail thereunto. I won't quarrel with the public, however, for the " Bulgars " are generally right; and if I miss now, I may hit another time :— and so, the " gods give us joy ".

You like *Beppo*, that's right. I have not had the Fudges[1] yet, but live in hopes. I need not say that your successes are mine. By the way, Lydia White is here, and has just borrowed my copy of *Lalla Rookh*. * *

Hunt's letter is probably the exact piece of vulgar coxcombry you might expect from his situation. He is a good man, with some poetical elements in his chaos; but spoilt by the Christ-Church Hospital and a Sunday newspaper,—to say nothing of the Surrey gaol, which conceited him into a martyr. But he is a good man. When I saw *Rimini* in MS., I told him that I deemed it good poetry at bottom, disfigured only by a strange style. His answer was, that his style was a system, or *upon system*, or some such cant; and, when a man talks of system, his case is hopeless : so I said no more to him, and very little to any one else.

He believes his trash of vulgar phrases tortured into compound barbarisms to be *old* English; and we may say of it as Aimwell says of Captain Gibbet's regiment, when the Captain calls it an " old corps ",—" the *oldest* in Europe, if I may judge by your uniform ". He sent out his *Foliage* by Percy Shelley * * *, and, of all the ineffable Centaurs that were ever begotten by Self-love upon a Night-mare, I think " this monstrous Sagittary " the most prodigious. *He* (Leigh H.) is an honest charlatan, who has persuaded himself into a belief of his own impostures, and talks Punch in pure simplicity of heart, taking himself (as poor Fitzgerald said of *him*self in the *Morning Post*) for *Vates* in both senses, or nonsenses, of the word. Did you look at the translations of his own which he prefers to Pope and Cowper, and says so?—Did you read his skimble-skamble about Wordsworth being at the head of his own *profession*, in the *eyes* of *those* who followed it? I thought that poetry was an *art*, or an *attribute*, and not a *profession*;—but be it one, is that * * * * * * at the head of *your* profession in *your* eyes? I'll be curst if he is of *mine*, or ever shall be. He is the only one of us (but of us he is not) whose coronation I would oppose. Let them take Scott, Campbell, Crabbe, or you, or me, or any of the living, and throne him;—but not this new Jacob Behmen, this * * * * * * whose pride might have kept him true, even had his principles turned as perverted as his *soi-disant* poetry.

[1] The reference is to Moore's *Fudge Family in Paris*, etc.

But Leigh Hunt is a good man, and a good father—see his Odes to all the Masters Hunt;—a good husband—see his Sonnet to Mrs. Hunt;—a good friend—see his Epistles to different people;—and a great coxcomb and a very vulgar person in every thing about him. But that's not his fault, but of circumstances.

    *   *   *   *   *   *   *
    *   *   *   *   *   *   *

I do not know any good model for a life of Sheridan but that of *Savage*. Recollect, however, that the life of such a man may be made far more amusing than if he had been a Wilberforce;—and this without offending the living, or insulting the dead. The Whigs abuse him; however, he never left them, and such blunderers deserve neither credit nor compassion.—As for his creditors,—remember, Sheridan *never had* a shilling, and was thrown, with great powers and passions, into the thick of the world, and placed upon the pinnacle of success, with no other external means to support him in his elevation. Did Fox * * * *pay his* debts?—or did Sheridan take a subscription? Was the * *'s drunkenness more excusable than his? Were his intrigues more notorious than those of all his contemporaries? and is his memory to be blasted, and theirs respected? Don't let yourself be led away by clamour, but compare him with the coalitioner Fox, and the pensioner Burke, as a man of principle, and with ten hundred thousand in personal views, and with none in talent, for he beat them all *out* and *out*. Without means, without connexion, without character, (which might be false at first, and make him mad afterwards from desperation,) he beat them all, in all he ever attempted. But alas, poor human nature! Good night or rather, morning. It is four, and the dawn gleams over the Grand Canal, and unshadows the Rialto. I must to bed; up all night—but, as George Philpot says, " it's life, though, damme it's life ! "

Ever yours, B.

Excuse errors—no time for revision. The post goes out at noon, and I shan't be up then. I will write again soon about your *plan* for a publication.

TO THE HON. DOUGLAS KINNAIRD * *Venice, July 15th, 1818*

DEAR DOUGLAS,—I hear wonders of your popular eloquence [1] and speeches to the mobility, from all quarters, and I see by the papers that Captain Lemchen [2] has been well nigh slain by a *potatoe*, so the Italian Gazettes have it; it serves him right, a fellow who has lost three ships, an Orang-outang, a Boa Constrictor (they both died in the passage), and an Election—he be damned. How came Burdett not to be at the head of the poll?

Murray's letters and the credits are come, laud we the Gods! If I did not know of old, Wildman [3] to be a Man of honour, and Spooney a damned tortoise in all his proceeds, I should suspect foul play in this delay of the man and papers; now that your politics are a little subsided, for God his sake, row the man of law, spur him, kick him on the Crickle, do something, any thing, you are my power of Attorney, and I thereby empower you to use it and abuse Hanson, till the fellow says or does something as a gentleman should do.

I am in Venice, instead of summering it at Este, writing for the Clerk and the conveyances, but, " why tarry the wheels of his Chariot? "

I hear of Scrope and his jests, and Hobhouse and his toils; I wish you all the pleasure such pursuits can afford, and as much success as usually attends them.

I have lately had a long swim (beating an Italian all to bubbles) of more than four miles, from Lido to the other end of the Grand Canal, that is the part which enters from Mestri. I won by a good three quarters of a mile, and as many quarters of an hour, knocking the Chevalier up, and coming in myself quite fresh; the fellow had swum the Beresina in the Bonaparte Campaign, and thought of coping with " our Youth ", but it would not do.

Give my love to Scrope and the rest of us ragmuffins, and believe me yours ever and truly,

BYRON

Pray look very sharp after Spooney; I have my suspicions, my suspicions, Sir, my Suspicions.

---

[1] Kinnaird, like Hobhouse, took an active part in the Westminster election.

[2] Captain Sir Murray Maxwell, R.N., the Tory candidate.

[3] Newstead was purchased by Byron's old school-fellow, Colonel Wildman, in November 1817 for £94,500.

TO THOMAS MOORE   *Venice, September 19, 1818*

An English newspaper here would be a prodigy, and an opposition one a monster; and except some extracts *from* extracts in the vile, garbled Paris gazettes, nothing of the kind reaches the Veneto-Lombard public, who are, perhaps, the most oppressed in Europe. My correspondences with England are mostly on business, and chiefly with my attorney, who has no very exalted notion, or extensive conception, of an author's attributes; for he once took up an *Edinburgh Review*, and, looking at it a minute, said to me, " So, I see you have got into the magazine ",—which is the only sentence I ever heard him utter upon literary matters, or the men thereof.

My first news of your Irish Apotheosis has, consequently, been from yourself. But, as it will not be forgotten in a hurry, either by your friends or your enemies, I hope to have it more in detail from some of the former, and, in the mean time, I wish you joy with all my heart. Such a moment must have been a good deal better than Westminster Abbey,—besides being an assurance of *that* one day (many years hence, I trust), into the bargain.

I am sorry to perceive, however, by the close of your letter, that even *you* have not escaped the *surgit amari*, etc., and that your damned deputy has been gathering such " dew from the still *vext* Bermoothes "—or rather *vexatious*. Pray, give me some items of the affair, as you say it is a serious one; and, if it grows more so, you should make a trip over here for a few months, to see how things turn out. I suppose you are a violent admirer of England by your staying so long in it. For my own part, I have passed, between the age of one-and-twenty and thirty, half the intervenient years out of it without regretting any thing, except that I ever returned to it at all, and the gloomy prospect before me of business and parentage obliging me, one day, to return to it again,—at least, for the transaction of affairs, the signing of papers, and inspecting of children.

I have here my natural daughter, by name Allegra,—a pretty little girl enough, and reckoned like papa. Her mamma is English,—but it is a long story, and—there's an end. She is about twenty months old.   * * *

434

I have finished the first canto (a long one, of about 180 octaves) of a poem in the style and manner of *Beppo*, encouraged by the good success of the same. It is called *Don Juan*, and is meant to be a little quietly facetious upon everything. But I doubt whether it is not—at least, as far as it has yet gone—too free for these very modest days. However, I shall try the experiment, anonymously; and if it don't take, it will be discontinued. It is dedicated to Southey in good, simple, savage verse, upon the Laureat's politics, and the way he got them. But the bore of copying it out is intolerable; and if I had an amanuensis he would be of no use, as my writing is so difficult to decipher.

> My poem's Epic, and is meant to be
>   Divided in twelve books, each book containing,
> With love and war, a heavy gale at sea—
>   A list of ships, and captains, and kings reigning—
> New characters, etc., etc.

The above are two stanzas, which I send you as a brick of my Babel, and by which you can judge of the texture of the structure.

In writing the *Life* of Sheridan, never mind the angry lies of the humbug Whigs. Recollect that he was an Irishman and a clever fellow, and that *we* have had some very pleasant days with him. Don't forget that he was at school at Harrow, where, in my time, we used to show his name—R. B. Sheridan, 1765,—as an honour to the walls. Remember * * * * * * *. Depend upon it that there were worse folks going, of that gang, than ever Sheridan was.

What did Parr [1] mean by "haughtiness and coldness"? I listened to him with admiring ignorance, and respectful silence. What more could a talker for fame have?—they don't like to be answered. It was at Payne Knight's I met him, where he gave me more Greek than I could carry away. But I certainly meant to (and *did*) treat him with the most respectful deference.

I wish you a good night, with a Venetian benediction, "*Benedetto te, e la terra che ti fara!* "—" May you be blessed, and the *earth* which you will *make*! "—is it not pretty? You would think it still prettier if you had heard it, as I did two hours ago,

---

[1] Dr. Samuel Parr, the celebrated pedagogue.

from the lips of a Venetian girl, with large black eyes, a face like Faustina's, and the figure of a Juno—tall and energetic as a Pythoness, with eyes flashing, and her dark hair streaming in the moonlight—one of those women who may be made any thing. I am sure if I put a poniard into the hand of this one, she would plunge it where I told her,—and into *me*, if I offended her. I like this kind of animal, and am sure that I should have preferred Medea to any woman that ever breathed. You may, perhaps, wonder that I don't in that case. * * * I could have forgiven the dagger or the bowl,—any thing, but the deliberate desolation piled upon me, when I stood alone upon my hearth, with my household gods shivered around me. * * Do you suppose I have forgotten it? It has comparatively swallowed up in me every other feeling, and I am only a spectator upon earth, till a tenfold opportunity offers. It may come yet. There are others more to be blamed than * * * *, and it is on these that my eyes are fixed unceasingly.

TO THE HON. AUGUSTA LEIGH   *Venice, Sep^{tr} 21st 1818*

DEAREST AUGUSTA,—I particularly beg that you will contrive to get the enclosed letter safely delivered to Lady Frances, and if there is an answer to let me have it. You can write to her first and state that you have such a letter—at my request—for there is no occasion for any concealment at least with· *her*—and pray oblige me so far, for many reasons.

If the Queen dies you are no more a Maid of Honour—is it not so? Allegra is well, but her mother (whom the Devil confound) came prancing the other day over the Appennines—to see her *shild*; which threw my Venetian loves (who are none of the quietest) into great combustion; and I was in a pucker till I got her to the Euganean hills, where she and the child now are, for the present. I declined seeing her for fear that the consequence might be an addition to the family; she is to have the child a month with her and then to return herself to Lucca, or Naples, where she was with her relatives (she is English you know), and to send Allegra to Venice again. I lent her my house at Este for her maternal holidays. As troubles don't come single, here is another confusion. The chaste wife of a baker—having quarrelled with her tyrannical husband—has run away *to* me (God knows without being invited), and resists all the tears and penitence and beg-pardons of her disconsolate Lord, and the threats of the police, and the priest of the parish besides; and swears she won't give up her unlawful love (myself), for any body, or any thing. I assure you I have begged her in all possible ways too to go back to her husband, promising her all kinds of eternal fidelity into the bargain, but she only flies into a fury; and as she is a very tall and formidable Girl of three and twenty, with the large black eyes and handsome face of a pretty fiend, a correspondent figure and a carriage as haughty as a Princess—with the violent passions and capacities for mischief of an Italian when they are roused—I am a little embarrassed with my unexpected acquisition. However she keeps my household in rare order, and has already frightened the learned Fletcher out of his remnants of wits more than once; we have turned her into a housekeeper. As the morals of this place are very lax, all the women commend her and say she has done right—especially her own relations. You need not be alarmed—I know how to manage her—and can deal with anything but a cold blooded animal such as Miss Milbanke. The worst is that she won't let a woman come into the house, unless she is as old and frightful as possible; and has sent so many to the right about that my former female acquaintances are equally frightened and angry. She is extremely fond of the child, and is very cheerful and good-natured, when not jealous; but Othello himself was a fool to her in that respect. Her soubriquet in her family was *la Mora* from her colour, as she is very dark (though clear of complexion), which literally means *the Moor* so that I have " the Moor of Venice " in propria persona as part of my household. She has been here this month. I had known her (and fifty others) more than a year, but did not anticipate this escapade, which was the fault of her booby husband's treatment—who now runs about repenting and roaring like a bull calf. I told him to take her in the devil's name, but she would not stir; and made him a long speech in the Venetian dialect which was more entertaining to anybody than to him to whom it was addressed. You see Goose—that there is no quiet in this world —so be a good woman—and repent of y^r sins.——

437

TO LADY BYRON   *Venice, Novr 18th 1818*

Sir Samuel Romilly has cut his throat for the loss of his wife.[1]
It is now nearly three years since he became, in the face of his
compact (by a retainer—previous, and, I believe, general),
the advocate of the measures and the Approver of the proceedings, which deprived me of mine. I would not exactly,
like Mr. Thwackum, when Philosopher Square bit his own
tongue—" saddle him with a Judgement "; but

> " This even-handed Justice
> Commends the ingredients of our poisoned Chalice
> To our own lips."

This Man little thought, when he was lacerating my heart
according to law, while he was poisoning my life at its sources,
aiding and abetting in the blighting, branding, and exile that
was to be the result of his counsels in their indirect effects,
that in less than thirty-six moons—in the pride of his triumph
as the highest candidate for the representation of the Sister-
City of the mightiest of Capitals—in the fullness of his professional career—in the greenness of a healthy old age—in the
radiance of fame, and the complacency of self-earned riches—
that a domestic affliction would lay him in the earth, with the
meanest of malefactors, in a cross-road with the stake in his
body, if the verdict of insanity did not redeem his ashes from
the sentence of the laws he had lived upon by interpreting or
misinterpreting, and died in violating.

This man had eight children, lately deprived of their
mother: could he not live? Perhaps, previous to his annihilation, he felt a portion of what he contributed his legal mite to
make me feel; but I have lived—lived to see him a Sexagenary
Suicide.

It was not in vain that I invoked Nemesis in the midnight
of Rome from the awfullest of her ruins.

Fare you well.   B.

---

[1] Sir Samuel Romilly had incurred Byron's enmity because, having accepted
a retaining-fee from the poet at the beginning of the separation-proceedings, he
had subsequently acted against him.

TO JOHN CAM HOBHOUSE AND
THE HON. DOUGLAS KINNAIRD †   *Venice, January 19th, 1819*

DEAR H. AND DEAR K.,—I approve and sanction all your legal proceedings with regard to my affairs, and can only repeat my thanks and approbation. If you put off the payments of debts "till *after* Lady Noel's death", it is well; if till *after* her damnation, better, for that will last for ever; yet I hope not; for her sake as well as the creditors I am willing to believe in purgatory.

With regard to the Poeshie, I will have no "cutting and slashing", as Perry calls it; you may omit the stanzas on Castlereagh, indeed it is better, and the two "*Bobs*" at the end of the 3rd stanza of the dedication, which will leave "high" and "a-dry" good rhymes without any "*double* (or single) entendre", but no more. I appeal, not "to Philip fasting", but to Alexander drunk; I appeal to Murray at his ledger, to the people, in short, Don Juan shall be an entire horse, or none. If the objection be to the indecency, the Age which applauds the "Bath Guide", and Little's poems, and reads Fielding and Smollett still, may bear with that. If to the poetry, I will take my chance. I will not give way to all the cant of Christendom. I have been cloyed with applause, and sickened with abuse; at present I care for little but the copyright; I have imbibed a great love for money, let me have it; if Murray loses this time, he won't the next; he will be cautious, and I shall learn the decline of his customers by his epistolary indications. But in no case will I submit to have the poem mutilated. There is another Canto written, but not copied, in two hundred and odd Stanzas, if this succeeds; as to the prudery of the present day, what is it? Are we more moral than when Prior wrote? Is there anything in "Don Juan" so strong as in Ariosto, or Voltaire, or Chaucer?

Tell Hobhouse his letter to Di Breme has made a great sensation, and is to be published in the Tuscan and other gazettes. Count R. came to consult with me about it last Sunday; we think of Tuscany; for Florence and Milan are in literary war; but the Lombard league is headed by Marti, and would make a difficulty of insertion in the Lombard gazettes; once published in the Pisan, it will find its way through Italy by translation or reply.

So Lauderdale has been telling a story! I suppose this is my reward for presenting him at Countess Benzoni's and showing him what attention I could. Which " piece " does he mean? Since last year I have run the gauntlet. Is it the Tarruscelli—the Da Mosto—the Spineda—the Lotti—the Rizzato—the Eleanora—the Carlotta—the Giulietta—the Aloisi—the Zambieri—the Eleanora da Bezzi (who was the King of Naples' Gioachino's mistress—at least one of them)—the Theresina of Mazzurati—the Glettenheim and her sister—the Luigia and her mother—the Fornaretta—the Santa—the Caligara—the Portiera Vedova—the Bolognese figurante—the Tentora and her sister—cum multis aliis? Some of them are countesses and some of them cobbler's wives, some noble, some middling, some low, and all whores. Which does the damned old " Ludro and porco fottuto " mean? Since *he* tells a story about me, I will tell one about him. When he landed at the *Custom House* from Corfu, he called for " *Post horses, directly* ". He was told that there were no horses except mine nearer than Lido, unless he wished for the four bronze coursers of St. Mark, which *were at his service*.

I am, yours ever, B.

Let me have H.'s election immediately. I mention it *last* as being what I was least likely to forget.

P.S.—Whatever brain-money you get on my account from Murray, pray remit me. I will never consent to pay away what I *earn*. That is *mine*, and what I get by my brains I will spend <u>* * *</u>, as long as I have a tester or a * remaining. I shall not live long, and for that reason I must live while I can. So let him disburse, and me receive. " For the night cometh." If I had but had twenty thousand a year I should not have been living now. But all men are not born with a silver or gold spoon in their mouths. My balance also—my balance—and a copyright. I have another Canto, too, ready; and then there will be my half year in June. Recollect I care for nothing but " monies ".

January 20^{the}, 1819

You say nothing of Mazeppa. Did it arrive, with one other, besides that you mention?

TO JOHN CAM HOBHOUSE †   *Venice, April 6th, 1819*

My dear Hobhouse,—I have not derived from the Scriptures of Rochefoucault that consolation which I expected " in the misfortunes of our best friends ".

I had much at heart your gaining the Election, but from " the filthy puddle " into which your patriotism had run you, I had, like Croaker, my bodings, but like old " Curry-comb " you make " so handsome a corpse ", that my wailing is changed into admiration. With the Burdettites divided, and the Whigs and Tories united, what else could be expected? If I had guessed at your opponent, I would have made one among your Cortes, and have * Caroline Lamb out of her " two hundred votes " * * * * *. I think I could have neutralised her zeal with a little management. But alas! who would have thought of that cuckoldy family's *standing* for a *member*. I suppose it is the first time that George Lamb ever *stood* for anything;—and William with his " Corni ". " Cazzo da Seno ! " (as we Venetians say. It means : * * * * * *in earnest*— a sad way of swearing). But that you who know them should have to *concur* with such dogs—well—did I ever—no I never etc. etc. etc.

I have sent my second Canto ; but I will have no gelding. Murray has my order of the day. Douglas Kinnaird with more than usual politeness writes me vivaciously that Hanson or I willed the *three per cent*, instead of the five—as if I could prefer *three* to *five* per cent !—death and fiends !—and then *he* lifts up his leg against the publication of Don Juan. " Et tu *Brute* " (*the e mute* recollect). I shall certainly hitch our dear friend into some d—d story or other, " my dear, Mr. Sneer—Mr. Sneer— my dear ". I must write again in a few days, it being now past four in the morning ; it is Passion week, and rather dull. I am dull too, for I have fallen in love with a Romagnola Countess from Ravenna,[1] who is nineteen years old, and has a Count of fifty—whom she seems disposed to qualify, the first year of marriage being just over. I knew her a little last year at her starting, but they always wait a year, at least generally. I met her first at the Albrizzi's, and this spring at the Benzona's —and I have hopes, sir,—hopes, but she wants me to come to

[1] Teresa Guiccioli.

Ravenna, and then to Bologna. Now this would be all very well for certainties; but for mere hopes; if she should plant me, and I should make a "fiasco", never could I show my face on the Piazza. It is nothing that money can do, for the Conte is awfully rich, and would be so even in England,—but he is fifty and odd; has had two wives and children before this his third (a pretty fair-haired girl last year out of a convent; now making her second tour of the Venetian Conversazioni) and does not seem so jealous this year as he did last—when he stuck close to her side—even at the Governor's.

She is pretty, but has no tact; answers aloud, when she should whisper—talks of age to old ladies who want to pass for young; and this blessed night horrified a correct company at the Benzona's, by calling out to me " *mio Byron* " in an audible key, during a dead silence of pause in the other prattlers, who stared and whispered their respective *serventi*. One of her preliminaries is that I must never leave Italy. I have no desire to leave it, but I should not like to be frittered down into a regular Cicisbeo. What shall I do? I am in love, and tired of promiscuous concubinage, and have now an opportunity of settling for life.

Yours, B.

FRAGMENT OF A LETTER
TO JOHN CAM HOBHOUSE†   [*FPO Postmark April 20 1819*]

. . . P.S.—We have had, a fortnight ago, the devil's own row with an elephant who broke loose, ate up a fruit shop, killed his keeper; broke into a church; and was at last killed by a cannon-shot brought from the Arsenal. I saw him the day he broke open his own house; he was standing in the Riva, and his keepers trying to persuade him with *peck loaves* to go on board of a sort of ark they had got. I went close up to him that afternoon in my gondola, and he amused himself with flinging great beams that flew about over the water in all directions; he was then not *very* angry, but towards midnight he became furious, and displayed the most extraordinary strength, pulling down everything before him. All musketry proved in vain; and when he charged, the Austrians threw down their muskets and ran. At last they broke a hole and brought a field piece, the first shot missed, the second entered behind, and came out *all but* the skin at his shoulder. I saw him dead the next day, a stupendous fellow. He went mad for want of a She, it being his rutting month.

Fletcher is well. I have got two monkeys, a fox, and two new mastiffs, Mutz is still in high old age. The monkeys are charming. Last month I had a business about a Venetian girl who wanted to marry me, a circumstance prevented, like Dr. Blifil's espousals, not only by my previous marriage, but by Mr. Allworthy's being acquainted with the existence of Mrs. Dr. Blifil. I was very honest, and gave her no hopes, but there was a scene, I having been found at her window at midnight, and they sent me a priest, and a friend of the family's, to talk with me the next day, both of whom I treated with coffee.

TO THE HON. DOUGLAS KINNAIRD †   *Venice,*
April 24th, 1819

DEAR DOUGLAS,—

" When that the Captain came for to know it
He very much applauded what she had done "

and I only want the command " of the gallant Thunder Bomb " to make you my " first Lieutenant ". I meant " five thousand pounds " and never intend to have so much meaning again. In short, I refer you Gentlemen to my original letter of instructions which, by the blessing of God, seems to bear as many constructions as a Delphic Oracle; I say I refer you to that when you are at a loss how to avoid paying my money away; I hate paying and you are quite right to encourage me. As to Hanson & *Son,* I make no distinctions—it would be a sort of blasphemy—I should as soon think of untwisting the Trinity. What do they mean by separate bills? With regard to the Rochdale suit—and the " large discretion " or Indiscretion of " a thousand pounds "—what could I do? I want to gain my suit; but I will be guided by you. If you think " pounds Scottish " will do better, let me know—I am docile.

Pray what could make Farebrother say that Seventeen thousand pounds had been bidden for the undisputed part of Rochdale manor? It may be so, but I never heard of it before, not even from Spooney. If anybody bids, take it, and send it me by post; but don't pay away to those low people of tradesmen. They may survive Lady Noel, or me, and get it from the executors and heirs. But I don't approve of any living liquidations—a damned deal too much has been paid already—the fact is that the villains owe me money—and not I to them. Damn " *the Vampire* ". What do I know of Vampires ?[1] It must be some bookselling imposture; contradict it in a solemn paragraph.

I sent off on April 3rd the 2nd canto of " Don Juan " addressed to Murray, I hope it is arrived—by the Lord it is a Capo d'Opera, so " full of pastime and prodigality ", but you sha'n't decimate nor mutilate, no—" rather than that, come critics into the list, and champion me to the uttermost ".

Nor you, nor that rugged rhinoceros Murray, have ever told me, in answer to *fifty* times the question, if he ever received the additions to Canto *first*, entitled " Julia's letter " and also some four stanzas for the beginning.

I have fallen in love, within the last month, with a Romagnuola Countess from Ravenna, the spouse of a year of Count Guiccioli, who is sixty—the girl twenty. He has eighty thousand ducats of rent, and has had two wives before. But he is sixty. He is the first of Ravenna nobles, but he is sixty. She is as fair as sunrise, and warm as noon, we had but ten days to manage all our little matters in beginning, middle and end; and we managed them; and I have done my duty with the proper consummation. But she is young, and was not content with what she had done, unless it was to be turned to the advantage of the public, and so she made an éclat, which rather astonished even the Venetians, and electrified the Conversazioni of the Benzona, the Albrizzi, and the Michelli, and made her husband look embarrassed. They have been gone back to Ravenna some time, but they return in the winter. She is the queerest woman I ever met with, for in general they cost one something in one way or other, whereas by an odd combina-

---

[1] Polidori's romance, *The Vampyre*, published in 1819, was popularly credited to Byron.

tion of circumstances, I have proved an expense to *her*, which is not *my* custom, but an accident ; however it don't matter. She is a sort of Italian Caroline Lamb, except that she is much prettier, and not so savage. But she has the same red-hot head, the same noble disdain of public opinion, with the superstructure of all that Italy can add to such natural dispositions. To be sure, they may go much further here with impunity, as her husband's rank ensured them reception at all societies including the Court ; and as it was her first outbreak since marriage, the sympathizing world was liberal. She is also of the Ravenna noblesse, educated in a convent, sacrifice to wealth, filial duty, and all that. I am damnably in love, but they are gone—gone—for many months—and nothing but Hope keeps me alive *seriously*.

Yours ever, B.

TO THE COUNTESS GUICCIOLI * 1   *Venice, 25th April, 1819*

MY LOVE,—I hope you have received my letter of the 22nd, addressed to the person in Ravenna of whom you told me, before leaving Venice. You scold me for not having written to you in the country—but—how could I ? My sweetest treasure, you gave me no other address but that of Ravenna. If you knew how great is the love I feel for you, you would not believe me capable of forgetting you for a single instant ; you must become better acquainted with me. Perhaps one day you will know that, although I do not deserve you, I do indeed love you.

You want to know whom I most enjoy seeing, since you have gone away ? who makes me tremble and feel—not what you alone can arouse in my soul—but something like it ? Well, I will tell you—it is the *old porter* whom Fanny 2 used to send with your notes when you were in Venice, and who now brings your letters—still dear, but not so dear as those which brought the hope of seeing you that same day at the usual

---

1 This and the letter of August 7, 1820, in the Gamba collection, have been translated from the Italian by the Marchesa Origo, and are included in her study of Teresa Guiccioli and Byron, *The Last Attachment* (Murray and Cape, 1949).

2 Fanny Silvestrini, Teresa Guiccioli's confidante.

time. My Teresa, where are you? Everything here reminds
me of you, everything is the same, but you are not here and
I still am. In separation the one who goes away suffers less
than the one who stays behind. The distraction of the journey,
the change of scene, the landscape, the movement, perhaps
even the separation, distracts the mind and lightens the heart.
But the One who stays behind is surrounded by the same
things, tomorrow as yesterday, while only that is lacking which
made me forget that a tomorrow would ever come. When I
go to the Conversazione I give myself up to tedium, too happy
to suffer ennui, rather than grief. I see the same faces—hear
the same voices—but no longer dare to look towards the sofa
where I shall not see *you* any more, but instead some old crone
who might be Calumny personified. I hear, without the
slightest emotion, the opening of that door which I used to
watch with so much anxiety when I was there before you,
hoping to see you come in. I will not speak of *much dearer* places
still, for *there* I shall not go—unless you return; I have no other
pleasure than thinking of you, but I do not see how I could see
again the places where we have been together—especially those
most consecrated to our love—without dying of grief.

Fanny is now in Treviso, and God knows when I shall
have any more letters from you; but meanwhile I have
received three; you must by now have arrived in Ravenna—I
long to hear of your arrival; my fate depends upon your
decision. Fanny will be back in a few days; but tomorrow
I shall send her a note by a friend's hand to ask her not to
forget to send me your news, if she receives any letters before
returning to Venice.

My Treasure, my life has become most monotonous and
sad; neither books, nor music, nor *horses* (rare things in Venice
—but you know that mine are at the Lido), nor dogs, give me
any pleasure; the society of women does not attract me; I
won't speak of the society of men, for that I have always
despised. For some years I have been trying systematically to
avoid strong passions, having suffered too much from the
tyranny of Love. *Never to feel* admiration [1]—and to enjoy myself
without giving too much importance to the enjoyment in itself—
to feel indifference toward human affairs—contempt for many—

[1] "Not to admire is all the art I know."—*Don Juan.*

but hatred for none, this was the basis of my philosophy. I did not mean to love any more, nor did I hope to receive Love. You have put to flight all my resolutions; now I am all yours; I will become what you wish—perhaps happy in your love, but never at peace again. You should not have re-awakened my heart, for (at least in my own country) my love has been fatal to those I love—and to myself. But these reflections come too late. You have been mine—and whatever the outcome—I am, and eternally shall be, entirely yours. I kiss you a thousand and a thousand times—but—

> Che giova a te, cor mio, l' esser amato?
> Che giova a me l' aver si caro amante?
> Perchè crudo destino—
> Ne disunisci tu s' Amor ne stringe? [1]

Love me—as always your tender and faithful,

B

TO THE LORD KINNAIRD*   *Venice, May 15, 1819*

MY DEAR *LORD*,[2]—Three years and some months ago, when you were reading " Bertram " at your brother's, on my exclaiming in the words of Parson Adams to his Son, " *Lege Dick, Lege* " (on occasion of some interruption that had occurred) you replied to me " my name is *not Richard*, my Lord ", thus converting my luckless quotation into an intentional liberty, and reproving me there*for*. This was a hint to me to address you in future with all Aristocratical decorum as becomes our birth, parentage, and education, and now I pay you back in your own coin, and say unto you, my dear Lord, " my name is *not Lady* " with which you commence your letter, which I am nevertheless as glad to receive, as I shall be to see the writer.

" Your Lordship will be right welcome back to Denmark."
Your good nature to the chaste [? Arpalice] has been very serviceable to her, for without it she would have never rejoined

---

[1] " What does it profit you, my heart, to be beloved?
    What good to me, to have so dear a lover?
    Why should a cruel fate
    Separate those whom love has once united? "
                 —Guarini, *Il Pastor Fido.*
[2] The brother of Douglas Kinnaird.

her principal Performer. I had a letter from her soon after her arrival at Milan, but have heard nothing since. She may probably write from Munich.

It was my intention to have left Venice tomorrow, on my journey to R. but the Lady has miscarried, and her recovery seems more remote than was expected, being still in bed. I have been ordered to come at all events, but what the deuce should I do in the mean time without the possibility of seeing her, or at least of seeing her to any purpose in her present state. However, on the mere chance of seeing her only, I shall set out about the 20th and leave the rest to the protecting deities.

I hope that you will arrive in Venice before I set out, and would wait a day or two on purpose, if you will let me know by return of post, where are you going? To *Reggio*? I should like greatly to see you on your route, and will lay to till you come within hail, if you will make the Signal. But pray respond by the first ordinary.

There is the devil to do here at present, an Englishman— son of a Baronet—robbed a Baronet (Sir W. Drummond) at his " Hostel or Inn " of goods and monies, and is like " to be troubled at Size " about it; the young man is a damned Rascal and is to be treated accordingly, by being permitted to get off. At least I suppose so.

Don't forget to answer and believe me, dear Kinnaird, very truly

and affectly.,   yrs., BYRON

P.S.—If they open our letters at the post they will be edified by the correspondence—it is all hitherto about whores and rogues.

TO JOHN MURRAY   *Venice, May 15, 1819*

DEAR SIR,—I have received and return by this post, under another Cover, the first proof of *Don Juan*. Before the Second can arrive, it is probable that I may have left Venice, and the length of my absence is so uncertain, that you had better proceed to the publication without boring me with more proofs.

I send by last post an addition—and a new copy of "Julia's Letter", perceiving or supposing the former one in winter did not arrive.

Mr. Hobhouse is at it again about indelicacy. There is *no indelicacy*; if he wants *that*, let him read Swift, his great Idol; but his Imagination must be a dunghill, with a Viper's nest in the middle, to engender such a supposition about this poem. For my part, I think you are all crazed. * * * Request him not "to put me in a phrenzy", as Sir Anthony Absolute says, "though he was not the indulgent father that I am."

I have got your extract, and the *Vampire*. I need not say it is *not mine*. There is a rule to go by: you are my publisher (till we quarrel), and what is not published by you is not written by me.

The story of Shelley's agitation is true.[1] I can't tell what seized him, for he don't want courage. He was once with me in a gale of Wind, in a small boat, right under the rocks between Meillerie and St. Gingo. We were five in the boat— a servant, two boatmen, and ourselves. The sail was mismanaged, and the boat was filling fast. He can't swim. I stripped off my coat—made him strip off his and take hold of an oar, telling him that I thought (being myself an expert swimmer) I could save him, if he would not struggle when I took hold of him—unless we got smashed against the rocks, which were high and sharp, with an awkward surf on them at that minute. We were then about a hundred yards from shore, and the boat in peril. He answered me with the greatest coolness, that " he had no notion of being saved, and that I would have enough to do to save myself, and begged not to trouble me ". Luckily, the boat righted, and, baling, we got round a point into St. Gingo, where the inhabitants came down and embraced the boatmen on their escape, the Wind having been high enough to tear up some huge trees from the Alps above us, as we saw next day.

And yet the same Shelley, who was as cool as it was possible to be in such circumstances, (of which I am no judge myself,

[1] During the summer of 1816, when they were both in Switzerland, Shelley, after an evening of ghost-stories, had been seized with sudden panic. Later, he explained that, while gazing at Mary, he had remembered a tale he had been told of a woman who " had eyes instead of nipples, which taking hold of his mind horrified him. . . ."

as the chance of swimming naturally gives self possession when near shore), certainly had the fit of phantasy which Polidori describes, though *not exactly* as he describes it.

The story of the agreement to write the Ghost-books is true; but the ladies are *not* sisters. One is Godwin's daughter by Mary Wolstonecraft, and the other the *present* Mrs. Godwin's daughter by a former husband. So much for Scoundrel Southey's story of " *incest* "; neither was there *any promiscuous intercourse* whatever. Both are an invention of that execrable villain Southey, whom I will term so as publicly as he deserves. Mary Godwin (now Mrs. Shelley) wrote *Frankenstein*, which you have reviewed, thinking it Shelley's. Methinks it is a wonderful work for a girl of nineteen,—*not* nineteen, indeed, at that time. I enclose you the beginning of mine, by which you will see how far it resembles Mr. Colburn's publication. If you choose to publish it in the *Edinburgh Magazine* (*Wilson's and Blackwood's*) you may, *stating why*, and with such explanatory proem as you please. I never went on with it, as you will perceive by the date. I began it in an old account-book of Miss Milbanke's, which I kept because it contains the word " Household ", written by her twice on the inside blank page of the covers, being the only two scraps I have in the world in her writing, except her name to the Deed of Separation. Her letters I sent back except those of the quarrelling correspondence, and those, being documents, are placed in possession of a third person (Mr. Hobhouse), with copies of several of my own; so that I have no kind of memorial whatever of her, but these *two* words,—and her actions. I have torn the leaves containing the part of the Tale out of the book, and enclose them with this sheet.

Next week I set out for Romagna—at least in all probability. You had better go on with the publications without waiting to hear farther, for I have other things in my head. " Mazeppa " and " The Ode " *Separate*—what think you? *Juan anonymously*, without the dedication, for I won't be shabby and attack Southey under Cloud of night.

What do you mean? First you seem hurt by my letter, and then, in your next, you talk of its " power ", and so forth. " This is a damned blind story, Jack; but never mind, go on." You may be sure I said nothing *on purpose* to plague you; but if you will put me " in a phrenzy, I will never call you Beck [*sic*] again ". I remember nothing of the epistle at present.

What do you mean by Polidori's *Diary*? [1] Why, I defy him to say any thing about me, but he is welcome. I have nothing to reproach me with on his score, and I am much mistaken if that is not his *own* opinion. But why publish the names of the two girls? and in such a manner?—what a blundering piece of exculpation ! *He* asked Pictet, etc., to dinner, and of course was left to entertain them. I went into Society *solely* to present *him* (as I told him), that he might return into good company if he chose ; it was the best thing for his youth and circumstances : for myself, I had done with Society, and, having presented him, withdrew to my own " way of life ". It is true that I returned without entering Lady Dalrymple Hamilton's, because I saw it full. It is true that Mrs. Hervey (she writes novels) fainted at my entrance into Coppet, and then came back again. On her fainting, the Duchesse de Broglie exclaimed, " This is *too much*—at *sixty-five* years of age ! "—I never gave " the English " an opportunity of " avoiding " me ; but I trust that, if ever I do, they will seize it.

I am, yours very truly, B.

TO ——[2]   *Venice [Monday], May 17th 1819*

My dearest Love,—I have been negligent in not writing, but what can I say ? Three years absence—and the total change of scene and habit make such a difference—that we have now nothing in common but our affections and our relationship.—

But I have never ceased nor can cease to feel for a moment that perfect and boundless attachment which bound and binds me to you—which renders me utterly incapable of *real* love for any other human being—for what could they be to me after *you*? My own xxxx we may have been very wrong—but I repent of nothing except that cursed marriage—and your

---

[1] Dr. Polidori had originally been commissioned by Murray to produce a journal of his journey with the poet. His *Diary* was eventually published under the editorship of W. M. Rossetti.

[2] This letter, originally published by Lord Lovelace in *Astarte*, was addressed, it has been assumed, to Augusta Leigh.

refusing to continue to love me as you had loved me—I can neither forget nor *quite forgive* you for that precious piece of reformation.—but I can never be other than I have been—and whenever I love anything it is because it reminds me in some way or other of yourself—for instance I not long ago attached myself to a Venetian for no earthly reason (although a pretty woman) but because she was called xxxx and she often remarked (without knowing the reason) how fond I was of the name.—It is heart-breaking to think of our long Separation—and I am sure more than punishment enough for all our sins—Dante is more humane in his " Hell " for he places his unfortunate lovers (Francesca of Rimini and Paolo whose case fell a good deal short of *ours*—though sufficiently naughty) in company—and though they suffer—it is at least together.—If ever I return to England—it will be to see you—and recollect that in all time—and place—and feelings—I have never ceased to be the same to you in heart—Circumstances may have ruffled my manner—and hardened my spirit—you may have seen me harsh and exasperated with all things around me ; grieved and tortured with *your new resolution,*—and the soon after persecution of that infamous fiend who drove me from my Country and conspired against my life—by endeavouring to deprive me of all that could render it precious—but remember that even then *you* were the sole object that cost me a tear? and *what tears* ! do you remember *our* parting? I have not spirits now to write to you upon other subjects—I am well in health—and have no cause of grief but the reflection that we are not together—When you write to me speak to me of yourself—and say that you love me—never mind commonplace people and topics—which can be in no degree interesting—to me who see nothing in England but the country which holds *you*—or around it but the sea which divides us.—They say absence destroys weak passions—and confirms strong ones—Alas ! *mine* for you is the union of all passions and of all affections—Has strengthened itself but will destroy me—I do not speak of *physical* destruction—for I have endured and can endure much —but of the annihilation of all thoughts feelings or hopes—which have not more or less a reference to you and to *our recollections*—

Ever dearest.   [Signature erased]

TO JOHN MURRAY   *Venice, May 18, 1819*

DEAR SIR,—Yesterday I wrote to Mr. Hobhouse and returned the proof under cover to you. Tell Mr. Hobhouse that in the Ferrara Story I told him, the phrase was *Vi riveresco Signor Cognato* and *not Cognato mio* as I stated yesterday by mistake.

I wrote to you in haste and at past two in the morning having besides had an accident. In going, about an hour and a half ago, to a rendezvous with a Venetian girl (unmarried and the daughter of one of their nobles), I tumbled into the Grand Canal, and, not choosing to miss my appointment by the delays of changing, I have been perched in a balcony with my wet clothes on ever since, till this minute that on my return I have slipped into my dressing-gown. My foot slipped in getting into my Gondola to set out (owing to the cursed slippery steps of their palaces), and in I flounced like a Carp, and went dripping like a Triton to my Sea nymph and had to scramble up to a grated window :—

> Fenced with iron within and without
> Lest the lover get in or the Lady get out.

She is a very dear friend of mine, and I have undergone some trouble on her account, for last winter the truculent tyrant her flinty-hearted father, having been informed by an infernal German, Countess Vorsperg (their next neighbour), of our meetings, they sent a priest to me, and a Commissary of police, and they locked the Girl up, and gave her prayers and bread and water, and our connection was cut off for some time ; but the father hath lately been laid up, and the brother is at Milan, and the mother falls asleep, and the Servants are naturally on the wrong side of the question, and there is no Moon at Midnight just now, so that we have lately been able to recommence ; the fair one is eighteen ; her name, Angelina ; the family name, of course, I don't tell you.

She proposed to me to divorce my mathematical wife, and I told her that in England we can't divorce except for *female* infidelity. " And pray, (said she), how do you know what she may have been doing these last three years? " I answered that I could not tell, but that the state of Cuckoldom was not quite so flourishing in Great Britain as with us here. "But", she said, "can't you get rid of her?" "Not more than is done already (I answered): You would not have me *poison her*?" Would you believe it? She made me *no answer*. Is not that a true and odd national trait? It spoke more than a thousand words, and yet this is a little, pretty, sweet-tempered, quiet feminine being as ever you saw, but the Passions of a Sunny Soil are paramount to all other considerations. An unmarried Girl naturally wishes to be married: if she can marry and love at the same time it is well, but at any rate she must love. I am not sure that my pretty paramour was herself fully aware of the inference to be drawn from her dead Silence, but even the unconsciousness of the latent idea was striking to an observer of the Passions; and I never strike out a thought of another's or of my own without trying to trace it to its Source.

I wrote to Mr. H. pretty fully about our matters. In a few days I leave Venice for Romagna. Excuse this scrawl, for I write in a state of shivering from having sat in my dripping drapery, and from some other little accessories which affect this husk of our immortal Kernel.

Tell Augusta that I wrote to her by yesterday's post, addressed to your care. Let me know if you come out this Summer that I may be in the way, and come to me; don't go to an Inn. I do not know that I can promise you any pleasure; " our way of life " is so different in these parts, but I insure to myself a great deal in seeing you, and in endeavouring (however vainly) to prove to you that I am, very truly

Yours ever, B.

P.S.—I have read Parson Hodgson's *Friends* in which he seems to display his knowledge of the subject by a Covert attack or two on some of his own. He probably wants another Living; at least I judge so by the prominence of his piety, although he was always pious—even when he was kept by a Washerwoman on the New Road. I have seen him cry over her picture, which he generally wore under his left Armpit. But he is a good man, and I have no doubt does his duty by his Parish. As to the poetry of his New-fangled Stanza, I wish they would write the octave or the Spenser; we have no other legitimate measure of that kind. He is right in defending *Pope* against the bastard Pelicans of the poetical winter day, who add insult to their Parricide by sucking the blood of the parent of English *real* poetry—poetry without fault,—and then spurning the bosoms which fed them.

TO THE LORD KINNAIRD *   *Venice, May 26th, 1819*

MY DEAR KINNAIRD,—I saw in the papers the attack you mention, which is blackguard enough, but what you ought naturally to have expected as the consequence of having endeavoured to do a good action, by discovering a bad one. You remember the Scotch proverb " The Redder aye gets the worst lick o' the fray ", so the next time that anyone is to be shot, pray, don't interrupt them ; it appeared to have equally displeased the gentleman missed, the gentleman missing, and the un-gentleman prosecuting, who has lavished upon you such gratuitous and absurd calumny. For my own part (so you were out of it) I feel no curiosity about the matter, unless to know whether Julia [Gramont ?] the Dalilah of that very bad shot (who missed a whole Coach and horses : we could have taught him better at Joe Manton's) was a good piece. I have no patience for the rest of their trash, and if you don't lose yours, the thing can do you no real harm, though it is hard enough to be sure, to be treated in such a manner for having wished to expose an assassin and discover a conspiracy.

It is my intention to leave Venice on Saturday next, perhaps you had better address to me " ferma in posta, Bologna ". I will do my best to meet you on my return, as I shall probably remain but a few days at Ravenna. I leave you your choice of time, place etc. as a few posts in or out of the way will make no difference. I mean to proceed to Ravenna and Rimini, and to stay a few days at Bologna on my way back again to Venice. You may be very sure that I shall have great pleasure in meeting you.

My departure would have taken place before, but our abortion has not yet let us out of our chamber at Ravenna, except once, when we fell ill again. I was still required to set out, but my instructions were a little confused, and though I am really very much in love, yet I see no great use in not adopting a little caution ; we had already terminated the *Essential* part of the business *four* continuous days previous to her setting out from V. (the whole affair was of a week) so that there is nothing very new before us. I can't tell whether I was the involuntary cause of the miscarriage, but certes I was not the father of the foetus, for she was three months advanced before our first passade, and whether the Count was the parent or not I can't imagine ; perhaps he might ; they are but a year married, and she miscarried once before.

Pray let me have your news. I have heard of your " campaigning at the King of Bohemy " as Jerry Sneak says of Major Sturgeon, and of Reggio, and Turin also. I recollect seeing your charmer dance three years ago, but never saw her off the stage. Believe me, my dear K., ever yours very truly and affectly.,

BYRON

TO JOHN MURRAY *Bologna, June 7, 1819*

DEAR SIR,—Tell Mr. Hobhouse that I wrote to him a few days ago from Ferrara. It will therefore be idle in him or you to wait for any further answers or returns of proofs from Venice, as I have directed that no English letters be sent after me. The publication can be proceeded in without, and I am already sick of your remarks, to which I think not the least attention ought to be paid.

Tell Mr. Hobhouse that, since I wrote to him, I had availed myself of my Ferrara letters, and found the society much younger and better there than at Venice. I was very much pleased with the little the shortness of my stay permitted me to see of the Gonfaloniere Count Mosti, and his family and friends in general.

I have been picture-gazing this morning at the famous Domenichino and Guido, both of which are superlative. I afterwards went to the beautiful Cimetery of Bologna, beyond the walls, and found, besides the superb Burial-ground, an original of a *Custode*, who reminded me of the grave-digger in

Hamlet. He has a collection of Capuchins' skulls, labelled on the forehead, and taking down one of them, said, " This was Brother Desiderio Berro, who died at forty—one of my best friends. I begged his head of his brethren after his decease, and they gave it me. I put it in lime and then boiled it. Here it is, teeth and all, in excellent preservation. He was the merriest, cleverest fellow I ever knew. Wherever he went, he brought joy ; and when any one was melancholy, the sight of him was enough to make him cheerful again. He walked so actively, you might have taken him for a dancer—he joked—he laughed—oh ! he was such a Frate as I never saw before, nor ever shall again ! "

He told me that he had himself planted all the Cypresses in the Cimetery ; that he had the greatest attachment to them and to his dead people ; that since 1801 they had buried fifty three thousand persons. In showing some older monuments, there was that of a Roman girl of twenty, with a bust by Bernini. She was a Princess Barberini, dead two centuries ago : he said that, on opening her grave, they had found her hair complete, and " as yellow as gold ". Some of the epitaphs at Ferrara pleased me more than the more splendid monuments of Bologna ; for instance :—

> " Martini Luigi
>   Implora pace."

> " Lucrezia Picini
>   Implora eterna quiete."

Can any thing be more full of pathos? Those few words say all that can be said or sought : the dead had had enough of life ; all they wanted was rest, and this they " *implore* ". There is all the helplessness, and humble hope, and deathlike prayer, that can arise from the grave—" *implora pace* ". I hope, who-ever may survive me, and shall see me put in the foreigners' burying-ground at the Lido, within the fortress by the Adriatic, will those two words, and no more, put over me. I trust they won't think of " pickling, and bringing me home to Clod or Blunderbuss Hall ". I am sure my bones would not rest in an English grave, or my clay mix with the earth of that country. I believe the thought would drive me mad on my deathbed, could I suppose that any of my friends would be base enough to convey my carcase back to your soil. I would not even feed your worms, if I could help it.

So, as Shakespeare says of Mowbray, the banished Duke of Norfolk, who died at Venice (see Richard II.), that he, after fighting

> " Against black pagans, Turks, and Saracens,
> And toil'd with works of war, retir'd himself
> To Italy; and there, at *Venice*, gave
> His body to that *pleasant* country's earth,
> And his pure soul unto his Captain Christ,
> Under whose colours he had fought so long."

Before I left Venice, I had returned to you your late, and Mr. Hobhouse's, sheets of *Juan*. Don't wait for further answers from me, but address yours to Venice, as usual. I know nothing of my own movements; I may return there in a few days, or not for some time. All this depends on circumstances. I left Mr. Hoppner very well, as well as his son and Mrs. Hoppner. My daughter Allegra was well too, and is growing pretty; her hair is growing darker, and her eyes are blue. Her temper and her ways, Mr. Hoppner says, are like mine, as well as her features: she will make, in that case, a manageable young lady.

I never hear any thing of Ada, the little Electra of my Mycenæ; the moral Clytemnestra is not very communicative of her tidings, but there will come a day of reckoning, even if I should not live to see it.

I have at least seen Romilly shivered who was one of the assassins. When that felon, or lunatic (take your choice he must be one and might be both), was doing his worst to uproot my whole family tree, branch, and blossoms; when, after taking my retainer, he went over to them; when he was bringing desolation on my hearth and destruction on my household Gods, did he think that, in less than three years, a natural event—a severe domestic—but an expected and common domestic calamity,—would lay his carcase in a cross road, or stamp his name in a verdict of Lunacy? Did he (who in his drivelling sexagenary dotage had not the courage to survive his Nurse—for what else was a wife to him at his time of life?)—reflect or consider what my feelings must have been, when wife, and child, and sister, and name, and fame, and country were to be my sacrifice on his legal altar—and this at a moment when my health was declining, my fortune embarrassed, and my mind had been shaken by many kinds of disappointment, while I was yet young and might have reformed what might be wrong in my conduct, and retrieved what was perplexing in my affairs. But the wretch is in his grave. I detested him living, and I will not affect to pity him dead; I still loathe him—as much as we can hate dust—but that is nothing.

What a long letter I have scribbled!

Yours truly, B.

P.S.—Here, as in Greece, they strew flowers on the tombs. I saw a quantity of rose-leaves, and entire roses, scattered over the graves at Ferrara. It has the most pleasing effect you can imagine.

TO RICHARD BELGRAVE HOPPNER † *Ravenna, June 20*th *1819*

MY DEAR HOPPNER,—I wrote to you a week ago (particularly begging a line in answer by return of post) to request you would send off Augustine with the two Grey saddle horses, and the Carriage and Carriage horses, saddles, etc., to wait for me at the *Pellegrino*—(the Inn there) in *Bologna*. To this letter and one of the same purport to Mr. Scott, I have had no answer, which makes me uneasy as I shall probably not return to Venice for some time. I wished my English letters also to be forwarded with Augustine to Bologna. If there was any want of Money, Siri and Willhalm would equip him.

Pray write to me here (*Ravenna*) by next post; it will reach me in time, and do not let Augustine delay a moment for the nonsense of that son of a bitch Edgecombe, who may probably be the cause of his dawdling.

I wrote to you from Padua, and from Bologna, and since from Ravenna. I find my situation very agreeable, but want my horses very much, there being good riding in the environs. I can fix no time for my return to Venice—it may be soon or late—or not at all—it all depends on the *Dama* [Teresa

Guiccioli], whom I found very seriously in *bed* with a cough and spitting of blood, etc., all of which has subsided, and something else has recommenced.   Her miscarriage has made her a good deal thinner ; and I found all the people here firmly persuaded that she would never recover ;—they were mistaken, however.

My letters were useful as far as I employed them ; and I like both the place and people, though I don't trouble the latter more than I can help. *She* manages very well, though the *local* is inconvenient (no *bolts* and be d—d to them) and we run great risks (were it not at sleeping hours—after dinner) and *no* place but the great Saloon of his own palace. So that if I come away with a Stiletto in my gizzard some fine afternoon, I shall not be astonished.

I can't make *him* out at all—he visits me frequently, and takes me out (like Whittington, the Lord Mayor) in a coach and *six* horses. The fact appears to be, that he is completely *governed* by her—for that matter, so am I. The people here don't know what to make of us, as he had the character of jealousy with all his wives—this is the third. He is the richest of the Ravennese, by their own account, but is not popular among them.

By the aid of a Priest, a Chambermaid, a young Negro-boy, and a female friend, we are enabled to carry on our un-lawful loves, as far as they can well go, though generally with some peril, especially as the female friend and priest are at present out of town for some days, so that some of the pre-cautions devolve upon the Maid and Negro.

Now do pray—send off Augustine—and carriage—and cattle to Bologna without fail or delay—or I shall lose my remaining Shred of senses.

Don't forget this. My coming—going—and every thing depends upon *her* entirely just as Mrs. Hoppner—(to whom I remit my reverences) said, in the true spirit of female prophecy.

You are but a shabby fellow not to have written before—and I am,

Truly yours, B.

P.S.—Address by return of Post to me—at *Ravenna*.

TO THE LORD KINNAIRD *   *Ravenna, July 5th, 1819*

MY DEAR KINNAIRD,—The G[uiccioli] has been very unwell (not ill enough though to induce any amatory abstinence, except that single day when the *Chat* awoke a little prematurely) and I persuaded *him* to have Aglietti from Venice. He came yesterday; they have put on leeches, and prescribed a regimen, and say that she may be cured if she likes. Will she like? I doubt her liking anything for very long, except one thing, and I presume she will soon arrive at varying even that, in which case I should be at liberty to repass the Po, and perhaps the Alps; but as yet I can say nothing.

I had a letter from W. Webster the other day; he is at Nantes Loire Nif, and I have half a mind to go back in search of *La Fanchette*, but I know nothing of the geography of the place. Where the devil is Nantes? And what is Loire *Nif*? A river, I suppose, an't it?

La Geltruda is gone to Bologna; after pinching her left thigh one evening, I was never permitted to set eyes on her *not no more*. It is no fault of mine, her not coming to Faenza; she did not set off till yesterday.

I have been exchanging visits with the Cardinal Legate who called on me to day. He is a fine old fellow, Malvasia by name, and has been rather loose in his youth, without being much tighter in his age. He and I took very kindly to each other.

How am I to get the books, and to leave yours? Is the Bianchi to be visible, or my *Aunt* only? Of course, you could not doubt the lady and still less your friend; but I suppose, nevertheless, I shall see my aunt only. Well, it is hard, but I agree, only adding that my green carriage has lost much of its splendour and consequently I am shorn of one of the principal seductive qualities of an accomplished gentleman. I am, as I said, in perfect indecision, depending upon the *will* of a woman who has none, and on whom I never calculate for more than twelve hours. She will do as she pleases, and then so will I. A young Italian, married to a rich old Patrician, with only one man besides for a lover, is not likely to embarrass either with a long Constancy; and in that case, you know, there could be no great harm in my beginning the world again, or giving it up for good.

Will you tell me where this *Nantes* is? I can't find it in
the road book.

Addio. I am just going to take a canter into the pine forest
with Ferdinando.

Yours ever and truly, B.

P.S.—I approve your intentions about the books and the
Sequins also.

TO LADY BYRON   *Ravenna, July 20th 1819*
[Enclosing verses of a German poet]

I have received from Holstein (I believe) the annexed
paper of the Baroness of Hohenhausen etc. and the inclosed
letter of a Mr. Jacob (or Jacobssen) and as they " ardently
wish it could reach you " I transmit it. You will smile, as I
have done, at the importance which they attach to such things,
and the effect which they conceive capable of being produced
by composition, but the Germans are still a young and a
romantic people, and live in an ideal world. Perhaps it may
not offend you, however it may surprise, that the good people
on the frontiers of Denmark have taken an interest in your
domestic Affairs, which have now, I think, nearly made the
tour of Europe, and been discussed in most of its languages, to
as little purpose as in our own. If you like to retain the enclosed, you can do so, an indication to my Sister that you have
received the letter will be a sufficient answer. I will not close
this sheet without a few words more. Fletcher has complained
to me of your declining to give his wife a character, on account
of your " doubts of her veracity in some circumstances a short
time before she left you ". If your doubts allude to her testimony on your case during the then discussion, you *must* or at
least ought to be the best judge how far she spoke truth or not;
I can only say that She never had directly or indirectly, through
me or mine, the slightest inducement to the contrary, nor am I
indeed perfectly aware of what her Evidence was, never having
seen her nor communicated with her at that period or since.
I presume that you will weigh well your justice before you
deprive the woman of the means of obtaining her bread. No

one can be more fully aware than I am of the utter inefficacy
of any words of mine to you on this or on any other subject,
but I have discharged my duty to Truth in stating the above,
and now do yours.

The date of my letter, indeed my letter itself, may surprize
you, but I left Venice in the beginning of June, and came down
into Romagna ; there is the famous forest of Boccaccio's Story
and Dryden's fable hardby, the Adriatic not far distant, and the
Sepulchre of Dante within the walls. I am just going to take a
Canter (for I have resumed my Tartar habits since I left
England) in the cool of the Evening, and in the shadow of the
forest till the Ave Maria. I have got both my saddle and
Carriage horses with me, and don't spare them, in the cooler
part of the day. But I shall probably return to Venice in a
short time. Ravenna itself preserves perhaps more of the old
Italian manners than any City in Italy. It is out of the way of
travellers and armies, and thus they have retained more of their
originality. They make love a good deal, and assassinate a
little. The department is governed by a Cardinal Legate
(Alberoni was once legate here) to whom I have been presented and who told me some singular anecdotes of past times
—of Alfieri etc. and others. I tried to discover for Leigh
Hunt some traces of Francesca, but except her father Guido's
tomb, and the mere notice of the fact in the Latin commentary
of Benvenuto da Imola in M.S. in the library, I could discover
nothing for him. He (Hunt) has made a sad mistake about
" old Ravenna's *clear-shewn towers* and *bay* " the city lies so low
that you must be close upon it before it is " shewn " at all, and
the Sea had retired *four miles* at least, long before Francesca
was born, and as far back as the Exarchs and Emperors. They
tell me that at Rimini they know as little about her now—as
they do here—so I have not gone there, it lies in the way to
Rome, but I was at Rome in 1817. This is odd, for at Venice
I found many traditions of the old Venetians, and at Ferrara a
plentiful assortment of the House of Este, with the remains of
the very Mirror, whose reflection cost at least a dozen lives,
including those of Parisina and Ugo. I was wrong in placing
those two naughty people in a garden. Parisina was a Malatesta of Rimini, and her daughter by Niccolo of Este was
also put to death by some Italian Chief her husband in nearly

the same manner as her mother. Her name was Ginevra. So that including the alliance of Francesca with Launcelot Malatesta of Rimini, that same Malatesta family appears to have been but indifferently fortunate in their matrimonial speculations——I have written to you thus much, because in writing to you at all I may as well write much as little. I have not heard of Ada for many months but they say " no news is good news " she must now be three years and almost eight months old. You must let her be taught Italian as soon as she can be taught any language but her own, and pray let her be musical, that is if She has a turn that way. I presume that Italian being a language of mine, will not prevent you from recollecting my request at the proper time.

I am etc. B.

TO THE HON. AUGUSTA LEIGH †   *Ravenna, July 26th, 1819*

MY DEAREST AUGUSTA,—I am at too great a distance to scold you, but I *will* ask you whether *your* letter of the *1st* July *is an answer* to the letter I wrote you before I quitted Venice? What? is it come to *this?* Have you no memory? or no heart? You *had* both—and I *have* both—at least for *you.*

I write this presuming that you received *that* letter. Is it that you fear? Do not be afraid of the past ; the world has its own affairs without thinking of *ours* and you may write safely. If you do, address as usual to *Venice*. My house is not in St. Marc's but on the Grand Canal, within sight of the Rialto Bridge.

I do not like at all this pain in your side and always think of your mother's constitution. You must always be to me the first consideration in the world. Shall I come to *you?* or would a warm climate do you good? If so say the word, and I will provide you and your whole family (including that precious luggage your husband) with the means of making an agreeable journey. You need not fear about *me*. I am much altered and should be little trouble to you, nor would I give you more of my company than you like. I confess after three years and a half— and *such years* ! and *such a year* as preceded those three years ! —it would be a relief to me to see you again, and if it would be so to you I will come to you. Pray answer me, and recollect that I will do as you like in everything, even to returning to England, which is not the pleasantest of residences were *you* out of it.

I write from Ravenna. I came here on account of a Countess Guiccioli, a girl of twenty married to a very rich old man of sixty about a year ago. With her last winter I had a *liaison* according to the good old Italian custom. She miscarried in May and sent for me here, and here I have been these two months. She is pretty, a great coquette, extremely vain, excessively affected, clever enough, without the smallest principle, with a good deal of imagination and some passion. She had set her heart on carrying me off from Venice out of vanity, and succeeded, and having made herself the subject of general conversation has greatly contributed to her recovery. Her husband is one of the richest nobles of Ravenna, threescore years of age. This is his third wife. You may suppose what *esteem* I entertain for *her*. Perhaps it is about equal on both sides. I have my saddle-horses here and there is good riding in the forest. With these, and my carriage which is here also, and the sea, and my books, and the lady, the time passes. I am very fond of riding and always *was out* of England. But I hate your Hyde Park, and your turnpike roads, and must have forests, downs, or desarts to expatiate in. I detest *knowing* the road one is to go, and being interrupted by your damned finger-posts, or a blackguard roaring for twopence at a turnpike.

I send you a sonnet which this faithful lady had made for the nuptials of one of her relations in which she swears the most *alarming constancy* to her husband. Is not this good? You may suppose my *face* when she shewed it to me. I could not help laughing—one of *our* laughs. All this is very absurd, but you see that I have good morals at bottom.

She is an equestrian too, but a bore in her rides, for she can't guide her horse and he runs after mine, and tries to bite him, and then she begins screaming in a high hat and sky-blue riding habit, making a most absurd figure, and embarrassing me and both our grooms, who have the devil's own work to keep her from tumbling, or having her clothes torn off by the trees and thickets of the pine forest. I fell a little in love with her intimate friend, a certain Geltruda (that is *Gertrude*) who is very young and seems very well disposed to be perfidious; but alas! *her* husband is jealous, and the G. also detected me in an illicit squeezing of hands, the consequence of which was that the friend was whisked off to Bologna for a few days, and since her return I have never been able to see her but twice, with a dragon of a mother in law and a barbarian husband by her side, besides my own dear precious *Amica*, who hates all flirting but her own. But I have a priest who befriends me and the Gertrude says a good deal with her great black eyes, so that perhaps . . . but alas! I mean to give up these things altogether. I have now given you some account of my present state. The guide-book will tell you about Ravenna. I can't tell how long or short may be my stay. Write to me—love me —as ever

Yours most affectly B.

P.S.—*This* affair is *not* in the least expensive, being all in the wealthy line, but troublesome, for the lady is imperious, and exigeante. However there are hopes that we may quarrel. When we do you shall hear.

TO JOHN CAM HOBHOUSE † *Ravenna, July 30th, 1819*

DEAR HOBHOUSE,—Your last letter was of the beginning of June. How is it with you?—are you slain by Major Cartwright? [1] or ill of a quinsey? or are you writing a pamphlet in rejoinder to Erskine? I understand that a tailor and you are amongst the most strenuous writers in favour of the *measures* taken by the reformers. I sometimes get a glimpse of your speeches with the names of the tavern and company, in a stray newspaper, " Galignani ", or the " Lugano Gazette "; there is Mr. *Bicker*-stith, the man-midwife, and several other worthies of the like calibre; " there never was a set of more amicable officers ", as Major Sturgeon says. Pray let me hear how you go on.

My sister writes to me that " Scrope looks ill and out of spirits ", and has not his wonted air of prosperity, and that she fears his pursuits have not had all their former success. Is it even so? I suppose there is no knowing, and that the only

[1] Major Cartwright, a veteran supporter of parliamentary reform, had challenged Hobhouse, after a dispute arising out of the Westminster Election of 1819, in which Hobhouse was defeated.

way in which his friends will be apprized will be by some con-founded thing or other happening to him. He has not written to me since the winter, in last year's last month. What is he about?

The Dougal Creature [1] has written to mention the pact with Murray; if *it* (*i.e.*, D[on] J[uan]) fails, the sum is too much; if it succeeds, it is too little by five hundred guineas in coin or ingots. Donny Johnny will either succeed greatly, or tumble flatly; there will be no medium—at least I think not. Galignani announces " Mazeppa " as stamped, but I know nothing, and hear nothing of it, nor of " Juan "; what is become of the " Ode to Venice "? I am endeavouring here to get a tran-script of Benevento da Imola's Latin commentary on Dante, never yet stamped, quite " inedita ". They promise it me.

I have been swimming in the Adriatic, and cantering through Boccaccio's Pinery; it is a fine forest, " so full of pastime and prodigality ", and I have persuaded my contessa to put a side-saddle upon a pony of her sposo's, and we ride together—she in a hat shaped like Punch's and the merry Mrs. Ford's of Windsor, and a sky-blue tiffany riding-habit, like the ghost of Prologue's grandmother. I bought an English horse of Capt. Fyler some time ago (which, with my others, is here), and he is a famous leaper, and my amusement has been to make her groom, on a huge coach-horse, follow me over certain ditches and drain-lets, an operation in which he is considerably incommoded by a pair of jack-boots, as well as by the novelty of the undertaking. You would like the forest; it reaches from here to Rimini.

I have been here these two months, and hitherto all hath *gone on well*, with the usual *excerpta* of some " gelosie ", which are the fault of the climate, and of the conjunction of two such capricious people as the Guiccioli and the Inglese, but here hath been no stabbing nor drugging of possets. The last person assassinated here was the Commissary of Police, three months ago; they *kilt* him from an alley one evening, but he is recovering from the slugs with which they sprinkled him, from an " Archibugia " that shot him round a corner, like the Irishman's gun. He and Manzoni, who was stabbed dead going to the theatre at Forli, not long before, are the only

[1] Douglas Kinnaird.

recent instances. But it is the custom of the country, and not much worse than duelling, where one undertakes, at a certain personal risk of a more open nature, to get rid of a disagreeable person, who is injurious or inconvenient, and if such people become insupportable, what is to be done? It is give and take, like everything else—you run the same risk, and they run the same risk; it has the same object with duelling, but adopts a different means. As to the trash about *honour*, that is all stuff; a man offends, you want to kill him, this is amiable and natural, but *how*? The natural mode is obvious, but the artificial varies according to education.

I am taking the generous side of the question, seeing I am much more exposed here to become the patient than the agent of such an experiment. I know but one man whom I should be tempted to put to rest, and he is not an Italian nor in Italy, therefore I trust that he won't pass through Romagna during my sojourn, *because* 'gin he did, there is no saying what the fashionable facilities might induce a vindictive gentleman to meditate; besides, there are injuries where the balance is so greatly against the offender, that you are not to risk life against his (excepting always the law, which is originally a convention), but to trample as [you] would on any other venomous animal.

To return to Dante (where you will find a pretty eulogy on revenge): his tomb is within fifty yards of my " locanda ", the effigy and tombstone well preserved, but the outside is a mere modern cupola.

The house flanking this house, but divided by a street, is said to have been inhabited by him, but that is mere *say-so*, as far as I can make out; it is old enough to have been inhabited by Honorius, for that matter. The Polentani, his patrons, are buried in a church behind his grave, but there are no tidings nor tradition of Francesca, here or at Rimini, except the mere fact, which, to be sure, is a thumper, as they were actually killed in it. Hunt made a devil of a mistake about—

" Old Ravenna's clear shewn towers and bay."

There has been no bay nor sea within five miles since long before the time of the Exarchs, and as to " *clear shewn* ", the town lies so low that you must be close upon it before it is seen at all, and then there is no comprehensive view unless you climb the steeple.

I was introduced to the Cardinal Legate, a fine old boy, and I might have known all the world, but I prefer a private life, and have lived almost entirely with my paramour, her husband, *his* son by a former marriage, and her father, with her confidante, " in white linen ", a very pretty woman, noble also as her friend, called Gertrude Vicari, who has, however, a jealous husband, " a strange Centaur ", as Gibbon calls a philosophical theologian. But he is a profane historian.

I also fell in love with a promised bride, named Ursula——something, one of the prettiest creatures I ever saw ; but her barbarous mother, suspecting her of smiling from a window upon me, has watched her ever since, and she won't be married till September so there be no hopes ; however, I am trying my best with a priest (*not* to marry me, you may believe) and others to bring about some-at.

A precious epistle of gossip this is. But these are all I can say of " fatti miei ". I have had the G—— (whom I came for) in any case. And what more I can get I know not, but will try. It is much better for beauty than Lombardy. Canova is now in the Austrian states.

Ever, etc., very truly yours, B.

P.S. *July 31st.*—Considerable *lusinghe* that Ursula will be obtained, she being well-disposed. Do you know what happened to Lord Kinnaird at Faenza? When he went back to Milan, they stopped his carriage to search for the Bianchi (the dancer he keeps) thinking she had broke her engagement for the Fair of Sinigaglia to return into Lombardy. Lege, Dick, lege. But it was not so. She *is* dancing at the Fair.

An old woman at Rome, reading Boccaccio, exclaimed, " I wish to God that this was saying one's prayers ".

TO ALEXANDER SCOTT*   *Ravenna, July 31st, 1819*

DEAR SCOTTIN,[1]—You were right. I *will* consider first. But the truth is I *do* like terra firma a little after the long

---

[1] With Alexander Scott and the Cavaliere Mengaldo, "a gentleman of Bassano ", Byron had set out to swim from the Lido to Venice in 1818. The Italian was outdistanced and gave up the contest.

absence from it. As to the G[uiccioli] she has not much to do with my resolution, as I have something besides her on my hands—and in my eye. But I shall say nothing more now, till I am more sure. There are better things in that line, in this part of the world, than at Venice. Besides, like the preserve of a manor, this part has not yet been shot over.

It would be very unpleasant to me that you should quit Venice without our meeting again. I would almost take a flight there again on purpose to see you rather than this should be, and arrange my concerns in person. Where do you think of going? How are the cows? You are wrong about H's letter. There was nothing in it to offend *her*—but me. For instance telling her that *she* would be the *planter*. That *she* was voluble—what is all this? If I had told her that she was called and thought an absurd woman (which I carefully avoided) there indeed I should have been thoroughly Hoppnerian. You may tell a man that he is thought libertine, profligate, a villain, but not that his nose wants blowing or that his neckcloth is ill tied. Suppose you were to say to that Coxcomb Mengaldo that he was dangerous, disaffected, a severe disciplinarian in his regiment, that he had ill used Carlotta Aglietti, that he had been guilty of atrocities in his retreat from *Moscow* (*Moscow* would sweeten him) he would affect but feel nothing. But if you told him that his father sold eggs not very fresh he would be wrath to a degree.

I do not know whether I make myself understood; but it is in the little nooks of character where your true tormentors play the mosquito and the gadfly, and where such fellows as M. and H. distil their little drop of venom. Now I do maintain that I have always avoided this, which is never necessary unless in cases where your fame or fortunes may be seriously attacked. I could have driven Hoppner mad had I ever told him a 10,000th part of the things that I knew and the buffone Cavaliere little less so. But I resisted the pettiness of repaying them in kind. In future I shall be less kind to them and you may tell Mengaldo so—a little tittle tattle boasting parvenu, who never could forgive one's beating him in his own narrow field as we did hollow besides in the wider one of waters. I wish you had heard the account he had left at Ferrara of the swimming match. *You* were sunk and omitted altogether, and *he* had passed the Rialto and was only beaten by me by some accident! We knew him to be a liar before but would think the complete drubbing we both gave him in the swimming match would have silenced him on that score. I could not help saying, on hearing it, to his friends, " this story is Mengaldo all over ".

I enclose a letter which I beg you to forward to Siri and Willhalm. I wish them to remit the 23 francs to Genoa as I know not how.

I have as yet decided nothing, but have a general idea of quitting Venice altogether, particularly if I can get this other girl. But in the meantime the establishment may remain as it is, except that I wish they enquire on what terms the landlords of the houses would take them back again supposing me to be so disposed. Edgecombe may have a hint of my thoughts and Mr. Dorville also. As to the " baron fottuto ", as he is not the only thing " fottuto " (by me) in his family, I overlook that for his wife's sake. What *can* he do unless I buy or sell with him?—And I don't mean to do either. If *she plants*—let her. " There are as good fish in the sea as ever came out of it." There is a Scotch proverb for you hot as haggis. By the way how many *t*'s are there in " fottuto "—one or two? " Fotuto "— eh? Continue to write. Remember me to Missiaglia and *Peppi*, and Marina, and all the Conversaziners. I regret to have missed Canova at Venice, having missed him also at Rome, and in London. Believe me ever and truly yours affectly

                                                                    BYRON

TO JOHN MURRAY †   *Ravenna, August 1, 1819*
                (Address your answer to Venice, however.)

DEAR SIR,—Don't be alarmed. You will see me defend myself gaily—that is, if I happen to be in Spirits; and by *Spirits*, I don't mean your meaning of the word, but the spirit of a bull-dog when pinched, or a bull when pinned—it is then that they make best sport—and as my Sensations under an attack are probably a happy compound of the united energies of those amiable animals, you may perhaps see what Marrall calls " rare sport ", and some good tossing and goring, in the course of the controversy. But I must be in the right cue first, and I doubt I am almost too far off to be in a sufficient fury for the purpose; and then I have effeminated and enervated myself with love and the summer in these last two months.

I wrote to Mr. Hobhouse the other day, and foretold that Juan would either fail entirely or succeed completely—there will be no medium: appearances are not favourable; but as you write the day after publication, it can hardly be decided what opinion will predominate. You seem in a fright, and doubtless with cause. Come what may, I never will flatter the million's canting in any shape: circumstances may or may not have placed me at times in a situation to lead the public opinion, but the public opinion never led, nor ever shall lead, me. I will not sit " on a degraded throne "; so pray put Messrs. Southey, or Sotheby, or Tom Moore, or Horace Twiss upon it—they will all of them be transported with their coronation.

You have bought Harlow's drawings of Margarita and me rather dear methinks; but since you desire the story of Margarita Cogni, you shall be told it, though it may be lengthy.

Her face is of the fine Venetian cast of the old Time, and her figure, though perhaps too tall, not less fine—taken altogether in the national dress.

In the summer of 1817, Hobhouse and myself were sauntering on horseback along the Brenta one evening, when, amongst a group of peasants, we remarked two girls as the prettiest we had seen for some time. About this period, there had been great distress in the country, and I had a little relieved some of the people. Generosity makes a great figure at very little cost in Venetian livres, and mine had probably been exaggerated—as an Englishman's. Whether they remarked us looking at them or no, I know not; but one of them called out to me in Venetian, " Why do not you, who relieve others, think of us also? " I turned round and answered her—" *Cara, tu sei troppo bella e giovane per aver' bisogno del' soccorso mio* ". She answered, " If you saw my hut and my food, you would not say so ". All this passed half jestingly, and I saw no more of her for some days.

A few evenings after, we met with these two girls again, and they addressed us more seriously, assuring us of the truth of their statement. They were cousins; Margarita married, the other single. As I doubted still of the circumstances, I took the business up in a different light, and made an appointment with them for the next evening. Hobhouse had taken a fancy to the single lady, who was much shorter in stature, but a very pretty girl also. They came attended by a third woman, who was cursedly in the way, and Hobhouse's charmer took fright (I don't mean at Hobhouse, but at not being married—for here no woman will do anything under adultery), and flew off; and mine made some bother—at the propositions, and wished to consider of them. I told her, " if you really are in want, I will relieve you without any conditions whatever, and you may make love with me or no just as you please—*that* shall make no difference; but if you are not in absolute necessity, this is naturally a rendezvous, and I presumed that you understood this when you made the appointment ". She said that she had no objection to make love with me, as she was married, and all married women did it : but that her husband (a baker) was somewhat ferocious, and would do her a mischief. In short, in a few evenings we arranged our affairs, and for two years, in the course of which I had more women than I can count or recount, she was the only one who preserved over me an ascendancy which was often disputed, and never impaired. As she herself used to say publicly, " It don't matter, he may have five hundred ; but he will always come back to me ".

The reasons of this were, firstly, her person—very dark, tall, the Venetian face, very fine black eyes—and certain other qualities which need not be mentioned. She was two and twenty years old, and, never having had children, had not spoilt her figure, nor anything else—which is, I assure you, a great desideration in a hot climate where they grow relaxed and doughy, and flumpity a short time after breeding. She was, besides, a thorough Venetian in her dialect, in her thoughts, in her countenance, in every thing, with all their naïveté and Pantaloon humour. Besides, she could neither read nor write, and could not plague me with letters,—except twice that she paid sixpence to a public scribe, under the piazza, to make a letter for her, upon some occasion, when I was ill and could not see her. In other respects she was somewhat fierce and *prepotente*, that is, overbearing, and used to walk in whenever it suited her, with no very great regard to time, place, nor persons; and if she found any women in her way, she knocked them down.

When I first knew her, I was in *relazione* (*liaison*) with la Signora Segati, who was silly enough one evening at Dolo, accompanied by some of her female friends, to threaten her; for the Gossips of the Villeggiatura had already found out, by the neighing of my horse one evening, that I used to " ride late in the night " to meet the Fornarina. Margarita threw back her veil (*fazziolo*), and replied in very explicit Venetian, " *You* are *not* his *wife*: *I* am *not* his *wife*: *you* are his *Donna*, and *I* am his *Donna*: *your* husband is a cuckold, and *mine* is another. For the rest, what *right* have you to reproach me? if he prefers what is mine to what is yours, is it my fault? if you wish to secure him, tie him to your petticoat-string; but do not think to speak to me without a reply, because you happen to be richer than I am." Having delivered this pretty piece of eloquence (which I translate as it was related to me by a bye-stander), she went on her way, leaving a numerous audience with Madame Segati, to ponder at her leisure on the dialogue between them.

When I came to Venice for the Winter, she followed. I never had any regular *liaison* with her, but whenever she came I never allowed any other connection to interfere with her; and as she found herself out to be a favourite, she came pretty often. But she had inordinate Self-love, and was not tolerant of other women, except of the Segati, who was, as she said, my regular *Amica*, so that I, being at that time somewhat promiscuous, there was great confusion and demolition of head-dresses and handkerchiefs; and sometimes my servants, in " redding the fray " between her and other feminine persons, received more knocks than acknowledgements for their peaceful endeavours. At the *Cavalchina*, the masqued ball on the last night of the Carnival, where all the World goes, she snatched off the mask of Madame Contarini, a lady noble by birth, and decent in conduct, for no other reason, but because she happened to be leaning on my arm. You may suppose what a cursed noise this made; but this is only one of her pranks.

At last she quarrelled with her husband, and one evening ran away to my house. I told her this would not do : she said she would lie in the street, but not go back to him ; that he beat her (the gentle tigress), spent her money, and scandalously neglected his Oven. As it was Midnight I let her stay, and next day there was no moving her at all. Her husband came, roaring and crying, and entreating her to come back :—*not* she ! He then applied to the Police, and they applied to me : I told them and her husband to *take* her ; I did not want her ; she had come, and I could not fling her out of the window ; but they might conduct her through that or the door if they chose it. She went before the Commissary, but was obliged to return with that *becco ettico* (" consumptive cuckold "), as she called the poor man, who had a Ptisick. In a few days she ran away again. After a precious piece of work, she fixed herself in my house, really and truly without my consent, but, owing to my indolence, and not being able to keep my countenance ; for if I began in a rage, she always finished by making me laugh with some Venetian pantaloonery or another ; and the Gipsy knew this well enough, as well as her other powers of persuasion, and exerted them with the usual tact and success of all She-things—high and low, they are all alike for that.

Madame Benzone also took her under her protection, and then her head turned. She was always in extremes, either crying or laughing ; and so fierce when angered, that she was the terror of men, women, and children—for she had the strength of an Amazon, with the temper of Medea. She was a fine animal, but quite untameable. *I* was the only person that could at all keep her in any order, and when she saw me really angry (which they tell me is rather a savage sight), she subsided. But she had a thousand fooleries : in her *fazziolo*, the dress of the lower orders, she looked beautiful ; but, alas ! she longed for a hat and feathers, and all I could say or do (and I said much) could not prevent this travestie. I put the first into the fire ; but I got tired of burning them, before she did of buying them, so that she made herself a figure—for they did not at all become her.

Then she would have her gowns with a *tail*—like a lady, forsooth : nothing would serve her but " *l' abito colla coua* ", or *cua*, (that is the Venetian for " *la Coda* ", the tail or train,) and as her cursed pronunciation of the word made me laugh, there was an end of all controversy, and she dragged this diabolical tail after her every where.

In the meantime, she beat the women and stopped my letters. I found her one day pondering over one : she used to try to find out by their shape whether they were feminine or no ; and she used to lament her ignorance, and actually studied her Alphabet, on purpose (as she declared) to open all letters addressed to me and read their contents.

I must not omit to do justice to her housekeeping qualities : after she came into my house as *donna di governo*, the expences were reduced to less than half, and every body did their duty better—the apartments were kept in order, and every thing and every body else, except herself.

That she had a sufficient regard for me in her wild way, I had many reasons to believe. I will mention one. In the autumn, one day, going to the Lido with my Gondoliers, we were overtaken by a heavy Squall, and the Gondola put in peril—hats blown away, boat filling, oar lost, tumbling sea, thunder, rain in torrents, night coming, and wind increasing. On our return, after a tight struggle, I found her on the open steps of the Mocenigo palace, on the Grand Canal, with her great black eyes flashing through her tears, and the long dark hair, which was streaming drenched with rain over her brows and breast. She was perfectly exposed to the storm ; and the wind blowing her hair and dress about her tall thin figure, and the lightning flashing round her, with the waves rolling at her feet, made her look like Medea alighted from her chariot, or the Sibyl of the tempest that was rolling around her, the only living thing within hail at that moment except ourselves. On seeing me safe, she did not wait to greet me, as might be expected, but calling out to me—*Ah! can' della Madonna, xe esto il tempo per andar' al' Lido ?* (Ah ! Dog of the Virgin, is this a time to go to Lido?) ran into the house, and solaced herself with scolding the boatmen for not foreseeing the " *temporale* ". I was told by the servants that she had only been prevented from coming in a boat to look after me, by the refusal of all the Gondoliers of the Canal to put out into the harbour in such a moment : and that then she sate down on the steps in all the thickest of the Squall, and would neither be removed nor comforted. Her joy at seeing me again was moderately mixed with ferocity, and gave me the idea of a tigress over her recovered Cubs.

But her reign drew near a close. She became quite ungovernable some months after; and a concurrence of complaints, some true, and many false—" a favourite has no friend " —determined me to part with her. I told her quietly that she must return home, (she had acquired a sufficient provision for herself and mother, etc., in my service,) and She refused to quit the house. I was firm, and she went, threatening knives and revenge. I told her that I had seen knives drawn before her time, and that if she chose to begin, there was a knife, and fork also, at her service on the table, and that intimidation would not do. The next day, while I was at dinner, she walked in, (having broke open a glass door that led from the hall below to the staircase, by way of prologue,) and, advancing strait up to the table, snatched the knife from my hand, cutting me slightly in the thumb in the operation. Whether she meant to use this against herself or me, I know not—probably against neither—but Fletcher seized her by the arms, and disarmed her. I then called my boatmen, and desired them to get the Gondola ready, and conduct her to her own house again, seeing carefully that she did herself no mischief by the way. She seemed quite quiet, and walked down stairs. I resumed my dinner.

We heard a great noise: I went out, and met them on the staircase, carrying her up stairs. She had thrown herself into the Canal. That she intended to destroy herself, I do not believe; but when we consider the fear women and men who can't swim have of deep or even of shallow water, (and the Venetians in particular, though they live on the waves,) and that it was also night, and dark, and very cold, it shows that she had a devilish spirit of some sort within her. They had got her out without much difficulty or damage, excepting the salt water she had swallowed, and the wetting she had undergone.

I foresaw her intention to refix herself, and sent for a Surgeon, enquiring how many hours it would require to restore her from her agitation; and he named the time. I then said, " I give you that time, and more if you require it; but at the expiration of the prescribed period, if *She* does not leave the house, *I* will ".

All my people were consternated—they had always been frightened at her, and were now paralyzed : they wanted me to apply to the police, to guard myself, etc., etc., like a pack of sniveling servile boobies as they were. I did nothing of the kind, thinking that I might as well end that way as another ; besides, I had been used to savage women, and knew their ways.

I had her sent home quietly after her recovery, and never saw her since, except twice at the opera, at a distance amongst the audience. She made many attempts to return, but no more violent ones. And this is the story of Margarita Cogni, as far as it belongs to me.

I forgot to mention that she was very devout, and would cross herself if she heard the prayer-time strike—sometimes when that ceremony did not appear to be much in unison with what she was then about.

She was quick in reply ; as, for instance—One day when she had made me very angry with beating somebody or other, I called her a *Cow* (*Cow*, in Italian, is a sad affront and tantamount to the feminine of dog in English). I called her " *Vacca* ". She turned round, curtesied, and answered, " *Vacca tua*, *'Celenza* " (*i.e. Eccelenza*). " *Your* Cow, please your Excellency." In short, she was, as I said before, a very fine Animal, of considerable beauty and energy, with many good and several amusing qualities, but wild as a witch and fierce as a demon. She used to boast publicly of her ascendancy over me, contrasting it with that of other women, and assigning for it sundry reasons, physical and moral, which did more credit to her person than her modesty. True it was, that they all tried to get her away, and no one succeeded till her own absurdity helped them. Whenever there was a competition, and sometimes one would be shut in one room and one in another to prevent battle, she had generally the preference.

Yours very truly and affectionately, B.

P.S.—The Countess G[uiccioli] is much better than she was. I sent you, before leaving Venice, a letter containing the real original sketch which gave rise to the *Vampire*, etc.: did you get it?

TO JOHN MURRAY   *Bologna, August 12, 1819*

DEAR SIR,—I do not know how far I may be able to reply
to your letter, for I am not very well to-day. Last night I
went to the representation of Alfieri's *Mirra*,[1] the two last acts
of which threw me into convulsions. I do not mean by that
word a lady's hysterics, but the agony of reluctant tears, and
the choaking shudder, which I do not often undergo for fiction.
This is but the second time for anything under reality; the
first was on seeing Kean's Sir Giles Overreach. The worst
was, that the " *dama* ", in whose box I was, went off in the
same way, I really believe more from fright than any other
sympathy—at least with the players : but she has been ill, and
I have been ill, and we are all languid and pathetic this morning, with great expenditure of Sal Volatile. But, to return to
your letter of the 23d of July.

You are right, Gifford is right, Crabbe is right, Hobhouse
is right—you are all right, and I am all wrong; but do, pray,
let me have that pleasure. Cut me up root and branch;
quarter me in the *Quarterly*; send round my *disjecti membra
poetæ*, like those of the Levite's Concubine; make me, if you
will, a spectacle to men and angels; but don't ask me to alter,
for I can't :—I am obstinate and lazy—and there's the truth.

But, nevertheless, I will answer your friend C[ohen],[2] who
objects to the quick succession of fun and gravity, as if in that
case the gravity did not (in intention, at least) heighten the
fun. His metaphor is, that " we are never scorched and
drenched at the same time ". Blessings on his experience!
Ask him these questions about " scorching and drenching ".
Did he never play at Cricket, or walk a mile in hot weather?
Did he never spill a dish of tea over himself in handing the cup
to his charmer, to the great shame of his nankeen breeches?
Did he never swim in the sea at Noonday with the Sun in his
eyes and on his head, which all the foam of Ocean could not
cool? Did he never draw his foot out of a tub of too hot water,
damning his eyes and his valet's? * * * * * Was he ever in a
Turkish bath, that marble paradise of sherbet and Sodomy?
Was he ever in a cauldron of boiling oil, like St. John? or in

---

[1] Alfieri's tragedy concerns a young woman smitten with passion for her father.
[2] Afterwards Sir Francis Palgrave.

the sulphureous waves of hell? (where he ought to be for his
" scorching and drenching at the same time "). Did he never
tumble into a river or lake, fishing, and sit in his wet cloathes
in the boat, or on the bank, afterwards " scorched and
drenched ", like a true sportsman? " Oh for breath to utter ! "
—but make him my compliments ; he is a clever fellow for
all that—a very clever fellow.

You ask me for the plan of Donny Johnny : I *have* no plan
—I *had* no plan ; but I had or have materials ; though if,
like Tony Lumpkin, I am " to be snubbed so when I am in
spirits ", the poem will be naught, and the poet turn serious
again. If it don't take, I will leave it off where it is, with all
due respect to the Public ; but if continued, it must be in my
own way. You might as well make Hamlet (or Diggory)
" act mad " in a strait waistcoat as trammel my buffoonery, if
I am to be a buffoon : their gestures and my thoughts would
only be pitiably absurd and ludicrously constrained. Why,
Man, the Soul of such writing is its licence ; at least the *liberty*
of that *licence*, if one likes—*not* that one should abuse it : it is
like trial by Jury and Peerage and the Habeas Corpus—a very
fine thing, but chiefly in the *reversion* ; because no one wishes to
be tried for the mere pleasure of proving his possession of the
privilege.

But a truce with these reflections. You are too earnest and
eager about a work never intended to be serious. Do you
suppose that I could have any intention but to giggle and make
giggle?—a playful satire, with as little poetry as could be helped,
was what I meant : and as to the indecency, do, pray, read in
Boswell what *Johnson*, the sullen moralist, says of *Prior* and
Paulo Purgante.

Will you get a favour done for me? *You* can, by your
Government friends, Croker, Canning, or my old Schoolfellow
Peel, and I can't. Here it is. Will you ask them to appoint
(*without salary or emolument*) a noble Italian [1] (whom I will name
afterwards) Consul or Vice-Consul for Ravenna? He is a
man of very large property,—noble, too ; but he wishes to
have a British protection, in case of changes. Ravenna is near
the sea. He wants *no emolument* whatever : that his office might

---

[1] Count Guiccioli, a secret Liberal, had solicited Byron's interest in obtaining
such employment.

be useful, I know; as I lately sent off from Ravenna to Trieste a poor devil of an English Sailor, who had remained there sick, sorry, and penniless (having been set ashore in 1814), from the want of any accredited agent able or willing to help him home-wards. Will you get this done? It will be the greatest favour to me. If you do, I will then send his name and condition, subject, of course, to rejection, if *not* approved when known.

I know that in the Levant you make consuls and Vice-Consuls, perpetually, of foreigners. This man is a Patrician, and has twelve thousand a year. His motive is a British protec-tion in case of new Invasions. Don't you think Croker would do it for us? To be sure, *my interest* is rare !! but, perhaps a brother-wit in the Tory line might do a good turn at the re-quest of so harmless and long absent a Whig, particularly as there is no *salary* nor *burthen* of any sort to be annexed to the office.

I can assure you, I should look upon it as a great obliga-tion; but, alas! that very circumstance may, very probably, operate to the contrary—indeed, it ought. But I have, at least, been an honest and an open enemy. Amongst your many splendid Government Connections, could not you, think you, get our Bibulus made a Consul? Or make me one, that I may make him my Vice. You may be assured that, in case of accidents in Italy, he would be no feeble adjunct—as you would think if you knew his property.

What is all this about Tom Moore? but why do I ask? since the state of my own affairs would not permit me to be of use to him, although they are greatly improved since 1816, and may, with some more luck and a little prudence, become quite Clear. It seems his Claimants are *American* merchants? *There* goes *Nemesis!* Moore abused America. It is always thus in the long run :—Time, the Avenger. You have seen every trampler down, in turn, from Buonaparte to the simplest individuals. You saw how some were avenged even upon my insignificance, and how in turn Romilly paid for his atrocity. It is an odd World; but the Watch has its mainspring, after all.

So the Prince has been repealing Lord Ed. Fitzgerald's forfeiture? [1] *Ecco un' Sonnetto!*

---

[1] Lord Edward Fitzgerald, the Irish rebel, had met his death, while resisting arrest, in 1798. His attainder was repealed in 1819.

To be the father of the fatherless,
To stretch the hand from the throne's height, and raise
  His offspring, who expired in other days
To make thy Sire's Sway by a kingdom less,—
This is to be a Monarch, and repress
  Envy into unutterable praise.
Dismiss thy Guard, and trust thee to such traits,
For who would lift a hand, except to bless?
Were it not easy, Sir, and is't not sweet
To make thyself beloved? and to be
Omnipotent by Mercy's means? for thus
Thy Sovereignty would grow but more complete,
A Despot thou, and yet thy people free,
And by the Heart, not Hand, enslaving us.

There, you dogs: there's a Sonnet for you: you won't
have such as that in a hurry from Mr. Fitzgerald. You may
publish it with my name, an ye wool. He deserves all praise,
bad and good; it was a very noble piece of principality.
Would you like an epigram—a translation?

> If for silver, or for gold,
>   You could melt ten thousand pimples
>   Into half a dozen dimples,
> Then your face we might behold,
>   Looking, doubtless, much more smugly,
>   Yet even then 'twould be damned ugly.

This was written on some Frenchwoman, by Rulhières, I
believe. And so " good morrow t' ye, good Master lieutenant ".

Yours, BYRON

TO JOHN CAM HOBHOUSE   *Bologna, August 20th, 1819*

My dear Hobhouse,—I have not lately had of your news,
and shall not reproach you because I think that if you had good
to send me, you would be the first. I wrote to you twice or
thrice from Ravenna, and now I am at Bologna. Address to
me, however, at Venice.

My time has been passed viciously and agreeably; at thirty-one so few years, months, days remain, that " Carpe diem " is not enough. I have been obliged to crop even the seconds, for who can trust *to-morrow?—to-morrow* quotha? to-hour, to-*minute*. I can not repent me (I try very often) so much of anything I have done, as of anything I have left undone. Alas! I have been but idle, and have the prospect of an early decay, without having seized every available instant of our pleasurable years. This is a bitter thought, and it will be difficult for me ever to recover the despondency into which this idea naturally throws one. Philosophy would be in vain—let us try action.

In England I see and read of reform, " and there never were such troublesome times, especially for *constables* "; they have wafered Mr. Birch of Stockport. There is much of Hunt and Harrison, and Sir Charles (Linsey) Woolsey but we hear nothing of you and Burdett? The " Venerable Cartwright ", too—why did you not shorten that fellow's longevity? I do assure you (though that lust for duelling of which you used to accuse me in the Stevens's Coffee-house has long subsided into a moderate desire of killing one's more personal enemies) that I would have Mantoned [1] old Cartwright most readily. I have no notion of an old fool like that drivelling defiance, and coughing a challenge at his youngers and his betters. " *Solder him up* ", as Francis said of his defunct wife.

And now what do you think of doing? I have two notions : one to visit England in the spring, the other to go to South America. Europe is grown decrepit ; besides, it is all the same thing over again ; those fellows are fresh as their world, and fierce as their earthquakes. Besides, I am enamoured of General Paer, who has proved that my grandfather spoke truth about the Patagonians, with his gigantic cavalry.

Would that the Dougal of Bishop's Castle would find a purchaser for Rochdale.

I would embark (with Fletcher as a breeding beast of burthen) and possess myself of the pinnacle of the Andes, or a spacious plain of unbounded extent in an eligible earthquake situation.

---

[1] Manton's was a famous shooting-gallery, frequented by Byron and his friends.

Will my wife always live? will her mother never die? is her father immortal? What are you about? married and settled in the country, I suppose by your silence.

Yours, B.

P.S.—I hear nothing of Don Juan but in two letters from Murray; the first very tremulous, the second in better spirits.

Of the fate of the " pome " I am quite uncertain, and do not anticipate much brilliancy from your silence. But I do not care. I am as sure as the Archbishop of Grenada that I never wrote better, and I wish you all better taste, but will not send you any pistoles.

TO JOHN CAM HOBHOUSE   *Bologna, August 23rd, 1819*

MY DEAR HOBHOUSE,—I have received a letter from Murray containing the " British Review's " eleventh article. Had you any conception of a man's tumbling into such a trap as Roberts [1] has done? Why it is precisely what he was wished to do. I have enclosed an epistle for publication with a queer signature (to Murray, who should keep the anonymous still about D. Juan) in answer to Roberts, which pray approve if you can. It is written in an evening and morning in haste, with ill-health and worse nerves. I am so bilious, that I nearly lose my head, and so nervous that I cry for nothing; at least to-day I burst into tears, all alone by myself, over a cistern of gold-fishes, which are not pathetic animals. I can assure you it is not Mr. Roberts, or any of his crew that can affect me; but I have been excited and agitated, and exhausted mentally and bodily all this summer, till I really sometimes begin to think not only " that I shall die at top first ", but that the moment is not very remote. I have had no particular cause of griefs, except the usual accompaniments of all unlawful passions.

I have to do with a woman rendered perfectly disinterested by her situation in life, and young and amiable and pretty; in short as good, and at least as attractive as anything of the sex can be, with all the advantages and disadvantages of being

---

[1] William Roberts, editor of the *British Review*, which had suggested that *Don Juan* could not be by Byron.

scarcely twenty years old, and only two out of her Romagnuolo convent at Faenza.

But I feel—and I feel it bitterly—that a man should not consume his life at the side and on the bosom of a woman, and a stranger; that even the recompense, and it is much, is not enough, and that this Cicisbean existence is to be condemned. But I have neither the strength of mind to break my chain, nor the insensibility which would deaden its weight. I cannot tell what will become of me—to leave, or to be left would at present drive me quite out of my senses; and yet to what have I conducted myself? I have, luckily, or unluckily, no ambition left; it would be better if I had, it would at least awake me; whereas at present I merely start in my sleep.

I think I wrote to you last week, but really (like Lord Grizzle) cannot positively tell.

Why don't you write? pray do—never mind " Don Juan ", let him tumble—and let me too—like Jack and Gill.

Write, and believe me—as long as I can keep my sanity, ever yours most truly and affect^ly,

B.

TO JOHN MURRAY   *Bologna, August 24, 1819*

DEAR SIR,—I wrote to you by last post, enclosing a buffooning letter for publication, addressed to the buffoon Roberts, who has thought proper to tie a cannister to his own tail. It was written off hand, and in the midst of circumstances not very favourable to facetiousness, so that there may, perhaps, be more bitterness than enough for that sort of small acid punch. You will tell me.

Keep the *anonymous*, in every case : it helps what fun there may be; but if the matter grows serious about *Don Juan*, and you feel *yourself* in a scrape, or *me* either, *own that I am the author*. *I* will never *shrink*; and if *you* do, I can always answer you in the question of Guatimozin to his minister—each being on his own coals.

I wish that I had been in better spirits, but I am out of sorts, out of nerves; and now and then (I begin to fear) out of my senses. All this Italy has done for me, and not England : I defy all of you, and your climate to boot, to make me mad.

But if ever I do really become a Bedlamite, and wear a strait waistcoat, let me be brought back among you; your people will then be proper compagny.

I assure you what I here say and feel has nothing to do with England, either in a literary or personal point of view. All my present pleasures or plagues are as Italian as the Opera. And after all, they are but trifles, for all this arises from my *dama's* being in the country for three days (at Capofiume); but as I could never live for but one human being at a time, (and, I assure you, *that one* has never been *myself*, as you may know by the consequences, for the *Selfish* are *successful* in life,) I feel alone and unhappy.

I have sent for my daughter from Venice, and I ride daily, and walk in a Garden, under a purple canopy of grapes, and sit by a fountain, and talk with the Gardener of his toils, which seem greater than Adam's, and with his wife, and with his Son's wife, who is the youngest of the party, and, I think, talks best of the three. Then I revisit the Campo Santo, and my old friend, the Sexton, has two—but *one* the prettiest daughter imaginable; and I amuse myself with contrasting her beautiful and innocent face of fifteen with the skulls with which he has peopled several cells, and particularly with that of one skull dated 1766, which was once covered (the tradition goes,) by the most lovely features of Bologna—noble and rich. When I look at these, and at this girl—when I think of what *they were*, and what *she* must be—why, then, my dear Murray, I won't shock you by saying what I think. It is little matter what becomes of us " bearded men ", but I don't like the notion of a beautiful woman's lasting less than a beautiful tree—than her own picture—her own shadow, which won't change so to the Sun as her face to the mirror. I must leave off, for my head aches consumedly: I have never been quite well since the night of the representation of Alfieri's *Mirra*, a fortnight ago.

Yours ever, B.

TO THE COUNTESS GUICCIOLI   *Bologna, August 25, 1819*

MY DEAR TERESA,—I have read this book in your garden; —my love, you were absent, or else I could not have read it.

It is a favourite book of yours, and the writer was a friend of mine. You will not understand these English words, and *others* will not understand them—which is the reason I have not scrawled them in Italian. But you will recognise the hand-writing of him who passionately loved you, and you will divine that, over a book which was yours, he could only think of love. In that word, beautiful in all languages, but most so in yours—*Amor mio*—is comprised my existence here and hereafter. I feel I exist here, and I fear that I shall exist hereafter,—to *what* purpose you will decide; my destiny rests with you, and you are a woman, seventeen years of age, and two out of a convent. I wish that you had stayed there, with all my heart,—or, at least, that I had never met you in your married state.

But all this is too late. I love you, and you love me,—at least, you *say so*, and *act* as if you *did* so, which last is a great consolation in all events. But *I* more than love you, and cannot cease to love you.

Think of me, sometimes, when the Alps and the ocean divide us,—but they never will, unless you *wish* it.

BYRON

TO CAPT. HAY *   *Venice, Sept. 1819*

MY DEAR HAY,[1]—It is said that when Sir Isaac Newton delivered an opinion which any one chose to controvert, he never was at the pains to defend it, but contented himself with saying—" I believe, Sir, if you will be at the trouble of examin-ing my opinion, you will find that I have very good reason for it."—In making the assertion you allude to, I, too, have a most potent reason. Having been an eye and ear witness though an involuntary one, I ought to know what passed behind the curtain. There is nothing new under the sun, nay, under the moon neither. The mystical tradition of Apollo flaying his competitor is related by Diodorus Siculus with such praises of

---

[1] Captain John Hay, an acquaintance both of Byron and of Shelley, was involved with them and Trelawny in the scuffle which occurred at the gates of Pisa in 1822, when Sergeant-Major Masi claimed that he had been assaulted by the English party and afterwards stabbed by one of the Gambas' servants. This incident led to the Gambas' exile.

the musical skill of Marsyas, and with such imputations of trickery and cruelty on the God of Poetry, that it was probably an allegory, not so much of the chastisement merited by presumptuous ignorance as of the vindictive jealousy of *gens de plume.*—Damn the old sentimental serpent.—Lives there that being with wit enough to keep him from putrifying who doubts the rascality of the fellow ?—

To my extreme mortification I grow wiser every day—though Venice be not exactly the place for turning Solomon in a hurry—if you come over to the city of the winged lion you will soon convince yourself of it . . . 3 o'clock A.M. Good morrow !

ever yours, Byron

TO JOHN CAM HOBHOUSE   *Venice, Oct. 3rd, 1819*

DEAR HOBHOUSE,—I wrote to Murray last week and begged him to reassure you of my health and sanity, as far as I know at present. At Bologna I was out of sorts in health and spirits. Here—I have health at least. My South American project, of which I believe I spoke to you (as you mention it)—was this. I perceived by the inclosed paragraphs that advantageous offers were—or are to be held out to settlers in the Venezuela territory. My affairs in England are nearly settled or in prospect of settlement ; in Italy I have no debts, and I could leave it when I choose. The Anglo-Americans are a little too coarse for me, and their climate too cold, and I should prefer the others. I could soon grapple with the Spanish language. Ellice or others would get me letters to Bolivar and his government, and if men of little, or no property are encouraged there, surely with present income, and—if I could sell Rochdale —with some capital, I might be suffered as a landholder there, or at least a tenant, and if possible, and legal—a Citizen. I wish you would speak to *Perry* of the *M[orning] C[hronicle]*— who is their Gazetteer—about this, and ask like Jeremy Diddler—not for eighteen pence—but information on the subject. I assure you that I am very *serious* in the idea, and that the notion has been about me for a long time, as you will see

by the worn state of the advertisement. I should go there
with my natural daughter, Allegra,—now nearly three years
old, and with me here,—and pitch my tent for good and all.

I am not tired of Italy, but a man must be a Cicisbeo and
a Singer in duets, and a connoisseur of Operas—or nothing—
here. I have made some progress in all these accomplishments,
but I can't say that I don't feel the degradation. Better be
an unskilful Planter, an awkward settler,—better be a hunter,
or anything, than a flatterer of fiddlers, and fan carrier of a
woman. I like women—God he knows—but the more their
system here developes upon me, the worse it seems, after
Turkey too; here the *polygamy* is all on the female side. I
have been an intriguer, a husband, a whoremonger, and now
I am a Cavalier Servente—by the holy! it is a strange sensation. After having belonged in my own and other countries
to the intriguing, the married, and the keeping parts of the
town,—to be sure an honest arrangement is the best, and I
have had that too, and have—but they expect it to be for *life*,
thereby, I presume, excluding longevity. But let us be serious,
if possible.

You must not talk to me of England, that is out of the
question. I had a house and lands, and a wife and child, and
a name there—once—but all these things are transmuted or
sequestered. Of the last, and best, ten years of my life, nearly
six have been passed out of it. I feel no love for the soil after
the treatment I received before leaving it for the last time, but
I do not hate it enough to wish to take a part in its calamities,
as on either side harm must be done before good can accrue;
revolutions are not to be made with rosewater. My taste for
revolution is abated, with my other passions.

Yet I want a country, and a home, and—if possible—a free
one. I am not yet thirty-two years of age. I might still be a
decent Citizen, and found a house, and a family as good—or
better—than the former. I could at all events occupy myself
rationally, my hopes are not high, nor my ambition extensive,
and when tens of thousands of our countrymen are colonizing
(like the Greeks of old in Sicily and Italy) from so many causes,
does my notion seem visionary or irrational? There is no
freedom in Europe—that's certain; it is besides a worn out
portion of the globe. What I should be glad of is *information*

as to the encouragement, the means required, and what is accorded, and what would be my probable reception. Perry —or Ellice or many merchants would be able to tell you this for me. I won't go there to travel, but to settle. Do not laugh at me; you will, but I assure you I am quite in earnest if the thing be practicable. I do not want to have anything to do with war projects, but to go there as a settler, and if as a citizen all the better, my own government would not, I think, refuse me permission, if they know their own interest; such fellows as I am are no desideratum for Sidmouth at present, I think. Address to me at Venice. I should of course come to Liverpool, or some town on your coast, to take my passage and receive my credentials. Believe me,

Ever yours most truly, BYRON

TO THE HON. DOUGLAS KINNAIRD †   *Venice, Octr 26, 1819*[1]

MY DEAR DOUGLAS,—My late expenditure has arisen from living at a distance from Venice and being obliged to keep up two establishments, from frequent journeys and buying some furniture and books as well as a horse or two—and not from any renewal of the *Epicurean* system as you suspect.

I have been faithful to my honest liaison with Countess Guiccioli and I can assure you that she has never cost me directly or indirectly a sixpence, indeed the circumstances of herself and family render this no merit. I never offered her but one present—a broach of brilliants and she sent it back to me with her *own hair* in it (* * * * * * * but *that* is an Italian custom) and a note to say that she was not in the habit of receiving presents of that value, but hoped that I would not consider her sending it back as an affront, nor the value diminished by the enclosure.   * * * * * * * * * * * * * *

Why should you prevent Hanson from making a *peer* if he likes it. I think the " *garrotting* " would be by far the best parliamentary privilege I know of. Damn your delicacy. It is a low commercial quality and very unworthy a man who prefixes " honourable " to his nomenclature. If you say that I must sign the bonds, I suppose that I must, but it is very

[1] Wrongly dated as Oct. 26th, 1818, by Byron.

iniquitous to make me pay my debts—you have no idea of the pain it gives me.

Pray do three things, get my property out of the *funds*, get Rochdale sold, get me some information from Parry about *South* America, and 4thly ask Lady Noel not to live so very long. As to subscribing to Manchester—if I do that I will write a letter to Burdett for publication to accompany the Subscription which shall be more radical than anything yet rooted—but I feel lazy. I have thought of this for some time but, alas, the air of this cursed Italy enervates and disfranchises the thoughts of a man after nearly four years of respiration to say nothing of emission.

As to " Don Juan ", confess, confess—you dog and be candid—that it is the sublime of *that there* sort of writing—it may be bawdy but is it not good English? It may be profligate but is it not *life*, is it not *the thing*? Could any man have written it who has not lived in the world?—and [f]ooled in a post-chaise?—in a hackney coach?—in a gondola?—against a wall?—in a court carriage?—in a vis à vis?—on a table?—and under it? I have written about a hundred stanzas of a third Canto, but it is a damned modest—the outcry has frighted me. I have such projects for the Don but the Cant is so much stronger than the *, nowadays, that the benefit of experience in a man who had well weighed the worth of both monosyllables must be lost to despairing posterity. After all what stuff this outcry is—Lalla Rookh and Little are more dangerous than my burlesque poem can be. Moore has been here, we got tipsy together and were very amicable ; he is gone to Rome. I put my life (in M.S.) into his hands (not for publication), you or anybody else may see it at his return. It only comes up to 1816. He is a noble fellow and looks quite fresh and poetical, nine years (the age of a poem's education) my senior. He looks younger. This comes from marriage and being settled in the country. I want to go to South America— I have written to Hobhouse all about it. I wrote to my wife, three months ago, under cover to Murray. Has she got the letter—or is the letter got into Blackwood's Magazine?

You ask after my christmas pye. Remit it anyhow— *circulars* is the best. You are right about *income*—I must have it all. How the devil do I know that I may live a year or a month? I wish I knew, that I might regulate my spending in more ways than one. As it is one always thinks there is but a span. A man may as well break or be damned for a large sum as a small one. I should be loath to pay the devil or any other creditor more than six pence in the pound.

B.

TO RICHARD BELGRAVE HOPPNER† *October 29, 1819*

MY DEAR HOPPNER,—The Ferrara Story is of a piece with all the rest of the Venetian manufacture; you may judge. I only changed horses there since I wrote to you after my visit in June last. " *Convent* "—and " *carry off* " quotha !—and " *girl* "—I should like to know *who* has been carried off— except poor dear *me*. I have been more ravished myself than any body since the Trojan war; but as to the arrest and it's causes—one is as true as the other, and I can account for the invention of neither. I suppose it is some confusion of the tale of the F[ornarina]—and of Mᵉ Guiccioli—and half a dozen more—but it is useless to unravel the web, when one has only to brush it away.

I shall settle with Muster Edgecombe who looks very blue at your *in-decision*, and swears that he is the best arithmetician in Europe; and so I think also, for he makes out two and two to be five.

You may see me next week. I have a horse or two more (five in all) and I shall repossess myself of Lido, and I will rise earlier, and we will go and shake our livers over the beach as heretofore—if you like, and we will make the Adriatic roar again with our hatred of that now empty Oyster shell without it's pearl—the city of Venice.

Murray sent me a letter yesterday; the impostors have published *two* new *third* Cantos of *Don Juan*; the devil take the impudence of some blackguard bookseller or other there*for*.

Perhaps I did not make myself understood. He told me the sale had not been great—1200 out of 1500 quarto I believe (which is nothing after selling 13000 of *The Corsair* in one day) but that the " best judges, etc.", had said it was very fine, and clever, and particularly good English, and poetry, and all those consolatory things which are not, however, worth a single copy to a bookseller;—and as to the author—of course I am in a damned passion at the bad taste of the times, and swear there is nothing like posterity, who of course must know more of the matter than their Grandfathers.

There has been an eleventh commandment to the women not to read it—and what is still more extraordinary they seem not to have broken it. But that can be of little import to them, poor things, for the reading or non-reading a book will never keep down a single petticoat;—but it is of import to Murray, who will be in scandal for his aiding as publisher.

He is bold howsomedever—wanting two more cantos against the winter. I think that he had better not, for by the larkins! it will only make a new row for him.

Edgecombe is gone to Venice to-day to consign my chattels to t'other fellow.

Count G[uiccioli] comes to Venice next week and I am requested to consign his wife to him, which shall be done—with all her linen.

What you say of the long evenings at the Mira, or Venice, reminds me of what *Curran* said to Moore—" so—I hear—you have married a pretty woman—and a very good creature too —an excellent creature—pray—um—*how do you pass your evenings?* " it is a devil of a question that, and perhaps as easy to answer with a wife as with a mistress; but surely they are longer than the nights. I am all for morality now, and shall confine myself henceforward to the strictest adultery, which you will please to recollect is all that that virtuous wife of mine has left me.

If you go to Milan, pray leave at least a *Vice-Consul*—the only Vice that will ever be wanting in Venice. D'Orville is a good fellow. But you should go to England in the Spring with me, and plant Mrs. Hoppner at Berne with her relations for a few months.

I wish you had been here (at Venice I mean not the Mira) when Moore was here; we were very merry and tipsy—he *hated* Venice by the way, and swore it was a sad place.

So—Madame Albrizzi's death is in danger, poor woman. Saranzo is of course in the crazy recollection of their rancid amours.

Moore told me that at Geneva they had made a devil of a story of the Fornaretta—" young lady seduced—subsequent abandonment—leap into the grand canal—her being in the hospital of *fous* in consequence ". I should like to know who was nearest being made "*fou*" and be damned to them. Don't you think me in the interesting character of a very ill used gentleman?

I hope your little boy is well. Allegrina is flourishing like a pome-granate blossom.

Yours ever, BYRON

TO LADY BYRON *[Ravenna, December 31ˢᵗ 1819]*

Augusta can tell you all about me and mine if you think either worth the enquiry ;—But the object of my writing is to come—

It is this.—I saw Moore three months ago and gave to his care—a long Memoir written up to the Summer of 1816, of my life—which I had been writing since I left England.—It will not be published till after my death—and in fact it is a " Memoir " and not " confessions " I have omitted the most important and decisive events and passions of my existence not to compromise others.—But it is not so with the part you occupy—which is long and minute—and I could wish you to see, read—and mark any part or parts that do not appear to coincide with the truth.—The truth I have always stated—but there are two ways of looking at it—and your way may be not mine.—I have never revised the papers since they were written —You may read them—and mark what you please—I wish you [to] know what I think and say of you and yours.—You will find nothing to flatter you—nothing to lead you to the most remote supposition that we could ever have been—or be happy together.—But I do not choose to give to another generation statements which we cannot arise from the dust to prove or disprove—without letting you see fairly and fully what I look upon you to have been—and what I depict you as being.—If seeing this—you can detect what is false—or answer what is charged—do so—*your mark*—shall not be erased.

You will perhaps say *why* write my life?—Alas ! I say so too—but they who have traduced it—and blasted it—and branded me—should know—that it is they—and not I—are the cause—It is no great pleasure to have lived—and less to live over again the details of existence—but the last becomes sometimes a necessity and even a duty.—

If you choose to see this you may—if you do not—you have at least had the option.

[Finished] January 1st—[1820].

TO RICHARD BELGRAVE HOPPNER   *Ravenna, Dec. 31, 1819*

MY DEAR HOPPNER,—Will you have the goodness to ask or cause to be asked of Siri and Willhalm, if they have not *three* sabres of mine in custody according to the enclosed note? if not, they must have lost two for they never sent them back.

And will you desire Missiaglia to subscribe for and send me the *Minerva*, a Paris paper, as well as *Galignani*.

I have been here this week, and was obliged to put on my armour and go the night after my arrival to the Marquis Cavalli's, where there were between two and three hundred of the best company I have seen in Italy,—more beauty, more youth, and more diamonds among the women than have been seen these fifty years in the Sea-Sodom. I never saw such a difference between two places of the same latitude, (or *p*latitude, it is all one,)—music, dancing, and play, all in the same *salle*. The G.'s object appeared to be to parade her foreign lover as much as possible, and, faith, if she seemed to glory in the Scandal, it was not for me to be ashamed of it. Nobody seemed surprised;—all the women, on the contrary, were, as it were, delighted with the excellent example. The Vice-legate, and all the other Vices, were as polite as could be ;— and I, who had acted on the reserve, was fairly obliged to take the lady under my arm, and look as much like a Cicisbeo as I could on so short a notice,—to say nothing of the embarrassment of a cocked hat and sword, much more formidable to me than ever it will be to the enemy.

I write in great haste—do you answer as hastily. I can

understand nothing of all this; but it seems as if the G. had been presumed to be *planted*, and was determined to show that she was not,—*plantation*, in this hemisphere, being the greatest moral misfortune. But this is mere conjecture, for I know nothing about it—except that every body are very kind to her, and not discourteous to me. Fathers, and all relations, quite agreeable.

Yours ever and truly, B.

P.S.—Best respects to Mrs. H.

I would send the *compliments* of the season; but the season itself is so little complimentary with snow and rain that I wait for sunshine.

5

Teresa Guiccioli

January 1820 to July 1823

yron's life in Ravenna was as placid and humdrum as his career in Venice had been feverish. He occupied rooms in the Guiccioli palace, was cordially received by Teresa's husband, " a very polite personage ", and in conjunction with Count Gamba, her father, and Pietro Gamba, her youthful and enthusiastic brother, played some part in revolutionary intrigues against the Austrian government. Then, during the summer of 1821, the revolutionary movement was unmasked, and the Gambas banished from Ravenna. Byron, as in duty bound, followed them to Pisa, where he installed his cumbrous household at the Palazzo Lanfranchi. But the Tuscan authorities became suspicious: a scuffle in which Byron's servants were involved gave them the pretext that they needed: and, though they hesitated to meddle with a celebrated Englishman, his Italian friends were advised that they would do well to leave the city. Byron thereupon took a villa at Montenero near Leghorn, sent the Gambas on ahead, and removed thither himself during the early summer months of 1822. Two deaths, which occurred in the course of that year, affected him profoundly. In April he learned that Allegra, his natural daughter, had died of fever at her convent: on June 8th Shelley was drowned while sailing in the Gulf of Spezzia. A few days before Shelley's death, Leigh Hunt, who had agreed to edit a paper which Byron and Shelley thought of founding, reached Italy with his wife and children. The Liberal was doomed to early extinction; and Leigh Hunt and his good-natured, but indolent and capricious, patron were very soon at variance. Byron was growing bored and restive, and at moments talked of emigrating to the New World and " buying a principality in one of the South American States—Chili or Peru ", when the news that a Whig committee had been formed in London to assist the Greek insurgents gave his imagination a fresh interest and his plans a new direction.

TO THE HON. DOUGLAS KINNAIRD *   *January 2nd, 1820*

DEAR DOUGLAS,—In the present state of the funds and of the country, you will hardly wonder at my anxiety to be informed whether you have succeeded in investing the settled property elsewhere, or what has been done towards that object. I wrote to you twice lately to tell you that I had postponed my intention of return for some time. Neither the season nor the length of the journey would have suited my daughter's health after her illness.

You will do me a great favour in letting me know all about any steps that may have been or are to be taken. You do not write, nor like to receive, long letters; so I will not trail this further. I read your speeches in Galignani. Is H. or is he not the author of " a trifling mistake ", or is the House mistaken and not H.? ¹ I always said that I should " have to bail my old friend out of the round-house ", and so it seems. What will be the issue of it all? He has not written to me these four months. But it is no time to reproach his silence when he is in a scrape. Don't forget to let me know all about him.

Yours ever truly and [indecipherable], B.

P.S.—You may remit my half year to the usual address— Venice—in *circulars* as most universal.

TO JOHN MURRAY   *Ravenna, February 21, 1820*

DEAR MURRAY,—The Bulldogs will be very agreeable: I have only those of this country, who, though good, and ready to fly at any thing, yet have not the tenacity of tooth and Stoicism in endurance of my canine fellow-citizens : then pray send them by the readiest conveyance—perhaps best by Sea. Mr. Kinnaird will disburse for them, and deduct from the amount on your application or on that of Captain Fyler.

I see the good old King is gone to his place : one can't

---

¹ During December 1819, Hobhouse's pamphlet, *A Trifling Mistake in Thomas Lord Erskine's Recent Preface,* was brought to the notice of the House of Commons and voted a breach of privilege. He was committed to Newgate, where he remained till February. At the next election he finally entered the House as one of the representatives for Westminster.

help being sorry, though blindness, and age, and insanity, are supposed to be drawbacks on human felicity; but I am not at all sure that the latter, at least, might not render him happier than any of his subjects.

I have no thoughts of coming to the Coronation, though I should like to see it, and though I have a right to be a puppet in it; but my division with Lady Byron, which has drawn an equinoctial line between me and mine in all other things, will operate in this also to prevent my being in the same procession.

By Saturday's post I sent you four packets, containing Cantos third and fourth of D[on] J[uan]; recollect that these two cantos reckon only as *one* with you and me, being, in fact, the third Canto cut into two, because I found it too long. Remember this, and don't imagine that there could be any other motive. The whole is about 225 Stanzas, more or less, and a lyric of 96 lines, so that they are no longer than the first *single* cantos: but the truth is, that I made the first too long, and should have cut those down also had I thought better. Instead of saying in future for so many cantos, say so many *Stanzas* or pages: it was Jacob Tonson's way, and certainly the best: it prevents mistakes. I might have sent you a dozen cantos of 40 Stanzas each,—those of *the Minstrel* (Beattie's) are no longer, —and ruined you at once, if you don't suffer as it is; but recollect you are not *pinned down* to anything you say in a letter, and that, calculating even these two cantos as *one* only (which they were and are to be reckoned), you are not bound by your offer: act as may seem fair to all parties.

I have finished my translation of the first Canto of the " *Morgante Maggiore* " of Pulci, which I will transcribe and send: it is the parent, not only of *Whistle-craft*,[1] but of all jocose Italian poetry. You must print it side by side with the original Italian, because I wish the reader to judge of the fidelity: it is stanza for stanza, and often line for line, if not word for word.

You ask me for a volume of manners, etc., on Italy: perhaps I am in the case to know more of them than most Englishmen, because I have lived among the natives, and in parts of the country where Englishmen never resided before (I

---

[1] John Hookham Frere's *Prospectus and Specimen of an intended National Work, by William and Robert Whistlecraft*, is said to have inspired Byron's *Beppo*. Frere was also a brilliant translator of Aristophanes.

speak of Romagna and this place particularly) ; but there are many reasons why I do not choose to touch in print on such a subject. I have lived in their houses and in the heart of their families, sometimes merely as " *amico di casa* ", and sometimes as " *Amico di cuore* " of the *Dama*, and in neither case do I feel myself authorized in making a book of them. Their moral is not your moral ; their life is not your life ; you would not understand it : it is not English, nor French, nor German, which you would all understand. The Conventual education, the Cavalier Servitude, the habits of thought and living are so entirely different, and the difference becomes so much more striking the more you live intimately with them, that I know not how to make you comprehend a people, who are at once temperate and profligate, serious in their character and buffoons in their amusements, capable of impressions and passions, which are at once *sudden* and *durable* (what you find in no other nation), and who actually have *no society* (what we would call so), as you may see by their Comedies : they have no real comedy, not even in Goldoni ; and that is because they have no Society to draw it from.

Their Conversazioni are not Society at all. They go to the theatre to talk, and into company to hold their tongues. The *women* sit in a circle, and the men gather into groupes, or they play at dreary *Faro* or " *Lotto reale* ", for small sums. Their Academie are Concerts like our own, with better music and more form. Their best things are the Carnival balls and masquerades, when every body runs mad for six weeks. After their dinners and suppers, they make extempore verses and buffoon one another ; but it is in a humour which you would not enter into, ye of the North.

In their houses it is better. I should know something of the matter, having had a pretty general experience among their women, from the fisherman's wife up to the *Nobil' Donna*, whom I serve. Their system has its rules, and its fitnesses, and decorums, so as to be reduced to a kind of discipline or game at hearts, which admits few deviations, unless you wish to lose it. They are extremely tenacious, and jealous as furies ; not permitting their lovers even to marry if they can help it, and keeping them always close to them in public as in private whenever they can. In short, they transfer marriage to adultery, and strike the *not* out of that commandment. The reason is, that they marry for their parents, and love for themselves. They exact fidelity from a lover as a debt of honour, while they pay the husband as a tradesman, that is, not at all. You hear a person's character, male or female, canvassed, not as depending on their conduct to their husbands or wives, but to their mistress or lover. And—and—that's all. If I wrote a quarto, I don't know that I could do more than amplify what I have here noted. It is to be observed that while they do all this, the greatest outward respect is to be paid to the husbands, not only by the ladies, but by their *Serventi*—particularly if the husband serves no one himself (which is not often the case, however): so that you would often suppose them relations— the *Servente* making the figure of one adopted into the family. Sometimes the ladies run a little restive and elope, or divide, or make a scene; but this is at starting, generally, when they know no better, or when they fall in love with a foreigner, or some such anomaly,—and is always reckoned unnecessary and extravagant.

You enquire after " Dante's prophecy ": I have not done more than six hundred lines, but will vaticinate at leisure.

Of the bust I know nothing. No Cameos or Seals are to be cut here or elsewhere that I know of, in any good style. Hobhouse should write himself to Thorwalsen: the bust was made and paid for three years ago.

Pray tell Mrs. Leigh to request Lady Byron to urge forward the transfer from the funds, which Hanson is opposing, because he has views of investment for some Client of his own, which I can't consent to. I wrote to Lady B. on business this post, addressed to the care of Mr. D. Kinnaird.

Somebody has sent me some American abuse of *Mazeppa* and " the Ode ": in future I will compliment nothing but Canada, and desert to the English.

By the king's death Mr. H[obhouse], I hear, will stand for Westminster: I shall be glad to hear of his standing any where except in the pillory, which, from the company he must have lately kept (I always except Burdett, and Douglas K., and the genteel part of the reformers), was perhaps to be apprehended. I was really glad to hear it was for libel instead of larceny; for, though impossible in his own person, he might have been taken up by mistake for another at a meeting. All reflections on his present case and place are so *Nugatory*, that it would be useless to pursue the subject further. I am out of all patience to see my friends sacrifice themselves for a pack of black-guards, who disgust one with their Cause, although I have always been a friend to and a Voter for reform. If Hunt had addressed the language to me which he did to Mr. H. last election, I would not have descended to call out such a mis-creant who won't fight; but have passed my sword-stick through his body, like a dog's, and then thrown myself on my Peers, who would, I hope, have weighed the provocation: at any rate, it would have been as public a Service as Walworth's chastisement of Wat. Tyler. If we must have a tyrant, let him at least be a gentleman who has been bred to the business, and let us fall by the axe and not by the butcher's cleaver.

No one can be more sick of, or indifferent to, politics than I am, if they let me alone; but if the time comes when a part must be taken one way or the other, I shall pause before I lend myself to the views of such ruffians, although I cannot but approve of a Constitutional amelioration of long abuses.

Lord George Gordon, and Wilkes, and Burdett, and Horne Tooke, were all men of education and courteous deportment: so is Hobhouse; but as for these others, I am convinced that Robespierre was a Child, and Marat a Quaker in comparison of what they would be, could they throttle their way to power.

Yours ever, B.

TO JOHN CAM HOBHOUSE †   *Ravenna, March 3rd, 1820*

My dear Hobhouse,—I have paused thus long in replying to your letter not knowing well in what terms to write; because though I approve of the object, yet, with the exception of Burdett and Doug. K. and one or two others, I dislike the companions of your labours as much as the place to which they have brought you.

I perceive by the papers that " ould Apias Kerkus " has not extricated you from the " puddle " into which your wit hath brought you. However, if this be but a prologue to a seat

for Westminster I shall less regret your previous ordeal ; but
I am glad that I did not come to England, for it would not have
pleased me to find on my own return from transportation my
best friends in Newgate. " Did I ever—no I never ",—but
I will say no more, all reflections being quite *Nugatory* on the
occasion, still I admire your gallantry, and think you could
not do otherwise, *having* written the pamphlet, but "*why bitch*
Mr. Wild? " why write it? why lend yourself to Hunt and
Cobbett, and the bones of Tom Paine? " Death and fiends ! "
You used to be thought a prudent man, at least by me, whom
you favoured with so much good counsel ; but methinks you
are waxed somewhat rash, at least in politics. However, the
king is dead, so get out of Mr. Burn's apartments, and get into
the House of Commons ; and then abuse it as much as you
please, and I'll come over and hear you. Seriously ; I did
not " laugh " as you supposed I would ; no more did Fletcher ;
but we looked both as grave as if we had got to have been your
bail, particularly that learned person who pounced upon the
event in the course of spelling the Lugano Gazette.

So Scrope is gone [1]—down-*diddled*—as Doug. K. writes it,
the said Doug. being like the man who, when he lost a friend,
went to the Saint James's Coffee House and took a new one ;
but to you and me the loss of Scrope is irreparable ; we could
have better spared not only a " better man ", but the " best
of men ". Gone to Bruges where he will get tipsy with
Dutch beer and shoot himself the first foggy morning. Brummell at Calais ; Scrope at Bruges, Buonaparte at St. Helena,
you in your new apartments, and I at Ravenna, only think !
so many great men ! There has been nothing like it since
Themistocles at Magnesia, and Marius at Carthage.

But times change, and they are luckiest who get over their
first rounds at the beginning of the battle.

The other day, February 25th, we plucked violets by the
wayside *here*, at Ravenna ; and now, March 3rd, it is snowing
for all the world as it may do in Cateaton St.

We have nothing new here but the Cardinal from Imola
and the news of the berri-cide in France by a sadler ; I suppose
the Duke had not paid his bill.

I shall let " dearest duck " waddle alone at the Corona-

---

[1] Scrope Davies had escaped from his creditors by leaving the country.

tion; a ceremony which I should like to see, and have a right to act Punch in; but the crown itself would not bribe me to return to England, unless business or actual urgency required it. I was very near coming, but that was because I had been very much " agitato " with some circumstances of a domestic description, here in Italy, and not from any love of the tight little Island.

Tell Doug. K. that I answered his last letter long ago, and enclosed in the letter an order peremptory to Spooney, to make me an Irish Absentee, according to Doug.'s own directions.

I like the security in Dublin houses, " an empty house on Ormond Quay ", but pray, are they insured in case of conflagration? Deliver me that, and let us be guaranteed, otherwise what becomes of my fee?

My Clytemnestra stipulated for the security of her jointure; it was delicately done, considering that the poor woman will only have ten thousand a year, more or less, for life, on the death of her mother.

I sent Murray two more cantos of Donny Johnny, but they are only to reckon as *one* in arithmetic, because they are but one long one, cut into *two*, whilk was expedient on account of tedium. So don't let him be charged for these two but as one. I sent him also a translation, close and rugged, of the first canto of the Morgante Maggiore, to be published with the original text, side by side, " cheek by jowl gome ", on account of the superlative merits of both. All these are to be corrected by you by way of solace during your probation.

William Bankes came to see me twice, once at Venice and he since came a second time from Bologna to Ravenna on purpose, so I took him to a Ball here, and presented him to all the Ostrogothic Nobility, and to the Dama whom I serve. I have settled into regular *serventismo*, and find it the happiest state of all, always excepting scarmentado's. I double a shawl with considerable alacrity; but have not yet arrived at the perfection of putting it on the right way; and I hand in and out, and know my post in a conversazione, and theatre; and play at cards as well as a man can do who of all the Italian pack can only distinguish " Asso " and " Re ", the rest for me are hieroglyphics. Luckily the play is limited to " Papetti ", that is pieces of four Pauls, somewhere in, or about two shillings.

I am in favour and respect with the Cardinal, and Vice-legato, and in decent intercourse with the Gonfaloniere and all the Nobilità of the middle ages. Nobody has been stabbed this winter, and few new liaisons formed—there is Sposa Fiorentina, a pretty girl yet in abeyance, but no one can decide yet who is to be her servante, most of the men being already adulterated, and she showing no preferences to any who are not. There is a certain Marchese who I think would run a chance if he did not take matters rather too phi[lo]sophically.

Syricci is here improvising away with great success * * *

B.

TO JOHN CAM HOBHOUSE† *Ravenna, March 29th, 1820*

My dear Hobhouse,—I congratulate you on your change of residence, which, I perceive by the papers, took place on the dissolution of king and parliament. The other day I sent (through Murray) a song for you—you dog—to pay you off for them there verses which you compounded in April 1816.

> " No more shall Mr. Murray
> Pace Piccadilly in a hurry,
> Nor Holmes with not a few grimaces
> Beg a few pounds for a few faces,
> Nor Douglas——"

but I won't go on, though you deserve it, but you see I forget nothing—but good.

I suppose I shall soon see your speeches again, and your determination " not to be saddled with wooden shoes as the Gazetteer says ", but do pray get into Parliament, and out of the company of all these fellows, except Burdett and Douglas Kinnaird, and don't be so very violent. I doubt that Thistle-wood [1] will be a great help to the ministers in all the elections, but especially in the Westminster. What a set of desperate fools these Utican conspirators seem to have been. As if in London, after the disarming acts, or indeed at any time, a

---

[1] Thistlewood was one of the ringleaders of the " Cato Street Conspiracy ", to assassinate the whole Cabinet at a dinner-party at Lord Harrowby's house.

secret could have been kept among thirty or forty. And if they had killed poor Harrowby—in whose house I have been five hundred times, at dinners and parties; his wife is one of " the Exquisites "—and t'other fellows, what end would it have answered? " They understand these things better in France ", as Yorick says, but really, if these sort of awkward butchers are to get the upper hand, *I* for one will declare *off*. I have always been (*before* you were, as you well know) a well-wisher to, and voter for reform in parliament; but " such fellows as these, who will never go to the gallows with any credit ", such infamous scoundrels as Hunt and Cobbett, in short, the whole gang (always excepting you, B. and D.) disgust, and make one doubt of the virtue of any principle or politics which can be embraced by similar ragamuffins. I know that revolutions are not to be made with rose water, but though some blood may, and must be shed on such occasions, there is no reason it should be *clotted*; in short, the Radicals seem to be no better than Jack Cade or Wat Tyler, and to be dealt with accordingly.

I perceive you talk *Tacitus* to them sometimes; what do they make of it? It is a great comfort, however, to see you termed " *young Mr. Hobhouse* ", at least to me who am a year and a half younger, and had given up for these two years all further idea of being

> " Gentle and juvenile, curly and gay,
>   In the manner of Ackermann's dresses for May."

And now, my man—my parliament man I hope—what is become of Scrope? Is he at Bruges? or have you gone to " the St. James's coffee-house to take another "?

You will have been sadly plagued by this time with some new packets of poesy and prose for the press; but Murray was so pressing and in such a hurry for something for the *Season*, that I e'en sent him a cargo; otherwise I had got sulky about Juan, and did not mean to print any more, at least " *before term ends* ". You will see that I have taken up the *Pope* question (in prose) with a high hand, and *you* (when you can spare yourself from *Party* to Mankind) must help me. You know how often, under the Mira elms, and by the Adriatic on the Lido, we have discussed that question, and lamented the villainous cant which at present would decry him. It is my intention to give battle to the blackguards and try if the " little Nightingale " can't be heard again.

But at present you are on the hustings, or in the chair. Success go with you.

P.S.—Items of " Poeshie of the King your Master ". Sent last Moon.

Cantos of Don Juan—two. To reckon as one only, however, with Murray on account of their brevity.
First Canto of Morgante Maggiore translated.
Prophecy of Dante—*four short* Cantos.
Prose Observations on an article in B.d's Edin : Magazine.
Poeshie—Episode of Francesca of Rimini translated.

For all these matters you will request the honourable Dougal to arrange the elements with Mr. Murray. Tell the Dougal I answered him peremptorily in favour of the Irish Mortgage long ago, and *against* Spooney, and hope that he hath done the needful ; but yr. damned parliaments cut up all useful friendship.

[Note on the margin of the first sheet]

Ask Dougal to get Spooney's bill and try to bring Rochdale to the hammer. I want to buy an Annuity like.

TO RICHARD BELGRAVE HOPPNER †   *Ravenna,*
March 31st, 1820

DEAR HOPPNER,—Laziness has kept me from answering your letter. It is an inveterate vice, which grows stronger, and I feel it in my pen at this moment. . . . With regard to Mr. Gnoatto, I doubt that the Chevalier is too honest a man to make a good lawyer. Castelli is a bustling, sly, sharp Atornato, and will be more likely to make the rascal wince. But I mean to do thus,—that is to say, with your approbation. . . . You will inform Madame Mocenigo, that till Mr. Gnoatto's money is paid, I *shall deduct that sum* from her rent in

June, till she compels her Servant to pay it. She may make a cause of it, if she likes *so will I* and carry it through all the tribunals so as to give her as many years work of it, as she pleases. At the same time I will prosecute *him* also. I am not even sure that I will pay her *at all*, till she compels her Scoundrelly dependant to do me justice, which a word from *her* would do. All this you had better let *her* know as soon as can be.

By the way, I should like to have my *Gondola* sold, for what it will bring and do you carry the money to the account of expences. If Mother Mocenigo does as she ought to do, I may perhaps give up her house, and pay her rent into the bargain. If not, I'll pay nothing and we'll go to law—I *loves* a " lité." . . .

What you tell me of Mrs. Strephon is very amusing, but all private matters must be suppressed at present by the public plots, and so forth. I wonder what it will all end in. I should probably have gone to England for the Coronation, but for my wife—I don't wish to walk in such company under present circumstances. . . . Ravenna continues much the same as I described it—Conversazioni all Lent, and much better even than any at Venice. There are small games at hazard—that is Faro—where nobody can point more than a shilling or two—other Card-tables—and as múch talk and Coffee as you please. Everybody does and says what they please, and I do not recollect any disagreeable events, except being three times falsely accused of flirtation, and once being robbed of six sixpences by a nobleman of the city—a Count Bozzi. I did not suspect the illustrious delinquent, but the Countess Vitelloni and the Marquess Lovatelli told me of it directly, and also that it was a way he had—of filching money, when he saw it before him. But I did not ax him for the cash, but contented myself with telling him that if he did it again I should anticipate the law. . . . There is to be a theatre in April, and a fair, and an Opera, and another Opera in June, besides the fine weather of Nature's giving, and the ride in the Forest of Pine. . . . Augustine overturned the carriage a fortnight ago, and smashed it, and himself and me, and Tita, and the horses, into a temporary hodge-podge. He pleaded against the horses, but it was his own bad driving. Nobody was hurt—a few slight bruises—the escape was tolerable—being between a river on one side and a steep bank on the other. I was luckily alone—Allegra being with Madame Guiccioli. With my best respects to Mrs Hoppner,

Believe me ever most truly yrs.

BYRON

P.S.—Could you give me an Item of what books remain at Venice. I *don't* want them, but merely to know whether the few that are not here are there, and were not lost by the way. . . . I hope and trust you have got all your wine safe—and that it is drinkable. . . .

Allegra is prettier I think, but as obstinate as a Mule, and as ravenous as a Vulture. Health good to judge by the complexion, temper tolerable, but for vanity and pertinacity. She thinks herself handsome, and will do as she pleases. . . .

TO RICHARD BELGRAVE HOPPNER   *Ravenna, April 22ᵈ 1820*

MY DEAR HOPPNER,—With regard to Gnoatto, I cannot relent in favour of Madame Mocenigo, who protects a rascal and retains him in her service. Suppose the case of your Servant or mine, you having the same claim upon F[letche]r or I upon your Tim, would either of us retain them an instant unless they paid the debt? As " there is no force in the decrees of Venice ", no Justice to be obtained from the tribunals,— because even conviction does not compel payment, nor enforce punishment,—you must excuse me when I repeat *that not one farthing of the rent shall be paid*, till either Gnoatto pays me his debt, or quits Madame Mocenigo's service. I will abide by the consequences; but I could wish that no time was lost in apprizing her of the affair. You must not mind her relation Seranzo's statement; he may be a very good man, but he is but a Venetian, which I take to be in the present age the *ne plus ultra* of human abasement in all moral qualities whatsoever. I dislike differing from you in opinion; but I have no other course to take, and either Gnoatto pays me, or quits her Service, or I will resist to the uttermost the liquidation of her rent. I have nothing against her, nor for her; I owe her neither ill will, nor kindness;—but if she protects a Scoundrel, and there is no other redress, I will *make* some.

It has been and always will be the case where there is *no law*. Individuals must then right themselves. They have set the example " and it shall go hard but I will better the Instruction ". Two words from her would suffice to make the villain do his duty ; if they are not said, or if they have no effect, let him be dismissed ; if not, as I have said, so will I do.

I wrote last week to Siri to desire *Vincenzo* to be sent to take charge of the beds and Swords to this place by Sea. I am in no hurry for the books,—none whatever,—and don't want them.

Pray has not Mingaldo the Biography of living people? —it is not here, nor in your list. I am not at all sure that *he* has it either, but it may be possible.

Let Castelli go on to the last. I am determined to see Merryweather *out* in this business, just to discover what is or is not to be done in their tribunals, and if ever I cross him, as I have tried the law in vain, (since it has but convicted him and then done nothing in consequence)—I will try a shorter process with that personage.

About Allegra, I can only say to Claire—that I so totally disapprove of the mode of Children's treatment in their family,[1] that I should look upon the Child as going into a hospital. Is it not so? Have they *reared* one? Her health here has hitherto been *excellent*, and her temper not bad ; she is sometimes vain and obstinate, but always clean and cheerful, and as, in a year or two, I shall either send her to England, or put her in a Convent for education, these defects will be remedied as far as they can in human nature. But the Child shall not quit me again to perish of Starvation, and green fruit, or be taught to believe that there is no Deity. Whenever there is convenience of vicinity and access, her Mother can always have her with her ; otherwise no. It was so stipulated from the beginning.

The Girl is not so well off as with you, but far better than with them ; the fact is she is spoilt, being a great favourite with every body on account of the fairness of her skin, which shines among their dusky children like the milky way, but there is no comparison of her situation now, and that under Elise, or with them. She has grown considerably, is very clean, and

[1] The Shelleys.

lively. She has plenty of air and exercise at home, and she goes out daily with Me Guiccioli in her carriage to the Corso.

The paper is finished and so must the letter be.

Yours ever, B.

My best respects to Mrs. H. and the little boy—and Dorville.

TO THE HON. DOUGLAS KINNAIRD *   *Ravenna, May 3rd, 1820*

MY DEAR DOUGLAS,—I have written to you twice lately, once enclosing a letter of Hanson's, and secondly a letter of Murray's. I shall therefore not trouble you now at great length on the subject of yours of the 18th ult?. It holds out no great inducements to visit England, which you say you yourself would like to quit.

I see the funds are improving. If they get high enough to enable us to sell out without loss, do so, and place the money any where or how rather than have it in the three per cents. I have already given my consent to complete the Mortgage for Ireland, if it can be done without a heavy loss, and so that the house property is ensured. I once more recommend *Rochdale* to your notice, the more so, that you will perceive that Hanson particularly alludes to it and to the proposal of accommodation made by the other party.

I have had no letter from Murray since the one I sent to you, with my opinions thereupon, and shall therefore not intrude upon the man of books for the present with my correspondence. I will just repeat that my *prose* (an Answer to the Galin. Magazine) is *not* for present publication, but I wish you to read it, because as how I think you will find it very smart in the invective line.

I sometimes think of making one among you (not among the radicals by the way) in the coming Autumn, *after the Coronation*, for I won't waddle with " dearest duck " ; [1] but really the encouragement you hold out is not very great, and I don't know how my finances may stand for an English visit unless a

---

[1] A day after leaving her husband in London, Lady Byron wrote him an affectionate letter, beginning " Dearest Duck ".

better interest of the settled property, or a sale of Rochdale, take place.

I have been obliged to be at expenses in changing my sea-residence for a land house, much as a Triton would on coming ashore. I have had to buy me a landau in lieu of a Conch or Gondola, to get me horses, to alter my tarpaulin liveries into terra firma fashions, and to leave nothing of the Sea about us but the crest on my carriage, a Mermaid, as you may remember. I have bought me furniture and new Saddles and all that from Milan, and chairs and tables from various parts of the Globe, at some cost and great trouble. However, I am still in respectable cash, having no occasion to spend money except upon *myself* and *family*, which only consists of my daughter and servant.

Sir Humphrey Davy was here the other day, and much pleased with the *primitive Italian* character of the people, who like strangers because they see so few of them. He will tell you himself all about it being on his way to England.

I am glad to hear any good of any body, and particularly of our Hobhouse. Pray get in for Bishop's Castle, and let me hear from you, how you are and all that, and what you may have settled or *not* settled with Spooney, and Moray " the *dear*."

Yours ever and truly,   BYRON

TO THOMAS MOORE   *Ravenna, May 24, 1820*

I wrote to you a few days ago. There is also a letter of January last for you at Murray's, which will explain to you why I am here. Murray ought to have forwarded it long ago. I enclose you an epistle from a countrywoman of yours at Paris, which has moved my entrails. You will have the goodness, perhaps, to enquire into the truth of her story, and I will help her as far as I can,—though not in the useless way she proposes. Her letter is evidently unstudied, and so natural, that the orthography is also in a state of nature.

Here is a poor creature, ill and solitary, who thinks, as a last resource, of translating you or me into French! Was there ever such a notion? It seems to me the consummation of despair. Pray enquire, and let me know, and, if you could draw a bill on me *here* for a few hundred francs, at your banker's, I will duly honour it,—that is, if she is not an impostor. If not, let me know, that I may get something remitted by my banker Longhi, of Bologna, for I have no correspondence myself at Paris : but tell her she must not translate ;—if she does, it will be the height of ingratitude.

I had a letter (not of the same kind, but in French and flattery) from a Madame Sophie Gail, of Paris, whom I take to be the spouse of a Gallo-Greek of that name. Who is she ? and what is she ? and how came she to take an interest in my *poeshie* or its author? If you know her, tell her, with my compliments, that, as I only *read* French, I have not answered her letter, but would have done so in Italian, if I had not thought it would look like an affectation. I have just been scolding my monkey for tearing the seal of her letter, and spoiling a mock book, in which I put rose leaves. I had a civet-cat the other day, too; but it ran away, after scratching my monkey's cheek, and I am in search of it still. It was the fiercest beast I ever saw, and like * * in the face and manner.

I have a world of things to say; but, as they are not come to a *dénouement*, I don't care to begin their history till it is wound up. After you went, I had a fever, but got well again without bark. Sir Humphry Davy was here the other day, and liked Ravenna very much. He will tell you any thing you may wish to know about the place and your humble servitor.

Your apprehensions (arising from Scott's) were unfounded. There are *no damages* in this country, but there will probably be a separation between them, as her family, which is a principal one, by its connections, are very much against *him*, for the whole of his conduct;—and he is old and obstinate, and she is young and a woman, determined to sacrifice every thing to her affections. I have given her the best advice, viz. to stay with him,—pointing out the state of a separated woman, (for the priests won't let lovers live openly together, unless the husband sanctions it,) and making the most exquisite moral reflections,—but to no purpose. She says, " I will stay with him, if he will let you remain with me. It is hard that I should be the only woman in Romagna who is not to have her *Amico* ; but, if not, I will not live with him ; and as for the consequences, love, etc., etc., etc."—you know how females reason on such occasions.

He says he has let it go on till he can do so no longer. But he wants her to stay, and dismiss me; for he doesn't like to pay back her dowry and to make an alimony. Her relations are rather for the separation, as they detest him,—indeed, so does every body. The populace and the women are, as usual, all for those who are in the wrong, viz. the lady and her lover. I should have retreated, but honour, and an erysipelas which has attacked her, prevent me,—to say nothing of love, for I love her most entirely, though not enough to persuade her to sacrifice every thing to a frenzy. " I see how it will end; she will be the sixteenth Mrs. Shuffleton."

My paper is finished, and so must this letter.

Yours ever, B.

P.S.—I regret that you have not completed the Italian Fudges. Pray, how come you to be still in Paris? Murray has four or five things of mine in hand—the new *Don Juan*, which his back-shop synod don't admire;—a translation of the first canto of Pulci's *Morgante Maggiore*, excellent;—a short ditto from Dante, not so much approved: the *Prophecy of Dante*, very grand and worthy, etc., etc., etc.:—a furious prose answer to Blackwood's " Observations on *Don Juan* ", with a savage Defence of Pope—likely to make a row. The opinions above I quote from Murray and his Utican senate;—you will form your own, when you see the things.

You will have no great chance of seeing me, for I begin to think I must finish in Italy. But, if you come my way, you shall have a tureen of macaroni. Pray tell me about yourself, and your intents.

My trustees are going to lend Earl Blessington sixty thousand pounds (at six per cent.) on a Dublin mortgage. Only think of my becoming an Irish absentee!

TO JOHN CAM HOBHOUSE *   *Ravenna, June 8th, 1820*

MY DEAR HOBHOUSE,—You are right. The *prose* must not be published—at least the merely *personal part*; and how the portion on Pope may be divided I do not know. I wish you would ferret out at Whitton the " Hints from Horace ". I think it (the Pope part) might be appended to that Popean poem—for publication or no, as you decide. I care not a damn. Murray was in a violent hurry for poetry. I sent it— and now he is reluctant. I don't *pin* him ; I am quite equal upon the subject. I do not even require his own offers. About Don Juan—as I said before, you may lock up the whole— Dante and all—in your desk ; it is to me the same. The only thing that mattered was the " conscription "—lawyer Scout's object of respect—his fee. But I won't dispute about dirty elements in such matters, least of all with Murray. Anything disagreeable is his own fault. He bored me for something all the winter, and I sent him what I had. But I am not at all persuaded of the merits of aught but the translation from Pulci, which is verse for verse, and word for word, an't it? I am tired of scribbling, and nothing but the convenience of an occasional extra thousand pounds would have induced me to go on. But even that will not weigh with me, if it is to be cavilled upon. I don't know whether the *Danticles* [1] be good or no ; for my opinions on my poeshie are always those of the last person I hear speak about them. Murray's costivity is a bad sign of their merits, and your notion is probably the right one ; for my own part I don't understand a word of the whole four cantos, and was therefore lost in admiration of their sublimity.

Tell Dougal that by this post I expedite a *full and unconditional* consent to the Mortgage. He is sullen, but must cheer up. If I quarrel with my banker as well as the bookseller, it would be troppo.

It is quite unlikely that the poeshies should be popular ; but in case of non-publication you can take care of the M.S.S. They will do for a posthumous—someday or other. I can't promise to be in England in autumn. I don't much affect that paese.

You say the Po verses are fine. I thought so little of them that they lay by me a year uncopied. But they were written in *red-hot Earnest* ; and that makes them good.

The best news you could send me, would be the translation

<hr>

[1] *The Prophecy of Dante.*

of Lady N., the adjustment and sale of Rochdale, the conclusion of the Irish Mortgage and, though last not least, your own *Succes* (as Madame D. had it) which will be ensured by " *delicaci* ". I have quite lost all personal interest about anything except money to supply my own indolent expences; and when I rouse up to appear to take an interest about anything, it is a temporary irritation like Galvanism upon Mutton. The life of an Epicurean, and the philosophy of one, are merely prevented by " that rash humour which my Mother gave me " that makes one restless and nervous, and can overthrow all tranquillity with a Sirocco. Surely you agree with me about the real *vacuum* of human pursuits, but one must face an object of attainment, not to rust in the Scabbard altogether.

Yrs. ever most truly, B.

TO THOMAS MOORE   *Ravenna, July 13, 1820*

To remove or increase your Irish anxiety about my being " in a wisp ", I answer your letter forthwith; premising that, as I am a " *Will* of the wisp ", I may chance to flit out of it. But, first, a word on the Memoir; [1]—I have no objection, nay, I would rather that *one* correct copy was taken and deposited in honourable hands, in case of accidents happening to the original; for you know that I have none, and have never even *re*-read, nor, indeed, *read* at all what is there written; I only know that I wrote it with the fullest intention to be " faithful and true " in my narrative, but *not* impartial—no, by the Lord! I can't pretend to be that, while I feel. But I wish to give every body concerned the opportunity to contradict or correct me.

I have no objection to any proper person seeing what is there written,—seeing it was written, like every thing else, for the purpose of being read, however much many writings may fail in arriving at that object.

With regard to " the wisp ", the Pope has pronounced *their*

---

[1] Byron's autobiographical manuscript, afterwards destroyed by Byron's executors, had been handed to Moore, to dispose of as he pleased, at Venice during the autumn of 1819.

separation. The decree came yesterday from Babylon,—it was *she* and *her friends* who demanded it, on the grounds of her husband's (the noble Count Cavalier's) extraordinary usage. *He* opposed it with all his might because of the alimony, which has been assigned, with all her goods, chattels, carriage, etc., to be restored by him. In Italy they can't divorce. He insisted on her giving me up, and he would forgive every thing,—even the adultery, which he swears that he can prove by " famous witnesses ". But, in this country, the very courts hold such proofs in abhorrence, the Italians being as much more delicate in public than the English, as they are more passionate in private.

The friends and relatives, who are numerous and powerful, reply to him—" *You*, yourself, are either fool or knave,—fool, if you did not see the consequences of the approximation of these two young persons,—knave, if you connive at it. Take your choice,—but don't break out (after twelve months of the closest intimacy, under your own eyes and positive sanction) with a scandal, which can only make you ridiculous and her unhappy."

He swore that he thought our intercourse was purely amicable, and that *I* was more partial to him than to her, till melancholy testimony proved the contrary. To this they answer, that " Will of *this* wisp " was not an unknown person, and that " *clamosa Fama* " had not proclaimed the purity of my morals;—that *her* brother, a year ago, wrote from Rome to warn him that his wife would infallibly be led astray by this *ignis fatuus*, unless he took proper measures, all of which he neglected to take, etc., etc.

Now he says that he encouraged my return to Ravenna, to see " *in quanti piedi di acqua siamo* ", and he has found enough to drown him in. In short,

> " Ce ne fut pas le tout ; sa femme se plaignit—
> Procès—La parenté se joint en excuse et dit
> Que du *Docteur* venoit tout le mauvais ménage ;
> Que cet homme étoit fou, que sa femme étoit sage.
> On fit casser le mariage."

It is best to let the women alone, in the way of conflict, for they are sure to win against the field. She returns to her father's house, and I can only see her under great restrictions—such is the custom of the country. The relations behave very well :— I offered any settlement, but they refused to accept it, and swear she *shan't* live with G[uiccioli] (as he has tried to prove her faithless), but that he shall maintain her ; and, in fact, a judgment to this effect came yesterday. I am, of course, in an awkward situation enough.

I have heard no more of the carabiniers who protested against my liveries. They are not popular, those same soldiers, and, in a small row, the other night, one was slain, another wounded, and divers put to flight, by some of the Romagnuole youth, who are dexterous, and somewhat liberal of the knife. The perpetrators are not discovered, but I hope and believe that none of my ragamuffins were in it, though they are somewhat savage, and secretly armed, like most of the inhabitants. It is their way, and saves sometimes a good deal of litigation.

There is a revolution at Naples. If so, it will probably leave a card at Ravenna in its way to Lombardy.

Your publishers seem to have used you like mine. M. has shuffled, and almost insinuated that my last productions are *dull*. Dull, sir !—damme, dull ! I believe he is right. He begs for the completion of my tragedy of *Marino Faliero*, none of which is yet gone to England. The fifth act is nearly completed, but it is dreadfully long—40 sheets of long paper of 4 pages each—about 150 when printed ; but " so full of pastime and prodigality " that I think it will do.

Pray send and publish your *Pome* upon me ; and don't be afraid of praising me too highly. I shall pocket my blushes.

" Not actionable ! "—*Chantre d'enfer !*—by * * that's " a speech ", and I won't put up with it. A pretty title to give a man for doubting if there be any such place !

So my Gail is gone—and Miss Mah*o*ny won't take *mo*ney. I am very glad of it—I like to be generous, free of expense. But beg her not to translate me.

Oh, pray tell Galignani that I shall send him a screed of doctrine if he don't be more punctual. Somebody *regularly detains two*, and sometimes *four*, of his Messengers by the way. Do, pray, entreat him to be more precise. News are worth money in this remote kingdom of the Ostrogoths.

Pray, reply. I should like much to share some of your

Champagne and La Fitte, but I am too Italian for Paris in
general.   Make Murray send my letter to you—it is full of
epigrams.

Yours, etc.

TO THE HON. DOUGLAS KINNAIRD*   *Ravenna, July 20th, 1820*
11 o'clock at night

DEAR DOUGLAS,—Some weeks ago you will have received
my consent to the Mortgage to be lent to Ld Blessington.   What
have you done upon it?   My half year's fee from the funds,
where is it?   Messrs. Hanson write that the Rochdale Cause
has been heard.   Is it decided?   I shall be glad to hear on
these and other points at your imperial leisure.

There is a Revolution at Naples, and one is expected
throughout Italy daily.   I have completed (but have to copy
out) a tragedy in five acts, on Marino Faliero Doge of Venice.
The fever has attacked me again but slightly.   I caught it
riding in the forest, part of which is agueish and marshy.

Madame Guiccioli has been separated from her husband
who has been sentenced (by the Pope) to pay her twelve
hundred crowns a year of alimony, a handsome allowance for
a lone woman in these parts—almost three hundred pounds
sterling a year, and worth about a thousand in England.   The
story is a long one.   He wanted to bully, and failed with
both lady and gentleman.   They say here that he will have me
taken off, it is the custom.   There were two [perished last] week,
a priest and a factor, one by a political club, and the other by
a private hand, for revenge; nobody fights, but they pop
at you from behind trees, and put a knife into you in
company, or in turning a corner, while you are blowing your
nose.   He may do as he pleases; I only recommend him not
to miss, for if such a thing is attempted, and fails, he shan't
have another opportunity; " Sauce for the Goose is sauce for
the Gander ".   It would be easy to know the quarter whence
it came, and I would pistol him on the spot on my return
from the escape.   I have taken no precautions, (which indeed
would be useless) except taking my pistols when I ride out in

the woods every evening. You know I used to be a pretty good shot, and that if the rogues missed, that I should probably hit.

All these fooleries are what the people of the place say (who detest him by the way) and, whether true or not, I shan't stir a step out of my way; a man's life is not worth holding on such a tenure as the fear of such fellows, and what must be will, if it be decreed but not otherwise.

While I am in *the very act of writing* to you, my Steward Lega has come to tell me that this moment, a quarter of an hour past, a brigadier of the Gens d'armes has been shot in the thigh (I heard the pistol and thought it was ·my servants cleaning my own and firing them first) by no one knows who ; all we know is that they had a quarrel with the populace two weeks ago, who warned them and had already wounded two before.

They had also a squabble (the Gens d'armes) with my servants about the lace of my liveries as resembling their uniforms, but they were reduced to order by the decision of the police in favour of the liveries.

I hope none of my ragamuffins have been in this matter.

Here is a state of society for you ! It is like the middle ages. Grand uncertainty, but very dramatic.

                                        Yours ever, B.

P.S.—all *fact* I assure you. It is moonlight. A fortnight ago a similar thing happened to these soldiers, but they were only [wounded] (two of them) with knives. One lost his hat in the scuffle.

TO JOHN MURRAY   *Ravenna, July 22nd 1820*

DEAR MURRAY,—The tragedy is finished, but when it will be copied is more than can be reckoned upon. We are here upon the eve of evolutions and revolutions. Naples is revolutionized, and the ferment is among the Romagnuoles, by far the bravest and most original of the present Italians, though still half savage. Buonaparte said the troops from Romagna were the best of his Italic corps, and I believe it. The Neapolitans are not worth a curse, and will be beaten if it comes to fighting: the rest of Italy, I think, might stand. The Cardinal is at his wits' end; it is true that he had not far to go. Some papal towns on the Neapolitan frontier have already revolted. Here there are as yet but the sparks of the volcano; but the ground is hot, and the air sultry. Three assassinations last week here and at Faenza—an anti-liberal priest, a factor, and a trooper last night,—I heard the pistol-shot that brought him down within a short distance of my own door. There had been quarrels between the troops and people of some duration : this is the third soldier wounded within the last month. There is a great commotion in people's minds, which will lead to nobody knows what—a row probably. There are secret Societies all over the country as in Germany, who cut off those obnoxious to them, like the Free tribunals, be they high or low ; and then it becomes impossible to discover or punish the assassins—their measures are taken so well.

You ask me about the books. *Jerusalem* is the best; *Anastasius* good, but no more written by a Greek than by a Hebrew ; the *Diary of an Invalid* good and true, bating a few mistakes about *Serventismo*, which no foreigner can understand or really know without residing years in the country. I read that part (translated that is) to some of the ladies in the way of knowing how far it was accurate, and they laughed, particularly at the part where he says that " they must not have children by their lover ". " Assuredly " (was the answer), " we don't pretend to say that it is right; but *men* cannot conceive the repugnance that a *woman* has to have children *except by the man she loves* ". They have been known even to obtain abortions when it was by the *other*, but that is rare. I know one instance, however, of a woman making herself miscarry, because she wanted to meet her lover (they were in two different cities) in the lying-in month (hers was or should have been in October). She was a very pretty woman—young and clever—and brought on by it a malady which she has not recovered to this day : however, she met her *Amico* by it at the proper time. It is but fair to say that he had dissuaded her from this piece of amatory atrocity, and was very angry when he knew that she had committed it ; but the " it was for your sake, to meet you at the time, which could not have been otherwise accomplished ", applied to his

Self love, disarmed him ; and they set about supplying the loss.

I have had a little touch of fever again ; but it has receded. The heat is 85 in the shade.

I remember what you say of the Queen : it happened in Lady Ox——'s boudoir or dressing room, if I recollect rightly ; but it was not her Majesty's fault, though very laughable at the time : a minute sooner, she might have stumbled on something still more awkward.   How the *Porcelain* came there I cannot conceive, and remember asking Lady O. afterwards, who laid the blame on the Servants.   I think the Queen will win—I wish she may : she was always very civil to me.   You must not trust Italian witnesses : nobody believes them in their own courts ; why should you ?   For 50 or 100 Sequins you may have any testimony you please, and the Judge into the bargain.

Yours ever, B.

Pray forward my letter of January to Mr. Moore.

TO THE COUNTESS GUICCIOLI *   *Ravenna, August 7th, 1820*

MY LOVE + + + " Forget what has happened ", you say—a fine forgetfulness—but what then did happen ?   The woman is as ugly as an ogre—a thing of Lega's [1]—not very young— not of bad reputation—not adorned with the slightest quality that might arouse a caprice.   But you have condescended to be jealous—which I shall not so easily forget, as you so *generously* forgive yourself.   It is a very naughty *O* :   I feel it.

Allegrina has already spoiled your present—breaking one of the little carriages.   Her fever is a little better ;   I shall not go to my " fair country " of *NO*—unless you are jealous of filthy maids—in which case I shall.

I think you should neither accept nor refuse Guiccioli's proposal without thinking it over.   Perhaps one could do this —reply—that he should *assign you 2000 scudi* after his death —and in return you would be prepared to give up 400 of the 1200 decreed by the most just of all Popes.   Freedom would be a

---

[1] Antonio Lega Zambelli, Byron's Secretary at Ravenna.

great thing no doubt—with that head of yours—but 400 scudi is a respectable sum in this country—and not to be given up without any compensation. For the rest—you can trust me— I will make you independent of everyone—at least during my lifetime. But you are made angry with the mere idea—and want to be independent on your own and to write " *Cantate* " in lengthy epistles in the style of Santa Chiara—the convent where you were said to be always in a rage.[1]

I am reading the second volume of the proposal of that classic cuckold Perticari.[2]—It may be well-written—in a style worthy of Santa Chiara and the *trecento*—but it would be more à propos if the Count, instead of proving that *Dante* was the greatest of men (which no one at present wishes to deny, as he is now all the fashion), could prove to his contemporaries that his father-in-law Monti [3] is not the most vile and infamous of men ; it is such a dishonour to talent itself that a man of ability ought to blush to belong to the same century as that Judas of Parnassus.

This seems to have become a peroration, or at least would be in English, but my thoughts fail me when I must express myself in the effeminate words of the language of musicians. I am in a rage this evening—as you were in the convent.—I kiss and embrace you 100000000 . . . times. Love me.

P.S.—There is a certain O—I feel it in the note itself— and very much yes—Greet both the G[amba]s—I value their good graces. That blessed villa is being got ready—as quickly as possible on account of the two little girls—Allegra —and *you*.

[1] Byron wrote " rabbiosa " (in a rage), which Teresa has attempted to change into " studiosa " (studious).

[2] Count Giulio Perticari (1790–1822), the son-in-law of the poet Vincenzo Monti, whose wife was notoriously unfaithful to him, was one of the defenders of the classicists, against the new-fangled romantics. The work referred to is " *Dell' amor patrio di Dante* " (1820).

[3] The reference is to Monti's political unreliability. He was also, like his son-in-law, unfortunate in his matrimonial relations, a fact on which Byron commented in his *Prophecy of Dante*, in lines omitted in the earlier editions of Byron's Poems, but quoted by Moore :

> " The prostitution of his Muse and wife,
> Both beautiful, and both by him debased,
> Shall salt his bread and give him means of life."

TO THE HON. AUGUSTA LEIGH   *Ravenna, August 19ᵗʰ 1820*

My dearest Augusta,—I always loved you better than
any earthly existence, and I always shall unless I go mad.
And if I did *not* so love you—still I would not persecute or
oppress any one wittingly—especially for debts, of which I
know the *agony by experience*. Of Colonel Leigh's bond, I really
have forgotten all particulars, except that it was *not* of *my*
wishing. And I never would nor ever will be *pressed* into the
Gang of his creditors. I would *not take the money* if he had it. You
may judge if I would dun him having it not ——

Whatever measure I can take for his extrication will be
taken. Only tell me how—for I am ignorant, and far away.
Who does and *who can* accuse *you* of " interested views " ? I
think people must have gone into Bedlam such things appear
to me so very incomprehensible. Pray explain ——

yors ever and truly   Byron.

TO JOHN MURRAY   *Ravenna, September 7, 1820*

Dear Murray,—In correcting the proofs you must refer
to the *Manuscript*, because there are in it *various readings*. Pray
attend to this, and choose what Gifford thinks best. Let me
know what he thinks of the whole.

You speak of Lady Noel's illness : she is not of those who
die :—the amiable only do ; and those whose death would *do*
good live. Whenever she is pleased to return, it may be presumed that she will take her " *divining rod* " along with her ;
it may be of use to her at home, as well as to the " *rich man* "
of the Evangelists.

Pray do not let the papers paragraph me back to England :
they may say what they please—any loathsome abuse—but
that. Contradict it.

My last letters will have taught you to expect an explosion
here : it was primed and loaded, but they hesitated to fire the
train. One of the Cities shirked from the league. I cannot
write more at large for a thousand reasons. Our " *puir hill*
folk " offered to strike, and to raise the first banner. But

Bologna paused—and now 'tis Autumn, and the season half over. " Oh Jerusalem, Jerusalem ! " the Huns are on the Po ; but if once they pass it on their march to Naples, all Italy will rise behind them : the Dogs—the Wolves—may they perish like the Host of Sennacherib ! If you want to publish the *Prophecy of Dante*, you never will have a better time.

Thanks for books—but as yet no *Monastery* of Walter Scott's, the ONLY book except *Edinburgh* and *Quarterly* which I desire to see. Why do you send me so much *trash* upon Italy—such tears, etc., which I know *must be false* ? Matthews is good— very good : all the rest are like Sotheby's " *Good* ", or like Sotheby himself, that old rotten Medlar of Rhyme. The Queen—how is it ? prospers She ?

TO RICHARD BELGRAVE HOPPNER   *Ravenna, Sept.* 10^*th* *1820*

MY DEAR HOPPNER,—*Ecco* Advocate Fossati's letter. No paper has nor will be signed. Pray *draw* on me for the Napoleons, for I have no mode of remitting them otherwise ; Missiaglia would empower some one here to receive them for you, as it is not a *piazza bancale*.

I regret that you have such a bad opinion of Shiloh ; [1] you used to have a good one. Surely he has talent and honour, but is crazy against religion and morality. His tragedy is sad work ; but the subject renders it so. His *Islam* had much poetry. You seem lately to have got some notion against him.

Clare writes me the most insolent letters about Allegra ; see what a man gets by taking care of natural children ! Were it not for the poor little child's sake, I am almost tempted to send her back to her atheistical mother, but that would be too bad ; you cannot conceive the excess of her insolence, and I know not why, for I have been at great care and expense,— taking a house in the country on purpose for her. She has *two* maids and every possible attention. If Clare thinks that she shall ever interfere with the child's morals or education, she mistakes ; she never shall. The girl shall be a Christian and

[1] Shelley.

a married woman, if possible. As to seeing her, she may see
her—under proper restrictions ; but she is not to throw every
thing into confusion with her Bedlam behaviour. To express
it delicately, I think Madame Clare is a damned bitch. What
think you ?

> Yours ever and truly, B.ⁿ

TO THE HON. DOUGLAS KINNAIRD*[1]   *Ravenna,*
                                    September 17th, 1820

DEAR DOUGLAS,—I got your letter—why, man ! what are
ye aboot? What makes you so careful of your paper? Is it
for the sake of contrast? This is the Paper Age. The Golden,
the Silver and the Iron ages are long since past, the two former
never to return ! We are now happily arrived at the *Age of Rags.*
The *He*-mans [2] and *She*-mans of our literature are as plenty as
blackberries as we of the North say. They have made a *litter-*
ature of literature, which at this moment is more extensively
spread ; but 'tis grown shallow, it seems, in proportion to its
diffusion. Our age is in everything an affected age, and where
affectation prevails the *fair* sex—or rather the *blue*—are always
strongly tinctured with it. A little learning may be swelled to
an enormous size by artifice. Madam de Stael, I grant, is a
clever woman ; but all the other *madams* are no Staels. The
philosophical petticoats of our times surpass even those of the
age of Elizabeth who pretended to cultivate an acquaintance
with the classics. Roger Asham tells us that, going to wait on
Lady Jane Grey at her father's house in Leicestershire, he
found her reading Plato's works in the Greek, while the rest
of the family were hunting in the park. Possibly the lady had
no objection to be interrupted in her studies—*she* was *hunting*
for applause. I shall be at them one of these days—there is
nothing like ridicule, the only weapon that the English climate
cannot rust.

I have to acknowledge the receipt of sundry books which at
present I have no inclination to anatomize—they are rather

---

[1] Since first printing of this edition the authenticity of this letter is in doubt.

[2] Felicia Dorothea Hemans, authoress of *Domestic Affections, and other
Poems,* etc.

stale. But why do you send anything to the Foreign Office—
that den of thieves? Your friend with his young spouse arrived
safely in this place. He has just remitted your letter of introduction. I shall invade him in the cause of [indecipherable]—
out of envy—as Lucifer looked at Adam and Eve.

Sta sempre umilissimo servitore   BIRON

TO RICHARD BELGRAVE HOPPNER   *Ravenna, 8bre. 1°. 1820*

MY DEAR HOPPNER,—Your letters and papers came very
safely, though slowly, missing one post.

The Shiloh story is true no doubt,[1] though Elise is but a sort
of *Queen's evidence.* You remember how eager she was to return
to them, and then she goes away and abuses them. Of the
facts, however, there can be little doubt ; it is just like them.
You may be sure that I keep your counsel.

I have not remitted the 30 Napoleons (or *what* was it ?), till
I hear that Missiaglia has received his safely, when I shall do
so by the like channel.

What you say of the Queen's affair is very just and true ;
but the event seems not very easy to anticipate.

I enclose an epistle from Shiloh.

Yours ever and truly, BYRON

TO THE HON. AUGUSTA LEIGH *   *Ravenna, 8bre 1820*

MY DEAREST AUGUSTA,—I suppose by this time that you
will be out of your fidget, and that the dilatory Hanson will
have set Colonel L[eigh] at rest upon the subject of the bond,
etc.

Ada's picture is very like her mother—I mean the prints,
for I have not received the picture, neither has Murray sent it,
I presume. She seems stout of her age, which is five years on
the 10th. of 10bre,—is it not so ? It is almost as long since I
have seen her, all but a month. What day of January was it,

---

[1] Elise Foggi, a Swiss nursemaid dismissed by the Shelleys, had spread stories
to their discredit, alleging that Claire Clairmont had had an intrigue with Shelley,
and that he had consigned their child to the Foundlings' Hospital.

when Lady B. marched upon Kirkby? which was the Signal of war. Sir Walter Scott says in the beginning of *the Abbot*, that " every *five* years we find ourselves another and yet the same, with a change of views and no less of the light in which we regard them; a change of motives as well as of actions." This I presume applies still more to those who have past their *five* years in foreign countries, for my part I suppose that I am *two* others, for it seems that some fool has been betting that he saw me in London the other day in a *Curricle*. If he said a *Canoe*, it would have been much more likely. And *you*? What have *your* " five years " done?—made your house like a Lying-in Hospital;—there never was such a creature, except a rabbit, for increase and multiplication. In short we are five years older in fact, and I at least *ten* in appearance. The Lady B——, I suppose, retains her old starch obstinacy, with a deeper dash of Sternness from the dint of time, and the effort it has cost her to be " magnanimous ", as they called her mischief-making. People accused somebody of painting her in " Donna *Inez* "; did it strike you so? I can't say it did me, there might be something of her in the outline; but the Spaniard was only a silly woman, and the other is a cut-and-dry, made-up character, which is another matter.

Time and Events will one day or the other revenge her past conduct, without any interference of mine.

So—Joe Murray is gathered to his Masters; as you say, the very Ghosts have died with him. Newstead and he went almost together, and now the B's must carve them out another inheritance. If Ada had been a Son, I do not think that I should have parted with it after all; but I dislike George B[yro]n for his behaviour in 1816, and I am unacquainted with the others who may be in the line of the title, and, being myself abroad, and at feud with the whole of the Noels, and with most of the B's except yourself, of course these concurring with other and pressing circumstances, rendered the disposal of the Abbey necessary and not improper. Somebody said the other day that " Lady Noel had been ill "; she is too troublesome an old woman ever to die while her death can do any good, but, if she ever does march, it is to be presumed that she will take her " water-divining rod " with her; it may be a useful twig to her, and the devil too, when she gets home again.

I can say little to you of Italy, except that it is a very distracted State.

In England the Queen has been bountiful to the Scandal-mongers. She has got the Noel batch of Counsellors, it seems (except Romilly—who cut his throat); you see what *those* sort of fellows *are*, and how they prey on a cause of this kind, like crows on carrion. Her Majesty's innocence is probably something like another person's guilt. However she has been an ill-used woman; that's the truth on't, and, in the nature of things, the woman ought to get the better. They generally do, whether they ought or not.

I did not come over,—for fifty reasons,—and amongst others, that I do not think it a very creditable thing to be one of the Judges even, upon such matters.

I have got a flourishing family, (besides my daughter Allegra); here are two Cats, six dogs, a badger, a falcon, a tame Crow, and a Monkey. The fox died, and a Civet Cat ran away. With the exception of an occasional civil war about provisions, they agree to admiration, and do not make more noise than a well-behaved Nursery.

I have also eight horses,—four carriage, and four saddle,—and go prancing away daily, at present up to the middle in mire, for here have been the Autumnal rains, and drenched every thing, amongst others myself yesterday. I got soaked through, cloak and all, and the horse through his skin, I believe.

I have now written to you a long family letter.[1]

Ever yours, B.

TO JOHN MURRAY   *Ravenna, 8bre 6, 1820*

DEAR Mᵞ,—You will have now received all the acts, corrected, of the *M[arino] F[aliero]*. What you say of the " Bet of 100 guineas ", made by some one who says that he saw me last week, reminds me of what happened in 1810. You can easily ascertain the fact, and it is an odd one.

In the latter end of 1811, I met one evening at the Alfred my old School and form-fellow, (for we were within two of each other—*he* the higher, though both very near the top of our

----
[1] Here a line has been cut out.

remove,) *Peel*, the Irish Secretary. He told me that, in 1810, he met me, as he thought, in St. James's Street, but we passed without speaking. He mentioned this, and it was denied as impossible, I being then in Turkey. A day or two after, he pointed out to his brother a person on the opposite side of the way; " there ", said he, " is the man whom I took for Byron " : his brother instantly answered, " why, it *is* Byron, and no one else ". But this is not all : I was *seen* by somebody to *write down my name* amongst the Enquirers after the King's health, then attacked by insanity. Now, at this very period, as nearly as I could make out, I was ill of a *strong fever* at Patras, caught in the marshes near Olympia, from the *Malaria*. If I had died there, this would have been a new Ghost Story for you. You can easily make out the accuracy of this from Peel himself, who told it in detail. I suppose you will be of the opinion of Lucretius, who (denies the immortality of the Soul, but) asserts that from the " flying off of the Surfaces of bodies perpetually, these surfaces or cases, like the Coats of an onion, are sometimes seen entire when they are separated from it, so that the shapes and shadows of both the dead and absent are frequently beheld ".

But if they are, are their coats and waistcoats also seen ? I do not disbelieve that we may be *two* by some unconscious process, to a certain sign ; but which of these two I happen at present to be, I leave you to decide. I only hope that *t'other me* behaves like a Gemman.

I wish you would get Peel asked how far I am accurate in my recollection of what he told me ; for I don't like to say such things without authority.

I am not sure that I was *not spoken* with ; but this also you can ascertain. I have written to you such lots that I stop.

                                        Yours, B.

P.S.—Send me the proofs of the " *Hints from H., etc.*".

P.S.—Last year (in June, 1819), I met at Count Mosti's, at Ferrara, an Italian who asked me " if I knew Lord Byron ? " I told him *no* (no one knows himself, *you* know) : " then ", says he, " I do ; I met him at Naples the other day ". I pulled out my card and asked him if that was the way he spelt his name : and he answered, *yes*. I suspect that it was a blackguard Navy Surgeon, named *Bury* or *Berry*, who attended a young travelling

Madman about, named Graham, and passed himself for a
Lord at the Posthouses : he was a vulgar dog—quite of the
Cockpit order—and a precious representative I must have had
of him, if it was even so ; but I don't know. He passed himself
off as a Gentleman, and squired about a Countess Zinnani (of
this place), then at Venice, an ugly battered woman, of bad
morals even for Italy.

TO JOHN MURRAY   *Ravenna, 9ᵇʳᵉ 4°, 1820*

I have received from Mr. Galignani the enclosed letters,
duplicates and receipts, which will explain themselves. As the
poems are your property by purchase, right, and justice, *all
matters of publication*, etc., etc., *are for you to decide upon*. I know
not how far my compliance with Mr. G.'s request might be
legal, and I doubt that it would not be honest. In case you
choose to arrange with him, I enclose the permits to *you*, and
in so doing I wash my hands of the business altogether. I sign
them merely to enable you to exert the power you justly possess
more properly. I will have nothing to do with it further,
except, in my answer to Mr. Galignani, to state that the letters,
etc., etc., are sent to you, and the causes thereof.

If you can check those foreign Pirates, do ; if not, put the
permissive papers in the fire : *I* can have no view nor object
whatever, but to secure to you your property.

Yours, BYRON

P.S.—There will be shortly " *the Devil to pay* " *here* ; and,
as there is no saying that I may not form an *Item in his bill*, I
shall not now write at greater length : *you* have *not answered* my
late letters ; and you have acted foolishly, as you will find out
some day.

P.S.—I have read part of the *Quarterly* just arrived : Mr.
Bowles shall be answered ; he is not *quite* correct in his statement about *E[nglish] B[ards] and S[cotch] R[eviewers]*. They support
Pope, I see, in the *Quarterly*. Let them continue to do so : it is
a Sin, and a Shame, and a *damnation* to think that *Pope!!* should
require it—but he does. Those miserable mountebanks of the
day, the poets, disgrace themselves and deny God, in running
down Pope, the most *faultless* of Poets, and almost of men.

The *Edinburgh* praises Jack Keats or Ketch, or whatever his names are: why, his is the * of Poetry—something like the pleasure an Italian fiddler extracted out of being suspended daily by a Street Walker in Drury Lane. This went on for some weeks: at last the Girl went to get a pint of Gin—met another, chatted too long, and Cornelli was *hanged outright before she returned*. Such like is the trash they praise, and such will be the end of the *outstretched* poesy of this miserable Self-polluter of the human mind.

W. Scott's *Monastery* just arrived: many thanks for that Grand Desideratum of the last six months.

P.S.—You have cut up old Edgeworth, it seems, amongst you. You are right: he was a bore. I met the whole batch— Mr., Mrs., and Miss—at a blue breakfast of Lady Davy's in Blue Square; and he proved but bad, in taste and tact and decent breeding. He began by saying that *Parr* (Dr. Parr) had attacked him, and that he (the father of Miss E.) had *cut him up* in his answer. Now, Parr would have annihilated him; and if he had not, why tell *us* (a long story) *who* wanted to break- fast? I saw them different times in different parties, and I thought him a very tiresome coarse old Irish half-and-half Gentleman, and her a pleasant reserved old woman—* * *

* * * * * * * * *

TO JOHN MURRAY   *R[avenn]a, 9bre 9°, 1820*

DEAR MORAY,—The talent you approve of is an amiable one and as you say might prove " a national Service ", but unfor- tunately I must be angry with a man before I draw his real portrait; and I can't deal in " *generals* ", so that I trust never to have provocation enough to make a *Gallery*. If " *the* person " had not by many little dirty sneaking traits provoked it, I should have been silent, though I *had observed* him. Here follows an alteration. Put—

> Devil with *such* delight in damning,
> That if at the resurrection
> Unto him the free selection
> Of his future could be given,
> 'Twould be rather Hell than Heaven.

That is to say, if these two new lines do not too much lengthen out and weaken the amiability of the original thought and expression. You have a discretionary power about showing: I should think that Croker and D'Israeli would not disrelish a sight of these light little humorous things, and may be indulged now and then.

D'Israeli wrote the article on Spence: I know him by the mark in his mouth. I am glad that the *Quarterly* has had so much Classical honesty as to insert it: it is good and true.

Hobhouse writes me a facetious letter about my *indolence* and love of Slumber. It becomes him : he is in active life; he writes pamphlets against Canning, to which he does not put his name; he gets into Newgate and into Parliament—both honourable places of refuge; and he " greatly daring dines " at all the taverns (why don't he set up a *tap* room at once), and then writes to quiz my laziness.

Why, I do like one or two vices, to be sure; but I can back a horse and fire a pistol " without winking or blinking " like Major Sturgeon; I have fed at times for two months together on *sheer biscuit and water* (without metaphor); I can get over seventy or eighty miles a day *riding* post upon [?] of all sorts, and *swim five* at a Stretch, taking a *piece* before and after, as at Venice, in 1818, or at least I *could do*, and have done it ONCE, and I never was ten minutes in my life over a *solitary* dinner.

Now, my friend Hobhouse, when we were wayfaring men, used to complain grievously of hard beds and sharp insects, while I slept like a top, and to awaken me with his swearing at them : he used to damn his dinners daily, both quality and cookery and quantity, and reproach me for a sort of " brutal " indifference, as he called it, to these particulars; and now he writes me facetious sneerings because I *do not* get up early in a morning, when there is no occasion—if there were, *he* knows that I was always *out* of bed before him, though it is true that my ablutions detained me longer in dressing than his noble contempt of that " oriental scrupulosity " permitted.

Then he is still sore about " *the ballad* "—he !! why, he lampooned me at Brighton, in 1808, about Jackson the boxer and bold Webster, etc.: in 1809, he turned the death of my friend E^d *Long* into ridicule and rhyme, because his name was susceptible of a *pun*; and, although he saw that I was distressed

at it, before I left England in 1816, he wrote rhymes upon *D.*
Kinnaird, you, and *myself*; and at Venice he parodied the lines
" Though the day of my destiny's over " in a comfortable
quizzing way: and now he harps on my ballad about his
election! Pray tell him all this, for I will have no underhand
work with my " old Cronies ". If he can deny the facts, let
him. I maintain that he is more *carnivorously* and *carnally
sensual* than I am, though I am bad enough too for that matter;
but not in eating and haranguing at the Crown and Anchor,
where I never was but twice—and those were at " Whore's
Hops " when I was a younker in my teens; and, Egad, I think
them the most respectable meetings of the two. But he is a
little wroth that I would not come over to the *Queen's* trial:
lazy, quotha! it is so true that he should be ashamed of asserting it. He counsels me not to " get into a Scrape "; but, as
Beau Clincher says, " How melancholy are Newgate reflections! " To be sure, his advice is worth following; for experience teacheth: he has been in a dozen within these last two
years. *I pronounce me the more temperate of the two.*

Have you gotten *The Hints* yet?

I know Henry Matthews: he is the image, to the very
voice, of his brother Charles, only darker: his *laugh* his in
particular. The first time I ever met him was in Scrope
Davies's rooms after his brother's death, and I nearly dropped,
thinking that it was his Ghost. I have also dined with him
in his rooms at King's College. Hobhouse once purposed a
similar memoir; but I am afraid that the letters of Charles's
correspondence with me (which are at Whitton with my other
papers) would hardly do for the public: for our lives were not
over strict, and our letters somewhat lax upon most subjects.

His Superiority over all his contemporaries was quite indisputable and acknowledged: none of us ever thought of being
at all near Matthews; and yet there were some high men of his
standing—Bankes, Bob Milnes, Hobhouse, Bailey, and many
others—without numbering the *mere Academical* men, of whom
we hear little out of the University, and whom he beat *hollow*
on *their own* Ground.

His gaining the Downing Fellowship was the completest
thing of the kind ever known. He carried off both declamation prizes: in short, he did whatever he chose. He was

three or four years my Senior, but I lived a good deal with him latterly, and with his friends. He wrote to me the very day of his death (I believe), or at least a day before, if not the very day. He meant to have stood for the University Membership. He was a very odd and humourous fellow besides, and spared nobody : for instance, walking out in Newstead Garden, he stopped at Boatswain's monument inscribed " Here lies Boatswain, a Dog ", etc., and then observing a *blank* marble tablet on the other side, " So (says he) there is room for another friend, and I propose that the Inscription be ' Here lies H—bh—se, a Pig '," etc. You may as well not let *this* transpire to the worthy member, lest he regard neither his dead friend nor his living one, with his wonted Suavity.

Rose's *lines* must be at his own option : *I* can have no objection to their publication. Pray salute him from me.

Mr. Keats, whose poetry you enquire after, appears to me what I have already said : such writing is a sort of mental masturbation—* * * * * * * * his *Imagination*. I don't mean he is *indecent*, but viciously soliciting his own ideas into a state, which is neither poetry nor any thing else but a Bedlam vision produced by raw pork and opium. Barry Cornwall would write well, if he would let himself. Croly is superior to many, but seems to think himself inferior to Nobody.

Last week I sent you a correspondence with Galignani, and some documents on your property. You have now, I think, an opportunity of *checking*, or at least *limiting*, those *French re-publications*. You may let all your authors publish what they please *against me* or *mine* : a publisher is not, and cannot be, responsible for all the works that issue from his printer's.

The " White Lady of Avenel " is not quite so good as a *real well-authenticated* (" Donna bianca ") *White Lady* of *Colalto*, or spectre in the Marca Trivigiana, who has been repeatedly seen : there is a man (a huntsman) now alive who saw her also. Hoppner could tell you all about her, and so can Rose perhaps. I myself have *no doubt* of the fact, historical and spectral. She always appeared on particular occasions, before the deaths of the family, etc., etc. I heard Mᵉ Benzoni say, that she knew a Gentleman who had seen her cross his room at Colalto Castle. Hoppner saw and spoke with the Huntsman who met her at the Chase, and never *hunted* afterwards. She was a Girl attendant, who, one day dressing the hair of a Countess Colalto, was seen by her mistress to smile upon her husband in the Glass. The Countess had her shut up in the wall at the Castle, like Constance de Beverley. Ever after, she haunted them and all the Colaltos. She is described as very beautiful and fair. It is well authenticated.

Yours, B.

TO THE HON. AUGUSTA LEIGH   *Ravenna, 9bre 18th 1820*

MY DEAREST AUGUSTA,—You will I hope have received a discreetly long letter from me—not long ago,—Murray has just written that *Waite* [1]—is dead—poor fellow—he and Blake—both deceased—what *is* to become of our hair and teeth.—The hair is less to be minded—any body can cut hair—though not so well—but the *mouth* is a still more serious concern.——

Has he no Successor?—pray tell me the next best—for what am I to do for brushes and powder?——And then the *Children* —only think—what will become of their jaws? Such men ought to be immortal—and not your stupid heroes—orators and poets.——

I am really so sorry—that I can't think of anything else just now.—Besides I liked him with all his Coxcombry.——

Let me know what we are all to do,—and to whom we can have recourse without damage for our cleaning—scaling and powder.—

How do you get on with your affairs?—and how does every body get on.——

How is all your rabbit-warren of a family? I gave you an account of mine by last letter.—The Child Allegra is well—but the Monkey has got a cough—and the tame Crow has lately suffered from the head ache.——Fletcher has been bled for a Stitch—and looks flourishing again——

Pray write—excuse this short scrawl—

yours ever   B

P.S.—Recollect about Waite's Successor—why he was only *married* the other day—and now I don't wonder so much that the poor man died of it.——

---

[1] Waite was a fashionable dentist, resident at 2 Old Burlington Street; Blake, an equally renowned barber.

TO JOHN MURRAY   *Ravenna, 9ᵇʳᵉ 19, 1820*

DEAR MURRAY,—What you said of the late Charles Skinner
Matthews has set me to my recollections; but I have not
been able to turn up any thing which would do for the purposed Memoir of his brother,—even if he had previously done
enough during his life to sanction the introduction of anecdotes
so merely personal. He was, however, a very extraordinary
man, and would have been a great one. No one ever succeeded
in a more surpassing degree than he did as far as he went. He
was indolent, too; but whenever he stripped, he overthrew all
antagonists. His conquests will be found registered at Cambridge, particularly his *Downing* one, which was hotly and
highly contested, and yet easily *won*. Hobhouse was his most
intimate friend, and can tell you more of him than any man.
William Bankes also a great deal. I myself recollect more of
his oddities than of his academical qualities, for we lived most
together at a very idle period of *my* life. When I went up to
Trinity, in 1805, at the age of seventeen and a half, I was
miserable and untoward to a degree. I was wretched at leaving
Harrow, to which I had become attached during the two last
years of my stay there; wretched at going to Cambridge
instead of Oxford (there were no rooms vacant at Christ-
church); wretched from some private domestic circumstances
of different kinds, and consequently about as unsocial as a
wolf taken from the troop. So that, although I knew Matthews,
and met him often *then* at Bankes's, (who was my collegiate
pastor, and master, and patron,) and at Rhode's, Milnes's,
Price's, Dick's, Macnamara's, Farrell's, Gally Knight's, and
others of that *set* of contemporaries, yet I was neither intimate
with him nor with any one else, except my old schoolfellow
Edward Long (with whom I used to pass the day in riding and
swimming), and William Bankes, who was good-naturedly
tolerant of my ferocities.

It was not till 1807, after I had been upwards of a year
away from Cambridge, to which I had returned again to *reside*
for my degree, that I became one of Matthews's familiars, by
means of Hobhouse, who, after hating me for two years, because I wore a *white hat*, and a *grey* coat, and rode a *grey* horse
(as he says himself), took me into his good graces because I

had written some poetry. I had always lived a good deal, and got drunk occasionally, in their company—but now we became really friends in a morning. Matthews, however, was not at this period resident in College. I met *him* chiefly in London, and at uncertain periods at Cambridge. Hobhouse, in the mean time, did great things: he founded the Cambridge " Whig Club " (which he seems to have forgotten), and the " Amicable Society ", which was dissolved in consequence of the members constantly quarrelling, and made himself very popular with " us youth ", and no less formidable to all tutors, professors, and heads of Colleges. William Bankes was gone; while he stayed, he ruled the roast—or rather the *roasting*— and was father of all mischiefs.

Matthews and I, meeting in London, and elsewhere became great cronies. He was not good tempered—nor am I— but with a little tact his temper was manageable, and I thought him so superior a man, that I was willing to sacrifice something to his humours, which were often, at the same time, amusing and provoking. What became of his *papers* (and he certainly had many), at the time of his death, was never known. I mention this by the way, fearing to skip it over, and *as he wrote* remarkably well, both in Latin and English. We went down to Newstead together, where I had got a famous cellar, and *Monks'* dresses from a masquerade warehouse. We were a company of some seven or eight, with an occasional neighbour or so for visiters, and used to sit up late in our friars' dresses, drinking burgundy, claret, champagne, and what not, out of the *skull-cup*, and all sorts of glasses, and buffooning all round the house, in our conventual garments. Matthews always denominated me " the Abbot ", and never called me by any other name in his good humours, to the day of his death. The harmony of these our symposia was somewhat interrupted, a few days after our assembling, by Matthews's threatening to throw Hobhouse out of a *window*, in consequence of I know not what commerce of jokes ending in this epigram. Hobhouse came to me and said, that " his respect and regard for me as host would not permit him to call out any of my guests, and that he should go to town next morning ". He did. It was in vain that I represented to him that the window was not high, and that the turf under it was particularly soft. Away he went.

Matthews and myself had travelled down from London together, talking all the way incessantly upon one single topic. When we got to Loughborough, I know not what chasm had made us diverge for a moment to some other subject, at which he was indignant. " Come," said he, " don't let us break through—let us go on as we began, to our journey's end " ; and so he continued, and was as entertaining as ever to the very end. He had previously occupied, during my year's absence from Cambridge, my rooms in Trinity, with the furniture ; and Jones, the tutor, in his odd way, had said, on putting him in, " Mr. Matthews, I recommend to your attention not to damage any of the moveables, for Lord Byron, Sir, is a young man of *tumultuous passions* ". Matthews was delighted with this ; and whenever anybody came to visit him, begged them to handle the very door with caution ; and used to repeat Jones's admonition in his tone and manner. There was a large mirror in the room, on which he remarked, " that he thought his friends were grown uncommonly assiduous in coming to *see him,* but he soon discovered that they only came to *see themselves* ". Jones's phrase of " *tumultuous passions* ", and the whole scene, had put him into such good humour, that I verily believe that I owed to it a portion of his good graces.

When at Newstead, somebody by accident rubbed against one of his white silk stockings, one day before dinner ; of course the gentleman apologised. " Sir," answered Matthews, " it may be all very well for you, who have a great many silk stockings, to dirty other people's ; but to me, who have only this *one pair*, which I have put on in honour of the Abbot here, no apology can compensate for such carelessness ; besides, the expense of washing." He had the same sort of droll sardonic way about every thing. A wild Irishman, named Farrell, one evening began to say something at a large supper at Cambridge, Matthews roared out " Silence ! " and then, pointing to Farrell, cried out, in the words of the oracle, " *Orson is endowed with reason* ". You may easily suppose that Orson lost what reason he had acquired, on hearing this compliment. When Hobhouse published his volume of poems, the *Miscellany* (which Matthews *would* call the " *Miss-sell-any* "), all that could be drawn from him was, that the preface was " extremely like *Walsh* ". Hobhouse thought this at first a compliment ; but we never could make out what it was, for all we know of *Walsh* is his Ode to King William, and Pope's epithet of "*knowing Walsh*". When the Newstead party broke up for London, Hobhouse and Matthews, who were the greatest friends possible, agreed, for a whim, to *walk together* to town. They quarrelled by the way, and actually walked the latter half of the journey, occasionally passing and repassing, without speaking. When Matthews had got to Highgate, he had spent all his money but three-pence halfpenny, and determined to spend that also in a pint of beer, which I believe he was drinking before a public-house, as Hobhouse passed him (still without speaking) for the last time on their route. They were reconciled in London again.

One of Matthews's passions was "the fancy"; and he sparred uncommonly well. But he always got beaten in rows, or combats with the bare fist. In swimming, too, he swam well; but with *effort* and *labour*, and *too high* out of the water; so that Scrope Davies and myself, of whom he was therein somewhat emulous, always told him that he would be drowned if ever he came to a difficult pass in the water. He was so; but surely Scrope and myself would have been most heartily glad that

> "the Dean had lived,
> And our prediction proved a lie".

His head was uncommonly handsome, very like what *Pope's* was in his youth.

His voice, and laugh, and features, are strongly resembled by his brother Henry's, if Henry be *he* of *King's College*. His passion for boxing was so great, that he actually wanted me to match him with Dogherty (whom I had backed and made the match for against Tom Belcher), and I saw them spar together at my own lodgings with the gloves on. As he was bent upon it, I would have backed Dogherty to please him, but the match went off. It was of course to have been a private fight, in a private room.

On one occasion, being too late to go home and dress, he was equipped by a friend (Mr. Baillie, I believe,) in a magnificently fashionable and somewhat exaggerated shirt and neckcloth. He proceeded to the Opera, and took his station in

Fop's Alley. During the interval between the opera and the ballet, an acquaintance took his station by him and saluted him: " Come round," said Matthews, " come round ".— " Why should I come round? " said the other ; " you have only to turn your head—I am close by you."—" That is exactly what I cannot do," said Matthews ; " don't you see the state I am in? " pointing to his buckram shirt collar and inflexible cravat,—and there he stood with his head always in the same perpendicular position during the whole spectacle.

One evening, after dining together, as we were going to the Opera, I happened to have a spare Opera ticket (as sub-scriber to a box), and presented it to Matthews. " Now, sir," said he to Hobhouse afterwards, " this I call *courteous* in the Abbot—another man would never have thought that I might do better with half a guinea than throw it to a door-keeper ;— but here is a man not only asks me to dinner, but gives me a ticket for the theatre." These were only his oddities, for no man was more liberal, or more honourable in all his doings and dealings, than Matthews. He gave Hobhouse and me, before we set out for Constantinople, a most splendid entertain-ment, to which we did ample justice. One of his fancies was dining at all sorts of out-of-the-way places. Somebody popped upon him in I know not what coffee-house in the Strand—and what do you think was the attraction? Why, that he paid a shilling (I think) to *dine with his hat on*. This he called his " *hat* house ", and used to boast of the comfort of being covered at meal times.

When Sir Henry Smith was expelled from Cambridge for a row with a tradesman named " Hiron ", Matthews solaced himself with shouting under Hiron's windows every evening,

> " Ah me ! what perils do environ
> The man who meddles with *hot Hirons* ".

He was also of that band of profane scoffers who, under the auspices of [Bankes], used to rouse Lort Mansel (late Bishop of Bristol) from his slumbers in the lodge of Trinity ; and when he appeared at the window foaming with wrath, and crying out, " I know you, gentlemen, I know you ! " were wont to reply, " We beseech thee to hear us, good *Lort* ! "—" Good *Lort* deliver us ! " (Lort was his Christian name.) As he was very

free in his speculations upon all kinds of subjects, although by
no means either dissolute or intemperate in his conduct, and
as I was no less independent, our conversation and correspondence used to alarm our friend Hobhouse to a considerable
degree.

You must be almost tired of my packets, which will have
cost a mint of postage.

Salute Gifford and all my friends.

Yours, B.

TO THE HON. DOUGLAS KINNAIRD †   *Ravenna, 9bre 22nd, 1820*

MY DEAR DOUGLAS,—You ask me to *make* Hanson *make
Claughton* pay *me*. I would willingly know how I am to make
Hanson do that or any thing else at this distance of time and
place? If you intimate to him that what is taken out of
Claughton's pocket will go into his own, in diminution of his
" bill of pains and penalties ", he may perhaps condescend to
do his duty. It is useless for me to say more. I have written,
and written, and *you* have spoken. I suppose he will end by
having his own way, and a pretty way it is.

The affairs of this part of Italy are simplifying ; the liberals
have delayed till it is too late for them to do anything to the
purpose. If the scoundrels of Troppau decide on a massacre
(as is probable) the Barbarians will march in by one frontier,
and the Neapolitans by the other. They have *both asked* permission of his Holiness so to do, which is equivalent to asking
a man's permission to give him a kick on the a—se ; if he grants
it, it is a sign he can't return it.

The worst of all is, that this devoted country will become,
for the six thousandth time, since God made man in his own
image, the seat of war. I recollect Spain in 1809, and the
Morea and part of Greece in 1810–1811, when Veli Pacha was
on his way to combat the Russians (the Turkish armies make
their *own country* like an enemy's on a march), and a small
stretch also of my own county of Nottingham under the
Luddites, when we were burning the frames, and sometimes
the manufactories, so that I have a tolerable idea of what may
ensue. Here all is suspicion and terrorism, bullying, arming,

and disarming; the priests scared, the people gloomy, and the merchants *buying* up corn to *supply the armies*. I am so pleased with the last piece of Italic patriotism, that I have underlined it for your remark; it is just as if our Hampshire farmers should prepare magazines for any two continental scoundrels, who could land and fight it out in New Forest.

I come in for my share of the *vigorous* system of the day. They have taken it into their heads that I am popular (which no one ever was in Italy but an opera singer, or ever will be till the resurrection of Romulus), and are trying by all kinds of petty vexations to disgust and make me retire. This I should hardly believe, it seems so absurd, if some of their priests did not avow it. They try to fix squabbles upon my servants, to involve me in scrapes (no difficult matter), and lastly they (the governing party) menace to shut Madame Guiccioli up in a *convent*. The last piece of policy springs from two motives; the one because her *family* are suspected of liberal principles, and the second because mine (although I do not preach them) are known, and were known when it was far less reputable to be a friend to liberty than it is now.

If I am proud of some of the poetry, I am much prouder of some of my predictions; they are as good as Fitzgerald's, the Literary Fund seer, and Murray's post poet.

If they should succeed in putting this poor girl into a convent for doing that with me which all the other countesses of Italy have done with everybody for these 1000 years, of course I would accede to a retreat on my part, rather than a prison on hers, for the former only is what they *really* want. She is, as women are apt to be by opposition, sufficiently heroic and obstinate; but as both these qualities may only tend the more to put her in monastic durance, I am at a loss what to do. I have seen the correspondence of half a dozen bigots on the subject, and perceive that they have set about it, merely as an indirect way of attacking part of her relations, and myself. You may imagine that I am, as usual, in warm water with this affair in prospect.

As for public affairs they look no better. [word torn out], parties have dawdled till it is too late. I question if they could get together twelve thousand men of their own, *now*. And some months ago it was different.

Pray write. Remember me to Hobhouse, and believe me
ever

Yours most truly, B.

P.S.—The police at present is under the Germans, or rather
the Austrians, who do not merit the name of Germans, who
open all letters it is supposed. I have no objection, so that they
see how I hate and utterly despise and detest those *Hun brutes*,
and all they can do in their temporary wickedness, for Time
and Opinion, and the vengeance of a roused-up people will at
length manure Italy with their carcases, it may not be for one
year, or two, or ten, but it *will* be, and so that it *could be* sooner,
I know not what a man ought *not* to do, but their antagonists
are no great shakes. The Spaniards are the boys after all.

TO JOHN MURRAY   *Ravenna, D^{ecr} 9th 1820*

DEAR MURRAY,—I intended to have written to you at
some length by this post, but as the Military Commandant is
now lying dead in my house, on Fletcher's bed, I have other
things to think of.

He was shot at 8 o'clock this evening about two hundred
paces from our door. I was putting on my great coat to pay a
visit to the Countess G., when I heard a shot, and on going into
the hall, found all my servants on the balcony exclaiming that
" a Man was murdered ". As it is the custom here to let people
fight it through, they wanted to hinder me from going out ;
but I ran down into the Street : Tita, the bravest of them,
followed me ; and we made our way to the Commandant, who
was lying on his back, with five wounds, of which three in the
body—one in the heart. There were about him Diego, his
Adjutant, crying like a Child ; a priest howling ; a surgeon
who dared not touch him ; two or three confused and frightened
soldiers ; one or two of the boldest of the mob ; and the Street
dark as pitch, with the people flying in all directions. As Diego
could only cry and wring his hands, and the Priest could only
pray, and nobody seemed able or willing to do anything except
exclaim, shake and stare, I made my servant and one of the
mob take up the body ; sent off Diego crying to the Cardinal,

the Soldiers for the Guard; and had the Commandant conveyed up Stairs to my own quarters. But he was quite gone. I
made the surgeon examine him, and examined him myself.
He had bled inwardly, and very little external blood was
apparent. One of the slugs had gone quite through—all but
the skin: I felt it myself. Two more shots in the body, one
in a finger, and another in the arm. His face not at all disfigured: he seems asleep, but is growing livid. The assassin
has not been taken; but the gun was found—a gun filed down
to half the barrel.

He said nothing but *O Dio!* and *O Gesu* two or three times.

The house was filled at last with soldiers, officers, police,
and military; but they are clearing away—all but the sentinels,
and the body is to be removed tomorrow. It seems that, if I
had not had him taken into my house, he might have lain in
the Streets till morning; as here nobody meddles with such
things, for fear of the consequences—either of public suspicion,
or private revenge on the part of the slayers. They may do as
they please: I shall never be deterred from a duty of humanity
by all the assassins of Italy, and that is a wide word.

He was a brave officer, but an unpopular man. The whole
town is in confusion.

You may judge better of things here by this detail, than by
anything which I could add on the Subject: communicate this
letter to Hobhouse and Douglas Kᵈ, and believe me

Yours ever truly, B.

P.S.—The poor Man's wife is not yet aware of his death:
they are to break it to her in the morning.

The Lieutenant, who is watching the body, is smoking
with the greatest *sangfroid*: a strange people.

TO LADY BYRON   *Ravenna, [Thursday], 10ᵇʳᵉ 28ᵗʰ 1820*

I acknowledge your note which is on the whole satisfactory
—the style a little harsh—but that was to be expected—it
would have been too great a peace-offering after nearly five
years—to have been gracious in the manner, as well as in the
matter.—Yet you might have been so—for communications

between *us*—are like " Dialogues of the Dead "—or " letters between this world and the next ". You have alluded to the " *past* " and I to the future.—As to Augusta—she knows as little of my request, as of your answer—Whatever She is or may have been—*you* have never had reason to complain of her—on the contrary—you are not aware of the obligations under which you have been to her.—Her life and mine—and yours and mine—were two things perfectly distinct from each other—when one ceased the other began—and now both are closed.

You must be aware of the reasons of my bequest in favour of Augusta and her Children which are the restrictions I am under by the Settlement, which death would make yours—at least the available portion.

I wrote to you on the 8th or ninth inst, I think.—Things here are fast coming to a Crisis.— — — War may be considered as nearly inevitable—though the King of N[aples] is gone to Congress, that will scarcely hinder it—the people are so excited, you must not mind what the English fools say of Italy—they know nothing—they go gaping from Rome to Florence and so on—which is like seeing England—in Saint James's Street.— — —

I live with the people and amongst them—and know them —and you may rely upon my not deceiving you, though I may myself. If you mean ever to extricate the Settlement from the funds now is the time to make the trustees act—while Stocks are yet up—and peace not actually broken. Pray attend to this—

Yours BYRON

P.S.—Excuse haste—I have scribbled in great quickness,— and do not attribute it to ill-humour—but to matters which are on hand—and which must be attended to—I am really obliged by your attention to my request.— — — You could not have sent me any thing half so acceptable but I have *burnt* your note that you may be under no restraint but your internal feeling.— It is a comfort to me *now*—beyond all comforts; that A— and her children will be thought of—after I am nothing; but five years ago—it would have been something more? why did you *then keep silence*? I told you that I was going *long*—and going *far* (not so *far* as I intended—for I meant to have gone to

Turkey and am not sure that I shall not finish with it—but *longer* than I meant to have made of existence—at least at that time—) and two words about her or hers would have been to me—like vengeance or freedom to an Italian—i.e. the " Ne plus ultra " of gratifications—She and two others were the only things I ever really loved—I may say it now—for we are young no longer.——

TO THOMAS MOORE   *Ravenna, January 2, 1821*

Your entering into my project for the *Memoir*, is pleasant to me. But I doubt (contrary to me my dear Mad^e Mac F * * ,[1] whom I always loved, and always shall—not only because I really *did* feel attached to her *personally*, but because she and about a dozen others of that sex were all who stuck by me in the grand conflict of 1815)—but I doubt, I say, whether the *Memoir* could appear in my lifetime;—and, indeed, I had rather it did not; for a man always *looks dead* after his Life has appeared, and I should certes not survive the appearance of mine. The first part I cannot consent to alter, even although Madame de S[tael]'s opinion of B. C. and my remarks upon Lady C.'s beauty (which is surely great, and I suppose that I have said so—at least, I ought) should go down to our grandchildren in unsophisticated nakedness.

As to Madame de S[tael], I am by no means bound to be her beadsman—she was always more civil to me in person than during my absence. Our dear defunct friend, Monk Lewis, who was too great a bore ever to lie, assured me upon his tiresome word of honour, that at Florence, the said Madame de S[tael] was open-*mouthed* against me; and when asked, in *Switzerland, why* she had changed her opinion, replied, with laudable sincerity, that I had named her in a sonnet with Voltaire, Rousseau, etc. and that she could not help it through decency. Now, I have not forgotten this, but I have been generous,—as mine acquaintance, the late Captain Whitby, of the navy, used to say to his seamen (when " married to the gunner's daughter ")—" two dozen and let you off easy ". The " two dozen " were with the cat-o'-nine tails;—the " let you off easy " was rather his own opinion than that of the patient.

My acquaintance with these terms and practices arises from my having been much conversant with ships of war and naval heroes in the year of my voyages in the Mediterranean. Whitby was in the gallant action off Lissa in 1811. He was brave, but a disciplinarian. When he left his frigate, he left a *parrot*, which was taught by the crew the following sounds— (it must be remarked that Captain Whitby was the image of

[1] Presumably Madame de Flahaut, the former Miss Mercer Elphinstone.

Fawcett the actor, in voice, face, and figure, and that he squinted).

The Parrot loquitur.

" Whitby! Whitby! funny eye! funny eye! two dozen, and let you off easy. Oh you——! "

Now, if Madame de B. has a parrot, it had better be taught a French parody of the same sounds.

With regard to our purposed Journal, I will call it what you please, but it should be a newspaper, to make it *pay*. We can call it " The Harp ", if you like—or any thing.

I feel exactly as you do about our " art ", but it comes over me in a kind of rage every now and then, like * * * *, and then, if I don't write to empty my mind, I go mad. As to that regular, uninterrupted love of writing, which you describe in your friend, I do not understand it. I feel it as a torture, which I must get rid of, but never as a pleasure. On the contrary, I think composition a great pain.

I wish you to think seriously of the Journal scheme—for I am as serious as one can be, in this world, about any thing. As to matters here, they are high and mighty—but not for paper. It is much about the state of things betwixt Cain and Abel. There is, in fact, no law or government at all; and it is wonderful how well things go on without them. Excepting a few occasional murders, (every body killing whomsoever he pleases, and being killed, in turn, by a friend, or relative, of the defunct,) there is as quiet a society and as merry a Carnival as can be met with in a tour through Europe. There is nothing like habit in these things.

I shall remain here till May or June, and, unless " honour comes unlooked for ", we may perhaps meet, in France or England, within the year.

Yours, etc.

Of course, I cannot explain to you existing circumstances, as they open all letters.

Will you set me right about your curst *Champs Elysées?*— are they " *és* " or " *ées* " for the adjective? I know nothing of French, being all Italian. Though I can read and understand French, I never attempt to speak it; for I hate it. From the second part of the Memoirs cut what you please.

EXTRACTS FROM A DIARY
JANUARY 4–FEBRUARY 27, 1821

Ravenna, January 4, 1821

"A SUDDEN thought strikes me." Let me begin a Journal once more. The last I kept was in Switzerland, in record of a tour made in the Bernese Alps, which I made to send to my sister in 1816, and I suppose that she has it still, for she wrote to me that she was pleased with it. Another, and longer, I kept in 1813–1814, which I gave to Thomas Moore in the same year.

This morning I gat me up late, as usual—weather bad— bad as England—worse. The snow of last week melting to the sirocco of to-day, so that there were two damned things at once. Could not even get to ride on horseback in the forest. Stayed at home all the morning—looked at the fire—wondered when the post would come. Post came at the Ave Maria, instead of half-past one o'clock, as it ought. Galignani's *Messengers*, six in number—a letter from Faenza, but none from England. Very sulky in consequence (for there ought to have been letters), and ate in consequence a copious dinner ; for when I am vexed, it makes me swallow quicker—but drank very little.

I was out of spirits—read the papers—thought what *fame* was, on reading, in a case of murder, that " Mr. Wych, grocer, at Tunbridge, sold some bacon, flour, cheese, and, it is believed, some plums, to some gipsy woman accused. He had on his counter (I quote faithfully) a *book*, the Life of *Pamela*, which he was *tearing* for *waste* paper, etc., etc. In the cheese was found, etc., and a *leaf* of *Pamela wrapt round the bacon*." What would Richardson, the vainest and luckiest of *living* authors (*i.e.* while alive)—he who, with Aaron Hill, used to prophesy and chuckle over the presumed fall of Fielding (the *prose* Homer of human nature) and of Pope (the most beautiful of poets)—what would he have said, could he have traced his pages from their place on the French prince's toilets (see Boswell's Johnson) to the grocer's counter and the gipsy-murderess's bacon ! ! !

What would he have said? What can any body say, save what Solomon said long before us? After all, it is but passing from one counter to another, from the bookseller's to the other tradesman's—grocer or pastry-cook. For my part, I have met with most poetry upon trunks; so that I am apt to consider the trunk-maker as the sexton of authorship.

Wrote five letters in about half an hour, short and savage, to all my rascally correspondents. Carriage came. Heard the news of three murders at Faenza and Forli—a carabinier, a smuggler, and an attorney—all last night. The two first in a quarrel, the latter by premeditation.

Three weeks ago—almost a month—the 7th it was—I picked up the commandant, mortally wounded, out of the street; he died in my house; assassins unknown, but presumed political. His brethren wrote from Rome last night to thank me for having assisted him in his last moments. Poor fellow! it was a pity; he was a good soldier, but imprudent. It was eight in the evening when they killed him. We heard the shot; my servants and I ran out, and found him expiring, with five wounds, two whereof mortal—by slugs they seemed. I examined him, but did not go to the dissection next morning.

Carriage at 8 or so—went to visit La Contessa G[uiccioli]— found her playing on the piano-forte—talked till ten, when the Count, her father, and the no less Count, her brother, came in from the theatre. Play, they said, Alfieri's *Fileppo*—well received.

Two days ago the King of Naples passed through Bologna on his way to congress. My servant Luigi brought the news. I had sent him to Bologna for a lamp. How will it end? Time will show.

Came home at eleven, or rather before. If the road and weather are comfortable, mean to ride to-morrow. High time —almost a week at this work—snow, sirocco, one day—frost and snow the other—sad climate for Italy. But the two seasons, last and present, are extraordinary. Read a Life of Leonardo da Vinci by Rossi [? Bossi]—ruminated—wrote this much, and will go to bed.

January 5, 1821

Rose late—dull and drooping—the weather dripping and dense. Snow on the ground, and sirocco above in the sky, like yesterday. Roads up to the horse's belly, so that riding (at least for pleasure) is not very feasible. Added a postscript to my letter to Murray. Read the conclusion, for the fiftieth time

(I have read all W. Scott's novels at least fifty times), of the third series of *Tales of my Landlord*—grand work—Scotch Fielding, as well as great English poet—wonderful man! I long to get drunk with him.

Dined *versus* six o' the clock. Forgot that there was a plum-pudding, (I have added, lately, *eating* to my " family of vices ",) and had dined before I knew it. Drank half a bottle of some sort of spirits—probably spirits of wine; for what they call brandy, rum, etc., etc., here is nothing but spirits of wine, coloured accordingly. Did *not* eat two apples, which were placed by way of dessert. Fed the two cats, the hawk, and the tame (but *not tamed*) crow. Read Mitford's *History of Greece*—Xenophon's *Retreat of the Ten Thousand*. Up to this present moment writing, 6 minutes before eight o' the clock—French hours, not Italian.

Hear the carriage—order pistols and great coat, as usual—necessary articles. Weather cold—carriage open, and in-habitants somewhat savage—rather treacherous and highly inflamed by politics. Fine fellows, though,—good materials for a nation. Out of chaos God made a world, and out of high passions comes a people.

Clock strikes—going out to make love. Somewhat perilous, but not disagreeable. Memorandum—a new screen put up to-day. It is rather antique, but will do with a little repair.

Thaw continues—hopeful that riding may be practicable to-morrow. Sent the papers to All[1].—grand events coming.

11 o' the clock and nine minutes. Visited La Contessa G[uiccioli] *nata* G[hisleri] G[amba]. Found her beginning my letter of answer to the thanks of Alessio del Pinto of Rome for assisting his brother the late Commandant in his last moments, as I had begged her to pen my reply for the purer Italian, I being an ultra-montane, little skilled in the set phrase of Tuscany. Cut short the letter—finish it another day. Talked of Italy, patriotism, Alfieri, Madame Albany, and other branches of learning. Also Sallust's *Conspiracy of Catiline*, and the *War of Jugurtha*. At 9 came in her brother, Il Conte Pietro—at 10, her father, Conte Ruggiero.

Talked of various modes of warfare—of the Hungarian and Highland modes of broad-sword exercise, in both whereof I was once a moderate " master of fence ". Settled that the

R. will break out on the 7th or 8th of March, in which appointment I should trust, had it not been settled that it was to have
broken out in October, 1820. But those Bolognese shirked the
Romagnuoles.

" It is all one to Ranger." One must not be particular, but
take rebellion when it lies in the way. Come home—read the
Ten Thousand again, and will go to bed.

Mem.—Ordered Fletcher (at four o'clock this afternoon)
to copy out seven or eight apophthegms of Bacon, in which I
have detected such blunders as a schoolboy might detect rather
than commit. Such are the sages! What must they be, when
such as I can stumble on their mistakes or misstatements? I
will go to bed, for I find that I grow cynical.

January 6, 1821

Mist—thaw—slop—rain. No stirring out on horseback.
Read Spence's *Anecdotes*. Pope a fine fellow—always thought
him so. Corrected blunders in *nine* apophthegms of Bacon—
all historical—and read Mitford's *Greece*. Wrote an epigram.
Turned to a passage in Guinguené—ditto in Lord Holland's
Lope de Vega. Wrote a note on *Don Juan*.

At eight went out to visit. Heard a little music—like
music. Talked with Count Pietro G[amba] of the Italian
comedian Vestris, who is now at Rome—have seen him often
act in Venice—a good actor—very. Somewhat of a mannerist;
but excellent in broad comedy, as well as in the sentimental
pathetic. He has made me frequently laugh and cry, neither
of which is now a very easy matter—at least, for a player to
produce in me.

Thought of the state of women under the ancient Greeks
—convenient enough. Present state a remnant of the barbarism of the chivalric and feudal ages—artificial and un-
natural. They ought to mind home—and be well fed and
clothed—but not mixed in society. Well educated, too, in
religion—but to read neither poetry nor politics—nothing but
books of piety and cookery. Music—drawing—dancing—also
a little gardening and ploughing now and then. I have seen
them mending the roads in Epirus with good success. Why not,
as well as haymaking and milking?

Came home, and read Mitford again, and played with my

mastiff—gave him his supper. Made another reading to the epigram, but the turn the same. To-night at the theatre, there being a prince on his throne in the last scene of the comedy,— the audience laughed, and asked him for a *Constitution*. This shows the state of the public mind here, as well as the assassinations. It won't do. There must be an universal republic,— and there ought to be.

The crow is lame of a leg—wonder how it happened— some fool trod upon his toe, I suppose. The falcon pretty brisk —the cats large and noisy—the monkeys I have not looked to since the cold weather, as they suffer by being brought up. Horses must be gay—get a ride as soon as weather serves. Deuced muggy still—an Italian winter is a sad thing, but all the other seasons are charming.

What is the reason that I have been, all my lifetime, more or less *ennuyé*? and that, if any thing, I am rather less so now than I was at twenty, as far as my recollection serves? I do not know how to answer this, but presume that it is constitutional,—as well as the waking in low spirits, which I have invariably done for many years. Temperance and exercise, which I have practised at times, and for a long time together vigorously and violently, made little or no difference. Violent passions did;—when under their immediate influence—it is odd, but—I was in agitated, but *not* in depressed, spirits.

A dose of salts has the effect of a temporary inebriation, like light champagne, upon me. But wine and spirits make me sullen and savage to ferocity—silent, however, and retiring, and not quarrelsome, if not spoken to. Swimming also raises my spirits,—but in general they are low, and get daily lower. That is *hopeless*; for I do not think I am so much *ennuyé* as I was at nineteen. The proof is, that then I must game, or drink, or be in motion of some kind, or I was miserable. At present, I can mope in quietness; and like being alone better than any company—except the lady's whom I serve. But I feel a something, which makes me think that, if I ever reach near to old age, like Swift, " I shall die at top " first. Only I do not dread idiotism or madness so much as he did. On the contrary, I think some quieter stages of both must be preferable to much of what men think the possession of their senses.

January 7, 1821, Sunday

Still rain—mist—snow—drizzle—and all the incalculable combinations of a climate where heat and cold struggle for mastery. Read Spence, and turned over Roscoe, to find a passage I have not found. Read the fourth vol. of W. Scott's second series of *Tales of my Landlord.* Dined. Read the *Lugano Gazette.* Read—I forget what. At eight went to conversazione. Found there the Countess Geltrude, Betti V. and her husband, and others. Pretty black-eyed woman that—*only* nineteen—same age as Teresa, who is prettier, though.

The Count Pietro G[amba] took me aside to say that the Patriots have had notice from Forli (twenty miles off) that to-night the government and its party mean to strike a stroke—that the Cardinal here has had orders to make several arrests immediately, and that, in consequence, the Liberals are arming, and have posted patroles in the streets, to sound the alarm and give notice to fight for it.

He asked me " what should be done? " I answered, " Fight for it, rather than be taken in detail " ; and offered, if any of them are in immediate apprehension of arrest, to receive them in my house (which is defensible), and to defend them, with my servants and themselves (we have arms and ammunition), as long as we can,—or to try to get them away under cloud of night. On going home, I offered him the pistols which I had about me—but he refused, but said he would come off to me in case of accidents.

It wants half an hour of midnight, and rains ;—as Gibbet says, " a fine night for their enterprise—dark as hell, and blows like the devil ". If the row don't happen *now*, it must soon. I thought that their system of shooting people would soon produce a re-action—and now it seems coming. I will do what I can in the way of combat, though a little out of exercise. The cause is a good one.

Turned over and over half a score of books for the passage in question, and can't find it. Expect to hear the drum and the musquetry momently (for they swear to resist, and are right,)– but I hear nothing, as yet, save the plash of the rain and the gusts of the wind at intervals. Don't like to go to bed, because I hate to be waked, and would rather sit up for the row, if there is to be one.

Mended the fire—have got the arms—and a book or two, which I shall turn over. I know little of their numbers, but think the Carbonari strong enough to beat the troops, even here. With twenty men this house might be defended for twenty-four hours against any force to be brought against it, *now* in this place, for the same time; and, in such a time, the country would have notice, and would rise,—if ever they *will* rise, of which there is some doubt. In the mean time, I may as well read as do any thing else, being alone.

January 8, 1821, Monday

Rose, and found Count P. G. in my apartments. Sent away the servant. Told me that, according to the best information, the Government had not issued orders for the arrests apprehended; that the attack in Forli had not taken place (as expected) by the *Sanfedisti*—the opponents of the *Carbonari* or Liberals—and that, as yet, they are still in apprehension only. Asked me for some arms of a better sort, which I gave him. Settled that, in case of a row, the Liberals were to assemble *here* (with me), and that he had given the word to Vincenzo G. and others of the *Chiefs* for that purpose. He himself and father are going to the chase in the forest; but V. G. is to come to me, and an express to be sent off to him, P. G., if any thing occurs, Concerted operations. They are to seize—but no matter.

I advised them to attack in detail, and in different parties, in different *places* (though at the *same* time), so as to divide the attention of the troops, who, though few, yet being disciplined, would beat any body of people (not trained) in a regular fight— unless dispersed in small parties, and distracted with different assaults. Offered to let them assemble here if they choose. It is a strongish post—narrow street, commanded from within— and tenable walls.

Dined. Tried on a new coat. Letter to Murray, with corrections of Bacon's *Apophthegms* and an epigram—the *latter not* for publication. At eight went to Teresa, Countess G. At nine and a half came in Il Conte P. and Count P. G. Talked of a certain proclamation lately issued. Count R. G. had been with * * (the * *), to sound him about the arrests. He, * *, is a *trimmer*, and deals, at present, his cards with both hands. If he don't mind, they'll be full. * * pretends (*I* doubt him —*they* don't,—we shall see) that there is no such order, and seems staggered by the immense exertions of the Neapolitans, and the fierce spirit of the Liberals here. The truth is, that * * cares for little but his place (which is a good one), and wishes to play pretty with both parties. He has changed his mind thirty times these last three moons, to my knowledge, for he corresponds with me. But he is not a bloody fellow—only an avaricious one.

It seems that, just at this moment (as Lydia Languish says), " there will be no elopement after all ". I wish that I had known as much last night—or, rather, this morning—I should have gone to bed two hours earlier. And yet I ought not to complain ; for, though it is a sirocco, and heavy rain, I have not *yawned* for these two days.

Came home—read *History of Greece*—before dinner had read Walter Scott's *Rob Roy*. Wrote address to the letter in answer to Alessio del Pinto, who has thanked me for helping his brother (the late Commandant, murdered here last month) in his last moments. Have told him I only did a duty of humanity —as is true. The brother lives at Rome.

Mended the fire with some *sgobole* (a Romagnuole word), and gave the falcon some water. Drank some Seltzer-water. Mem.—received to-day a print, or etching, of the story of Ugolino, by an Italian painter—different, of course, from Sir Joshua Reynolds's, and I think (as far as recollection goes) *no worse*, for Reynolds's is not good in history. Tore a button in my new coat.

I wonder what figure these Italians will make in a regular row. I sometimes think that, like the Irishman's gun (some-body had sold him a crooked one), they will only do for " shooting round a corner " ; at least, this sort of shooting has been the late tenor of their exploits. And yet there are materials in this people, and a noble energy, if well directed. But who is to direct them? No matter. Out of such times heroes spring. Difficulties are the hotbeds of high spirits, and Freedom the mother of the few virtues incident to human nature.

Tuesday, January 9, 1821

Rose—the day fine. Ordered the horses; but Lega (my *secretary*, an Italianism for steward or chief servant) coming to tell me that the painter had finished the work in fresco for the room he has been employed on lately, I went to see it before I set out. The painter has not copied badly the prints from Titian, etc., considering all things.

Dined. Read Johnson's *Vanity of Human Wishes*,—all the examples and mode of giving them sublime, as well as the latter part, with the exception of an occasional couplet. I do not so much admire the opening. I remember an observation of Sharpe's, (the *Conversationist*, as he was called in London, and a very clever man,) that the first line of this poem was super-fluous, and that Pope (the best of poets, *I* think,) would have begun at once, only changing the punctuation—

" Survey mankind from China to Peru ".

The former line, " Let observation ", etc., is certainly heavy and useless. But 'tis a grand poem—and *so true!*—true as the 10th of Juvenal himself. The lapse of ages *changes* all things—time—language—the earth—the bounds of the sea—the stars of the sky, and every thing " about, around, and underneath " man, *except man himself*, who has always been, and always will be, an unlucky rascal. The infinite variety of lives conduct but to death, and the infinity of wishes lead but to disappointment. All the discoveries which have yet been made have multiplied little but existence. An extirpated disease is succeeded by some new pestilence; and a discovered world has brought little to the old one, except the p— first and freedom afterwards —the *latter* a fine thing, particularly as they gave it to Europe in exchange for slavery. But it is doubtful whether " the Sovereigns " would not think the *first* the best present of the two to their subjects.

At eight went out—heard some news. They say the King of Naples has declared by couriers from Florence, to the *Powers* (as they call now those wretches with crowns), that his Constitution was compulsive, etc., etc., and that the Austrian barbarians are placed again on *war* pay, and will march. Let them—" they come like sacrifices in their trim ", the hounds of hell! Let it still be a hope to see their bones piled like those of the human dogs at Morat, in Switzerland, which I have seen.

Heard some music. At nine the usual visitors—news, *war*, or rumours of war. Consulted with P. G., etc., etc. They mean to *insurrect* here, and are to honour me with a call thereupon. I shall not fall back; though I don't think them in force or heart sufficient to make much of it. But, *onward!*— it is now the time to act, and what signifies *self*, if a single spark of that which would be worthy of the past can be bequeathed unquenchedly to the future? It is not one man, nor a million, but the *spirit* of liberty which must be spread. The waves which dash upon the shore are, one by one, broken, but yet the *ocean* conquers, nevertheless. It overwhelms the Armada, it wears the rock, and, if the *Neptunians* are to be believed,.it has not only destroyed, but made a world. In like manner, whatever the sacrifice of individuals, the great cause will gather strength, sweep down what is rugged, and fertilise (for *sea-weed* is *manure*) what is cultivable. And so, the mere selfish calculation ought never to be made on such occasions; and, at present, it shall not be computed by me. I was never a good arithmetician of chances, and shall not commence now.

January 10, 1821

Day fine—rained only in the morning. Looked over accounts. Read Campbell's *Poets*—marked errors of Tom (the author) for correction. Dined—went out—music—Tyrolese air, with variations. Sustained the cause of the original simple air against the variations of the Italian school.

Politics somewhat tempestuous, and cloudier daily. Tomorrow being foreign post-day, probably something more will be known.

Came home—read. Corrected Tom Campbell's slips of the pen. A good work, though—style affected—but his defence of Pope is glorious. To be sure, it is his *own cause* too,—but no matter, it is very good, and does him great credit.

Midnight

I have been turning over different *Lives* of the Poets. I rarely read their works, unless an occasional flight over the

classical ones, Pope, Dryden, Johnson, Gray, and those who
approach them nearest (I leave the *rant* of the rest to the *cant*
of the day), and—I had made several reflections, but I feel
sleepy, and may as well go to bed.

January 11, 1821

Read the letters. Corrected the tragedy and the *Hints from
Horace*. Dined, and got into better spirits. Went out—returned
—finished letters, five in number. Read *Poets*, and an anecdote
in Spence.

All[1]. writes to me that the Pope, and Duke of Tuscany, and
King of Sardinia, have also been called to Congress; but the
Pope will only deal there by proxy. So the interests of millions
are in the hands of about twenty coxcombs, at a place called
Leibach!

I should almost regret that my own affairs went well, when
those of nations are in peril. If the interests of mankind could
be essentially bettered (particularly of these oppressed Italians),
I should not so much mind my own " sma peculiar ". God
grant us all better times, or more philosophy!

In reading, I have just chanced upon an expression of Tom
Campbell's;—speaking of Collins, he says that " no reader
cares any more about the *characteristic manners* of his Eclogues
than about the authenticity of the tale of Troy ". 'Tis false—
we *do* care about " the authenticity of the tale of Troy ". I
have stood upon that plain *daily*, for more than a month in
1810; and if any thing diminished my pleasure, it was that the
blackguard Bryant had impugned its veracity. It is true I read
Homer Travestied (the first twelve books), because Hobhouse
and others bored me with their learned localities, and I love
quizzing. But I still venerated the grand original as the truth
of *history* (in the material *facts*) and of *place*. Otherwise, it
would have given me no delight. Who will persuade me,
when I reclined upon a mighty tomb, that it did not contain a
hero?—its very magnitude proved this. Men do not labour
over the ignoble and petty dead—and why should not the
dead be *Homer's* dead? The secret of Tom Campbell's defence
of *inaccuracy* in costume and description is, that his *Gertrude*, etc.,
has no more locality in common with Pennsylvania than with
Penmanmaur. It is notoriously full of grossly false scenery, as

all Americans declare, though they praise parts of the poem. It is thus that self-love for ever creeps out, like a snake, to sting anything which happens, even accidentally, to stumble upon it.

January 12, 1821

The weather still so humid and impracticable, that London, in its most oppressive fogs, were a summer-bower to this mist and sirocco, which has now lasted (but with one day's interval), chequered with snow or heavy rain only, since the 30th of December, 1820. It is so far lucky that I have a literary turn; —but it is very tiresome not to be able to stir out, in comfort, on any horse but Pegasus, for so many days. The roads are even worse than the weather, by the long splashing, and the heavy soil, and the growth of the waters.

Read the Poets—English, that is to say—out of Campbell's edition. There is a good deal of taffeta in some of Tom's prefatory phrases, but his work is good as a whole. I like him best, though, in his own poetry.

Murray writes that they want to act the Tragedy of *Marino Faliero*—more fools they, it was written for the closet. I have protested against this piece of usurpation, (which, it seems, is legal for managers over any printed work, against the author's will) and I hope they will not attempt it. Why don't they bring out some of the numberless aspirants for theatrical celebrity, now encumbering their shelves, instead of lugging me out of the library? I have written a fierce protest against any such attempt; but I still would hope that it will not be necessary, and that they will see, at once, that it is not intended for the stage. It is too regular—the time, twenty-four hours—the change of place not frequent—nothing *melo*-dramatic—no surprises, no starts, nor trap-doors, nor opportunities " for tossing their heads and kicking their heels "—and no *love*— the grand ingredient of a modern play.

I have found out the seal cut on Murray's letter. It is meant for Walter Scott—or *Sir* Walter—he is the first poet knighted since Sir Richard Blackmore. But it does not do him justice. Scott's—particularly when he recites—is a very intelligent countenance, and this seal says nothing.

Scott is certainly the most wonderful writer of the day.

His novels are a new literature in themselves, and his poetry as good as any—if not better (only on an erroneous system)—and only ceased to be so popular, because the vulgar learned were tired of hearing " Aristides called the Just ", and Scott the Best, and ostracised him.

I like him, too, for his manliness of character, for the extreme pleasantness of his conversation, and his good-nature towards myself, personally. May he prosper !—for he deserves it. I know no reading to which I fall with such alacrity as a work of W. Scott's. I shall give the seal, with his bust on it, to Madame la Comtesse G[uiccioli] this evening, who will be curious to have the effigies of a man so celebrated.

How strange are my thoughts !—The reading of the song of Milton, " Sabrina fair " has brought back upon me—I know not how or why—the happiest, perhaps, days of my life (always excepting, here and there, a Harrow holiday in the two latter summers of my stay there) when living at Cambridge with Edward Noel Long, afterwards of the Guards,—who, after having served honourably in the expedition to Copenhagen (of which two or three thousand scoundrels yet survive in plight and pay), was drowned early in 1809, on his passage to Lisbon with his regiment in the *St. George* transport, which was run foul of in the night by another transport. We were rival swimmers—fond of riding—reading—and of conviviality. We had been at Harrow together ; but—*there*, at least—his was a less boisterous spirit than mine. I was always cricketing—rebelling—fighting—*row*ing (from *row*, not *boat*-rowing, a different practice), and in all manner of mischiefs ; while he was more sedate and polished. At Cambridge—both of Trinity—my spirit rather softened, or his roughened, for we became very great friends. The description of Sabrina's seat reminds me of our rival feats in *diving*. Though Cam's is not a very translucent wave, it was fourteen feet deep, where we used to dive for, and pick up—having thrown them in on purpose—plates, eggs, and even shillings. I remember, in particular, there was the stump of a tree (at least ten or twelve feet deep) in the bed of the river, in a spot where we bathed most commonly, round which I used to cling, and " wonder how the devil I came there ".

Our evenings we passed in music (he was musical, and

played on more than one instrument, flute and violoncello), in which I was audience; and I think that our chief beverage was soda-water. In the day we rode, bathed, and lounged, reading occasionally. I remember our buying, with vast alacrity, Moore's new quarto (in 1806), and reading it together in the evenings.

We only passed the summer together;—Long had gone into the Guards during the year I passed in Notts, away from college. *His* friendship, and a violent, though *pure*, love and passion—which held me at the same period—were the then romance of the most romantic period of my life.

*   *   *   *   *   *   *

I remember that, in the spring of 1809, Hobhouse laughed at my being distressed at Long's death, and amused himself with making epigrams upon his name, which was susceptible of a pun—*Long, short*, etc. But three years after, he had ample leisure to repent it, when our mutual friend, and his, Hobhouse's, particular friend, Charles Matthews, was drowned also, and he himself was as much affected by a similar calamity. But *I* did not pay him back in puns and epigrams, for I valued Matthews too much myself to do so; and, even if I had not, I should have respected his griefs.

Long's father wrote to me to write his son's epitaph. I promised—but I had not the heart to complete it. He was such a good amiable being as rarely remains long in this world; with talent and accomplishments, too, to make him the more regretted. Yet, although a cheerful companion, he had strange melancholy thoughts sometimes. I remember once that we were going to his uncle's, I think—I went to accompany him to the door merely, in some Upper or Lower Grosvenor or Brook Street, I forget which, but it was in a street leading out of some square,—he told me that, the night before, he " had taken up a pistol—not knowing or examining whether it was loaded or no—and had snapped it at his head, leaving it to chance whether it might not be charged ". The letter, too, which he wrote me on leaving college to join the Guards, was as melancholy in its tenour as it could well be on such an occasion. But he showed nothing of this in his deportment, being mild and gentle;—and yet with much turn for the ludicrous in his disposition. We were both much attached to

Harrow, and sometimes made excursions there together from London to revive our schoolboy recollections.

Midnight

Read the Italian translation by Guido Sorelli of the German Grillparzer—a devil of a name, to be sure, for posterity; but they *must* learn to pronounce it. With all the allowance for a *translation*, and above all, an *Italian* translation (they are the very worst of translators, except from the Classics—Annibale Caro, for instance—and *there*, the bastardy of their language helps them, as, by way of *looking legitimate*, they ape their father's tongue) ;—but with every allowance for such a disadvantage, the tragedy of *Sappho* is superb and sublime! There is no denying it. The man has done a great thing in writing that play. And *who is he*? I know him not; but *ages will*. 'Tis a high intellect.

I must premise, however, that I have read *nothing* of Adolph Müllner's (the author of *Guilt*), and much less of Goethe and Schiller, and Wieland, than I could wish. I only know them through the medium of English, French, and Italian translations. Of the *real* language I know absolutely nothing,—except oaths learned from postillions and officers in a squabble! I can *swear* in German potently, when I like—" Sacrament—*Verfluchter—Hundsfott* "—and so forth; but I have little else of their energetic conversation.

I like, however, their women, (I was once *so desperately* in love with a German woman, Constance,) and all that I have read, translated, of their writings, and all that I have seen on the Rhine of their country and people—all, except the Austrians, whom I abhor, loathe, and—I cannot find words for my hate of them, and should be sorry to find deeds correspondent to my hate; for I abhor cruelty more than I abhor the Austrians—except on an impulse, and then I am savage—but not deliberately so.

Grillparzer is grand—antique—*not so simple* as the ancients, but very simple for a modern—too Madame de Stael*ish*, now and then—but altogether a great and goodly writer.

January 13, 1821, Saturday

Sketched the outline and Drams. Pers. of an intended tragedy of Sardanapalus, which I have for some time meditated. Took the names from Diodorus Siculus, (I know the history of Sardanapalus, and have known it since I was twelve years old,) and read over a passage in the ninth vol. octavo, of Mitford's *Greece*, where he rather vindicates the memory of this last of the Assyrians.

Dined—news come—the *Powers* mean to war with the peoples. The intelligence seems positive—let it be so—they will be beaten in the end. The king-times are fast finishing. There will be blood shed like water, and tears like mist; but the peoples will conquer in the end. I shall not live to see it, but I foresee it.

I carried Teresa the Italian translation of Grillparzer's *Sappho*, which she promises to read. She quarrelled with me, because I said that love was *not the loftiest* theme for true tragedy; and, having the advantage of her native language, and natural female eloquence, she overcame my fewer arguments. I believe she was right. I must put more love into *Sardanapalus* than I intended. I speak, of course, *if* the times will allow me leisure. That *if* will hardly be a peace-maker.

January 14, 1821

Turned over Seneca's tragedies. Wrote the opening lines of the intended tragedy of *Sardanapalus*. Rode out some miles into the forest. Misty and rainy. Returned—dined—wrote some more of my tragedy.

Read Diodorus Siculus—turned over Seneca, and some other books. Wrote some more of the tragedy. Took a glass of grog. After having ridden hard in rainy weather, and scribbled, and scribbled again, the spirits (at least mine) need a little exhilaration, and I don't like laudanum now as I used to do. So I have mixed a glass of strong waters and single waters, which I shall now proceed to empty. Therefore and thereunto I conclude this day's diary.

The effect of all wines and spirits upon me is, however, strange. It *settles*, but it makes me gloomy—gloomy at the very moment of their effect, and not gay hardly ever. But it composes for a time, though sullenly.

January 15, 1821

Weather fine. Received visit. Rode out into the forest—fired pistols. Returned home—dined—dipped into a volume of Mitford's *Greece*—wrote part of a scene of *Sardanapalus*. Went out—heard some music—heard some politics. More ministers from the other Italian powers gone to Congress. War seems certain—in that case, it will be a savage one. Talked over various important matters with one of the initiated. At ten and half returned home.

I have just thought of something odd. In the year 1814, Moore (" the poet ", *par excellence*, and he deserves it) and I were going together, in the same carriage, to dine with Earl Grey, the *Capo Politico* of the remaining Whigs. Murray, the magnificent (the illustrious publisher of that name), had just sent me a Java gazette—I know not why, or wherefore. Pulling it out, by way of curiosity, we found it to contain a dispute (the said Java gazette) on Moore's merits and mine. I think, if I had been there, that I could have saved them the trouble of disputing on the subject. But, there is *fame* for you at six and twenty! Alexander had conquered India at the same age; but I doubt if he was disputed about, or his conquests compared with those of Indian Bacchus, at Java.

It was a great fame to be named with Moore; greater to be compared with him; greatest—*pleasure*, at least—to be *with* him; and, surely, an odd coincidence, that we should be dining together while they were quarrelling about us beyond the equinoctial line.

Well, the same evening, I met Lawrence the painter, and heard one of Lord Grey's daughters (a fine, tall, spirit-looking girl, with much of the *patrician thoroughbred look* of her father, which I dote upon) play on the harp, so modestly and ingenuously, that she *looked music*. Well, I would rather have had my talk with Lawrence (who talked delightfully) and heard the girl, than have had all the fame of Moore and me put together.

The only pleasure of fame is that it paves the way to pleasure; and the more intellectual our pleasure, the better for the pleasure and for us too. It was, however, agreeable to have heard our fame before dinner, and a girl's harp after.

January 16, 1821

Read — rode — fired pistols — returned — dined — wrote —visited—heard music—talked nonsense—and went home.

567

Wrote part of a Tragedy—advanced in Act 1st with " all deliberate speed ". Bought a blanket. The weather is still muggy as a London May—mist, mizzle, the air replete with Scotticisms, which, though fine in the descriptions of Ossian, are somewhat tiresome in real, prosaic perspective. Politics still mysterious.

January 17, 1821

Rode i' the forest—fired pistols—dined. Arrived a packet of books from England and Lombardy—English, Italian, French, and Latin. Read till eight—went out.

January 18, 1821

To-day, the post arriving late, did not ride. Read letters— only two gazettes instead of twelve now due. Made Lega write to that negligent Galignani, and added a postscript. Dined.

At eight proposed to go out. Lega came in with a letter about a bill *unpaid* at Venice, which I thought paid months ago. I flew into a paroxysm of rage, which almost made me faint. I have not been well ever since. I deserve it for being such a fool—but it *was* provoking—a set of scoundrels ! It is, however, but five and twenty pounds.

January 19, 1821

Rode. Winter's wind somewhat more unkind than ingratitude itself, though Shakspeare says otherwise. At least, I am so much more accustomed to meet with ingratitude than the north wind, that I thought the latter the sharper of the two. I had met with both in the course of the twenty-four hours, so could judge.

Thought of a plan of education for my daughter Allegra, who ought to begin soon with her studies. Wrote a letter— afterwards a postscript. Rather in low spirits—certainly hippish—liver touched—will take a dose of salts.

I have been reading the Life, by himself and daughter, of Mr. R. L. Edgeworth, the father of *the* Miss Edgeworth.[1] It is altogether a great name. In 1813, I recollect to have met them in the fashionable world of London (of which I then formed an item, a fraction, the segment of a circle, the unit of a million, the nothing of something) in the assemblies of the hour, and at a breakfast of Sir Humphry and Lady Davy's, to which I was invited for the nonce. I had been the lion of 1812 : Miss Edge-

[1] Maria Edgeworth, the celebrated moralist and fashionable woman of letters.

worth and Madame de Stael, with " the Cossack ", towards the end of 1813, were the exhibitions of the succeeding year.

I thought Edgeworth a fine old fellow, of a clarety, elderly, red complexion, but active, brisk, and endless. He was seventy, but did not look fifty—no, nor forty-eight even. I had seen poor Fitzpatrick not very long before—a man of pleasure, wit, eloquence, all things. He tottered—but still talked like a gentleman, though feebly. Edgeworth bounced about, and talked loud and long; but he seemed neither weakly nor decrepit, and hardly old.

He began by telling " that he had given Dr. Parr a dressing, who had taken him for an Irish bogtrotter ", etc., etc. Now I, who know Dr. Parr, and who know (*not* by experience—for I never should have presumed so far as to contend with him— but by hearing him *with* others, and *of* others) that it is not so easy a matter to " dress him ", thought Mr. Edgeworth an assertor of what was not true. He could not have stood before Parr for an instant. For the rest, he seemed intelligent, vehement, vivacious, and full of life. He bids fair for a hundred years.

He was not much admired in London, and I remember a " ryghte merrie " and conceited jest which was rife among the gallants of the day,—viz. a paper had been presented for the *recall of Mrs. Siddons to the stage*, (she having lately taken leave, to the loss of ages,—for nothing ever was, or can be, like her,) to which all men had been called to subscribe. Whereupon Thomas Moore, of profane and poetical memory, did propose that a similar paper should be *sub*scribed and *circum*scribed " for the recall of Mr. Edgeworth to Ireland ".

The fact was—every body cared more about *her*. She was a nice little unassuming " Jeannie Deans-looking body ", as we Scotch say—and, if not handsome, certainly not ill-looking. Her conversation was as quiet as herself. One would never have guessed she could write *her name*; whereas her father talked, *not* as if he could write nothing else, but as if nothing else was worth writing.

As for Mrs. Edgeworth, I forget—except that I think she was the youngest of the party. Altogether, they were an excellent cage of the kind; and succeeded for two months, till the landing of Madame de Stael.

To turn from them to their works, I admire them; but

they excite no feeling, and they leave no love—except for some Irish steward or postillion. However, the impression of intellect and prudence is profound—and may be useful.

January 21, 1821

Rode—fired pistols. Read from Grimm's *Correspondence*. Dined—went out—heard music—returned—wrote a letter to the Lord Chamberlain to request him to prevent the theatres from representing the Doge, which the Italian papers say that they are going to act. This is pretty work—what! without asking my consent, and even in opposition to it!

January 21, 1821

Fine, clear, frosty day—that is to say, an Italian frost, for their winters hardly get beyond snow; for which reason nobody knows how to skate (or skait)—a Dutch and English accomplishment. Rode out, as usual, and fired pistols. Good shooting—broke four common, and rather small, bottles, in four shots, at fourteen paces, with a common pair of pistols and indifferent powder. Almost as good *wafering* or shooting—considering the difference of powder and pistol,—as when, in 1809, 1810, 1811, 1812, 1813, 1814, it was my luck to split walking-sticks, wafers, half-crowns, shillings, and even the *eye* of a walking-stick, at twelve paces, with a single bullet—and all by *eye* and calulation; for my hand is not steady, and apt to change with the very weather. To the prowess which I here note, Joe Manton and others can bear testimony; for the former taught, and the latter has seen me do, these feats.

Dined—visited—came home—read. Remarked on an anecdote in Grimm's *Correspondence*, which says that " Regnard et la plûpart des poëtes comiques étaient gens bilieux et mélancoliques; et que M. de Voltaire, qui est très gai, n'a jamais fait que des tragédies—et que la comédie gaie est le seul genre où il n'ait point réussi. C'est que celui qui rit et celui qui fait rire sont deux hommes fort différens."—Vol. VI.

At this moment I feel as bilious as the best comic writer of them all, even as Regnard himself, the next to Molière, who has written some of the best comedies in any language, and who is supposed to have committed suicide,) and am not in spirits to continue my proposed tragedy of *Sardanapalus*, which I have, for some days, ceased to compose.

To-morrow is my birth-day—that is to say, at twelve o' the clock, midnight, *i.e.* in twelve minutes, I shall have completed thirty and three years of age!!!—and I go to my bed with a heaviness of heart at having lived so long, and to so little purpose.

It is three minutes past twelve.—" 'Tis the middle of the night by the castle clock ", and I am now thirty-three!

> " Eheu, fugaces, Posthume, Posthume,
>   Labuntur anni " ;—

but I don't regret them so much for what I have done, as for what I *might* have done.

> Through life's road, so dim and dirty,
> I have dragged to three-and-thirty.
> What have these years left to me?
> Nothing—except thirty-three.

January 22, 1821

1821.
Here lies
interred in the Eternity
of the Past,
from whence there is no
Resurrection
for the Days—Whatever there may be
for the Dust—
the Thirty-Third Year
of an ill-spent Life,
Which, after
a lingering disease of many months
sunk into a lethargy,
and expired,
January 22d, 1821, A. D.
Leaving a successor
Inconsolable
for the very loss which
occasioned its
Existence.

January 23, 1821

Fine day. Read — rode — fired pistols, and returned. Dined — read. Went out at eight — made the usual visit. Heard of nothing but war,—" the cry is still, They come ". The Carbonari seem to have no plan—nothing fixed among themselves, how, when, or what to do. In that case, they will make nothing of this project, so often postponed, and never put in action.

Came home, and gave some necessary orders, in case of circumstances requiring a change of place. I shall act according to what may seem proper, when I hear decidedly what the Barbarians mean to do. At present, they are building a bridge of boats over the Po, which looks very warlike. A few days will probably show. I think of retiring towards Ancona, nearer the northern frontier; that is to say, if Teresa and her father are obliged to retire, which is most likely, as all the family are Liberals. If not, I shall stay. But my movements will depend upon the lady's wishes—for myself, it is much the same.

I am somewhat puzzled what to do with my little daughter, and my effects, which are of some quantity and value,—and neither of them do in the seat of war, where I think of going. But there is an elderly lady who will take charge of *her*, and T[eresa] says that the Marchese C. will undertake to hold the chattels in safe keeping. Half the city are getting their affairs in marching trim. A pretty Carnival! The blackguards might as well have waited till Lent.

January 24, 1821

Returned—met some masques in the Corso—*Vive la bagatelle!*—the Germans are on the Po, the Barbarians at the gate, and their masters in council at Leybach (or whatever the eructation of the sound may syllable into a human pronunciation), and lo! they dance and sing and make merry, " for tomorrow they may die ". Who can say that the Arlequins are not right? Like the Lady Baussiere, and my old friend Burton —I " rode on ".

Dined—(damn this pen!)—beef tough—there is no beef in Italy worth a curse; unless a man could eat an old ox with the hide on, singed in the sun.

The principal persons in the events which may occur in a

few days are gone out on a *shooting party*. If it were like a
" *highland* hunting ", a pretext of the chase for a grand re-union
of counsellors and chiefs, it would be all very well. But it is
nothing more or less than a real snivelling, popping, small-
shot, water-hen waste of powder, ammunition, and shot, for
their own special amusement : a rare set of fellows for " a man
to risk his neck with ", as " Marishall Wells " says in the
Black Dwarf.

If they gather,—" whilk is to be doubted ",—they will not
muster a thousand men. The reason of this is, that the populace
are not interested,—only the higher and middle orders. I wish
that the peasantry *were*; they are a fine savage race of two-
legged leopards. But the Bolognese won't—the Romagnuoles
can't without them. Or, if they try—what then? They will
try, and man can do no more—and, if he *would* but try his
utmost, much might be done. The Dutch, for instance, against
the Spaniards—*then* the tyrants of Europe, since, the slaves,
and, lately, the freedmen.

The year 1820 was not a fortunate one for the individual
me, whatever it may be for the nations. I lost a lawsuit, after
two decisions in my favour. The project of lending money on
an Irish mortgage was finally rejected by my wife's trustee
after a year's hope and trouble. The Rochdale lawsuit had
endured fifteen years, and always prospered till I married ;
since which, every thing has gone wrong—with me at least.

In the same year, 1820, the Countess T[eresa] G[uiccioli]
nata G[hisleri] G[amba], in despite of all I said and did to
prevent it, *would* separate from her husband, Il Cavalier Com-
mendatore G[amba], etc., etc., etc., and all on the account of
" P. P. clerk of this parish ". The other little petty vexations
of the year—overturns in carriages—the murder of people
before one's door, and dying in one's beds—the cramp in
swimming—colics—indigestions and bilious attacks, etc., etc.,
etc.—
> " Many small articles make up a sum,
> And hey ho for Caleb Quotem, oh ! "

January 25, 1821

Received a letter from Lord S[idney] O[sborne], state
secretary of the Seven Islands—a fine fellow—clever—dished

in England five years ago, and came abroad to retrench and to renew. He wrote from Ancona, in his way back to Corfu, on some matters of our own. He is son of the late Duke of L[eeds] by a second marriage. He wants me to go to Corfu. Why not?—perhaps I may, next spring.

Answered Murray's letter—read—lounged. Scrawled this additional page of life's log-book. One day more is over of it and of me:—but " which is best, life or death, the gods only know ", as Socrates said to his judges, on the breaking up of the tribunal. Two thousand years since that sage's declaration of ignorance have not enlightened us more upon this important point; for, according to the Christian dispensation, no one can know whether he is *sure* of salvation—even the most righteous—since a single slip of faith may throw him on his back, like a skaiter, while gliding smoothly to his paradise. Now, therefore, whatever the certainty of faith in the facts may be, the certainty of the individual as to his happiness or misery is no greater than it was under Jupiter.

It has been said that the immortality of the soul is a *grand peut-être*—but still it is a *grand* one. Every body clings to it— the stupidest, and dullest, and wickedest of human bipeds is still persuaded that he is immortal.

January 26, 1821

Fine day—a few mares' tails portending change, but the sky clear, upon the whole. Rode—fired pistols—good shooting. Coming back, met an old man. Charity—purchased a shilling's worth of salvation. If that was to be bought, I have given more to my fellow-creatures in this life—sometimes for *vice*, but, if not more *often*, at least more *considerably*, for virtue— than I now possess. I never in my life gave a mistress so much as I have sometimes given a poor man in honest distress; but no matter. The scoundrels who have all along persecuted me (with the help of * * who has crowned their efforts) will triumph;—and, when justice is done to me, it will be when this hand that writes is as cold as the hearts which have stung me.

Returning, on the bridge near the mill, met an old woman. I asked her age—she said " *Tre croci* ". I asked my groom (though myself a decent Italian) what the devil *her* three crosses meant. He said, ninety years, and that she had five years more to boot ! ! I repeated the same three times—not to mistake—ninety-five years ! ! !—and she was yet rather active— *heard* my question, for she answered it—*saw* me, for she advanced towards me ; and did not appear at all decrepit, though certainly touched with years. Told her to come to-morrow, and will examine her myself. I love phenomena. If she *is* ninety-five years old, she must recollect the Cardinal Alberoni, who was legate here.

On dismounting, found Lieutenant E. just arrived from Faenza. Invited him to dine with me to-morrow. Did *not* invite him for to-day, because there was a small *turbot*, (Friday, fast regularly and religiously,) which I wanted to eat all myself. Ate it.

Went out—found T. as usual—music. The gentlemen, who make revolutions and are gone on a shooting, are not yet returned. They don't return till Sunday—that is to say, they have been out for five days, buffooning, while the interests of a whole country are at stake, and even they themselves compromised.

It is a difficult part to play amongst such a set of assassins and blockheads—but, when the scum is skimmed off, or has boiled over, good may come of it. If this country could but be freed, what would be too great for the accomplishment of that desire? for the extinction of that Sigh of Ages? Let us hope. They have hoped these thousand years. The very revolvement of the chances may bring it—it is upon the dice.

If the Neapolitans have but a single Massaniello amongst them, they will beat the bloody butchers of the crown and sabre. Holland, in worse circumstances, beat the Spains and Philips ; America beat the English ; Greece beat Xerxes ; and France beat Europe, till she took a tyrant ; South America beats her old vultures out of their nest ; and, if these men are but firm in themselves, there is nothing to shake them from without.

January 28, 1821

Lugano Gazette did not come. Letters from Venice. It appears that the Austrian brutes have seized my three or four pounds of English powder. The scoundrels !—I hope to pay them in *ball* for that powder. Rode out till twilight.

Pondered the subjects of four tragedies to be written (life and circumstances permitting), to wit, Sardanapalus, already begun; Cain, a metaphysical subject, something in the style of Manfred, but in five *acts*, perhaps, with the chorus; Francesca of Rimini, in five acts; and I am not sure that I would not try Tiberius. I think that I could extract a something, of *my* tragic, at least, out of the gloomy sequestration and old age of the tyrant—and even out of his sojourn at Caprea—by softening the *details*, and exhibiting the despair which must have led to those very vicious pleasures. For none but a powerful and gloomy mind overthrown would have had recourse to such solitary horrors,—being also, at the same time, *old*, and the master of the world.

Memoranda.

What is Poetry?—The feeling of a Former world and Future.

Thought Second.

Why, at the very height of desire and human pleasure,—worldly, social, amorous, ambitious, or even avaricious,—does there mingle a certain sense of doubt and sorrow—a fear of what is to come—a doubt of what *is*—a retrospect to the past, leading to a prognostication of the future? (The best of Prophets of the future is the Past.) Why is this, or these?—I know not, except that on a pinnacle we are most susceptible of giddiness, and that we never fear falling except from a precipice —the higher, the more awful, and the more sublime; and, therefore, I am not sure that Fear is not a pleasurable sensation; at least, *Hope* is; and *what Hope* is there without a deep leaven of Fear? and what sensation is so delightful as Hope? and, if it were not for Hope, where would the Future be?—in hell. It is useless to say *where* the Present is, for most of us know; and as for the Past, *what* predominates in memory?—*Hope baffled*. Ergo, in all human affairs, it is Hope—Hope—Hope. I allow sixteen minutes, though I never counted them, to any given or supposed possession. From whatever place we commence, we know where it all must end. And yet, what good is there in knowing it? It does not make men better or wiser. During the greatest horrors of the greatest plagues, (Athens and Florence, for example—see Thucydides and Machiavelli,) men were more cruel and profligate than ever. It is all a mystery. I feel most things, but I know nothing, except

— — — — — — — —

— — — — — — — —

— — — — — — — —[1]

    Thought for a Speech of Lucifer, in the Tragedy of Cain :—
        Were *Death* an *evil*, would *I* let thee *live*?
        Fool ! live as I live—as thy father lives,
        And thy son's sons shall live for evermore.

                Past Midnight.   One o' the clock

I have been reading Frederick Schlegel (brother to the other of the name) till now, and I can make out nothing. He evidently shows a great power of words, but there is nothing to be taken hold of. He is like Hazlitt, in English, who *talks pimples*—a red and white corruption rising up (in little imitation of mountains upon maps), but containing nothing, and discharging nothing, except their own humours.

I dislike him the worse, (that is, Schlegel,) because he always seems upon the verge of meaning; and, lo, he goes down like sunset, or melts like a rainbow, leaving a rather rich confusion,—to which, however, the above comparisons do too much honour.

Continuing to read Mr. Frederick Schlegel. He is not such a fool as I took him for, that is to say, when he speaks of the North. But still he speaks of things *all over the world* with a kind of authority that a philosopher would disdain, and a man of common sense, feeling, and knowledge of his own ignorance, would be ashamed of. The man is evidently wanting to make an impression, like his brother,—or like George in the Vicar of Wakefield, who found out that all the good things had been said already on the right side, and therefore " dressed up some paradoxes " upon the wrong side—ingenious, but false, as he himself says—to which " the learned world said nothing, nothing at all, sir ". The " learned world ", however, *has* said something to the brothers Schlegel.

It is high time to think of something else. What they say of the antiquities of the North is best.

   [1] " Thus marked, with impatient strokes of the pen, by himself in the original." Moore.

January 29, 1821

Yesterday, the woman of ninety-five years of age was with me. She said her eldest son (if now alive) would have been seventy. She is thin—short, but active—hears, and sees, and talks incessantly. Several teeth left—all in the lower jaw, and single front teeth. She is very deeply wrinkled, and has a sort of scattered grey beard over her chin, at least as long as my mustachios. Her head, in fact, resembles the drawing in crayons of Pope the poet's mother, which is in some editions of his works.

I forgot to ask her if she remembered Alberoni (legate here), but will ask her next time. Gave her a louis—ordered her a new suit of clothes, and put her upon a weekly pension. Till now, she had worked at gathering wood and pine-nuts in the forest—pretty work at ninety-five years old! She had a dozen children, of whom some are alive. Her name is Maria Montanari.

Met a company of the sect (a kind of Liberal Club) called the *Americani* in the forest, all armed, and singing, with all their might, in Romagnuole—" *Sem* tutti soldat' per la liberta " (" we are all soldiers for liberty "). They cheered me as I passed—I returned their salute, and rode on. This may show the spirit of Italy at present.

My to-day's journal consists of what I omitted yesterday. To-day was much as usual. Have rather a better opinion of the writings of the Schlegels than I had four-and-twenty hours ago; and will amend it still further, if possible.

They say that the Piedmontese have at length arisen—*ça ira!*

Read Schlegel. Of Dante he says, " that at no time has the greatest and most national of all Italian poets ever been much the favourite of his countrymen ". 'Tis false! There have been more editors and commentators (and imitators, ultimately) of Dante than of all their poets put together. *Not* a favourite! Why, they talk Dante—write Dante—and think and dream Dante at this moment (1821) to an excess, which would be ridiculous, but that he deserves it.

In the same style this German talks of gondolas on the Arno—a precious fellow to dare to speak of Italy!

He says also that Dante's chief defect is a want, in a word, of gentle feelings. Of gentle feelings!—and Francesca of Rimini—and the father's feelings in Ugolino—and Beatrice—and " La Pia ! " Why, there is gentleness in Dante beyond all gentleness, when he is tender. It is true that, treating of the Christian Hades, or Hell, there is not much scope or site for gentleness—but who *but* Dante could have introduced any " gentleness " at all into *Hell*? Is there any in Milton's? No—and Dante's Heaven is all love, and glory and majesty.

One o'clock

I have found out, however, where the German is right—it is about the *Vicar of Wakefield*. " Of all romances in miniature (and, perhaps, this is the best shape in which Romance can appear) the *Vicar of Wakefield* is, I think, the most exquisite ". He *thinks!*—he might be sure. But it is very well for a Schlegel. I feel sleepy, and may as well get me to bed. To-morrow there will be fine weather.

" Trust on, and think to-morrow will repay."

January 30, 1821

The Count P[ietro] G[amba] this evening (by commission from the Ci.) transmitted to me the new *words* for the next six months. * * * and * * *. The new sacred word is * * *—the reply * * *—the rejoinder * * *. The former word (now changed) was * * *—there is also * * *—* * *. Things seem fast coming to a crisis—*ça ira!*

We talked over various matters of moment and movement. These I omit;—if they come to any thing, they will speak for themselves. After these, we spoke of Kosciusko. Count R. G. told me that he has seen the Polish officers in the Italian war burst into tears on hearing his name.

Something must be up in Piedmont—all the letters and papers are stopped. Nobody knows anything, and the Germans are concentrating near Mantua. Of the decision of Leybach nothing is known. This state of things cannot last long. The ferment in men's minds at present cannot be conceived without seeing it.

January 31, 1821

For several days I have not written any thing except a few answers to letters. In momentary expectation of an explosion of some kind, it is not easy to settle down to the desk for the higher kinds of composition. I *could* do it, to be sure, for, last summer, I wrote my drama in the very bustle of Madame la Contessa G[uiccioli]'s divorce, and all its process of accompaniments. At the same time, I also had the news of the loss of an important lawsuit in England. But these were only private and personal business; the present is of a different nature.

I suppose it is this, but have some suspicion that it may be laziness, which prevents me from writing; especially as Rochefoucalt says that " laziness often masters them all "— speaking of the *passions*. If this were true, it could hardly be said that " idleness is the root of all evil ", since this is supposed to spring from the passions only: *ergo*, that which masters all the passions (laziness, to wit) would in so much be a good. Who knows?

Midnight

I have been reading Grimm's *Correspondence*. He repeats frequently, in speaking of a poet, or a man of genius in any department, even in music, (Grétry, for instance,) that he must have *une ame qui se tourmente, un esprit violent*. How far this may be true, I know not; but if it were, I should be a poet " *per excellenza* "; for I have always had *une ame*, which not only tormented itself but every body else in contact with it; and an *esprit violent*, which has almost left me without any *esprit* at all. As to defining what a poet *should* be, it is not worth while, for what are *they* worth? what have they done?

Grimm, however, is an excellent critic and literary historian. His *Correspondence* forms the annals of the literary part of that age of France, with much of her politics, and still more of her " way of life ". He is as valuable, and far more entertaining than Muratori or Tiraboschi—I had almost said, than Ginguené— but there we should pause. However, 't is a great man in its line.

Monsieur St. Lambert has,

" Et lorsqu' à ses regards la lumière est ravie,
    Il n'a plus, en mourant, à perdre que la vie ".

This is, word for word, Thomson's

    " And dying, all we can resign is breath ",

without the smallest acknowledgment from the Lorrainer of a
poet. M. St. Lambert is dead as a man, and (for any thing I
know to the contrary) damned, as a poet, by this time. However, his *Seasons* have good things, and, it may be, some of his
own.

February 2, 1821

I have been considering what can be the reason why I
always wake, at a certain hour in the morning, and always in
very bad spirits—I may say, in actual despair and despondency,
in all respects—even of that which pleased me over night. In
about an hour or two, this goes off, and I compose either to
sleep again, or, at least, to quiet. In England, five years ago,
I had the same kind of hypochondria, but accompanied with
so violent a thirst that I have drank as many as fifteen bottles
of soda-water in one night, after going to bed, and been still
thirsty—calculating, however, some lost from the bursting out
and effervescence and overflowing of the soda-water, in drawing
the corks, or striking off the necks of the bottles from mere
thirsty impatience. At present, I have *not* the thirst; but the
depression of spirits is no less violent.

I read in Edgeworth's *Memoirs* of something similar (except
that his thirst expended itself on *small beer*) in the case of Sir
F. B. Delaval ;—but then he was, at least, twenty years older.
What is it?—liver? In England, Le Man (the apothecary)
cured me of the thirst in three days, and it had lasted as many
years. I suppose that it is all hypochondria.

What I feel most growing upon me are laziness, and a disrelish more powerful than indifference. If I rouse, it is into
fury. I presume that I shall end (if not earlier by accident,
or some such termination), like Swift—" dying at top ". I
confess I do not contemplate this with so much horror as he
apparently did for some years before it happened. But Swift
had hardly *begun life* at the very period (thirty-three) when I
feel quite an *old sort* of feel.

Oh! there is an organ playing in the street—a waltz, too!
I must leave off to listen. They are playing a waltz which I

have heard ten thousand times at the balls in London, between 1812 and 1815. Music is a strange thing.

February 5, 1821

At last, " the kiln's in a low ". The Germans are ordered to march, and Italy is, for the ten thousandth time to become a field of battle. Last night the news came.

This afternoon—Count P. G. came to me to consult upon divers matters. We rode out together. They have sent off to the C. for orders. To-morrow the decision ought to arrive, and then something will be done. Returned—dined—read—went out—talked over matters. Made a purchase of some arms for the new enrolled Americani, who are all on tiptoe to march. Gave order for some *harness* and portmanteaus necessary for the horses.

Read some of Bowles's dispute about Pope, with all the replies and rejoinders. Perceive that my name has been lugged into the controversy, but have not time to state what I know of the subject. On some " piping day of peace " it is probable that I may resume it.

February 9, 1821

Before dinner wrote a little ; also, before I rode out, Count P. G. called upon me, to let me know the result of the meeting of the Ci. at F. and at B. * * returned late last night. Every thing was combined under the idea that the Barbarians would pass the Po on the 15th inst. Instead of this, from some previous information or otherwise, they have hastened their march and actually passed two days ago ; so that all that can be done at present in Romagna is, to stand on the alert and wait for the advance of the Neapolitans. Every thing was ready, and the Neapolitans had sent on their own instructions and intentions, all calculated for the *tenth* and *eleventh*, on which days a general rising was to take place, under the supposition that the Barbarians could not advance before the 15th.

As it is, they have but fifty or sixty thousand troops, a number with which they might as well attempt to conquer the world as secure Italy in its present state. The artillery marches *last*, and alone, and there is an idea of an attempt to cut part of them off. All this will much depend upon the first steps of the

Neapolitans. *Here*, the public spirit is excellent, provided it be kept up. This will be seen by the event.

It is probable that Italy will be delivered from the Barbarians if the Neapolitans will but stand firm, and are united among themselves. *Here* they appear so.

February 10, 1821

Day passed as usual—nothing new. Barbarians still in march—not well equipped, and, of course, not well received on their route. There is some talk of a commotion at Paris.

Rode out between four and six—finished my letter to Murray on Bowles's pamphlets—added postscript. Passed the evening as usual—out till eleven—and subsequently at home.

February 11, 1821

Wrote—had a copy taken of an extract from Petrarch's Letters, with reference to the conspiracy of the Doge, Marino Faliero, containing the poet's opinion of the matter. Heard a heavy firing of cannon towards Comacchio—the Barbarians rejoicing for their principal pig's birthday, which is to-morrow —or Saint day—I forget which. Received a ticket for the first ball to-morrow. Shall not go to the first, but intend going to the second, as also to the Veglioni.

February 13, 1821

To-day read a little in Louis B.'s *Hollande*, but have written nothing since the completion of the letter on the Pope controversy. Politics are quite misty for the present. The Barbarians still upon their march. It is not easy to divine what the Italians will now do.

Was elected yesterday *Socio* of the Carnival Ball Society. This is the fifth carnival that I have passed. In the four former, I racketed a good deal. In the present, I have been as sober as Lady Grace herself.

February 14, 1821

Much as usual. Wrote, before riding out, part of a scene of *Sardanapalus*. The first act nearly finished. The rest of the day and evening as before—partly without, in conversazione —partly at home.

Heard the particulars of the late fray at Russi, a town not far from this. It is exactly the fact of Romēo and Giulietta—*not* Romĕo, as the Barbarian writes it. Two families of *Contadini* (peasants) are at feud. At a ball, the younger part of the families forget their quarrel, and dance together. An old man of one of them enters, and reproves the young men for dancing with the females of the opposite family. The male relatives of the latter resent this. Both parties rush home and arm themselves. They meet directly, by moonlight, in the public way, and fight it out. Three are killed on the spot, and six wounded, most of them dangerously,—pretty well for two families, methinks—and all *fact*, of the last week. Another assassination has taken place at Cesenna—in all about *forty* in Romagna within the last three months. These people retain much of the middle ages.

February 15, 1821

Last night finished the first act of *Sardanapalus*. To-night, or to-morrow, I ought to answer letters.

February 16, 1821

Last night Il Conte P. G. sent a man with a bag full of bayonets, some muskets, and some hundreds of cartridges to my house, without apprizing me, though I had seen him not half an hour before. About ten days ago, when there was to be a rising here, the Liberals and my brethren C^1. asked me to purchase some arms for a certain few of our ragamuffins. I did so immediately, and ordered ammunition, etc., and they were armed accordingly. Well—the rising is prevented by the Barbarians marching a week sooner than appointed; and an *order* is issued, and in force, by the Government, " that all persons having arms concealed, etc., etc., shall be liable to, etc., etc."—and what do my friends, the patriots, do two days afterwards? Why, they throw back upon my hands, and into my house, these very arms (without a word of warning previously) with which I had furnished them at their own request, and at my own peril and expense.

It was lucky that Lega was at home to receive them. If any of the servants had (except Tita and F. and Lega) they would have betrayed it immediately. In the mean time, if they are denounced or discovered, I shall be in a scrape.

At nine went out—at eleven returned. Beat the crow for stealing the falcon's victuals. Read *Tales of my Landlord*— wrote a letter—and mixed a moderate beaker of water with other ingredients.

February 18, 1821

The news are that the Neapolitans have broken a bridge, and slain four pontifical carabiniers, whilk carabiniers wished to oppose. Besides the disrespect to neutrality, it is a pity that the first blood shed in this German quarrel should be Italian. However, the war seems begun in good earnest: for, if the Neapolitans kill the Pope's carabiniers, they will not be more delicate towards the Barbarians. If it be even so, in a short time " there will be news o' thae craws ", as Mrs. Alison Wilson says of Jenny Blane's " unco cockernony " in the *Tales of my Landlord*.

In turning over Grimm's *Correspondence* to-day, I found a thought of Tom Moore's in a song of Maupertuis to a female Laplander

> " Et tous les lieux
> Où sont ses yeux,
> Font la zone brûlante ".

This is Moore's,

> " And those eyes make my climate, wherever I roam."

But I am sure that Moore never saw it; for this was published in Grimm's *Correspondence*, in 1813, and I knew Moore's by heart in 1812. There is also another, but an antithetical coincidence—

> " Le soleil luit,
> Des jours sans nuit
> Bientôt il nous destine ;
> Mais ces longs jours
> Seront trop courts,
> Passés près de Christine ".

This is the *thought reversed*, of the last stanza of the ballad on Charlotte Lynes, given in Miss Seward's *Memoirs of Darwin*, which is pretty—I quote from memory of these last fifteen years.

" For my first night I'd go
To those regions of snow,
Where the sun for six months never shines;
And think, even then,
He too soon came again,
To disturb me with fair Charlotte Lynes."

To-day I have had no communication with my Carbonari cronies; but, in the mean time, my lower apartments are full of their bayonets, fusils, cartridges, and what not. I suppose that they consider me as a depôt, to be sacrificed, in case of accidents. It is no great matter, supposing that Italy could be liberated, who or what is sacrificed. It is a grand object— the very *poetry* of politics. Only think—a free Italy !!! Why, there has been nothing like it since the days of Augustus. I reckon the times of Cæsar (Julius) free; because the commotions left every body a side to take, and the parties were pretty equal at the set out. But, afterwards, it was all prætorian and legionary business—and since !—we shall see, or, at least, some will see, what card will turn up. It is best to hope, even of the hopeless. The Dutch did more than these fellows have to do, in the Seventy Years' War.

February 19, 1821

Came home *solus*—very high wind—lightning—moonshine —solitary stragglers muffled in cloaks—women in masks— white houses—clouds hurrying over the sky, like spilt milk blown out of the pail—altogether very poetical. It is still blowing hard—the tiles flying, and the house rocking—rain splashing—lightning flashing—quite a fine Swiss Alpine evening, and the sea roaring in the distance.

Visited—conversazione. All the women frightened by the squall : they *won't* go to the masquerade because it lightens— the pious reason !

Still blowing away. A. has sent me some news to-day. The war approaches nearer and nearer. Oh those scoundrel sovereigns ! Let us but see them beaten—let the Neapolitans but have the pluck of the Dutch of old, or the Spaniards of now, or of the German Protestants, the Scotch Presbyterians, the Swiss under Tell, or the Greeks under Themistocles—*all* small and solitary nations (except the Spaniards and German

Lutherans), and there is yet a resurrection for Italy, and a hope for the world.

February 20, 1821

The news of the day are, that the Neapolitans are full of energy. The public spirit *here* is certainly well kept up. The *Americani* (a patriotic society here, an under branch of the *Carbonari*) give a dinner in *the Forest* in a few days, and have invited me, as one of the C¹. It is to be in *the Forest* of Boccacio's and Dryden's " Huntsman's Ghost " ; and, even if I had not the same political feelings, (to say nothing of my old convivial turn, which every now and then revives,) I would go as a poet, or, at least, as a lover of poetry. I shall expect to see the spectre of " Ostasio degli Onesti " (Dryden has turned him into Guido Cavalcanti—an essentially different person, as may be found in Dante) come " thundering for his prey in the midst of the festival ". At any rate, whether he does or no, I will get as tipsy and patriotic as possible.

Within these few days I have read, but not written.

February 21, 1821

As usual, rode—visited, etc. Business begins to thicken. The Pope has printed a declaration against the patriots, who, he says, meditate a rising. The consequence of all this will be, that, in a fortnight, the whole country will be up. The proclamation is not yet published, but printed, ready for distribution. * * sent me a copy privately—a sign that he does not know what to think. When he wants to be well with the patriots, he sends to me some civil message or other.

For my own part, it seems to me, that nothing but the most decided success of the Barbarians can prevent a general and immediate rise of the whole nation.

February 23, 1821

Almost ditto with yesterday—rode, etc.—visited—wrote nothing—read Roman History.

Had a curious letter from a fellow, who informs me that the Barbarians are ill-disposed towards me. He is probably a spy, or an impostor. But be it so, even as he says. They cannot bestow their hostility on one who loathes and execrates them more than I do, or who will oppose their views with more zeal, when the opportunity offers.

February 24, 1821

Rode, etc., as usual. The secret intelligence arrived this morning from the frontier to the C^1. is as bad as possible. The *plan* has missed—the Chiefs are betrayed, military, as well as civil—and the Neapólitans not only have *not* moved, but have declared to the P. government, and to the Barbarians, that they know nothing of the matter ! ! !

Thus the world goes; and thus the Italians are always lost for lack of union among themselves. What is to be done *here*, between the two fires, and cut off from the N^n. frontier, is not decided. My opinion was,—better to rise than be taken in detail; but how it will be settled now, I cannot tell. Messengers are despatched to the delegates of the other cities to learn their resolutions.

I always had an idea that it would be *bungled*; but was willing to hope, and am so still. Whatever I can do by money, means, or person, I will venture freely for their freedom; and have so repeated to them (some of the Chiefs here) half an hour ago. I have two thousand five hundred scudi, better than five hundred pounds, in the house, which I offered to begin with.

February 25, 1821

Came home—my head aches—plenty of news, but too tiresome to set down. I have neither read nor written, nor thought, but led a purely animal life all day. I mean to try to write a page or two before I go to bed. But, as Squire Sullen says, " My head aches consumedly : Scrub, bring me a dram ! " Drank some Imola wine, and some punch !

Log-book continued

February 27, 1821

I have been a day without continuing the log, because I could not find a blank book. At length I recollected this.

Rode, etc.—wrote down an additional stanza for the 5th canto of *D[on J[uan]* which I had composed in bed this morning. Visited *l'Amica*. We are invited, on the night of the

Veglione (next Dominica) with the Marchesa Clelia Cavalli and the Countess Spinelli Rasponi. I promised to go. Last night there was a row at the ball, of which I am a *socio*. The Vice-legate had the imprudent insolence to introduce *three* of his servants in masque—*without tickets*, too! and in spite of remonstrances. The consequence was, that the young men of the ball took it up, and were near throwing the Vice-legate out of the window. His servants, seeing the scene, withdrew, and he after them. His reverence Monsignore ought to know, that these are not times for the predominance of priests over decorum. Two minutes more, two steps further, and the whole city would have been in arms, and the government driven out of it.

Such is the spirit of the day, and these fellows appear not to perceive it. As far as the simple fact went, the young men were right, servants being prohibited always at these festivals.

Yesterday wrote two notes on the " Bowles and Pope " controversy, and sent them off to Murray by the post. The old woman whom I relieved in the forest (she is ninety-four years of age) brought me two bunches of violets. *Nam vita gaudet mortua floribus.* I was much pleased with the present. An English woman would have presented a pair of worsted stockings, at least, in the month of February. Both excellent things; but the former are more elegant. The present, at this season, reminds one of Gray's stanza, omitted from his elegy :—

" Here scatter'd oft, the *earliest* of the year,
    By hands unseen, are showers of violets found ;
  The red-breast loves to build and warble here,
    And little footsteps lightly print the ground ".

As fine a stanza as any in his elegy. I wonder that he could have the heart to omit it.

Last night I suffered horribly—from an indigestion, I believe. I *never* sup—that is, never at home. But, last night, I was prevailed upon by the Countess Gamba's persuasion, and the strenuous example of her brother, to swallow, at supper, a quantity of boiled cockles, and to dilute them, *not* reluctantly, with some Imola wine. When I came home, apprehensive of the consequences, I swallowed three or four glasses of spirits, which men (the venders) call brandy, rum, or hollands, but which gods would entitle spirits of wine, coloured or sugared. All was pretty well till I got to bed, when I became somewhat swollen, and considerably vertiginous. I got out, and mixing some soda-powders, drank them off. This brought on temporary relief. I returned to bed; but grew sick and sorry once and again. Took more soda-water. At last I fell into a dreary sleep. Woke, and was ill all day, till I had galloped a few miles. Query—was it the cockles, or what I took to correct them, that caused the commotion? I think both. I remarked in my illness the complete inertion, inaction, and destruction of my chief mental faculties. I tried to rouse them, and yet could not —and this is the *Soul!!!* I should believe that it was married to the body, if they did not sympathise so much with each other. If the one rose, when the other fell, it would be a sign that they longed for the natural state of divorce. But as it is, they seem to draw together like post-horses.

Let us hope the best—it is the grand possession.

TO THE HON. DOUGLAS KINNAIRD *
Ravenna,
February 1st, 1821

DEAR DOUGLAS,—Murray's offer is not a liberal one, nor in proportion to what he offered for Ld. W[aldegrave]'s trash of memoirs ; Lord Orford's may and must be better—he was a truly clever fellow. Besides it was my intention to deal with Mr. M. for the *whole*, and not in parts. Murray certainly has shuffled a little with me of late ; when Galignani wrote to offer me in an indirect manner to purchase the *Copyright in France* of my works I *enclosed his letters with the instrument signed* to Murray, desiring him to *make use of them for himself only*, as I thought it fair that *he* should have the advantage. He never wrote for *three months*, even to acknowledge, far less to thank me, but after repeated letters of mine he at last owns that he had the letters and offered the *instruments* to Galignani—for " a reasonable sum ". In this he only did as I meant him to do, but it was not very liberal [*erased*: a dirty trick] to say nothing about it till it was wrung from him. I can name no sum for the *whole* of the poems. I have been five years out of England ; things may be altered, the sale of books different, my writings less popular. What can I say? You must be in the way of judging better than I can by a little enquiry or by consulting with mutual friends. Had it been five years ago (when I was in my zenith) I certainly would not have taken three thousand guineas for the *whole* of the M.S.S. now in his hands ; and I speak of the very lowest. But still I will not swerve from any agreement *you* may make with him. With *me* he always avoids the subject, and always has done whenever he could.

With Mr. Hanson I shall henceforward be *two*. I sent my answer to him enclosed to *you* the other day ; and I beg you to advise him that from henceforward there is an end to all *personal* friendship between him and me, and that the sooner we close our professional connection also the better. Of course I desire a mortgage, but this their last piece of rascality makes me despair. You may give my compliments to Mr. Bland and tell him that I have no *personal* pique against him, for I do not even know him ; but if the funds ever fail and I lose my property in them it is through *him* and his formalities and by all that is dear to man I will *blow his brains out* and take what fortune may afterwards send me. I am perfectly serious, and pray tell him so, for as I have said so will I do. I address this to Pall Mall, anticipating your return.

yours ever and most truly, BYRON

P.S.—I had heard through your brother the other day something of what you tell me about the boy. But you know by experience that I never interfere in any matters with the women or children of my friends. It is the only quiet course.

P.P.S.—I wrote to desire you to interfere to oppose any representation of " the Doge ", and have written ditto to Mr. Murray.

TO JOHN CAM HOBHOUSE *   *Ravenna, Fy. 22nd, 1821*

MY DEAR HOBHOUSE,—Why the devil don't you write? Are you out of humour? And why? I am not, and shall therefore favour you with one epistle and two requests. The first is to make a short note to a letter I have written to Murray for publication (in any Magazine or in the Examiner) on the remarks of a diplomatic puppy called Turner who, having *failed* in swimming the Hellespont, says that Ekenhead and I succeeded because the *current* was in our favour!! From the *European* side was it so? Were we not obliged to *swim up* against it to pass at all?

My next request is that you will be personally polite—and request Douglas K. to be so—to Mr. Curioni (an Opera Singer) and Madame Taruscelli, a Venetian fair (the same that Kinnaird wanted to be introduced to and was refused) who will arrive in London early in March from Barcelona for the Opera. I am sure that you would like the Lady's society vastly, and oblige her by yours; she is an old friend of mine, and very pretty. She has written to me the enclosed epistle [1] which will explain her. Now an't I a good fellow? I am not like those Venetian fellows who, when their own liaisons are over with a piece, would prevent all others from partaking of the public property, as they did by Kinnaird and *would* have done by me; but I introduced myself, being piqued by their " Dog in a Manger " behaviour.

As to politics, I enclose you the Pope's proclamation. Of course, I cannot write at length, all letters being opened. The Germans are within hail of the Neapolitans by this time. They will get their gruel. They marched ten days sooner than expected, which prevented a general rising. But they are in a situation that, if they do not win their first battle, they will have all Italy upon them. They are damned rascals and deserve it. It is, however, hard upon the poor Pope—in his old age to have all this row in his neighbourhood.

Yours ever and truly, B.

TO THE HON. DOUGLAS KINNAIRD *   *Ravenna, Fy. 26th, 1821*

MY DEAR DOUGLAS,—You will have seen, or will soon see, a greater number of your circular billets than usual from my

---

[1] In the enclosed letter, Signora Taruscelli, who addresses Byron as " Amico piu che carissimo ", besides announcing her projected visit to London and asking for letters of introduction, remarks that she is " always in enamoured of, and always faithful to Curioni " and blesses the day when she left Venice. She understands that the delights of Ravenna still occupy all her friend's attention. " So much constancy in Byron ? "

quarter; and that you may not suppose me more extravagant than usual I will let you know the reason. In the present confusion, and approaching convulsion, of all these countries, Mr. Ghigi (my banker here) has taken a fancy to your notes, and is continually giving me *cash* for them, which cash is still in my strong box, and not more of it spent than usual. I believe·that Ghigi is speculating upon grain etc. on account of the war, or that he finds your notes *better paper* than the country bills of exchange. This is all I know, and the reason of this apparent extravagance of mine.

I have a favour to ask you. Curioni, the Opera Singer, will arrive in England from Barcelona in March. He is accompanied by the Signora Arpalice Taruscelli of Venice, a very pretty woman, and an old acquaintance of mine. They have written to me for letters. Will you call upon them? and introduce them to such of the theatrical people and Editors— Perry etc.—as may be useful to them? You may perhaps *not* have to repent of it; for she is very pretty, and no less gallant, and grateful for any attention. You will find them out by enquiring at the Opera House. I have lately written to you on various matters. On politics I can say nothing; but you will hear strange things soon probably. The confusion is as great as it can well be. I am going to put my daughter into a convent, and for myself I shall take what fortune is pleased to send; you may imagine what sort of scene Italy is likely to present in a row.

If you can do anything by way of purchase or mortgage to lay my money out on while the funds are high, let me know. Hanson's rascality throws me into despair. You will have received my message *for* him, which I beg of you to repeat. I am anxious to have done with him. Could we not purchase or find an English mortgage? In the course of time land must get up again, and now might be the time to buy. As I want no *mansion house* nor ornamental grounds—nothing but *rental* land—what think you? I shall be guided by your opinion in all such matters; but if the funds fail I will blow Bland's brains out.

Yours ever and truly, B.

P.S.—I answered you about Murray.

DEAR MORAY,—In my packet of the 12th Instant, in the last sheet (*not* the *half* sheet), last page, *omit* the sentence which (defining, or attempting to define, what and who are gentlemanly) begins, " I should say at least in life, that most military men have it, and few naval ; that several men of rank have it, and few lawyers," etc., etc. I say, omit the whole of that Sentence, because, like the " Cosmogony, or Creation of the World," in the *Vicar of Wakefield*, it is not much to the purpose.

In the Sentence above, too, almost at the top of the same page, after the words " that there ever was, or can be, an Aristocracy of poets," add and insert these words—" I do not mean that they should write in the Style of the Song by a person of Quality, or *parle Euphuism* ; but there is a *Nobility* of thought and expression to be found no less in Shakespeare, Pope, and Burns, than in Dante, Alfieri, etc., etc.," and so on. Or, if you please, perhaps you had better omit the whole of the latter digression on the *vulgar* poets, and insert only as far as the end of the Sentence upon Pope's Homer, where I prefer it to Cowper's, and quote Dr. Clarke in favour of its accuracy.

Upon all these points, take an opinion—take the Sense (or nonsense) of your learned visitants, and act thereby. I am very tractable—in PROSE.

Whether I have made out the case for Pope, I know not ; but I am very sure that I have been zealous in the attempt. If it comes to the proofs, we shall beat the Blackguards. I will show more *imagery* in twenty lines of Pope than in any equal length of quotation in English poesy, and that in places where they least expect it : for instance, in his lines on *Sporus*,—now, do just *read* them over—the subject is of no consequence (whether it be Satire or Epic)—we are talking of *poetry* and *imagery* from *Nature and Art*. Now, mark the images separately and arithmetically :—

1. The thing of *Silk*.
2. *Curd* of *Ass's* milk.
3. The *Butterfly*.
4. The *Wheel*.

5. Bug with gilded wings.
6. *Painted* Child of dirt.
7. Whose *Buzz*.
8. Well-bred *Spaniels*.
9. *Shallow streams run dimpling.*
10. *Florid impotence.*
11. *Prompter. Puppet squeaks.*
12. *The Ear of Eve.*
13. *Familiar toad.*
14. *Half-froth, half-venom, spits* himself abroad.
15. *Fop* at the *toilet*.
16. *Flatterer* at the *board*.
17. *Amphibious thing.*
18. Now *trips a lady*.
19. Now *struts a Lord*.
20. A *Cherub's face*.
21. A *reptile* all the rest.
22. The *Rabbins*.
23. Pride that *licks the dust*.

> " Beauty that shocks you, parts that none will trust,
> Wit that can creep, and *Pride* that *licks* the *dust*."

Now, is there a line of all the passage without the most *forcible* imagery (for his purpose) ?   Look at the *variety*, at the *poetry*, of the passage—at the *imagination* : there is hardly a line from which a *painting* might not be made, and *is*.   But this is nothing in comparison with his higher passages in the *Essay on Man*, and many of his other poems, serious and comic. There never was such an unjust outcry in this world as that which these Scoundrels are trying against Pope.

In the letter to you upon Bowles, etc., insert *these* which follow (*under* the place, as a Note, where I am speaking of Dyer's " Grongar Hill ", and the use of *artificial* imagery in illustrating *Nature*) :—" Corneille's celebrated lines on Fortune—

> " ' Et comme elle a l'éclat du *Verre*,
> Elle en a la fragilité '—

are a further instance of the noble use which may be made of artificial imagery, and quite equal to any taken from Nature."

Ask Mr. Gifford if, in the 5th act of *The Doge*,[1] you could not contrive (where the Sentence of the *Veil* is past) to insert the following lines in Marino Faliero's answer :—

> But let it be so.   It will be in vain :
> The Veil which blackens o'er this blighted name,
> And hides, or seems to hide, these lineaments,
> Shall draw more Gazers than the thousand portraits
> Which glitter round it in their painted trappings,
> *Your* delegated Slaves—the people's tyrants.

Which will be best? " painted trappings ", or " pictured purple ", or " pictured trappings ", or " painted purple " ? Perpend, and let me know.

I have not had any letter from you, which I am anxious for, to know whether you have received my letters and packets, the letter on Bowles's Pope, etc., etc.   Let me hear from you.

Yours truly, B.

P.S.—Upon *public* matters here I say little : You will all hear soon enough of a general row throughout Italy.   There never was a more foolish step than the Expedition to N. by these fellows.

I wish you to propose to *Holmes*, the miniature painter, to come out to me this spring.   I will pay his expences, and any sum in reason.   I wish him to take my daughter's picture (who is in a convent) and the Countess G.'s, and the head of a peasant Girl, which latter would make a study for Raphael. It is a complete *peasant* face, but an *Italian* peasant's, and quite in the Raphael Fornarina style.   Her figure is tall, but rather large, and not at all comparable to her face, which is really superb.   She is not seventeen, and I am anxious to have her likeness while it lasts.   Madame G. is also very handsome, but it is quite in a different style—completely blonde and fair— very uncommon in Italy : yet not an *English* fairness, but more like a Swede or a Norwegian.   Her figure, too, particularly the bust, is uncommonly good.   It must be *Holmes* : I like him because he takes such inveterate likenesses.   There is a war here ; but a solitary traveller, with little baggage, and nothing

---

[1] *Marino Faliero, a Tragedy*, finished July 1820, was published at the end of the year, together with the *Prophecy of Dante*.

to do with politics, has nothing to fear. Pack him up in the diligence. Don't forget.

MY DEAR DOUGLAS,—I shall consent to nothing of the kind. Our good friends must have the goodness to " bide a wee ". One of three events must occur :—Lady Noel will die—or Lady B.—or myself. In the first case they will be paid out of the incoming : in the second my property will be so far liberated (the offspring being a daughter) as to leave a surplus to cover more than any outstanding present debts : in the third, my executors will of course see their claims liquidated. But as to my parting at this present with a thousand guineas—I wonder if you take me for an Atheist, to make me so unchristian a proposition. It is true that I have reduced my expences in *that* line ; but I have had others to encounter. On getting to dry land, I have had to buy carriages, and some new horses, and to furnish my house, for here you find only walls, *no furnished* apartments—it is not the custom. Besides, though I do not subscribe to liquidate the sum of two thousand pounds for a man of twenty thousand a year, nor write me down a contributor to the English radical societies, yet wherever I find a poor man suffering for his opinions—and there are many such in this country—I always let him have a shilling out of a guinea. You speak with some facetiousness of the *Haus*—etc. Wait till the play is played out. Whatever happens, no tyrant nor tyranny nor barbarian army shall make me change my tone or thoughts or actions, or alter anything but my temper. I say so *now*, as I said so then—now that they are at their butcherwork, as before when they were merely preparing for it.

As to Murray, I presume that you forwarded my letter. I acquiesce in what you say about the arrangement with him, but not at all in the appropriation of the fee. Let me see it in circulars, and then I will tell you whether I will pay them away or no. You must have a very bad opinion of my principles to hint at such a thing. If you pay anything, pay them the interest, provided it is not above a hundred and fifty pounds.

You persuaded me to give those bonds and now you see the consequence. It would have been better to have stood a suit at [law]. At the worst, Rochdale will always in any case bring enough to cover the bonds, and they may seize and sell it for anything I care. I have had more trouble than profit with it. As to Lady Noel, what you say of her declining health would be very well to any one else; but the way to be immortal (I mean *not* to die at all) is to have me for your heir. I recommend you to put me in your will; and you will see that (as long as *I* live at least) you will never even catch cold.

I have written to you twice or thrice lately—and so on. I could give you some curious and interesting details on things here; but they open all letters, and I have no wish to gratify any curiosity, except that of my friends and gossips. Some day or other when we meet (if we meet) I will make your hair stand on end, and Hobhouse's wig (does he wear one still) start from its frame, and leave him under *bare poles*. There is one thing I wish particularly to propose to you patriots; and yet it can't be, without this letter went in a balloon—and, as Moleda [?] says, " *thaut's* impossible ". Let me hear from you —and as good news as you can send in that agreeable soft conciliatory style of yours——

TO RICHARD BELGRAVE HOPPNER   *Ravenna, April 3, 1821*

Thanks for the translation. I have sent you some books, which I do not know whether you have read or no—you need not return them, in any case. I enclose you also a letter from Pisa. I have neither spared trouble nor expense in the care of the child; and as she was now four years old complete, and quite above the control of the servants—and as a *man* living without any woman at the head of his house cannot much attend to a nursery—I had no resource but to place her for a time (at a high pension too) in the convent of Bagna-Cavalli (twelve miles off), where the air is good, and where she will, at least, have her learning advanced, and her morals and religion inculcated. I had also another reason;—things were and are in such a state here, that I had no reason to look upon my own personal safety as particularly insurable; and I thought the infant best out of harm's way, for the present.

It is also fit that I should add that I by no means intended, nor intend, to give a *natural* child an *English* education, because with the disadvantages of her birth, her after settlement would be doubly difficult. Abroad, with a fair foreign education and a portion of five or six thousand pounds, she might and may marry very respectably. In England such a dowry would be a pittance, while elsewhere it is a fortune. It is, besides, my wish that she should be a Roman Catholic, which I look upon as the best religion, as it is assuredly the oldest of the various branches of Christianity. I have now explained my notions as to the *place* where she now is—it is the best I could find for the present; but I have no prejudices in its favour.

I do not speak of politics, because it seems a hopeless subject, as long as those scoundrels are to be permitted to bully states out of their independence. Believe me,

Yours ever and truly.

P.S.—There is a report here of a change in France; but with what truth is not yet known.

P.S.—My respects to Mrs. H. I *have* the " best opinion " of her countrywomen; [1] and at my time of life, (three and thirty, 22d January, 1821,) that is to say, after the life I have led, a *good* opinion is the only rational one which a man should entertain of the whole sex—up to *thirty*, the worst possible opinion a man can have of them in *general*, the better for himself. Afterwards, it is a matter of no importance to *them*, nor to him either, *what opinion* he entertains—his day is over, or, at least, should be.

You see how sober I am become.

TO THE HON. DOUGLAS KINNAIRD*   *Ra. April 26th, 1821*

MY DEAR DOUGLAS,—" The Mystery is resolved " as Mrs. Malaprop says. You were not taken in—but I was. However, I cannot laugh at the joke for sundry reasons—some of them personal. If ever we meet, I can tell you a few things which

[1] Mrs. Hoppner was of Swiss origin.

may perhaps amuse you for a moment. In the meantime I have been disappointed, and you are amused without me. So that there is no loss to you at least.

I have received your letters, all very kind and sensible—nobody like you for business. But I cannot part with more of the produce than the 150—for the present. As for Claughton, why don't he pay? I wrote to desire that he might be proceeded with weeks ago. I hear from Mrs. L[eigh] that Lady N[oel] *has been* " dangerously ill " ; but it should seem by *her* letter that she is now getting dangerously well again. Your letter seems more dubious. Your approval of *the B.'s Letter* is gratifying. I shall be glad to hear as much on the part of the general reader. I did not mean you to be " *passive* " with Murray. On the contrary, I shall thank you to be *active*; for I will not treat with him except through *you* or Hobhouse. *Judge* for yourself, according to the appearance of the impression made by the M.S.S. on their publication, or consult any honest men who understand such matters, and I will abide by your decision. Murray complains to me that you are *brusque* with him. For that matter, so you are at times with most people; and I see no reason for any exception in his favour. I gave in about the D. Juans because you all seemed to think them heavy. You say I was tractable ; but, if you had taken the other line, I should have been as acquiescent in your decision.

I do not know how far your new Opera Acquaintances may answer your expectations ; but any civility to them will be an addition to the many you have conferred on your *trusting* client —and affectionate friend.

B.

P.S.—What's that you say about " *Yolk of Egg for the hair* " ? The receipt—the receipt immediately. Does *the Letter take*? Love to Hobhouse.

Why should Rogers take the " Venerable " ill? He was sixty-three years, eleven months and fourteen days old when I first knew him ten years ago come next November. I meant him a compliment. As for his age, I have seen the certificate from Bow Church dated " 1747—October 10th. Baptized Samuel son of Peter Rogers, Scrivener, Furnivals Inn ". He and Dryden and Chaucer are the oldest upon record to have written so well at that advanced period. His age is a credit to him. I wonder what you mean.

Don't forget the " recipe ". . . .

TO PERCY BYSSHE SHELLEY *Ravenna, April 26, 1821*

The child continues doing well, and the accounts are regular and favourable. It is gratifying to me that you and Mrs. Shelley do not disapprove of the step which I have taken, which is merely temporary.

I am very sorry to hear what you say of Keats—is it *actually* true? I did not think criticism had been so killing. Though I differ from you essentially in your estimate of his performances, I so much abhor all unnecessary pain, that I would rather he had been seated on the highest peak of Parnassus than have perished in such a manner. Poor fellow! though with such inordinate self-love he would probably have not been very happy. I read the review of *Endymion* in the *Quarterly*. It was severe,—but surely not so severe as many reviews in that and other journals upon others.

I recollect the effect on me of the *Edinburgh* on my first poem; it was rage, and resistance, and redress—but not despondency nor despair. I grant that those are not amiable feelings; but, in this world of bustle and broil, and especially in the career of writing, a man should calculate upon his powers of *resistance* before he goes into the arena.

> " Expect not life from pain nor danger free,
> Nor deem the doom of man reversed for thee."

You know my opinion of *that second-hand* school of poetry. You also know my high opinion of your own poetry,—because it is of *no* school. I read *Cenci*—but, besides that I think the *subject* essentially *un*dramatic, I am not an admirer of our old dramatists *as models*. I deny that the English have hitherto had a drama at all. Your *Cenci*, however, was a work of power, and poetry. As to *my* drama, pray revenge yourself upon it, by being as free as I have been with yours.

I have not yet got your *Prometheus*, which I long to see. I have heard nothing of mine, and do not know that it is yet published. I have published a pamphlet on the Pope controversy, which you will not like. Had I known that Keats was dead—or that he was alive and so sensitive—I should have omitted some remarks upon his poetry, to which I was provoked by his *attack* upon *Pope*, and my disapprobation of *his own* style of writing.

You want me to undertake a great poem—I have not the inclination nor the power. As I grow older, the indifference—*not* to life, for we love it by instinct—but to the stimuli of life, increases. Besides, this late failure of the Italians has latterly disappointed me for many reasons,—some public, some personal. My respects to Mrs. S.

Yours ever, B.

P.S.—Could not you and I contrive to meet this summer? Could not you take a run here *alone*?

TO THOMAS MOORE *Ravenna, April 28, 1821*

You cannot have been more disappointed than myself, nor so much deceived. I have been so at some personal risk also, which is not yet done away with. However, no time nor circumstances shall alter my tone nor my feelings of indignation against tyranny triumphant. The present business has been as much a work of treachery as of cowardice,—though both may have done their part. If ever you and I meet again, I will have a talk with you upon the subject. At present, for obvious reasons, I can write but little, as all letters are opened. In *mine* they shall always find *my* sentiments, but nothing that can lead to the oppression of others.

You will please to recollect that the Neapolitans are now nowhere more execrated than in Italy, and not blame a whole people for the vices of a province. That would be like condemning Great Britain because they plunder wrecks in Cornwall.

And now let us be literary;—a sad falling off, but it is always a consolation. If " Othello's occupation be gone ", let us take to the next best; and, if we cannot contribute to make mankind more free and wise, we may amuse ourselves and those who like it. What are you writing? I have been scribbling at intervals, and Murray will be publishing about now.

Lady Noel has, as you say, been dangerously ill; but it may console you to learn that she is dangerously well again.

I have written a sheet or two more of Memoranda for you; and I kept a little Journal for about a month or two, till I had filled the paper-book. I then left it off, as things grew busy, and, afterwards, too gloomy to set down without a painful feeling. This I should be glad to send you, if I had an opportunity; but a volume, however small, don't go well by such posts as exist in this Inquisition of a country.

I have no news. As a very pretty woman said to me a few nights ago, with the tears in her eyes, as she sat at the harpsichord, "Alas! the Italians must now return to making operas". I fear *that* and maccaroni are their forte, and " motley their only wear ". However, there are some high spirits among them still. Pray write.

And believe me, etc.

"MY DICTIONARY," MAY, 1821—DETACHED
THOUGHTS, OCTOBER 15, 1821–MAY 18, 1822

Ravenna, May 1ˢᵗ 1821

AMONGST various journals, memoranda, diaries, etc., which I have kept in the course of my living, I began one about three months ago, and carried it on till I had filled one paper-book (thinnish), and two sheets or so of another. I then left off, partly because I thought we should have some business here, and I had furbished up my arms, and got my apparatus ready for taking a turn with the Patriots, having my drawers full of their proclamations, oaths, and resolutions, and my lower rooms of their hidden weapons of most calibres; and partly because I had filled my paper book. But the Neapolitans have betrayed themselves and all the World, and those who would have given their blood for Italy can now only give her their tears.

Some day or other, if dust holds together, I have been enough in the Secret (at least in this part of the country) to cast perhaps some little light upon the atrocious treachery which has replunged Italy into Barbarism. At present I have neither the time nor the temper. However, the *real* Italians are *not* to blame—merely the scoundrels at the *Heel of the Boot*, which the *Hun* now wears, and will trample them to ashes with for their Servility.

I have risked myself with the others *here*, and how far I may or may not be compromised is a problem at this moment : some of them like " Craigengelt " would " tell all and more than all to save themselves " ; but, come what may, the cause was a glorious one, though it reads at present as if the Greeks had run away from Xerxes.

Happy the few who have only to reproach themselves with believing that these rascals were less *rascaille* than they proved. *Here* in Romagna the efforts were necessarily limited to pre-parations and good intentions, until the Germans were fairly engaged in *equal* warfare, as we are upon their very frontiers without a single fort, or hill, nearer than San Marino. Whether " Hell will be paved with " those " good intentions ", I know not ; but there will probably be good store of Neapolitans to walk upon the pavement, whatever may be its composition. Slabs of lava from their mountain, with the bodies of their own damned Souls for cement, would be the fittest causeway for Satan's *Corso*.

But what shall I write? another Journal? I think not. Anything that comes uppermost—and call it " my Dictionary ".

MY DICTIONARY

Augustus.—I have often been puzzled with his character. Was he a great Man? Assuredly. But not one of *my* great men. I have always looked upon Sylla as the greatest Char-acter in History, for laying down his power at the moment when it was

" too great to keep or to resign ",

and thus despising them all. As to the retention of his power by Augustus, the thing was already settled. If he had given it up, the Commonwealth was gone, the republic was long past all resuscitation. Had Brutus and Cassius gained the battle of Philippi, it would not have restored the republic—its days ended with the Gracchi, the rest was a mere struggle of parties. You might as well cure a Consumption, restore a broken egg, as revive a state so long a prey to every uppermost Soldier as Rome had long been.

As for a despotism, if Augustus could have been sure that all his Successors would have been like himself (I mean *not* as *Octavius*, but Augustus), or Napoleon would have insured the world that *none* of his Successors would have been like himself, the antient or modern World might have gone on like the Empire of China—in a state of lethargic prosperity.

Suppose, for instance, that, instead of Tiberius and Caligula, Augustus had been immediately succeeded by Nerva, Trajan, the Antonines, or even by Titus and his father, what a difference in our estimate of himself? So far from gaining by the *contrast*, I think that one half of our dislike arises from his having been heired by Tiberius, and one half of Julius Cæsar's fame from his having had his empire consolidated by Augustus.

Suppose that there had been *no Octavius*, and Tiberius had " jumped the life " between, and at once succeeded Julius? And yet it is difficult to say whether hereditary right, or popular choice, produce the worse Sovereigns. The Roman Consuls make a goodly show, but then they only reigned for a year, and were under a sort of personal obligation to distinguish themselves. It is still more difficult to say which form of Government is the *worst*—all are so bad. As for democracy, it is the worst of the whole; for what is (*in fact*) democracy? an Aristocracy of Blackguards.

ABERDEEN—OLD AND NEW, OR THE AULDTOUN AND NEWTOUN

For several years of my earliest childhood I was in that City, but have never revisited it since I was ten years old. I was sent at five years old, or earlier, to a School kept by a Mr. *Bowers*, who was called " *Bodsy* Bowers " by reason of his dapperness. It was a School for both sexes. I learned little there, except to repeat by rote the first lesson of Monosyllables —" God made man, let us love him "—by hearing it often repeated, without acquiring a letter. Whenever proof was made of my progress at home, I repeated these words with the most rapid fluency; but on turning over a new leaf, I continued to repeat them, so that the narrow boundaries of my first year's accomplishments were detected, my ears boxed (which they did not deserve, seeing that it was by *ear* only that I had acquired my letters), and my intellects consigned to a new preceptor. He was a very decent, clever, little Clergyman, named Ross, afterwards Minister of one of the Kirks (*East* I think). Under *him* I made an astonishing progress, and I recollect to this day his mild manners and good-natured pains-taking.

The moment I could read, my grand passion was *history*; and why, I know not, but I was particularly taken with the battle near the Lake Regillus in the Roman History, put into my hands the first.

Four years ago, when standing on the heights of Tusculum, and looking down upon the little round Lake, that was once Regillus, and which dots the immense expanse below, I remembered my young enthusiasm and my old instructor.

Afterwards I had a very serious, saturnine, but kind young man, named Paterson, for a Tutor: he was the son of my Shoemaker, but a good Scholar, as is common with the Scotch. He was a rigid Presbyterian also. With him I began Latin in Ruddiman's Grammar, and continued till I went to the " Grammar School " (*Scotice* " Schule "—*Aberdonice* " Squeel "), where I threaded all the Classes to the *fourth*, when I was recalled to England (where I had been hatched) by the demise of my Uncle.

I acquired this handwriting, which I can hardly read myself, under the fair copies of Mr. Duncan of the same city. I don't think that he would plume himself upon my progress. However, I wrote much better then than I have ever done since. Haste and agitation of one kind or another have quite spoilt as pretty a scrawl as ever scratched over a frank.

The Grammar School might consist of a hundred and fifty of all ages under age. It was divided into five classes, taught by four masters, the Chief teaching the fifth and fourth himself, as in England the fifth, sixth forms, and Monitors are heard by the Head Masters.

DETACHED THOUGHTS

Octr 15th 1821

I have been thinking over the other day on the various comparisons, good or evil, which I have seen published of myself in different journals English and foreign. This was suggested to me by accidentally turning over a foreign one lately; for I have made it a rule latterly never to *search* for anything of the kind, but not to avoid the perusal if presented by Chance.

To begin then—I have seen myself compared personally or poetically, in English, French, *German* (*as* interpreted to me), Italian, and Portuguese, within these nine years, to Rousseau—Göethe—Young—Aretino—Timon of Athens—" An Alabaster Vase lighted up within "—Satan—Shakespeare—Buonaparte — Tiberius — Aeschylus — Sophocles — Euripides — Harlequin—The Clown—Sternhold and Hopkins—to the Phantasmagoria—to Henry the 8th—to Chenies—to Mirabeau—to young R. Dallas (the Schoolboy)—to Michael Angelo—to Raphael—to a *petit maître*—to Diogenes—to Childe Harold—to Lara—to the Count in Beppo—to Milton—to Pope—to Dryden—to Burns—to Savage—to Chatterton—to " oft have I heard of thee my Lord Biron " in Shakespeare—to Churchill the poet—to Kean the Actor—to Alfieri, etc., etc., etc. The likeness to Alfieri was asserted very seriously by an Italian, who had known him in his younger days : it of course related merely to our apparent personal dispositions. He did not assert it to *me* (for we were not then good friends), but in society.

The Object of so many contradictory comparisons must probably be like something different from them all ; but what *that* is, is more than *I* know, or any body else.

My Mother, before I was twenty, would have it that I was like Rousseau, and Madame de Staël used to say so too in 1813, and the *Edin^h Review* has something of the sort in its critique on the 4th Canto of *Ch^e Ha^d*. I can't see any point of resemblance : he wrote prose, I verse : he was of the people, I of the Aristocracy : he was a philosopher, I am none : he published his first work at forty, I mine at eighteen : his first essay brought him universal applause, mine the contrary : he married his housekeeper, I could not keep house with my wife : he thought all the world in a plot against *him*, my little world seems to think *me* in a plot against it, if I may judge by their abuse in print and coterie : he liked Botany, I like flowers, and herbs, and trees, but know nothing of their pedigrees : he wrote Music, I limit my knowledge of it to what I catch by *Ear*—I never could learn any thing by *study*, not even a language, it was all by rote and ear and memory : he had a bad memory, I *had* at least an excellent one (ask Hodgson the poet, a good judge, for he has an astonishing one) : he wrote with hesitation and care, I with rapidity and rarely with pains : *he* could never ride nor swim " nor was cunning of fence ", *I* am an excellent swimmer, a decent though not at all a dashing rider (having staved in a rib at eighteen in the course of scampering), and was sufficient of fence—particularly of the Highland broadsword ; not a bad boxer when I could keep my temper, which was difficult, but which I strove to do ever since I knocked down Mr. Purling and put his knee-pan out (with the gloves on) in Angelo's and Jackson's rooms in 1806 during the sparring ; and I was besides a very fair cricketer—one of the Harrow Eleven when we play[ed] against Eton in 1805. Besides, Rousseau's way of life, his country, his manners, his whole character, were so very different, that I am at a loss to conceive how such a comparison could have arisen, as it has done three several times, and all in rather a remarkable manner. I forgot to say, that *he* was also short-sighted, and that hitherto my eyes have been the contrary to such a degree, that, in the largest theatre of Bologna, I distinguished and read some busts and inscriptions painted near the stage, from a box so distant, and so *darkly* lighted, that none of the company (composed of young and very bright-eyed people—some of them in the same box) could make out a letter, and thought it was a trick, though I had never been in that theatre before.

Altogether, I think myself justified in thinking the comparison not well founded. I don't say this out of pique, for Rousseau was a great man, and the thing if true were flattering enough ; but I have no idea of being pleased with a chimera.

I

When I met old Courtenay, the Orator, at Rogers the poet's in 1811-1812, I was much taken with the portly remains of his fine figure, and the still acute quickness of his conversation. It was *he* who silenced Flood in the English House by a crushing reply to a hasty début of the rival of Grattan in Ireland. I asked Courtenay (for I like to trace motives), if he had not some personal provocation ; for the acrimony of his answer seemed to me (as I had read it) to involve it. Courtenay said " he had—that when in Ireland (being an Irishman) at the *bar* of the Irish house of Commons that Flood had made a personal and unfair attack upon *himself*, who, not being a member of that house, could not defend himself; and that some years afterwards, the opportunity of retort offering in the English Parliament, he could not resist it ". He certainly repaid F. with interest, for Flood never made any figure, and only a speech or two afterwards in the E. H. of Commons. I must except, however, his speech on Reform in 1790, which " Fox called the best he ever heard upon that Subject ".

2

When Fox was asked what he thought the best speech he had ever heard, he replied " Sheridan's on the Impeachment of Hastings in the house of Commons " (*not* that in Westminster Hall). When asked what he thought of his *own* speech on the breaking out of the War? he replied " that was a damned good speech too ".—From Ld Holland.

3

When Sheridan made his famous speech already alluded to, Fox advised him to speak it over again in Westminster Hall on the trial, as nothing better *could* be made of the subject ; but Sheridan made his new speech as different as possible, and, according to the best Judges, very inferior to the former, notwithstanding the laboured panegyric of Burke upon his *Colleague*.—L^d H.

4

Burke spoilt his own speaking afterwards by an imitation of Sheridan's in Westminster Hall : this Speech he called always " the grand desideratum, which was neither poetry nor eloquence, but something *better* than both ".

5

I have never heard any one who fulfilled my Ideal of an Orator. Grattan would have been near it but for his Harlequin delivery. Pitt I never heard. Fox but once, and then he struck me as a debater, which to me seems as different from an Orator as an Improvisatore or a versifier from a poet. Grey is great, but it is not oratory. Canning is sometimes very like one. Windham I did not admire, though all the world did : it seemed such sophistry. Whitbread was the Demosthenes of bad taste and vulgar vehemence, but strong and English. Holland is impressive from sense and sincerity. Lord Lansdowne good, but still a debater only. Grenville I like vastly, if he would prune his speeches down to an hour's delivery. Burdett is sweet and silvery as Belial himself, and *I* think the greatest favourite in Pandemonium ; at least I always heard the Country Gentlemen and the ministerial devilry praise his *speeches* upstairs, and run down from Bellamy's when he was upon his legs. I heard Bob. Milnes make his *second* speech : it made no impression. I like Ward—studied, but keen, and sometimes eloquent. Peel, my School and form-fellow (we sate within two of each other) strange to say I have never heard, though I often wished to do so ; but, from what I remember of him at Harrow, he *is*, or *should* be, amongst the best of them. Now, I do *not* admire Mr. Wilberforce's speaking ; it is nothing but a flow of *words*—" words, words alone ".

I doubt greatly if the English *have* any eloquence, properly so called, and am inclined to think that the Irish *had* a great deal, and that the French *will* have, and have had in Mirabeau. Lord Chatham and Burke are the nearest approaches to Orators in England. I don't know what Erskine may have been at the *bar*, but in the house I wish him at the Bar once more. Lauderdale is shrill, and Scotch, and acute. Of Brougham I shall say nothing, as I have a personal feeling of dislike to the man.

But amongst all these—good, bad, and indifferent—I never heard the speech which was not too long for the auditors, and not very intelligible except here and there. The whole thing is a grand deception, and as tedious and tiresome as may be

to those who must be often present. I heard Sheridan only
once, and that briefly ; but I liked his voice, his manner, and
his wit : he is the only one of them I ever wished to hear at
greater length. In society I have met him frequently : he was
superb ! He had a sort of liking for me, and never attacked me
—at least to my face, and he did every body else—high names,
and wits, and orators, some of them poets also. I have seen
[him] cut up Whitbread, quiz Me de Stael, annihilate Colman,
and do little less by some others (whose names as friends I
set not down), of good fame and abilities. Poor fellow ! he
got drunk very thoroughly and very soon. It occasionally fell
to my lot to convoy him home—no sinecure, for he was so
tipsy that I was obliged to put on his cock'd hat for him : to
be sure it tumbled off again, and I was not myself so sober as
to be able to pick it up again.

6

There was something odd about Sheridan. One day at a
dinner he was slightly praising that pert pretender and impostor, Lyttelton (The Parliament puppy, still alive, I believe).
I took the liberty of differing from him : he turned round
upon me, and said, " Is that your real opinion? " I confirmed
it. Then said he, " Fortified by this concurrence, I beg leave
to say that it in fact is also *my* opinion, and that he is a person
whom I do absolutely and utterly despise, abhor, and detest ".
He then launched out into a description of his despicable
qualities, at some length, and with his usual wit, and evidently
in earnest (for he hated Lyttelton). His former compliment
had been drawn out by some preceding one, just as its reverse
was by my hinting that it was unmerited.

7

One day I saw him take up his own " Monody on Garrick ".
He lighted upon the dedication to the Dowager Lady Spencer :
on seeing it he flew into a rage, and exclaimed " that it must
be a forgery—that he had never dedicated anything of his to
such a d—d canting b—h ", etc., etc., etc. ; and so went on
for half an hour abusing his own dedication, or at least the
object of it. If all writers were equally sincere, it would be
ludicrous.

8

He told me that, on the night of the grand success of his
S[*chool*] *for* S[*candal*], he was knocked down and put into the
watch house for making a row in the Street, and being found
intoxicated by the watchmen.

9

Latterly, when found drunk one night in the kennel, and
asked his *Name* by the Watchmen, he answered " *Wilberforce* ".
The last time I met him was, I think, at Sir Gilbert Elliot's,
where he was as quick as ever. No, it was not the last time :
the last time was at Douglas K^d's. I have met him in all places
and parties—at Whitehall with the Melbournes, at the Marquis
of Tavistock's, at Robins the Auctioneer's, at Sir Humphrey
Davy's, at Sam Rogers's, in short, in most kinds of company,
and always found him very convivial and delightful.

10

Sheridan's liking for me (whether he was not mystifying
me I do not know ; but Lady C^e L. and others told me he said
the same both before and after he knew me) was founded upon
English Bards and S. Reviewers. He told me that he did not care
about poetry (or about mine—at least, any but *that* poem of
mine), but he was sure, from *that* and other symptoms, I should
make an Orator, if I would but take to speaking, and grow a
parliament man. He never ceased harping upon this to me,
to the last ; and I remember my old tutor Dr. Drury had the
same notion when I was a *boy* : but it never was my turn of
inclination to try. I spoke once or twice as all young peers
do, as a kind of introduction into public life ; but dissipation,
shyness, haughty and reserved opinions, together with the
short time I lived in England—after my majority (only about
five years in all)—prevented me from resuming the experiment.
As far as it went, it was not discouraging—particularly my
first speech (I spoke three or four times in all) ; but just after
it my poem of C^e H^d was published, and nobody ever thought
about my *prose* afterwards : nor indeed did I ; it became to
me a secondary and neglected object, though I sometimes
wonder to myself *if* I should have succeeded?

11

The Impression of Parliament upon me was that it's members are not formidable as *Speakers*, but very much so as an *audience*; because in so numerous a body there may be little Eloquence (after all there were but *two* thorough Orators in all Antiquity, and I suspect still *fewer* in modern times), but must be a leaven of thought and good sense sufficient to make them *know* what is right, though they can't express it nobly.

12

Horne Tooke and Roscoe both are said to have declared, that they left Parliament with a higher opinion of its aggregate integrity and abilities than that with which they had entered it. The general amount of both in most parliaments is probably about the same, as also the number of *Speakers* and their *talent*. I except *Orators*, of course, because *they* are things of Ages and not of Septenniaĺ or triennial reunions.

Neither house ever struck me with more awe or respect than the same number of Turks in a Divan, or of Methodists in a barn would have done. Whatever diffidence or nervousness I felt (and I felt both in a great degree) arose from the number rather than the quality of the assemblage, and the thought rather of the *public without* than the persons within— knowing (as all know) that Cicero himself, and probably the Messiah, could never have alter'd the vote of a single Lord of the Bedchamber or Bishop.

I thought *our* house dull, but the other animating enough upon great days.

12 [so repeated by Byron]

Sheridan dying was requested to undergo " an Operation " : he replied that he had already submitted to *two*, which were enough for one man's life time. Being asked what they were, he answered, " having his hair cut, and sitting for his picture ".

13

Whenever an American requests to see me (which is *not* unfrequently), I comply : 1stly, because I respect a people who acquired their freedom by firmness without excess ; and

2^{ndly}, because these trans-atlantic visits, " few and far between ", make me feel as if talking with Posterity from the other side of the Styx. In a century or two, the new English and Spanish Atlantides will be masters of the old Countries in all probability, as Greece and Europe overcame their Mother Asia in the older, or earlier ages as they are called.

14

Sheridan was one day offered a bet by M. G. Lewis. " I will bet you, Mr. Sheridan, a very large sum : I will bet you what you *owe me* as Manager, for my ' Castle Spectre '." " I never make *large bets*," said Sheridan : " but I will lay you a *very small one* ; I will bet you *what it is* WORTH ! "

15

Lewis, though a kind man, hated Sheridan ; and we had some words upon that score when in Switzerland in 1816. Lewis afterwards sent me the following epigram upon Sheridan from Saint Maurice :—

> " For worst abuse of finest parts
>   Was Misophil begotten ;
> There might indeed be *blacker* hearts,
>   But none could be more *rotten* ".

16

Lewis at Oatlands was observed one morning to have his eyes red, and his air sentimental : being asked why? replied, " that when people said any thing *kind* to him, it affected him deeply ; and just now the Duchess has said something *so* kind to me that . . ." here " tears began to flow " again. " Never mind, Lewis," said Col. Armstrong to him, " never mind, don't cry. *She could not mean it.*"

17

Lewis was a good man, a clever man, but a bore, a damned bore, one may say. My only revenge or consolation used to be, setting him by the ears with some vivacious person who hated Bores, especially Me de Stael, or Hobhouse, for example. But I liked Lewis : he was a Jewel of a Man had he been better set.

I don't mean *personally*, but less *tiresome*; for he was tedious, as well as contradictory, to every thing and every body.

Being short-sighted, when we used to ride out together near the Brenta in the twilight in Summer, he made me go *before* to pilot him. I am absent at times, especially towards evening; and the consequence of this pilotage was some narrow escapes to the Monk on horseback. Once I led him *into* a ditch, over which I had passed as usual forgetting to warn my convoy. Once I led him nearly into the river, instead of *on* the *moveable* bridge which *in*commodes passengers; and twice did we both run against the diligence, which, being heavy and slow, did communicate less damage than it received in its leaders, who were *terrassé*'d by the charge. Thrice did I lose him in the gray of the Gloaming, and was obliged to bring to to his distant signals of distance and distress. All the time he went on talking without intermission, for he was a man of many words.

Poor fellow, he died, a martyr to his new riches, of a second visit to Jamaica—

> " I'll give the lands of Deloraine
> Dark Musgrave were alive again ! "

that is

> I would give many a Sugar Cane
> Monk Lewis were alive again !

18

Lewis said to me, " Why do you talk *Venetian* " (such as I could talk, not very fine to be sure) " to the Venetians? and not the usual Italian? " I answered, partly from habit, and partly to be understood, if possible. " It may be so," said Lewis, " but it sounds to me like talking with a *brogue* to an *Irishman*."

19

Baillie (commonly called Long Baillie, a very clever man, but odd), complained in riding to our friend Scrope B. Davies, " that he had a *stitch* in his side ". " I don't wonder at it " (said Scrope) " for you ride *like* a *tailor*." Whoever had seen B. on horseback, with his very tall figure on a small nag, would not deny the justice of the repartée.

20

In 1808, Scrope and myself being at Supper at Steevens's (I think Hobhouse was there too) after the Opera, young Goulburne (of the Blues and of the Blue-viad) came in full of the praises of his horse, Grimaldi, who had just won a race at Newmarket. " Did he win easy? " said Scrope. " Sir," replied Goulburne, " he did not even condescend to *puff* at coming in." " No " (said Scrope), " and so *you puff for* him."

21

Captain Wallace, a notorious character of that day, and *then* intimate with most of the more dissipated young men of the day, asked me one night at the Gaming table, where I thought *his Soul* would be found after death? I answered him, " In *Silver Hell* " (a cant name for a second rate Gambling house).

22

When the Honble J. W. Ward quitted the Whigs, he facetiously demanded, at Sir James Macintosh's table, in the presence of Made de Staël, Malthus, and a large and goodly company of all parties and countries, " what it would take to *re-whig him*, as he thought of turning again ". " Before you can be *re-whigged* " (said I), " I am afraid you must be *re-Warded*." This pun has been attributed to others : they are welcome to it ; but it was mine notwithstanding, as a numerous company and Ward himself doth know. I believe Luttrel versified it afterwards to put into the *M. Chronicle*—at least the late Lady Melbourne told me so. Ward took it good-humouredly at the time.

23

When Sheridan was on his death-bed, Rogers aided him with purse and person : this was particularly kind in Rogers, who always spoke ill of Sheridan (to me at least) ; but indeed he does that of every-body to any body. Rogers is the reverse of the line

" The *best good man* with the *worst natured* Muse ",
being

" The *worst* good man with the *best* natured Muse ".

His Muse being all Sentiment and Sago and Sugar, while he himself is a venomous talker. I say " *worst good* man " because he is (perhaps) a *good* man—at least he does good now and then, as well he may, to purchase himself a shilling's worth of Salvation for his Slanders. They are so *little* too—small talk, and old Womanny; and he is malignant too, and envious, and—he be damned!

24

Curran! Curran's the Man who struck me most. Such Imagination! There never was any thing like it, that ever I saw or heard of. His *published* life, his published speeches, give you *no* idea of the Man—none at all. He was a *Machine* of Imagination, as some one said that Piron was an " Epigrammatic Machine ".

I did not see a great deal of Curran—only in 1813; but I met him at home (for he used to call on me), and in society, at Mac'Intosh's, Holland House, etc., etc., etc., and he was wonderful, even to me, who had seen many remarkable men of the time.

25

A young American, named Coolidge, called on me not many months ago: he was intelligent, very handsome, and not more than twenty years old according to appearances. A little romantic, but that sits well upon youth, and mighty fond of poesy as may be suspected from his approaching me in my cavern. He brought me a message from an old Servant of my family (Joe Murray), and told me that *he* (Mr. Coolidge) had obtained a copy of my bust from Thorwal[d]sen at Rome, to send to America. I confess I was more flattered by this young enthusiasm of a solitary trans-atlantic traveller, than if they had decreed me a Statue in the Paris Pantheon (I have seen Emperors and demagogues cast down from their pedestals even in my own time, and Grattan's name razed from the Street called after him in Dublin) I say that I was more flattered by it, because it was *single*, *un-political*, and was without motive or ostentation—the pure and warm feeling of a boy for the poet he admired. It must have been expensive though. *I* would not pay the price of a Thorwaldsen bust for any human head and shoulders, except Napoleon's, or my children's, or

some " *absurd Womankind's* " as Monkbarns calls them, or my
Sister's.   If asked, *why* then I sate for my own—answer, that it
was at the request particular of J. C. Hobhouse, Esqre, and for
no one else.   A *picture* is a different matter—every body sits
for their picture ; but a bust looks like putting up pretensions
to permanency, and smacks something of a hankering for *public*
fame rather than private remembrance.

26

One of the cleverest men I ever knew in Conversation was
Scrope Beardmore Davies.   Hobhouse is also very good in that
line, though it is of less consequence to a man who has other
ways of showing his talents than in company.   Scrope was
always ready, and often witty : Hobhouse is witty, but not
always so ready, being more diffident.

27

A drunken man ran against Hobhouse in the Street.   A
companion of the Drunkard, not much less so, cried out to
Hobhouse, " *An't* you ashamed to run against a drunken man?
couldn't you see that he was *drunk*? "   " Damn him " (answered
Hobhouse) " isn't *he* ashamed to run against *me*? couldn't he
see that *I* was *sober*? "

28

When Brummell was obliged (by that affair of poor Meyler,
who thence acquired the name of " Dick the Dandy-killer "—
it was about money and debt and all that) to retire to France,
he knew no French ; and having obtained a Grammar for the
purposes of Study, our friend Scrope Davies was asked what
progress Brummell had made in French, to which he responded, " that B. had been stopped like Buonaparte in
Russia by the *Elements* ".   I have put this pun into " Beppo ",
which is " a fair exchange and no robbery " ; for Scrope made
his fortune at several dinners (as he owned himself), by repeating occasionally as his own some of the buffooneries with
which I had encountered him in the Morning.

29

I liked the Dandies ; they were always very civil to *me*,
though in general they disliked literary people, and persecuted

and mystified Me de Staël, Lewis, Horace Twiss, and the like, damnably. They persuaded Me de Staël that Alvanley [1] had a hundred thousand a year, etc., etc., till she praised him to his *face* for his *beauty*! and made a set at him for Albertine (*Libertine*, as Brummell baptized her, though the poor Girl was and is as correct as maid or wife can be, and very amiable withal), and a hundred fooleries besides.

The truth is, that, though I gave up the business early, I had a tinge of Dandyism in my minority, and probably retained enough of it, to conciliate the great ones; at four and twenty. I had gamed, and drank, and taken my degrees in most dissipations; and having no pedantry, and not being overbearing, we ran quietly together. I knew them all more or less, and they made me a Member of Watier's (a superb Club at that time), being, I take it, the only literary man (except *two others*, both men of the world, M. and S.) in it.

Our Masquerade was a grand one; so was the Dandy Ball, too, at the Argyle, but *that* (the latter) was given by the four Chiefs, B., M., A., and P., if I err not.

30

I was a Member of the Alfred too, being elected while in Greece. It was pleasant—a little too sober and literary, and bored with Sotheby and Sir Francis D'Ivernois! but one met Peel, and Ward, and Valentia, and many other pleasant or known people; and was upon the whole a decent resource on a rainy day, in a dearth of parties, or parliament, or an empty season.

31

I belonged, or belong, to the following Clubs or Societies:—to the Alfred, to the Cocoa tree, to Watier's, to the Union, to Racket's (at Brighton), to the Pugilistic, to the Owls or " Fly by Night ", to the *Cambridge* Whig Club, to the Harrow Club, Cambridge, and to one or two private Clubs, to the Hampden political Club, and to the Italian Carbonari, etc., etc., etc., " though last *not least* ". I got into all these, and never stood for any other—at least to my own knowledge. I declined being proposed to several others; though pressed to stand Candidate.

---

[1] Lord Alvanley was a renowned dandy and wit, but notably ill-favoured: see Dighton's caricature " Going to White's ".

32

If the papers lie not (which they generally do), Demetrius Zograffo of Athens is at the head of the Athenian part of the present Greek Insurrection. He was my Servant in 1809, 1810, 1811, 1812, at different intervals in those years (for I left him in Greece when I went to Constantinople), and accompanied me to England in 1811. He returned to Greece, Spring 1812. He was a clever, but not *apparently* an enterprizing, man; but Circumstances make men. His two sons (*then* infants) were named Miltiades and Alcibiades. May the Omen be happy!

33

I have a notion that Gamblers are as happy as most people, being always *excited*. Women, wine, fame, the table, even Ambition, *sate* now and then; but every turn of the card, and cast of the dice, keeps the Gamester alive: besides one can Game ten times longer than one can do any thing else.

I was very fond of it when young, that is to say, of "Hazard"; for I hate all *Card* Games, even Faro. When Macco (or whatever they spell it) was introduced, I gave up the whole thing; for I loved and missed the *rattle* and *dash* of the box and dice, and the glorious uncertainty, not only of good luck or bad luck, but of *any luck at all*, as one had sometimes to throw *often* to decide at all.

I have thrown as many as fourteen mains running, and carried off all the cash upon the table occasionally; but I had no coolness or judgement or calculation. It was the *delight* of the thing that pleased me. Upon the whole, I left off in time without being much a winner or loser. Since one and twenty years of age, I played but little, and then never above a hundred or two, or three.

34

As far as Fame goes (that is to say *living* Fame) I have had my share—perhaps, indeed, *certainly* more than my *deserts*. Some odd instances have occurred to my own experience of the wild and strange places, to which a name may penetrate, and where it may impress. Two years ago (almost three, being in August or July 1819), I received at Ravenna a letter in *English* verse from *Drontheim* in Norway, written by a Norwegian, and full of the usual compliments, etc., etc. It is still somewhere amongst my papers. In the same month, I received an invitation into *Holstein* from a Mr. Jacobsen (I think), of Hamburgh; also (by the same medium), a translation of Medora's song in the " Corsair " by a Westphalian Baroness (not " Thunderton-tronck "), with some original verses of hers (very pretty and Klopstock-ish), and a prose translation annexed to them, on the subject of my wife. As they concerned *her* more than me, I sent them to her together with Mr. J.'s letter. It was odd enough to receive an invitation to pass the *summer* in *Holstein*, while in *Italy*, from people I never knew. The letter was addressed to Venice. Mr. J. talked to me of the " wild roses growing in the Holstein summer " : why then did the Cimbri and Teutones emigrate?

What a strange thing is life and man? Were I to present myself at the door of the house, where my daughter now is, the door would be shut in my face, unless (as is not impossible) I knocked down the porter; and if I had gone in that year (and perhaps now) to Drontheim (the furthest town in Norway), or into Holstein, I should have been received with open arms into the mansions of Stranger and foreigners, attached to me by no tie but that of mind and rumour.

As far as *Fame* goes, I have had my share: it has indeed been leavened by other human contingencies, and this in a greater degree than has occurred to most literary men of a *decent* rank in life; but on the whole I take it that such equipoise is the condition of humanity.

I doubt sometimes whether, after all, a quiet and unagitated life would have suited me: yet I sometimes long for it. My earliest dreams (as most boys' dreams are) were martial; but a little later they were all for *love* and retirement, till the hopeless attachment to M. C. began, and continued (though sedulously concealed) *very* early in my teens; and so upwards for a time. *This* threw me out again " alone on a wide, wide sea ".

In the year 1804, I recollect meeting my Sister at General Harcourt's in Portland Place. I was then *one* thing, and *as* she had always till then found me. When we met again in 1805 (she told me since), that my temper and disposition were so completely altered, that I was hardly to be recognized. I was not then sensible of the change, but I can believe it, and account for it.

35

A private play being got up at Cambridge, a Mr. *Tulk*, greatly to the inconvenience of Actors and audience, declined his part on a sudden, so that it was necessary to make an apology to the Company. In doing this, Hobhouse (indignant like all the rest at this inopportune caprice of the Seceder) stated to the audience " that in consequence of *a* Mr. Tulk having unexpectedly thrown up his part, they must request their indulgence, etc., etc." Next day, the furious Tulk demanded of Hobhouse, " did you, Sir, or did you not use *that* expression? " " Sir," (said Hobhouse) " I *did* or *did not* use that expression." " Perhaps " (said Scrope Davies, who was present), " you object to the *indefinite article*, and prefer being entitled *the Mr. Tulk*? " *The* Tulk eyed Scrope indignantly; but aware, probably, that the said Scrope, besides being a profane Jester, had the misfortune to be a very good shot, and had already fought two or three duels, he retired without further objections to either article, except a conditional menace—*if* he should ascertain that an intention, etc., etc., etc.

36

I have been called in as Mediator or Second at least twenty times in violent quarrels, and have always contrived to settle the business without compromising the honour of the parties, or leading them to mortal consequences; and this too sometimes in very difficult and delicate circumstances, and having to deal with very hot and haughty Spirits—Irishmen, Gamesters, Guardsmen, Captains and Cornets of horse, and the like. This was of course in my youth, when I lived in hot-headed company. I have had to carry challenges from Gentlemen to Noblemen, from Captains to Captains, from lawyers to Counsellors, and once from a Clergyman to an officer in the Life-guards. It may seem strange, but I found the latter by far the most difficult

> " . . . to compose
> The bloody duel without blows ".

The business being about a woman. I must add too that I never saw a *woman* behave so ill, like a cold-blooded heartless

whore as she was; but very handsome for all that. A certain
Susan C. was she called. I never saw her but once, and that
was to induce her but to say two words (which in no degree
compromised herself), and which would have had the effect of
saving a priest or a Lieutenant of Cavalry. She would *not* say
them, and neither N. or myself (the Son of Sir E. N. and a
friend of one of the parties) could prevail upon her to say them,
though both of us used to deal in some sort with Womankind.
At last I managed to quiet the combatants without her talis-
man, and, I believe, to her great disappointment. She was
the d—st b—h that I ever saw, and I have seen a great many.
Though my Clergyman was sure to lose either his life or his
living, he was as warlike as the Bishop of Beauvais, and would
hardly be pacified: but then he was in love, and that is a
martial passion.

37

[Scrawled out by Byron]

38

Somebody asked Schlegel (the Dousterswivel of Madame
de Stael) " whether he did not think *Canova* a great Sculptor? "
" Ah ! " replied the modest Prussian, " did you ever see *my bust*
by *Tiecke*? "

39

At Venice, in the year 1817, an order came from Vienna
for the Archbishop to go in State to Saint Mark's in his Carriage
and four horses, which is much the same as commanding the
Lord Mayor of London to proceed through Temple Bar in his
Barge.

40

When I met Hudson Lowe, the Jailor, at Lord Holland's,
before he sailed for Saint Helena, the discourse turned on the
battle of Waterloo. I asked him whether the dispositions of
Napoleon were those of a great General: he answered dis-
paragingly, " that they were very *simple* ". I had always
thought that a degree of Simplicity was an ingredient of
Greatness.

41

I was much struck with the simplicity of Grattan's manners
in private life: they were odd, but they were natural. Curran

used to take him off bowing to the very ground, and " thanking
God that he had no peculiarities of gesture or appearance ",
in a way irresistibly ludicrous.   And Rogers used to call him
" a Sentimental Harlequin ";   but Rogers back-bites every
body; and Curran, who used to quiz his great friend Godwin
to his very face, would hardly respect a fair mark of mimicry
in another.   To be sure, Curran *was* admirable !   To hear his
description of the examination of an Irish witness, was next to
hearing his own speeches : the latter I never heard, but I have
the former.

42

I have heard that, when Grattan made his first speech in
the English Commons, it was for some minutes doubtful
whether to laugh at or cheer him.   The debût of his predecessor, Flood, had been a complete failure, under nearly
similar circumstances.   But when the ministerial part of our
Senators had watched Pitt (their thermometer) for their cue,
and saw him nod repeatedly his stately nod of approbation,
they took the hint from their huntsman, and broke out into the
most rapturous cheers.   Grattan's speech indeed deserved
them : it was a *chef d'œuvre*.   I did not hear *that* speech of his
(being then at Harrow), but heard most of his others on the same
question ; also that on the war of 1815.   I differed from his
opinion on the latter question, but coincided in the general
admiration of his eloquence.

43

At the Opposition Meeting of the peers in 1812 at Lord
Grenville's, when Ld Grey and he read to us the correspondence
upon Moira's negociation, I sate next to the present Duke of
Grafton.   When it was over, I turned to him, and said, " What
is to be done next? "   " Wake the Duke of Norfolk " (who was
snoring near us) replied he, " I don't think the Negociators
have left anything else for us to do this turn."

44

In the debate, or rather discussion, afterwards in the
House of Lords upon that very question, I sate immediately
behind Lord Moira, who was extremely annoyed at G.'s speech

upon the subject, and while G. was speaking, turned round to me repeatedly, and asked me whether I agreed with him? It was an awkward question to me who had not heard both sides. Moira kept repeating to me, " it was *not so*, it was so and so, etc." I did not know very well what to think, but I sympathized with the acuteness of his feelings upon the subject.

45

Lord Eldon affects an Imitation of two very different Chancellors, Thurlow and Loughborough, and can indulge in an oath now and then. On one of the debates on the Catholic question, when we were either equal or within one (I forget which), I had been sent for in great haste to a Ball, which I quitted, I confess, somewhat reluctantly, to emancipate five Millions of people. I came in late, and did not go immediately into the body of the house, but stood just behind the Woolsack. Eldon turned round, and, catching my eye, immediately said to a peer (who had come to him for a few minutes on the Woolsack, as is the custom of his friends), " Damn them! they'll have it now, by G—d! The vote that is just come in will give it them."

46

When I came of age, some delays on account of some birth and marriage certificates from Cornwall occasioned me not to take my seat for several weeks. When these were over, and I had taken the Oaths, the Chancellor apologized to me for the delay, observing " that these forms were a part of his *duty* ". I begged of him to make no apology, and added (as he certainly had shown no violent hurry) " Your Lordship was exactly like ' Tom Thumb ' (which was then being acted), You did your *duty*, and you did *no more* ".

47

In a certain Capital abroad, the Minister's Secretary (the Minister being then absent) was piqued that I did not call upon him. When I was going away, Mr. W., an acquaintance of mine, applied to him for my passport, which was sent, but at the same time accompanied by a formal note from the Secretary stating " that at *Mr. W.'s request* he had granted, etc.", and in such a manner as appeared to *hint* that it was only to oblige *Mr. W.* that he had given me that which in fact he had no right to refuse to Any-body. I wrote to him the following answer :—" Lord B. presents his Compliments to L., and is extremely obliged to *Mr. W.* for the passport ".

48

There was a Madman of the name of Battersby, that frequented Steevens's and the Prince of Wales's Coffee-houses, about the time when I was leading a loose life about town, before I was of age. One night he came up to some hapless Stranger, whose coat was not to his liking, and said, " Pray, Sir, did the tailor cut your coat in that fashion, or the rats gnaw it? "

49

The following is (I believe) better known. A beau (*dandies* were not then christened) came into the P. of W.'s, and exclaimed, "Waiter, bring me a glass of Madeira Negus with a Jelly, and rub my plate with a Chalotte ". This in a very soft tone of voice. A Lieutenant of the Navy, who sate in the next box, immediately roared out the following rough parody : " Waiter, bring me a glass of d—d stiff Grog, and rub my a—e with a brick-bat."

50

Sotheby is a good man, rhymes well (if not wisely), but is a bore. He seizes you by the button. One night of a route at Mrs. Hope's, he had fastened upon me (something about Agamemnon, or Orestes, or some of his plays), notwithstanding my symptoms of manifest distress (for I was in love, and had just nicked a minute, when neither mothers, nor husbands, nor rivals, nor gossips, were near my then idol, who was beautiful as the Statues of the Gallery where we stood at the time)— Sotheby I say had seized upon me by the button and the heart-strings, and spared neither. W. Spencer, who likes fun, and don't dislike mischief, saw my case, and coming up to us both, took me by the hand, and pathetically bade me farewell : " for," said he, " I see it is all over with you ". Sotheby then went away. " Sic me servavit Apollo."

51

It is singular how soon we lose the impression of what ceases to be *constantly* before us. A year impairs, a lustre obliterates. There is little distinct left without an *effort* of memory : *then* indeed the lights are rekindled for a moment; but who can be sure that Imagination is not the torch-bearer? Let any man try at the end of *ten* years to bring before him the features, or the mind, or the sayings, or the habits, of his best friend, or his *greatest* man (I mean his favourite—his Buona-parte, his this, that or 'tother), and he will be surprized at the extreme confusion of his ideas. I speak confidently on this point, having always past for one who had a good, aye, an excellent memory. I except indeed our recollections of Womankind : there is no forgetting *them* (and be d—d to them) any more than any other remarkable Era, such as " the revolution ", or " the plague ", or " the Invasion ", or " the Comet ", or " the War " of such and such an Epoch—being the favourite dates of Mankind, who have so many *blessings* in their lot, that they never make their Calendars from them, being too common. For instance, you see " the great drought ", " the Thames frozen over ", " the Seven years war broke out ", the E. or F. or S. " Revolution commenced ", " The Lisbon Earthquake ", " the Lima Earthquake ", " The Earthquake of Calabria ", the " Plague of London ", " Ditto of Constantin-ople ", " the Sweating Sickness ", " The Yellow fever of Philadelphia ", etc., etc., etc. ; but you don't see " the abund-ant harvest ", " the fine Summer ", " the long peace ", " the wealthy speculation ", the " wreckless voyage ", recorded so emphatically? By the way, there has been a. *thirty years war*, and a *Seventy years war* : was there ever a *Seventy or a thirty years Peace*? Or was there ever even a *day's Universal* peace, except perhaps in China, where they have found out the miserable happiness of a stationary and unwarlike mediocrity? And is all this, because Nature is niggard or savage? or Mankind un-grateful? Let philosophers decide. I am none.

52

In the year 1814, as Moore and I were going to dine with Lord Grey in P. Square, I pulled out a " Java Gazette " (which

Murray had sent to me), in which there was a controversy on our respective merits as poets. It was amusing enough that we should be proceeding peaceably on the same table, while they were squabbling about us in the Indian Seas (to be sure, the paper was dated six months before), and filling columns with Batavian Criticism. But this is fame, I presume.

53

In general, I do not draw well with literary men : not that I dislike them, but I never know what to say to them after I have praised their last publication. There are several exceptions, to be sure; but then they have either been men of the world, such as Scott, and Moore, etc., or visionaries out of it, such as Shelley, etc. : but your literary every day man and I never went well in company—especially your foreigner, whom I never could abide. Except Giordani, and—and—and—(I really can't name any other) I do not remember a man amongst them, whom I ever wished to see twice, except perhaps Mezzophanti, who is a Monster of Languages, the Briareus of parts of Speech, a walking Polyglott and more, who ought to have existed at the time of the tower of Babel as universal Interpreter. He is indeed a Marvel—unassuming also : I tried him in all the tongues of which I knew a single oath (or adjuration to the Gods against Postboys, Lawyers, Tartars, boatmen, Sailors, pilots, Gondoliers, Muleteers, Camel-drivers, Vetturini, Postmasters, post-horses, post-houses, post-everything), and Egad ! he astounded me even to my English.

54

Three Swedes came to Bologna, knowing no tongue but Swedish. The inhabitants in despair presented them to Mezzophanti. Mezzophanti (though a great Linguist) knew no more Swedish than the Inhabitants. But in two days, by dint of dictionary, he talked with them fluently and freely, so that they were astonished, and every body else, at his acquisition of another tongue in forty eight hours. I had this anecdote first from Me Albrizzi, and afterwards confirmed by *himself*—and he is not a boaster.

55

I sometimes wish that I had studied languages with more attention : those which I know, even the classical (Greek and Latin, in the usual proportion of a sixth form boy), and a smattering of modern Greek, the Armenian and Arabic Alphabets, a few Turkish and Albanian phrases, oaths, or requests, Italian tolerably, Spanish less than tolerably, French to read with ease but speak with difficulty—or rather not at all—all have been acquired by ear or eye, and never by anything like Study. Like " Edie Ochiltree ", " I never dowed to bide a hard turn o' wark in my life ".

To be sure, I set in zealously for the Armenian and Arabic, but I fell in love with some absurd womankind both times, before I had overcome the Characters ; and at Malta and Venice left the profitable Orientalists for—for—(no matter what), notwithstanding that my master, the Padre Pasquale Aucher (for whom, by the way, I compiled the major part of two Armenian and English Grammars), assured me " that the terrestrial Paradise had been certainly in *Armenia* ". I went seeking it—God knows where—did I find it? Umph! Now and then, for a minute or two.

56

Of Actors, Cooke was the most natural, Kemble the most supernatural, Kean a medium between the two, but Mrs. Siddons worth them all put together, of those whom I remember to have seen in England.

57

I have seen Sheridan weep two or three times : it may be that he was maudlin ; but this only renders it more impressive, for who would see—

> " From Marlborough's eyes the tears of dotage flow,
>   And Swift expire a driveller and a show? "

Once I saw him cry at Robins's, the Auctioneer's, after a splendid dinner full of great names and high Spirits. I had the honour of sitting next to Sheridan. The occasion of his tears was some observation or other upon the subject of the sturdiness of the Whigs in resisting Office, and keeping to their principles. Sheridan turned round—" Sir, it is easy for my Lord G., or Earl G., or Marquis B., or Lᵈ H., with thousands upon thousands a year—some of it either *presently* derived or *inherited* in Sinecures or acquisitions from the public money—to boast of their patriotism, and keep aloof from temptation ; but they do not know from what temptations those have kept aloof, who had equal pride—at least equal talents, and not unequal passions, and nevertheless knew not in the course of their lives what it was to have a shilling of their own ". And in saying this he wept.

58

I have more than once heard Sheridan say, that he never " had a shilling of his own " : to be sure, he contrived to extract a good many of other people's.

In 1815, I had occasion to visit my Lawyer in Chancery Lane : he was with Sheridan. After mutual greetings, etc., Sheridan retired first. Before recurring to my own business, I could not help enquiring *that* of S. " Oh " (replied the Attorneo), " the usual thing—to stave off an action from his Wine-Merchant, my Client." " Well " (said I), " and what do you mean to do? " " Nothing at all for the present ", said he : " would you have us proceed against old Sherry? What would be the use of it? " And here he began laughing, and going over Sheridan's good gifts of Conversation. Now, from personal experience, I can vouch that my Attorneo is by no means the tenderest of men, or particularly accessible to any kind of impression out of the Statute or record. And yet Sheridan, in half an hour, had found the way to soften and seduce him in such a manner, that I almost think he would have thrown his Client (an honest man with all the laws and some justice on his side) out of the window, had he come in at the moment. Such was Sheridan ! He could soften an Attorney ! There has been nothing like it since the days of Orpheus.

59

When the Bailiffs (for I have seen most kinds of life) came upon me in 1815, to seize my chattels (being a peer of parliament my person was beyond him), being curious (as is my habit), I first asked him " what Extents elsewhere he had for Government? " upon which he showed me one upon *one house only* for *seventy thousand pounds!* Next I asked him, if he had nothing for Sheridan? " Oh, Sheridan," said he: " aye, I have this " (pulling out a pocket-book, etc.). " But, my L., I have been in Mr. Sheridan's house a twelve-month at a time: a civil gentleman—knows how to deal with *us*, etc., etc., etc." Our own business was then discussed, which was none of the easiest for me at that time. But the Man was civil, and, (what I valued more), communicative. I had met many of his brethren years before in affairs of my friends (commoners, that is), but this was the first (or second) on my own account. A civil Man, feed accordingly: probably he anticipated as much.

60

No man would live his life over again, is an old and true saying, which all can resolve for themselves. At the same time, there are probably *moments* in most men's lives, which they would live over the rest of life to *regain*? Else, why do we live at all? Because Hope recurs to Memory, both false; but—but—but—but—and this *but* drags on till—What? I do not know, and who does? " He that died o' Wednesday." By the way, there is a poor devil to be shot tomorrow here (Ravenna) for murder. He hath eaten half a Turkey for his dinner, besides fruit and pudding; and he refuses to confess? Shall I go to see him exhale? No. And why? Because it is to take place at *Nine*. Now, could I *save* him, or a fly even from the same catastrophe, I would out-match years; but as I cannot, I will not get up earlier to see another man shot, than I would to run the same risk in person. Besides, I have seen more men than one die that death (and other deaths) before to-day.

It is not cruelty which actuates mankind, but excitement, on such occasions; at least, I suppose so. It is detestable to *take* life in that way, unless it be to preserve two lives.

61

Old Edgeworth, the fourth or fifth Mrs. Edgeworth, and *the* Miss Edgeworth were in London, 1813. Miss Edgeworth liked, Mrs. Edgeworth not disliked, old Edgeworth a bore—

the worst of bores—a boisterous Bore. I met them in society
once at a breakfast of Sir H. D.'s. Old Edgeworth came in
late, boasting that he had given " Dr. Parr a dressing the night
before " (no such easy matter by the way). I thought *her*
pleasant. They all abused Anna Seward's memory.

62

When on the road, they heard of *her* brother's, and *his*
Son's, death. What was to be done? Their *London* Apparel
was all ordered and made ! So they sunk his death for the six
weeks of their Sojourn, and went into mourning on their way
back to Ireland. *Fact!*

63

While the Colony were in London, there was a book, with
a Subscription for the " recall of Mrs. Siddons to the Stage ",
going about for signatures. Moore moved for a similar subscription for the " recall of *Mr. Edgeworth to Ireland!* "

64

Sir Humphrey Davy told me, that the Scene of the French
Valet and Irish postboy in " Ennui " was taken from *his* verbal
description to the Edgeworths in Edgeworthtown of a similar
fact on the road occurring to himself. So much the better—
being *life*.

65

When I was fifteen years of age, it happened that in a
Cavern in Derbyshire I had to cross in a boat (in which two
people only could lie down) a stream which flows under a rock,
with the rock so close upon the water, as to admit the boat only
to be pushed on by a ferry-man (a sort of Charon), who wades
at the stern stooping all the time. The Companion of my
transit was M. A. C[haworth], with whom I had been long in
love, and never told it, though *she* had discovered it without. I
recollect my sensations, but cannot describe them—and it is as
well.

We were a party—a Mr. W., two Miss W.'s, Mr. and Mrs.
Cl—ke, Miss M., and *my* M. A. C. Alas ! why do I say *My*?
Our Union would have healed feuds, in which blood had been
shed by our fathers ; it would have joined lands, broad and rich ;

it would have joined at least *one* heart, and two persons not ill-matched in years (she is two years my elder) ; and—and—and —what has been the result? *She* has married a man older than herself, been wretched, and separated. I have married, and am separated : and yet *We* are *not* united.

66

One of my notions, different from those of my contemporaries, is, that the present is not a high age of English Poetry : there are *more* poets (soi-disant) than ever there were, and proportionally *less* poetry.

This *thesis* I have maintained for some years, but, strange to say, it meeteth not with favour from my brethren of the Shell. Even Moore shakes his head, and firmly believes that it is the grand Era of British Poesy.

67

When I belonged to the D[rury] L[ane] Committee, and was one of the S. C. of Management, the number of plays upon the shelves were about *five* hundred. Conceiving that amongst these there must be *some* of merit, in person and by proxy I caused an investigation. I do not think that, of those which I saw, there was one which could be conscientiously tolerated. There never were such things as most of them.

Mathurin [1] was very kindly recommended to me by Walter Scott, to whom I had recourse ; firstly, in the hope that he would do something for us himself; and secondly, in my despair, that he would point out to us any young (or old) writer of promise. Mathurin sent his Bertram, and a letter *without* his address, so that at first I could give him no answer. When I at last hit upon his residence, I sent him a favourable answer, and something more substantial. His play succeeded, but I was at that time absent from England.

I tried Coleridge, too ; but he had nothing feasible in hand at the time. Mr. Sotheby obligingly offered *all* his tragedies, and I pledged myself; and, notwithstanding many squabbles with my Committe[e]d Brethren, did get " Ivan " accepted, read, and the parts distributed. But lo ! in the very heart of

---

[1] The Rev. Charles Robert Maturin, author of *Bertram, or The Castle of Aldobrand, Manuel*, etc., etc. : a dramatist admired by Walter Scott.

the matter, upon some *tepid*-ness on the part of Kean, or warmth on that of the Authour, Sotheby withdrew his play.

Sir J. B. Burgess did also present four tragedies and a farce, and I moved Green-room and S. Committee; but they would not.

Then the Scenes I had to go through! The authours, and the authoresses, the Milliners, the wild Irishmen, the people from Brighton, from Blackwall, from Chatham, from Cheltenham, from Dublin, from Dundee, who came in upon me! To all of whom it was proper to give a civil answer, and a hearing, and a reading. Mrs. Glover's father, an Irish dancing-Master of Sixty years, called upon me to request to play "*Archer*", drest in silk stockings on a frosty morning, to show his legs (which were certainly good and Irish for his age, and had been still better). Miss Emma Somebody, with a play entitled the "Bandit of Bohemia", or some such title or production. Mr. O'Higgins, then resident at Richmond, with an Irish tragedy, in which the unities could not fail to be observed, for the protagonist was chained by the leg to a pillar during the chief part of the performance. He was a wild man, of a salvage [*sic*] appearance; and the difficulty of *not* laughing at him was only to be got over by reflecting upon the probable consequences of such cachinnation.

As I am really a civil and polite person, and *do* hate giving pain, when it can be avoided, I sent them up to Douglas Kinnaird, who is a man of business, and sufficiently ready with a negative, and left them to settle with him. And, as at the beginning of next year, I went abroad, I have since been little aware of the progress of the theatres.

68

Players are said to be an impracticable people. They are so. But I managed to steer clear of any disputes with them, and, excepting one debate with the Elder Byrne about Miss Smith's Pas de (Something—I forget the technicals), I do not remember any litigation of my own. I used to protect Miss Smith, because she was like Lady Jane Harley in the face; and likenesses go a great way with me. Indeed, in general, I left such things to my more bustling colleagues, who used to reprove me seriously for not being able to take such things in hand without buffooning with the Histrions, and throwing things into confusion by treating light matters with levity.

69

Then the Committee!—then the Sub-Committee! We were but few, and never agreed! There was Peter Moore who contradicted Kinnaird, and Kinnaird who contradicted everybody: then our two managers, Rae and Dibdin, and our Secretary, Ward! And yet we were all very zealous and in earnest to do good, and so forth. Hobhouse furnished us with prologues to our revived Old English plays, but was not pleased with me for complimenting him as " the *Upton* " of our theatre (Mr. Upton is or was the poet who writes the songs for Astley's), and almost gave up prologuizing in consequence.

70

In the Pantomime of 1815–16, there was a Representation of the Masquerade of 1814, given by " us Youth " of Watier's Club to Wellington and Co. Douglas Kinnaird, and one or two others with myself, put on Masques, and went *on* the Stage amongst the " οἱ πολλοί ", to see the effect of a theatre from the Stage. It is very grand. Douglas danced among the figuranti, too; and they were puzzled to find out who we were, as being more than their number. It was odd enough that D. K. and I should have been both at the *real* Masquerade, and afterwards in the Mimic one of the same on the stage of D. L. Theatre.

71

When I was a youth, I was reckoned a good actor. Besides " Harrow Speeches " (in which I shone) I enacted " Penruddock " in the " Wheel of Fortune ", and " Tristram Fickle " in Allingham's farce of " the Weathercock ", for three nights (the duration of our compact), in some private theatricals at Southwell in 1806, with great applause. The occasional prologue for our volunteer play was also of my composition. The other performers were young ladies and gentlemen of the neighbourhood; and the whole went off with great effect upon our good-natured audience.

72

When I first went up to College, it was a new and a heavy
hearted scene for me. Firstly, I so much disliked leaving
Harrow, that, though it was time (I being seventeen), it
broke my very rest for the last quarter with counting the days
that remained. I always *hated* Harrow till the last year and
half, but then I liked it. Secondly, I wished to go to Oxford
and not to Cambridge. Thirdly, I was so completely alone in
this new world, that it half broke my Spirits. My companions
were not unsocial, but the contrary—lively, hospitable, of rank,
and fortune, and gay far beyond my gaiety. I mingled with,
and dined and supped, etc., with them; but, I know not how,
it was one of the deadliest and heaviest feelings of my life to
feel that I was no longer a boy. From that moment I began to
grow old in my own esteem; and in my esteem age is not
estimable. I took my gradations in the vices with great
promptitude, but they were not to my taste; for my early
passions, though violent in the extreme, were concentrated,
and hated division or spreading abroad. I could have left or
lost the world with or for that which I loved; but, though my
temperament was naturally burning, I could not share in the
common place libertinism of the place and time without disgust. And yet this very disgust, and my heart thrown back
upon itself, threw me into excesses perhaps more fatal than those
from which I shrunk, as fixing upon one (at a time) the passions,
which, spread amongst many, would have hurt only myself.

73

People have wondered at the Melancholy which runs
through my writings. Others have wondered at my personal
gaiety; but I recollect once, after an hour, in which I had
been sincerely and particularly gay, and rather brilliant, in
company, my wife replying to me when I said (upon her remarking my high spirits) " and yet, Bell, I have been called
and mis-called Melancholy—you must have seen how falsely,
frequently ". " No, B.," (she answered) " it is not so : at *heart*
you are the most melancholy of mankind, and often when
apparently gayest."

74

If I could explain at length the *real* causes which have contributed to increase this perhaps *natural* temperament of mine, this Melancholy which hath made me a bye-word, nobody would wonder; but this is impossible without doing much mischief. I do not know what other men's lives have been, but I cannot conceive anything more strange than some of the earlier parts of mine. I have written my memoirs, but omitted *all* the really *consequential* and *important* parts, from deference to the dead, to the living, and to those who must be both.

75

I sometimes think that I should have written the *whole* as a *esson*, but it might have proved a *lesson* to be *learnt* rather than avoided; for passion is a whirlpool, which is not to be viewed nearly without attraction from its Vortex.

76

I must not go on with these reflections, or I shall be letting out some secret or other to paralyze posterity.

77

One night, Scrope Davies at a gaming house (before I was of age), being tipsy as he usually was at the Midnight hour, and having lost monies, was in vain intreated by his friends, one degree less intoxicated than himself, to come or go home. In despair, he was left to himself, and to the demons of the dice-box. Next day, being visited, about two of the Clock, by some friends just risen with a severe headache and empty pockets (who had left him losing at four or five in the morning), he was found in a sound sleep, without a night-cap, and not particularly encumbered with bed-cloathes: a Chamber-pot stood by his bed-side, *brim-full* of —— *Bank Notes!* all won, God knows how, and crammed, Scrope knew not where; but *there* they were, all good legitimate notes, and to the amount of some thousand pounds.

78

At Brighthelmstone (I love orthography at length), in the year 1808, Hobhouse, Scrope Davies, Major Cooper, and myself, having dined together with Lord Delvin, Count (I forget the french Emigrant nomenclature) and others, did about the middle of the night (we *four*) proceed to a house of Gambling, being then *amongst us* possest of about *twenty guineas* of ready cash, with which we had to maintain as many of your whorson horses and servants, besides house-hold and whore-hold expenditure. We had, I say, twenty guineas or so, and we lost them, returning home in bad humour. Cooper went home. Scrope and Hobhouse and I (it being high Summer), did firstly strip and plunge into the Sea, whence, after half an hour's swimming of those of us (Scrope and I) who could swim, we emerged in our dressing-gowns to discuss a bottle or two of Champaigne and Hock (according to choice) at our quarters. In course of this discussion, words arose; Scrope seized H. by the throat; H. seized a knife in self-defence, and stabbed Scrope in the shoulder to avoid being throttled. Scrope fell bathed in blood and wine—for the *bottle* fell with him, being infinitely intoxicated with Gaming, Sea-bathing at two in the morning, and Supplementary Champaigne. The skirmish had past before I had time or thought to interfere. Of course I lectured against gambling—

" Pugnare Thracum est ",

and then examined Scrope's wound, which proved to be a gash long and broad, but not deep nor dangerous. Scrope was furious : first he wanted to fight, then to go away in a post-chaise, and then to *shoot* himself, which latter intention I offered to forward, provided that he did not use *my pistols*, which, in case of suicide, would become a deo-dand to the King. At length, with many oaths and some difficulty, he was gotten to bed. In the morning, Cool reflection and a Surgeon came, and, by dint of loss of blood, and sticking plaister, the quarrel (which Scrope had begun), was healed as well as the wound, and we were all friends as for years before and after.

79

My first dash into poetry was as early as 1800. It was the ebullition of a passion for my first Cousin Margaret Parker (daughter and grand-daughter of the two Admirals Parker), one of the most beautiful of evanescent beings. I have long forgotten the verses, but it would be difficult for me to forget her. Her dark eyes! her long eye-lashes! her completely Greek cast of face and figure! I was then about twelve—She rather older, perhaps a year. She died about a year or two afterwards, in consequence of a fall which injured her spine and induced consumption. Her Sister, Augusta (by some thought still more beautiful), died of the same malady; and it was indeed in attending her that Margaret met with the accident, which occasioned her own death. My Sister told me that, when she went to see her shortly before her death, upon accidentally mentioning my name, Margaret coloured through the paleness of mortality to the eyes, to the great astonishment of my Sister, who (residing with her Grandmother, Lady Holderness) saw at that time but little of me for family reasons, knew nothing of our attachment, nor could conceive why my name should affect her at such a time. I knew nothing of her illness (being at Harrow and in the country), till she was gone.

Some years after, I made an attempt at an Elegy. A very dull one. I do not recollect scarcely any thing equal to the *transparent* beauty of my cousin, or to the sweetness of her temper, during the short period of our intimacy. She looked as if she had been made out of a rainbow—all beauty and peace.

My passion had its usual effects upon me: I could not sleep, could not eat; I could not rest; and although I had reason to know that she loved me, it was the torture of my life to think of the time which must elapse before we could meet again—being usually about *twelve hours* of separation! But I was a fool then, and am not much wiser now.

80

My passions were developed very early—so early, that few would believe me, if I were to state the period, and the facts which accompanied it. Perhaps this was one of the reasons which caused the anticipated melancholy of my thoughts—having anticipated life.

My earlier poems are the thoughts of one at least ten years older than the age at which they were written: I don't mean for their solidity, but their Experience. The two first Cantos of Ce Hd were completed at twenty two, and they are written as if by a man older than I shall probably ever be.

[81 omitted by Byron]

82

Upon Parnassus, going to the fountain of Delphi (Castri), in 1809, I saw a flight of twelve Eagles (Hobhouse says they are Vultures—at least in conversation), and I seized the Omen. On the day before, I composed the lines to Parnassus (in Childe Harold), and, on beholding the birds, had a hope that Apollo had accepted my homage. I have at least had the name and fame of a Poet during the poetical period of life (from twenty to thirty) : whether it will last is another matter ; but I *have been* a votary of the Deity and the place, and am grateful for what he has done in my behalf, leaving the future in his hands as I left the past.

83

Like Sylla, I have always believed that all things depend upon Fortune, and nothing upon ourselves. I am not aware of any one thought or action worthy of being called good to myself or others, which is not to be attributed to the Good Goddess, Fortune !

84

Two or three years ago, I thought of going to one of the Americas, English or Spanish. But the accounts sent from England, in consequence of my enquiries, discouraged me. After all, I believe most countries, properly balanced, are equal to *a Stranger* (by no means to the *native*, though). I remembered General Ludlow's domal inscription :—

" Omne solum forti patria "—

And sate down free in a country of Slavery for many centuries. But there is *no* freedom, even for *Masters*, in the midst of slaves : it makes my blood boil to see the thing. I sometimes wish that I was the Owner of Africa, to do at once, what Wilberforce will do in time, viz.—sweep Slavery from her desarts, and look on upon the first dance of their Freedom.

As to *political* slavery—so general—it is man's own fault ; if they *will* be slaves, let them ! Yet it is but " a word and a blow ". See how England formerly, France, Spain, Portugal,

America, Switzerland, freed themselves! There is no one instance of a *long* contest, in which *men* did not triumph over Systems. If Tyranny misses her *first* spring, she is cowardly as the tiger, and retires to be hunted.

85

An Italian (the younger Count Ruota), writing from Ravenna to his friend at Rome in 1820, says of me, by way of compliment, " that in society no one would take me for an Englishman, though he believes that I *am* English at bottom—my manners were so different ". This he meant as a grand eulogy, and I accept it as such. The letter was shown to me this year by the Correspondent, Count P. G., or by his Sister.

86

I have been a reviewer. In " the Monthly Review " I wrote some articles, which were inserted. This was in the latter part of 1811. In 1807, in a Magazine called " Monthly Literary Recreations ", I reviewed Wordsworth's trash of that time. Excepting these, I cannot accuse myself of anonymous Criticism (that I recollect), though I have been *offered* more than one review in our principal Journals.

87

Till I was eighteen years old (odd as it may seem), I had never read a review. But, while at Harrow, my general information was so great on modern topics, as to induce a suspicion that I could only collect so much information from *reviews*, because I was never *seen* reading, but always idle and in mischief, or at play. The truth is that I read eating, read in bed, read when no one else reads; and had read all sorts of reading since I was five years old, and yet never *met* with a review, which is the only reason that I know of why I should not have read them. But it is true; for I remember when Hunter and Curzon, in 1804, told me this opinion at Harrow, I made them laugh by my ludicrous astonishment in asking them, " *what is* a review? " To be sure, they were then less common. In three years more, I was better acquainted with that same, but the first I ever read was in 1806–7.

88

At School, I was (as I have said) remarked for the extent and readiness of my *general* information; but in all other respects idle; capable of great sudden exertions (such as thirty or forty Greek Hexameters—of course with such prosody as it pleased God), but of few continuous drudgeries. My qualities were much more oratorical and martial, than poetical; and Dr. D., my grand patron (our head-master), had a great notion that I should turn out an Orator, from my fluency, my turbulence, my voice, my copiousness of declamation, and my action. I remember that my first declamation astonished him into some unwonted (for he was economical of such), and sudden compliments, before the declaimers at our first rehearsal. My first Harrow verses (that is, English as exercises), a translation of a chorus from the Prometheus of Aeschylus, were received by him but cooly: no one had the least notion that I should subside into poesy.

89

Peel, the Orator and Statesman ("that was, or is, or is to be"), was my form fellow, and we were both at the top of our remove (a public School Phrase). We were on good terms, but his brother was my intimate friend. There were always great hopes of Peel amongst us all—Masters and Scholars, and he has not disappointed them. As a Scholar, he was greatly my superior: as a declaimer, and Actor, I was reckoned at least his equal. As a school boy *out* of school, I was always *in* scrapes, and *he never*; and *in School* he *always* knew his lesson, and I rarely; but when I knew it, I knew it nearly as well. In general information, history, etc., etc., I think I was *his* Superior, as also of most boys of my standing.

89 [twice]

The prodigy of our School days was George Sinclair (son of Sir John): he made exercises for half the School (*literally*), verses at will, and themes without it. When in the Shell, he made exercises for his Uncle, Dudley Macdonald (a dunce who could only play upon the flute), in the sixth. He was a friend of mine, and in the same remove, and used at times to beg me to let him do my exercise—a request always most readily accorded, upon a pinch, or when I wanted to do something else, which was usually once an hour. On the other hand, he was pacific, and I savage; so I fought for him, or thrashed others for him, or thrashed himself to make him thrash others, whom it was necessary, as a point of honour and stature, that he should so chastise. Or, we talked politics, for he was a great politician, and were very good friends. I have some of his letters, written to me from School, still.

90

Clayton was another School Monster of learning, and talent, and hope; but what has become of him I do not know: he was certainly a Genius.

91

My School friendships were with *me passions* (for I was always violent), but I do not know that there is one which has endured (to be sure, some have been cut short by death) till now. That with Lord Clare began one of the earliest and lasted longest, being only interrupted by distance, that I know of. I never hear the word " *Clare* " without a beating of the heart even *now*, and I write it with the feelings of 1803-4-5 ad infinitum.

92

In 1812, at Middelton (Lord Jersey's), amongst a goodly company of Lords, Ladies, and wits, etc., there was poor old Vice Leach, the lawyer, attempting to play off the fine gentleman. His first exhibition—an attempt on horseback, I think, to escort the women—God knows where, in the month of November, ended in a fit of the Lumbago—as Lord Ogleby says, " a grievous enemy to Gallantry and address "—and if he could but have heard Lady Jersey quizzing him (as I did) next day for the *cause* of his malady, I don't think that he would have turned a " Squire of dames " in a hurry again. He seemed to me the greatest fool (in that line) I ever saw. This was the last I saw of old Vice Leach, except in town, where he was creeping into assemblies, and trying to look young and gentlemanly.

93

Erskine too! Erskine was there—good, but intolerable. He jested, he talked, he did every thing admirably, but then he *would* be applauded for the same thing twice over : he would read his own verses, his own paragraphs, and tell his own story, again and again—and then " the trial by Jury !!! " I almost wished it abolished, for I sate next him at dinner. As I had read his published speeches, there was no occasion to repeat them to me.

Chester (the fox hunter), surnamed " *Cheeks Chester* ", and I sweated the Claret, being the only two who did so. Cheeks, who loves his bottle, and had no notion of meeting with a " bon vivant " in a scribbler, in making my eulogy to somebody one evening, summed it up in—" By G—d, he *drinks like a Man!* "

94

Nobody drank, however, but Cheeks and I. To be sure, there was little occasion, for we swept off what was on the table (a most splendid board, as may be supposed, at Jersey's) very sufficiently. However, we carried our liquor discreetly, like " the Baron of Bradwardine ".

95

If I had to live over again, I do not know what I would change in my life, unless it were *for not to have lived at all*. All history and experience, and the rest, teaches us that the good and evil are pretty equally balanced in this existence, and that what is most to be desired is an easy passage out of it.

What can it give us but *years*? and those have little of good but their ending.

96

Of the Immortality of the Soul, it appears to me that there can be little doubt, if we attend for a moment to the action of Mind. It is in perpetual activity. I used to doubt of it, but reflection has taught me better. It acts also so very independent of body : in dreams for instance incoherently and madly, I grant you ; but still it is *Mind*, and much more *Mind* than when we are awake. Now, that *this* should not act *separately*, as well as jointly, who can pronounce? The Stoics, Epictetus and Marcus Aurelius, call the present state " a Soul which drags a Carcase " : a heavy chain, to be sure ; but all chains, being material, may be shaken off.

How far our future life will be individual, or, rather, how far it will at all resemble our *present* existence, is another question; but that the *Mind* is *eternal*, seems as probable as that the body is not so. Of course, I have ventured upon the question without recurring to Revelation, which, however, is at least as rational a solution of it as any other.

A *material* resurrection seems strange, and even absurd, except for purposes of punishment; and all punishment, which is to *revenge* rather than *correct*, must be *morally wrong*. And *when* the *World is at an end*, what moral or warning purpose *can* eternal tortures answer? Human passions have probably disfigured the divine doctrines here, but the whole thing is inscrutable. It is useless to tell me *not* to *reason*, but to *believe*. You might as well tell a man not to wake but *sleep*. And then to *bully* with torments! and all that! I cannot help thinking that the *menace* of Hell makes as many devils, as the severe penal codes of inhuman humanity make villains.

Man is born *passionate* of body, but with an innate though secret tendency to the love of Good in his Mainspring of Mind. But God help us all! It is at present a sad jar of atoms.

97

Matter is eternal, always changing, but reproduced, and, as far as we can comprehend Eternity, Eternal; and why not *Mind*? Why should not the Mind act with and upon the Universe? as portions of it act upon and with the congregated dust called Mankind? See, how one man acts upon himself and others, or upon multitudes? The same Agency, in a higher and purer degree, may act upon the Stars, etc., ad infinitum.

98

I have often been inclined to Materialism in philosophy but could never bear its introduction into *Christianity*, which appears to me essentially founded upon the *Soul*. For this reason, Priestley's Christian Materialism always struck me as deadly. Believe the resurrection of the body, if you will, but *not without* a *Soul*. The devil's in it, if, after having had a Soul (as surely the *Mind*, or whatever you call it, *is*) in this world, we must part with it in the next, even for an Immortal Materiality. I own my partiality for *Spirit*.

99

I am always most religious upon a sun-shiny day; as if there was some association between an internal approach to greater light and purity, and the kindler of this dark lanthorn of our eternal existence.

100

The Night is also a religious concern; and even more so, when I viewed the Moon and Stars through Herschell's telescope, and saw that they were worlds.

101

If, according to some speculations, you could prove the World many thousand years older than the Mosaic Chronology, or if you could knock up Adam and Eve and the Apple and Serpent, still what is to be put up in their stead? or how is the difficulty removed? Things must have had a beginning, and what matters it *when* or *how*?

I sometimes think that *Man* may be the relic of some higher material being, wrecked in a former world, and degenerated in the hardships and struggle through Chaos into Conformity— or something like it; as we see Laplanders, Esquimaux, etc., inferior in the present state, as the Elements become more inexorable. But even then this higher pre-Adamite supposititious Creation must have had an Origin and a *Creator*; for a *Creator* is a more natural imagination than a fortuitous concourse of atoms. All things remount to a fountain, though they may flow to an Ocean.

102

What a strange thing is the propagation of life! A bubble of Seed which may be spilt in a whore's lap—or in the orgasm of a voluptuous dream—might (for aught we know) have formed a Caesar or a Buonaparte: there is nothing remarkable recorded of their Sires, that I know of.

103

Lord Kames has said (if I misquote not), " that a power to call up agreeable ideas at will would be something greater for mortals than all the boons of a fairy tale ".

I have found increasing upon me (without sufficient cause at times) the depression of Spirits (with few intervals), which I have some reason to believe constitutional or inherited.

104

Plutarch says, in his life of Lysander, that Aristotle observes, " that in general great Geniuses are of a melancholy turn, and instances Socrates, Plato, and Hercules (or Heracleitus), as examples, and Lysander, though not *while* young, yet as inclined to it when approaching towards age ". Whether I am a Genius or not, I have been called such by my friends as well as enemies, and in more countries and languages than one, and also within a no very long period of existence. Of my Genius, I can say nothing, but of my melancholy, that it is " increasing and ought to be diminished "—but how?

105

I take it that most men are so at bottom, but that it is only remarked in the remarkable. The Duchesse de Broglie, in reply to a remark of mine on the errors of clever people, said, " that they were not *worse* than others, only being more in view, more noted, especially in all that could reduce them to the rest, or raise the rest to them ". In 1816, this was.

106

In fact (I suppose that), if the follies of fools were all set down like those of the wise, the wise (who seem at present only a better sort of fools), would appear almost intelligent.

107

I have met George Colman occasionally, and thought him extremely pleasant and convivial. Sheridan's humour, or rather wit, was always saturnine, and sometimes savage : he never laughed (at least that *I* saw, and I watched him), but Colman did. I have got very drunk with them both ; but, if I had to *choose*, and could not have both at a time, I should say, " let me begin the evening with Sheridan, and finish it with Colman ". Sheridan for dinner—Colman for Supper. Sheridan for Claret or port ; but Colman for every thing, from the Madeira and Champaigne at dinner—the Claret with a

layer of *port* between the Glasses—up to the Punch of the Night,
and down to the Grog or Gin and water of day-break. All
these I have threaded with both the same. Sheridan was a
Grenadier Company of Life-Guards, but Colman a whole
regiment—of *light Infantry*, to be sure, but still a *regiment*.

108

Alcibiades is said to have been " successful in all his
battles "; but *what* battles? Name them! If you mention
Caesar, or Annibal, or Napoleon, you at once rush upon
Pharsalia, Munda, Alesia, Cannae, Thrasimene, Trebia, Lodi,
Marengo, Jena, Austerlitz, Friedland, Wagram, Moskwa;
but it is less easy to pitch upon the victories of Alcibiades,
though they may be named too—though not so readily as the
Leuctra and Mantinea of Epaminondas, the Marathon of
Miltiades, the Salamis of Themistocles, and the Thermopylae
of Leonidas.

Yet upon the whole it may be doubted, whether there be a
name of Antiquity, which comes down with such a general
charm as that of *Alcibiades*. *Why?* I cannot answer: who can?

109

The vanity of Victories is considerable. Of all who fell at
Waterloo or Trafalgar, ask any man in company to *name you
ten off hand*: they will stick at Nelson; the other will survive
himself. *Nelson was* a hero: the other is a mere Corporal,
dividing with Prussians and Spaniards the luck, which he
never deserved. He even—but I hate the fool, and will be
silent.

110

The Miscreant Wellington is the Cub of Fortune, but she
will never lick him into shape: if he lives, he will be beaten—
that's certain. Victory was never before wasted upon such an
unprofitable soil, as this dunghill of Tyranny, whence nothing
springs but Viper's eggs.

111

I remember seeing Blucher in the London Assemblies, and
never saw anything of his age less venerable. With the voice
and manners of a recruiting Sergeant, he pretended to the

honours of a hero; just as if a stone could be worshipped, because a Man had stumbled over it.

112

There is nothing left for Mankind but a Republic, and I think that there are hopes of such. The two Americas (South and North) have it; Spain and Portugal approach it; all thirst for it. Oh Washington!

113

Pisa, Novr 5th 1821

" There is a strange coincidence sometimes in the little things of this world, Sancho ", says Sterne in a letter (if I mistake not) ; and so I have often found it.

Page 128, article 91, of this collection of scattered things, I had alluded to my friend Lord Clare in terms such as my feelings suggested. About a week or two afterwards, I met him on the road between Imola and Bologna, after not having met for seven or eight years. He was abroad in 1814, and came home just as I set out in 1816.

This meeting annihilated for a moment all the years between the present time and the days of *Harrow*. It was a new and inexplicable feeling, like rising from the grave, to me. Clare, too, was much agitated—*more* in appearance than even myself; for I could feel his heart beat to his fingers' ends, unless, indeed, it was the pulse of my own which made me think so. He told me that I should find a note from him, left at Bologna. I did. We were obliged to part for our different journeys—he for Rome, I for Pisa ; but with the promise to meet again in Spring. We were but five minutes together, and in the public road ; but I hardly recollect an hour of my existence which could be weighed against them. He had heard that I was coming on, and had left his letter for me at B., because the people with whom he was travelling could not wait longer.

Of all I have ever known, he has always been the least altered in every thing from the excellent qualities and kind affections which attached me to him so strongly at School. I should hardly have thought it possible for Society (or the World as it is called), to leave a being with so little of the leaven of bad passions. I do not speak from personal experience only, but from all I have ever heard of him from others during absence and distance.

114

I met with Rogers at Bologna : staid a day there, crossed the Appennines with him. He remained at Florence ; I went on to Pisa—8bre 29, 30th etc., 1821.

115

I re-visited the Florence Gallery, etc. My former impressions were confirmed ; but there were too many visitors there, to allow me to *feel* any thing properly. When we were (about thirty or forty) all stuffed into the Cabinet of Gems, and knick-knackeries, in a corner of one of the Galleries, I told R. that it " felt like being in the Watch-house ". I left him to make his obeisances to some of his acquaintances, and strolled on alone—the only few minutes I could snatch of any feeling for the works around me. I do not mean to apply this to a *tête à tête* scrutiny with Rogers, who has an excellent taste and deep feeling for the Arts (indeed much more of both than I can possess ; for of the *former* I have not much) ; but to the crowd of jostling starers and travelling talkers around me.

I heard one bold Briton declare to the woman on his arm, looking at the Venus of Titian, " Well, now, this is really very fine indeed ",—an observation, which, like that of the landlord in Joseph Andrews " on the certainty of death ", was (as the landlord's wife observed), " extremely true ".

In the Pitti palace, I did not omit Goldsmith's prescription for a Connoisseur, viz : " that the pictures would have been better, if the painter had taken more pains, and to praise the works of Pietro Perugino ".

116

I have lately been reading Fielding over again. They talk of Radicalism, Jacobinism, etc., in England (I am told), but they should turn over the pages of " Jonathan Wild the Great ". The inequality of conditions, and the littleness of the great, were never set forth in stronger terms ; and his contempt for Conquerors and the like is such, that, had he lived *now*, he would have been denounced in " the Courier " as the grand

Mouth-piece and Factionary of the revolutionists. And yet I never recollect to have heard this turn of Fielding's mind noticed, though it is obvious in every page.

117

The following dialogue passed between me and a very pretty peasant Girl (Rosa Benini, married to Domenico Ovioli, or Oviuoli, the Vetturino) at Ravenna.

Rosa. " *What* is the Pope? "

I. " Don't *you* know? "

Rosa. " No, I don't know. What or who is he? Is he a *Saint*? "

I. " He is an old man."

Rosa. " What nonsense to make such a fuss about an old man. Have you ever seen him? "

I. " Yes, at Rome."

Rosa. " You English don't obey the Pope ? "

I. " No, we don't; but you do."

Rosa. " I don't know what I believe, but the priests talk about him. I am sure I did not know what he was."

This dialogue I have translated nearly verbatim, and I don't think that I have either added to or taken away from it. The speaker was under eighteen, and an old acquaintance of mine. It struck me as odd that I should have to instruct her *who* the Pope was: I think they might have found it out without me by this time. The fact is indisputable, and occurred but a few weeks ago, before I left Ravenna.

Pisa, Novr 6th 1821

118

1

Oh! talk not to me of a name great in story
The days of our Youth are the days of our Glory,
And the myrtle and ivy of sweet two and twenty
Are worth all your laurels though ever so plenty.

2

What are garlands and crowns to the brow that is wrinkled?
'Tis but as a dead flower with May-dew besprinkled:
Then away with all such from the head that is hoary,
What care I for the wreaths that can *only* give Glory?

3

Oh! Fame! if I e'er took delight in thy praises,
'Twas less for the sake of thy high-sounding phrases,
Than to see the bright eyes of the dear One discover
She thought that I was not unworthy to love her.

4

There chiefly I sought thee, *there* only I found thee;
Her Glance was the best of the rays that surround thee,
When it sparkled o'er aught that was bright in my story,
I knew it was love, and I felt it was Glory.

I composed these stanzas (except the fourth added now) a few days ago, on the road from Florence to Pisa.

Pisa, Novr 6th 1821

119

My daughter Ada, on her recent birthday the other day (the 10th of December 1821), completed her sixth year. Since she was a Month old, or rather better, I have not seen her. But I hear that she is a fine child, with a violent temper.

I have been thinking of an odd circumstance. My daughter, my wife, my half sister, my mother, my sister's mother, my natural daughter, and myself, are or were all *only* children. My sister's Mother (Lady Conyers) had only my half *sister* by that second marriage (herself too an only child), and my father had only me (an only child) by his second marriage with my Mother (an only child too). Such a complication of *only* children, all tending to *one family*, is singular enough, and looks like fatality almost. But the fiercest Animals have the rarest numbers in their litters, as Lions, tigers, and even Elephants which are mild in comparison.

120

May 18th 1822

I have not taken up this sort of Journal for many months: shall I continue it? " Chi lo sa? "

I have written little this year, but a good deal last (1821). *Five* plays in all (two yet unpublished), some Cantos, etc. I have begun one or two things since, but under some discouragement, or rather indignation at the brutality of the attacks, which

I hear (for I have seen but few of them) have been multiplied in every direction against me and my recent writings. But the English dishonour themselves more than me by such conduct. It is strange, but the Germans say that I am more popular in Germany by far than in England, and I have heard the Americans say as much of America. The French, too, have printed a considerable number of translations—in prose! with good success; but *their* predilection (if it exists) depends, I suspect, upon their belief that I have no great passion for England or the English. It would be singular if I had; however, I wish them no harm.

121[1]

TO THOMAS MOORE   *May 14, 1821*

If any part of the letter to Bowles has (unintentionally, as far as I remember the contents) vexed you, you are fully avenged; for I see by an Italian paper that, notwithstanding all my remonstrances through all my friends (and yourself among the rest), the managers persisted in attempting the tragedy,[2] and that it has been " unanimously hissed!! " This is the consolatory phrase of the Milan paper, (which detests me cordially, and abuses me, on all occasions, as a Liberal,) with the addition, that *I* " brought the play out " of my own good will.

All this is vexatious enough, and seems a sort of dramatic Calvinism—predestined damnation, without a sinner's own fault. I took all the pains poor mortal could to prevent this inevitable catastrophe—partly by appeals of all kinds, up to the Lord Chamberlain, and partly to the fellows themselves. But, as remonstrance was vain, complaint is useless. I do not understand it—for Murray's letter of the 24th, and all his preceding ones, gave me the strongest hopes that there would be no representation. As yet, I know nothing but the fact, which I presume to be true, as the date is Paris, and the 30th.

[1] Here the manuscript ends.
[2] *Marino Faliero*, in spite of an injunction obtained by John Murray's solicitor against the actor Robert William Elliston, was " dragged on to the stage " at the Surrey Theatre during Easter 1821. It proved less unsuccessful there than first reports suggested.

They must have been in a *hell* of a hurry for this damnation, since I did not even know that it was published; and, without its being first published, the histrions could not have got hold of it. Any one might have seen, at a glance, that it was utterly impracticable for the stage; and this little accident will by no means enhance its merit in the closet.

Well, patience is a virtue, and, I suppose, practice will make it perfect. Since last year (spring, that is) I have lost a lawsuit, of great importance, on Rochdale collieries—have occasioned a divorce—have had my poesy disparaged by Murray and the critics—my fortune refused to be placed on an advantageous settlement (in Ireland) by the trustees;—my life threatened last month (they put about a paper here to excite an attempt at my assassination, on account of politics, and a notion which the priests disseminated that I was in a league against the Germans,)—and, finally, my mother-in-law recovered last fortnight, and my play was damned last week! These are like " the eight-and-twenty misfortunes of Harlequin ". But they must be borne. If I give in, it shall be after keeping up a spirit at least. I should not have cared so much about it, if our southern neighbours had not bungled us all out of freedom for these five hundred years to come.

Did you know John Keats? They say that he was killed by a review of him in the *Quarterly*—if he be dead, which I really don't know. I don't understand that *yielding* sensitiveness. What I feel (as at this present) is an immense rage for eight-and-forty hours, and then, as usual—unless this time it should last longer. I must get on horseback to quiet me.

Yours, etc.

Francis I. wrote, after the battle of Pavia, " All is lost except our honour ". A hissed author may reverse it— " *Nothing* is lost, except our honour ". But the horses are waiting, and the paper full. I wrote last week to you.

TO THE HON. AUGUSTA LEIGH   *Ravenna, June 22d. 1821*

MY DEAREST A.,—What was I to write about? I live in a different world. You knew from others that I was in tolerable plight, and all that. However write I will since you desire it. I have put my daughter in a convent for the present to begin her accomplishments by reading, to which she had a learned aversion, but the arrangement is merely temporary till I can settle some plan for her; if I return to England, it is likely that she will accompany me—if not—I sometimes think of Switzerland, and sometimes of the Italian Conventual education; I shall hear both sides (for I have Swiss Friends—through Mr. Hoppner the Consul General, he is connected by marriage with that country) and choose what seems most rational. My menagerie—(which you enquire after) has had some vacancies by the elopement of one cat, the decease of two monkies and a crow, by indigestion—but it is still a flourishing and somewhat obstreperous establishment.

You may suppose that I was sufficiently provoked by Elliston's behaviour, the more so as the foreign Journals, the Austrian ones at least (who detest me for my politics) had misrepresented the whole thing. The moment I knew the real facts from England, I made these Italical Gentry contradict themselves and tell the truth—the former they are used to— the latter was a sad trial to them, but they did it, however, by dint of Mr. Hoppner's and my own remonstrances.

Tell Murray that I enclosed him a month ago (on the 2d.) another play, which I presume that he has received (as I ensured it at the post Office) *you* must help him to decypher it, for I sent the only copy, and you can better make out my *griffonnage*; tell him it *must* be printed (aye and published too) immediately, and copied out, for I do not choose to have only that *one* copy.

Will you for the hundredth time apply to Lady B. about the *funds*, they are now *high*, and I could sell out to a great advantage. Don't forget this, that cursed connection crosses at every turn my fortunes, my feelings and my fame. I had no wish to nourish my detestation of her and her family, but they pursue, like an Evil Genius. I send you an Elegy upon Lady Noel's *recovery*—(made too [here about fourteen lines of the autograph are cut off] the parish register—I will reserve my tears for the demise of Lady Noel, but the old —— will live forever because she is so amiable and useful.

Yours ever and [illegible.], B

P.S.—Let me know about Holmes.   Oh La !—is he as great a mountebank as ever?

TO JOHN CAM HOBHOUSE   *Ravenna, July 6th, 1821*

MY DEAR H.,—I have written by this post to Murray to omit the stanza to which you object.[1]   In case he should forget, you can jog his memory.   I have also agreed to a request of Madame Guiccioli's *not* to continue that poem further.   She had read the French translation, and thinks it a detestable production.   This will not seem strange even in Italian morality, because women all over the world always retain their freemasonry, and as that consists in the illusion of the sentiment which constitutes their sole empire (all owing to chivalry and the Goths—the Greeks knew better), all works which refer to the *comedy* of the passions, and laugh at senti-mentalism, of course are proscribed by the whole *sect*.   I never knew a woman who did not admire Rousseau, and hate Gil Blas, and de Grammont and the like, for the same reason.   And I never met with a woman, English or foreign, who did not do as much by D[on] J[uan].   As I am docile, I yielded, and promised to confine myself to the " highflying of Buttons ", —(you remember Pope's phrase)—for the time to come.   You will be very glad of this, as an earlier opponent of that poem's publication.

I only read your Canningippic in the papers, but even there it was worthy of anything since those against Anthony.

You must not give letters to me ; I have taken an oath against being civil ever since —— but you will see my reason in the last note to Marino Faliero.

I have sent to England a tragedy a month ago, and I am in the *fifth* act of another.   Murray has not acknowledged its arrival.   I must one day break with that gentleman, if he is not the civiler.

Of Burdett's affair I cannot judge, so I made an epigram

[1] " By the way, do not cut at poor Queeney in your Don Juan about Semi-ramis and her Courser courier.   She would feel it very much I assure you." Hobhouse to Byron, June 19th, 1821.

on it, which I sent to Douglas K^d. By the way, now the *funds are up, stir him* up, and the bloody trustees. It would give me pleasure to see some of you, that I might gossip over the late revolt (or rather revolt*ing*) transactions of these parts. Things are far from quiet even now. Have you seen my " Elegy on the recovery of Lady Noel "?

> " Behold the blessings of a lucky lot !
> My play is damned—and Lady Noel *not*."

Do you know that your bust was sent to England (viâ Livorno) months ago?

Let me hear from or of you.　　　　　　　　　　　　Yours, B.

P.S.—Fletcher is turned money-lender, and puts out money (*here*) at 20 per cent. Query, will he get it again? *Who* knows?

TO RICHARD BELGRAVE HOPPNER　　　*Ravenna, July 23, 1821*

This country being in a state of proscription, and all my friends exiled or arrested—the whole family of Gamba obliged to go to Florence for the present—the father and son for politics —(and the Guiccioli, because menaced with a *convent*, as her father is *not* here,) I have determined to remove to Switzerland, and they also. Indeed, my life here is not supposed to be particularly safe—but that has been the case for this twelve-month past, and is therefore not the primary consideration.

I have written by this post to Mr. Hentsch, junior, the banker of Geneva, to provide (if possible) a house for me, and another for Gamba's family, (the father, son, and daughter,) on the *Jura* side of the lake of Geneva, furnished, and with stabling (for *me* at least) for eight horses. I shall bring Allegra with me. Could you assist me or Hentsch in his researches? The Gambas are at Florence, but have authorised me to treat for them. You know, or do not know, that they are great patriots—and both—but the son in particular—very fine fellows. *This* I know, for I have seen them lately in very awkward situations—*not* pecuniary, but personal—and they behaved like heroes, neither yielding nor retracting.

You have no idea what a state of oppression this country is in—they arrested above a thousand of high and low throughout Romagna—banished some and confined others, without *trial*, *process*, or even *accusation!!* Every body says they would have done the same by me if they dared proceed openly. My motive, however, for remaining, is because *every one* of my acquaintance, to the amount of hundreds almost, have been exiled.

Will you do what you can in looking out for a couple of houses *furnished*, and conferring with Hentsch for us? We care nothing about society, and are only anxious for a temporary and tranquil asylum and individual freedom.

Believe me, etc.

P.S.—Can you give me an idea of the comparative expenses of Switzerland and Italy? which I have forgotten. I speak merely of those of decent *living*, *horses*, etc., and not of luxuries or high living. Do *not*, however, decide any thing positively till I have your answer, as I can then know how to think upon these topics of transmigration, etc., etc., etc.

TO THE HON. DOUGLAS KINNAIRD* *July 24th* [14th?] *1821*

MY DEAR DOUGLAS,—You perhaps did right in not forwarding the letter, which was none of the tenderest. Open, and read it, and forward it not. You must excuse my impatience about the funds. You *forget* that you must have a further power of attorney to sell out; and, in the intervals of a courier's expedition, the funds may fall, or the courier may fall, or—what can I say? I should approve of the Exchequer bills.

So my lady has been civil—that's news—and new. However, it is her child's interest, and as such no great stretch of politeness.

With regard to M., you will please to recollect that I never meant any *comparison*. I sent his letter to show you his way of thinking. Mine is this. I believe M[urray] to be a good man with a personal regard for me. But a bargain is in its very essence a *hostile* transaction. If I were to come to you, Douglas, and say " lend me five hundred pounds ", you would either do it, or give a good reason why you would not.   But if I come and say " Douglas, I have a carriage and horses, or a library or what you will.   Give me five hundred pounds for them ", you first enquire if they are worth it.   And, even if they are, do not all men try to abate the price of all they buy ?   I contend that a bargain, even between brethren, is a declaration of war.   Now this must be much more so in a man like M. whose business is nothing but a perpetual speculation on what will or will not succeed, and can have no steady returns, being a matter of opinion.   I have no doubt that he would lend or give—freely —what he would refuse for value received in M.S.S.   So do not think too hardly of him.   I do not know myself to what he alludes, nor do I wish to know.   Your manner is quick, as is the case with all men of any vivacity ;   and *he* might feel perhaps a turn of the lip, or a short reply, which Hobhouse would only make a long letter about, and I should only keep in mind for six months, and then pay you off in your own coin on a fit opportunity.   Now these are resources which the great M. has not.   Neither is he on that equality of feeling with you (as doubtless neither in cash) which can admit of that agreeable give and take, which you and I and all of our Chorus have long reciprocated.   It is different with me.   A publisher becomes identified almost with his authors, and can say any-thing, or hear anything.

And now there approacheth new barter.   By this post is forwarded (with the returned proofs of " Sardanapalus ") the tragedy M.S.S. of " the two Foscari " in five acts.   When you have read both and formed your opinion, I leave to you the discretionary power of poundage and pence.   Perhaps it were as well to publish them first and settle afterwards according to success—if there be any.   You will perceive that I have kept aloof from the Stage as before.   By the time you receive this the Coronation will have subsided and you may have leisure to think of such things.

I write out of spirits ;   for they have been banishing (without trial) half the inhabitants—and many of my friends amongst them—of this country, as politicians.   I hope that this will find you in good humour.

Yours ever—B.

TO JOHN MURRAY *R^a July 30th 1821*

DEAR SIR,—Enclosed is the best account of the Doge
Faliero, which was only sent to me from an old MSS. the
other day. Get it translated, and append it as a note to the
next edition. You will perhaps be pleased to see that my
conceptions of his character were correct, though I regret not
having met with this extract before. You will perceive that he
himself said exactly what he is made to say, about the Bishop of
Treviso. You will see also that he spoke very little, and those
only words " of rage and disdain ", *after* his arrest, which is the
case in the play, except when he breaks out at the close of Act
fifth. But his speech to the Conspirators is better in the MSS.
than in the play : I wish that I had met with it in time. Do not
forget this note, with a translation.

In a former note to the Juans, speaking of Voltaire, I have
quoted his famous " Zaire, tu pleures ", which is an error ; it
should be " Zaire, *vous pleurez* " ; recollect this ; and recollect
also that your *want* of *recollection* has permitted you to publish
the note on the Kelso traveller, which *I had positively desired you
not*, for proof of which I refer you to my letters. I presume that
you are able to lay your hand upon these letters, as you are
accused publicly, in a pamphlet, of showing them about. I
wait your acknowledgement of the packets containing *The
Foscaris*, notes, etc., etc. : now your Coronation is over, perhaps
you will find time. I have also written to Mr. Kinnaird, to say
that I expect the two tragedies to be published speedily, and
to inform him that I am willing to make any abatement, on
your statement of loss liable to be incurred by publishing at an
improper season.

I am so busy here about these poor proscribed exiles, who
are scattered about, and with trying to get some of them
recalled, that I have hardly time or patience to write a short
preface, which will be proper for the two plays. However, I
will make it out, on receiving the next proofs.

Yours ever and truly, B.

P.S.—Please to append the letter about *the Hellespont* as a
note to your next opportunity of the verses on Leander, etc.,
etc., etc., in *Childe Harold*. Don't forget it amidst your multi-

tudinous avocations, which I think of celebrating in a dithyrambic ode to Albemarle Street.

Are you aware that Shelley has written an elegy on Keats,
and accuses the *Quarterly* of killing him?

> " Who killed John Keats? "
> " I," says the Quarterly,
> So savage and Tartarly;
> " 'Twas one of my feats."

> " Who shot the arrow? "
> " The poet-priest Milman
> (So ready to kill man),
> Or Southey or Barrow."

You know very well that I did not approve of Keats's
poetry, or principles of poetry, or of his abuse of Pope; but,
as he is dead, omit *all* that is said *about him* in any *MSS.* of
mine, or publication. His *Hyperion* is a fine monument, and
will keep his name. I do not envy the man who wrote the
article : your review people have no more right to kill than any
other foot pads. However, he who would die of an article in a
review would probably have died of something else equally
trivial. The same thing nearly happened to Kirke White, who
afterwards died of a consumption.

TO JOHN MURRAY　　　　　　　　*Rᵃ August 23ᵈ 1821*

DEAR SIR,—Enclosed are the two acts corrected. With
regard to the charges about the Shipwreck,—I think that I
told both you and Mr. Hobhouse, years ago, that [there] was
not a *single circumstance* of it *not* taken from *fact*; not, indeed,
from any *single* shipwreck, but all from *actual* facts of different
wrecks. Almost all *Don Juan* is *real* life, either my own, or
from people I knew. By the way, much of the description of
the *furniture*, in Canto 3ᵈ, is taken from *Tully's Tripoli* (pray
note this), and the rest from my own observation. Remember,
I never meant to conceal this at all, and have only not stated
it, because *Don Juan* had no preface nor name to it. If you

think it worth while to make this statement, do so, in your own way. *I* laugh at such charges, convinced that no writer ever borrowed less, or made his materials more his own. Much is coincidence: for instance, Lady Morgan (in a really *excellent* book, I assure you, on Italy) calls Venice an *Ocean Rome*; I have the very same expression in *Foscari*, and yet *you* know that the play was written months ago, and sent to England. The *Italy* I received only on the 16th in^st.

Your friend, like the public, is not aware, that my dramatic simplicity is *studiously* Greek, and must continue so: *no* reform ever succeeded at first. I admire the old English dramatists; but this is quite another field, and has nothing to do with theirs. I want to make a *regular* English drama, no matter whether for the Stage or not, which is not my object,--but a *mental theatre*.

Yours ever, B.

Is the bust arrived?

P.S.—*Can't* accept your courteous offer.

> For Orford and for Waldegrave
> You give much more than me you *gave*;
> Which is not fairly to behave
>   My Murray!
>
> Because if a live dog, 'tis said,
> Be worth a Lion fairly sped,
> A *live lord* must be worth *two* dead,
>   My Murray!
>
> And if, as the opinion goes,
> Verse hath a better sale than prose—
> Certes, I should have more than those,
>   My Murray!
>
> But now this sheet is nearly crammed,
> So, if *you will*, *I* shan't be shammed,
> And if you *won't*,—*you* may be damned,
>   My Murray!

These matters must be arranged with Mr. Douglas K. He is my trustee, and a man of honour. To him you can state all your mercantile reasons, which you might not like to state

to me personally, such as " heavy season "—" flat public "—
" don't go off "—" Lordship writes too much "—" won't
take advice "—" declining popularity "—" deductions for
the trade "—" make very little "—" generally lose by him "—
" pirated edition "—" foreign edition "—" severe criticisms ",
etc., with other hints and howls for an oration, which I leave
Douglas, who is an orator, to answer.

You can also state them more freely to a third person, as
between you and me they could only produce some smart
postscripts, which would not adorn our mutual archives.

I am sorry for the Queen, and that's more than you are.

TO THE HON. DOUGLAS KINNAIRD *   *Ra. August 23rd 1821*

MY DEAR DOUGLAS,—I have received the enclosed proposal
from Mr Murray which I can *not* accept. He offers me for *all*
the sum he once offered for *two* cantos of D. Juan. I will
accept nothing of the kind unless he advances very considerably, and unless the things have completely failed. This *you*
can inform yourself of, and act accordingly. With regard to
what his friend says of " *Simplicity* ",[1] I study to be so. It is
an experiment whether the English *Closet* or *mental* theatre
will or will not bear a *regular* drama instead of the melo-drama.
Murray's offer falls short by *one half* of the fair proposal, all
things considered. However I leave you a free discretion and
will ratify any agreement of *yours*, confident that it will be honest
and loyal to both parties.

Yours ever and truly, B.

[1] Preserved with this letter is a letter to Byron from John Murray, offering
a thousand guineas for " the Two Tragedies " (which will make " a handsome
and interesting volume ") and the same sum for the Third, Fourth, and Fifth
Cantos of *Don Juan*. Murray also quotes from a letter he has received from William
Gifford, to whom " two Acts of ' the Foscari ' " have been submitted: " Never
mind his plays not being stage-worthy : in these times it signifies not much—
but he has the true dramatic turn, and fails only in his plots. If he could but
get a little into the bustle of our old dramatists, absurd as it sometimes was, it
would do : otherwise he must die a martyr to his simplicity or singleness. . . .
After all [Gifford concludes] he is a wonderful creature—if I had him, I would
keep him up carefully, and shew him only on high days and holy days."

P.S.—Enclosed is a letter from Miss Boyce.[1] She was a transient piece of mine; but I owe her little on that score, * * * * *. Advance the poor creature some money and *deduct* it from your books quoad banker for me.

[On a separate half-sheet]

Allow me to remind you that up to 1819 *all* the *offers* came from *our* part, and *not* from Murray's. *He* offered for the third Canto of Cᵉ H. *twelve hundred* and then came up to two thousand. For the 4th he gave at once two thousand five hundred; and both yourself and Hᵉ and your brother thought that I might have obtained more. If *we* are *down* in the scribbling world, say so *at once*, and I will withdraw from the Arena without a word further. Excuse my ignorance, which comes from my foreign residence.

As I am about it, take one more quotation from your *own* letters : " I think that Murray ought to offer you *more* than *any other bookseller*. Now it is my belief that he bids you *less*. You may be *sure* that I have *good authority* for *what I say* ", etc. etc. etc. Now, my dear Dougal, these are your own words, and after them *what can* " *I say* " ?, when not *three months* after you write to me something sounding very like the reverse of your former expressions so recently transmitted?

TO OCTAVIUS GILCHRIST*   *Ravenna, September 5th, 1821*

SIR,[2]—I have to acknowledge the arrival of yr. three pamphlets " from the author " whom I thank very sincerely for the attention. The tone which Mr. Bowles has taken in this controversy has been so different with the different parties, that we are perhaps none of us fair personal judges of the subject. Long before I had seen Mr. B's answers to myself,

[1] Writing from No. 5 Church Hill, St. Pancras, Byron's petitioner, who signs herself " the wretched but *unchanged* Susan Boyce ", speaks of the misery she has endured " for the last 3 years in consequence of my so cruelly being turned from my situation at Drury Lane ". She begs Byron to repeat his former kindnesses and " save *me* and my *poor Boy* from perishing. I am at the Haymarket Theatre for £2 per week : it was the *only* vacant situation. . . ." For further light on Susan Boyce, see " *To Lord Byron* ", by George Paston and Peter Quennell.

[2] Octavius Graham Gilchrist, a poetical grocer of Stamford, had attempted to " rescue Pope from the rancorous persecution of his editor, the Rev. Mr. Bowles ".

or the last pamphlet of the three which you have sent to me,
I had written an answer to his attack upon yourself, which
perhaps you may have seen (or at any rate may see if you
think it worth the trouble) at Mr. Murray's. . . . As it was
somewhat savage, on reading Mr. Bowles's mild reply to me,
I suppressed its publication, recollecting also that you were
perfectly competent to your own defence, and might probably
look upon my interference as impertinent. . . . I have not
read Mr. Bowles's " Sequel " to which your third pamphlet
refers.   Mr. Bowles has certainly not set *you* an example of
forbearance in *controversy*; but in *society* he really is what I have
described him, but as we are all mad upon some subject or
other, and the only reason why it does not appear in *all* is that
their insane chord has not been struck upon, our Editor seems
to have been touched upon the score of Pope, and for that
reason it is a thousand pities that he ever meddled with him.
By the way, to refer to myself, I think you might as well have
omitted the mention of Don Juan and Beppo and Little etc. as
more indecent than the " Imitation from Horace " of Pope,
for two reasons—firstly they are *not so* indecent by any means,
as for example,

> " And if a tight young girl will serve the turn
>   In arrant pride continues still to *churn* "

> *or*

> " What pushed poor Q—— on the imperial whore
>   T'was but to be where Charles had been before."

and in the next place, as I had been fighting Pope's battles as
well as I could, it was rather hard in an *ally* to bring in an
" odious comparison " at the expence of his auxiliary.   However this is a trifle, and if Pope's moral reputation can be still
further elevated at the expence of mine, I will yield it as
freely, as I have always admired him sincerely—much more
indeed than you yourself in all probability, for *I* do not think
him inferior to Milton—although to state such an opinion
publicly in the present day would be equivalent to saying that
I do not think Shakespeare without the grossest of faults, which
is another heterodox notion of my entertainment.   Indeed I look
upon a proper appreciation of Pope as a touchstone of taste,

and the present question as not only whether Pope is or is not in the first rank of our literature, but whether *that* literature shall or shall not relapse into the Barbarism from which it has scarcely emerged for above a century and a half. I do not deny the natural powers of Mind of the earlier dramatists, but I think that their service as a *standard* is doing irreparable mischief. It is also a great error to suppose the *present* a *high* age of English poetry—it is equivalent to the age of *Statius* or *Silius Italicus* except that instead of imitating the Virgils of our language they are " trying back " (to use a hunting phrase) upon the Ennius's and Lucilius's who had better have remained in their obscurity. Those poor idiots of the Lakes, too, are diluting our literature as much as they can. In short, all of us more or less (except Campbell and Rogers) have much to answer for, and I don't see any remedy. But I am wandering from the subject—which is to thank you for your present and to beg you to believe me your obliged and very faithl. serv^t,

BYRON

Is it not odd that hitherto Pope has been edited only by *priests*? Warburton—Warton—Bowles?—at least I know no others.

P.S.—I saw Mr. Mawman the other day;—he tells me that the Booksellers have engaged Roscoe to edite Pope, and I think the choice is a very judicious one. Roscoe has all the elegance and classical turn of mind requisite to do Pope justice. Hitherto he has only been edited by his enemies or by Warburton who was a polemical parson and as fit to edite Poetry as Pope to preach in Gloucester Cathedral. The Attorney-bishop did him no good, and Warton and Bowles have done him harm. Mr. Murray tells me that Roscoe is requested (by the publishers) to keep the controversy with Mr. Bowles etc. quite out of sight and not to allude to it at all. This is the *quietest* way, but whether it is the best I know not. I suppose it is. . . . Mr. Mawman seemed indignant at Bowles's edition which he said " was a treachery to his employers who had paid him to edite Pope—and not to blame him ". He wondered that I had not put this more strongly in my letter. But how was I to know it? . . . It seemed to me inconceivable that they could publish such an edition without being aware of its *tendency*—and thus tacitly approving it with their "Imprimatur". . . .

TO JOHN MURRAY   *Ravenna, September 12ᵗʰ 1821*

DEAR SIR,—By Tuesday's post, I forwarded, in three packets, the drama of "*Cain*", in three acts, of which I request the acknowledgement when arrived. To the last speech of *Eve*, in the last act (*i.e.* where she curses Cain), add these three lines to the concluding one—

> May the Grass wither from thy foot! the Woods
> Deny thee shelter! Earth a home! the Dust
> A Grave! the Sun his light! and Heaven her God!

There's as pretty a piece of Imprecation for you, when joined to the lines already sent, as you may wish to meet with in the course of your business. But don't forget the addition of the above three lines, which are clinchers to Eve's speech.

Let me know what Gifford thinks (if the play arrives in safety); for I have a good opinion of the piece, as poetry: it is in my gay metaphysical style, and in the *Manfred* line.

You must at least commend my facility and variety, when you consider what I have done within the last fifteen months, with my head, too, full of other and of mundane matters. But no doubt you will avoid saying any good of it, for fear I should raise the price upon you: that's right—stick to business! Let me know what your other ragamuffins are writing, for I suppose you don't like starting too many of your Vagabonds at once. You may give them the start, for any thing I care.

If this arrives in time to be added to the other two dramas, publish them *together*: if not, publish it separately, in the *same* form, to tally for the purchasers. Let me have a proof of the whole speedily. It is longer than *Manfred*.

Why don't you publish my *Pulci*?[1] the best thing I ever wrote, with the Italian to it. I wish I was alongside of you: nothing is ever done in a man's absence; every body runs counter, because they *can*. If ever I *do* return to England,

---

[1] Byron's translation of the first Canto of Luigi Pulci's *Morgante Maggiore*, with the Italian, was published in the *Liberal*.

(which I shan't though,) I will write a poem to which *English Bards*, etc., shall be New Milk, in comparison. Your present literary world of mountebanks stands in need of such an Avatar ; but I am not yet quite bilious enough : a season or two more, and a provocation or two, will wind me up to the point, and then, have at the whole set !

I have no patience with the sort of trash you send me out by way of books ; except Scott's novels, and three or four other things, I never saw such work or works. Campbell is lecturing, Moore idling, Southey twaddling, Wordsworth driveling, Coleridge muddling, Joanna Baillie piddling, Bowles quibbling, squabbling, and sniveling. Milman will *do*, if he don't cant too much, nor imitate Southey : the fellow has poesy in him ; but he is envious, and unhappy, as all the envious are. Still he is among the best of the day. Barry Cornwall will do better by and bye, I dare say, if he don't get spoilt by green tea, and the praises of Pentonville and Paradise Row. The pity of these men is, that they never lived either in *high life*, nor in *solitude* : there is no medium for the knowledge of the *busy* or the *still* world. If admitted into high life for a season, it is merely as *spectators*—they form no part of the Mechanism thereof. Now Moore and I, the one by circumstances, and the other by birth, happened to be free of the corporation, and to have entered into its pulses and passions, *quarum partes fuimus*. Both of us have learnt by this much which nothing else could have taught us.

Yours, B.

P.S.—I saw one of your brethren, another of the Allied Sovereigns of Grub-Street, the other day, viz. : Mawman the Great, by whom I sent due homage to your imperial self. To-morrow's post may perhaps bring a letter from you ; but you are the most ungrateful and ungracious of correspondents. But there is some excuse for you, with your perpetual levee of politicians, parson-scribblers, and loungers : some day I will give you a *poetical* Catalogue of them.

The post is come : no letter, but never mind.

How is Mrs. Murray, and Gifford ? Better ? Say *well*.

My Compliments to Mr. Heber [1] upon his Election.

---

[1] Richard Heber (1773–1833) was elected M.P. for the University of Oxford, August 24th, 1821.

TO THOMAS MOORE   *Ravenna, September 19, 1821*

I am in all the sweat, dust, and blasphemy of an universal packing of all my things, furniture, etc., for Pisa, whither I go for the winter. The cause has been the exile of all my fellow Carbonics, and, amongst them, of the whole family of Madame G.; who, you know, was divorced from her husband last week, " on account of P.P. clerk of this parish ",[1] and who is obliged to join her father and relatives, now in exile there, to avoid being shut up in a monastery, because the Pope's decree of separation required her to reside in *casa paterna*, or else, for decorum's sake, in a convent. As I could not say with Hamlet, " Get thee to a nunnery ", I am preparing to follow them.

It is awful work, this love, and prevents all a man's projects of good or glory. I wanted to go to Greece lately (as every thing seems up here) with her brother, who is a very fine, brave fellow (I have seen him put to the proof), and wild about liberty. But the tears of a woman who has left her husband for a man, and the weakness of one's own heart, are paramount to these projects, and I can hardly indulge them.

We were divided in choice between Switzerland and Tuscany, and I gave my vote for Pisa, as nearer the Mediterranean, which I love for the sake of the shores which it washes, and for my young recollections of 1809. Switzerland is a curst selfish, swinish country of brutes, placed in the most romantic region of the world. I never could bear the inhabitants, and still less their English visitors; for which reason, after writing for some information about houses, upon hearing that there was a colony of English all over the cantons of Geneva, etc., I immediately gave up the thought, and persuaded the Gambas to do the same.

By the last post I sent you " The Irish Avatar ",[2]—what think you? The last line—" a name never spoke but with curses or jeers "—must run either " a name only uttered with curses or jeers ", or, " a wretch never named but with curses or jeers ". Be*case* as *how*, " spoke " is not grammar, except in

---

[1] Alluding to Pope's *Memoirs of P. P. Clerk of this Parish.*

[2] " Lord B.'s tremendous verses against the King and the Irish " (as Moore called them) were inspired by George IV's triumphal expedition to Dublin, soon after the Queen's death.

the House of Commons; and I doubt whether we can say " a name *spoken* ", for *mentioned*. I have some doubts, too, about " repay ",—" and for murder repay with a shout and a smile ". Should it not be, " and for murder repay him with shouts and a smile ", or " *reward* him with shouts and a smile "?

So, pray put your poetical pen through the MS. and take the least bad of the emendations. Also, if there be any further breaking of Priscian's head, will you apply a plaster? I wrote in the greatest hurry and fury, and sent it to you the day after ; so, doubtless, there will be some awful constructions, and a rather lawless conscription of rhythmus.

With respect to what Anna Seward calls " the liberty of transcript ",—when complaining of Miss Matilda Muggleton, the accomplished daughter of a choral vicar of Worcester Cathedral, who had abused the said " liberty of transcript ", by inserting in the *Malvern Mercury* Miss Seward's " Elegy on the South Pole ", as her *own* production, with her *own* signature, two years after having taken a copy, by permission of the authoress—with regard, I say, to the " liberty of transcript ", I by no means oppose an occasional copy to the benevolent few, provided it does not degenerate into such licentiousness of Verb and Noun as may tend to " disparage my parts of speech " by the carelessness of the transcribblers.

I do not think that there is much danger of the " King's Press being abused " upon the occasion, if the publishers of journals have any regard for their remaining liberty of person. It is as pretty a piece of invective as ever put publisher in the way to " Botany ". Therefore, if *they* meddle with it, it is at *their* peril. As for myself, I will answer any jontleman—though I by no means recognise a " right of search " into an unpublished production and unavowed poem. The same applies to things published *sans* consent. I hope you like, at least the concluding lines of the *Pome*?

What are you doing, and where are you? in England? Nail Murray—nail him to his own counter, till he shells out the thirteens. Since I wrote to you, I have sent him another tragedy—*Cain* by name—making three in MS. now in his hands, or in the printer's. It is in the *Manfred* metaphysical style, and full of some Titanic declamation ;—Lucifer being one of the *dram. pers.*, who takes Cain a voyage among the stars, and afterwards to " Hades ", where he shows him the phantoms of a former world, and its inhabitants. I have gone upon the notion of Cuvier, that the world has been destroyed three or four times, and was inhabited by mammoths, behemoths, and what not; but *not* by man till the Mosaic period, as, indeed, is proved by the strata of bones found ;—those of all unknown animals, and known, being dug out, but none of mankind. I have, therefore, supposed Cain to be shown, in the *rational* Preadamites, beings endowed with a higher intelligence than man, but totally unlike him in form, and with much greater strength of mind and person. You may suppose the small talk which takes place between him and Lucifer upon these matters is not quite canonical.

The consequence is, that Cain comes back and kills Abel in a fit of dissatisfaction, partly with the politics of Paradise, which had driven them all out of it, and partly because (as it is written in Genesis) Abel's sacrifice was the more acceptable to the Deity. I trust that the Rhapsody has arrived—it is in three acts, and entitled " *A Mystery* ", according to the former Christian custom, and in honour of what it probably will remain to the reader.

Yours, etc.

TO JOHN MURRAY   *R^a Septr 20th 1821*

DEAR MURRAY,—You need not send " *The Blues* ", which is a mere buffoonery, never meant for publication.

The papers to which I allude, in case of Survivorship, are collections of letters, etc., since I was sixteen years old, contained in the trunks in the care of Mr. Hobhouse. This collection is at least doubled by those I have now here; all received since my last Ostracism. To these I should wish the Editor to have access, *not* for the purpose of *abusing confidences*, nor of *hurting* the feelings of correspondents living, or the memories of the dead; but there are things which would do neither, that I have left unnoticed or unexplained, and which (like all such things) Time only can permit to be noticed or explained, though some are to my credit. The task will, of course, require delicacy; but that will not be wanting, if

Moore and Hobhouse survive me, and, I may add, yourself;
and that you may all three do so, is, I assure you, my very
sincere wish. I am not sure that long life is desirable for one
of my temper and constitutional depression of Spirits, which of
course I suppress in society; but which breaks out when alone,
and in my writings, in spite of myself. It has been deepened,
perhaps, by some long past events (I do not allude to my
marriage, etc.—on the contrary, *that* raised them by the
persecution giving a fillip to my Spirits); but I call it constitutional, as I have reason to think it. You know, or you do
not know, that my maternal Grandfather (a very clever man,
and amiable, I am told) was strongly suspected of Suicide (he
was found drowned in the Avon at Bath), and that another
very near relative of the same branch took poison, and was
merely saved by antidotes. For the first of these events there
was no apparent cause, as he was rich, respected, and of
considerable intellectual resources, hardly forty years of age, and
not at all addicted to any unhinging vice. It was, however,
but a strong suspicion, owing to the manner of his death and
to his melancholy temper. The *second had* a cause, but it does
not become me to touch upon it; it happened when I was far
too young to be aware of it, and I never heard of it till after the
death of that relative, many years afterwards. I think, then,
that I may call this dejection *constitutional*. I had always been
told that in *temper* I more resembled my maternal Grandfather
than any of my *father's* family—that is, in the gloomier part of
his temper, for he was what you call a good natured man, and
I am not.

The Journal here I sent by Mawman to Moore the other
day; but as it is a mere diary, only *parts* of it would ever do for
publication. The other Journal, of the tour in 1816, I should
think Augusta might let you have a copy of; but her nerves
have been in such a state since 1815, that there is no knowing.
Lady Byron's people, and L^y Caroline Lamb's people, and a
parcel of that set, got about her and frightened her with all
sorts of hints and menaces, so that she has never since been
able to write to *me* a *clear common letter*, and is so full of mysteries
and miseries, that I can only sympathize, without always
understanding her. All my loves, too, make a point of calling
upon her, which puts her into a flutter (no difficult matter);

and, the year before last I think, Lady F. W. W. marched in upon her, and Lady Oxford, a few years ago, spoke to her at a party; and these and such like calamities have made her afraid of her shadow. It is a very odd fancy that they all take to her: it was only six months ago, that I had some difficulty in preventing the Countess G. from invading her with an Italian letter. I should like to have seen Augusta's face, with an Etruscan Epistle, and all its Meridional style of *issimas*, and other superlatives, before her.

I am much mortified that Gifford don't take to my new dramas: to be sure, they are as opposite to the English drama as one thing can be to another; but I have a notion that, if understood, they will in time find favour (though *not* on the stage) with the reader. The Simplicity of plot is intentional, and the avoidance of *rant* also, as also the compression of the Speeches in the more severe situations. What I seek to show in *The Foscaris* is the *suppressed* passion, rather than the rant of the present day. For that matter—

> " Nay, if thou'lt mouth,
> I'll rant as well as thou "—

would not be difficult, as I think I have shown in my younger productions—*not dramatic* ones, to be sure. But, as I said before, I am mortified that Gifford don't like them; but I see no remedy, our notions on the subject being so different. How is he? well, I hope: let me know. I regret his demur the more that he has been always my grand patron, and I know no praise which would compensate me in my own mind for his censure. I do not mind *reviews*, as I can work them at their own weapons.

Yours ever and truly, B.

P.S.—By the way, on our next settlement (which will take place with Mr. Kinnaird), you will please to deduct the various sums for *books*, packages *received* and *sent*, the *bust*, tooth-powder, etc., etc., expended by you on my account.

Hobhouse, in his preface to " *Rimini* ", will probably be better able to explain my dramatic system, than I could do, as he is well acquainted with the whole thing. It is more upon the Alfieri School than the English.

I hope that we shall not have Mr. Rogers here: there is a mean minuteness in his mind and tittle-tattle that I dislike, ever since I *found him out* (which was but slowly); besides he is not a good man: why don't he go to bed? What does he do travelling?

The Journal of 1814 I dare say Moore will give, or a copy.

Has *Cain* (the dramatic third attempt), arrived yet? Let me know.

Address to me at *Pisa*, whither I am going. The reason is, that all my Italian friends here have been exiled, and are met there for the present; and I go to join them, as agreed upon, for the Winter.

TO JOHN MURRAY   *Ravenna, September 24ᵗʰ 1821*

DEAR MURRAY,—I have been thinking over our late correspondence, and wish to propose to you the following articles for our future :—

1ˢᵗˡʸ That you shall write to me of yourself, of the health, wealth, and welfare of all friends; but of *me* (*quoad me*) little or nothing.

2ᵈˡʸ That you shall send me Soda powders, tooth-powder, tooth-brushes, or any such anti-odontalgic or chemical articles, as heretofore, *ad libitum*, upon being re-imbursed for the same.

3ᵈˡʸ That you shall *not* send me any modern, or (as they are called) *new*, publications in *English whatsoever*, save and excepting any writing, prose or verse, of (or reasonably presumed to be of) Walter Scott, Crabbe, Moore, Campbell, Rogers, Gifford, Joanna Baillie, *Irving* (the American), Hogg, Wilson (*Isle of Palms* Man), or *any* especial *single* work of fancy which is thought to be of considerable merit; *Voyages* and *travels*, provided that they are *neither in Greece, Spain, Asia Minor, Albania, nor Italy*, will be welcome: having travelled the countries mentioned, I know that what is said of them can convey nothing further which I desire to know about them. No other English works whatsoever.

4ᵗʰˡʸ That you send me *no periodical works* whatsoever— *no Edinburgh, Quarterly, Monthly*, nor any Review, Magazine, Newspaper, English or foreign, of any description.

5^{thly} That you send me *no* opinions whatsoever, either *good*, *bad*, or *indifferent*, of yourself, or your friends, or others, concerning any work, or works, of mine, past, present, or to come.

6^{thly} That all negotiations in matters of business between you and me pass through the medium of the Honble Douglas Kinnaird, my friend and trustee, or Mr. Hobhouse, as *Alter Ego*, and tantamount to myself during my absence, or presence.

Some of these propositions may at first seem strange, but they are founded. The quantity of trash I have received as books is incalculable, and neither amused nor instructed. Reviews and Magazines are at the best but ephemeral and superficial reading: *who thinks* of the *grand article* of *last year* in any *given review?* in the next place, if they regard *myself*, they tend to increase *Egotism*; if favourable, I do not deny that the praise *elates*, and if unfavourable, that the abuse *irritates*— the latter may conduct me to inflict a species of Satire, which would neither do good to you nor to your friends: *they* may smile *now*, and so may *you*; but if I took you all in hand, it would not be difficult to cut you up like gourds. I did as much by as powerful people at nineteen years old, and I know little as yet, in three and thirty, which should prevent me from making all your ribs Gridirons for your hearts, if such were my propensity. But it is *not*. Therefore let me hear none of your provocations. If any thing occurs so very *gross* as to require my notice, I shall hear of it from my personal friends. For the rest, I merely request to be left in ignorance.

The same applies to opinions, *good*, *bad*, or *indifferent*, of persons in conversation or correspondence: these do not *interrupt*, but they *soil* the *current* of my *Mind*. I am sensitive enough, but *not* till I am *touched*; and *here* I am beyond the touch of the short arms of literary England, except the few feelers of the Polypus that crawl over the Channel in the way of Extract.

All these precautions *in* England would be useless: the libeller or the flatterer would there reach me in spite of all; but in Italy we know little of literary England, and think less, except what reaches us through some garbled and brief extract in some miserable Gazette. For *two years* (excepting two or three articles cut out and sent to *you*, by the post) I never read a newspaper which was not forced upon me by some accident, and know, upon the whole, as little of England as you all do of Italy, and God knows *that* is little enough, with all your travels, etc., etc., etc. The English travellers *know Italy* as *you* know Guernsey : how much is *that*?

If any thing occurs so violently gross or personal as to require notice, Mr. D⁸ Kinnaird will let me *know* ; but of *praise* I desire to hear *nothing*.

You will say, " to what tends all this? " I will answer THAT ;—to keep my mind *free and unbiassed* by all paltry and personal irritabilities of praise or censure ;—to let my Genius take its natural direction, while my feelings are like the dead, who know nothing and feel nothing of all or aught that is said or done in their regard.

If you can observe these conditions, you will spare yourself and others some pain : let me not be worked upon to rise up ; for if I do, it will not be for a little : if you can *not* observe these conditions, we shall cease to be correspondents, but *not friends* ; for I shall always be

Yours ever and truly, BYRON

P.S.—I have taken these resolutions not from any irritation against *you* or *yours*, but simply upon reflection that all reading, either praise or censure, of myself has done me harm. When I was in Switzerland and Greece, I was out of the way of hearing either, and *how I wrote there!* In Italy I am out of the way of it too ; but latterly, partly through my fault, and partly through your kindness in wishing to send me the *newest* and most periodical publications, I have had a crowd of reviews, etc., thrust upon me, which have bored me with their jargon, of one kind or another, and taken off my attention from greater objects. You have also sent me a parcel of trash of poetry, for no reason that I can conceive, unless to provoke me to write a new *English Bards*. Now *this* I wish to avoid ; for if ever I *do*, it will be a strong production ; and I desire peace, as long as the fools will keep their nonsense out of my way.

TO JOHN MURRAY   *Septr 28th 1821*

DEAR MORAY,—I add another cover to request you to ask Moore to obtain (if possible) my letters to the late Lady

Melbourne from Lady Cowper. They are very numerous, and
ought to have been restored long ago, as I was ready to give
back Lady M.'s in exchange: these latter are in Mr. Hobhouse's custody with my other papers, and shall be punctually
restored if required. I did not choose before to apply to Lady
Cowper, as her mother's death naturally kept me from in-
truding upon her feelings at the time of its occurrence. Some
years have now elapsed, and it is essential that I should have
my own epistles. They are essential as confirming that part
of the " Memoranda " which refer to the two periods (1812 and
1814) when my marriage with her niece was in contemplation,
and will tend to show what my real views and feelings were
upon that subject, which have been so variously represented.
You need not let *this motive* be stated to L*y* C*r*, as it in no degree
concerns *her* particularly; but *if* they refuse to give them up
(or keep back *any*—recollect that they are in *great quantity*),
it would become the duty of the Editor and my Executors to
refer to parts of Lady Melbourne's letters—so that the thing is
as broad as it is long. They involve also many other topics,
which may or may not be referred to, according to the discretion of Moore, etc., when the time comes.

You need not be alarmed: the "*fourteen years*" will hardly
elapse without some mortality amongst us; it is a long lease of
life to speculate upon. So your Cent per Cent Shylock Calculation will not be in so much peril, as the " Argosie " will sink
before that time, and " the pound of flesh " be withered
previously to your being so long out of a return.

I also wish to give you a hint or two (as you have really
behaved very handsomely to M. in the business, and are a
fine fellow in your line) for your advantage. *If* by your own
management you can extract any of my epistles from L*y*
Caroline Lamb (mind she don't give you *forgeries* in my *hand*:
she has done as much you *know* before now) they might be of
use in your collection (sinking of course the *names* and *all such
circumstances* as might hurt *living* feelings, or *those* of *survivors*);
they treat of more topics than love occasionally.

As to those to other correspondents (female, etc.), there
are plenty scattered about in the world; but how to direct
you to recover them, I know not: most of them have kept
them—I hear at least that L*y* O[xford] and F. W[ebster] have

kept theirs; but these letters are of course inaccessible (and perhaps not desirable), as well as those of some others.

I will tell you who may *happen* to have some letters of mine in their possession : Lord Powerscourt, some to his late brother; Mr. Long of—(I forget his place)—but the father of Edward Long of the Guards, who was drowned in going to Lisbon early in 1809; Miss Elizabeth Pigot, of Southwell, Notts (she *may* be *Mistress* by this time, for she had more years than I) : *they* were *not* love-letters, so that you might have them without scruple. There are, or might be, some to the late Rev⁰ J. C. Tattersall, in the hands of his brother (half-brother) Mr. Wheatley, who resides near Canterbury, I think. There are some to Charles Gordon, now of Dulwich; and some few to Mrs. Chaworth; but these latter are probably destroyed or inaccessible.

All my letters to Lady B., before and since her marriage, are in her possession, as well as her own which I sent to her : she had not the courtesy to restore me *mine*; but never mind; though they were too much to my credit for her to give them back, we can do without them.

I mention these people and particulars merely as *chances* : most of them have probably destroyed the letters, which in fact were of little import, most of them written when very young, and several at School and College.

Peel (the *second* brother of the Secretary) was a correspondent of mine, and also Porter, the son of the Bishop of Clogher; Lord Clare a very voluminous one; William Harness (a friend of Jew Milman's) another; Charles Drummond (son of the Banker); William Bankes (the Voyager); your friend R. C. Dallas, Esqʳᵉ. Hodgson, Henry Drury, Hobhouse, you were already aware of.

I have gone through this long list of

" The cold, the faithless, and the dead ",

because I know that, like " the curious in fish sauce ", you are a researcher of such things.

Besides these, there are other occasional ones to literary men and so forth, complimentary, etc., etc., etc., not worth much more than the rest. There are some hundreds, too, of Italian notes of mine, scribbled with a noble contempt of the grammar and dictionary, and in very English Etruscan; for I *speak* Italian very fluently but write it carelessly and incorrectly to a degree.

TO THE HON. AUGUSTA LEIGH   *Octr 5th, 1821*

My dearest Augusta,—Has there been nothing to make it grey? to be sure the *years* have not. Your *parcel* will not find me here—I am going to *Pisa*, for the winter. The late political troubles here have occasioned the exile of all my friends and connections, and I am going there to join them. You know or you do not know that Madame La Comtesse G. was separated from her husband last year (on account of P.P. Clerk of this parish), that the Pope decided in her favor and gave her a separate maintenance and that we lived very quietly and decently—she at her father's (as the Pope decided) and I at home—till this Summer. When her father was exiled, she was obliged either to accompany him or retire into a Convent—such being the terms of His Holiness's deed of divorcement. They went to Pisa by my recommendation and there I go to join them.

So there's a *romance* for you. I assure you it was not my wish nor fault altogether. Her husband was old—rich—and must have left her a large jointure in a few years; but he was jealous, and insisted etc, and *she* like all the rest *would* have her own way. You know that all my loves go crazy, and make scenes—and so—" She is the sixteenth Mrs. Shuffleton ". Being very young—very romantic—and odd—and being contradicted by her husband besides, and being of a country where morals are no better than in England, (though elopements and divorces are rare—and *this* made an uncommon noise—the first that had occurred at Ravenna for two hundred years—that is in a *public* way with appeals to the Pope etc) you are not to wonder much at it; she being too a beauty and the great Belle of the four Legations, and married not quite a year (at our first acquaintance) to a man *forty* years older than herself who had had two wives already and a little suspected of having poisoned his first.

We have been living hitherto decently and quietly. These

things here do not exclude a woman from all society as in y^r hypocritical country. It is very odd that all my *fairs* are such romantic people; and always daggering or divorcing—or making scenes.

But this is " positively the last time of performance " (as the playbills say), or of my getting into such scrapes for the future. Indeed—I have had my share. But this is a finisher; for you know when a woman is separated from her husband for her *Amant*, he is bound both by honour (and inclination at least I am), to live with her all his days; as long as there is no misconduct.

So you see that I have closed as papa *begun*, and *you* will probably never see me again as long as you live. Indeed you don't deserve it—for having behaved so *coldly—when I was ready to have sacrificed every thing for you—and after [you had] taken the farther* [indecipherable] *always* [indecipherable] [1]

It is nearly three years that this " liaison " has lasted. I was dreadfully in love—and she blindly so—for she has sacrificed every thing to this headlong passion. That comes of being romantic. I can say that, without being so *furiously* in love as at first, I am more attached to her than I thought it possible to be to any woman after three years—(*except one and who was she can* YOU *guess*) [1] and have not the least wish nor prospect of separation from her.

She herself, (and it is now a year since her separation, a year too of all kinds of vicissitudes et^c) is still more decided. Of course the *step* was a decisive one. If Lady B. would but please to die, and the Countess G.'s husband (for Catholics can't marry though divorced), we should probably have to marry—though I would rather *not*—thinking it the way to hate each other—for all people whatsoever.

However you need not calculate upon seeing me again in a hurry, if ever. How have you sent the *parcel*, and how am I to receive it at Pisa? I am anxious about the Seal—not about Hodgson's nonsense. What is the fool afraid of the *post* for? it is the *safest*—the only *safe* conveyance. They never meddle but with political packets.

Yours.

[1] The words in italics have been erased—apparently not by Byron.

P.S.—*You* ought to be a great admirer of the *future* Lady B. for *three* reasons, 1^{stly} She is a grand patroness of the present Lady B. and always says " that she has no doubt that " she was exceedingly ill-used by me—2dly She is an admirer of yours ; and I have had great difficulty in keeping her from writing to you eleven pages, (for she is a grand Scribe), and 3dly she having read " Don Juan " in a *French* translation—made me promise to write *no more* of it, declaring that it was abominable etc etc that *Donna Inez* WAS meant for Lady B. and in short made me vow *not* to continue it—(this occurred lately) and since the last cantos were sent to England last year). Is this not altogether odd enough? She has a good deal of *us* too. I mean that turn for ridicule like Aunt Sophy and you and I and all the B's. Desire Georgiana to write me a letter. I suppose she can by this time.

Opened by me—and the Seal taken off—so—don't accuse the post-office without cause.

B—that's a sign—a written one where the wax was.

TO LADY BYRON [1]   *Pisa, November 17, 1821*
(To the care of the Hon. Mrs. Leigh, London.)

I have to acknowledge the receipt of " Ada's hair ", which is very soft and pretty, and nearly as dark already as mine was at twelve years old, if I may judge from what I recollect of some in Augusta's possession, taken at that age. But it don't curl,—perhaps from its being let grow.

I also thank you for the inscription of the date and name, and I will tell you why ;—I believe that they are the only two or three words of your hand-writing in my possession. For your letters I returned ; and except the two words, or rather the one word, " Household ", written twice in an old account book, I have no other. I burnt your last note, for two reasons :— firstly, it was written in a style not very agreeable ; and, secondly, I wished to take your word without documents,

---

[1] This letter, never sent to Lady Byron, was enclosed by Byron in a letter to Lady Blessington (May 6th, 1823).

which are the worldly resources of suspicious people.

I suppose that this note will reach you somewhere about Ada's birthday—the 10th of December, I believe. She will then be six, so that in about twelve more I shall have some chance of meeting her;—perhaps sooner, if I am obliged to go to England by business or otherwise. Recollect, however, one thing, either in distance or nearness;—every day which keeps us asunder should, after so long a period, rather soften our mutual feelings, which must always have one rallying-point as long as our child exists, which I presume we both hope will be long after either of her parents.

The time which has elapsed since the separation has been considerably more than the whole brief period of our union, and the not much longer one of our prior acquaintance. We both made a bitter mistake; but now it is over, and irrevocably so. For, at thirty-three on my part, and a few years less on yours, though it is no very extended period of life, still it is one when the habits and thought are generally so formed as to admit of no modification; and as we could not agree when younger, we should with difficulty do so now.

I say all this, because I own to you, that, notwithstanding every thing, I considered our re-union as not impossible for more than a year after the separation;—but then I gave up the hope entirely and for ever. But this very impossibility of re-union seems to me at least a reason why, on all the few points of discussion which can arise between us, we should preserve the courtesies of life, and as much of its kindness as people who are never to meet may preserve perhaps more easily than nearer connections. For my own part, I am violent, but not malignant; for only fresh provocations can awaken my resentments. To you, who are colder and more concentrated, I would just hint, that you may sometimes mistake the depth of a cold anger for dignity, and a worse feeling for duty. I assure you that I bear you *now* (whatever I may have done) no resentment whatever. Remember, that *if you have injured me* in aught, this forgiveness is something; and that, if I have *injured you*, it is something more still, if it be true, as the moralists say, that the most offending are the least forgiving.

Whether the offence has been solely on my side, or reciprocal, or on yours chiefly, I have ceased to reflect upon any but two things,—viz. that you are the mother of my child, and that we shall never meet again. I think if you also consider the two corresponding points with reference to myself, it will be better for all three.

> Yours ever,
> NOEL BYRON [1]

TO JOHN MURRAY   *Pisa, December 4, 1821*

DEAR SIR,—By extracts in the English papers,—in your holy Ally, Galignani's *Messenger*,—I perceive that " the two greatest examples of human vanity in the present age " are, firstly, " the ex-Emperor Napoleon ", and secondly, " his Lordship, etc., the noble poet ", meaning your humble servant, " poor guiltless I ".

Poor Napoleon ! he little dreamed to what " vile comparisons " the turn of the Wheel would reduce him ! I cannot help thinking, however, that had our learned brother of the newspaper office seen my very moderate answer to the very scurrile epistle of my radical patron, John Hobhouse, M.P., he would have thought the thermometer of my " Vanity " reduced to a very decent temperature. By the way you do not happen to know whether Mrs. Fry had commenced her reform of the prisoners at the time when Mr. Hobhouse was in Newgate? there are some of his phrases, and much of his style (in that same letter), which led me to suspect that either she had not, or that he had profited less than the others by her instructions. Last week I sent back the deed of Mr. Moore signed and witnessed. It was inclosed to Mr. Kinnaird with a request to forward it to you. I have also transmitted to him my opinions upon your proposition, etc., etc., but addressed them to himself.

I have got here into a famous old feudal palazzo, on the Arno, large enough for a garrison, with dungeons below and cells in the walls, and so full of *Ghosts*, that the learned Fletcher (my valet) has begged leave to change his room, and then refused to occupy his *new* room, because there were more ghosts

---

[1] When, on the death of her mother, Lady Byron succeeded to the Wentworth estate, Byron adopted the additional name of Noel.

there than in the other. It is quite true that there are most extraordinary noises (as in all old buildings), which have terrified the servants so as to incommode me extremely. There is one place where people were evidently *walled up*; for there is but one possible passage, *broken* through the wall, and then meant to be closed again upon the inmate. The house belonged to the Lanfranchi family, (the same mentioned by Ugolino in his dream, as his persecutor with Sismondi,) and has had a fierce owner or two in its time. The staircase, etc., is said to have been built by Michel Agnolo. It is not yet cold enough for a fire. What a climate!

I am, however, bothered about these spectres, (as they say the last occupants were, too,) of whom I have as yet seen nothing, nor, indeed, heard (*myself*); but all the other ears have been regaled by all kinds of supernatural sounds. The first night I thought I heard an odd noise, but it has not been repeated. I have now been here more than a month.

Yours, BYRON

P.S.—Pray send me two or three dozen of " *Acton's corn-rubbers* " in a parcel by the post—*packed dry* and well—if you can.

I have received safely the parcel containing the Seal—the *E. Review*—and some pamphlets, etc. The others are I presume upon their way.

Are there not designs from *Faust*? Send me some, and a translation of it,—if such there is. Also of Goethe's life if such there be; if not—the original German.

Pisa, January 12, 1822

My dear Sir Walter,—I need not say how grateful I am for your letter, but I must own my ingratitude in not having written to you again long ago. Since I left England (and it is not for all the usual term of transportation) I have scribbled to five hundred blockheads on business, etc., without difficulty, though with no great pleasure; and yet, with the notion of addressing you a hundred times in my head, and always in my heart, I have not done what I ought to have done. I can only account for it on the same principle of tremulous anxiety with which one sometimes makes love to a beautiful woman of our own degree, with whom one is enamoured in good earnest; whereas, we attack a fresh-coloured housemaid without (I speak, of course, of earlier times) any sentimental remorse or mitigation of our virtuous purpose.

I owe to you far more than the usual obligation for the courtesies of literature and common friendship; for you went out of your way in 1817 to do me a service, when it required not merely kindness, but courage to do so: to have been recorded by you in such a manner, would have been a proud memorial at any time, but at such a time, when " all the world and his wife ", as the proverb goes, were trying to trample upon me, was something still higher to my self-esteem,—I allude to the *Quarterly Review* of the Third Canto of *Childe Harold*, which Murray told me was written by you,—and, indeed, I should have known it without his information, as there could not be *two* who *could* and *would* have done this at the time. Had it been a common criticism, however eloquent or panegyrical, I should have felt pleased, undoubtedly, and grateful, but not to the extent which the extraordinary good-heartedness of the whole proceeding must induce in any mind capable of such sensations. The very *tardiness* of this acknow-ledgment will, at least, show that I have not forgotten the obligation; and I can assure you that my sense of it has been out at compound interest during the delay. I shall only add one word upon the subject, which is, that I think that you, and Jeffrey, and Leigh Hunt, were the only literary men, of numbers whom I know (and some of whom I had served), who dared venture even an anonymous word in my favour just then : and that, of those three, I had never seen *one* at all —of the second much less than I desired—and that the third was under no kind of obligation to me, whatever ; while the other *two* had been actually attacked by me on a former occasion ; *one*, indeed, with some provocation, but the other wantonly enough. So you see you have been heaping " coals of fire ", etc., in the true gospel manner, and I can assure you that they have burnt down to my very heart.

I am glad that you accepted the Inscription. I meant to have inscribed *The Foscarini* to you instead ; but, first, I heard that *Cain* was thought the least bad of the two as a composition ; and, 2dly, I have abused Southey like a pickpocket, in a note to *The Foscarini*, and I recollected that he is a friend of yours (though not of mine), and that it would not be the handsome thing to dedicate to one friend any thing containing such matters about another. However, I'll work the Laureate before I have done with him, as soon as I can muster Billingsgate therefor. I like a row, and always did from a boy, in the course of which propensity, I must needs say, that I have found it the most easy of all to be gratified, personally and poetically. You disclaim " jealousies " ; but I would ask, as Boswell did of Johnson, " of *whom could* you be *jealous?* "—of none of the living certainly, and (taking all and all into consideration) of which of the dead? I don't like to bore you about the Scotch novels, (as they call them, though two of them are wholly English, and the rest half so), but nothing can or could ever persuade me, since I was the first ten minutes in your company, that you are *not* the man. To me those novels have so much of " Auld lang syne " (I was bred a canny Scot till ten years old), that I never move without them ; and when I removed from Ravenna to Pisa the other day, and sent on my library before, they were the only books that I kept by me, although I already have them by heart.

January 27, 1822

I delayed till now concluding, in the hope that I should have got *The Pirate*, who is under way for me, but has not yet hove in sight. I hear that your daughter is married, and I suppose by this time you are half a grandfather—a young one, by the way. I have heard great things of Mrs. Lockhart's

personal and mental charms, and much good of her lord:
that you may live to see as many novel Scotts as there are
Scott's novels, is the very bad pun, but sincere wish of

Yours ever most affectionately, etc.

P.S.—Why don't you take a turn in Italy? You would
find yourself as well known and as welcome as in the Highlands among the natives. As for the English, you would be with
them as in London; and I need not add, that I should be
delighted to see you again, which is far more than I shall ever
feel or say for England, or (with a few exceptions " of kith,
kin, and allies ") any thing that it contains. But my " heart
warms to the tartan ", or to anything of Scotland, which reminds me of Aberdeen and other parts, not so far from the
Highlands as that town, about Invercauld and Braemar,
where I was sent to drink goat's *whey* in 1795–6, in consequence
of a threatened decline after the scarlet fever. But I am
gossiping, so, good night—and the gods be with your dreams!

Pray, present my respects to Lady Scott, who may, perhaps,
recollect having seen me in town in 1815.

I see that one of your supporters (for, like Sir Hildebrand,
I am fond of Guillim,) is a *mermaid*; it is my *crest* too, and with
precisely the same curl of tail. There's concatenation for you:
—I am building a little cutter at Genoa, to go a cruising in the
summer. I know *you* like the sea too.

TO ROBERT SOUTHEY*   *Pisa, Fy 7th, 1822*

SIR,[1]—My friend, the Honourable Douglas Kinnaird, will
deliver to you a message from me, to which an answer is
requested.

I have the honour to be
Your very obedt. humble Servnt. BYRON

TO THE HON. DOUGLAS KINNAIRD*   [*Feb. 7th 1822*]

P.S.—I give you a " Carte blanche " in Southey's business.
If you agree with me that he ought to be called to account, I

---

[1] As a result of calumnious statements he was alleged to have made, Byron
proposed to call out Southey.

beg you to convey my invitation to meet when and where he may appoint, to settle this with him and his friend, and to let me know in as few posts as possible, that I may join you. This will (or ought) to prevent unnecessary delay. I wish you to observe that if I come to England with this object, *before* my message is delivered and the preliminaries fixed, my arrival would transpire in the interim of the arrangement; whereas, if all is settled before hand, we may bring the affair to a decision on the day of my landing.

Better on the coast of France, as less liable to interruption or publicity, but I presume Mr. S. is too great a patriot to come off the soil for such a purpose. The grounds are, that after the language he has both used and preached, this is the only honourable way of deciding the business.

I enclose your credentials in a note to Mr. Southey. I require satisfaction for the expression in his letter in the Newspapers; that will be the tenor of the Message, as you are well aware. Of course you will suspend the publication of " the Vision " [of Judgement] till we know whether the business can be settled in a more proper manner.

TO THOMAS MOORE *Pisa, March 4, 1822*

Since I wrote the enclosed, I have waited another post, and now have your answer acknowledging the arrival of the packet—a troublesome one, I fear, to you in more ways than one, both from weight external and internal.

The unpublished things in your hands, in Douglas K.'s, and Mr. John Murray's, are, *Heaven and Earth*, a lyrical kind of Drama upon the Deluge, etc.;—*Werner, now with you*;—a translation of the First Canto of the *Morgante Maggiore*;—*ditto* of an Episode in Dante;—some stanzas to the Po, June 1st, 1819;—*Hints from Horace*, written in 1811, but a good deal, *since*, to be omitted; several prose things, which may, perhaps, as well remain unpublished;—*The Vision*, etc., of Quevedo Redivivus, in verse.

Here you see is " more matter for a May morning "; but how much of this can be published is for consideration. The

Quevedo (one of my best in that line) has appalled the Row already, and must take its chance at Paris, if at all. The new Mystery is less speculative than *Cain*, and very pious; besides, it is chiefly lyrical. The *Morgante* is the *best* translation that ever was or will be made; and the rest are—whatever you please to think them.

I am sorry you think *Werner* even *approaching* to any fitness for the stage, which, with my notions upon it, is very far from my present object. With regard to the publication, I have already explained that I have no exorbitant expectations of either fame or profit in the present instances; but wish them published because they are written, which is the common feeling of all scribblers.

With respect to " Religion ", can I never convince you that *I* have no such opinions as the characters in that drama, which seems to have frightened every body? Yet *they* are nothing to the expressions in Goethe's *Faust* (which are ten times hardier), and not a whit more bold than those of Milton's Satan. My ideas of a character may run away with me: like all imaginative men, I, of course, embody myself with the character while I *draw* it, but not a moment after the pen is from off the paper.

I am no enemy to religion, but the contrary. As a proof, I am educating my natural daughter a strict Catholic in a convent of Romagna; for I think people can never have *enough* of religion, if they are to have any. I incline, myself, very much to the Catholic doctrines; but if I am to write a drama, I must make my characters speak as I conceive them likely to argue.

As to poor Shelley, who is another bugbear to you and the world, he is, to my knowledge, the *least* selfish and the mildest of men—a man who has made more sacrifices of his fortune and feelings for others than any I ever heard of. With his speculative opinions I have nothing in common, nor desire to have.

The truth is, my dear Moore, you live near the *stove* of society, where you are unavoidably influenced by its heat and its vapours. I did so once—and too much—and enough to give a colour to my whole future existence. As my success in society was *not* inconsiderable, I am surely not a prejudiced judge upon the subject, unless in its favour; but I think it, as now constituted, *fatal* to all great original undertakings of every kind. I never courted it *then*, when I was young and high in blood, and one of its " curled darlings " ; and do you think I would do so *now*, when I am living in a clearer atmosphere? One thing *only* might lead me back to it, and that is, to try once more if I could do any good in *politics* ; but *not* in the petty politics I see now preying upon our miserable country.

Do not let me be misunderstood, however. If you speak your *own* opinions, they ever had, and will have, the greatest weight with *me*. But if you merely *echo* the *monde*, (and it is difficult not to do so, being in its favour and its ferment,) I can only regret that you should ever repeat any thing to which I cannot pay attention.

But I am prosing. The gods go with you, and as much immortality of all kinds as may suit your present and all other existence.

Yours, etc.

TO THOMAS MOORE *Pisa, March 6, 1822*

The enclosed letter from Murray hath melted me ; though I think it against his own interest to wish that I should continue his connection. You may, therefore, send him the packet of *Werner*, which will save you all further trouble. And pray, *can you* forgive me for the bore and expense I have already put upon you? At least, *say* so—for I feel ashamed of having given you so much for such nonsense.

The fact is, I cannot *keep* my *resentments*, though violent enough in their onset. Besides, now that all the world are *at* Murray on my account, I neither can nor ought to leave him ; unless, as I really thought, it were better for *him* that I should.

I have had no other news from England, except a letter from Barry Cornwall, the bard, and my old school-fellow.[1] Though I have sickened you with letters lately, believe me

Yours, etc.

P.S.—In your last letter you say, speaking of Shelley, that you would almost prefer the " damning bigot " to the " annihilating infidel ". Shelley believes in immortality, how-

---

[1] "Barry Cornwall was the pen-name of Bryan Waller Procter, the literary man of law.

ever—but this by the way. Do you remember Frederick the Great's answer to the remonstrance of the villagers whose curate preached against the eternity of hell's torments? It was thus:—
" If my faithful subjects of Schrausenhaussen prefer being eternally damned, let them ".

Of the two, I should think the long sleep better than the agonised vigil. But men, miserable as they are, cling so to any thing *like* life, that they probably would prefer damnation to quiet. Besides, they think themselves so *important* in the creation, that nothing less can satisfy their pride—the insects!

TO JOHN MURRAY   *Pisa, April 22ᵈ 1822*

DEAR SIR, You will regret to hear that I have received intelligence of the death of my daughter Allegra of a fever in the Convent of Bagna Cavallo, where she was placed for the last year, to commence her education. It is a heavy blow for many reasons, but must be borne,—with time.

It is my present intention to send her remains to England for sepulture in Harrow Church (where I once hoped to have laid my own), and this is my reason for troubling you with this notice. I wish the funeral to be very private. The body is embalmed, and in lead. It will be embarked from Leghorn. Would you have any objection to give the proper directions on its arrival?

I am yours, etc., N. B.

P.S.—You are aware that protestants are not allowed holy ground in Catholic countries.

TO PERCY BYSSHE SHELLEY   *April 23, 1822*

The blow was stunning and unexpected ; for I thought the danger over, by the long interval between her stated amelioration and the arrival of the express. But I have borne up against it as I best can, and so far successfully, that I can go about the usual business of life with the same appearance of composure,

and even greater. There is nothing to prevent your coming
to-morrow; but, perhaps, to-day, and yester-evening, it was
better not to have met. I do not know that I have any thing
to reproach in my conduct, and certainly nothing in my feelings
and intentions towards the dead. But it is a moment when we
are apt to think that, if this or that had been done, such event
might have been prevented,—though every day and hour
shows us that they are the most natural and inevitable. I
suppose that Time will do his usual work—Death has done his.

Yours ever, N. B.

TO SIR WALTER SCOTT *Pisa, May 4, 1822*

MY DEAR SIR WALTER,—Your account of your family is
very pleasing: would that I " could answer this comfort with
the like " ! but I have just lost my natural daughter, Allegra,
by a fever. The only consolation, save time, is the reflection
that she is either at rest or happy; for her few years (only five)
prevented her from having incurred any sin, except what we
inherit from Adam.

" Whom the gods love die young."

I need not say that your letters are particularly welcome,
when they do not tax your time and patience; and now that
our correspondence is resumed, I trust it will continue.

I have lately had some anxiety, rather than trouble, about
an awkward affair here, which you may perhaps have heard
of; but our minister has behaved very handsomely, and the
Tuscan Government as well as it is possible for such a government to behave, which is not saying much for the latter.
Some other English and Scots, and myself, had a brawl with a
dragoon, who insulted one of the party, and whom we mistook
for an officer, as he was medalled and well mounted, etc.; but
he turned out to be a serjeant-major. He called out the
guard at the gates to arrest us (we being unarmed); upon
which I and another (an Italian) rode through the said guard;
but they succeeded in detaining others of the party. I rode to
my house, and sent my secretary to give an account of the

attempted and illegal arrest to the authorities, and then, without dismounting, rode back towards the gates, which are near my present mansion. Half-way I met my man vapouring away and threatening to draw upon me (who had a cane in my hand, and no other arms). I, still believing him an officer, demanded his name and address, and gave him my hand and glove thereupon. A servant of mine thrust in between us (totally without orders), but let him go on my command. He then rode off at full speed; but about forty paces further was stabbed, and very dangerously (so as to be in peril), by some *Callum Beg* or other of my people (for I have some rough-handed folks about me), I need hardly say without my direction or approval. The said dragoon had been sabring our unarmed countrymen, however, at the *gate, after they were in arrest,* and held by the guards, and wounded one, Captain Hay, very severely. However, he got his paiks—having acted like an assassin, and being treated like one. *Who* wounded him, though it was done before thousands of people, they have never been able to ascertain, or prove, nor even the *weapon*; some said a *pistol,* an *air-gun,* a stiletto, a sword, a lance, a pitchfork, and what not. They have arrested and examined servants and people of all descriptions, but can make out nothing. Mr. Dawkins, our minister, assures me that no suspicion is entertained of the man who wounded him having been instigated by me, or any of the party. I enclose you copies of the depositions of those with us, and Dr. Crauford, a canny Scot (*not* an acquaintance), who saw the latter part of the affair. They are in Italian.

These are the only literary matters in which I have been engaged since the publication and row about *Cain*;—but Mr. Murray has several things of mine in his obstetrical hands. Another *Mystery*—a *Vision*—a Drama—and the like. But *you won't* tell me what *you* are doing—however, I shall find you out, write what you will. You say that I should like your son-in-law—it would be very difficult for me to dislike any one connected with you; but I have no doubt that his own qualities are all that you describe.

I am sorry you don't like Lord Orford's new work. My aristocracy, which is very fierce, makes him a favourite of mine. Recollect that those " little factions " comprised Lord

Chatham and Fox, the father; and that *we* live in gigantic and exaggerated times, which make all under Gog and Magog appear pigmean. After having seen Napoleon begin like Tamerlane and end like Bajazet in our own time, we have not the same interest in what would otherwise have appeared important history. But I must conclude.

Believe me ever and most truly yours, NOEL BYRON

TO LORD HOLLAND*   *Pisa, May 11th, 1822*

MY DEAR LORD HOLLAND,—Let me thank you for your kind letter. What you say respecting poor Allegra is but too true. Her death, I confess, chilled my blood with horror. It was perhaps the most lively sorrow I have ever felt. With respect to the calumnies heaped upon me, I confess, though I am accustomed to all sorts of accusations, there are calumnies against which innocence itself loses courage. What of the— but the subject is too painful to me to touch upon. Great as my affliction may be, I beg to assure you, that I neither seek for, nor require the pity of any man; and, although I by no means reject the sympathy of my friends, yet I feel that, if it were not expressed with greater delicacy of sentiment than *the party* appears to possess, it would be more chilling to my heart than the blasts of a Siberian winter.

The war of " *Church and State* " has astonished me more than it disturbs; for I really thought " *Cain* " a speculative and hardy—but still a harmless—production. That crazy forgotten book, the " Pursuits of Literature ", contains one observation insisting notice. " Literature ", says the writer, " well or ill conducted, is the great engine by which all civilized states must ultimately be supported or overthrown." It were a difficult point to decide whether religion, education or litera- ture, in the hands of power, would tend most to its stability. It is certain, however, if by any means it could obtain all three, its influence would be unbounded, and a nation so enslaved would enjoy only an automaton existence, following every impulse of its rulers.

Let me hear from you when convenient, and believe me
Yours ever most affectionately, N. BYRON

TO JOHN MURRAY   *Montenero, May 26ᵗʰ 1822, near Leghorn*

DEAR SIR,—The body is embarked, in what ship I know not, neither could I enter into the details; but the Countess G. G. has had the goodness to give the necessary orders to Mr. Dunn, who superintends the embarkation, and will write to you. I wish it to be buried in Harrow Church: there is a spot in the Churchyard, near the footpath, on the brow of the hill looking towards Windsor, and a tomb under a large tree (bearing the name of Peachie, or Peachey), where I used to sit for hours and hours when a boy: this was my favourite spot; but, as I wish to erect a tablet to her memory, the body had better be deposited in the Church. Near the door, on the left hand as you enter, there is a monument with a tablet containing these words:—

> " When Sorrow weeps o'er Virtue's sacred dust,
> Our tears become us, and our Grief is just:
> Such were the tears she shed, who grateful pays
> This last sad tribute of her love and praise ".

I recollect them (after seventeen years), not from any thing remarkable in them, but because from my seat in the Gallery I had generally my eyes turned towards that monument: as near it as convenient I could wish Allegra to be buried, and on the wall a marble tablet placed, with these words:—[1]

In memory of
Allegra,
daughter of G. G. Lord Byron,
who died at Bagnacavallo,
in Italy, April 20th, 1822,
aged five years and three months.

" I shall go to her, but she shall not return to me."
2d Samuel, xii. 23

The funeral I wish to be as private as is consistent with decency; and I could hope that Henry Drury will, perhaps, read the service over her. If he should decline it, it can be done by the usual Minister for the time being. I do not know that I need add more just now.

---

[1] Byron's wishes were not carried out.

I will now turn to other subjects. Since I came here, I have been invited by the Americans on board of their Squadron, where I was received with all the kindness which I could wish, and with *more ceremony* than I am fond of. I found them finer ships than your own of the same class, well manned and officered. A number of American gentlemen also were on board at the time, and some ladies. As I was taking leave, an American lady asked me for a *rose* which I wore, for the purpose, she said, of sending to America something which I had about me, as a memorial. I need not add, that I felt the compliment properly. Captain Chauncey showed me an American and very pretty edition of my poems, and offered me a passage to the United States, if I would go there. Commodore Jones was also not less kind and attentive. I have since received the enclosed letter, desiring me to sit for my picture for some Americans. It is singular that, in the same year that Lady Noel leaves by will an interdiction for my daughter to see her father's portrait for many years, the individuals of a nation, not remarkable for their liking to the English in particular, nor for flattering men in general, request me to sit for my "pourtraicture", as Baron Bradwardine calls it. I am also told of considerable literary honours in Germany. Goethe, I am told, is my professed patron and protector. At Leipsic, this year, the highest prize was proposed for a translation of two Cantos of *Childe Harold*. I am not sure that this was at *Leipsic*, but Mr. Bancroft was my authority—a good German Scholar (a young American), and an acquaintance of Goethe's.

Goethe and the Germans are particularly fond of *Don Juan*, which they judge of as a work of Art. I had heard something like this before through Baron Lutzerode. The translations have been very frequent of several of the works, and Goethe made a comparison between *Faust* and *Manfred*.

All this is some compensation for your English native brutality, so fully displayed this year (I mean *not your* individually) to its brightest extent.

I forgot to mention a little anecdote of a different kind. I went over the Constitution (the Commodore's flag ship), and saw, among other things worthy of remark, a little boy *born* on board of her by a sailor's wife. They had christened him "Constitution Jones". I, of course, approved the name;

and the woman added, " Ah, Sir, if he turns out but half as good as his name! "

Yours ever and truly, N. B.

TO THE HON. DOUGLAS KINNAIRD *   *Montenero, Leghorn,*
May 27th, 1822

MY DEAR DOUGLAS,—My above address, as at Pisa, may probably be the same in Sept., and I need not add that you will be welcome there, as any where else that may happen to [be] my residence.

I have received the enclosed letter from Mr. Hanson Jr. When I constituted you my *Power of* Attorney, I meant it to be also *Power over* my Attorney. And so deal with the Attornd according to your despotism. Does he mean that the *whole* balance, or *his separate* balance, is £600? For if I recollect rightly, they set up a sort of *separate* claim, and a double claim besides. I see no use in their appealing to me, because if I empowered you to act during my absence, it was with the wish that you should do so. Else *why* make you my Potestas at all?

You see they are getting on but slowly with that eternal mortgage. If the funds fall, (and war seems imminent) I shall lose all owing to the cursed dilatoriness of trustees and Solicitors, and yet he seems eager enough for his bill. Hanson is always too sanguine about Rochdale matters. However, the sum obtained for the tolls is better than nothing. I wonder when that blessed Appeal on the minerals will be heard and decided. I suppose my politics will prevent its success. " Well, Heaven's above all! " As to the temporary and precarious tenure of the Noel affairs, manage it as you please. With those two fellows for trustees, I expect little profit, and less comfort.

Hobhouse proposed to ensure *her* life for *twenty* instead of *ten* thousand pounds. What think you? *When* and *how* and *where* are the *rents* paid, or to be paid when they are due, or are they overdue? What sum do you think I should set aside for liquidations etc.? On all these points I desiderate illumination.

What *is* Lady N. B.'s *complaint*? For of this even I know

nothing. There is another thing I wish to say. As Mr. Murray should not run risks unnecessarily while I am going down hill in the world of scribbling, I will be at the *whole* expense of the publications of the things in hand, and any little profit which may accrue, I can take, or at any rate undergo the probable loss. I care nothing about the Edinburgh Review (which I have not seen), though it will do much harm. I have no hesitation in saying that the late volume contains by far the best of my writings, and the time will come when it will be thought so.

You must also advance for me to Murray the expense of poor little Allegra's funeral. I have directed that she may be buried at Harrow on the Hill, and committed the care of the funeral (which I wish to be as private as is consistent with decency) to Mr. M. not wishing to trouble *you*.

Yours ever,   N. B.

TO THOMAS MOORE   *Montenero, Villa Dupuy, near Leghorn,*
                               June 8, 1822

I have written to you twice through the medium of Murray, and on one subject, *trite* enough,—the loss of poor little Allegra by a fever : on which topic I shall say no more—there is nothing but time.

A few days ago, my earliest and dearest friend, Lord Clare, came over from Geneva on purpose to see me before he returned to England. As I have always loved him (since I was thirteen, at Harrow) better than any (*male*) thing in the world, I need hardly say what a melancholy pleasure it was to see him for a *day* only; for he was obliged to resume his journey immediately. * * * I have heard, also, many other things of our acquaintances which I did not know; amongst others, that * * * Do you recollect, in the year of revelry 1814, the pleasantest parties and balls all over London? and not the least so at * *'s. Do you recollect your singing duets with Lady * *, and my flirtation with Lady * *, and all the other fooleries of the time? while * * was sighing, and Lady * * ogling him with her clear hazel eyes. *But* eight years have passed, and, since that time, * * has * * * * * * ;—— has run away with * * * * * ; and *mysen* (as my Nottinghamshire friends call themselves) might as well have thrown myself out of the window while you were singing, as intermarried where I did. You and * * * * have come off the best of us. I speak merely of my marriage, and its consequences, distresses, and calumnies ; for I have been much more happy, on the whole, *since*, than I ever could have been with * * * * * *.

I have read the recent article of Jeffrey in a faithful transcription of the impartial Galignani. I suppose the long and short of it is, that he wishes to provoke me to reply. But I won't, for I owe him a good turn still for his kindness by-gone. Indeed, I presume that the present opportunity of attacking me again was irresistible ; and I can't blame him, knowing what human nature is. I shall make but one remark :—what does he mean by elaborate? The whole volume was written with the greatest rapidity, in the midst of evolutions, and revolutions, and persecutions, and proscriptions of all who interested me in Italy. They said the same of *Lara*, which, *you* know, was written amidst balls and fooleries, and after coming home from masquerades and routs, in the summer of the sovereigns. Of all I have ever written, they are perhaps the most carelessly composed ; and their faults, whatever they may be, are those of negligence, and not of labour. I do not think this a merit, but it is a fact.

Yours ever and truly, N. B.

P.S.—You see the great advantage of my new signature ;— it may either stand for " Nota Bene " or " Noel Byron ", and, as such, will save much repetition, in writing either books or letters. Since I came here, I have been invited on board of the American squadron, and treated with all possible honour and ceremony. They have asked me to sit for my picture ; and, as I was going away, an American lady took a rose from me (which had been given to me by a very pretty Italian lady that very morning), because, she said, " She was determined to send or take something which I had about me to America ". *There* is a kind of Lalla Rookh incident for you ! However, all these American honours arise, perhaps, not so much from their enthusiasm for my " Poeshie ", as their belief in my dislike to the English,—in which I have the satisfaction to coincide with them. I would rather, however, have a nod from an American, than a snuff-box from an emperor.

TO ISAAC D'ISRAELI [1]   *Montenero, Villa Dupuy, n^r Leghorn,*
(to ye care of John Murray, Esqre)   *June 10th 1822*

DEAR SIR,—If you will permit me to call you so. I had some time ago taken up my pen at Pisa to thank you for the present of your new Edition of the *Literary Character*, which has often been to me a consolation, and always a pleasure. I was interrupted, however, partly by business, and partly by vexations of different kinds, for I have not very long ago lost a child by a fever, and I have had a good deal of petty trouble with the laws of this lawless country, on account of the prosecution of a servant for an attack upon a cowardly Scoundrel of a dragoon, who drew his Sword upon some unarmed Englishmen ; and whom I had done the honour to mistake for an officer, and to treat like a Gentleman. He turned out to be neither—like many others with medals and in uniform ; but he paid for his brutality with a severe and dangerous wound inflicted by nobody knows whom : for of three suspected and two arrested they have been able to identify neither, which is strange, since he was wounded in the presence of thousands in a public Street during a feast day and full promenade.

But to return to things more analogous to the *Literary Character*. I wish to say that had I known that the book was to fall into your hands, or that the MSS. notes you have thought worthy of publication would have attracted your attention, I would have made them more copious and perhaps not so careless.

I really cannot know whether I am or am not the Genius you are pleased to call me, but I am very willing to put up with the mistake, if it be one. It is a title dearly enough bought by most men, to render it endurable, even when not quite clearly

[1] Author of *Curiosities of Literature, Calamities of Authors*, etc., etc., father of the statesman.

made out, which it never *can* be till the Posterity, whose decisions are merely dreams to ourselves, has sanctioned or denied it, while it can touch us no further.

Mr. Murray is in possession of an MSS. Memoir of mine (not to be published till I am in my grave) which, strange as it may seem, I never read over since it was written and have no desire to read over again. In it I have told what, as far as I know, is the *truth—not* the *whole* truth—for if I had done so I must have involved much private and some dissipated history ; but, nevertheless, nothing but the truth, as far as regard for others permitted it to appear.

I do not know whether you have seen those MSS. ;   but as you are curious in such things as relate to the human mind, I should feel gratified if you had.

I also sent him (Murray) a few days since, a commonplace book, by my friend Lord Clare, containing a few things which may perhaps aid his publication in case of his surviving me.

If there are any questions which you would like to ask me as connected with your Philosophy of the literary Mind (*if* mine be a literary mind), I will answer them fairly or give a reason for *not*—good, bad, or indifferent.   At present I am paying the penalty of having helped to spoil the public taste, for, as long as I wrote in the false exaggerated style of youth and the times in which we live, they applauded me to the very echo ;   and within these few years, when I have endeavoured at better things and written what I suspect to have the principle of duration in it, the Church, the Chancellor, and all men— even to my grand patron Francis Jeffrey Esqre of the *E.R.*— have risen up against me and my later publications.   Such is Truth !   Men dare not look her in the face, except by degrees : they mistake her for a Gorgon, instead of knowing her to be a Minerva.

I do not mean to apply this mythological simile to my own endeavours.   I have only to turn over a few pages of your volumes to find innumerable and far more illustrious instances.

It is lucky that I am of a temper not to be easily turned aside though by no means difficult to irritate.   But I am making a dissertation instead of writing a letter.   I write to you from the Villa Dupuy, near Leghorn, with the islands of Elba and Corsica visible from my balcony, and my old friend

the Mediterranean rolling blue at my feet. As long as I retain
my feeling and my passion for Nature, I can partly soften or
subdue my other passions and resist or endure those of others.

I have the honour to be, truly, your obliged

and faithful Ser^t, NOEL BYRON

TO E. J. DAWKINS *   *Pisa, July 4th 1822*
[British Minister at Florence]

DEAR SIR,—I regret to say that my anticipations were well
founded. The Gamba family received on Tuesday an order
to quit the Tuscan States in four days.[1] Of course this is
virtually my own exile, for where they go I am no less bound
by honour than by feeling to follow. I believe we shall try
to obtain leave to remain at Lucca—if that fails, Genoa—and,
failing that, possibly America; for both Captain Chauncey of
the American Squadron (which returns in September) and
Mr. Bruen an American Merchant now at Leghorn offered
me a passage in the handsomest manner—the latter sent to
me to say that he would even send his vessel round to Genoa
for us, if we chose to accept his offer. With regard to the
interpretation which will be put upon my departure at this
time, I hope that you will do me the favour of letting the truth
be known, as my own absence will deprive me of the power of
doing so for myself, and I have little doubt that advantage will
be taken of that circumstance.

This letter will be presented to you by Mr. Taaffe, who is
in considerable confusion at a measure to which his own heed-
lessness has a good deal contributed. But—poor fellow—I
suppose that he meant no harm. He wanted the Countess
Guiccioli to go to Florence and fling herself at the feet of the
Grand Duchess—

a supplicant to wait
While Ladies interpose, and Slaves debate

I can only say, that if she did anything of the kind, I would
never fling myself at *her* feet again.

Collini's office has now become a Sinecure, and I wish him

---

[1] For an account of the affray which led to the Gambas being exiled from the
Tuscan States, see Byron's letter to Sir Walter Scott, May 4th, 1822.

joy of it.   The inconvenience and expense to me will be very
considerable, as I have two houses, furniture, Wines, Dinner
Services—linen,—books, my Schooner—and in short—a whole
establishment for a family—to leave at a moment's warning—
and this without knowing where the Gambas will be permitted
to rest, and of course where I can rest also.

The whole thing—the manner in which it was announced,
by the Commissary etc. was done in the most insulting manner.
The Courier treated as if he were a delinquent, and sent away
with Soldiers to take charge of him and lodged in the prison of
Pisa, by way of Hostel.

I trust that this just Government is now content, my
countrymen have been insulted and wounded by a rascal,
and my Servants treated like Criminals though guiltless, while
a noble and respectable family including a sick lady are
ordered away like so many felons, without a shadow of justice,
or even a *pretence* of *proof*.

With regard to yourself, I can only add that my obligations
and feelings towards you are the same as if your exertions had
been attended with Success.   I certainly did at one time think,
that whether they considered the person who applied in our
behalf, or the persons in whose behalf the application was
made, we should at least have had a *fair* trial, as I afforded
every facility for the investigation.   As it is, I will *not* express
my sentiments—at least for the present I cannot—as no words
could be at all adequate to describe my Sense of the manner
in which the whole has been conducted by these people who
call themselves a Government.

TO E. J. DAWKINS *   *Pisa, July 6th 1822*
[British Minister at Florence]

DEAR SIR,—Certainly, if anything will be of use at Lucca,
it is probable that a letter from you may have that effect.   I
should be sorry to give you the personal trouble of a journey,
on any account.   With regard to the Gambas I beg leave to
observe that the Countess Guiccioli is *not* an exile, and her
passport is or *was* given in the usual manner.   When she was
separated from her husband in 1820, by the Pope's decree,

it was enjoined by His Holiness that she was to reside with her father—or otherwise to forfeit the alimony or *any* money (or whatever the word may be in the Roman or Romagnole Doctors' Commons) allotted to her from her husband's estates by the Papal order. When her father and brother were exiled for political reasons, Count Guiccioli as was natural and conjugal applied to have her shut up in a Convent, on the plea that she was no longer residing with her family. A Minister of the Legation gave me notice of this application and its probable result in time for her to rejoin her relations in Tuscany. I could not then accompany her in person, as it would have [been] construed into an Elopement; but I joined her afterwards at Pisa. If you can obtain permission for *them* or for *her* at least to reside within the Lucchese territory, it would be a great service, till I can make arrangements for the removal of my establishment. I shall go with them, but could then return here to settle my business.—I do not even know upon what pretext She was ordered to quit Tuscany, or even if she really was so, since her name is not in the letter, nor is she an exile, and is besides in very delicate health as Sr Vacca testified and can testify.

Believe me yrs very truly
and obliged

NOEL BYRON

P.S.—Would you like to take a cruise in my little Schooner? it would console me for not being allowed to use it myself, if it could be of any pleasure to you while at Leghorn.

TO THOMAS MOORE *Pisa, August 8, 1822*

You will have heard by this time that Shelley and another gentleman (Captain Williams) were drowned about a month ago (a *month* yesterday), in a squall off the Gulf of Spezia. There is thus another man gone, about whom the world was ill-naturedly, and ignorantly, and brutally mistaken. It will, perhaps, do him justice *now*, when he can be no better for it.

I have not seen the thing you mention, and only heard of it casually, nor have I any desire. The price is, as I saw in some advertisements, fourteen shillings, which is too much to pay for a libel on oneself. Some one said in a letter, that it was a Dr. Watkins, who deals in the life and libel line. It must have diminished your natural pleasure, as a friend (*vide* Rochefoucault), to see yourself in it.

With regard to the Blackwood fellows, I never published any thing against them; nor, indeed, have seen their magazine (except in Galignani's extracts) for these three years past. I once wrote, a good while ago, some remarks on their review of *Don Juan*, but saying very little about themselves, and these were *not* published. If you think that I ought to follow your example (and I like to be in your company when I can) in contradicting their impudence, you may shape this declaration of mine into a similar paragraph for me. It is possible that you may have seen the little I *did* write (and never published) at Murray's :—it contained much more about Southey than about the Blacks.

If you think that I ought to do any thing about Watkins's book, I should not care much about publishing *my Memoir now*, should it be necessary to counteract the fellow. But, in *that* case, I should like to look over the *press* myself. Let me know what you think, or whether I had better *not* :—at least, not the second part, which touches on the actual confines of still existing matters.

I have written three more cantos of *Don Juan*, and am hovering on the brink of another (the ninth). The reason I want the stanzas again which I sent you is, that as these cantos contain a full detail (like the storm in Canto Second) of the siege and assault of Ismael, with much of sarcasm on those butchers in large business, your mercenary soldiery, it is a good opportunity of gracing the poem with * * *. With these things and these fellows, it is necessary, in the present clash of philosophy and tyranny, to throw away the scabbard. I know it is against fearful odds; but the battle must be fought; and it will be eventually for the good of mankind, whatever it may be for the individual who risks himself.

What do you think of your Irish bishop? Do you remember Swift's line, " Let me have a *barrack*—a fig for the *clergy* "? This seems to have been his reverence's motto.
* * * * *

Yours, etc.

TO THOMAS MOORE *Pisa, August 27, 1822*

It is boring to trouble you with " such small gear " ; but it must be owned that I should be glad if you would enquire whether my Irish subscription ever reached the committee in Paris from Leghorn. My reasons, like Vellum's, " are three-fold " :—First, I doubt the accuracy of all almoners, or re-mitters of benevolent cash ; second, I do suspect that the said Committee, having in part served its time to time-serving, may have kept back the acknowledgment of an obnoxious politician's name in their lists ; and third, I feel pretty sure that I shall one day be twitted by the government scribes for having been a professor of love for Ireland, and not coming forward with the others in her distresses.

It is not, as you may opine, that I am ambitious of having my name in the papers, as I can have that any day in the week gratis. All I want is to know if the Reverend Thomas Hall did or did not remit my subscription (200 scudi of Tuscany, or about a thousand francs, more or less,) to the Committee at Paris.

The other day at Viareggio, I thought proper to swim off to my schooner (the Bolivar) in the offing, and thence to shore again—about three miles, or better, in all. As it was at mid-day, under a broiling sun, the consequence has been a feverish attack, and my whole skin's coming off, after going through the process of one large continuous blister, raised by the sun and sea together. I have suffered much pain ; not being able to lie on my back, or even side ; for my shoulders and arms were equally St. Bartholomewed. But it is over,—and I have got a new skin, and am as glossy as a snake in its new suit.

We have been burning the bodies of Shelley and Williams on the sea-shore, to render them fit for removal and regular interment. You can have no idea what an extraordinary effect such a funeral pile has, on a desolate shore, with moun-tains in the back-ground and the sea before, and the singular appearance the salt and frankincense gave to the flame. All of Shelley was consumed, except his *heart*, which would not take the flame, and is now preserved in spirits of wine.

Your old acquaintance Londonderry has quietly died at North Cray ! and the virtuous De Witt was torn in pieces by the populace! What a lucky * * the Irishman has been in his life and end. In him your Irish Franklin *est mort*!

Leigh Hunt is sweating articles for his new Journal; and both he and I think it somewhat shabby in *you* not to contribute. Will you become one of the *properrioters*? " Do, and we go snacks." I recommend you to think twice before you respond in the negative.

I have nearly (*quite three*) four new cantos of *Don Juan* ready. I obtained permission from the female Censor Morum of *my* morals to continue it, provided it were immaculate; so I have been as decent as need be. There is a deal of war—a siege, and all that, in the style, graphical and technical, of the shipwreck in Canto Second, which " took ", as they say in the Row.

Yours, etc.

P.S.—That * * * Galignani has about ten lies in one paragraph. It was not a Bible that was found in Shelley's pocket, but John Keats's poems. However, it would not have been strange, for he was a great admirer of Scripture as a composition. *I* did not send my bust to the academy of New York; but I sat for my picture to young West, an American artist, at the request of some members of that Academy to *him* that he would take my portrait,—for the Academy, I believe.

I had, and still have, thoughts of South America, but am fluctuating between it and Greece. I should have gone, long ago, to one of them, but for my liaison with the Countess G[uiccioli]; for love, in these days, is little compatible with glory. *She* would be delighted to go too; but I do not choose to expose her to a long voyage, and a residence in an unsettled country, where I shall probably take a part of some sort.

TO MRS. SHELLEY   *6ᵗʰ October, 1822*

The sofa—which I regret is *not* of your furniture—it was purchased by me at Pisa since you left it.

It is convenient for my room, though of little value (about 12 pauls), and I offered to send another (now sent) in its stead. I preferred retaining the purchased furniture, but always intended that you should have as good or better in its place. I have a particular dislike to anything of Shelley's being within the same walls with Mrs. Hunt's children. They are dirtier and more mischievous than Yahoos. What they can't destroy with their filth they will with their fingers. I presume you received ninety and odd crowns from the wreck of the *Don Juan,* and also the price of the boat purchased by Captain R., if not, you will have *both.* Hunt has these in hand.

With regard to any difficulties about money, I can only repeat that I will be your banker till this state of things is cleared up, and you can see what is to be done ; so there is little to hinder you on that score. I was confined for four days to my bed at Lerici. Poor Hunt, with his six little blackguards, are coming slowly up ; as usual he turned back once—was there ever such a *kraal* out of the Hottentot country.

N. B.

TO THE HON. AUGUSTA LEIGH   *Albaro, Genoa, Nov. 7ᵗʰ 1822*

My DEAREST A.,—I have yours of the 25ᵗʰ. My illness is quite gone, it was only at Lerici. On the fourth night I had got a little sleep, and was so wearied, that, though there were three slight shocks of an Earthquake that frightened the whole town into the streets, neither they nor the tumult awakened me.

We have had a deluge here, which has carried away half the country between this and Genoa (about two miles or less distant) but being on a hill we were only nearly knocked down by the lightning and battered by columns of rain, and our lower floor afloat, with the comfortable view of the whole landscape under water, and people screaming out of their garret windows ; *two bridges* swept down, and our next door neighbours, a Cobbler, a Wigmaker, and a Ginger-bread baker, delivering up their whole stock to the elements, which marched away with a quantity of shoes, several Perukes, and Gingerbread in all its branches. The whole came on so suddenly that there was no time to prepare. Think only, at the *top* of a hill of the road being an impassable cascade, and a child being drowned a few yards from its own door (as we heard say) in a place where Water is in general a rare commodity.

Well, after all this comes a preaching Friar and says that
the day of Judgement will take place positively on the *4th* with
all kinds of tempest and what not, in consequence of which the
whole City (except some impious Scoffers) sent him presents to
avert the wrath of Heaven by his prayers, and even the *public
authorities* had warned the Captains of Ships, who, to mend the
matter, almost all bought *new Cables* and anchors by way of
weathering the Gale.

But the fourth turned out a very fine day. All those who
had paid their money are excessively angry, and insist either
upon having the day of judgement or their cash again. But the
Friar's device seems to be " no money to be returned ", and
he says that he merely made a mistake in the time, for the day
of Judgement will certainly come for all that, either here or in
some other part of Italy.

This has a little pacified the expectants. You will think
this a fiction. Enquire further then. The populace actually
used to kiss the fellow's feet in the streets. His Sermon, however, had small effect upon some, for they gave a ball on the
3^d, and a tradesman brought me an *over*charge on the same day,
upon which I threatened him with the friar; but he said that
was a reason for being paid on the 3^d as he had a sum to make
up for his last account.

There seem [1] * * *

to lady [hardy]   *Albaro, November 10, 1822*

    *   *   *   *   *   *   *

The Chevalier [2] persisted in declaring himself an ill-used
gentleman, and describing you as a kind of cold Calypso, who
lead astray people of an amatory disposition without giving
them any sort of compensation, contenting yourself, it seems,
with only making *one* fool instead of two, which is the more
approved method of proceeding on such occasions. For my
part, I think you are quite right; and be assured from me that

[1] The conclusion of this letter is missing.
[2] James Wedderburn Webster, who was now separated from his wife, Lady
Frances. Byron's correspondent was the widow of the naval officer who attended
Nelson's death-bed.

a woman (as society is constituted in England) who gives any advantage to a man may expect a lover, but will sooner or later find a tyrant; and this is not the man's fault either, perhaps, but is the necessary and natural result of the circumstances of society, which, in fact, tyrannise over the man equally with the woman; that is to say, if either of them have any feeling or honour.

You can write to me at your leisure and inclination. I have always laid it down as a maxim, and found it justified by experience, that a man and a woman make far better friendships than can exist between two of the same sex; but *these* with this condition, that they never have made, or are to make, love with each other. Lovers may, and, indeed, generally *are* enemies, but they never can be friends; because there must always be a spice of jealousy and a something of self in all their speculations.

Indeed, I rather look upon love altogether as a sort of hostile transaction, very necessary to make or to break matches, and keep the world going, but by no means a sinecure to the parties concerned.

Now, as my love perils are, I believe, pretty well over, and yours, by all accounts, are never to begin, we shall be the best friends imaginable, as far as both are concerned; and with this advantage, that we may both fall to loving right and left through all our acquaintance, without either sullenness or sorrow from that amiable passion, which are its inseparable attendants.

Believe me, etc., N. B.

TO THE HON. DOUGLAS KINNAIRD [?]   *Genoa,*
November, 1822

MY DEAR [DOUGLAS],—I have finished the twelfth canto of *Don Juan*, which I will forward when copied. With the sixth, seventh, and eighth in one volume, and the ninth, tenth, eleventh, and twelfth in another, the whole may form two volumes, of about the same size as the two former. There are some good things in them, as perhaps may be allowed. Perhaps one volume had better be published with one publisher, and the other with another; it would be a new experiment: or one in one month, and another in the next; or both at once. What thinkest thou?

Murray, long after the " piracies ", offered me a thousand pounds (guineas) a canto for as many as I might choose to write. He has since departed from this proposal, for it was too much, and I would not take advantage of it.

You must, however, use your own judgement with regard to the MSS. and let me know what you propose; presuming always (what may at last be but a presumption) that the seven new cantos are, on the whole, equal to the five former.

Suppose Hunt, or somebody else, were to publish one canto a week, upon the same size and paper, to correspond with the various former editions?—but this is merely as a vision, and may be very foolish, for aught I know.

I have read the defence of *Cain*, which is very good; who can be the author? As to myself I shall not be deterred by any outcry; your present public hate me, but they shall not interrupt the march of my mind, nor prevent me from telling those who are attempting to trample on all thought, that their thrones shall yet be rocked to their foundations. It is Madame de Stael who says, that " all talent has a propensity to attack the strong ". *I* have never flattered—whether it be or be not a proof of talent.

I have just seen the illustrious * * * [Wedderburn Webster] who came to visit me here. I had not seen him these ten years. He had a black wig, and has been made a knight for writing against the queen. He wants a diplomatic situation, and seems likely to want it.

He found me thinner even than in 1813; for since my late illness at Lerici, in my way here, I have subsided into my more meagre outline, and am obliged to be very abstinent by medical advice, on account of liver and what not.

But to the point—or at least my point in mentioning this new chevalier. Ten years ago I lent him a thousand pounds on condition that he would not go to the Jews; he took the moneys, and went to the Jews. Now, as Mr. —— [Hanson] is a purchaser of bonds, will he purchase this of me? or will any body else, at a discount?

I have been invited by the Americans on board of their squadron here, and received with the greatest kindness, and rather *too much* ceremony. They have asked me to sit for my picture to an American artist now in Florence. As I was preparing to depart, an American lady took a rose which I wore, from me, and said that she wished to send something which I had about me to America. They showed me, too, American editions of my poems, and all kinds of attention and good-will.

I also hear that, as an author, I am in high request in Germany. All this is some compensation for the desertion of the English.

Would you write a German line to Goethe for me, explaining the omission of the dedication to *Sardanapalus*, by the fault of the publisher, and asking his permission to prefix it to the forthcoming volume of *Werner* and the *Mystery*.

Are you quite well yet? I hope so. I am selling two more horses, and dismissing two superfluous servants. My horses now amount to *four*, instead of *nine* : and I have arranged my establishment on the same footing. So you perceive that I am in earnest in my frugalities.

Yours ever affectionately, N. B.

TO JOHN MURRAY [FRAGMENT]   [*Genoa, 10ᵇʳᵉ 9, 1822*]

Very willing to lighten any losses (" go to " ; thou art " a fellow that hath had losses ", like Dogberry, is it not so?) which you may experience from my becoming obnoxious to the Blue people.

I hope that you have a milder winter than we have here. We have had inundations worthy of the Trent or Po, and the Conductor (Franklin's) of my house was struck (or supposed to be stricken) by a thunderbolt. I was so near the window that I was dazzled and my eyes hurt for several minutes, and every body in the house felt an electric shock at the moment. Madame Guiccioli was frightened, as you may suppose.

I have thought since, that your bigots would have " saddled me with a judgement " (as Thwackum did Square when he

bit his tongue in talking Metaphysics), if any thing had
happened of consequence. These fellows always forget Christ
in their Christianity, and what he said when " the tower of
Siloam fell ".

To-day is the 9th, and the 10th is my surviving daughter's
birthday. I have ordered, as a regale, a mutton chop and a
bottle of ale. She is seven years old, I believe. Did I ever tell
you that the day I came of age I dined on eggs and bacon and a
bottle of ale for once in a way? They are my favourite dish
and drinkable; but as neither of them agree with me, I never
use them but on great jubilees—once in four or five years or so.

I see some booby represents the Hunts and Mrs. Shelley as
living in my house: it is a falsehood. They reside at some
distance, and I do not see them twice in a month. I have not
met Mr. H[unt] a dozen times since I came to Genoa, or near it.

> Yours ever, N. B.

TO JOHN CAM HOBHOUSE   *Genoa, 10ᵇʳᵉ 14th, 1822*

My dear H.,—Y[ou]rs of Turin arrived yesterday. If
Lady M[organ] arrives safely, she will be received; but I
suspect the Dogana will detain her. We are all in great surprise and displeasure at the Marchesa's mancanza, which is
the more extraordinary as she is a particular friend of the
Count G[amba] (the father who gave the letter), who, it is
supposed, went still further than Pius 6th with her in their
Gioventù, and at this very time, as all along, she has been a
staunch supporter of Me. Guiccioli's suit against her sposo,
still pending in appeal before his Papal Majesty. Be this as it
may, Count G[amba] writes to enquire and remonstrate. She
must have known you, as being herself a friend, and what's
more, a witness of the late Queen's; and must have heard
your name, in the course of that conflict of testimonies. But
we have had a complaint from Florence from Madame Regnier,
that you either did not or would not avail yourself of your letter
to Madame Regnier, who says she would have been glad to
see you. By my own experience, and that of all I ever heard of,
I know what Italian introductions [are]; the stranger pays the

visit, and invites to dinner; and perhaps the *visit* is repaid. This is generally the case, unless you settle in a place, and then you may have enough of mummery and maccaroni, opera boxes, and conversazioni (criminal ditto included); but a flying stranger must take " Folly as it flies ".

You ask after my health; it has been worse since I saw you, is better now, and may be better still, without being what Scrope used to call " rude health ". I never quite recovered that stupid long swim in the broiling sun and saline sea of August. At Lerici I was in my bed for four days; and it is not the best place for beds, and physicians. The doctor made his debut by talking of *Hippocratè*; in consequence of which, I sent him away; but the women being clamorous as usual, and myself, as Fribble says, in " exquisite torter ", he was recalled; and after several formidable administrations of medicines which would not remain in the stomach; and of glysters which could not be persuaded to quit it again, Nature, I presume, did the business, and saved me from a threatened inflammation of the bowels; during which (by way of rocking my cradle) we had a slight shock of an earthquake, such as we felt at Athens, probably an echo of that of Aleppo. Well, I scuttled out of bed the moment I was convalescent, got to Sestri by dint of rowing, in twelve hours; and came on per terra, to Genoa the same night; verily believing that the journey did me more good than the physic, or the physician. All went on very well till about a month ago, when I had, and have a *cutaneous* and very uncomfortable eruption, for which, by the advice of an English physician, I am taking what he calls a " *decoction of Woods* " (and of *Forests* too, I should think by its variety of tastes), and I am so pleased with the name that I swallow a pint daily with more faith than effect hitherto.

Since I have been here I have seen Dick Fitzgibbon (Lord Clare's brother, and your brother M.P.), Lady Hardy, and various of your country-people, and lastly, that little and insane James Wedderburn Webster, now converted into a Knight (but of no order—a regular Address and City Knight), yclept Sir James Wedderburn. I saw little change in him, except that his countenance rather more resembled his *backside* (do you remember Mr. Frank, of the coffee house's, accentuation of that injured word?) than heretofore; and that he had gotten

a new wig, and says he means to marry, having a wife living,
from whom he cannot get divorced.

You will have heard before this reaches you that our friend
D[ouglas] K[innaird] has had *another* fall, from *another* horse,
and thereby brake his collar-bone, besides being grievously
contused; but he is getting well, and I wish that he would
choose his stud better. I should look in vain for such another
Potestas of Attorneo, and still more vainly for a similar friend;
that is to say, who could unite the power and the will to undergo the drudgery he has done for " P.P., Clerk of this Parish ".

I trust that this will find you flourishing, in speech as in
health. I doubt if the Congressors will be so pacific as you
anticipate.

Henry Hunt is out of prison, and John Hunt is in a fair way
of going into it, by what I hear; all you predicted has come to
pass. I have gotten myself into a scrape with the very best
intentions (i.e., to do good to these Sunday paper patriots).
Doug. will narrate as much as you care to listen to. Leigh
Hunt is discomposed because said Murray showed (and be
d—d to him) a letter in which I qualified that illustrious editor
as " a bore ", and I have offended everybody, like the old man
and his ass. What is to be done with mine?

Pray excuse this long epistle. All here salute you with
meridian cordiality; remember me to Burdett, and the
Dougal, and etc., etc., believing me

Ever yours and faithfully, N. B.

TO JOHN MURRAY   *Genoa, 10bre 25°, 1822*

I had sent you back the *Quarterly*, without perusal, having
resolved to read no more reviews, good, bad, or indifferent;
but " who can control his fate? " Galignani, to whom my
English studies are confined, has forwarded a copy of at least
one half of it, in his indefatigable Catch-penny weekly compilation; and as, " like Honour, it came unlooked for ", I have
looked through it. I must say that, upon the *whole*, that is, the
whole of the *half* which I have read (for the other half is to be
the Segment of Gal.'s next week's Circular), it is extremely

handsome, and any thing but unkind or unfair. As I take the good in good part, I must not, nor will not, quarrel with the bad : what the Writer says of *Don Juan* is harsh, but it is inevitable. He must follow, or at least not directly oppose, the opinion of a prevailing, and yet not very firmly seated, party : a review may and will direct or " turn awry " the Currents of opinion, but it must not directly oppose them. *Don Juan* will be known by and bye, for what it is intended,—a *Satire* on *abuses* of the present states of Society, and not an eulogy of vice : it may be now and then voluptuous : I can't help that. Ariosto is worse; Smollett (see Lord Strutwell in vol. 2ᵈ of *R[oderick] R[andom]*) ten times worse; and Fielding no better. No Girl will ever be seduced by reading *D.J.* :—no, no ; she will go to Little's poems and Rousseau's romans for that, or even to the immaculate De Stael : they will encourage her, and not the Don, who laughs at that, and—and—most other things. But never mind—Ça ira !

And now to a less agreeable topic, of which *pars magna es*— you Murray of Albemarle Sᵗ and the other Murray of Bridge Street—" Arcades Ambo " (" *Murrays both* ") " et *cant*-are pares " : ye, I say, between you, are the Causes of the prosecution of John Hunt, Esqʳᵉ on account of the *Vision*.[1] You, by sending him an incorrect copy, and the other, by his function. Egad, but H.'s Counsel will lay it on you with a trowel for your tergiversifying as to the MSS., etc., whereby poor H. (and, for anything I know, myself—I am willing enough) is likely to be impounded.

Now, do you see what you and your friends do by your injudicious rudeness?—actually cement a sort of connection which you strove to prevent, and which, had the H.'s *prospered*, would not in all probability have continued. As it is, I will not quit them in their adversity, though it should cost me character, fame, money, and the usual et cetera.

My original motives I already explained (in the letter which you thought proper to show) : they are the *true* ones, and I abide by them, as I tell you, and I told Lʰ Hᵗ when he

---

[1] *The Vision of Judgement*, which Byron had presented to Leigh Hunt and his brother. When John was prosecuted for publishing it—at the instance of a society called the Constitutional Association, to which Charles Murray of Bridge Street acted as legal adviser—Byron provided funds for his defence. Hunt was convicted and fined.

questioned me on the subject of that letter. He was violently hurt, and never will forgive me at bottom; but I can't help that. I never meant to make a parade of it; but if he chose to question me, I could only answer the plain truth: and I confess I did not see anything in the letter to hurt him, unless I said he was "a *bore*", which I don't remember. Had their Journal gone on well, and I could have aided to make it better for them, I should then have left them, after my safe pilotage off a lee shore, to make a prosperous voyage by themselves. As it is, I can't, and would not, if I could, leave them amidst the breakers.

As to any community of feeling, thought, or opinion, between L. H. and me, there is little or none: we meet rarely, hardly ever; but I think him a good principled and able man, and must do as I would be done by. I do not know what world he has lived in, but I have lived in three or four; and none of them like his Keats and Kangaroo *terra incognita*. Alas! poor Shelley! how he would have laughed had he lived, and how we used to laugh now and then, at various things, which are grave in the Suburbs!

You are all mistaken about Shelley. You do not know how mild, how tolerant, how good he was in Society; and as perfect a Gentleman as ever crossed a drawing-room, when he liked, and where he liked.

I have some thoughts of taking a run down to Naples (*solus*, or, at most, *cum solâ*) this Spring, and writing, when I have studied the Country, a fifth and sixth Canto of *Ch^e Harolde*: but this is merely an idea for the present, and I have other excursions and voyages in my mind. The busts are finished: are you worthy of them?

Yours, etc., N. B.

P.S.—Mrs. Shelley is residing with the Hunts at some distance from me: I see them very seldom, and generally on account of their business. Mrs. S., I believe, will go to England in the Spring.

Count Gamba's family, the father and Son and daughter, are residing with me by Mr. Hill's (the minister's) recommendation, as a safer asylum from the political persecutions than they could have in another residence; but they occupy one part of a large house, and I the other, and our establishments are quite separate.

Since I have read the Q[*uarterly*], I shall erase two or three passages in the latter 6 or 7 Cantos, in which I had lightly stroked over two or three of your authors; but I will not return evil for good. I liked what I read of the article much.

Mr. J. Hunt is most likely the publisher of the new Cantos; with what prospects of success I know not, nor does it very much matter, as far as I am concerned; but I hope that it may be of use to him, for he is a stiff, sturdy, conscientious man, and I like him : he is such a one as Prynne or Pym might be. I bear you no ill will for declining the *D. Js.*, but I cannot commend your conduct to the H.'s.

Have you aided Madame de Yossy, as I requested? I sent her 300 francs. Recommend her, will you, to the Literary F[und], or to some benevolence within your Circles.

TO THE HON. AUGUSTA LEIGH   *Genoa. J^{y} 27th 1823*

MY DEAREST AUGUSTA,—Your informant was as usual in
error. Do not believe all the lies you may hear. Hobhouse
can tell you that I have *not* lost *any* of my *teeth hitherto*, since I
was 12 years old, and had a back one taken out by Dumergue
to make room for others growing, and so far from being fatter
—at *present* I am much thinner than when I left England,
when I was not very stout—the *latter* you will regret, the *former*
you will be glad to hear. Hobhouse can tell you all particulars,
though I am much reduced since he saw me, and more than
you would like. I write to you these few lines in haste, perhaps
we may meet in Spring, either *here*, or in England. Hobhouse
says your coming out would be the best thing which you could
do, for yourself and me too—ever yrs most affectly

N. B.

TO THOMAS MOORE   *Genoa, April 2, 1823*

I have just seen some friends of yours, who paid me a visit
yesterday, which, in honour of them and of you, I returned
to-day;—as I reserve my bear-skin and teeth, and paws and
claws, for our enemies.

I have also seen Henry Fox, Lord Holland's son, whom I
had not looked upon since I left him a pretty, mild boy, without
a neck-cloth, in a jacket, and in delicate health, seven long
years agone, at the period of mine eclipse—the third, I believe,
as I have generally one every two or three years. I think that
he has the softest and most amiable expression of countenance I
ever saw, and manners correspondent. If to those he can add
hereditary talents, he will keep the name of Fox in all its freshness for half a century more, I hope. I speak from a transient
glimpse—but I love still to yield to such impressions; for I
have ever found that those I liked longest and best, I took to
at first sight; and I always liked that boy—perhaps, in part,
from some resemblance in the less fortunate part of our
destinies—I mean, to avoid mistakes, his lameness. But there
is this difference, that *he* appears a halting angel, who has
tripped against a star; whilst I am *Le Diable Boiteux*,—a

soubriquet, which I marvel that, amongst their various *nominis umbræ*, the Orthodox have not hit upon.

Your other allies, whom I have found very agreeable personages, are Milor Blessington and *épouse*, travelling with a very handsome companion, in the shape of a " French Count " [1] (to use Farquhar's phrase in the *Beaux Stratagem*), who has all the air of a *Cupidon déchaîné*, and is one of the few specimens I have seen of our ideal of a Frenchman *before* the Revolution—an old friend with a new face, upon whose like I never thought that we should look again. Miladi seems highly literary, to which, and your honour's acquaintance with the family, I attribute the pleasure of having seen them. She is also very pretty even in a morning,—a species of beauty on which the sun of Italy does not shine so frequently as the chandelier. Certainly, English women wear better than their continental neighbours of the same sex. Mountjoy seems very good-natured, but is much tamed, since I recollect him in all the glory of gems and snuff-boxes, and uniforms, and theatricals, and speeches in our house—" I mean, of peers ",—(I must refer you to Pope—whom you don't read and won't appreciate —for that quotation, which you must allow to be poetical,) and sitting to Stroelling, the painter, (so you remember our visit, with Leckie, to the German?) to be depicted as one of the heroes of Agincourt, " with his long sword, saddle, bridle, Whack fal de ", etc., etc.

I have been unwell—caught a cold and inflammation, which menaced a conflagration, after dining with our ambassador, Monsieur Hill,—not owing to the dinner, but my carriage broke down in the way home, and I had to walk some miles, up hill partly, after hot rooms, in a very bleak, windy evening, and over-hotted, or over-colded myself. I have not been so robustious as formerly, ever since the last summer, when I fell ill after a long swim in the Mediterranean, and have never been quite right up to this present writing. I am thin,—perhaps thinner than you saw me, when I was nearly transparent, in 1812,—and am obliged to be moderate of my mouth ; which, nevertheless, won't prevent me (the gods willing) from dining with your friends the day after to-morrow.

[1] Count Alfred d'Orsay.

They give me a very good account of you, and of your nearly Emprisoned *Angels*. But why did you change your title?—you will regret this some day. The bigots are not to be conciliated; and, if they were—are they worth it? I suspect that I am a more orthodox Christian than you are; and, whenever I see a real Christian, either in practice or in theory, (for I never yet found the man who could produce either, when put to the proof,) I am his disciple. But, till then, I cannot truckle to tithe-mongers,—nor can I imagine what has made *you* circumcise your Seraphs.

I have been far more persecuted than you, as you may judge by my present decadence,—for I take it that I am as low in popularity and bookselling as any writer can be. At least, so my friends assure me—blessings on their benevolence! This they attribute to Hunt; but they are wrong—it must be, partly at least, owing to myself; be it so. As to Hunt, I prefer *not* having turned him to starve in the streets to any personal honour which might have accrued from some genuine philanthropy. I really act upon principle in this matter, for we have nothing much in common; and I cannot describe to you the despairing sensation of trying to do something for a man who seems incapable or unwilling to do any thing further for himself,—at least, to the purpose. It is like pulling a man out of a river who directly throws himself in again. For the last three or four years Shelley assisted, and had once actually extricated him. I have since his demise,—and even before,—done what I could: but it is not in my power to make this permanent. I want Hunt to return to England, for which I would furnish him with the means in comfort; and his situation *there*, on the whole, is bettered, by the payment of a portion of his debts, etc.; and he would be on the spot to continue his Journal, or Journals, with his brother, who seems a sensible, plain, sturdy, and enduring person. * *

TO THE EARL OF BLESSINGTON   *April 5, 1823*

MY DEAR LORD,—How is your gout? or rather, how are you? I return the Count D'Orsay's Journal, which is a very extraordinary production, and of a most melancholy truth in all that regards high life in England. I know, or knew personally, most of the personages and societies which he describes; and after reading his remarks, have the sensation fresh upon me as if I had seen them yesterday. I would however plead in behalf of some few exceptions, which I will mention by and by. The most singular thing is, *how* he should have penetrated *not* the *fact*, but the *mystery* of the English *ennui* at two-and-twenty. I was about the same age when I made the same discovery, in almost precisely the same circles,—(for there is scarcely a person mentioned whom I did not see nightly or daily, and was acquainted more or less intimately with most of them,)—but I never could have described it so well. *Il faut être Français*, to effect this.

But he ought also to have been in the country during the hunting season, with " a select party of distinguished guests ", as the papers term it. He ought to have seen the gentlemen after dinner (on the hunting days), and the soirée ensuing thereupon,—and the women looking as if they had hunted, or rather been hunted; and I could have wished that he had been at a dinner in town, which I recollect at Lord Cowper's—small, but select, and composed of the most amusing people. The dessert was hardly on the table, when, out of twelve, I counted *five asleep*; of that five, there were *Tierney*, Lord Lansdowne, and Lord Darnley—I forget the other two, but they were either wits or orators—perhaps poets.

My residence in the East and in Italy has made me somewhat indulgent of the siesta;—but then they set regularly about it in warm countries, and perform it in solitude (or at most in a tête-à-tête with a proper companion), and retire quietly to their rooms to get out of the sun's way for an hour or two.

Altogether, your friend's Journal is a very formidable production. Alas! our dearly beloved countrymen have only discovered that they are tired, and not that they are tiresome; and I suspect that the communication of the latter unpleasant verity will not be better received than truths usually are. I have read the whole with great attention and instruction. I am too good a patriot to say *pleasure*—at least I won't say so, whatever I may think. I showed it (I hope no breach of confidence) to a young Italian lady of rank, *très instruite* also;

and who passes, or passed, for being one of the three most celebrated belles in the district of Italy, where her family and connections resided in less troublesome times as to politics, (which is not Genoa, by the way,) and she was delighted with it, and says that she has derived a better notion of English society from it than from all Madame de Stael's metaphysical disputations on the same subject, in her work on the Revolution. I beg that you will thank the young philosopher, and make my compliments to Lady B. and her sister.

Believe me your very obliged and faithful　N.B.

P.S.—There is a rumour in letters of some disturbance or complot in the French Pyrenean army—generals suspected or dismissed, and ministers of war travelling to see what's the matter. " Marry (as David says), this hath an angry favour."

Tell Count D'Orsay that some of the names are not quite intelligible, especially of the clubs; he speaks of *Watts*—perhaps he is right, but in my time *Watier's* was the Dandy Club, of which (though no dandy) I was a member, at the time too of its greatest glory, when Brummel and Mildmay, Alvanley and Pierrepoint, gave the Dandy Balls; and we (the club, that is,) got up the famous masquerade at Burlington House and Garden, for Wellington. He does not speak of the *Alfred*, which was the most *recherché* and most tiresome of any, as I know, by being a member of that too.

TO THE EARL OF BLESSINGTON　　　　*April 14, 1823*

I am truly sorry that I cannot accompany you in your ride this morning, owing to a violent pain in my face, arising from a wart to which I by medical advice applied a caustic. Whether I put too much, I do not know; but the consequence is, that not only I have been put to some pain, but the peccant part and its immediate environ are as black as if the printer's devil had marked me for an author. As I do not wish to frighten your horses, or their riders, I shall postpone waiting upon you until six o'clock, when I hope to have subsided into a more christian-like resemblance to my fellow-creatures. My infliction has partially extended even to my fingers; for on trying to get the black from off my upper lip at least, I have only transferred a portion thereof to my right hand, and neither lemon-juice nor eau de Cologne, nor any other eau, have been able as yet to redeem it also from a more inky appearance than is either proper or pleasant. But " out, damn'd spot "— you may have perceived something of the kind yesterday; for on my return, I saw that during my visit it had increased, was increasing, and ought to be diminished; and I could not help laughing at the figure I must have cut before you. At any rate, I shall be with you at six, with the advantage of twilight.

Ever most truly, etc.

Eleven o'clock

P.S.—I wrote the above at three this morning. I regret to say that the whole of the skin of about an *inch* square above my upper lip has come off, so that I cannot even shave or masticate, and I am equally unfit to appear at your table, and to partake of its hospitality. Will you therefore pardon me, and not mistake this rueful excuse for a " *make-believe* ", as you will soon recognise whenever I have the pleasure of meeting you again, and I will call the moment I am, in the nursery phrase, " fit to be seen ". Tell Lady B., with my compliments, that I am rummaging my papers for a MS. worthy of her acceptation. I have just seen the younger Count Gamba; and as I cannot prevail on his infinite modesty to take the field without me, I must take this piece of diffidence on myself also, and beg your indulgence for both.

TO THE COUNT D'ORSAY   *April 22, 1823*

My dear Count D'Orsay (if you will permit me to address you so familiarly),—You should be content with writing in your own language, like Grammont, and succeeding in London as nobody has succeeded since the days of Charles the Second and the records of Antonio Hamilton, without deviating into our barbarous language,—which you understand and write, however, much better than it deserves.

My " approbation ", as you are pleased to term it, was very sincere, but perhaps not very impartial; for, though I love my country, I do not love my countrymen—at least, such as they now are. And, besides the seduction of talent and wit in your work, I fear that to me there was the attraction of vengeance. I have *seen* and *felt* much of what you have described so well. I have known the persons, and the re-unions so described,— (many of them, that is to say,) and the portraits are so like that I cannot but admire the painter no less than his performance.

But I am sorry for you; for if you are so well acquainted with life at your age, what will become of you when the illusion is still more dissipated ? But never mind—*en avant !*—live while you can; and that you may have the full enjoyment of the many advantages of youth, talent, and figure, which you possess, is the wish of an—Englishman,—I suppose, but it is no treason; for my mother was Scotch, and my name and my family are both Norman; and as for myself, I am of no country. As for my " Works ", which you are pleased to mention, let them go to the Devil, from whence (if you believe many persons) they came.

I have the honour to be your obliged, etc., etc.

TO THE EARL OF BLESSINGTON   *April 22nd, 1823*

MILOR,—I received your billet at dinner, which was a good one—with a sprinkling of female foreigners, who, I dare say, were very agreeable. As I have formed a sullen resolution about presentations, which I never break (above once a month), I begged —— to dispense me from being introduced, and intrigued for myself a place as far remote as possible from his fair guests, and very near a bottle of the best wine to confirm my misogyny. After coffee, I had accomplished my retreat as far as the hall, on full tilt towards your *thé*, which I was very eager to partake of, when I was arrested by —— requesting that I would make my bow to the French Ambassadress, who it seems is a Dillon, Irish, but born or bred in America; has been pretty, and is a *blue*, and of course entitled to the homage of all persons who have been printed. I returned, and it was then too late to detain Miss P——[1] over the tea-urn. I beg you to accept my regrets, and present my regards to Milady, and Miss P——, and Comte Alfred, and believe me

Ever yours, NOEL BYRON

TO THE COUNTESS OF BLESSINGTON   *May 3, 1823*

DEAR LADY BLESSINGTON,—My request would be for a copy of the miniature of Lady B. which I have seen in possession of the late Lady Noel, as I have no picture, or indeed memorial of any kind of Lady B., as all her letters were in her own possession before I left England, and we have had no correspondence since—at least on her part.

My message, with regard to the infant, is simply to this effect—that in the event of any accident occurring to the mother, and my remaining the survivor, it would be my wish to have her plans carried into effect, both with regard to the education of the child, and the person or persons under whose care Lady B. might be desirous that she should be placed. It is not my intention to interfere with her in any way on the subject during her life; and I presume that it would be some consolation to her to know, (if she is in ill health, as I am given to understand,) that in *no* case would any thing be done, as far as I am concerned, but in strict conformity with Lady B.'s own wishes and intentions—left in what manner she thought proper.

Believe me, dear Lady B., your obliged, etc.

TO THE COUNTESS OF BLESSINGTON   *Albaro, May 6, 1823*

MY DEAR LADY ——,—I send you the letter which I had forgotten, and the book, which I ought to have remembered. It contains (the book, I mean,) some melancholy truths; though I believe that it is too triste a work ever to have been popular. The first time I ever read it (not the edition I send

---

[1] Miss Power, Lady Blessington's sister.

you,—for I got it since,) was at the desire of Madame de Stael, who was supposed by the good-natured world to be the heroine ; —which she was not, however, and was furious at the supposition. This occurred in Switzerland, in the summer of 1816, and the last season in which I ever saw that celebrated person.

I have a request to make to my friend Alfred (since he has not disdained the title), viz. that he would condescend to add a *cap* to the gentleman in the jacket,—it would complete his costume,—and smooth his brow, which is somewhat too in-veterate a likeness of the original, God help me !

I did well to avoid the water-party,—*why*, is a mystery, which is not less to be wondered at than all my other mysteries. Tell Milor that I am deep in his MS., and will do him justice by a diligent perusal.

The letter which I enclose I was prevented from sending by my despair of its doing any good. I was perfectly sincere when I wrote it, and am so still. But it is difficult for me to withstand the thousand provocations on that subject, which both friends and foes have for seven years been throwing in the way of a man whose feelings were once quick, and whose temper was never patient. But " returning were as tedious as go o'er ". I feel this as much as ever Macbeth did ; and it is a dreary sensation, which at least avenges the real or imaginary wrongs of one of the two unfortunate persons whom it concerns.

But I am going to be gloomy ;—so " to bed, to bed ". Good night,—or rather morning. One of the reasons why I wish to avoid society is, that I can never sleep after it, and the pleasanter it has been the less I rest.

Ever most truly, etc., etc.

TO JOHN BOWRING [1]   *Genoa, May 12, 1823*

Sir,—I have great pleasure in acknowledging your letter, and the honour which the Committee have done me :—I shall endeavour to deserve their confidence by every means in my power. My first wish is to go up into the Levant in person, where I might be enabled to advance, if not the cause, at least

---

[1] Sir John Bowring, secretary of the Greek Committee founded to assist the cause of Greek freedom.

the means of obtaining information which the Committee might be desirous of acting upon; and my former residence in the country, my familiarity with the Italian language, (which is there universally spoken, or at least to the same extent as French in the more polished parts of the Continent,) and my *not* total ignorance of the Romaic, would afford me some advantages of experience. To this project the only objection is of a domestic nature, and I shall try to get over it;—if I fail in this, I must do what I can where I am; but it will be always a source of regret to me, to think that I might perhaps have done more for the cause on the spot.

Our last information of Captain Blaquiere is from Ancona, where he embarked with a fair wind for Corfu, on the 15th ult.; he is now probably at his destination. My last letter *from* him personally was dated Rome; he had been refused a passport through the Neapolitan territory, and returned to strike up through Romagna for Ancona:—little time, however, appears to have been lost by the delay.

The principal material wanted by the Greeks appears to be, first, a park of field artillery—light, and fit for mountain-service; secondly, gunpowder; thirdly, hospital or medical stores. The readiest mode of transmission is, I hear, by Idra, addressed to Mr. Negri, the minister. I meant to send up a certain quantity of the two latter—no great deal—but enough for an individual to show his good wishes for the Greek success, —but am pausing, because, in case I should go myself, I can take them with me. I do not want to limit my own contribution to this merely, but more especially, if I can get to Greece myself, I should devote whatever resources I can muster of my own, to advancing the great object. I am in correspondence with Signor Nicolas Karrellas (well known to Mr. Hobhouse), who is now at Pisa; but his latest advice merely stated, that the Greeks are at present employed in organising their *internal* government, and the details of its administration: this would seem to indicate *security*, but the war is however far from being terminated.

The Turks are an obstinate race, as all former wars have proved them, and will return to the charge for years to come, even if beaten, as it is to be hoped they will be. But in no case can the labours of the Committee be said to be in vain; for in the event even of the Greeks being subdued, and dispersed, the funds which could be employed in succouring and gathering together the remnant, so as to alleviate in part their distresses, and enable them to find or make a country (as so many emigrants of other nations have been compelled to do), would " bless both those who gave and those who took ", as the bounty both of justice and of mercy.

With regard to the formation of a brigade, (which Mr. Hobhouse hints at in his short letter of this day's receipt, enclosing the one to which I have the honour to reply,) I would presume to suggest—but merely as an opinion, resulting rather from the melancholy experience of the brigades embarked in the Columbian service than from any experiment yet fairly tried in GREECE,—that the attention of the Committee had better perhaps be directed to the employment of *officers* of experience than the enrolment of *raw British* soldiers, which latter are apt to be unruly, and not very serviceable, in irregular warfare, by the side of foreigners. A small body of good officers, expecially artillery; an engineer, with quantity (such as the Committee might deem requisite) of stores of the nature which Captain Blaquiere indicated as most wanted, would, I should conceive, be a highly useful accession. Officers, also, who had previously served in the Mediterranean would be preferable, as some knowledge of Italian is nearly indispensable.

It would also be as well that they should be aware, that they are not going " to rough it on a beef-steak and bottle of port ",—but that Greece—never, of late years, very plentifully stocked for a *mess*—is at present the country of all kinds of *privations*. This remark may seem superfluous ; but I have been led to it, by observing that many *foreign* officers, Italian, French, and even Germans (but *fewer* of the *latter*), have returned in disgust, imagining either that they were going up to make a party of pleasure, or to enjoy full pay, speedy promotion, and a very moderate degree of duty. They complain, too, of having been ill received by the Government or inhabitants ; but numbers of these complainants were mere adventurers, attracted by a hope of command and plunder, and disappointed of both. Those Greeks I have seen strenuously deny the charge of inhospitality, and declare that they shared their pittance to the last crum[b] with their foreign volunteers.

I need not suggest to the Committee the very great advantage which must accrue to Great Britain from the success of the Greeks, and their probable commercial relations with England in consequence; because I feel persuaded that the first object of the Committee is their EMANCIPATION, without any interested views. But the consideration might weigh with the English people in general, in their present passion for every kind of speculation,—they need not cross the American seas for one much better worth their while, and nearer home. The resources even for an emigrant population, in the Greek islands alone, are rarely to be paralleled; and the cheapness of every kind of, not *only necessary*, but *luxury*, (that is to say, *luxury* of *nature*,) fruits, wine, oil, etc., in a state of peace, are far beyond those of the Cape, and Van Diemen's Land, and the other places of refuge, which the English people are searching for over the waters.

I beg that the Committee will command me in any and every way. If I am favoured with any instructions, I shall endeavour to obey them to the letter, whether conformable to my own private opinion or not. I beg leave to add, personally, my respect for the gentleman whom I have the honour of addressing,

> And am, Sir, your obliged, etc.

P.S.—The best refutation of Gell [1] will be the active exertions of the Committee;—I am too warm a controversialist; and I suspect that if Mr. Hobhouse have taken him in hand, there will be little occasion for me to " encumber him with help ". If I go up into the country, I will endeavour to transmit as accurate and impartial an account as circumstances will permit.

I shall write to Mr. Karrellas. I expect intelligence from Captain Blaquiere, [2] who has promised me some early intimation from the seat of the Provisional Government. I gave him a letter of introduction to Lord Sydney Osborne, at Corfu; but as Lord S. is in the government service, of course his reception could only be a *cautious* one.

---

[1] Sir William Gell, in his *Narrative of a Journey in the Morea*, had suggested that the substitution of Russian for Turkish rule might, from the Greek point of view, be not without its advantages.

[2] At the first meeting of the Greek Committee, Edward Blaquiere, author and translator, had volunteered to visit Greece and collect information.

TO THE HON. DOUGLAS KINNAIRD †   *Genoa, May 21st, 1823*

MY DEAR DOUGLAS,—I enclose you another corrected proof of D. J., and also a note of Mr. Barry, the acting partner of Messrs. Webbs, on the proposed credit in case I go up to the Levant. I do not quite know what to name as the amount —undoubtedly about 5000, in addition to what I already have in your circular notes, and in Webb's bank, would be more than sufficient for my own personal wants for *good four years*, for my habits are simple, and you are aware that I have lately reduced my other expences of every kind. But, if I do go up among the Greeks, I may have occasion to be of service to them. There may be prisoners to ransom, some cash to advance, arms to purchase, or if I was to take an angry turn some sulky morning, and raise a troop of my own (though this is unlikely), any or all of these would require a command of credit and require my resources. You will let me have what you think proper *not under* the sum above stated ; but there is no *immediate* hurry, as I shall not sail till about July, if at all. It is to be understood that the *letter of credit for two thousand pounds* which I have *now untouched* is to be *returned* or left to be returned *untouched* in the hands of Messrs. Webb for your house the moment I receive the more extended credit. It is also [to] be understood that, if I receive this extended credit, and from any circumstances do not go up into the Levant, then that credit is to be null and void as it would then become quite superfluous to my present occasion. I am doing all I can to get away, but I have all kinds of obstacles thrown in my way by the " absurd womankind ", who seems determined on sacrificing herself in every way, and preventing me from doing any good, and all without reason ; for her relations, and her husband (who is moving the Pope and the Government here to get her to live with him again) and everybody, are earnest with her to return to Ravenna. She wants to go up to Greece too ! forsooth, a precious place to go to at present ! Of course the idea is ridiculous, as everything must there be sacrificed to seeing her out of harm's way. It is a case too, in which interest does not enter, and therefore hard to deal with ; for I have no kind of control in that way, and if she makes a scene (and she has a turn that way) we shall have another romance, and tale of ill-usage, and abandonment, and Lady Carolining, and Lady Byroning, and Glenarvoning, all cut and dry. There never was a man who gave up so much to women, and all I have gained by it has been the character of treating them harshly. However I shall do what I can, and have hopes; for her father has been recalled from his political exile; but with this proviso, that he do not return without his daughter. If I left a woman for another woman, she might have cause to complain, but really when a man merely wishes to go on a great duty, for a good cause, this selfishness on the part of the " feminie " is rather too much.

Ever yrs., N. B.

I add the enclosed letter from Mr. J. M. which does him credit : also another M.S.S. for a proof from the same.

TO HENRI BEYLE[1]   *Genoa, May 29, 1823*

SIR,—At present, that I know to whom I am indebted for a very flattering mention in the *Rome, Naples, and Florence*, in 1817, by Mons. Stendhal, it is fit that I should return my thanks (however undesired or undesirable) to Mons. Beyle, with whom I had the honour of being acquainted at Milan, in 1816. You only did me too much honour in what you were pleased to say in that work; but it has hardly given me less pleasure than the praise itself, to become at length aware (which I have done by mere accident) that I am indebted for it to one of whose good opinion I was really ambitious. So many changes have taken place since that period in the Milan circle, that I hardly dare recur to it;—some dead, some banished, and some in the Austrian dungeons.—Poor Pellico ! I trust that, in his iron solitude, his Muse is consoling him in part—one day to delight us again, when both she and her Poet are restored to freedom.

Of your works I have only seen *Rome*, etc., the Lives of Haydn and Mozart, and the *brochure* on Racine and Shakespeare. The *Histoire de la Peinture* I have not yet the good fortune to possess.

---

[1] The novelist had originally encountered Byron at Milan in 1816.

There is one part of your observations in the pamphlet which I shall venture to remark upon;—it regards Walter Scott. You say that " his character is little worthy of enthusiasm ", at the same time that you mention his productions in the manner they deserve. I have known Walter Scott long and well, and in occasional situations which call forth the *real* character—and I can assure you that his character *is* worthy of admiration—that of all men he is the most *open*, the most *honourable*, the most *amiable*. With his politics I have nothing to do : they differ from mine, which renders it difficult for me to speak of them. But he is *perfectly sincere* in them : and Sincerity may be humble, but she cannot be servile. I pray you, therefore, to correct or soften that passage. You may, perhaps, attribute this officiousness of mine to a false affectation of *candour*, as I happen to be a writer also. Attribute it to what motive you please, but *believe* the *truth*. I say that Walter Scott is as nearly a thorough good man as man can be, because I *know* it by experience to be the case.

If you do me the honour of an answer, may I request a speedy one?—because it is possible (though not yet decided) that circumstances may conduct me once more to Greece. My present address is Genoa, where an answer will reach me in a short time, or be forwarded to me wherever I may be.

I beg you to believe me, with a lively recollection of our brief acquaintance, and the hope of one day renewing it,

Your ever obliged

And obedient humble servant, NOEL BYRON

TO THE COUNTESS OF BLESSINGTON   *Albaro, June 2, 1823*

MY DEAR LADY BLESSINGTON,—I am *superstitious*, and have recollected that memorials with a *point* are of less fortunate augury ; I will, therefore, request you to accept, instead of the *pin*, the enclosed chain, which is of so slight a value that you need not hesitate. As you wished for something *worn*, I can only say, that it has been worn oftener and longer than the other. It is of Venetian manufacture ; and the only peculiarity about it is, that it could only be obtained at or from Venice. At Genoa they have none of the same kind. I also enclose a ring, which I would wish *Alfred* to keep; it is too large to *wear*; but is formed of *lava*, and so far adapted to the fire of his years and character. You will perhaps have the goodness to acknowledge the receipt of this note, and send back the pin (for good luck's sake), which I shall value much more for having been a night in your custody.

Ever and faithfully your obliged, etc.

P.S.—I hope your *nerves* are well to-day, and will continue to flourish.

TO J. J. COULMANN *Genoa, July 12* [?], *1823*

MY DEAR SIR,—Your letter, and what accompanied it, have given me the greatest pleasure. The glory and the works of the writers who have deigned to give me these volumes, bearing their names, were not unknown to me, but still it is more flattering to receive them from the authors themselves. I beg you to present my thanks to each of them in particular; and to add, how proud I am of their good opinion, and how charmed I shall be to cultivate their acquaintance, if ever the occasion should occur. The productions of M. Jouy have long been familiar to me. Who has not read and applauded *The Hermit* and *Scylla*? But I cannot accept what it has pleased your friends to call their *homage*, because there is no sovereign in the republic of letters; and even if there were, I have never had the pretension or the power to become a usurper.

I have also to return you thanks for having honoured me with your own compositions; I thought you too young, and probably too amiable, to be an author. As to the Essay, etc., I am obliged to you for the present, although I had already seen it joined to the last edition of the translation. I have nothing to object to it, with regard to what concerns myself personally, though naturally there are some of the facts in it discoloured, and several errors into which the author has been led by the accounts of others. I allude to facts, and not criticisms. But the same author has cruelly calumniated my father and my grand-uncle, but more especially the former. So far from being " brutal ", he was, according to the testimony of all those who knew him, of an extremely amiable and (*enjoué*) joyous character, but careless (*insouciant*) and dissipated. He had, consequently, the reputation of a good officer, and showed himself such in the Guards, in America. The facts themselves refute the assertion. It is not by " brutality " that a young Officer in the Guards seduces and carries off a Marchioness, and marries two heiresses. It is true that he was a very handsome man, which goes a great way. His first wife (Lady Conyers and Marchioness of Carmarthen) did not die of grief, but of a malady which she caught by having imprudently insisted upon accompanying my father to a hunt, before she was completely recovered from the accouchement which gave birth to my sister Augusta.

His second wife, my respected mother, had, I assure you, too proud a spirit to bear the ill-usage of any man, no matter who he might be; and this she would have soon proved. I should add, that he lived a long time in Paris, and was in habits of intimacy with the old Marshal Biron, Commandant of the French Guards; who, from the similitude of names, and Norman origin of our family, supposed that there was some distant relationship between us. He died some years before the age of forty, and whatever may have been his faults, they were certainly not those of harshness and grossness (*dureté et grossièreté*). If the notice should reach England, I am certain that the passage relative to my father will give much more pain to my sister (the wife of Colonel Leigh, attached to the Court of the late Queen, *not* Caroline, but Charlotte, wife of George III.), even than to me; and this she does not deserve, for there is not a more angelic being upon earth. Augusta and I have always loved the memory of our father as much as we loved each other, and this at least forms a presumption that the stain of harshness was not applicable to it. If he dissipated his fortune, that concerns us alone, for we are his heirs; and till we reproach him with it, I know no one else who has a right to do so. As to Lord Byron, who killed Mr. Chaworth in a duel, so far from retiring from the world, he made the tour of Europe, and was appointed Master of the Staghounds after that event, and did not give up society until his son had offended him by marrying in a manner contrary to his duty. So far from feeling any remorse for having killed Mr. Chaworth, who was a fire-eater (*spadassin*), and celebrated for his quarrelsome disposition, he always kept the sword which he used upon that occasion in his bed-chamber, where it still was *when he died*. It is singular enough, that when very young, I formed a strong attachment for the grand-niece and heiress of Mr. Chaworth, who stood in the same degree of relationship [to him] as myself to Lord Byron; and at one time it was thought that the two families would have been united in us. She was two years older than me, and we were very much together in our youth. She married a man of an ancient and respectable family; but her marriage was not a happier one than my own. Her conduct, however, was irreproachable, but there was no sympathy between their characters, and a separation took place. I had not seen her for many years. When an occasion offered, I was upon the point, with her consent, of paying her a visit, when my sister, who has always had more influence over me than anyone else, persuaded me not to do it. " For," said she, " if you go, you will fall in love again, and then there will be a scene; one step will lead to another, *et cela fera un éclat* ", etc. I was guided by these reasons, and shortly after I married; with what success it is useless to say. Mrs. C. some time after, being separated from her husband, became insane; but she has since recovered her reason, and is, I believe, reconciled to her husband. This is a long letter, and principally about my family, but it is the fault of M. Pichot, my benevolent biographer. He may say of me whatever of good or evil pleases him, but I desire that he should speak of my relations only as they deserve. If you could find an occasion of making him, as well as M. Nodier, rectify the facts relative to my father, and publish them, you would do me a great service, for I cannot bear to have him unjustly spoken of. I must conclude abruptly, for I have occupied you too long. Believe me to be very much honoured by your esteem, and always your obliged and obedient servant,

NOEL BYRON

P.S.—The tenth or twelfth of this month I shall embark for Greece. Should I return, I shall pass through Paris, and shall be much flattered in meeting you and your friends. Should I not return, give me as affectionate a place in your memory as possible.

6

Greece

September 1823 to April 1824

Byron did not expect that he would return from Greece—so he declared to his last confidante, the garrulous Lady Blessington; nor did he suppose that, while he still existed to further the cause of Hellenic freedom, his service would be easy. But he had accepted the Committee's invitation to represent them, and was resolved to do his utmost. Unfortunately neither was he a diplomatist, nor had he the training of a straightforward man of action. From the outset he encountered reverses. The Greeks were divided among themselves; each party was eager to lay hold of Byron's war-chest; and, having reached Cephalonia at the beginning of August 1823, he remained there till the end of the year, endeavouring to assess the claims and compose the differences of various rival parties. On January 5th, 1824, he at length gained Missolonghi, a squalid and inhospitable town among unhealthy marshlands. The story of Byron's life at Missolonghi is one of unending exasperation and ceaseless disappointment. He died of fever, after a brief but painful illness, on April 19th. His body was shipped to England and buried near Nottingham, in the village church of Hucknall Torkard.

JOURNAL IN CEPHALONIA

June 19th 1823

The dead have been awakened—shall I sleep?
  The World's at war with tyrants—shall I crouch?
The harvest's ripe—and shall I pause to reap?
  I slumber not; the thorn is in my Couch;
Each day a trumpet soundeth in mine ear,
  Its echo in my heart—

1823

Mataxata, Cephalonia, Sep^t 28

On the sixteenth (I think) of July, I sailed from Genoa in the English brig *Hercules*: J^{no} Scott, Master. On the 17th, a Gale of wind occasioning confusion and threatening damage to the horses in the hold, we bore up again for the same port, where we remained four and twenty hours longer, and then put to sea, touched at Leghorn, and pursued our voyage by the straits of Messina for Greece. Passing within sight of Elba, Corsica, the Lipari islands including Stromboli, Sicily, Italy, etc., about the 4th of August we anchored off Argostoli, in the chief harbour of the Island of Cephalonia.

Here I had some expectation of hearing from Capt. B[laquiere], who was on a mission from the G^k Committee in London to the Provisional Gov^t of the Morea, but, rather to my surprise, learned that he was on his way home, though his latest letters to me from the peninsula, after expressing an anxious wish that I should come up without delay, stated further that he intended to remain in the country for the present. I have since received various letters from him addrest to Genoa, and forwarded to the Islands, partly explaining the cause of his unexpected return, and also (contrary to his former opinion) requesting me not to proceed to Greece *yet*, for sundry reasons, some of importance. I sent a boat to Corfu in the hopes of finding him still there, but he had already sailed for Ancona.

In the island of Cephalonia, Colonel Napier commanded in chief as Resident, and Col. Duffie the 8th, a King's Regiment then forming the Garrison. We were received by both those Gentlemen, and indeed by all the officers, as well as the

Civilians, with the greatest kindness and hospitality, which, if we did not deserve, I still hope that we have done nothing to forfeit, and it has continued unabated, even since the Gloss of new Acquaintance has been worn away by frequent intercourse.

We here learned, what has since been fully confirmed, that the Greeks were in a state of political dissention amongst themselves; that Mavrocordato was dismissed, or had resigned (*L'un vaut bien l'autre*); and that Colocotroni, with I know not what or whose party, was paramount in the Morea. The Turks were in force in Acarnania, etc., and the Turkish fleet blockaded the coast from Messolonghi to Chiarenza, and subsequently to Navarino. The Greek fleet, from the want of means or other causes, remained in port in Hydra, Ipsara, and Spetzas, and, for aught that is yet certainly known, may be there still. As, rather contrary to my expectations, I had no advices from Peloponnesus, and had also letters to receive from England from the Committee, I determined to remain for the interim in the Ionian Islands, especially as it was difficult to land on the opposite coast without risking the confiscation of the vessel and her contents, which Captn Scott, naturally enough, declined to do, unless I would ensure to him the full amount of his possible damage.

To pass the time we made a little excursion over the mountain to Saint Euphemia, by worse roads than I ever met in the course of some years of travel in rough places of many countries. At Santa Euphemia we embarked for Ithaca, and made the tour of that beautiful Island, which I had visited several years before. The hospitality of Capt. Knox (the Resident) and his lady was in no respect inferior to that of our military friends of Cephalonia. That gentleman, with Mrs. K., and some of their friends, conducted us to the fountain of Arethusa, which alone would be worth the voyage; but the rest of the Island is not inferior in attractions to the admirers of Nature. The arts and traditions I leave to the Antiquaries, and so well have those Gentlemen contrived to settle such questions, that, as the existence of Troy is disputed, so that of Ithaca (as Homer's Ithaca, *i.e.*) is not yet admitted.

Though the month was August, and we had been cautioned against travelling in the sun, yet, as I had during my former experience never suffered from the heat as long as I continued in *motion*, I was unwilling to lose so many hours of the day on account of a sunbeam more or less, and, though our party was rather numerous, no one suffered either illness or inconvenience, as far as could be observed, though one of the servants (a Negro) declared that it was as hot as in the West Indies. I had left our thermometer on board, so could not ascertain the precise degree. We returned to Saint Euphemia, and passed over to the monastery of Samos on the opposite part of the bay, and proceeded next day to Argostoli by a better road than the path to Saint Euphemia. The land journey was made on mules.

Some day after our return, I heard that there were letters for me at Zante; but a considerable delay took place before the Greek, to whom they were consigned, had them properly forwarded, and I was at length indebted to Col. Napier for obtaining them for me; *what* occasioned the demur or delay was never explained.

I learned, by my advices from England, the request of the Committee that I would act as their representative near the Greek Gov^t, and take charge of the proper disposition and delivery of certain stores, etc., etc., expected by a vessel which has not yet arrived up to the present date (Septr 28).

Soon after my arrival, I took into my own pay a body of forty Suliotes under their chiefs Photomara, Giavella, and Drako, and would probably have increased the number, but I found them not quite united among themselves in any thing except raising their demands on me, although I had given a dollar per man more each month than they could receive from the G^k Gov^t, and they were destitute, at the time I took them, of everything. I had acceded to their own demand, and paid them a month in advance. But, set on probably by some of the trafficking shopkeepers with whom they were in the habit of dealing on credit, they made various attempts at what I thought extortion, so that I called them together, stating my view of the case, and declining to take them on with me. But I offered them another month's pay, and the price of their passage to Acarnania, where they could now easily go, as the Turkish fleet was gone, and the blockade removed.

This part of them accepted, and they went accordingly. Some difficulty arose about restoring their arms by the Septinsular Gov^t, but these were at length obtained, and they are now with their compatriots in Etolia or Acarnania.

I also transferred to the resident in Ithaca the sum of two hundred and fifty dollars for the refugees there, and I had conveyed to Cephalonia a Moreote family who were in the greatest helplessness, and provided them with a house and decent maintenance under the protection of Messrs. Corgialegno, wealthy merchants of Argostoli, to whom I had been recommended by my correspondents.

I had caused a letter to be written to Marco Bozzaris, the acting commander of a body of troops in Acarnania, for whom I had letters of recommendation. His answer was probably the last he ever signed, or dictated, for he was killed in action the very day after its date, with the character of a good soldier, and an honourable man, which are not always found together nor indeed separately. I was also invited by Count Metaxa, the Governor of Messolonghi, to go over there ; but it was necessary, in the present state of parties, that I should have some communication with the existing Gov^t on the subject of their opinion *where* I might be, if not *most* useful, at any rate *least* obnoxious.

As I did not come here to join a faction but a nation, and to deal with honest men and not with speculators or peculators, (charges bandied about daily by the Greeks of each other) it will require much circumspection to avoid the character of a partizan, and I perceive it to be the more difficult as I have already received invitations from more than one of the contending parties, always under the pretext that *they* are the " real Simon Pure ". After all, one should not despair, though all the foreigners that I have hitherto met with from amongst the Greeks are going or gone back disgusted.

Whoever goes into Greece at present should do it as Mrs. Fry went into Newgate—not in the expectation of meeting with any especial indication of existing probity, but in the hope that time and better treatment will reclaim the present burglarious and larcenous tendencies which have followed this General Gaol delivery.

When the limbs of the Greeks are a little less stiff from the shackles of four centuries, they will not march so much " as if they had gyves on their legs ". At present the Chains are broken indeed; but the links are still clanking, and the Saturnalia is still too recent to have converted the Slave into a sober Citizen. The worst of them is that (to use a coarse but the only expression that will not fall short of the truth) they are such damned liars; there never was such an incapacity for veracity shown since Eve lived in Paradise. One of them found fault the other day with the English language, because it had so few shades of a Negative, whereas a Greek can so modify a " No " to a " Yes ", and *vice versa*, by the slippery qualities of his language, that prevarication may be carried to any extent and still leave a loop-hole through which perjury may slip without being perceived. This was the Gentleman's own talk, and is only to be doubted because in the words of the Syllogism " Now Epimenides was a Cretan ". But they may be mended by and bye.

Sept. 30th.

After remaining here some time in expectation of hearing from the G^k G^t I availed myself of the opportunity of Messrs. B[rowne] and T[relawny] proceeding to Tripolitza, subsequently to the departure of the Turkish fleet, to write to the acting part of the Legislature. My object was not only to obtain some accurate information so as to enable me to proceed to the Spot where I might be, if not most safe, at least more serviceable, but to have an opportunity of forming a judgement on the real state of their affairs. In the meantime I hear from Mavrocordato and the Primate of Hydra, the latter inviting me to that island, the former hinting that he should like to meet me there or elsewhere.

1823.

10bre 17th

My Journal was discontinued abruptly and has not been resumed sooner, because on the day of its former date I received a letter from my sister Augusta, that intimated the illness of my daughter, and I had not then the heart to continue it. Subsequently I had heard through the same channel that she was better, and since that she is well; if so, for me all is well.

But although I learned this early in 9th 9bre, I know not why I have not continued my journal, though many things which would have formed a curious record have since occurred.

I know not why I resume it even now, except that, standing at the window of my apartment in this beautiful village, the calm though cool serenity of a beautiful and transparent Moonlight, showing the Islands, the Mountains, the Sea, with a distant outline of the Morea traced between the double Azure of the waves and skies, has quieted me enough to be able to write, from which (however difficult it may seem for one who has written so much publicly to refrain) is, and always has been, to me a task and a painful one. I could summon testimonies, were it necessary; but my hand-writing is sufficient. It is that of one who thinks much, rapidly, perhaps deeply, but rarely with pleasure.

But—*En avant*. The Greeks are advancing in their public progress, but quarrelling amongst themselves. I shall probably, *bon grè mal grè*, be obliged to join one of the factions, which I have hitherto strenuously avoided in the hope to unite them in one common interest.

Mavrocordato has appeared at length with the Hydriote Squadron in these seas, which apparition would hardly have taken place had I not engaged to pay two hundred thousand piastres (10 piastres per dollar being the present value on the Greek continent) in aid of Messolonghi, and has commenced operations somewhat successfully but not very prudently.

Fourteen (some say seventeen) Greek ships attacked a Turkish vessel of 12 Guns, and took her. This is not quite an Ocean Thermopylæ, but *n'importe*; they (*on dit*) have found on board 50,000 dollars, a sum of great service in their present exigencies, if properly applied. This prize, however, has been made within the bounds of Neutrality on the coast of Ithaca, and the Turks were (it is said) pursued on shore, and some slain. All this may involve a question of right and wrong with the not very tolerant Thomas Maitland, who is not very capable of distinguishing either. I have advanced the sum above noted to pay the said Squadron; it is not very large but is double that which Napoleon, the Emperor of Emperors, began his campaign in Italy withal—*vide Las Cases, passim*, vol. i. (*tome premier*).

The Turks have retired from before Messolonghi—nobody knows why—since they left provisions and ammunition behind them in quantities, and the Garrison made no sallies, or none to any purpose. They never invested Messolonghi this year, but bombarded Anatoliko (a sort of village which I recollect well, having passed through the whole of that country with fifty Albanians in 1809, Messolonghi included) near the Achelous. Some say Vrioni Pacha heard of an insurrection near Scutari, some one thing, some another. For my part, I have been in correspondence with the Chiefs, and their accounts are not unanimous.

The Suliotes, both there, here, and elsewhere, having taken a kind of liking *to*, or at least formed or renewed a sort of acquaintance *with*, me—(as I have aided them and their families in all that I could, according to circumstances) are apparently anxious that I should put myself forward as their Chief (if I may so say). I would rather not for the present, because there are too many divisions and Chiefs already. But if it should appear necessary, why—as they are admitted to be the best and bravest of the present combatants—it might, or may, so happen that I could, would, should, or shall take to me the support of such a body of men, with whose aid I think something might be done both *in* Greece and *out* of it (for there is a good deal to put to rights in both). I could maintain them out of my own present means (always supposing my present income and means to be permanent). They are not above a thousand, and of these not six hundred *real* Suliotes ; but then they are allowed to be equal (that seems a bravado though, but it is in print recently) *one* to 5 European Moslems, and ten Asiatics ! Be it as it may, they are in high esteem, and my very good friends.

A soldier may be maintained on the Mainland for 25 piastres (rather *better than two* dollars a month) monthly, and find his rations out of the country, or for *five dollars*, including his paying for his rations. Therefore for between two and three thousand dollars a month (and the dollar here is to be had for 4 and 2 pence instead of 4 and 6 pence, the price in England), I could maintain between five hundred and a thousand of these warriors for as long as necessary, and I have more means than are (supposing them to last) [sufficient] to do so. For my own personal wants are very simple (except in horses as I am no great pedestrian), and my income considerable for any country but England (being equal to the President's of the United

745

States! the English Secretaries of States or the French Ambassador's at Vienna and the greater Courts—150,000 Francs, I believe), and I have hope to have sold a Manor besides for nearly 3,000,000 francs more. Thus I could (with what we should extract according to the usages of war also), keep on foot a respectable clan, or Sept, or tribe, or horde, for some time, and, as I have not any motive for so doing but the well-wishing to Greece, I should hope with advantage.

TO THE COUNTESS GUICCIOLI [1]   *October 7*

Pietro has told you all the gossip of the island,—our earthquakes, our politics, and present abode in a pretty village. As his opinions and mine on the Greeks are nearly similar, I need say little on that subject. I was a fool to come here; but, being here, I must see what is to be done.

October ——

We are still in Cephalonia, waiting for news of a more accurate description; for all is contradiction and division in the reports of the state of the Greeks. I shall fulfil the object of my mission from the Committee, and then return into Italy; for it does not seem likely that, as an individual, I can be of use to them;—at least no other foreigner has yet appeared to be so, nor does it seem likely that any will be at present.

Pray be as cheerful and tranquil as you can; and be assured that there is nothing here that can excite any thing but a wish to be with you again,—though we are very kindly treated by the English here of all descriptions. Of the Greeks, I can't say much good hitherto, and I do not like to speak ill of them, though they do of one another.

October 29

You may be sure that the moment I can join you again, will be as welcome to me as at any period of our recollection. There is nothing very attractive here to divide my attention; but I must attend to the Greek cause, both from honour and inclination. Messrs. B[rowne] and T[relawny] are both in the Morea, where they have been very well received, and both of

[1] Extracts from letters to the Countess Guiccioli, printed in Moore's *Life*.

them write in good spirits and hopes. I am anxious to hear how the Spanish cause will be arranged, as I think it may have an influence on the Greek contest. I wish that both were fairly and favourably settled, that I might return to Italy, and talk over with you *our*, or rather Pietro's adventures, some of which are rather amusing, as also some of the incidents of our voyages and travels. But I reserve them, in the hope that we may laugh over them together at no very distant period.

TO THE HON. AUGUSTA LEIGH †   *Cephalonia, 8bre 12th 1823*

MY DEAREST AUGUSTA,—Your three letters on the subject of Ada's indisposition have made me very anxious to hear further of her amelioration. I have been subject to the same complaint, but not at so early an age, nor in so great a degree. Besides, it never affected my eyes but rather my hearing, and that only partially and slightly and for a short time. I had dreadful and almost periodical headaches till I was fourteen, and sometimes since; but abstinence and a habit of bathing my head in cold water every morning cured me, I think, at least I have been less molested since that period. Perhaps she will get quite well when she arrives at womanhood. But that is some time to look forward to, though if she is of so sanguine a habit it is probable that she may attain to that period earlier than is usual in our colder climate; * * * * * * You will excuse me touching on this topic *medically* and " en passant " because I cannot help thinking that the determination of blood to the head so early unassisted may have some connection with a similar tendency to earlier maturity. Perhaps it is a phantasy. At any rate let me know how she is. I need not say how *very* anxious I am (at this distance particularly) to hear of her welfare.

You ask why I came up amongst the Greeks? It was stated to me that my so doing might tend to their advantage in some measure in their present struggle for independence, both as an individual and as a member for the Committee now in England. How far this may be realized I cannot pretend to anticipate, but I am willing to do what I can. They have at length found leisure to quarrel among themselves, after repelling their other enemies, and it is no very easy part that I may have to play to avoid appearing partial to one or other of their factions. They have turned out Mavrocordato, who was the only *Washington* or *Kosciusko* kind of man amongst them, and they have not yet sent their deputies to London to treat for a loan, nor in short done themselves so much good as they might have done. I have written to Mr. Hobhouse three several times with a budget of documents on the subject, from which he can extract all the present information for the Committee. I have written to their Gov^t at Tripolizza and Salamis, and am waiting for instructions *where* to proceed, for things are in such a state amongst them, that it is difficult to conjecture where one could be useful to them, if at all. However, I have some hopes that they will see their own interest sufficiently not to quarrel till they have received their national independence, and then they can fight it out among them in a domestic manner—and welcome. You may suppose that I have something to *think* of at least, for you can have no idea what an intriguing cunning unquiet generation they are, and as emissaries of all parties come to me at present, and I must act impartially, it makes me exclaim, as Julian did at his military exercises, " Oh! Plato, what a task for a Philosopher! "

However, *you* won't think much of *my philosophy*; nor do I, *entre nous*———

If you think this epistle or any part of it worth transmitting to L^y B. you can send her a copy, as I suppose—unless she is become I know not what—she cannot be altogether indifferent as to my " whereabouts " and *what*abouts.

I am at present in a very pretty village (Metaxata in Cephalonia) between the mountains and the sea, with a view of Zante and the Morea, waiting for some more decisive intelligence from the provisional Gov^t in Salamis.—— But here come some visitors.

I was interrupted yesterday by Col. Napier and the Captain of a King's ship now in the harbour. Col. N. is Resident or Governor here and has been extremely kind and hospitable, as indeed have been all the English here. When their visit was over a Greek arrived on business about this eternal siege of Mesalonghi (on the Coast of Acarnania or Etolia) and some convoys of provisions which we want to throw in; and after this was discussed, I got on horseback (I brought up my horses with me on board and troublesome neighbours they were in blowing weather) and rode to Argostoli and back; and then I had one of my *thunder* headaches (*you* know how my head acts like a barometer when there is electricity in the air) and I could not resume till this morning. Since my arrival in August I made a tour to Ithaca (which you will take to be Ireland, but if you look into Pope's *Odyssey*, you will discover to be the antient name of the Isle of Wight) and also over some parts of Cephalonia.

We are pretty well in health, the Gods be thanked! By the way, who is this Dr. Tipperary or Mayo or whatever his name is? I never heard of anything of the name except an Irish County. Laurence the Surgeon, if he be the man who has been persecuted for his metaphysics, is, I have heard, an excellent professional man. But I wonder Ldy. B. should employ (so tell her) a Papist or a Sceptic. I thought that like " douce David Deans " she would not have allowed " a Goutte of physic to go through any of the family " unless she was sure that the prescriber was a Cameronian.

There is a clever but eccentric man here, a Dr. Kennedy, who is very pious and tries in good earnest to make converts; but his Christianity is a queer one, for he says that the priesthood of the Church of England are no more Christians than " Mahound or Termagant " are. He has made some converts, I suspect rather to the beauty of his wife (who is pretty as well as pious) than of his theology. I like what I have seen of him, of *her* I know nothing, nor desire to know, having other things to think about. *He* says that the dozen shocks of an Earthquake we had the other day are a sign of his doctrine, or a judgement on his audience, but this opinion has not acquired proselytes. One of the shocks was so prolonged that, though not very heavy, we thought the house would come down, and as we have a staircase to dismount *out* of the house (the buildings here are different from ours), it was judged expedient by the inmates (all *men* please to recollect, as if there had been females we must have helped them out or broken our heads for company) to make an expeditious retreat into the court-yard. *Who* was *first* out of the door I know not, but when I got to the bottom of the stairs I found several arrived before me, which could only have happened by their jumping out of the windows or down *over* or from the stairs (which had no balustrade or bannisters) rather than in the regular way of descent. The scene was ludicrous enough, but we had several more slight shocks in the night but stuck quietly to our beds, for it would have been of no use moving, as the house would have been down first, had it been to come down at all.

There was no great damage done in the Island (except an old house or two cracking in the middle), but the soldiers on parade were lifted up as a boat is by the tide, and you could have seen the whole line waving (though no one was in motion) by the heaving of the ground on which they were drawn up. You can't complain of this being a brief letter.

I wish you would obtain from Lady B. some account of Ada's disposition, habits, studies, moral tendencies, and temper, as well as of her personal appearance, for except from the miniature drawn five years ago (and she is now double that age nearly) I have no idea of even her aspect. When I am advised on these points, I can form some notion of her character and what way her dispositions or indispositions ought to be treated. At *her* present age I have an idea that I had many feelings and notions which people would not believe if I stated them *now*, and therefore I may as well keep them to myself. Is she social or solitary, taciturn or talkative, fond of reading or otherwise? And what is her *tic*?—I mean her foible. Is she passionate? I hope that the Gods have made her anything save *poetical*—it is enough to have one such fool in a family. You can answer all this at your leisure : address to *Genoa* as usual, the letters will be forwarded better by my Correspondents there.

Yours ever, N. B.

P.S.—Tell Douglas K^d I have only just got his letter of August 19th, and not only approve of his accepting a sum not under ten or twelve thousand pounds for the property in question, but also of his getting as much as can be gotten *above* that price.

TO DAVID GRANT*   *Cephalonia, 9ᵇʳᵉ 13th, 1823*

SIR,—I answered your obliging letter of the 12th of August by Capt. Symonds, and have now to avail myself of the advantage of your correspondence.

I yesterday drew bills for four thousand pounds sterling on my bankers in London, Messrs. Ransom and Co., Pall Mall East, in favour of the Greek Provisional Government to enable part of their fleet to succour Missolonghi now in a state of blockade. My letter of credit on Messrs. Ransom and the bills will be presented to your house by Mr Hamilton Browne, who is authorized to receive the amount in dollars and to convey these to this Island, the Greek Deputies paying the insurance and other expences incidental to business. I have to request that you will have the goodness to remit the sum as soon as possible. The bills are thirty days after sight, and I believe that Messrs. Webb can and have assured you of the goodness of the house on which they are drawn. I do not know what the present exchange is at Malta; but I should prefer infinitely negotiating with your house to transacting any business with the merchants of the Ionian Islands.

I have the honour to be your obliged and
very obedt. humble Sevt., NOEL BYRON

TO THE HON. DOUGLAS KINNAIRD*   *10ᵇʳᵉ 10th, 1823*

DEAR DOUGLAS,—This will be delivered by Col. Napier, whom I request you to present to the Committee. He is too well known to require me to say more than I have already said in my letter to Mr. Bowring—which see.

I have had only *two* letters from you, both (I think) of August: one, however, is without date. I have often written to acknowledge both, and to sanction or approve your acceptance of the Rochdale proposition.

I have been expending monies on the Greek cause. I shall probably have to expend *more*, and therefore require *more* to *expend*. As I hope that you have gotten together the Kirkby Mallory dues—also arrears—also mine own especial fees and

funds, the Rochdale produce and my income for the ensuing
year (and I have still of the present year something in hand,
including my Genoese credit) ought to make a pretty sufficient
sort of sum to take the field withal; and I like to do so with all
I can muster, in case of anything requiring the same. I shall
be as saving of my purse and person as you recommend; but
you know that [it] is as well to be in readiness with one or both
in the event of either being required.

Yrs, ever and faithfully, N. B.

P.S.—Col. Napier will tell you the recent events.

TO THE HON. DOUGLAS KINNAIRD [?]*   *10bre 11th, 1823*
[P.S. to a letter not preserved]

P.S.—I presume that you have also come to some agreement
with Mr. M. about " Werner ". The year is more than out
since he published it. Although the copyright should only be
worth two or three hundred pounds, I will tell you what can
be done with them. For three hundred pounds I can maintain
in Greece at more than *fullest pay* of the Provisional Govt.,
rations included, one hundred armed men *for three months*! It
is not that I am in any pressing need of monies, especially of
this kind, but it is better to have all financial matters arranged
of whatever description—rents, funds, purchase-monies or
printer's products. I presume that there is or will be something
from " the Island " also, and from the sale of the other writings;
but I do not reckon much on anything of that kind. H. ought
to have collected the works by this time, as before directed,
and published the whole eleven new D.J.s.

I am particular on this point only because a sum of trifling
account even for a Gentleman's *personal* expences in *London* or
Paris in Greece can arm and maintain hundreds of men. You
may judge of this when I tell you that the four thousand pounds
advanced by me is likely to set a fleet and an army in motion
for some months.

I request you to avoid all unnecessary disbursements
(excepting for the Insurances) in England. Whatever remains
to be paid to lawyers and creditors (and you yourself say that it
is but a sum not exceeding much my *whole*, Kirkby Mallory

included, *half* year's income) can be settled after the Greek war, or the Greek Kalends ; for the dogs, especially the lawyers, have already had more than ever was justly owing to them. But they shall have fair play—and I too, I hope and trust ; but prithee look to these recommended affairs.

TO THE HON. DOUGLAS KINNAIRD †   *10ᵇʳᵉ 23ʳᵈ, 1823*

DEAR DOUGLAS,—A quarter of a year has elapsed since I have heard from you, but I have written through various channels to approve of your *Rochdale proposition* which I hope has gone on *well*.

A Greek vessel has arrived from the squadron to convey me to Missolonghi, where Mavrocordato now is, and has assumed the command, so that I expect to embark immediately. Address, however, to Cephalonia, (through Messrs. Webb and Barry of Genoa, as usual) ; and get together all the means and credit of mine you can, to face the war establishment, for it is " in for a penny, in for a pound ", and I must do all that I can for the Ancients. I have advanced them four thousand pounds, which got the squadron to sea, and I made them forward the Deputies for the Loan, who ought to be soon in England, having sailed some weeks ago. I have already transmitted to you a copy of their agreement etc.—and to Hobhouse and Bowring various dispatches with copies or originals of correspondence more or less important. I am labouring to reconcile their parties, and there is some hope *now* of succeeding. Their *public* affairs go on well. The Turks have retreated from Acarnania without a battle, after a few fruitless attempts on Anatoliko and Corinth is taken, and the Greeks have gained a battle in the Archipelago and the squadron here, too, has taken a Turkish corvette with some money and a cargo. In short, if they can obtain a Loan, I am of opinion that matters will assume and preserve a steady and favourable aspect for their independence.

In the mean time I stand paymaster, and what not ; and lucky it is that, from the nature of the warfare and of the country, the resources even of an individual can be of partial and temporary service.

Colonel Stanhope is at Messolonghi. Probably we shall attempt Patras next. The Suliotes, who are friends of mine, seem anxious to have me with them, and so is Mavrocordato. If I can but succeed in reconciling the two parties (and I have left no stone unturned therefor), it will be something; and if not, why we must go over to the Morea with the Western Greeks—who are the bravest, and at present the strongest, now that they have beaten back the Turks—and try the effect of a little *physical* advice, should they persist in rejecting *moral* persuasion. I suppose you know the state and names of the parties from my letters to Hobhouse and Bowring. Once more (as usual) recommending to you the reinforcement of my strong box and credit from all lawful sources and *re*sources of mine to their practicable extent (and after all, it is better playing at nations than gaming at Almack's or Newmarket or piecing or dinnering) and also requesting Your Honour to write now and then one of those pithy epistles " touching the needful " so agreeable to the distant traveller,

I remain ever yours, N. B.

P.S.—Please to transmit any further credits through Messrs. Webb and Barry who have been very civil and useful, all throughout.

Dragomestri, January 2, 1824

MY DEAR MUIR,[1]—I wish you many returns of the season, and happiness therewithal. Gamba and the Bombard (there is a strong reason to believe) are carried into Patras by a Turkish frigate, which we saw chase them at dawn on the 31st : we had been close under the stern in the night, believing her a Greek till within pistol shot, and only escaped by a miracle of all the Saints (our captain says), and truly I am of his opinion, for we should never have got away of ourselves. They were signalising their consort with lights, and had illuminated the ship between decks, and were shouting like a mob ;—but then why did they not fire? Perhaps they took us for a Greek brûlot, and were afraid of kindling us—they had no colours flying even at dawn nor after.

At daybreak my boat was on the coast, but the wind unfavourable for *the port* ;—a large vessel with the wind in her favour standing between us and the Gulf, and another in chase of the Bombard about twelve miles off, or so. Soon after they stood (*i.e.* the Bombard and frigate) apparently towards Patras and, a Zantiote boat making signals to us from the shore to get away, away we went before the wind, and ran into a creek called Scrofes, I believe, where I landed Luke and another (as Luke's life was in most danger), with some money for themselves, and a letter for Stanhope, and sent them up the country to Messolonghi, where they would be in safety, as the place where we were could be assailed by armed boats in a moment, and Gamba had all our arms except two carbines, a fowling-piece, and some pistols.

In less than an hour the vessel in chase neared us, and we dashed out again, and showing our stern (our boat sails very well), got in before night to Dragomestri, where we now are. But where is the Greek fleet? I don't know—do you? I told our master of the boat that I was inclined to think the two large vessels (there were none else in sight) Greeks. But he answered, " They are too large—why don't they show their colours? " and his account was confirmed, be it true or false, by several boats which we met or passed, as we could not at any rate have got in with that wind without beating about for a long time; and as there was much property, and some lives to risk (the boy's especially) without any means of defence, it was necessary to let our boatmen have their own way.

I despatched yesterday another messenger to Messolonghi for an escort, but we have yet no answer. We are here (those of my boat) for the fifth day without taking our clothes off, and sleeping on deck in all weathers, but are all very well, and in good spirits. It is to be supposed that the Government will send, for their own sakes, an escort, as I have 16,000 dollars on board, the greater part for their service. I had (besides personal property to the amount of about 5000 more) 8000 dollars in specie of my own, without reckoning the Committee's stores: so that the Turks will have a good thing of it, if the prize be good.

I regret the detention of Gamba, etc., but the rest we can make up again; so tell Hancock[1] to set my bills into cash as soon as possible, and Corgialegno to prepare the remainder of my credit with Messrs. Webb to be turned into monies. I shall remain here, unless something extraordinary occurs, till Mavrocordato sends, and then go on, and act according to circumstances. My respects to the two colonels, and remembrances to all friends. Tell " *Ultima Analise* " that his friend [P]raidi did not make his appearance with the brig, though I think that he might as well have spoken with us *in* or *off* Zante, to give us a gentle hint of what we had to expect.

Yours ever affectionately, N. B.

P.S.—Excuse my scrawl on account of the pen and the frosty morning at daybreak. I write in haste, a boat starting for Kalamo. I do not know whether the detention of the Bombard (if she be detained, for I cannot swear to it, and I can only judge from appearances, and what all these fellows say), be an affair of the Government, and neutrality, and, etc.—but *she was stopped at least* twelve miles distant from any port, and had all her papers regular from *Zante* for *Kalamo* and *we also*. I did not land at Zante, being anxious to lose as little time as possible; but Sir F. S. came off to invite me, etc., and every body was as kind as could be, even in Cephalonia.

---

[1] Messrs. Samuel Barff and Charles Hancock were bankers of Zante and Argostoli.

TO CHARLES HANCOCK   *Missolonghi, February 5, 1824*

DEAR SIR,—Dr. Muir's letter and yours of the 23d reached me some days ago. Tell Muir that I am glad of his promotion for his sake, and of his remaining near us for our sakes ; though I cannot but regret Dr. Kennedy's departure, which accounts for the previous earthquakes and the present English weather in this climate. With all respect to my medical pastor, I have to announce to him, that amongst other fire-brands, our fire-master Parry (just landed) has disembarked an elect black-smith, entrusted with three hundred and twenty-two Greek Testaments. I have given him all facilities in my power for his works spiritual and temporal ; and if he can settle matters as easily with the Greek Archbishop and hierarchy, I trust that neither the heretic nor the supposed sceptic will be accused of intolerance.

By the way, I met with the said Archbishop at Anatolico (where I went by invitation of the Primates a few days ago, and was received with a heavier cannonade than the Turks, probably), for the second time (I had known him here before) ; and he and P. Mavrocordato, and the Chiefs and Primates and I, all dined together, and I thought the metropolitan the merriest of the party, and a very good Christian for all that. But Gamba (we got wet through on our way back) has been ill with a fever and colic ; and Luke (not the Evangelist, but a disciple of mine) has been out of sorts too, and so have others of the people, and I have been very well,—except that I caught cold yesterday, with swearing too much in the rain at the Greeks, who would not bear a hand in landing the Committee stores, and nearly spoiled our combustibles ; but I turned out in person, and made such a row as set them in motion, blas-pheming at them all from the Government downwards, till they actually did *some* part of what they ought to have done several days before, and this is esteemed, as it deserves to be, a wonder.

Tell Muir that, notwithstanding his remonstrances, which I receive thankfully, it is perhaps best that I should advance with the troops ; for if we do not do something soon, we shall only have a third year of defensive operation and another siege, and all that. We hear that the Turks are coming down in force, and sooner than usual : and as these fellows do mind me a little, it is the opinion that I should go,—firstly, because they will sooner listen to a foreigner than one of their own people, out of native jealousies : secondly, because the Turks will sooner treat or capitulate (if such occasion should happen) with a Frank than a Greek ; and, thirdly, because nobody else seems disposed to take the responsibility—Mavrocordato being very busy here, the foreign military men too young or not of authority enough to be obeyed by the natives, and the Chiefs (as aforesaid) inclined to obey any one except, or rather than, one of their own body. As for me, I am willing to do what I am bidden, and to follow my instructions. I neither seek nor shun that nor any thing else that they may wish me to attempt : as for personal safety, besides that it ought not to be a considera-tion, I take it that a man is on the whole as safe in one place as another ; and, after all, he had better end with a bullet than bark in his body. If we are not taken off with the sword, we are like to march off with an ague in this mud basket ; and to conclude with a very bad pun, to the ear rather than to the eye, better *martially* than *marsh-ally* ;—the situation of Messolonghi is not unknown to you. The dykes of Holland when broken down are the Deserts of Arabia for dryness, in comparison.

And now for the sinews of war. I thank you and Mr. Barff for your ready answer, which, next to ready money, is a pleasant thing. Besides the assets and balance, and the relics of the Corgialegno correspondence with Leghorn and Genoa, (I sold the dog's flour, tell him, but not at *his* price,) I shall request and require, from the beginning of March ensuing, about five thousand dollars every two months, *i.e.* about twenty-five thousand within the current year, at regular intervals, independent of the sums now negotiating. I can show you documents to prove that these are considerably *within* my supplies for the year in more ways than one ; but I do not like to tell the Greeks *exactly what* I *could* or would advance on an emergency, because, otherwise, they will double and triple their demands (a disposition that they have already sufficiently shown) : and though I am willing to do all I can *when* necessary, yet I do not see *why* they should not help a little ; for they are not quite so bare as they pretend to be by some accounts.

February 7, 1824

I have been interrupted by the arrival of Parry,[1] and afterwards by the return of Hesketh, who has not brought an answer to my epistles, which rather surprises me. You will write soon, I suppose. Parry seems a fine rough subject, but will hardly be ready for the field these three weeks : he and I will (I think) be able to draw together,—at least, *I* will not interfere with or contradict him in his own department. He complains grievously of the mercantile and *enthusymusy*, as Braham pronounces enthusiasm, part of the Committee, but greatly praises Gordon and Hume. Gordon *would* have given three or four thousand pounds and come out *himself*, but Kennedy or somebody else disgusted him, and thus they have spoiled part of their subscription and cramped their operations. Parry says Blaquière is a humbug, to which I say nothing. He sorely laments the printing and civilising expenses, and wishes that there was not a Sunday-school in the world, or *any* school *here* at present, save and except always an academy for artilleryship.

He complained also of the cold, a little to my surprise ; firstly, because, there being no chimneys, I have used myself to do without other warmth than the animal heat and one's cloak, in these parts ; and, secondly, because I should as soon have expected to hear a volcano sneeze, as a firemaster (who is to burn a whole fleet) exclaim against the atmosphere. I fully expected that his very approach would have scorched up the town like the burning-glasses of Archimedes.

Well, it seems that I am to be Commander-in-Chief, and the post is by no means a sinecure, for we are not what Major Sturgeon calls " a set of the most amicable officers ". Whether we shall have " a boxing bout between Captain Sheers and the Colonel ", I cannot tell ; but, between Suliote chiefs, German barons, English volunteers, and adventurers of all nations, we are likely to form as goodly an allied army as ever quarrelled beneath the same banner.

February 8, 1824

Interrupted again by business yesterday, and it is time to conclude my letter. I drew some time since on Mr. Barff for

---

[1] William Parry, firemaster R.N., had been sent out to Greece by the Committee, with eight English workmen, to help prepare the insurgents' artillery.

a thousand dollars, to complete some money wanted by the Government. The said Government got cash on that bill *here*, and at a profit; but the very same fellow who gave it to them, after proposing to give me money for other bills on Barff to the amount of thirteen hundred dollars, either could not, or thought better of it. I had written to Barff advising him, but had afterwards to write to tell him of the fellow's having not come up to time. You must really send me the balance soon. I have the artillerists and my Suliotes to pay, and Heaven knows what besides; and as every thing depends upon punctuality, all our operations will be at a stand-still unless you use despatch. I shall send to Mr. Barff or to you further bills on England for three thousand pounds, to be negotiated as speedily as you can. I have already stated here and formerly the sums I can command at home within the year,—without including my credits, or the bills already negotiated or negotiating, or Corgialegno's balance of Messrs. Webb's letter,—and my letters from my friends (received by Mr. Parry's vessel) confirm what I already stated. How much I may require in the course of the year I can't tell, but I will take care that it shall not exceed the means to supply it.

Yours ever, N. B.

P.S.—I have had, by desire of a Mr. *Gerosstati*, to draw on Demetrius Delladecima (is it our friend *in ultima analise*?) to pay the Committee expenses. I really do not understand what the Committee mean by some of their proceedings. Parry and I get on well *hitherto*: how long this may last, Heaven knows, but I hope it will, for a good deal for the Greek service depends upon it; but he has already had some *miffs* with Col. S[tanhope], and I do all I can to keep the peace amongst them. However, Parry is a fine fellow, extremely active, and of strong, sound, practical talent, by all accounts. Enclosed are bills for three thousand pounds, drawn in the mode directed (*i.e.* parcelled out in smaller bills). A good opportunity occurring for Cephalonia to send letters on, I avail myself of it. Remembrances to Stevens and all friends. Also my compliments and every thing kind to the colonels and officers.

February 9, 1824

P.S.—2d or 3d. I have reason to expect a person from

England directed with papers (on business) for me to sign, somewhere in the Islands, by and by : if such should arrive, would you forward him to me by a safe conveyance, as the papers regard a transaction with regard to the adjustment of a lawsuit, and a sum of several thousand pounds, which I, or my. bankers and trustees for me, may have to receive (in England) in consequence. The time of the probable arrival I cannot state, but the date of my letters is the 2d. Nov., and I suppose that he ought to arrive soon.

FROM THE MANUSCRIPT BOOK CONTAIN-
ING THE JOURNAL IN CEPHALONIA *Febry. 15th, 1824*

Upon February 15th—(I write on the 17th of the same month) I had a strong shock of a convulsive description, but whether Epileptic, Paralytic, or Apoplectic, is not yet decided by the two medical men, who attend me; or whether it be of some other nature (if such there be). It was very painful, and, had it lasted a minute longer, must have extinguished my mortality—if I can judge by sensations. I was speechless with the features much distorted, but *not* foaming at the mouth, they say, and my struggles so violent that several persons— two of whom, Mr. Parry the engineer, and my Servant Tita the Chasseur, are very strong men—could not hold me. It lasted about ten minutes, and came on immediately after drinking a tumbler of Cider mixed with cold water in Col. Stanhope's apartments. This is the first attack that I have had of the kind to the best of my belief. I never heard that any of my family were liable to the same, though my mother was subject to *hysterical affections*.

Yesterday (the 16th) leeches were applied to my temples. I had previously recovered a good deal, but with some feverish and variable symptoms. I bled profusely, and, as they went too near the temporal artery, there was some difficulty in stopping the blood even with the Lunar Caustic. This, how- ever, after some hours was accomplished about eleven o'clock at night, and this day (the 17th), though weakly, I feel tolerably convalescent.

With regard to the presumed causes of this attack, as far as I know, there might be several. The state of the place and the weather permit little exercise at present. I have been violently agitated with more than one passion recently, and a good deal occupied, politically as well as privately, and amidst conflicting parties, politics, and (as far as regards public matters) circumstances. I have also been in an anxious state with regard to things which may be only interesting to my own private feelings, and, perhaps, not uniformly so temperate as I may generally affirm that I was wont to be. How far any or all of these may have acted on the mind or body of one who had already undergone many previous changes of place and passion during a life of thirty-six years, I cannot tell, nor—— But I am interrupted by the arrival of a report from a party returned from reconnoitring a Turkish Brig of War, just stranded on the Coast, and which is to be attacked the moment we can get some guns to bear upon her. I shall hear what Parry says about it. Here he comes——

TO THE HON. AUGUSTA LEIGH   *Missolonghi,*
[Monday] Feb^v 23^d 1824

MY DEAREST AUGUSTA,[1]—I received a few days ago yours and Lady B's report of Ada's health, with other letters from England for which I ought to be and am (I hope) sufficiently thankful, as they were of great comfort and I wanted some, having been recently unwell, but am now much better. So that you need not be alarmed.

You will have heard of our journeys and escapes, and so forth, perhaps with some exaggeration; but it is all very well now, and I have been for some time in Greece, which is in as good a state as could be expected considering circumstances. But I will not plague you with politics, wars, or *earthquakes*, though we had another very smart one three nights ago, which produced a scene ridiculous enough, as no damage was done except to those who stuck fast in the scuffle to get first out of the doors or windows, amongst whom some recent importations,

[1] This letter was found unfinished on Byron's writing-table after his death.

fresh from England, who had been used to quieter elements, were rather squeezed in the press for precedence.

I have been obtaining the release of about nine and twenty Turkish prisoners—men, women, and children—and have sent them at my own expense home to their friends, but one, a pretty little girl of nine years of age named Hato or Hatagée, has expressed a strong wish to remain with me, or under my care, and I have nearly determined to adopt her. If I thought that Lady B. would let her come to England as a Companion to Ada—(they are about the same age), and we could easily provide for her; if not, I can send her to Italy for education. She is very lively and quick, and with great black oriental eyes, and Asiatic features. All her brothers were killed in the Revolution; her mother wishes to return to her husband who is at Prevesa, but says that she would rather entrust the child to me in the present state of the Country. Her extreme youth and sex have hitherto saved her life, but there is no saying what might occur in the course of the *war* (and of *such* a war), and I shall probably commit her to the charge of some English lady in the islands for the present. The Child herself has the same wish, and seems to have a decided character for her age. You can mention this matter if you think it worth while. I merely wish her to be respectably educated and treated, and, if my years and all things be considered, I presume it would be difficult to conceive me to have any other views.

With regard to Ada's health, I am glad to hear that it is so much better. But I think it right that Lady B. should be informed, and guard against it accordingly, that her description of much of her indisposition and tendencies very nearly resemble my *own* at a similar age, except that I was much more impetuous. Her preference of *prose* (strange as it may seem) *was* and indeed *is* mine (for I hate *reading* verse, and always did), and I never invented anything but " *boats—ships* " and generally relating to the Ocean. I shewed the report to Col. Stanhope, who was struck with the resemblance of *parts* of it to the *paternal* line even *now*. But it is also fit, though unpleasant, that I should mention that my recent attack, and a very severe one, had a strong appearance of *epilepsy*. *Why*— I know not, for it is late in life—its first appearance at thirty-six—and, as far as I *know*, it is not *hereditary*, and it is that it may not *become* so, that you should tell Lady B. to take some precautions in the case of Ada. My attack has not yet returned, and I am fighting it off with abstinence and exercise, and thus far with success; if merely casual, it is all very well.

TO JOHN MURRAY   *Missolonghi, February 25, 1824*

I have heard from Mr. Douglas Kinnaird that you state " a report of a satire on Mr. Gifford having arrived from Italy, *said* to be written by *me*! but that *you* do not believe it ". I dare say you do not, nor any body else, I should think. Whoever asserts that I am the author or abetter of anything of the kind on Gifford lies in his throat. I always regarded him as my literary father, and myself as his prodigal son; if any such composition exists, it is none of mine. *You* know as well as any body upon *whom* I have or have not written; and *you* also know whether they do or did not deserve that same. And so much for such matters.

You will perhaps be anxious to hear some news from this part of Greece (which is the most liable to invasion); but you will hear enough through public and private channels. I will, however, give you the events of a week, mingling my own private peculiar with the public; for we are here jumbled a little together at present.

On Sunday (the 15th, I believe), I had a strong and sudden convulsive attack, which left me speechless, though not motionless—for some strong men could not hold me; but whether it was epilepsy, catalepsy, cachexy, or apoplexy, or what other *exy* or *epsy*, the doctors have not decided; or whether it was spasmodic or nervous, etc.; but it was very unpleasant, and nearly carried me off, and all that. On Monday, they put leeches to my temples, no difficult matter, but the blood could not be stopped till eleven at night (they had gone too near the temporal artery for my temporal safety), and neither styptic nor caustic would cauterise the orifice till after a hundred attempts.

On Tuesday, a Turkish brig of war ran on shore. On Wednesday, great preparations being made to attack her, though protected by her consorts, the Turks burned her and retired to Patras. On Thursday, a quarrel ensued between the Suliotes and the Frank guard at the arsenal : a Swedish officer was killed, and a Suliote severely wounded, and a general fight expected, and with some difficulty prevented. On Friday, the officer was buried; and Captain Parry's English artificers mutinied, under pretence that their lives were in danger, and are for quitting the country :—they may.

On Saturday we had the smartest shock of an earthquake which I remember, (and I have felt thirty, slight or smart, at different periods ; they are common in the Mediterranean,) and the whole army discharged their arms, upon the same principle that savages beat drums, or howl, during an eclipse of the moon :—it was a rare scene altogether—if you had but seen the English Johnnies, who had never been out of a cockney workshop before !—or will again, if they can help it—and on Sunday we heard that the Vizier is come down to Larissa, with one hundred and odd thousand men.

In coming here, I had two escapes ; one from the Turks, (*one* of my vessels was taken, but afterwards released,) and the other from shipwreck. We drove twice on the rocks near the Scrofes (Islands near the coast).

I have obtained from the Greeks the release of eight-and-twenty Turkish prisoners, men, women, and children, and sent them to Patras and Prevesa at my own charges. One little girl of nine years old, who prefers remaining with me, I shall (if I live) send, with her mother, probably, to Italy, or to England, and adopt her. Her name is Hato, or Hatagée. She is a very pretty lively child. All her brothers were killed by the Greeks, and she herself and her mother merely spared by special favour and owing to her extreme youth, she being then but five or six years old.

My health is now better, and I ride about again. My office here is no sinecure, so many parties and difficulties of every kind ; but I will do what I can. Prince Mavrocordato is an excellent person, and does all in his power ; but his situation is perplexing in the extreme. Still we have great hopes of the success of the contest. You will hear, however, more of public news from plenty of quarters : for I have little time to write.

Believe me, yours, etc., etc., N. Bn.

TO THE EARL OF CLARE   *Missolonghi, March 31, 1824*

My dearest Clare,—This will be presented to you by a live Greek deputy, for whom I desiderate and solicit your countenance and goodwill. I hope that you do not forget that I always regard you as my dearest friend and love you as when we were Harrow boys together; and if I do not repeat this as often as I ought, it is that I may not tire you with what you so well know.

I refer you to Signor Zaimie, the Greek deputy, for all news, public and private. He will do better than an epistle in this respect.

I was sorry to hear that Dick had exported a married woman from Ireland, not only on account of morals but monies. I trust that the jury will be considerate. I *thought* that Richard looked sentimental when I saw him at Genoa, but little expected what he was to land in. Pray who *is* the lady? The papers merely inform us by dint of asterisks that she is somebody's wife and has children, and that Dick (as usual) was the intimate friend of the confiding husband. It is to be hoped that the jury will be bachelors.

Pray take care of *yourself* Clare, my dear, for in some of your letters I had a glimpse of a similar intrigue of yours. Have a care of an *éclat*. Your Irish juries lay it on heavy; and then besides you would be fixed for life with a *second-hand épouse*, whereas I wish to see you lead a virgin heiress from Saville Row to Mount Shannon.

Let me hear from you at your best leisure, and believe me ever and most truly, my dearest Clare,

Yours, Noel Byron

P.S.—The Turkish fleet are just bearing down to blockade this port; so how our deputy is to get by is a doubt, but the island boats frequently evade them.

The sight is pretty, but much finer for a limner than a lodger. It is the Squadron from the Gulf of Corinth (Hooke-Gulf of Lepanto); they (the Greeks, I mean) are all busy enough, as you may suppose, as the campaign is expected to commence next month. But as aforesaid I refer you for news to the bearer.

TO CHARLES F. BARRY   *April 9th 1824*

DEAR BARRY,[1]—The Account up to 11th July was 40,541,
etc., Genoese livres in my favour : since then I have had a
letter of Credit of Messrs. Webb for 60,000 Genoese livres, for
which I have drawn ; but how the account stands *exactly*, you
do not state. The balance will of course be replaced by my
London Correspondent, referring more particularly to the
Honble Douglas Kinnaird, who is also my Agent and trustee,
as well as banker, and a friend besides since we were at College
together—which is favourable to business, as it gives confidence,
or ought to do so.

I had hoped that you had obtained the price of the Schooner
from Ld Blessington : you must really tell him that I must make
the affair public, and take other steps which will be agreeable
to neither, unless he speedily pays the money, so long due, and
contracted by his own headstrong wish to purchase. You
know how fairly I treated him in the whole affair.

Every thing except the best (*i.e.* the Green travelling
Chariot) may be disposed of, and that speedily, as it will assist
to balance our accompt. As the Greeks have gotten their loan,
they may as well repay mine, which they no longer require :
and I request you to forward a copy of the agreement to Mr.
Kinnaird, and direct him from me to claim the money from the
Deputies. They were welcome to it in their difficulties, and
also for good and all, supposing that they had not got out of
them ; but, as it is, they can afford repayment, and I assure you
that, besides *this*, they have had many " a strong and long pull "
at my purse, which has been (and still is) disbursing pretty
freely in their cause : besides, I shall have to *re-expend* the same
monies, having some hundred men under orders, at my own
expense, for the Gk. Government and National service.

Of all their proceedings here, health, politics, plans, acts,
and deeds, etc.—good or otherwise, Gamba or others will tell
you—truly or not truly, according to their habits.

Yours ever, N. B^N

---

[1] On the evening of the day on which this letter was written, Byron came home
wet after a ride, and complained of feeling feverish. He died on April 19th, 1824.

APPENDIX

LETTERS HITHERTO UNPUBLISHED
Marked in the text with *

TO MRS. BYRON	[?] 1804	*Sir John Murray*
,, LORD CLARE	AUG. 20, 1807	*Yale University Library*
,, JOHN CAM HOBHOUSE	MAR. 26, 1808	*Sir John Murray*
,, JOHN CAM HOBHOUSE	APR. 15, 1808	*Sir John Murray*
,, EDWARD ELLICE	JUNE 25, 1809	*Russell Ellice, Esq.*
,, EDWARD ELLICE	JULY 4, 1810	*Russell Ellice, Esq.*
,, JOHN CAM HOBHOUSE	MAR. 5, 1811	*Sir John Murray*
,, JOHN CAM HOBHOUSE	FEB. 10, 1812	*Sir John Murray*
,, MISS MERCER ELPHINSTONE	JULY 29, 1812	*The Marquess of Lansdowne*
,, LADY MELBOURNE	[AUG. 12. 1812]	*Sir John Murray*
,, LADY CAROLINE LAMB	JAN. 1813	*Sir John Murray*
,, JOHN CAM HOBHOUSE	JAN. 17, 1813	*Sir John Murray*
,, MISS MERCER ELPHINSTONE	MAY 3, 1814	*The Marquess of Lansdowne*
,, HENRIETTA D'USSIÈRES	JUNE 8, 1814	*Sir John Murray*
,, S. T. COLERIDGE	OCT. 18, 1815	*Yale University Library*
,, MISS MERCER ELPHINSTONE	APR. 11, 1816	*The Marquess of Lansdowne*
,, THE HON. DOUGLAS KINNAIRD	JULY 20, 1816	*Lord Kinnaird*
,, THE HON. DOUGLAS KINNAIRD	JAN. 12, 1817	*Lord Kinnaird*
,, THE HON. DOUGLAS KINNAIRD	JULY 15, 1818	*Lord Kinnaird*
,, THE COUNTESS GUICCIOLI	APR. 25, 1819	*Count Carlo Gamba (translated by the Marchesa Origo)*
,, THE LORD KINNAIRD	MAY 15, 1819	*Lord Kinnaird*
,, THE LORD KINNAIRD	MAY 26, 1819	*Lord Kinnaird*
,, THE LORD KINNAIRD	JULY 5, 1819	*Lord Kinnaird*
,, ALEXANDER SCOTT	JULY 31, 1819	*The Pierpont Morgan Library, New York*
,, CAPTAIN HAY	SEPT. 1819	*From a copy, made in Nantes in 1925, in Sir John Murray's Collection*
,, THE HON. DOUGLAS KINNAIRD	JAN. 2, 1820	*Sir John Murray*
,, THE HON. DOUGLAS KINNAIRD	MAY 3, 1820	*Lord Kinnaird*
,, JOHN CAM HOBHOUSE	JUNE 8, 1820	*Sir John Murray*
,, THE HON. DOUGLAS KINNAIRD	JULY 20, 1820	*Lord Kinnaird*
,, THE COUNTESS GUICCIOLI	AUG. 7, 1820	*Count Carlo Gamba (translated by the Marchesa Origo)*

TO	THE HON. DOUGLAS KINNAIRD	SEPT. 17, 1820	*Yale University Library*
,,	THE HON. AUGUSTA LEIGH	OCT. 1820	*Sir John Murray (from a copy)*
,,	THE HON. DOUGLAS KINNAIRD	FEB. 1, 1821	*Sir John Murray*
,,	JOHN CAM HOBHOUSE	FEB. 22, 1821	*Sir John Murray*
,,	THE HON. DOUGLAS KINNAIRD	FEB. 26, 1821	*Sir John Murray*
,,	THE HON. DOUGLAS KINNAIRD	MAR. 23, 1821	*Sir John Murray*
,,	THE HON. DOUGLAS KINNAIRD	APR. 26, 1821	*Sir John Murray*
,,	THE HON. DOUGLAS KINNAIRD	JULY 24 [? 14] 1821	*Sir John Murray*
,,	THE HON. DOUGLAS KINNAIRD	AUG. 23, 1821	*Sir John Murray*
,,	OCTAVIUS GILCHRIST	SEPT. 5, 1821	*Henry E. Huntingdon Library*
,,	ROBERT SOUTHEY	FEB. 7, 1822	*Lord Kinnaird*
,,	THE HON. DOUGLAS KINNAIRD	[FEB. 7, 1822]	*Lord Kinnaird*
,,	LORD HOLLAND	MAY 11, 1822	*Historical Society of Pennsylvania*
,,	THE HON. DOUGLAS KINNAIRD	MAY 27, 1822	*Lord Kinnaird*
,,	E. J. DAWKINS	JULY 4, 1822	*University of Texas*
,,	E. J. DAWKINS	JULY 6, 1822	*University of Texas*
,,	DAVID GRANT	NOV. 13, 1823	*Sir John Murray*
,,	THE HON. DOUGLAS KINNAIRD	DEC. 10, 1823	*Sir John Murray*
,,	THE HON. DOUGLAS KINNAIRD [?]	DEC. 11, 1823	*Sir John Murray*

LETTERS INCLUDING HITHERTO UNPUBLISHED PASSAGES

Marked in the text with †

,,	JOHN CAM HOBHOUSE	FEB. 27, 1808	*Sir John Murray*
,,	MRS. BYRON	JUNE 28, 1810	*Correspondence of Lord Byron, edited by R. C. Dallas (suppressed)*
,,	JOHN CAM HOBHOUSE	JULY 29 AND 30, 1810	*Sir John Murray*
,,	JOHN CAM HOBHOUSE	AUG. 16, 1810	*Sir John Murray*
,,	JOHN CAM HOBHOUSE	AUG. 23, 1810	*Sir John Murray*
,,	JOHN CAM HOBHOUSE	SEPT. 25, 1810	*Sir John Murray*
,,	JOHN CAM HOBHOUSE	OCT. 2, 1810	*Sir John Murray*
,,	JOHN CAM HOBHOUSE	OCT. 4, 1810	*Sir John Murray*
,,	JOHN CAM HOBHOUSE	JUNE 19, 1811	*Sir John Murray*
,,	JOHN CAM HOBHOUSE	OCT. 22, 1811	*Sir John Murray*
,,	LADY CAROLINE LAMB	MARCH OR APRIL 1812	*Sir John Murray*
,,	LADY MELBOURNE	SEPT. 21, 1813	*Sir John Murray*
,,	JOHN CAM HOBHOUSE	MAY 1, 1816	*Sir John Murray*

TO THE HON. AUGUSTA LEIGH	NOV. 6, 1816	*Sir John Murray*
,, THE HON. AUGUSTA LEIGH	DEC. 19, 1816	*Sir John Murray*
,, JOHN MURRAY	JAN. 2, 1817	*Sir John Murray*
,, JOHN CAM HOBHOUSE	MAR. 31, 1817	*British Museum*
,, JOHN MURRAY	APR. 2, 1817	*Sir John Murray*
,, JOHN MURRAY	AUG. 21, 1817	*Sir John Murray*
,, JOHN MURRAY	JAN. 27, 1818	*Sir John Murray*
,, JOHN CAM HOBHOUSE AND		
THE HON. DOUGLAS KINNAIRD	JAN. 19, 1819	*Sir John Murray*
,, JOHN CAM HOBHOUSE	APR. 6, 1819	*Sir John Murray*
,, JOHN CAM HOBHOUSE	[APR. 20 1819]	*Sir John Murray*
,, THE HON. DOUGLAS KINNAIRD	APR. 24, 1819	*Sir John Murray*
,, RICHARD BELGRAVE HOPPNER	JUNE 20, 1819	*Sir John Murray*
,, THE HON. AUGUSTA LEIGH	JULY 26, 1819	*The Pierpont Morgan Library, New York*
,, JOHN CAM HOBHOUSE	JULY 30, 1819	*Sir John Murray*
,, JOHN MURRAY	AUG. 1, 1819	*Sir John Murray*
,, THE HON. DOUGLAS KINNAIRD	OCT. 26, 1819	*British Museum*
,, RICHARD BELGRAVE HOPPNER	OCT. 29, 1819	*Sir John Murray*
,, JOHN CAM HOBHOUSE	MAR. 3, 1820	*British Museum*
,, JOHN CAM HOBHOUSE	MAR. 29, 1820	*Sir John Murray*
,, RICHARD BELGRAVE HOPPNER	MAR. 31, 1820	*Henry E. Huntingdon Library*
,, THE HON. DOUGLAS KINNAIRD	NOV. 22, 1820	*Sir John Murray*
,, THE HON. DOUGLAS KINNAIRD	MAY 21, 1823	*Sir John Murray*
,, THE HON. AUGUSTA LEIGH	OCT. 12, 1823	*Sir John Murray*
,, THE HON. DOUGLAS KINNAIRD	DEC. 23, 1823	*Sir John Murray*

INDEX

asks Byron to write no more *Don Juan*, 656, 681; "menaced with convent", 657; female Censor Morum, 707; comment on d'Orsay journal, 722-3; on Byron going to Greece, 731-2; Byron's letters to, 445 and n., 486, 523, 746 and n.

Guiccioli Palace, 498

Guido, 456

Guilford, Francis North, 4th Earl of, 403

Guilford, Frederick North, 5th Earl of, 403

Guilt. See Müllner, Adolf

Gysbrecht van Amstel. See Vondel, J. van

Hall, Rev. Thomas, British Chaplain at Leghorn, 706

Halnaby, 348; Byron's letter from, 311

Hamilton, Anthony, 724

Hamilton, Lady Dalrymple, 372, 451

Hamilton, Mr. (F. O.), 417

Hammond, George, 416

Hamlet. See Shakespeare

Hampden Club, 619

Hancock, Charles, 756 and n.; Byron's letter to, 757

Hannibal, 316, 648

Hanson, Charles, 5 n., 697

Hanson, Hargreaves, 5 and n.

Hanson, John; Byron's solicitor, 5 n., 8, 10, 23, 42, 62-3, 84, 86-8, 92-3, 98, 110-11, 116-18, 123, 132, 154, 163, 210, 235, 244, 249, 303, 305, 334, 337, 378, 414, 423-5 and n., 427, 433-4, 441, 443-4, 490, 502, 505, 508, 512-13, 520, 528, 543, 591, 593, 630, 711; Byron's letters to, 16, 20, 26, 45

Hanson, Mrs. John, 21, 46

Hanson, Mary Anne. *See* Portsmouth, Countess of

Hanson, Newton, 5 n.

Harcourt, General William, Earl, 621

Harcourt, Mrs., 8

Hardwicke, 46

Hardwicke, Lady, 252, 278

Hardy, 709 n.

Hardy, Lady, 714; Byron's letter to, 709

Harley, Lady Jane, 634

Harlow, George Henry, painter, 472

Harness, Rev. William, 678; Byron's letters to, 48 and n., 128

Harris, Harry, 320

Harrow; Byron at, ix, 2-5, 8-13, 16, 21, 25, 37, 44, 48 n., 128, 211, 435, 538, 563, 565, 610, 624, 636, 639, 641-3, 649; Speech Day, 15-16; Eton and Harrow match, 17, 19, 608; portrait of Byron's friends at, 49; his speeches at, 635, 642; Allegra buried in churchyard of, 691, 695, 698; Byron's letters from, 4, 9-12, 16

Harrow Club, Cambridge, 619

Harrowby, Lady, 168, 260, 507

Harrowby, Lord, 135, 154, 168, 260, 506 n., 507

Hartington, William Spencer, Marquess of. *See* Devonshire, Duke of

Hastings, 299; Byron's letter from, 295

Hastings, Warren, 609

Hato, Hatadjé *or* Hatagée, 763, 765

Hay, Captain John, 693; Byron's letter to, 487 and n.

Haygarth, Mr., at Athens, 89-90

Haymarket Theatre, 17, 127, 129, 664 n.

Haynes, Mr., 43

Hayreddin, Algerine pirate, 214

Hazlitt, 577

Headfort, Marchioness of, 35

Heathcote, Sir Gilbert, 320

Heathcote, Lady (Katherine Sophia Manners), 164, 253-4, 402, 405

Heaven and Earth, 688

Heber, Richard, 668 and n.

Hebrides, the, 35

Hellespont, 66, 319; Byron's swim across, 64, 67, 70, 73, 90, 99, 101, 148, 592, 660

Héloïse. See Rousseau, J.-J.

Hemans, Felicia Dorothea, *Domestic Affections and other Poems*, 527 and n.

Henderson, John, the Bath Roscius, 251

Hentsch, Mons. (banker at Geneva), 361, 366, 387, 657-8

Heraclitus, 647

Herbert, Baron, 57

Hercules, 647

Hercules, the, 739

Hermit, The. See Jouy, Victor J. E. de

OXFORD

MORE OXFORD PAPERBACKS

Details of a selection of other Oxford Paperbacks follow. A complete list of Oxford Paperbacks, including The World's Classics, Twentieth-Century Classics, OPUS, Past Masters, Oxford Authors, Oxford Shakespeare, and Oxford Paperback Reference, is available in the UK from the General Publicity Department, Oxford University Press (RS), Walton Street, Oxford, OX2 6DP.

In the USA, complete lists are available from the Paperbacks Marketing Manager, Oxford University Press, 200 Madison Avenue, New York, NY 10016.

Oxford Paperbacks are available from all good bookshops. In case of difficulty, customers in the UK can order direct from Oxford University Press Bookshop, 116 High Street, Oxford, Freepost, OX1 4BR, enclosing full payment. Please add 10 per cent of the published price for postage and packing.

THE ROMANTIC IMAGINATION

Maurice Bowra

This is a classic and illuminating study of the major poets of the Romantic movement and their followers: Blake, Coleridge, Wordsworth, Shelley, Keats, Byron, Poe, and Christina and Dante Gabriel Rossetti, and Swinburne. Originally delivered as a series of lectures at a time when the Romantics were to some extent in critical opprobrium, *The Romantic Imagination* sought to reassess the literary values of these poets.

THE ROMANTIC AGONY

Mario Praz

Second Edition

Foreword by Frank Kermode

In this remarkable study Mario Praz describes Romantic literature under one of its most characteristic aspects, that of erotic sensibility. It is, in effect, an analysis of a mood in literature— one which, however transient, was widespread. Expressed in dreams of 'luxurious cruelties', 'fatal women', corpse-passions, and sinful agonies of delight, the mood—as seen in the influence of Byron and de Sade—had a major effect on poets and painters of the nineteenth century.

'*The Romantic Agony* is now a classic in a sense which places it among such books as have, in the depth of their insights, power to alter a reader's understanding of the history of his society, and perhaps of his own history.' Frank Kermode

BYRON

Poetical Works

Edited by Frederick Page

New edition corrected by John Jump

Lord Byron, in many ways the archetype of the Romantic era and a poet whose moods swing between the cynical and the transcendental, has delighted subsequent generations with his poetry as he delighted and scandalized his own.

The text of this edition by Frederick Page, containing nearly all of Byron's published poems together with the poet's own notes, has been revised by John Jump. First published in The Oxford Poets in 1896, it was included in the Oxford Standard Authors series in 1904, and many times reprinted.

ELIZABETH GASKELL

Winifred Gérin

Winifred Gérin was the first biographer to make full use of the mass of material that became available with the publication of Elizabeth Gaskell's *Letters* in 1966. She reveals her as an admirable mother to her four daughters, a graceful and accomplished hostess, a dedicated social worker, a great traveller, and a delightful correspondent with a wide range of friends among the great political and literary figures of her day. The book won the Whitbread Literary Award in 1976.

'This biography of an enchanting woman who produced three wholly different literary masterpieces gives one all the available facts, interpreted with sympathy and intelligence.' *Daily Telegraph*

COLERIDGE

Poetical Works

Revised by Ernest Hartley Coleridge

This edition by Ernest Hartley Coleridge, grandson of the poet, contains a complete and authoritative text of Coleridge's poems. Here are his earliest extant teenage poems, his masterly meditative pieces, and the extraordinary supernatural poems— 'The Rime of the Ancient Mariner', 'Kubla Khan', and 'Christabel'.

The text follows that of the 1834 edition, the last published in the author's lifetime. The poems are printed, so far as is possible, in chronological order, with Coleridge's own notes as well as textual and bibliographical notes by the editor.

DOROTHY WORDSWORTH

Robert Gittings & Jo Manton

This brilliant biography is the first to treat Dorothy Wordsworth as a person in her own right rather than merely as an adjunct to her brother, or to Coleridge. Her devotion to her family and friends is well known, but she was also a woman of problems and contradictions, often connected with the changing social and political climate of her day. Her uncertain health and the nature of her final breakdown are fully examined for the first time, throwing light on several controversial actions in her life. She emerges as a more strange, wayward, and human figure than convention has portrayed.

'the authors have done what only the best biographers do; they re-create living people . . . it is a relief to have a real Dorothy presented' Patric Dickinson *The Times*

Oxford Lives

LINGUISTIC CRITICISM

Roger Fowler

A fruitful recent development in literary studies has been the application of ideas drawn from linguistics. Precise analytic methods help the practical criticism of texts, while at the same time the theory of language has illuminated literary theory. *Linguistic Criticism* is an introduction to the subject by one of its most experienced practitioners. Roger Fowler sets out clearly and simply a variety of analytic techniques whose application he demonstrates in discussion of a wide range of texts from fiction, poetry, and drama. He concentrates on structures which relate literature to ordinary language, stressing the importance of the reader's every-day language skills.

An OPUS book

THE COURTSHIP OF ROBERT BROWNING AND ELIZABETH BARRETT

Daniel Karlin

Daniel Karlin's exciting and imaginative book gives a fresh account of one of the most celebrated romances of literary history. Based on a much closer study of the love letters than has been attempted before, shows how significant they are for an interpretation of the work of both poets.

'A well written and very perceptive study of a love affair that was as much a literary event as a private emotional experience' *New Statesman*

'A rewarding study . . . Karlin's sensitive guidance enables us to appreciate the poignancy of what Browning achieved for Elizabeth.' *Times Higher Education Supplement*

SELECTED POEMS AND PROSE OF JOHN CLARE

Chosen and edited by
Eric Robinson and Geoffrey Summerfield

Illustrated by David Gentleman

This selection by Eric Robinson and Geoffrey Summerfield is based upon their study of Clare's original manuscripts and is an authentic reconstruction of what Clare actually wrote, in some cases going behind printed versions of his work to the primary sources, and in others presenting work never before published. It reveals the variety of Clare's writing, his poetic strengths and sensitivities, and defies the labelling of him as a 'peasant poet' or simple lyricist. Here is to be found also the best of Clare's prose—descriptive and political—which combines the traditions both of Cobbett and White of Selborne.

CHARLOTTE BRONTË

The Evolution of Genius

Winifred Gérin

Winner of the James Tait Black Memorial Prize, the William Heinemann Award, and the British Academy's Rose Mary Crawshay Prize.

'surely one of the great biographies of recent times' *Sunday Times*

'a book to end all books about the Brontës' *Sunday Telegraph*

Oxford Lives

EMILY BRONTË

A Biography

Winifred Gérin

Emily was perhaps the least accessible of the Brontë sisters, and Winifred Gérin goes a long way towards explaining her personality without becoming so dazzled by her strangeness that she does not also see her as human. She gives us a sharp impression of the sensitive Emily, tracing her development from unhappy schooldays, her love of the moors, the writing of *Gondal*, *Wuthering Heights*, the French essays, and her poems, to her death.

'a biographical landmark' *Observer*

'one of the monuments, scholarly, literary, intuitive, of our time' *Financial Times*

Philosophy

JOHN CLARE

Edited by Eric Robinson and David Powell

This selection of John Clare's writings, both verse and prose, is the most ambitious yet attempted. All aspects of Clare's genius—bird poems, nature, observations of all kinds, songs, ballads, social satire, reflections of English folk customs, intense expressions of Clare's search for his identity—are represented here. Clare is the finest poet of first love and also the saddest voice of isolation and despair.

The text is a result of more than thirty years' close study of Clare's manuscripts in England and the USA. It presents Clare's work with the minimum of editorial interference, selects the most authentic texts available, and allows the reader to encounter Clare's works exactly as he wrote them.

The Oxford Authors

THE FORCE OF POETRY

Christopher Ricks

Each of these scintillating essays asks how a poet's words reveal 'the force of poetry', that force—in Dr Johnson's words— 'which calls new powers into being, which embodies sentiment, and animates matter'. The poets range from John Gower to Geoffrey Hill, and among them are Marvell, Milton, Johnson, Wordsworth, Beddoes, Housman, Empson, Stevie Smith, Lowell, and Larkin. Concluding the book are four wider essays: on clichés; on lies; on misquotations; and on American English in its relation to the transitory.

'These essays show Christopher Ricks as the closest of close readers, conducting a series of master classes in how to read a poem—a work of enormous brilliance.' Bernard Bergonzi, *Encounter*

'The richness and variety of these essays is truly remarkable.' John Bayley, *Listener*

'Reading Professor Ricks's comments and observations convinces me that he is exactly the kind of critic every poet dreams of finding.' W. H. Auden

WORDSWORTH

Poetical Works

Revised by Ernest de Selincourt

This edition of Wordsworth's poems contains every piece of verse known to have been published by the poet himself, or of which he authorized the posthumous publication. The text, which Thomas Hutchinson based largely upon the 1849–50 standard edition—the last issued during the poet's lifetime— was revised in 1936 for the Oxford Standard Authors series by Ernest de Selincourt.

WILLIAM WORDSWORTH

Edited by Stephen Gill

'There are two reasons for acclaiming this book. The first is that it is simply the best students' edition of Wordsworth available . . . The second reason is that it makes available to the student and the general reader the original texts of the poems in chronological order . . . The selection is admirable . . . As well as clear uncluttered texts this edition offers us biographical and bibliographical notes on the poems, in which the standard of Dr Gill's scholarship is, as usual, excellent.' Michael Baron, *British Book News*

'Goes without saying that the introduction is of real value and the annotation copious and excellent . . . I did not find any poem that I wanted to add to the essential poems, but there is much that is of considerable interest and not widely known.' W. W. Robson, *Times Literary Supplement*

The Oxford Authors

GRAY AND COLLINS

Poetical Works

Edited by Roger Lonsdale

For this edition of the poems of Thomas Gray and William Collins, the text—which carefully retains the authors' original spelling and punctuation—has been completely revised and reset, and the work of the former arranged in chronological order of composition.

'A knowledge of the poetry of Gray and Collins is essential to an understanding of 18th-century literature. Consequently this admirable new edition by Dr Roger Lonsdale is especially welcome.' *British Book News*

'The narrow but genuine genius focused into a handful each of finely wrought poems of quiet but haunting reverberations.' *Birmingham Post*

THE OXFORD BOOK OF DREAMS

Chosen by Stephen Brook

This anthology draws on the dream material of a variety of novelists, poets, playwrights, and diarists to explore the dream experience in literature from pre-Christian times to the present day. It shows how the dream as a literary device has been exploited to the full by writers as diverse as Coleridge and Yeats, Dostoevsky and Proust, Tolstoy, Heller, and Franz Kafka. From dreams realistic and reminiscent to the world of nightmare and metamorphosis, from the ridiculous to the ridiculously funny, this collection is a fascinating reminder of the power and importance of dreams as a source of literary inspiration.

'splendid . . . Stephen Brook could hardly have done the job better' *Times Literary Supplement*

THE CONCISE OXFORD DICTIONARY OF QUOTATIONS

Nearly 6,000 of the most famous quotations have been selected from the latest edition of the best-selling *Oxford Dictionary of Quotations*. Over a thousand authors are represented, spanning a period of time from the eighth century BC to the 1980s, and covering countries as far apart as Russia and South Africa, China and Mexico. The generous index guides the searcher to a particular quotation or even to a selection of quotations on a particular topic; the main body of the book provides opportunity for endless browsing among varied company where Chekhov rubs shoulders with Chesterton, Lord Palmerston with Dorothy Parker, and Wodehouse with Wittgenstein.

Oxford Reference

THE OXFORD LITERARY GUIDE TO THE BRITISH ISLES

Edited by Dorothy Eagle and Hilary Carnell

This is the paperback edition of the best-selling *Oxford Literary Guide to the British Isles*. It lists hundreds of places in Britain and Ireland and gives details of their connections with the lives and works of famous writers. It provides maps, precise directions, and opening times for the tourist. Not only is it an indispensable companion to every journey, but also a delight for the armchair traveller with its endlessly fascinating facts and anecdotes.

'Anyone who can read or write will find the *Guide* a sure way of wallowing unashamedly in a rich nostalgia for . . . our literary heritage.' *Times Literary Supplement*

Oxford Reference

THE OXFORD BOOK OF SATIRICAL VERSE

Chosen by Geoffrey Grigson

'one of the best anthologies by the best modern anthologist' *New York Review of Books*

'An immense treasury of wit, exuberance, controlled malice and uncontrolled rage' *Times Literary Supplement*

THE NEW OXFORD BOOK OF
EIGHTEENTH-CENTURY VERSE

Chosen and Edited by Roger Lonsdale

'a major anthology: one of the best that Oxford has ever produced' *The Times*

'a major event . . . forces a reappraisal of what 18th-century poetry is' *Sunday Times*

'the most important anthology in recent years' *The Economist*

'indispensable' Kingsley Amis

COLERIDGE

Richard Holmes

Coleridge was not only a great poet, he was also a philosopher and explorer of the whole human condition. Richard Holmes describes Coleridge's work as a writer, explains his often difficult and fragmentary ideas, and shows that his concept of the creative imagination still shapes our notions of growth and culture.

'most attractive' *Listener*

'stylish, intelligent, and readable' *Irish Times*

Past Masters